275

299

383

p.236

244~45

The American War in Afghanistan

The American War in Afghanistan

A History

CARTER MALKASIAN

OXFORD
UNIVERSITY PRESS

OXFORD
UNIVERSITY PRESS

Oxford University Press is a department of the University of Oxford. It furthers
the University's objective of excellence in research, scholarship, and education
by publishing worldwide. Oxford is a registered trade mark of Oxford University
Press in the UK and certain other countries.

Published in the United States of America by Oxford University Press
198 Madison Avenue, New York, NY 10016, United States of America.

Library of Congress Cataloging-in-Publication Data
Names: Malkasian, Carter, 1975– author.
Title: The American war in Afghanistan: A History / Carter Malkasian.
Description: New York, NY : Oxford University Press, [2021] |
Includes bibliographical references and index. |
Identifiers: LCCN 2020056939 (print) | LCCN 2020056940 (ebook) |
ISBN 9780197550779 (hardback) | ISBN 9780197550793 (epub) | ISBN 9780197550809
Subjects: LCSH: Afghan War, 2001—United States. | Afghan War, 2001–
Classification: LCC DS371.412 .M327 2021 (print) | LCC DS371.412 (ebook) |
DDC 958.104/7373—dc23
LC record available at https://lccn.loc.gov/2020056939
LC ebook record available at https://lccn.loc.gov/2020056940

DOI: 10.1093/oso/9780197550779.001.0001

3 5 7 9 8 6 4 2

Printed by LSC Communications, United States of America

TABLE OF CONTENTS

LIST OF MAPS

LIST OF FIGURES

Thinking about America's War in Afghanistan

The heart of Afghanistan was the countryside, the *atraf*. There in small villages of mud-walled homes, surrounded by fields of wheat, corn, or poppy, most Afghans lived. Bearded men with worn hands worked the fields. Barefoot boys and girls played on dirt paths. Women toiled unseen within the walls, bounded in shroud. Every village had a simple, single-room mosque where men gathered to pray. Other than cell phones, cars, and assault rifles, the 21st century was invisible.

From 2001 to 2021, Americans passed through the countryside and its villages. Patrolling in green or tan camouflage, loaded with body armor, a helmet, ammunition, and water, with an M-4 or M-16 assault rifle or maybe a belt-fed machine gun cradled in their arms, they wound their way through fields and around the villages. Sometimes they staked a post out of brown dirt-filled HESCO barriers and squatted for a year or two. Sometimes with glowing green night vision they burst in during the small hours on a raid, and then disappeared. And sometimes rifles hammered, explosions cracked, and a brother was carried away. *Jang peh atraf kay die*, say the Afghans. "War is in the countryside."

On the outskirts of any village were mounds of gray rocks. They rested on a barren patch, or on high ground overlooking the fields, or shaded amid pine trees, or honored by a rickety wooden fence. A flag—a strip of cloth tied to a long bamboo pole—was planted in each. From afar, the whole plot was a fluttering multi-colored mass. It was the graveyard. For 40 years the graveyards grew. The tale of loss could be heard in Hamid Karzai's deep flowing Pashto when he sat face to face with the Taliban in 2019:

> You have all seen, since three, four, five, six years, nay longer, that upon
> our dear soil across Afghanistan . . . from Kunduz, to Khost, to Herat,
> to Badakhshan, to Faryab, to the environs of Kabul, that . . . two graves
> lie side by side—*dwa kabira tsang peh tsang prot dee*. On one is a black,

red, and green flag. On the other is a white flag. One in the name of the
Taliban entrusted to the soil. The other in the name of the Afghanistan
askar or soldier. . . . Around the graveyard, the graves of innocent
Afghans are in great number, every mother's heartfelt longing underground, every father's pride buried.[1]

Americans and Afghans fought in Afghanistan, against each other and side
by side, for more than 19 years. It was America's longest war. Through 2021,
it crossed four presidents—George W. Bush, Barack Obama, Donald Trump,
Joseph Biden. Fifteen US generals commanded there. Hundreds of thousands
of US troops and diplomats were deployed. Thousands were killed or wounded.
For a time it was "the good war." In the wake of the attacks of September 11,
Americans thought intervention just. In its latter years the war ceased to be
good. It became only long and futile.

I decided to write a book about the whole Afghan War in 2013 after reading
William Dalrymple's majestic *Return of a King: The Battle for Afghanistan*, about
Britain's first catastrophic foray into Afghanistan. His storytelling, thick with
Dari poems and Afghan viewpoints, captured my admiration. Though I knew
I could never match his skill, I wanted to follow his example and write a full his-
tory of America's war in Afghanistan. Such a history, that drew on wide-ranging
sources, had yet to be written.[2]

I had just become the political advisor to General Joseph Dunford, the commander of US and allied forces for all Afghanistan. I had already spent several
months in Kunar province and nearly two years in Garmser, Helmand province, where I learned Pashto. I had written a book on the latter, *War Comes to
Garmser: Thirty Years of War on the Afghan Frontier*. General Dunford asked me
to talk to Afghan leaders and visit the various regions to understand the local situation. The new job would allow me to see much of Afghanistan and meet with
Afghans from different backgrounds and allegiances. I had that job until the end
of August 2014 when General Dunford returned to the United States. A book on
the whole war seemed possible from this vista.

My problem was that the war did not end. In fact, I was actually witnessing the
beginning of a whole new phase. After 2014, I remained with General Dunford
as he became chairman of the joint chiefs of staff, senior officer for the entire US
Armed Forces. Serving as his advisor, I saw the war from an even higher viewpoint. I continued to visit Afghanistan regularly. In 2018 and 2019, I found myself spending months helping General Scott Miller, commander of US forces, in
Afghanistan, and participating in peace talks in Qatar with Ambassador Zalmay
Khalilzad, US special envoy for peace talks with the Taliban. The war escalated
and evolved—yet did not end. For years, I thought waiting for the end was going

to turn out to be unrealistic. Then, on April 14, 2021, President Joseph Biden declared the final US military withdrawal would be completed by September 11 of that year. That denouement is still fresh, too close for reasonable perspective. But the events leading up to it can be understood and reflected upon. In that sense, the book ended up being a full history of America's Afghan War from 2001 to 2021.

The Afghan War has a rich literature. Sarah Chayes's *The Punishment of Virtue*, published in 2006, is the best account of life in the first years of US intervention, inspiring because she lived in the middle of Kandahar and learned to speak Pashto. Over the following years, a library's worth of books hit the streets. Reporter Sebastian Junger's *War* about the Korengal Valley stands out among many good accounts of the experiences of Americans in combat; it is a vivid telling of the experiences of a single platoon in some of the worst fighting of the war. The best book by a high-ranking official is Stanley McChrystal's memoir, *My Share of the Task*, because it takes the reader straight into the misperceptions and contradictions of America's 2009–2011 surge, when nearly 100,000 US troops deployed to Afghanistan. Rajiv Chandrasekaran's *Little America* is a full treatment of those years. For a window into the Afghan people, Anand Gopal's *No Good Men among the Living* describes the hard lives of a warlord, a woman, and a Taliban. Then there are little-known gems such as Bette Dam's *A Man and a Motorcycle: How Hamid Karzai Came to Power* and David Edwards's *Caravan of Martyrs: Sacrifice and Suicide Bombing in Afghanistan*. Steve Coll's tome, *Directorate S: The C.I.A. and America's Secret Wars in Afghanistan and Pakistan*, is an authoritative text on what happened behind closed doors in the halls of power and is essential reading for the details of Pakistani policy and US peace efforts.

This book synthesizes earlier works into a single history while incorporating my own new research. The time in Kunar and Helmand and the 17 months with General Dunford and various visits since are sources of discussions, interviews, and firsthand observation of events. I have been to 15 provinces, with the most time spent in Helmand and Kunar, and Kandahar as a distant third. I have thoroughly reviewed Pashto written sources, including newspapers, books, and magazines. Friends have gone to Pakistan to bring me Taliban histories, documents, propaganda, and poems. I have mined key Pashto texts written by Taliban, hitherto unreferenced by Western scholars. These include the biography of Mullah Omar by his former spokesman, Abdul Hai Mutmain; the memoir of former Taliban foreign minister, Wakil Ahmed Mutawakil; and the history of the Taliban movement by Abdul Salam Zaeef, former ambassador to Pakistan and one of the most respected figures in Afghanistan. Additionally, I have conducted indirect surveys in which contacts interviewed dozens of Taliban fighters and commanders. And I have spoken directly to Taliban in Doha, in Kabul, and in the provinces.

The Afghan War's meanings for America have been subtle. It was not the all-encompassing experience of the Second World War or the American Civil War. Nor was it the searing national trauma of Vietnam. And it was not the shame of Iraq. The Afghan War's most direct impact was checking the terrorist threat to the United States. Afghanistan was the first front in the "war" on terrorism. Intervention prevented further harm to Americans. The war also changed the US military. Counterinsurgency, counterterrorism, special operations forces, and drone strikes are examples of new concepts, organizations, and tactics that emerged. Civil-military relations were tested in a way unseen since the Cold War. The war's meaning deepens when it comes to US foreign policy. It contributed to the Bush-era rush to fight terrorism and then later to the backlash against intervention that spawned the isolationism of the Trump years. There were macroeconomic implications as well. The war's formidable cost diverted funds from America's economic development at a time of slowdown. Above all, the Afghan War, along with Iraq, was the combat experience of a generation of US servicemen and women. For that reason alone, it matters.

The war's meaning was far greater for Afghanistan. It was the longest phase of a 40-year civil war that shook all walks of life, revolutionized politics and society, and reshaped culture. America's Afghan War was the second half of that civil war. Hundreds of thousands more Afghans died, millions fled their homes. From GPS-guided bombs to the cancer of suicide bombing, the Afghan people confronted new horrors. Over its long course, the war widened Afghanistan's divisions, between city and countryside, between Pashtuns and Dari-speakers, between haves and have-nots. Some good occurred, for infrastructure, education, freedom of the press, and women's rights; in a few lucky places, US soldiers, marines, and diplomats safeguarded years of tranquility. Democracy took root, sprouting elections and representation. At the same time Taliban Islamic rule entrenched itself. Worst of all, the war twisted the Afghan people. Extremism spread. The Islamic State appeared. Sacrifice, suicide, revenge, and killing ascended as values. Violence begat violence. In December 2001, Afghanistan's two decades of civil war appeared to be a passing nightmare. In December 2019, at the four-decade anniversary, violent disorder appeared to define a long-term reality.

The question of why we lost looms large. Or put another way for any who reject the verdict, why did the United States not prevail between 2001 and 2021? Although the al-Qaʻeda leader Osama bin Laden was killed and no major attack on the American homeland was carried out by a terrorist organization based in Afghanistan after 2001, the United States was unable to end the violence or hand the war to the Afghan authorities, which could not survive without US military backing. My goal when I started writing was to explain how the Afghan War came to a disappointing resolution, one that subjected the Afghan people to years of destruction. I especially wanted to highlight key mistakes and better paths that might have been taken.

I was already taken by several explanations for the direction of the war. The writings of Sarah Chayes, among others, founded a compelling argument that Afghanistan was suffering from unremitting violence because the government mistreated the Afghan people and Pakistan undermined peace. I sympathize with this argument. My own experiences also convince me that the tribalism underlying Afghan politics and society was so divisive that it encouraged instability.

A feeling that something more was going on nagged me as I left Afghanistan in August 2014. The United States had been in Afghanistan since 2001 and the country was still in trouble. Afghanistan's government by then had far more soldiers and equipment than the Taliban. Yet its forces were losing on the battlefield. The existing explanations helped but could not fully explain what I was seeing. Could I really lay what was military ineffectiveness on government mistreatment of the people or Pakistan? The logic felt forced. What do mistreatment and Pakistan have to do with the fact the government had the military tools to defend itself but was consistently losing to inferior numbers of Taliban? Tribal and political infighting offered a more compelling explanation but I could not tie it to every major case of battlefield defeat. All of these clearly were necessary conditions for what has transpired but their sum amounted to something less than the hardship that was playing out before my eyes.

In October 2014, I attended a small, closed-group discussion at the State Department with Michael McKinley, who had recently been appointed US ambassador to Afghanistan. We were having a lively debate on why the Taliban fight when the ambassador interjected, "Maybe I have read too much Hannah Arendt but I do not think this is about money or jobs. The Taliban are fighting for something larger." Ambassador McKinley's words captured what I was feeling but had not articulated.

The Taliban exemplified something that inspired, something that made them powerful in battle, something closely tied to what it meant to be Afghan. In simple terms, they fought for Islam and resistance to occupation, values enshrined in Afghan identity. Aligned with foreign occupiers, the government mustered no similar inspiration. It could not get its supporters, even if they outnumbered the Taliban, to go to the same lengths. Its claim to Islam was fraught. The very presence of Americans in Afghanistan trod on what it meant to be Afghan. It prodded at men and women to defend their honor, their religion, and their home. It dared young men to fight. It animated the Taliban. It sapped the will of Afghan soldiers and police. When they clashed, Taliban were more willing to kill and be killed than soldiers and police, or at least a good number of them. To the extent that this book has an overarching argument, it is that the Taliban's tie to what it meant to be Afghan was necessary to America's defeat in Afghanistan.

The literature to date has respectfully neglected this explanation. Although there are studies of Islam in Afghanistan, the possibility that Islam and resistance to occupation played a role in America's Afghan War has gone oddly unnoticed, almost shunned—in a country where people have eagerly tried to convert me to Islam, where religion defines daily life, and where insults to Islam instigate riots. The largest popular upheaval I witnessed in Afghanistan was not over the government's mistreatment of the people or Pakistani perfidy. It was over the possibility that an American had damaged a Koran. Thomas Barfield, a leading scholar on Afghanistan, best describes religion in Afghanistan: "There is no relationship, whether political, economic, or social, that is not validated by religion. . . . it is impossible to separate religion from politics because the two are so closely intertwined."[3]

The book that comes nearest to this explanation and has indeed influenced me is David Edwards's *Caravan of Martyrs: Sacrifice and Suicide Bombing in Afghanistan*. His thought-provoking work details how the act of martyrdom radicalized the war and war radicalized martyrdom. Edwards's most striking explanation for why suicide bombing became embedded in Afghan society, one that drives right to the heart of those of us who served in Afghanistan, is US occupation. Just as an Afghan tribesman was obligated to defend his family and land, so too was he obligated to do everything in his power to defend the Afghan homeland and seek revenge when that was not possible. A man who did otherwise was nothing. Prolonged US occupation tore at this obligation. Night raids, searches, ubiquitous armored convoys, mixing of men and women, and general ignorance of Afghan honor inflamed the humiliation. For Edwards, drones were the most pernicious. There was no defense against their distant strikes. The only recourse was revenge. Not all Afghans were driven to act. But enough were: "Some find that the way they can recover their honor and identity is by killing themselves in the process of killing those who have defiled their honor. . . . The bomber reclaims lost honor and standing in the community, he does his duty (*farz 'ain*) according to Islam (as interpreted by Taliban clerics), and he performs the political act of striking an unjust oppressor."[4]

The explanation of Islam and resistance to foreign occupation is powerful because it answers questions that arguments about grievances or Pakistan cannot. It is not the singular sufficient condition for the outcome of the Afghan War. It is a necessary one. Its impact is resounding: any Afghan government, however good and however democratic, was going to be imperiled as long as it was aligned with the United States. In turn, the United States was drawn to stay longer and longer: civil war in perpetual motion.

The explanation is also dangerous. It can be misinterpreted as meaning that all Muslims are bent on war or, worse, are fanatics. Such an interpretation would be wrong. Islam was a source of unity, justice, and inspiration. It was not the source of terrorism or atrocity. Although a few were extremists, unlike al-Qaʿeda, the Taliban as a whole were not and had no intention of plotting terrorist attacks on foreign countries. The point is that it is tougher to risk life for country when fighting alongside what some would call occupiers, especially when they believe in a different religion. To say that a people have sympathy for their countrymen and co-religionists over foreigners is hardly to label Islam a root of evil. Many people in many countries behave the same when faced with foreign intervention. As Samuel Huntington reminds us, "The principal impetus to . . . [revolutionary] movement is foreign war and foreign intervention. Nationalism is the cement of the revolutionary alliance and the engine of the revolutionary movement."[5]

The argument builds upon my earlier book on Afghanistan, *War Comes to Garmser*. In that book, I concluded that better decisions on the part of the United States would have led to a better outcome in Garmser. I thought we should have done more early on to build a stronger military, remove bad leaders, and manage tribal infighting. Evidence suggests that such actions may have led to greater stability, though the intervening years have left me more cynical. I have seen how hard it is to enact decisive new policies on a nationwide scale.

Like that book, this one too asks whether better decisions could have brought a better outcome, though it looks at the whole war instead of a single district. Themes of mistreatment, Pakistan, tribalism, and Islam and occupation run throughout. They set the war on a windy and rocky course. Was there anything the United States could have done to chart a calmer course? Could it have defeated its adversaries? Could it have fought a less costly war? Throughout the war, journalists, academics, experts, and officials fielded a host of criticisms: the Bush administration distracted itself with Iraq; US air strikes and night raids enraged the Afghan people; the Obama administration put a deadline on the surge; all three administrations permitted widespread government corruption. Were these really mistakes? Did they matter? Were there other mistakes?

When it comes to what could have been done differently, I suspect the biggest question for most Americans is: Why didn't we just leave? "The failure of American leaders—civilians and generals through three administrations, from the Pentagon to the State Department to Congress and the White House—to develop and pursue a strategy to end the war ought to be studied for generations," wrote the *New York Times* editorial board in 2019.[6] I have met few Americans who disagree that after September 11 we were right to go in, hunt down al-Qaʿeda, and overthrow the Taliban. To the end of 2019, Gallup and other credible public opinion polls find that a majority of Americans *never* believed that the US decision to invade Afghanistan was a mistake.[7] Yet, in my anecdotal experience, most Americans also assume we should have left some time after that. I have often been told that we were sacrificing American lives and treasure for very little. Over time, the terrorist threat, palpable at the outset of the war, became less tangible as al-Qaʻeda was pounded into the ground. The book will try to offer insight into why the United States did not withdraw until 2021 and instead committed to a faraway war in support of a fragile government; how, as the attacks of September 11 drifted farther and farther away, president after president decided to stick it out in a poor, landlocked country in the middle of Asia.

For the United States, Afghanistan was a long war but also an experience. It feels wrong to cast the entire experience as bad or evil. Better, I think, to see the good as well as the bad. I would not want to forget the friendships Americans forged with thousands of Afghans who were honestly trying to improve their country: whether a hard-working farmer, an idealistic technocrat, a heroic commando, an overburdened policeman, or a pathbreaking young woman. And I especially would not want to forget the kindness US servicemen and women brought to many Afghan lives and their dedication to protecting Americans at home. For me, America's Afghanistan experience is a dark, cloudy front with points of sunlight. The last thing I want to do is condemn it and all involved.

    With that in mind, we must confront a moral reality. The United States may have done more harm than good. Afghanistan's history since 1978 has been a story of trying to end civil war. The Taliban regime brought a few years of uneven respite before America's arrival jump-started the trauma. The Taliban were far from good. They oppressed women, hollowed out education, and silenced free speech. Our intervention did noble work in these spheres. But that good may not balance out the violence, death, and injury. Without our intervention, Afghans would have been deprived and oppressed, but alive. We should stand back and ask: In the name of stopping terrorism for our own sake, did we liberate, or oppress, the Afghan people?

The book looks at the war from the end of 2001 to the beginning of 2020. After this first chapter, chapters 2 and 3 briefly cover Afghanistan's culture and society, the Soviet-Afghan War, the ensuing civil war, and the first Taliban regime. The story really begins with the US invasion of Afghanistan in 2001 and Karzai's first years in power in chapters 4 and 5. The strategy of the Bush administration, the constitutional process and loya jirgas, and missed opportunities for peace talks with the Taliban are described in detail.

    The next chapters (6, 7, and 8) explain how the Taliban re-formed and instability returned, culminating in the Taliban offensive of 2006. Major battles in northern Helmand and western Kandahar comprise one of the most decisive events of the war. I also describe the Taliban movement under Mullah Omar and his lieutenants—Mullah Dadullah Lang and Mullah Abdul Ghani Baradar. Chapters 9 and 10 discuss the hard fighting Americans, British, and Canadians then experienced from 2007 to 2009 in long campaigns in the mountains of Kunar and Nuristan, throughout Helmand, and around the city of Kandahar. The battles American soldiers faced in the Korengal, Wanat, and other mountain outposts came to symbolize the war.

Then we turn to the surge of 2009 to 2011 in chapters 11 to 14. We examine Obama's painstaking decision to surge, General Stanley McChrystal's new counterinsurgency strategy, and the battles of Helmand and Kandahar—Marjah, Sangin, Arghandab, Panjwai, Zharey. This is the height of America's military experience in Afghanistan. It ends with the dramatic change in US strategy to drawing down and passing the war to the Afghan government.

The latter third of the book details the fighting of 2014 onward, after America had drawn down and the Afghan government tried to face the Taliban on its own. Chapters 15 to 18 discuss the unity government deal of 2014, the transition of Taliban leadership from Mullah Omar to Akhtar Mohammed Mansour, the Taliban offensives against Kunduz, Helmand, and other provincial capitals in 2015 and 2016, and the travails of the Afghan army and police. The results of America's efforts are truly evident here. Obama's strategy once more had to change. The rise of the Islamic State and the Taliban under the new leadership of Maulawi Haybatullah is also discussed. The book concludes in chapters 19 to 21 with the new policies of US president Donald Trump, the peace talks of 2019–2020, and a final summary of why we failed, what opportunities existed for a better ending, and why America never just got out.

Out of necessity the book has to focus on certain topics and regions to the detriment of others. US policy, military operations, and the Afghan side of the war (military and civilian, local and national) receive extensive attention. Events in the east, Kabul, and the south are described in detail. That the book has a bias toward Helmand and Kandahar, epicenters of the war and my experiences, should come as no surprise. The north and west, unfortunately, are less well attended, other than during dramatic events. Since the focus is on war, the story of democratic progress, institutional reforms, and international development assistance is presented only in broad brushstrokes. The same goes for the many advances experienced by the Afghan people. Kabul's youth movements and civil society are largely excluded. I also try to present the Taliban story. Pakistan is too important to be excluded but I withhold from delving into details of their internal politics or military operations. US allies and the coalition get the shortest shrift. Fifty-one countries joined the international military mission in Afghanistan at one point or another. They go unseen for long stretches. I habitually discuss

US strategy in isolation. Afghanistan is ripe for a proper international history. A foreigner in Afghanistan always has more to learn. On culture. On tradition. On families. On women. We never fully broke through the curtains segregating Afghans. The longer I study Afghanistan, the less I realize I know.

Writing this book has swallowed years. I am indebted to many. Derek Varble, historian and colleague at Oxford, rendered invaluable service commenting on the full manuscript. Thanks also go to Chris Kolenda, Matt Sherman, Dale Andrade, Daniel Marston, and Jerry Meyerle for graciously reviewing various chapters. Discussions with Stephen Biddle, Roger Myerson, John Nagl, David Edwards, Bruce Hoffman, Zach Constantino, Alison Kaufman, Robert Powell, Neill Joeck, and Tom Barfield were hugely beneficial. Teaching a yearly course on Afghanistan to dozens of insightful graduate students for Eliot Cohen at the School of Advanced International Studies, Johns Hopkins University, endlessly refined my ideas and conclusions. The think tank CNA and Bob Murray, Katherine McGrady, and Mark Geis were generous in allowing me the time to complete a book outside work (and that represents my own thoughts, not that of any organization). My final thanks go to David McBride, Emily MacKenzie, Cheryl Merritt, Elizabeth Bortka, and the team at Oxford University Press who once more patiently guided me through the writing of a book.

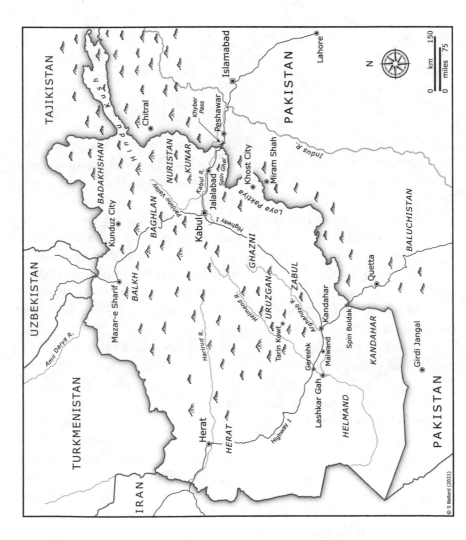

Map 1 Afghanistan

© S Ballard (2021)

The Country and Peoples
of Afghanistan

Afghanistan is a hard country, a land of desolate mountains and deserts, on the edge of the Middle East and South Asia, locked between Iran, Russia, and Pakistan. The towering Hindu Kush mountains break from the Himalayas and form a great massif across the center of the country. Rivers drain out of the Hindu Kush: the Kabul and Kunar in the east, the Amu Darya in the north, the Harirud in the west, and the Arghandab and Helmand in the south. They water valleys of farmland, widest around Jalalabad and Kandahar, in most other places less than a three-hour walk from either bank. Tributaries with thinner wisps of adjoining farmland feed the main rivers. Outside the mountains and fertile rivers lie deserts. The largest are in southern and western Afghanistan, stretching to Pakistan and Iran.

Afghanistan's population has risen over the years from roughly 12 million during most of the 20th century to 33 million in 2020, with the majority, 70 to 80 percent, living in the countryside.[1] The city of Kabul, nestled in a divide in the Hindu Kush, has been the seat of power for two centuries. At nearly 6,000 feet, for many the temperate climate is preferable to the summertime heat of Afghanistan's other cities.

Afghanistan is divided into provinces, 34 in 2020, each subdivided into five to fifteen districts. As Professor Thomas Barfield, don of Afghan studies, points out, it is easier to think in terms of four regions that circle Kabul. Moving clockwise, we can start with the north, where mountains and valleys descend to farmland along the Amu Darya. Mazar-e-Sharif, home of the Blue Mosque, a shrine to Ali, is the north's biggest city. Moving on, we go to the east, a land of high mountains and the Pakistan border. Its largest city is tree-lined Jalalabad, sited amid lush green farmland astride the Kabul River that flows into Pakistan. Next is the south, flatter and drier than any other region. Vast deserts blur the border with Pakistan. The ancient city of Kandahar is the south's capital, where Afghanistan was founded. Only Kabul surpasses its political weight. The last region is the west, bordering Iran's deserts. The city of Herat is a famous center of poetry and learning. Its people, sometimes called *roshan fikrai*, or "bright thinkers," are known for their education. In every region, a few smaller cities—probably better described as towns—exist as well, mostly at the center of bigger or more populous provinces, such as Khost city (eastern Afghanistan), Kunduz city (northern Afghanistan), and Lashkar Gah (southern Afghanistan).

Afghanistan has several ethnic groups. The Pashtuns are the biggest at about 40 percent of the population, roughly 13 million people at the beginning of the 21st century.[2] Pashtuns have traditionally ruled Afghanistan. Some elements of Afghan identity have been Pashtun characteristics that have been laid over the entire country. Pashtuns live primarily in the east and south, with substantial pockets in the north and west. A larger Pashtun population exists across the border in Pakistan, partitioned by the 1893 Durand Line. Pashtuns speak Pashto, one of Afghanistan's two national languages. The dialects of eastern Pashtuns are harsher than the southern dialects, and less influenced by Farsi. For example, *Pashtun* is *Pakhtun* in an eastern dialect. *Mooj* (we) is *mung*. *Sheh* (good) is *kheh*. Eastern Pashtuns insist that their *Pakhto* is the "real" *Pashto*.

The second-largest ethnic group is the Tajiks. They make up about 30 percent of the population and live primarily in the north and east of the country. Much of the population of Kabul has long been Tajik. They speak Dari, a dialect of Farsi, the other of Afghanistan's two national languages and the preferred one for official government business. Before 1978, Tajiks served the state as bureaucrats and soldiers but never held the political power of the Pashtuns. A Tajik had ruled Afghanistan only once, during the nine-month reign of Habibullah Kalakani in 1929. After 1978, Tajik prominence in the Soviet-Afghan War and ensuing civil war would enhance their political power. In 2009 and 2014, they would compete for the presidency.

After the Tajiks are the Hazaras. They are about 15 percent of the population, speak Dari, and, because of their East Asian features, are rumored to be descendants of the Mongols who invaded Afghanistan in the 1200s. They live primarily in the mountainous center of Afghanistan, though substantial communities formed in Kabul and Mazar-e-Sharif over the course of the 20th century. Unlike the Sunni Pashtuns and Tajiks, Hazaras follow Shi'a Islam. Over time, Hazaras have worked their way up in the cities from jobs as unskilled labor to the bureaucracy and are relatively educated. Pashtuns have sometimes discriminated against them because of their looks and devotion to Shi'ism.

The last of the large ethnic groups are the Uzbeks, about 10 percent of the population. They live in the north. They generally speak Dari but also have their own Uzbek language. Their community has ties to Central Asia, Russia, and Turkey.

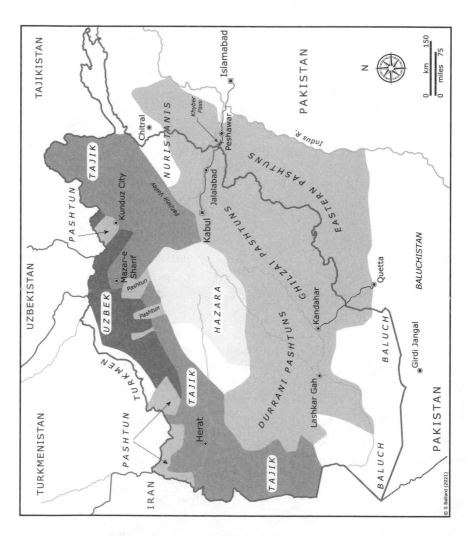

Map 2 Tribes and ethnic groups of Afghanistan

Outside these larger groups, Afghanistan is home to a variety of smaller ethnic groups, including Turkmen in the north, hardy Nuristanis in the high northeastern mountains, Pasha'i near Jalalabad, and Baluch in the south, who are another people with a large population in Pakistan, as well as in Iran. A few of the smaller ethnic groups, such as the Pasha'i and the Nuristanis, have at times had the solidarity to defend their interests. Others, such as the Baluch, have aligned themselves with larger groups for a political voice.

The country and people of Afghanistan have a long history that precedes the founding of the state in 1747 and includes three wars with Britain and one war with the Soviet Union. The communist revolution in 1978 and the subsequent Soviet intervention began 40 years of upheaval that affected politics, social structures, and culture. A basic understanding of Afghanistan's identity, culture, society, and history from the 18th to the late 20th century serves as a baseline for understanding those changes that Afghanistan would later experience. The following sections of this chapter go through that past, covering Afghan identity, tribal system, religious system, women's rights, economic development, relations with Pakistan, and finally the war with the Soviet Union.

The British spent nearly a century trying to control Afghanistan. Their efforts looked like one misadventure after another. Their first attempt to conquer the country was in 1839. It was a disaster. Only one man survived the retreat from Kabul. They tried again in 1879; things went not quite so bad. Their soldiers lost a major battle, the legendary Battle of Maiwand in 1880, but got out before there could be any catastrophic rout. Britain gave up on interfering in Afghan affairs in 1919 when Afghanistan attacked their forces—weary from the First World War—on the frontier.

In its century in Afghan affairs, Britain's one stroke of genius was allying with Emir Abdur Rahman Khan. Confronting mass resistance to its second invasion of Afghanistan, Britain scuttled plans to occupy and instead handed the country over to an adversary, the warlike Abdur Rahman, on the one condition that he run his foreign policy according to British interests. They funded his army and let him rule Afghanistan as he liked. For nearly 40 years, Britain was thus able to prevent Afghanistan from aligning with Russia or Germany.

The "Iron Emir," as he is sometimes known, created the modern Afghan state. He ushered in decades of stability. He reunited the country after years of civil war, crushing revolts and conquering autonomous regions and tribes. He established a centralized state structure and bureaucracy and a powerful army based on professional soldiers rather than tribal levies. He raised taxes, dug canals, and built roads and schools. In the words of Professor Barfield, "Abdur Rahman is justly credited with laying the foundation for a modern national state through his establishment of a highly centralized government. . . . Abdur Rahman's reign is seen as the beginning of Afghanistan as a nation-state."[3]

For Westerners, Abdur Rahman can seem like the quintessential state-builder. For Afghans during and after his reign, the Iron Emir was loathsome, guilty of taking money from the British and agreeing in 1893 to the Durand Line that recognized Peshawar, Quetta, and other eastern territory once under Kabul as part of British India. Ghazi Amanullah Khan, Abdur Rahman's grandson, who attacked British India in 1919, was, in contrast, praised. Amanullah had been a military failure. His forces were defeated on the battlefield. But the act of resistance compelled Britain to recognize Afghan independence. The rest of Amanullah's reign was disappointing. He pressed for so many liberal reforms that he was thrown out of power. Compared to his grandfather, his accomplishments were few. Yet from 1919 onward it was his picture that adorned Kabul on Afghan independence day and it was on his name that hung the title *ghazi*, warrior of Islam. As Professor Abdul Karim Talib Rahimi, a well-known Afghan scholar, notes, "The national history praises the heroes who have struggled to defend their father's soil . . . , such as Ghazi Akbar Khan, Ghazi Ayub Khan, and . . . Ghazi Amanullah Khan. . . . [E]veryone who is Afghan remembers the name of Amanullah . . . with shining stars of pride."[4]

Through the centuries, fighting invaders became part of what it meant to be Afghan. As Afghan historian M. Hasan Kakar wrote in 1993, "Afghans have a name for resisting invaders and protecting their freedom and independence."[5] Westerners tend to think of this reputation in terms of Afghanistan's victories over the British and Russians. For Afghans, the history went back to Alexander the Great and Genghis Khan, thence to revolts against the Mughals and toppling of the Safavid Empire, and only recently to the British and Russians. All were sources of identity.[6]

The Afghan state in many ways began with Pir Roshan and Khwashallah Khan Khattak, warrior-scholars who revolted against the Mughals in the 1500s and 1600s. They led long guerrilla campaigns across modern-day eastern Afghanistan and western Pakistan. Roshan supposedly created modern Pashto script. Khwashallah Khan is a beloved poet. Abdur Rahman Baba (born in approximately 1650), even more revered, wrote poems against the oppression of the Mughal emperors. The history of resistance reached new heights with the overthrow of the Safavid Persian Empire. Mir Wais Hotak, often given the title *Nika*, grandfather, freed Kandahar from the Safavids in 1709, defeating a Georgian governor (Georgi Khan) who had converted to Islam from Christianity, which made no difference to the Afghans. Mir Wais never built a state but he defeated an infidel. The famous poem *Hotaknama*, by Abdul Ghaffar, describes the overthrow of Georgi Khan:

> It was 700 men
> Such who were
> On their way to the shaykh
> Equal to the infidels
> To the next day, they fought
> They captured the place of the infidels
> The guns were cracking
> They awoke from their sleep
> Others the bright swords flashed
> The Hotaks filled the foreigners with war
> Heavy night that they fought
> The same Afghans rose to honor

Mir Wais's son then knocked over the faltering Safavid Empire in 1722 by capturing Isfahan, the empire's capital.

Mir Wais and his kin ruled briefly and never united Afghanistan. It would be Ahmed Shah Durrani who would actually found the state of Afghanistan. He ruled from 1747 to 1773 and is one of the few national heroes who fits the Western definition of a great leader. For Afghans, his greatness is framed by his independence from foreigners. He had no relations with the West, built an empire, lifted the Pashtun people into rule, and raided into northern India, which he cast as holy wars (jihads). Afghan history praises Ahmed Shah for leaving the Muslim Mughal emperor in place, winning battles against Hindus, and fighting the Sikhs.[7] Shortly before his death, he wrote a letter to his son and future successor, Timor Shah, on the virtues of kingship. In it, he advised, "To foreigners, never give any rights and way. If you give a little rights or way or turn, it is as if you have opened a way with your own hand for the destruction of the people."[8]

The wars against the British built upon the Afghan story of resistance, as would the war against the Soviets. Afghanistan never became a colony of a Western power. Maiwand, where Afghans defeated the British in 1880, became a symbol that appeared in daily speech and writing. One of Afghan history's few heroines is Maulali, who rallied the wavering Afghans at that battle. "We are a very proud people," reported an Afghan senior government official; "None of the surrounding countries can claim to never [have] been colonized or ruled by other nations in modern history. It is a wonderful point of satisfaction by all Afghans and a unifying force."[9]

Resistance was not a nationalist narrative limited to warriors or rabble-rousing politicians or extremist mullahs. Poets, scholars, bureaucrats, wives, and doctors shared it. At the end of the 20th century, Abdul Bari Jehani, Afghanistan's most famous contemporary poet, longed for the return of Afghanistan's martial accomplishments in his well-known poem, *Zma Kandahara*:

Once more we raise the shining sword
Come again, our legends, to our speech
Our Maulali and like to our speech
The stories of Maiwand to our speech
Part the gun, part the Jirga to our speech
We bring torches to the country's night
We bring lights to the dark cities.[10]

As resistance to occupation was a powerful part of what it meant to be Afghan through the 18th to the 20th centuries, so was Islam. Afghans prided themselves on their piety. Most Afghans scrupulously prayed five times per day, dutifully fasted during Ramadan (which they pronounced "*Ramadzan*"), and wanted to visit Mecca once in their life on *hajj*. In his letter on kingship, Ahmed Shah told his son, Timor Shah, to place Islam above all else: "For you, it is religious duty that your profit is drawn under the doctrines of religion. The first position will be specifically for religion. In front of your political business, have religious duty under your eyes, or in that expression that it is essential for you, for all your subjects, to become a good leader in religion and piety."[11]

The Koran offers certain values evident in Afghan identity and Afghanistan's struggles throughout the 18th to the 20th centuries. Two warrant discussion here.

First is oneness, or unity. There is one God and everyone should be united behind him. This truth stood over any other divisions, whether political or tribal, and gave Islam great power to rally people. In contrast, the Koran considers civil war, or *fitna*, highly destructive, one of the worst evils to befall a people. In the words of one former governor, "The Koran is about a social system. . . . Afghans believe that religion . . . is to keep the peace. War only protects peace. It cannot bring peace."[12] Through unity and oneness, Islam often provided Arab and Afghan leaders with a framework to overcome tribal divisions and internal conflict in society. The Prophet Mohammed and his followers succeeded by uniting against their superior yet fractious tribal opponents. Over 500 years ago, the famous Arab historian Mohammed ibn Khaldun noted how religious leaders, able to call on God's authority, were often more successful than tribal leaders in forming large movements.[13]

Second is the concept of *jihad*—holy war against nonbelievers (infidels) or a struggle to support Islam. Waging *jihad* against infidels is a theme in the Koran and the Hadith. For Westerners, the word *jihad* tends to be synonymous with terrorism. In Afghanistan, jihad against outside states and invaders could defend Islam and the Afghan way of life. It was not necessarily extreme. Indeed, several verses from the Koran guided believers to fight infidels. Tradition established that those who die in jihad were martyrs (*shahid*). Over centuries of war, Islamic religious scholars generally viewed jihad in defense against an infidel invasion as an individual duty for each and every Muslim.[14] It was a means of defense against the oppression of the outside and part of the Afghan people's endurance against empire after empire.

Afghanistan's history of resisting invasion and devotion to Islam has broad implications. It partly defined what it meant to be Afghan. Throughout Afghanistan's modern history, it helped bring Afghans together, transcending but not supplanting tribe or ethnicity.

From the beginning of the 18th to the end of the 20th century, tribes had much to do with politics and society in Afghanistan. Many of their features endured during the American war in Afghanistan and are likely to continue to do so in the future. Yet a variety of fluctuations occurred. Like identity, the tribal system is persistent but not constant, changing with time, which is why in this section we discuss the pre-war baseline before moving on to the chapters about the Taliban and the American war in Afghanistan.

During that period, for Pashtuns in particular, tribe was a natural source of pride, morale, and cohesion. Unlike Islam and resistance to invasion, however, tribe was not a source of cohesion across all Afghans. To the contrary, it was a source of disunity. Individual Afghans had some connection to their own tribe and community, rather than a common whole. The tribal system was naturally divided. Absence of hierarchy and an emphasis on revenge meant tribes were almost always at odds with each other.

Tribes pertained mainly to the Pashtuns and a few smaller ethnic groups, such as the Baluch and Nuristani. The Tajiks loosely identified themselves around communities—Herat, Mazar-e-Sharif, Badakhshan, Panjshir, Parwan, Kabul—and specific leaders rather than tribes. No hierarchy existed between the leaders. Hazaras were similar, with a stronger group feeling and stronger hierarchy within families in the villages. Due to their prevalence in the cities, a large number of Tajiks and Hazaras acted as individuals.[15]

Dozens of Pashtun tribes lived in Afghanistan. Pashtun tribes were known to be more divided—or, to use an anthropological term, "segmented"—than tribes in Arabia or Africa. A tribe is theoretically based on kinship, although there are plenty of exceptions to this rule. Pashtun tribes usually concentrated in clusters of villages across a few provinces and districts. Only a handful of tribes occupied a single block of territory. Most were a cluster of villages in one district and a cluster of villages in another district or province. Certain tribes had communities flung across the country. Consequently, tribes were fairly mixed together. A few districts but no provinces were dominated by one tribe. Many tribes also had expansive nomadic branches that migrated yearly with their flocks between provinces or between Afghanistan and Pakistan, India, or Iran.[16]

Pashtuns of Afghanistan could be parsed into three large Pashtun tribal groups: the eastern Pashtuns, Ghilzai, and Durrani. The eastern Pashtuns included the Zadran, Mangal, Wazir, and Mehsud tribes, their territory in a mountainous part of the east known as Loya Paktiya (the provinces of Paktiya, Khost, and Paktika) where tribal customs superseded the power of the state. The Mohmand, Shinwari, and Safi of Jalalabad and Kunar were often considered eastern Pashtuns as well, even though they had their own separate tribal lineages and dialect from the Loya Paktiya tribes.

The Ghilzai tribes spread from Kandahar to Kabul. They included the Hotak, Kharoti, Andar, Stanekzai, and Ahmedzai. Other tribes such as the Kakar were closely associated. Under Mir Wais, it was the Ghilzai that defeated the Iranian Safavid Empire. The Durranis later displaced them. The two confederations had a centuries-old rivalry. Of the Pashtuns, the Ghilzai tended to be viewed as the underdog. Large sections of Ghilzai tribes were nomads. During the 19th century, they manned much of the military and were at the forefront of resistance to the British while political spoils went to the Durranis. The Ghilzai finally rose to leadership in the late 20th century. Four successive communist presidents were Ghilzai. The last, Najibullah from the Ahmedzai, ruled from 1986 to 1992 and had the best reputation. Ghilzai tribes would also be leaders in the Taliban. Mullah Omar was a Hotak. And when it became a democracy, Afghanistan would elect Ashraf Ghani, another Ahmedzai, president in 2014.

The Durrani confederation included the great tribes of the south and west: the Barakzai, Achekzai, Alikozai, Noorzai, Ishaqzai, Alizai, and Popalzai. The Durrani were the aristocracy of Afghanistan. After 1747, much of the fertile land along the rivers in Helmand and Kandahar fell under their control, as did Kandahar City. Ahmed Shah Durrani, founder of the modern Afghan state, was a Popalzai. Durrani tribes ruled until 1978. As with all the tribal groups, the Durrani were hardly united. They competed with each other, and within each tribe. Indeed, it is important to remember that these tribal groupings—eastern Pashtun, Ghilzai, and Durrani—rarely acted as one or had a leader or any kind of ruling council. The individual tribes, how they worked, and how they were structured mattered much more than the larger groupings.

Tribal structure at that time in Afghanistan is simplest to explain from the bottom up. Villages were generally dominated by one tribe but contained laborers, shop-owners, and mullahs from others. Generally speaking, every village had a set of elders. An elder's standard duties were to resolve disputes within his family and village, win goods and services from the government, protect the community, and find as many jobs for villagers as possible. To varying degrees, depending on location, decisions for the village as a whole were made by the elders in council (called a *jirga* or *shura*). In the eastern provinces, consensus within the council was required. In the south (and in certain cases in the east), a single elder often was accepted as leader of a village. Even in this case, he was expected to consult with a council. Such an elder may have been the son of the last elder; or he may have been the most qualified man for the job.

A particularly powerful village elder influenced several villages or entire districts. Such a leader was known as *khan* or *qawmi misher* (tribal leader). I will refer to them as tribal leaders in order to distinguish these more powerful players from the average village elder. In the south, tribal leaders (khans) owned great tracts of land and large retinues of village elders heeded their guidance. At times, tribal leaders loosely coordinated to make decisions but as often acted independently. Each tribe had several tribal leaders. Decisions for the tribe as a whole were expected to be made in a shura with all the tribal leaders, if not with all the village elders. Rarely did a single tribal leader lead the entire tribe. Even fewer tribal leaders succeeded in having influence beyond their tribe, let alone reach across the people of a province. Tribal divisions were too strong.

Deeply rooted in the tribal system was Pashtunwali, the code of the Pashtuns. Much has been written about Pashtunwali and its customs, often more romantic than true. Pashtuns did not follow it as law. But it did guide what many elders and tribal leaders saw as obligations and responsibilities. Honor mattered to them, defined in terms of martial prowess, owning land, protecting one's family, confining the women of the family, giving to the community, offering hospitality, and being subservient to no man. The last point helps explain why shuras (or jirgas) were so important for decision-making. They placed men on equal public footing, even if the whole body knew which leader was really in charge.

Pashtunwali is most famous for the custom that a Pashtun must exact vengeance (*badal*) against his rivals. The emphasis on revenge easily turned slights into long-running feuds. For young men, a feud was a way of proving oneself. The greater the enemy, the greater the honor. Pashtuns often felt honor-bound to continue the feud until they received a sign of apology or outside mediation. The custom of revenge was one reason why dispute resolution through courts, tribal leaders, and religious leaders played such a large role in Afghan society.[17] It was also a reason why the tribes were so divided. Revenge creates enemies. Moreover, the danger of sparking a feud deterred tribal leaders from trying to enforce unity. A powerful tribal leader would restrain his own authority out of fear of inadvertently insulting another family and setting off an intractable feud.

Afghan rulers depended on the tribes to maintain order in the countryside. Without their cooperation, the state was often too weak to do so on its own. Afghan rulers artfully used carrots and sticks to keep tribal leaders in line: granting them authority over the affairs of their territory, offering goods and services, and sometimes taxing them. The tribes themselves viewed the state as another powerful actor—somewhat like another very powerful tribe—rather than an authority that deserved their allegiance. The government could be a source of patronage or punishment. From the tribal perspective, aligning against the state was not treacherous if it was necessary. Whatever was in the interest of the tribe was right: Pashtun realpolitik.

Another powerful group within society from 1747 onward were the religious leaders (also known as the *ulema*). More so than the tribes, the Taliban regime and the American war in Afghanistan would change aspects of their role in society. Again, the time before the civil wars that began in 1978 is our starting block so we can understand the changes to come in the later chapters. The religious system differed from the tribal system. It was not defined by territory or tribal hierarchy. The influence of religious leaders cut across tribes and regions. A Pashtun or Tajik religious leader had greater trouble influencing other ethnicities but it was not uncommon.

A *mullah* was the village religious leader. Every village had a mullah, independent from the elders and the khans.[18] Mullahs usually worked in a village far from their home, with a tribe other than their own. Education could amount to a few years of schooling in a madrasa, though often not. A mullah was chiefly to lead prayers, offer primary lessons to village children, and occasionally resolve local disputes. A village paid a mullah through donations, known as *zakat*, one of the five pillars of Islam. *Zakat* was usually 10 percent of the harvest.

Certain religious leaders carried the title *maulawi*, or religious scholar. They had years of formal education in addition to 12 years of primary and secondary education. Many religious scholars ran their own madrasas (religious schools), where they taught both children and young men seeking to become mullahs. Because of their education, religious scholars were highly regarded as authorities on Islam.

Scholars taught young men seeking to become mullahs how to speak, read, and write Arabic and about Islamic law (sharia). Derived from the Koran and the sayings of the Prophet Mohammed (Hadith), Islamic law deals with both criminal and civil issues, including punishments, marriage, divorce, and people's basic rights. Scholars taught about Islamic law so their students understood how to offer moral advice and deal with disputes brought to their door. Religious scholars could become judges (*qazi*), administering Islamic law. It was a powerful source of authority. The 1964 constitution recognized Islamic law as one source of law, alongside a secular legal code and customary (tribal) law.

Sufism also touched Afghanistan. Sufism is a mystical way of practicing Islam that stresses a personal connection with God, often through dreams. It could be more tolerant of music, dancing, and other activities that stricter forms of Islam prohibit. Religious leaders known as *pirs* taught Sufism and had followings of disciples. Shrines for *pirs* and other religious leaders were common and well-respected in Afghanistan. For the sake of simplicity, I do not delve into Sufism and treat *pirs* as another type of religious leader.

While status, lineage, money, weapons, and political power helped a tribesmen become an elder or tribal leader, such attributes were unnecessary for a man to become a religious leader. Any man could work under a mullah or study at a madrasa. Many mullahs came from poorer tribes. Consequently, religious leaders had a relationship with the poor and aggrieved.

Religious leaders in the various provinces and districts of Afghanistan lacked a formal governing structure but met regularly to discuss issues and Islam. Ties between them crossed tribal boundaries and districts and provinces. The ties could be based on family—many mullahs' brothers and fathers were also mullahs—or a common teacher or common view of Islam. Through them, religious leaders could spread their influence in ways tribal leaders could not. They had a unique ability to rally people behind a cause. In fact, given their sheer numbers, they could rival the government's ability to reach the people.[19]

Religious leaders united together to a greater degree than tribal leaders and the state, partly because of Islam's emphasis on unity and oneness, partly because madrasas taught common lessons on the Koran and the Hadith, and partly because religious norms called for a greater subservience among religious leaders than between tribesmen.[20] While tribesmen theoretically bowed to no man, religious students often swore obedience to their mentors. Known as the *bayt*, this oath is significant. A religious student or leader pledged to obey the guidance of his mentor. Mullah Abdul Salam Zaeef, one of the first members of the Taliban and later their ambassador to Pakistan, writes in his book, "Taliban students . . . respect their own mentors like a son respects his own father."[21] Though not always followed, the ideal of obedience reinforced the networks of a single religious leader, especially a scholar in a madrasa or well-known *pir*. A renowned teacher could have scores of students, many of whom would acquire their own students. All would bear some allegiance to the renowned teacher.[22]

The religious leaders' duties and learning granted authority independent from the tribal system or the state. Madrasas provided a role in education. The religious leaders' ability to interpret Islamic law provided a role in justice and as judges. Neither the state nor tribal leaders could revoke the roles of religious leaders without delegitimizing themselves. Indeed, a religious leader could threaten a ruler or tribal leader by questioning his dedication to Islam or issuing an edict (fatwa) that challenged his policies. They could also create momentum for a cause, such as a holy war (jihad), that a king or tribal leader would be compelled to support in order to protect his religious credentials. Religious leaders called forth and legitimized the jihads against Britain in 1840, 1880, 1896, and 1919, against the Soviet Union in 1980, and over and over again against Afghan rulers themselves.

Unsurprisingly, relations between rulers and religious leaders were often adversarial. Rulers wanted to minimize sources of opposition. Religious leaders did not want to surrender their authority over religion to the state. They generally distanced themselves from the state, lest they appear to be its tool.[23] Kings and presidents, parliamentarians and governors, tried to pay off religious leaders with varying degrees of success. In an attempt to ensure their blessings, rulers often put religious leaders on the state payroll or gave them official positions.[24] Rulers sometimes imprisoned religious leaders in order to cut them off from the people. Such action, however, risked turning the imprisoned religious leader into a hero or inciting revolt in the countryside. Religious leaders and the state, each with their own source of power, coexisted in a state of tension with each other.

Centuries of Afghan history highlight the deep roots of Islam, resistance to invasion, and tribalism in Afghanistan. These deep roots suggest a significance that might otherwise be missed. Again and again, resistance to invasion, Islam, and tribalism played a central role in war. They help explain cohesion, morale, and self-sacrifice—foundations of military effectiveness.

Women rarely appear in Afghan history. When they do, it is often as paragons of warrior spirit, Pashtunwali, and resistance to foreigners. Zarghona Ana, the mother of Ahmed Shah Durrani, is known for advising the great king on how to be a strong Pashtun leader. She is rumored to have said, "Victory and defeat are medals in hand. But let 'Ahmed' die and not bring back defeat."[25] Maulali symbolized the same spirit. Legend has it she rallied the faltering Afghans at the Battle of Maiwand with the fabled words, "If you return alive from Maiwand, I pray that God may keep you alive to taste disgrace."[26] At that moment, the tide turned and the British broke in rout. Maulali herself was one of the fallen.[27]

Glorious stories aside, women have been treated poorly in Afghanistan, even toward the end of the 20th century. Although reforms wedged out some basic rights, the vast majority of women still had little if any freedom. Islamic countries have been known for inhibiting women's rights. Afghanistan was especially conservative.

In the countryside, traditional customs denied freedom. Women rarely worked outside the home and received scant education. As the education system developed in the 20th century, girls could go to primary school, where available, usually segregated from the boys. Further education was unlikely. In Pashtun areas, the stress on tribal honor forced women to be covered, usually in powder blue head-to-toe burkas, and banned from travel without a male escort. In openminded villages, women could move between homes or work in the fields. Nomad women lived differently—without a burka and working outdoors—a function of their daily hardship. Women were usually married young and became part of the male household for life. Within the home, women sometimes supervised the household and enforced honor. Stories of Pashtun khans abiding the counsel of their wives and mothers are common. Pashtun poetry is filled with lines of women imploring men to fight, such as "Brotherless, I am certainly not. If you won't defend my honor then my brother will."[28] Few taunts were said to have greater power than "coward" from the lips of a woman. These stories should not be exaggerated. However many women had such influence, more had no say whatsoever and had to abide by what their husbands or fathers wanted.

In the cities, women enjoyed greater freedom by the latter half of the 20th century. It was there that reforms had taken place, especially in Kabul. Dress was less restrictive. Scarves and veils were acceptable. For education, secondary school and even college was possible. Women could hold jobs, especially in the government, though there was no upward mobility to speak of. Society shunned outspoken women. The most successful had to endure scorn and ridicule, including from their own families.

Relative to India, Pakistan, and its other neighbors, Afghanistan never modernized. At the end of the 1970s, on the eve of the wars that would engulf Afghanistan for 40 years, a third of Afghanistan's roughly 16 million people lived in the main river valleys and a handful of cities. The rest scratched out a living along the desert edge or rugged mountain valleys.[29]

The capital of Kabul then numbered 1.2 million people.[30] Its slightly off-center location placed it as the hub between Afghanistan's different regions and the dividing point between the Pashtun, Tajik, and Hazara populations. Kabul was a mixing bowl. All of Afghanistan's peoples were there. The city belonged to no group. Nor could any other city match its paved avenues, expansive neighborhoods, and all manner of businesses. As the center of government and the economy, a more liberal lifestyle prevailed than in the rest of the country, with greater education and rights for women. Suits, jeans, and unveiled faces mingled with turbans, pakols, and burkas. Kabul University thrived. If Afghanistan had a middle class, it was in Kabul. In later years, as war brought in influxes of people from the countryside, Afghans who had lived in Kabul before the end of the 1970s and the wars that followed would proudly called themselves *aslahee Kabuli*, real Kabulis.

Most Afghans lived outside Kabul or the other cities in mud villages in the countryside without sewage or running water. Pavement was limited to the major cities, the main ring road that arced from Herat to Kandahar to Kabul to Mazar-e-Sharif, and the five roads into Pakistan, Iran, and the Soviet Union. There were no railways. Electricity was intermittent in the cities and usually nonexistent in the countryside. A few dams produced hydroelectric power for a few of the cities. The countryside had to resort to diesel generators. Afghanistan's natural resources were undeveloped. Copper, iron, aluminum, uranium, and marble deposits, as well as natural gas in the north, were largely untouched. Besides Soviet investment in natural gas extraction, serious mining was barely attempted. Otherwise, Afghanistan had a few precious stones (the light blue lapis lazuli), a small marble industry, stocks of timber in the eastern mountains, and water.

Afghanistan's main economic activity was agriculture. The snowmelt-fed rivers irrigated stretches of farmland. Dam and canal projects in the 20th century expanded and improved irrigation so that new areas could be farmed. Throughout the 20th century, Afghanistan's agricultural products primarily went to its internal market. Afghanistan produced enough food to feed itself but distances and primitive conditions ruined perishables. Without railways, paved roads, and refrigeration, Afghans could not export their fruits and vegetables to the international market.

In addition to agriculture, Afghanistan's economy benefited from commerce. Afghanistan was a crossroads for trade passing back and forth between Europe and the Middle East and South and East Asia. Jalalabad, Kandahar, Mazar-e-Sharif, and Herat were all waypoints. The government, tribes, and other petty rulers historically taxed trade as a means of income.

Afghanistan had one other product relevant to its economy. Poppy. During most of the 20th century, illicit trade of poppy was the equivalent of roughly 10 percent of the total value of Afghanistan's licit imports. After 1979 and the Soviet invasion, poppy would become a major source of income for farmers, power brokers, the Taliban, and the government. Poppy is ideal for Afghanistan because it needs little water and the yield neither spoils nor damages on long trips across deserts and mountains.[31]

Pakistan, Afghanistan's eastern neighbor, was created out of the partition of British India in 1947. With mountainous tribal regions immediately lining an unmarked border, common Pashtun ties, and economic links, the country had major influence over Afghanistan.

The histories of the two countries were deeply intertwined. Opposite Jalalabad through the famous Khyber Pass, en route to the Pakistani capital of Islamabad, Ahmed Shah's successors had once wintered in Peshawar, Pakistan's Pashtun city, on the main road to India. During the late 20th century, "sandstone walls" and "crumbling gates" surrounded by craggy hills hinted at its history as the forward base of the British empire.[32] To its southwest, near the border with Khost, the town of Miram Shah and the lawless hills of North and South Waziristan were the sites of countless British adventures against the Waziri and Mehsud tribes. Drifting south through the hills to the desert in Baluchistan,

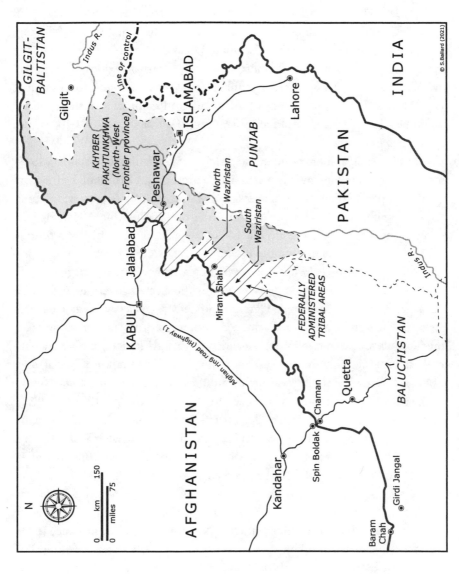

Map 3 Pakistan and the Afghan border

on the road to Kandahar, Quetta was a garrison town of low buildings and ordered streets, the location of the Pakistan military staff college.[33] Sheila Paine, a
British archaeologist, writes about the Quetta of 1991: "Quetta was a rootless,
shiftless place built on an unstable earthquake fault. In a haze of acrid exhaust
smoke and roads eddied with donkey carts, goats, men, auto rickshaws . . . aid
workers and refugees mingled in a temporary homeless restlessness, a medley of
faces . . . Afghan, Asian . . . Indian—all men, all capped, turbaned, scarfed."[34] Small
towns filled with smugglers, nomads, and refugees dotted the border: Chaman,
Girdi Jangal, Baram Chah. Further inland, outside the tribal regions, the massive
city of Karachi, which numbered 5.4 million in 1981 (quadrupling to 21 million
by 2011) was home to hundreds of thousands of Pashtuns.[35] All these places
would be where Afghans would form communities from 1978 to 2020, as war
engulfed their homes.

Pakistan was a far more populous and richer state than Afghanistan. Its 1947
population of 34 million people multiplied to more than 140 million by the turn
of the century, six times larger than Afghanistan's.[36] Pakistan's professional and
volunteer military was some 400,000 strong in the 1970s (the Afghan armed
forces at this time numbered around 100,000).[37] The military played a central
role in the state and in uniting the nation against external threat. From its independence in 1947, Pakistan was ostensibly a democracy, but beginning in
the 1958 the military staged coups whenever the elected government did not
meet their liking. They controlled foreign and defense policy even when elected
governments were in power, such that Pakistan was a democracy in name only.
The generals' outsized role inflated security threats. As military men, they naturally thought military threats were more important than political, social, and
economic issues. The result was a highly militarized set of national objectives.

The tribal regions, known as the Federally Administered Tribal Areas (FATA)
on the northeastern border with Afghanistan were semi-autonomous. They included the regions of North and South Waziristan and the Khyber Pass and were
largely Pashtun. The region was ruled directly by the federal government under
a set of laws created by the British, known as the frontier crimes regulations
(the system would end in 2018). The government allowed the tribes and local
peoples to manage their own business and kept order through punitive action
when necessary. The tribal regions buffered North-West Frontier province (later
renamed Khyber Pakhtunkhwa) from Afghanistan. Also largely Pashtun, the
North-West Frontier province was an official province with its own governor,
provincial assembly, and high court. Peshawar was the capital of the province.

From its creation, Pakistan maintained a unique interest in Afghanistan.
Pakistan's rival was India. The two countries fought three wars against each other
and skirmished in the disputed territory of Kashmir. India had the larger territory,
population, and military. Fewer than 100 kilometers stood between Islamabad

and Indian forces in Kashmir, a short drive for Indian tanks. These facts were overriding concerns for Pakistani leaders, who worried that Afghanistan might turn against them, leaving Pakistan surrounded and without any space to fall back—known as "strategic depth"—in the event of an Indian invasion. Nor did Pakistani leaders want the Soviet Union gaining influence in Afghanistan. The Soviet Union provided India with arms and supported India in the wars against Pakistan.

A related worry for Pakistan was Afghan nationalism. The creation of the Durand Line in 1893 had divided the Pashtun people between Afghanistan and Pakistan. Pashtun tribes in Afghanistan were strongly linked to those in Pakistan. Numerous tribes straddled the border, which was only clearly delineated at major crossing points, such as the Khyber Pass near Jalalabad and Chaman–Spin Boldak near Kandahar. Just about all Pashtun tribesmen viewed each other as part of a common shared culture and heritage. Afghans widely claimed that the tribal regions and Baluchistan, including the cities of Peshawar and Quetta in western Pakistan, were actually part of Afghanistan illegally divided out by the British.

The possibility that Pakistani Pashtuns might rebel and secede was a danger for Pakistan's leaders. The Afghan government in the 1950s called for uniting all Pashtuns under Afghanistan, a single "Pashtunistan." Such an action would have split the tribal regions from Pakistan and further narrowed Pakistan's strategic depth. For these reasons, Pakistani leaders paid careful attention to Afghanistan and the policies of its leaders.

In 1978, Afghanistan embarked on four decades of upheaval. That year, a communist coup overthrew the old Durrani dynastic government. The new communist government implemented a series of revolutionary reforms. The communists seized the land of tribal leaders, changed laws on marriage, and secularized education and the legal system. Tens of thousands of tribal leaders, religious leaders, and minority leaders were imprisoned or killed. Afghans, especially in the countryside, rejected the reforms. Uprisings prompted the Soviet Union to intervene at the end of 1979. The Soviets set up bases throughout the country and ultimately deployed 120,000 troops. The resistance, known as the mujahideen, launched guerrilla attacks on the Soviets, as well as on the communist government. The Soviets never had enough forces to suppress the mujahideen.

The Soviet-Afghan War lasted a decade. In Afghanistan, it was known to the mujahideen simply as the *jihad*. Religious leaders issued fatwas (edicts) blessing war against the Soviets as a religious duty. An estimated 150,000 Afghans, across all ethnic groups, fought as mujahideen. Afghan political parties exiled to Pakistan tried to lead the resistance. Famous ones were Jamiat Islami, led by the Tajik professor Burhanuddin Rabbani, and Hezb Islami, led by the Pashtun

Gulbuddin Hekmatyar. Powerful commanders emerged who would become central figures in Afghanistan for decades, such as Jalaluddin Haqqani, Ismael Khan, and Mohammed Atta. Most important was Ahmed Shah Massoud, the charismatic commander of the Tajiks of the Panjshir Valley, just north of Kabul. His forces were the best organized.

The United States viewed the war as an opportunity to wear down the Soviet Union. US interests in Afghanistan had previously been minimal. The United States had funded the damming of the Helmand and Arghandab Rivers and the digging of irrigation canals in Helmand and Kandahar in the 1950s and 1960s as a means of counterbalancing Soviet influence. Only one president had visited Afghanistan, President Dwight Eisenhower in 1959. When the Soviets invaded, President Jimmy Carter initiated a covert program to aid the mujahideen and sought to "make the Soviets see that this [aggression] was a major mistake."[38] After 1983, President Ronald Reagan dramatically ramped up aid. Director of Central Intelligence William Casey was convinced of the need to "make the Soviets bleed."[39] Administration officials thought a Soviet "Vietnam" in Afghanistan would be just retribution.

Afghanistan became a majoy policy initiative. Reagan's 1985 National Security Decision Directive instructed: "The two principal elements in our Afghanistan strategy are a program of covert action support to the Afghan resistance, and our diplomatic/political strategy to pressure the Soviet Union to withdraw its forces from Afghanistan and to increase international support for the Afghan resistance forces."[40] The United States provided limited training and $250 million to $300 million per year in funds and arms, including Stinger shoulder-launched surface-to-air missiles. Total US spending in Afghanistan in support of the mujahideen would top $1 billion.[41] The strategy naturally required the United States, in the language of the national security directive, to "maintain good working relations with Pakistan," in spite of the undemocratic military regime, because "in the absence of alternative routes of supply into Afghanistan, such relations are essential to the program."[42]

Along with the United States, Saudi Arabia, Pakistan, and other Arab and Western states supported the mujahideen with money and arms. Numerous refugee camps, madrasas, and training camps stood up in Pakistan. The Pakistan government, under General Zia al-Haq, funneled most of the assistance to the mujahideen, which served as its proxies in Afghanistan. The United States distributed its aid to the mujahideen via Pakistan. Consequently, Pakistan had tremendous say over the political and military fortunes of the different mujahideen.

Pakistan had started sheltering mujahideen political leaders in the mid-1970s, before the communist coup. Pakistani leaders, both civilian and military, saw Islam as a unifying force that could bring Afghanistan and Pakistan together and countervail Afghan nationalism. Zia al-Haq was a devout Muslim who hated communists and wanted Pakistan to embrace Islamic law. He viewed jihad in Afghanistan as a weapon against both the communists and Pashtun nationalism. He encouraged the funding of madrasas along the border where young Afghans could train to become mujahideen. Pakistani religious leaders and politicians from Pakistan's leading Islamist political party (Jamiat Islami) supported their Afghan counterparts.

Zia delegated support and supply of the mujahideen to the ISI (Inter-Services Intelligence), the military's intelligence branch. ISI officers dealt directly with the mujahideen and sometimes fought in Afghanistan. Many of these and other Pakistani officers had strong leanings toward Islamism and the idea that Islamic law should be the law of both Pakistan and Afghanistan. They felt a common bond with the mujahideen on the basis of religion and favored the harder line commanders, such as Gulbuddin Hekmatyar and Jalaluddin Haqqani. Other officers were Pashtuns and deeply committed to ensuring Afghanistan was run by Pashtuns who were pro-Pakistan.

The Soviet-Afghan War nurtured the insurgent small-unit organization and tactics that would underpin Taliban tactics in America's Afghan War. The basic mujahideen unit was a cadre of 10 to 50 men. They usually operated near their villages, although they often rested in the refugee camps in Pakistan. Their commander was usually from the local area. He could be a tribal leader, religious leader, or skilled fighter. The men shared tribal or community ties. Other units based on party loyalty, ethnic ties, or military professionalism existed but were the exception. Certain highly capable cadres were known to operate across districts and even provinces.

When the war started, cadres were armed with a smattering of old family-owned bolt-action rifles and new assault rifles captured from communist garrisons. As the war progressed, international support procured better weapons. Cadres were soon armed with Kalashnikov assault rifles, rocket-propelled-grenades (RPGs) and "PK" medium-machine guns. The mujahideen communicated over hand-held "ICOM" radios (walkie-talkies). This equipment allowed the lightly clad mujahideen to shoot up the slow-moving communist columns of trucks, tanks, and armored personnel carriers from a distance and escape before superior firepower could be brought to bear.

The mujahideen avoided seizing ground. They ambushed Soviet and communist units or raided their positions. At the edge of government control, sets of mujahideen cadres manned makeshift "front lines," where they would skirmish with Soviet and government soldiers from hidden positions in villages, irrigation ditches, and orchards. The mujahideen preferred to keep Soviet and government bases in the cities and towns beleaguered, in a state of constant harassment, than risk casualties by attempting an assault. Controlling the countryside was sufficient to keep the war going. Against a Soviet or communist offensive, they would fall back and abandon base areas if necessary. Upon this technological and tactical foundation, new innovations, such as improvised explosive devices (IEDs) and suicide car bombs, would be added over the next 30 years.[43]

The Soviet-Afghan War wrought dramatic social and economic change on Afghanistan. One million Afghans died. Another 4 million fled to Pakistan and Iran, where they lived in refugee camps. Certain districts in the Afghan countryside all but emptied of people. Education and medical care ground to a halt. A generation of Afghans had little chance at secondary education. For primary education, madrasas or schooling at a nearby mosque were often all that was possible. Agricultural production was disrupted. War stopped goods from getting to market. Canals and other infrastructure fell into disrepair. The social and economic effects of the war set the stage for decades of hardship.

During this time, in the absence of the state and with the disruption of traditional crops, poppy cultivation started to expand. Farmers planted poppy on large portions of Afghan farmland. At the same time, military commanders and tribal leaders developed networks to move or smuggle the product into Pakistan and Iran for either processing or onward shipment toward Russia and Europe. Poppy was turning into Afghanistan's major business, touching all levels of Afghan society.

The war upended the old balance between state, tribe, and religion. It tore down state structures painstakingly built over two centuries. Even with the Soviets present, the communist government became confined to the main roads and provincial capitals. In its place, tribal and religious leaders exerted greater power. These were not the old nobility or revered scholars. Within the tribes, established leaders were replaced by commanders who had gained their position through military prowess, guns, and money, later known as "warlords." Within the religious leaders, younger scholars, trained in Pakistani madrasas or militarized in the war, filled the role of older scholars who had fled or died. Religious leaders as a whole became more politically involved. Competition for power between mujahideen commanders and religious leaders would play out in the civil war and the Taliban regime.

In April 1988, Mikhail Gorbachev, leader of the Soviet Union, pulled the plug. Convinced the war was unwinnable, he withdrew all Soviet forces. The last Soviet soldiers crossed the Amu Darya on February 15, 1989. Gorbachev left Najibullah, the Afghan president, in place and continued to supply him with arms and money. Tough and energetic, Najibullah survived until the collapse of the Soviet Union in 1991, which severed Soviet money and guns. In April 1992, the communist regime fell and Ahmed Shah Massoud occupied Kabul.

American support for the mujahideen came to an end at the same time. It had dwindled after the Soviet withdrawal. It ceased altogether in September 1991 when the Soviet Union was on its last legs. The Cold War was over. President

George H.W. Bush wanted out. Congress generally opposed continued funding. Afghanistan was no longer of much importance to the United States.[44]

The end of the Cold War also contributed to a distancing in US-Pakistan relations. Because of Pakistan's nuclear weapons development, President Bush allowed the Pressler amendment to come into force in 1990, which cancelled delivery of F-16 fighters.[45] The cessation of aid to the mujahideen removed another basis for cooperation. Like Afghanistan, with the end of the Cold War, Pakistan became much less important for US foreign policy.

Afghan society was too broken after Najibullah for peace to emerge. The mujahideen may have won but they were deeply divided. The various ethnic groups and tribes were at odds. Without any common enemy, the different mujahideen parties turned on each other. A deeper civil war ensued: for many Afghans, it was the darkest chapter of their four decades of conflict, marked by widespread destruction and atrocities.

Kabul became a war zone, contested by the main mujahideen commanders. Massoud occupied the heart of the city and the strategic high ground. Hekmatyar occupied the southwestern Pashtun neighborhoods. Abdur Rashid Dostum, the ruthless Uzbek warlord, occupied the airport in the north. Hazaras occupied western neighborhoods. Fighting ravaged the city for four years. Indiscriminate rocket fire battered neighborhoods and killed as many as 25,000 civilians.[46] The only thing worse was the looting, killing, and rape that ruled the streets.

Meanwhile, the various mujahideen commanders fought out their own wars for control of provinces and regions. Certain provinces fell entirely to a single commander. Dostum controlled several Uzbek-dominated provinces in the north. Massoud controlled the northeastern block of Panjshir, Badakhshan, and Takhar. Hazaras controlled the central Hindu Kush. Ismael Khan, another powerful Tajik, controlled Herat. Other provinces were divided between warring commanders. Within their territory, commanders often taxed people or seized their land. Their militia and tribesmen were undisciplined. Certain groups were known to beat and even execute people. This was the environment that spawned the Taliban.

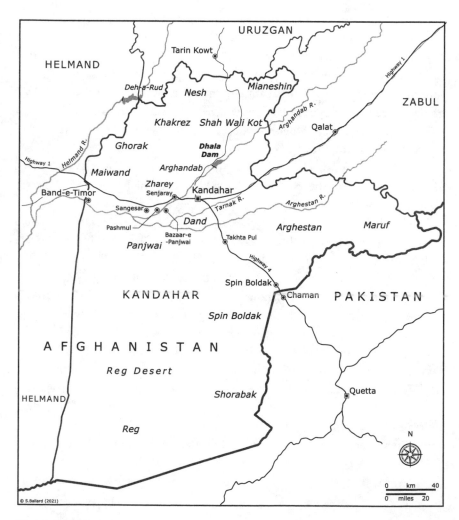

Map 4 Kandahar

‖ 3 ‖

The Taliban Emirate

Kandahar was the great city of the Pashtuns, a tan sprawl before the last low ridges of the Hindu Kush. Roads from Kabul, Uruzgan, Pakistan, and Iran met here. The city was a crossroads of commerce. Four archways marked ancient portes, facing each direction on the compass. Straight roads and dustier alleys neatly divided one-story mud buildings. Parks with dull *shin ghazi*—desert pine trees— dotted the city. At its heart, opposite the arched governor's palace, glistened the blue dome of the mosque of Ahmed Shah Durrani. The surrounding countryside was one of the most naturally fertile places in Afghanistan. Flat farmland and desert radiated south and west. Three thin rivers—the Arghandab, the Tarnak, and the Arghestan—irrigated a rich cropland, filled with wheat, grapes, melons, and pomegranates. The rivers converged well to the west of Kandahar City and flowed together into Helmand province.

Over the decades, Afghan rulers portioned Kandahar into 15 districts. The most fertile and populous were the three surrounding Kandahar City: Dand, Zharey-Panjwai, and Arghandab. The famous district of Maiwand, site of the great Afghan victory over the British in 1880, lay in the far west, adjacent to Helmand. Of strategic importance was Spin Boldak, on the border with Pakistan and the location of the main crossing point, where long caravans and convoys passed daily.

Kandahar's agricultural abundance, poppy, and concentration of political power fostered an easier lifestyle than elsewhere in the country. The average farmer led a harsh, calloused life but the tribal leaders might be called healthy, with weight on their bones from eating lamb. They wore baggy trousers and colorful loose-fitting blouses, tailored to be cool in the heat. The favored style of blouse was a "Kandahari chemise," collarless with an intricate embroidered pattern on the front. Older men wore turbans, younger men pillbox-shaped prayer caps sparkling with sequins. The vehicle of choice was a Toyota Land Cruiser, good for traversing the desert and smuggling poppy. Cheaper was the ubiquitous motorcycle. Year-round, they skipped along city streets and country dirt paths alike.

Kandahar is the birthplace of Afghanistan's modern rulers, starting with Mir Wais Nika and Ahmed Shah Durrani. And it is the birthplace of the Taliban. In the words of one esteemed religious scholar, "Kandahar is the father of Afghanistan. Peace starts here. War starts here. The Taliban started here."[1]

The Taliban rose to power during the mujahideen civil war that followed the Soviet withdrawal. Afghanistan was sliced up between warlords. In a few provinces, such as Panjshir under Ahmed Shah Massoud or Herat under Ismael Khan, a warlord enforced a degree of law and order. In others, disparate minor warlords vied for power in miniature versions of the larger civil war. Such was the case in Kandahar.[2] After the Soviets left, they controlled their tribal territory and clashed with each for power. Anarchy reigned. Their militias strung chains across the main roads to stop and tax passersby, so many chains that people could travel nowhere easily. Businessmen and smugglers lost a good deal of their earnings getting goods—including poppy—to market. In the worst cases, these militias murdered civilians and kidnapped boys and women and raped them.[3]

The founders of the Taliban were a group of religious leaders—mullahs and scholars—who had fought in the Soviet-Afghan War and were tied to each other through schooling, mentors, combat experience, and a shared view that Afghanistan should be ruled strictly according to Islam. Like most mullahs, they stood out. They preferred a black turban or plain prayer cap, and a simple blouse, in contrast to the Kandahari chemises or patterned turbans of the tribal leaders. They all had beards, frayed outward. Amid the excesses of the warlords, they looked authentic. Their network was densest in the countryside outside Kandahar City but extended to Helmand, Zabul, Uruzgan, Farah, and Ghazni. Many were from Ghilzai tribes, marginalized by the dominant southern tribal hierarchy.[4] These religious leaders were upset at the anarchy around them and compelled to act by the obligation in Islam to fight unjust oppression.[5]

For months, the religious leaders debated what to do in meetings in mosques in western Kandahar. In the first week of October 1994, they decided. Thirty-five gathered in Maiwand, west of Kandahar City, and issued a fatwa (edict) for a movement. Their goals were to: institute Islamic law, remove the warlords, form a single powerful and just government in accordance with the Koran, open the main road in Kandahar, implement social reforms and eliminate corruption, and restore the country's independence and territorial integrity.[6]

Abdul Salam Zaeef was an early member of the Taliban movement. He writes in his autobiography, *My Life with the Taliban*: "The *sharia* would be our guiding law and would be implemented by us. We would prosecute vice and foster virtue, and would stop those who were bleeding the land."[7] The participants of the meeting chose Maulawi Abdul Samad, a respected scholar, as overall leader and Mullah Mohammed Omar "Mujahed" as their military commander. Samad's leadership seems to have been titular. In all the histories, he is a minor figure whom Omar rapidly eclipses. He retired shortly after the movement formed.[8]

Abdul Salam Zaeef is one of our most important windows into the Taliban. The tall, broad man had been a mujahideen serving with other early Taliban against the Soviets and a religious student. His thoughtful face and thick black beard would become familiar to Americans in 2001 when as Taliban ambassador to Pakistan he held press conferences during the US invasion. The Pakistanis would eventually detain him and turn him over to the United States. The Americans incarcerated him in Guantanamo prison until 2005. After release from prison, Zaeef lived in Kabul, detached from the Taliban but a kind of unofficial ambassador, still in close contact with the movement's members. He wrote two books: *My Life with the Taliban*, an autobiography that was translated to English, and *Taliban: From Kandahar until Mazar*, a history of the Taliban movement in Pashto.

Mullah Mohammed Omar was a hard and pious man. At 35 years old, he had earned the sobriquet "Mujahed" from his time fighting the Soviets. He had been wounded several times. Shrapnel had taken an eye. His tribe was Hotak, the same as that of Mir Wais Nika, revered for driving the Iranians out of Afghanistan in 1709. Omar's father, a village mullah in Kandahar, had died when Omar was two and a half. Omar went to live with his uncle in the poor Deh-a-rud region of Uruzgan. One of his first teachers was a Sufi *pir*, a mystical religious leader. Those early teachings endowed Omar with a spiritual bent. He looked to his dreams for meaning and for the supernatural in events. The Soviet invasion drew him from religious studies to fight in Kandahar.[9] After the Soviets withdrew and the communist government fell, Omar retired to his mosque in the village of Sangesar, Maiwand district, and restarted life as a mullah.

It was the anarchy of the civil war that drove Omar to participate in the new movement. Legend has it that one day he came across the bodies of a carload of people that a militia had robbed, raped, murdered, and left on the side of the road (sacrilege in Islam). Omar decided he had to act.[10] Over the summer of 1994, he and a handful of loyal fighters helped Maulawi Pasanai, an Islamic scholar and judge, protect Sangesar.[11] Pasanai was admired for being foremost to rally the people of Kandahar to fight the communists in 1980. In a later radio broadcast, Mullah Omar recalled:

> We began visiting the students in the schools and the study circles. I . . . said to them: "The Religion of Allah is being stepped on. . . . The evil ones have taken control of the whole area; they steal the people's

money, they attack their honor on the main street, they kill people and put them against the rocks on the side of the road, and the cars pass by and see the dead body on the side of the road, and no one dares bury him in the earth." . . . We traveled . . . to the schools and study groups . . . until fifty-three People of the True Trust (in Allah) were ready. Then I returned to my school and said to them, "Come tomorrow morning," but they arrived at one a.m. . . . so this was the beginning.[12]

A mythology emerged around Mullah Omar, with stories of his Robin Hood–like exploits. One was that he and his men attacked a militia that had abducted and raped two young girls. Another is that they freed a boy whom two commanders were fighting over. These stories lifted his reputation—even if they have since proven apocryphal and go missing from Taliban writings and official histories.[13]

According to Wakil Ahmed Mutawakil, the future Taliban foreign minister, that first Taliban shura chose Mullah Omar as military commander because of his combat experience and his humility. Omar was tough. Original members of the Taliban often described him as "a simple man." A few went so far as to call him stupid, though in Afghanistan education does not mean much. Omar was said to be taciturn and willing to disregard detail and decree solutions to difficult problems.[14] Zaeef describes Omar's leadership style in his autobiography:

> He took a few moments to think after we had spoken, and then said nothing more for some time. This was one of Mullah Mohammed Omar's common habits, and he never changed this. He would listen to everybody with focus and respect for as long as they needed to talk, and never seek to cut them off. After he had listened, he then would answer with ordered, coherent thoughts.[15]

That Omar was from the tribe of Mir Wais added to his legitimacy.[16] Another dynamic was also at play. A few of the Taliban's founders misjudged Omar as so simple that he could serve as a temporary figurehead while a council of key founders controlled the real power.[17] The scheme would never transpire. After being selected as military commander, he acted to ensure the fighters answered to him. He brought together the handful of cadres in the movement and convinced their commanders to swear allegiance to him.[18] Soon after, his successes lifted him beyond the stature of any figurehead.

The structure of the movement was straightforward. Mullah Omar was the commander. A shura (council) of ten other key leaders worked beside him. Mullah Omar had authority over military appointments. The council had authority over civilian appointments, including governors and ministers, with Omar holding final approval.[19] Thus, early in the movement, Mullah Omar shared authority with other leaders. He used his authority rarely and deferred to the advice of the other leaders. Council meetings were often opened up to commanders and fighters. Ahmed Rashid, author of the most prominent history of the Taliban, witnessed early meetings: "On my early visits to Kandahar, I was impressed with the debates, which sometimes went on all night as commanders, mullahs, and ordinary fighters were called in to give their views, before Mullah Omar made a decision."[20] During this time, such a collaborative system succeeded because the infighting of the warlords impressed upon the movement's founders the need for common purpose.[21]

While the founders of the Taliban were experienced mujahideen, most of the foot soldiers had been children during the Soviet-Afghan War. In 1994, they were students at madrasas and mosques, often having grown up in refugee camps in Pakistan.[22] As word of the movement spread, they trickled into Afghanistan to join. Mullah Omar and other Taliban leaders used connections to fellow religious leaders in Pakistan to curry support. Madrasas encouraged their students to volunteer. Mullahs in refugee camps did the same thing. The Arabic and Pashto word for a religious student is "Talib" and the plural is "Taliban." Hence the name of the movement.

The Pakistan consulate in Kandahar under Major Pashtun Gul established relations with the new movement. Pakistan was having trouble getting caravans up to Herat. The militias were blocking and extorting the way. When one of their convoys was hijacked, Pakistan asked the Taliban for help. The Taliban freed the caravan. The action raised the Taliban's stock with the Pakistanis. Prime Minister Benazir Bhutto's civilian government and the military found common ground in backing the Taliban. Minister of interior, General Nazeerullah Babar, who answered to Bhutto, advocated for the Taliban while a group of Pashtun officers within the Pakistani army and ISI (Pakistani military intelligence) sympathized with the Taliban's Islamic goals. Bhutto, like the military, wanted a Pashtun ruling Afghanistan who would protect Pakistan's interests. No Pakistan government wanted an Afghan ruler to call for Pakistani Pashtuns to secede. Nor did any Pakistan government want an Afghan ruler to have good relations with their arch-rival, India. The Bhutto government especially opposed Ahmed Shah Massoud because he received some amount of support from India. In the conflict with Massoud, Pakistan's old Pashtun proxy, Gulbuddin Hekmatyar, leader of the Islamist group Hezb Islami, was falling short of expectations. The Taliban were an alternative.[23]

Existing documents and memoirs do not reveal how much Pakistan supported the Taliban with money, guns, and men during these early days. The Pakistani military treated the information as secret while the Taliban never wanted to appear dependent on a foreign power. Future Taliban foreign minister Mutawakil and various other Taliban founders later denied that Pakistan lifted the Taliban to power.[24] Indeed, Pakistan was unnecessary to the initial successes of 1994. At first, Pakistani generals and leaders doubted the movement's chances and hedged their bets. As the movement gained momentum, hedging fell aside. The consulate and a few Pakistani military officers started advising the Taliban. To boost recruiting, the ISI may have helped madrasa students travel to Kandahar. There are also indications that the ISI arranged for a group of several hundred former Afghan communist soldiers with technical skills who had been sheltering in Pakistan to serve the Taliban. Not until mid-1995, though, would Pakistan be providing the Taliban ample funds, ammunition, transport, supplies, and advisors.[25]

The Taliban captured Maiwand and the neighboring district of Zharey-Panjwai and began clearing the roads and instituting Islamic law. In Maiwand and Zharey-Panjwai, the Taliban's founders had the most influence. The Ishaqzai and Noorzai tribes dominated this area and Taliban founders knew the vast majority of the local leaders. Many had fought together against the Soviets. The traditional role of religious leaders within the community helped win over the villagers. From there, Mullah Omar, with a hundred or so Taliban, captured Spin Boldak, the all-important border crossing with Pakistan, along with the local militia's arms cache. Through that gate, thousands of refugees and madrasa students from Pakistan flocked to the movement.[26]

The Kandahar tribal leaders failed to unite against the Taliban. Tribal competition overrode common interest. Most passed the buck and did nothing. Several bandwagoned with the Taliban. Those who tried to balance were overwhelmed. Basher Khan, a Noorzai commander-smuggler, funded the Taliban from the beginning. In November, as the Taliban encircled Kandahar City, Mullah Naqib, the respected and powerful leader of the Alikozai tribe, aligned with them. With him, the Taliban were unstoppable. Gul Agha Sherzai, the Barakzai "governor" (in name only) of Kandahar, fled the city by its eastern gates for Pakistan.

The Kandahar warlords were minor, too divided by Pashtun tribalism to contend for power in Kabul. The great players in the civil war were in the north and west: Abdur Rashid Dostum, with his well-armed Uzbeks in the far north; Ismael Khan, the Tajik Jamiat Islami ruler of Herat; Gulbuddin Hekmatyar, with his Hezb Islami cadres of eastern Pashtuns, just south of Kabul; and Ahmed Shah Massoud, the renowned Jamiat Islami commander from the Panjshir, in the northeast and controlling most of Kabul. The Taliban would defeat them one by one, turning them against each other, just as they had defeated their Kandahar counterparts.

Immediately after capturing Kandahar in early November, Omar took over neighboring Helmand and Uruzgan. Within two months he moved against

Kabul. An official Taliban history tells how Mullah Omar came to this decision: "Mullah Mohammed Omar said to the Taliban that at night in his sleep he saw the Prophet Mohammed, may peace be upon him. He ordered Mullah Omar to consider the road to Kabul strategic and, for that reason, to move on Kabul."[27] Omar sent his fighters forward under Mullah Mohammed Rabbani and Mullah Bor Jan.

Fighting between Ahmed Shah Massoud and Gulbuddin Hekmatyar had torn Kabul apart. Hekmatyar, the fiery leader of Hezb Islami, considered himself the true ruler of Afghanistan because of his Pashtun ethnicity and Islamist background. Yet having fought the Soviets from Peshawar in Pakistan he had never won the support of the majority of Pashtuns. As the Taliban marched north through Zabul and Ghazni, religious leaders and former mujahideen rallied to their cause. This was the Ghilzai heartland and these tribes had as strong a tie to the Ghilzai-dominated Taliban leadership as they did to Hekmatyar. Hezb Islami cadres put up a fight but Hekmatyar, pinned between the Taliban and Massoud, decided he was outnumbered and fled to Pakistan and eventually Iran.

The Taliban now confronted Massoud at the gates of Kabul. Massoud had created a military machine. His 20,000 Tajik soldiers had extensive combat experience from their battles against the Soviets. Massoud had a group of capable subordinates who had grown up with him through the Soviet-Afghan War. The bulky Mohammed Fahim was his deputy and intelligence chief. He had worked with Massoud from the beginning and was close with the village leaders of Panjshir. Stories of his strongarm methods in Kabul colored his reputation. The leading frontline commander was the hard-working Bismullah Khan. He had been a member of the Parcham faction of the communist party until the Soviets invaded and he joined Massoud. In his mid-30s, he would frequently be Massoud's commander at the front line. On the political side were Yunis Qanooni, who had been injured in the leg, and the well-spoken and well-dressed Dr. Abdullah, an ophthalmologist who served as Massoud's advisor and emissary.

The Taliban would fight Massoud for seven years. That March of 1995, Massoud's forces, armed with tanks and artillery, smashed the first Taliban assault on Kabul, killing hundreds of Taliban. Mullah Omar's commanders fell back and a new battle line formed on the southern outskirts of the city.

Stalled in front of Kabul, Mullah Omar launched a second offensive westward from Kandahar against Ismael Khan in Herat. The offensive almost reached Herat but then Ismael Khan counterattacked in May. Heavy fighting cost the life of the experienced Taliban commander Mullah Mohammed Akhund. Ismael Khan got as far as Kandahar province. Panic struck Kandahar City. Omar hurriedly raised new cadres of fresh recruits. To lift morale, he walked among them, speaking with the fighters before they went out.[28] Abdul Hai Mutmain, future biographer of Mullah Omar, was a young cadre commander who raced to the front line in the bed of a packed Datsun pickup: "A black Isuzu was moving at great speed. It slowed upon seeing us. . . . A man stepped out. It was Mullah Mohammed Omar . . . *Tseera ee-ay roshana wa*. His face was shimmering. Traces of stress did not appear. Slowly, slowly Mullah Sahib spoke: 'I go. I must prepare other fighters and supplies. You all go too. We will ready ourselves rightly for battle tomorrow.' "[29]

Unfortunately for Ismael Khan, the other northern warlords turned against him. Massoud offered no assistance from Kabul while Dostum gifted the Taliban air strikes by his captured communist fighter jets. The Taliban defeated Ismael Khan in September 1995 and captured Herat. Together, the northern warlords would have had the numbers and resources to beat the Taliban, as Ismael Khan nearly did. Like the great powers facing Napoleon, the warlords competed with each other rather than ally together against a common enemy.

In these opening years of the movement, Mullah Omar won a reputation, in the words of the great Alizai tribal leader Raees Baghrani, as a "true mullah, a true Pashtun, and a true Afghan."[30] He ruled from a spare room in the Kandahar governor's building. He would sit on the ground with visitors, rendering decisions. He rarely left the building or conducted business elsewhere.[31] Mullah Omar had solidified his political position in the movement and could no longer easily be challenged..[32]

In April 1996, 1,500 religious leaders came to Kandahar to discuss the future of the movement and whether to consider peace talks or conquer all Afghanistan. The participants apparently rejected peace and declared jihad against Massoud and Rabbani.[33] They swore allegiance to Omar as "Emir al-Momineen," leader of the faithful. Omar donned the "cloak of the Prophet," the religious artifact venerated as having been worn by the Prophet Mohammed, stored next to the shrine of Ahmed Shah in Kandahar. The two acts granted Omar tremendous authority. Religious leaders, from village mullahs to esteemed scholars, were obliged under Islam to obey his orders.[34]

Henceforth Mullah Omar made more decisions on his own. Council members who had planned for him to be a figurehead were dismayed but did not rock the boat. One of these leaders later explained to me: "All Taliban accept unity, oneness, no matter who is the leader. This is the Taliban strength."[35] Likewise, in his book on the Taliban, Mutawakil says that rival parties never formed because of the imperative of unity amid the civil war—a concept found within the Koran itself. Mullah Omar took the next logical step and centralized a command structure.[36] According to Zaeef, Mullah Omar believed in a united chain of command.[37]

Mullah Omar pressed the war forward. Though he rarely left Kandahar, he was in constant communication with his commanders at the front via radio.

He firmly gripped his position as commander-in-chief. Thousands of Pashtuns were conscripted, barely trained, and shipped north to the front lines. A second Taliban offensive commenced against Kabul in September 1996 under Mullah Bor Jan. They outflanked Massoud by way of Jalalabad. While navigating the Taliban column up the Kabul River gorge, Mullah Bor Jan was killed by a lucky 82mm recoilless rifle shot from one of Massoud's young defenders. The other Taliban madly covered him up and bore him away, fearing a breakdown in morale. When Taliban were killed in battle, they were dubbed martyrs, *shahid*. So Mullah Bor Jan is forever known as Shahid Mullah Bor Jan. He had done enough. In danger of encirclement, Massoud withdrew his forces, steadily and calmly, with all their equipment, to the Tajik lands just north of Kabul.

In October, Rabbani, Massoud, Dostum, and Karim Khalili (a Hazara leader) at last united in what would eventually become the Northern Alliance. In May 1997, the Taliban attacked Dostum from Herat. To their good fortune, one of Dostum's rivals—General Malik Pahlawan—captured him and turned him over to the Taliban (he escaped to Iran a few months later). Malik, though, was as crafty as his erstwhile boss. The Taliban walked into Mazar-e-Sharif, the main city of the north, only to have Malik and the Hazaras of the city betray them. The whole city rose up. Hazaras hunted down Pashtuns in the streets. Thousands of Taliban were killed. Thousands were captured, tortured, stuffed into shipping containers, or thrown down wells. Ministers Akhtar Mohammed Mansour and Abdul Razziq were among those captured. Another 6,000 fled to Kunduz, where they held out under the leadership of Mullah Dadullah Lang, one of the Taliban's fiercest commanders. Mansour, Razziq, and Dadullah would survive the experience and go on to lead the Taliban in their future war with the United States. Mullah Omar went to Kabul to rally his commanders, preventing the defeat from demoralizing his larger forces. He also called religious leaders in Pakistan and asked them to send more young men from their madrasas. The madrasas supposedly rushed thousands of young reinforcements to Afghanistan.[38] The Taliban finally captured Mazar-e-Sharif for good in August 1998, massacring the 5,000 to 6,000 Hazara civilians in vengeance.[39] Massoud was the last man standing.

Mohammed Naim was a hard-bitten tribal leader and mujahideen commander from Paktiya. He had lost a leg fighting the Soviets. After the Soviets withdrew, he returned to his tribal lands. Eventually the Taliban came. "An unarmed Taliban could come to a village and everyone would respect him, even without a weapon," the wounded warrior noted. "They fought for beliefs and religion. That caused people to respect them tremendously."[40]

The Taliban regime lasted almost exactly seven years, from their capture of Kandahar in November 1994 to the city's fall in December 2001. With the capture of Kabul, Taliban referred to themselves as the "Islamic government of Afghanistan" and then modified that to the "Islamic Emirate of Afghanistan," the name they would insist upon for the next quarter century.

Harsh interpretation of Islamic law, oppression of women, executions, and stonings have draped the Taliban in infamy in the West. Their reputation in the east and south of Afghanistan—Pashtun Afghanistan—is less malevolent. If far from what Pashtuns consider good government, Taliban rule was bearable, even with its atrocities. After seizing power, the Taliban put down deep roots.

Taliban moral authority flowed from their leaders, who were mullahs and scholars. Religious leaders had always been respected as teachers and sources of knowledge. Many Afghans accepted that religious leaders might be a reasonable alternative to the anarchic rule of the warlords and tribal leaders; they appeared to be fair arbiters and unconcerned with personal power. Islam had an appeal that transcended tribe and ethnicity. The Taliban's unapologetic Pashtun chauvinism, though, often offended the Tajiks, Hazaras, and Uzbeks. Even within the Pashtuns, the Taliban captured a critical mass, but not the whole. It was the Taliban's unity that enabled them to rule over all the Pashtuns and eventually almost all Afghans in a fashion that had escaped the communists and mujahideen parties alike.

The Taliban government did not rely on the tribes to instill order. Mullah Omar preferred a hierarchy to mitigate against independent leaders with separate sources of power and questions of who was in charge of any province or district. Gone were the warlord baronies. Provincial governors had authority over military and civilian affairs in their provinces and reported directly to Omar. At the front lines, various unit commanders reported to an overall commander and he to Omar. Mullah Omar could remove his commanders, ministers, provincial governors, and district governors. No truly autonomous Taliban leaders existed.

The Islamic nature of the regime encouraged centralization. By placing Islam over tribalism, the Taliban were effectively placing oneness over division. Equally important was how religious leaders emphasized obedience as an Islamic duty. Low-level commanders tried to obey their superiors. In their minds, doing otherwise might be un-Islamic or even sinful. Mullah Dadullah Lang, feared as the best front line commander in the wars in the north, was known to lay down his arms on Mullah Omar's order. Zaeef writes that an early Taliban fighter was required to "swear obedience to his emir or commander, distance himself from tribal, party, and community prejudice, and without pay or weary serve only the will of Allah and the goodwill of the people."[41] Many of the Taliban fighters, who were young, schooled in Islam, and had grown up in refugee camps, were less tied to tribal loyalties than young men who had stayed in their villages and fought as part of a tribe. These fighters were more open to Taliban discipline and order.[42] The upshot of all this was that the Taliban were far more united than the tribal leaders, warlords, or government had ever been. Between hierarchy, the emphasis on loyalty, Islam, and the respect of low-level Taliban for their leaders, the Taliban were less prone to fighting with each other and thus better able to enforce their will upon the people.

The Taliban were, of course, far from the first Afghan Islamic movement. Hezb Islami, Jamiat Islami, and other mujahideen parties were Islamist. Yet they lacked the Taliban's credibility. Their leaders had mostly been taught at universities, not madrasas. And they were tainted by ambition, infighting, and corruption in the long years of exile in Peshawar or during the civil war. They did not represent the Islam of the village, the Islam of the vast majority of Afghans. Anthropologist David Edwards, who was in Peshawar at the time among the Islamist leaders, writes of the mujahideen parties, "Examples of heartfelt Islamic devotion were much in evidence . . . but so too was the sense of abiding suspicion conveyed by so many Afghans . . . that ambitious leaders were systematically corrupting the faith, that the Islam they represented was not the Islam the people as a whole believed in and practiced, that the struggles of the present were more about baser matters and concerns than the idealized struggles of the past."[43]

Islam blossomed under the Taliban. Adherence to its fundamental tenets had never before been so strong. The Taliban instituted and enforced Islamic law, encouraged prayer five times per day in a mosque, dictated payment of *zakat* (alms), and opened madrasas for tens of thousands of children. During Ramadan, few dared break the fast. Religious leaders were endowed with great authority. No longer simply leading prayers or teaching religious lessons, mullahs and maulawis were now political leaders for all society. The ranks of the government were open to them. They were the regime's preferred district governors, provincial governors, ministers, and military commanders.[44] They had more power in their own villages as well. Certain mullahs had retinues of armed men. Village mullahs were often responsible for tax collection and enforcing the regime's decisions in the village. A mullah was expected to resolve disputes, in effect becoming the village judge. The mullahs were also given greater influence over education. Most schools became madrasas or were closed. Secondary education was scarce.

The Taliban regime is most remembered for justice. Islamic courts stood up in almost every district to administer Islamic law. The Kandahar supreme Islamic court appointed provincial judges (all religious scholars). Its chief judge was Maulawi Pasanai, who had first allied with Omar to defend their village of Sangesar in the months before the Taliban movement had officially formed. As chief judge, Pasanai advised Mullah Omar and guided the institution of Islamic law throughout the country. The Taliban followed a harsh interpretation of Islamic law. Veils were mandatory, music was forbidden, punishments for crime were severe. Tough penalties deterred crime. Afghans tended to appreciate

Taliban quickness and fairness. Westerners tended to condemn their brutality, especially the public executions.

Taliban treatment of women was oppressive. Women were to play no role in open society, not even moving freely about their villages. Mullah Omar instructed that women should leave the home rarely and when they did to be fully covered and escorted.[45] They were banned from working. Young girls were not allowed to go to school. Women were barred from the remaining universities in Nangarhar, Mazar-e-Sharif, and Kandahar. The worst were the public stonings. Women found guilty of a crime, including adultery, were hauled out into stadiums in Kabul, Kandahar, and elsewhere, and executed with stones or gunshots in front of thousands of people. Video of a Taliban gunman executing a kneeling, burka-draped woman in a Kabul stadium was a defining act of evil for Westerners. Afghans, especially Pashtuns, accepted this extremism largely because it was just a gradation in their general oppression of women.

Taliban leaders decreed that these strictures were in line with Islamic law. They rejected Western notions of women's rights and claimed to be actually protecting women. In their minds, the atrocities of the civil war—*fitna*—demanded righteous purity.[46] Mullah Omar's 1998 "edict on women's rights in the community" stated he was aiming "to prevent injustice" and that "in Islamic law women have their own individual legal rights such that their . . . dignity and position becomes high and their modesty and concealment becomes secure. But unfortunately in Afghan society, because of the spread of the bad and unlawful, women from these their own lawful rights are being stripped and day by day are being oppressed."[47] A Taliban magazine explained, "These decisions and restrictions by Islamic government not only are in agreement with Islamic instructions but also indicate respect to the rights of women and human rights. In the context of human rights, education of women is not considered as important as the protection of honor and integrity of women . . . Is the protection of honor and dignity of women from sleazy eyes of voyeurs not considered respect to human rights?"[48]

Taliban leaders rationalized that the women who had been stoned and shot had actually committed crimes and been lawfully punished. They insisted that Afghans had to be punished in accordance with the orders of Allah and his Prophet, not Western laws: the victim's family had the right to kill or forgive a murderer; a hand of a thief was to be severed; an adulterer was to be stoned, whether male or female. They thought the West did not understand.[49]

To raise money, the Taliban promoted poppy cultivation. Production rose dramatically. By 1999, Afghanistan was the world's number one producer. Taxation of poppy was a major source of revenue, the most important for the regime. Farmers profited from the trade too, which probably made the Taliban's harsh law enforcement altogether acceptable. In 2000, the Taliban banned the production of poppy, deciding it un-Islamic. Unsurprisingly, punishment was so severe that few dared grow it.

Osama bin Laden first came to Pakistan in the mid-1980s, initially for charity work with Afghan refugees. There he associated with Abdullah Azam, an inspirational figure preaching global jihad who would become a founder of al-Qaʻeda. Bin Laden went on to set up training camps inside Afghanistan for Arabs who wanted to fight the Soviets. Bin Laden's fighters won a notable victory in 1987 at the Battle of Jaji. Soviet forces attempted to overrun their base in the mountains of Paktiya. Bin Laden fought in the battle himself. Legend has it he was on the front line firing his rifle. The victory attracted more recruits. Shortly after, al-Qaʻeda was founded. Training in the camps eventually included techniques for carrying out terrorist attacks in the West. Bin Laden left Afghanistan in 1989 following the failed mujahideen assault on Jalalabad that year. He lived in Saudi Arabia and then Sudan. In May 1996, he and about 50 men came back to Afghanistan. They went to Jalalabad, which fell to the Taliban a few months later. Bin Laden built a new base at Tora Bora, in the mountains south of the city, and spent much of his time there.[50]

Neither Mullah Omar nor any of the other senior Taliban leaders had ever met bin Laden. In August 1996, bin Laden issued "A Declaration of Jihad," his manifesto for action against the United States. The declaration drew international criticism upon the Taliban regime. Consequently, Omar summoned bin Laden to Kandahar in November. Face to face, sitting on a military cot before his guests, Omar permitted bin Laden to remain in Afghanistan but asked that he stop talking to the media about jihad against the United States. He promised to help al-Qaʻeda, but asked that he be patient: "Please wait; we are going to help you and help all the Muslims. But wait."[51] In keeping with the Pashtun custom of hospitality, Omar did not go the whole way and forbid bin Laden from pursuing terrorism against the United States, let alone speaking publicly. So bin Laden decided to ignore Omar's request and carry on. He deferred pledging allegiance to Omar as emir al-momineen until 1999 and then only did so through a colleague, not in person.[52]

If their personal relationship was strained, Omar appreciated bin Laden's money, development work, and military forces. Bin Laden established bases in Nangarhar, Kunar, Khost, and Kandahar. Eventually, a few hundred of his fighters took part in the war in the north, often committing the worst atrocities. Other foreign groups came to Afghanistan as well. The success of the jihad against the Soviets inspired groups seeking to establish a caliphate over the Muslim world.[53]

Mullah Omar never shut down al-Qaʻeda activities in Afghanistan even though he had proof of their terrorist operations. Taliban officials were in regular contact with bin Laden. From time to time, Omar saw him personally.

Omar displayed a degree of deference. He consulted with Pakistani religious leaders on how to improve relations with bin Laden. When bin Laden was in Kandahar, Omar visited his camp, which in Pashtun culture is a sign of respect. A ruler, tribal leader, or religious leader receives guests and supplicants. Going as a guest can imply that one is lesser than the host, in some way seeking the host's generosity.

Whether Omar was doing this because he valued bin Laden's assistance, feared insulting an Arab known widely as a defender of the faith, or simply wanted to avoid unneeded tensions is unclear. Omar may have been unwilling to risk the censure of someone who had so fervently fought in the name of Islam. Bin Laden's censure would have questioned the Islamic legitimacy of the Taliban regime and thus its hold on power and, indeed, the very meaning of the movement itself. Mustafa Hamid, an Arab in Afghanistan who had been working closely with bin Laden, writes that religious legitimacy is what won over the Taliban leadership: "It was also thought the presence of Arabs gave the Taliban religious legitimacy. In fact, the religious link is the strongest reason the Taliban allowed the Arabs to stay, in addition to the tribal customs."[54]

Al-Qaʻeda's ideas and support for the regime won sympathy from Taliban leaders and rank and file. Their fierce defense of the faith could be appealing. In the haunting words of Zaeef, the Taliban had never invited bin Laden into Afghanistan but nevertheless al-Qaʻeda eventually "became part of the Taliban culture."[55]

After the 1998 Kenya and Tanzania embassy bombings, the United States fired cruise missiles against the al-Qaʻeda camps in Khost. The United States and Saudi Arabia then tried to get the Taliban to turn over bin Laden. Mullah Omar refused. The cruise missile attacks prompted increased sympathy for bin Laden among Afghans. Mustafa Hamid believed, "Since America reacted, [Mullah Omar] could not stand with America strongly in one line against [bin Laden]; so he could not do anything."[56] Omar informed the United States and Saudi Arabia that bin Laden was his guest and under Islamic law and Pashtunwali he was obligated to protect him. Omar also thought surrendering bin Laden would prompt the United States to escalate its demands upon the Taliban regime and to try to change Afghanistan's religious character. Instead of turning him over, Omar promised, as their guest, bin Laden would do no harm to the outside world.

In 2000, Omar met with bin Laden and explicitly forbade him from attacking the United States.[57] Many Taliban leaders realized bin Laden was still plotting operations and warned Omar that he should be banished or surrendered to a specially convened international Islamic court. These ideas were broached to the United States and rejected. The Taliban regime found itself sanctioned by the West and Saudi Arabia.[58]

Friendship with bin Laden and oppressive domestic policies turned the Taliban Islamic Emirate of Afghanistan into an international pariah. Only Saudi Arabia, the United Arab Emirates, and Pakistan officially recognized the regime. The United Nations allowed them an unofficial ambassador, the English-speaking Maulawi Abdul Hakim Mujahed.

Pakistan continued to support the Taliban. After 1995, Pakistan gave them millions of dollars in aid ($30 million in 1997–1998, for example), including ammunition and military equipment. The ISI intelligence organization by no means controlled the Taliban. They trusted the Taliban to oppose Indian influence in Afghanistan. The Taliban had no relations with India. Chief of the army General Parvez Musharraf seized power from Prime Minister Nawaz Sharif in a military coup in 1999. He had commanded the Pakistani intrusion in the 1998–1999 Kargil War against India. Determined to counter India, he allowed Pakistani military advisors to deploy to northern Afghanistan to assist the Taliban against the Northern Alliance. Omar helpfully permitted Islamabad's Kashmir militant groups to use Afghanistan soil for training and preparations.

Afghanistan's other large neighbors supported their own clients. Russia was consumed with its own internal issues in the 1990s and provided only minor assistance to old connections, especially Dostum. When the Taliban captured Kabul and advanced toward Mazar-e-Sharif, they provided arms and airfield access (to receive supply shipments) to Ahmed Shah Massoud, who had a long history of Russian backdoor contacts. Vladimir Putin met with him in 2000.

The Iranians, historical players in Afghanistan, supported the Hazaras and Tajiks. The Hazaras were Shi'a Muslims, like the Iranian regime. Under the doctrine of *vilayet e-faqih*, the Iranian regime considered it an obligation to defend fellow Shi'a. The Tajiks spoke the same language as the Iranians, an important tie. The Taliban's strict belief in Sunni Islam and oppression of Hazaras hardened Iranian enmity. Iran nearly declared war on the Taliban regime when, during the 1998 fighting in Mazar-e-Sharif, Taliban fighters killed ten Iranian diplomats and one journalist at their consulate. Massoud traveled to Tehran and negotiated Iranian arms supplies. One of the Iranian liaisons to the Panjshir was Qassim Sulaymani, future leader of the elite Quds Force of the Islamic Revolutionary Guards Corps.

India also helped the Northern Alliance, particularly Massoud. Over the course of the conflict, Russia, Iran, and India gave more and more support to Massoud and the Northern Alliance in order to stem the Taliban tide and Pakistani influence.[59]

The United States eventually also opened relations with Massoud. During the Soviet War, Massoud had forged stronger relations with France and Britain than the United States. When the Soviet Union collapsed, so did American contact with Massoud. Contacts resumed after the Taliban seizure of Kabul. The growing threat from al-Qaʻeda then caused the United States to strengthen co-operation, especially after the 1998 embassy bombings in Kenya and Tanzania. The relationship mainly concerned intelligence and counterterrorism activities rather than provision of weapons or funding to fight the Taliban.[60]

Inside Afghanistan, the Taliban's luster dulled as the war dragged on. Afghans disliked conscription and the Taliban had trouble fielding forces in the north. Villages in Kandahar, Helmand, and Loya Paktiya (accustomed to exemptions from military service) sometimes revolted. The revolts were quashed but there was no question that the people were tired.

After 1997, roughly 25,000 to 30,000 Taliban operated around Kabul. They could not defeat Ahmed Shah Massoud and his army of 12,000 to 15,000 disciplined Tajiks.[61] The battle line between Massoud and the Taliban swayed to and fro just north of Kabul. The Taliban suffered stinging defeat at Massoud's hands in 1997 and then again in 1999 when his inspired counteroffensives pushed them back into Kabul. The Taliban repeatedly scorched the plain north of Kabul, driving out its Tajik people, poisoning wells, damaging irrigation ditches, and destroying homes. Massoud's lines near the Panjshir Valley never broke. The Taliban themselves, never prone to admit defeat, recognized Ahmed Shah Massoud as the sole foe they had been unable to beat, an honor accorded in one of their official publications: "But the enemy that the Islamic Emirate struggle continued against until the end was the Northern Alliance in north-east Afghanistan, the most important group of which, Shura-e-Nazar, was led by Ahmed Shah Massoud. Until the end, he fought off the Islamic Emirate in Parwan and Takhar."[62]

On September 9, 2001, two Arabs masquerading as journalists interviewed Massoud. When they met him, they blew up their camera, killing the famous leader. The Taliban did not claim responsibility. It was bin Laden's hit. Massoud was a hero for the Tajiks. Thirteen years later, I watched a Tajik general from Panjshir lament with tears in his eyes, "Massoud was ten times the leader of Fahim, Bismullah Khan, and Abdullah combined."[63] During Karzai's rule, posters of Massoud bedecked Kabul, often next to posters of Karzai. Massoud's military successes and his impressive Panjshiri fighting machine survived him and would give the Tajiks unprecedented political power and official standing in the Karzai era.

In spite of its many shortcomings, Taliban rule was effective. Violence within their territory was limited. Law and order prevailed. For those who claim that Afghanistan is ungovernable, the Taliban offer a striking counterexample. To the people in most of the country, the Taliban proved they could end the anarchy of warlords run amok. Taliban leaders long remembered their greatest successes as stopping the anarchy of the civil war and protecting the defenseless.[64]

This finding clashes with the standard narrative of Taliban rule, which paints them as brutally oppressive, narrow-minded, and backward when it came to the nuts and bolts of running a state. The Taliban were indeed many of these things, oppressive foremost among them. But they had a penchant for unity. In coming to power, the Taliban overwrote Islamic religious methods of discipline and subordination upon tribalism and thus stabilized the country and, aside from Massoud, effectively ended the civil war. Unlike the tribal leaders and warlords, they seldom fought with each other and instead accepted a hierarchy. Unity gave them the power to reorder society and mobilize it for seven years of war in the north. It allowed them to enforce harsh punishments and prevent opponents from pushing them out of power. Had their regime survived, peace may have persisted, if of an impoverished sort. In short, the Taliban could govern the "ungovernable" land.

The Taliban regime was a revolutionary event in Afghan history. Afghanistan had seen plenty of religious movements in its history. These earlier movements had usually occurred alongside tribal revolts or as the vanguard of larger nation-wide resistance to a foreign invader. In both cases, leadership usually fell to a great tribal leader or member of the royal family. Never before had a movement of religious leaders seized power. Never before had Islamic law been so rigorously implemented. The dissolution of the state and anarchy of the civil war had discredited other sources of authority. The Taliban's form of traditional Islam weathered the storm better than the tribes, new warlords, state, or educated Islamism.[65] Such strength portended the movement's perseverance on the political stage.

Up to 2001, the interests of the United States in Afghanistan had been minimal. The policies of the 1980s had been about damaging the Soviet Union rather than any intrinsic US interest in Afghanistan itself. The same could be said of the earlier and much smaller economic assistance efforts of the 1950s and 1960s; they were designed to counterbalance Soviet influence. The Taliban regime's excesses had drawn the attention of the administration of President Bill Clinton, which never recognized the Taliban emirate as the government of Afghanistan and curtailed unofficial relations from 1997 onward.

The Taliban's treatment of women was one reason for US disapproval. Secretary of State Madeleine Albright visited with Afghan female refugees in Central Asia and gave numerous speeches condemning the Taliban. "The Taliban seems determined to drag women back from the dawn of the 21st century to the 13th. The only human rights they appear to recognize are the rights to remain silent and invisible, uneducated and unemployed," she said in a talk in 1998 at Emory University in Georgia.[66] President Clinton himself assured the high profile Feminist Majority Foundation, which sponsored a campaign to

"Stop Gender Apartheid" in Afghanistan: "Let me be very clear about the position of the United States: The denial of basic human rights in Afghanistan or
anywhere else is simply unacceptable. If the leaders of the Taliban . . . want international acceptance, they must respect the rights of all their people. They must
treat women as human beings."[67]

Terrorism and Osama bin Laden attracted greater, albeit belated, concern.
The Clinton administration moved slowly to reopen relations with Massoud and
to track bin Laden. The harm a foreign terrorist might inflict on the United States
at home was largely theoretical. Although the truck bombing at the World Trade
Center in 1993 killed seven people, the scale of the threat was underestimated
and disregarded as a major defense issue.

Relations with Pakistan were also cool. Pakistan's 1998 nuclear tests caused
President Clinton to lay on new sanctions. Congress prohibited all economic
and military aid after Musharraf's coup. Pakistani generals came to view the
United States as untrustworthy.

President George W. Bush was elected in November 2000. Bush was aware
of terrorism as one of many threats within a broad national security strategy. He
was also concerned about rogue states with weapons of mass destruction. His
defense department embarked on a modernization effort that looked to exploit
a high-tech "revolution in military affairs" to redouble its conventional military
advantage against countries like North Korea, Iran, and, for a few hawks, China.
Afghanistan was rarely mentioned in policy discussions, let alone as a possible
battleground for the US military.[68] Bush had campaigned against nation-building
and unneeded foreign interventions. That was about to change.

|| 4 ||

The United States Enters Afghanistan

On September 11, 2001, two airliners crashed into the twin towers of the World Trade Center in New York City. Another struck the Pentagon. A fourth pitched into a field in Pennsylvania before it could strike its target, the US Capitol. Nearly 3,000 Americans were killed. About 6,000 more were injured. The attacks brought the United States into Afghanistan. The administration of President George W. Bush quickly confirmed that Osama bin Laden and al-Qaʻeda had perpetrated the attacks. Retaliation was underway within a month.

War came to Afghanistan as an external shock. The Soviet-Afghan War, the later civil war, and finally Taliban rule fostered an environment in which extremism could grow. Twenty years of disorder and outside intervention contributed to the rise of terrorism. Afghans themselves, however, were not international terrorists. The September 11 plot may have been supervised from Afghanistan but it was not Afghan. Al-Qaʻeda's brand of international terrorism was motivated by broader events in the Middle East, such as the policies of the government of Saudi Arabia and the presence of the United States in the Arabian Peninsula. Bin Laden, an Arab, had guided the operation. His role is pivotal. He wanted to attack the United States in spite of advice from his counselors to reconsider. Seldom in history has one man so singlehandedly provoked a war.

The dead hand of bin Laden haunts examination of America's early decisions in Afghanistan. As a side effect of September 11, bin Laden hoped to draw the United States into a long war in Afghanistan, where it would be defeated like the Soviet Union. Even before American bombs started falling, he was calling old mujahideen and religious scholars back to Afghanistan to wage a second jihad. He spoke about it again and again with his followers.[1] Bin Laden's dream would lead to his own death. But America would indeed find itself trapped in decades of war.

What happened in the weeks after September 11 had a dramatic effect on the course of the war. Many US decisions were brilliant. Others foreclosed opportunities. For their brilliance and for their lost opportunities, the opening months of America's Afghan War were among its most important.

The attack was a traumatic surprise for the United States. The heart of the American government and economy had been struck. The thousands of casualties exceeded those of Pearl Harbor and unlike 1941 were overwhelmingly civilian. President Bush addressed the nation that evening: "Today, our fellow citizens, our way of life, our very freedom came under attack in a series of deliberate and deadly terrorist acts. . . . Thousands of lives were suddenly ended by evil, despicable acts of terror. The pictures of airplanes flying into buildings, fires burning, huge structures collapsing, have filled us with disbelief, terrible sadness, and a quiet, unyielding anger." Alive to the possibility of follow-on attacks, Bush declared his resolve to "win the war against terrorism."[2]

The magnitude of the event convinced Americans far and wide that terrorism was a far deadlier threat than had been apparent and must be treated with the utmost seriousness. The September 12 *New York Times* headline was "U.S. ATTACKED." The editorial page exclaimed "The War against America," "An Unfathomable Attack," and "The National Defense." The column read, "Every routine, every habit . . . was fractured yesterday. If a flight full of commuters can be turned into a missile of war, everything is dangerous. If four planes can be taken over simultaneously by suicidal hijackers, then we can never be quite sure again that any bad intention can be thwarted, no matter how irrational or loathsome. . . . [It is] one of those moments in which history splits, and we define the world as 'before' and 'after.' "[3] It was a new era. Suddenly Afghanistan was America's foremost national security interest.

Immediately after the attacks, President Bush and his national security council (including Director of Central Intelligence George Tenet, Secretary of State Colin Powell, Secretary of Defense Donald Rumsfeld, National Security Advisor Condoleezza Rice, and Vice President Richard Cheney) agreed the United States would probably have to attack al-Qaʻeda—the most likely perpetrators of the attack—and Afghanistan. They suspected that the Taliban regime would have to be overthrown in the process. Rice writes in her memoir that hours after the attack occurred "we all knew that the outcome would be a declaration of war against the Taliban and an invasion of Afghanistan."[4] At that time, few Americans distinguished between al-Qaʻeda and the Taliban.

Still, Bush was not yet ready for regime change. He decided to issue an ultimatum to give the Taliban a chance to back down even though he was skeptical they would comply. The idea of launching a surprise attack was distasteful, especially since he was trying to hold the moral high ground.[5] On September 12, he told his national security council that the Taliban must surrender or kick out the entire al-Qaʻeda organization if it did not want war with the United States.[6] Bush would wait to publicly issue the ultimatum until the request could be passed in private to the Taliban. Bush's decision gave space to negotiate with the Taliban. If they agreed to turn over bin Laden, the United States could leave the regime in place. In retrospect, such a solution might have averted a US invasion of Afghanistan and the years of war that followed.

One of the administration's first steps was to talk to Pakistan. Because of its location and ties to the Taliban, Pakistan would be an essential ally. Secretary of State Colin Powell and his deputy Richard Armitage immediately pressured President Parvez Musharraf to change Pakistan's policies and provide military and diplomatic assistance against the Taliban and al-Qa'eda. On September 12 and 13, Armitage and Powell laid out a series of demands to General Mahmud, the director of the ISI (Pakistan military intelligence), and President Musharraf: Go after al-Qa'eda, shut down the border to al-Qa'eda, cut funding to al-Qa'eda, grant the United States basing and overflight rights, let the United States access Pakistan bases and borders, share intelligence, condemn and curb domestic support for the September 11 attacks, cut off fuel and volunteers going to the Taliban, and, finally, end support for the Taliban if they harbor al-Qa'eda. Impressed that a vengeful America might attack his own regime, Musharraf agreed to the demands.[7] He supposedly had met with his key generals at the army's general headquarters on September 12 ahead of speaking with Armitage and Powell and told them "the US will react like a wounded bear and it will attack Afghanistan."[8] Pakistan, he advised his generals, would have to turn away from the Taliban, at least for the time being.

Musharraf tried to preserve Pakistan's influence in Afghanistan by encouraging the Taliban to come to terms with the United States while also giving the United States the necessary military access. In the following weeks, he restrained Pakistani military support to the Taliban. General Mahmud and the ISI liked the Taliban. Mahmud had been providing arms and advisors to the Taliban's war against the Northern Alliance. He told Abdul Salam Zaeef, Afghanistan's ambassador to Pakistan, "We . . . know that an attack on Afghanistan from the United States . . . seems more and more likely. We want to assure you that you will not be alone in this *jihad* against America. We will be with you."[9] A few weeks later, Musharraf replaced Mahmud and recalled the ISI's chief officers with the Taliban. For the rest of 2001, the ISI would be divided. Some officers helped the United States with military operations. Others shipped the Taliban arms, ammunition, recruits, and advisors.[10]

In spite of his obstructionist ISI officers, Musharraf pressured the Taliban to turn over bin Laden. Mullah Omar had not been informed of the September 11 attack ahead of time. Bin Laden had disregarded Omar's instruction to consult with him on any international terrorist attack.[11] According to Taliban foreign minister Wakil Ahmed Mutawakil, many Taliban sympathized with bin

Laden and the Arabs but others questioned his attacks on other countries from Afghan soil. Before September 11, the council of Taliban ministers had stressed again and again that these guests must do no such thing.[12] After September 11, the Taliban publicly condemned the attacks and declared that those responsible must be brought to justice.[13] Nevertheless, Omar continued to harbor bin Laden. Before his removal, ISI director Mahmud called on Mullah Omar. At the meeting, Omar agreed to send an emissary to bin Laden to ask for his voluntary departure. Omar then told Pakistan he would be willing to surrender bin Laden to a third country. The United States refused, wanting bin Laden handed over directly.[14]

The other person in Pakistan searching for a deal with the Taliban was Robert Grenier, the CIA chief in Pakistan. On September 15, he met with Taliban southern zone commander Mullah Osmani. Osmani was open to giving up bin Laden but could not see how it could be done. He said Afghans would be so enraged that they would turn against the Taliban. Grenier nevertheless convinced Osmani to ask Mullah Omar to surrender bin Laden in order to avoid a US invasion.[15]

As Grenier tried to open a channel, Bush issued his ultimatum in a speech before Congress on September 20. He called for the Taliban to surrender bin Laden and al-Qaʻeda or share their fate. A few days earlier, Congress had given Bush authority to use "all necessary and appropriate force" against those behind the September 11 attacks or their supporters.[16]

The day of Bush's ultimatum, Taliban religious scholars were convening a large council in Kabul. The scholars ruled that if the United States invaded Afghanistan, jihad was obligated until the United States was forced out. That ruling would be the main justification for war against the United States for the next 20 years. It empowered Taliban leaders to call on all Afghans to rise up and fight the United States as a religious duty.[17]

The council also addressed the issue of bin Laden. Omar was still resistant to US demands. He had already told a delegation of Pakistani religious scholars that "turning over Osama would only be a disgrace for us and for Islamic thought and belief would be a weakness."[18] He was convinced that the United States would not "tolerate the Islamic Emirate or any other expression of rule by Islamic law" and argued that surrendering bin Laden would not end American schemes and unjustified demands.[19] The outcome of the Kabul council was a request that Mullah Omar ask bin Laden to leave Afghanistan.

The next day, Omar rejected the council's advice and refused Bush's ultimatum. Omar claimed bin Laden had not committed the attacks. As further justification, Omar cited bin Laden's oath of allegiance to him and the Afghan people's honorable commitment to protect guests.[20] It was a remarkable move that showcased his authority. Omar was not bound by obligations of consensual decision-making (a tribal leader would have been expected to heed the advice of other elders). The Taliban religious scholars, commanders, and rank and file accepted the decision, despite his rejection of their advice. Subordination for the sake of unity.

Sympathy existed within the Taliban toward bin Laden and al-Qaʻeda. Many Taliban were elated at the September 11 attacks and doubted the United States would retaliate. Zaeef, the Taliban ambassador to Pakistan, was watching the attacks on television as colleagues celebrated. "To them," he wrote, "America was our enemy, a country that had imposed sanctions on our country and one that had attacked us with missiles. The image on their screens—a symbol of that power burning on its own soil—was a reason for celebration."[21]

Grenier continued to speak with Mullah Osmani on giving up bin Laden or getting key leaders to break with Omar. Though no fan of bin Laden, on October 2, Osmani explained, "Bin Laden . . . has become synonymous in Afghanistan with Islam. The Taliban can't hand him over publicly any more than they can publicly reject Islam."[22] Grenier communicated with Osmani a few more times without any progress.[23] Omar, faithful, constrained by his view of his obligations to his people, with much of the movement behind him, was hurtling toward war.

An important factor in Mullah Omar's decision-making seems to have also been doubt that the United States would attack. Zaeef visited Omar during this time. Omar wanted the United States to present hard evidence of bin Laden's involvement in the September 11 attacks before he would take any steps to surrender him. In spite of information to the contrary from Zaeef and the ISI, Omar greatly underestimated the chances that the United States would attack. Zaeef writes in his autobiography, "In Mullah Mohammed Omar's mind there was a less than 10 percent chance that America would resort to anything beyond threats, and so an attack was unlikely."[24] Omar stayed in Kandahar, disregarding reports of an impending attack, believing the United States had no logical reason to strike.

Mustafa Hamid, as an Arab close to bin Laden, observed the same overconfidence throughout the Taliban leadership: "Strategically, the Taliban made a big mistake in their calculations. They did not think the Americans would come and bomb them the way they did."[25] Bin Laden misjudged that the United States could be defeated with the same tactics that had outlasted the Soviets, with fronts, bases, and other activities easily seen from the air and struck with a smart bomb.[26]

Through September, Bush and his cabinet left the door open for negotiations while planning moved forward. Other than Grenier's actions, effort to reach out to the Taliban was weak. Bush did not instruct Powell to open a line to the Taliban to work things out, which would have been the normal diplomatic course of action to avoid a war. Bush himself seems to have never asked about the details of outreach. He just waited for the Taliban response to his ultimatum. In meetings, the national security council discussed striking Mullah Omar. Their attention was as much on breaking up the Taliban and working with defectors as negotiating.[27] There was a sense, shared by Bush, of an imperative to attack, both to reassure the American people and to deter terrorists and their sponsors. Every few days Bush and his cabinet heard about a new terrorist plot. They worried the next attack could be imminent. Bush later said he believed that Americans felt another attack was certain.[28] His fear was that the next attack could be far worse, using chemical or biological weapons. In Bush's words, "What people forget is the number of threats that were pouring into the country. . . . We're saying to ourselves, what's the worst that could happen? And the worst that could happen was . . . not airplanes, but it's a chemical or biological weapon."[29] The September 11 attack had dispelled any doubt that al-Qa'eda would try to acquire such weapons and use them in the United States. In the 1990s, this was the stuff of movies. After September 11, it was real. It changed how American leaders thought about strategy.

Public opinion was equally concerned. Gallup polls in September and October showed that 60 to 80 percent of Americans believed another attack was somewhat or very likely. Roughly half of Americans were worried a family member would become a victim of terrorism. An impressive 73 percent viewed the Taliban "very unfavorably"; 67 percent favored military action involving ground troops. Only 28 percent opposed, a slim constituency for peace talks.[30] Like Omar, Bush was hurtling toward war.

As days passed, the window for negotiations closed. Planning for war progressed, pressure mounted, opinions hardened. Bush pushed to bomb, feeling war should have already begun. He wanted bin Laden on the run so as to disrupt any further attacks on the United States. Grenier's last proposals for negotiations were dismissed. Rice and Powell, who had been more open to negotiations, came to agree that the regime had to go. All looked at al-Qa'eda and the Taliban as one enemy. Omar's own obstinacy encouraged this kind of thinking.[31] Finally, on October 5, Bush decided time was up. The United States would attack on October 7.

Once US air strikes started, Taliban rallied to Omar and bin Laden. Grenier's Osmani channel dried up.[32] The chance to avoid war passed. Whether further attempts at negotiations could have succeeded is one of the big "what ifs" of 2001. More could have been done to find out. Bush was not focused on peace, looking at the ultimatum almost as a gesture of fair play before going to war, leaving negotiations to the CIA station chief instead of the Secretary of State, and waiting fewer than three weeks to find a solution. With more time and diplomatic effort, Taliban who were against war might have found a way to get Mullah Omar to give up bin Laden.

Afghans would have been left under a harsh regime—but without the death and disruption of war. The United States itself would have dodged years of sacrifice.

That said, the forces pressing toward war should not be underestimated. The attack on the United States created an imperative to strike back. "Such an insult to American honor was not to be dealt with by a long and meticulous police investigation," lectured the esteemed British military historian Michael Howard a few weeks after the war began. "It cried for immediate and spectacular vengeance. . . . And who can blame Americans? . . . It is a demand that can be satisfied only by military action—if possible, rapid and decisive military action. There must be catharsis: the blood of five thousand innocent civilians demands it."[33] Poor information between two extremely foreign peoples aided the press to war. The administration and the American people misunderstood the Taliban movement as inseparable from al-Qaʻeda. The Taliban misunderstood America's resolve to go to war. And the Taliban had their own domestic and religious imperatives. Mullah Omar, Emir al-Momineen, had to consider his own legitimacy as a defender of Islam. These conditions swept the United States and the Taliban toward war. In the end, a lot of patience and a lot of good fortune would have been needed to have avoided it.

As diplomacy idled, Bush and his team composed a war plan. The goal would be to capture or kill al-Qaʻeda members and overthrow the Taliban. Two days after September 11, CIA Director George Tenet ventured an idea to work with the Northern Alliance to destroy the Taliban and al-Qaʻeda. CIA paramilitary teams and US Army special forces teams would go into Afghanistan, embed with Northern Alliance forces, and call in air strikes in order to give the Northern Alliance a critical edge in combat. During subsequent discussions, Bush was enthusiastic about the idea.[34] The military could devise nothing equally imaginative. The chairman of the joint chiefs of staff, General Hugh Shelton, submitted a run-of-the-mill air campaign with cruise missiles and air strikes that Bush thought inadequate to defeat al-Qaʻeda. Bush was determined to have troops on the ground and break from the air-dominant military campaigns of the 1990s, which he believed signaled weakness to terrorists.[35]

Tenet tasked Grenier to turn the idea into a formal plan. Grenier's resulting plan was to deploy a few thousand US forces that would work as per Tenet's idea with the Northern Alliance and also some Pashtuns. It reasoned that excluding the Pashtuns would magnify resistance. As a general principle, the plan stressed that strategy should conform to rather than change Afghan culture. Somewhat optimistically, it called for casting the war as one of Afghans against Arab foreigners. On September 24, at a national security council meeting at Camp David, Bush approved Grenier's plan as the US war plan.[36]

The plan was refined and operationalized over the next two weeks. The CIA would send paramilitary teams into Afghanistan to run the US effort on the ground. US Army special forces teams would support them, directly advising Afghan units in combat and calling in air strikes. In all, approximately 500 CIA and special forces would go into Afghanistan. Two US Marine expeditionary units (2,000 men each) and additional special operations troops would later be added to the order of battle. An air campaign would precede the ground war with Afghan allies. The military planned for a variety of strikes with cruise missiles and precision bombs to disrupt al-Qa'eda and destroy the Taliban regime.[37] General Tommy Franks, the commander of central command (CENTCOM), who had jurisdiction over Afghanistan and Pakistan, would be in charge of the operation, including the CIA teams on the ground. Over Franks, Rumsfeld was empowered to oversee the whole war.

"Operation Enduring Freedom," the official name the US government used for the war, began on October 7, 2001, with a set of air and cruise missile strikes. Initial strikes quickly demolished Taliban airfields, radars, anti-aircraft weapons, and communications systems. The aircraft then turned to headquarters, ministries, bases, and other military targets. Mullah Omar's home was hit too.[38]

The United States applied the repertoire of precision weapons that had marked the American way of war since 1991. Precision bombs and Tomahawk cruise missiles could hit targets as small as a window. Laser-guided bombs, in which a bomb follows a laser designation provided by an aircraft or troops on the ground, had been prevalent since Vietnam. New GPS satellite guidance systems could track a bomb against any programmed coordinate, down to a square meter. The pilot could drop the bomb and forget about it, confident it would reach its target. The United States dropped hundreds of new GPS-guided 500-, 1,000-, and 2,000-pound bombs. Traditional unguided "dumb" bombs were also still in use.

Ordnance was released by a variety of aircraft: high performance F-15E strike fighters, carrier-based F-18C fighters, black B-2 stealth bombers, and 40-year-old Vietnam-era B-52G/H bombers. Especially well-known is the propeller-driven AC-130 Specter gunship. It carried a 150mm cannon, 25mm Gatling guns, and 40mm cannons. Computer systems allowed the gunship to hit targets precisely with more sustained fire than possible from a jet. With slight exaggeration, it was akin to a flying artillery battery. Manned aircraft were joined by new Predator drones flying out of Shamsi and Jacobabad air bases in Pakistan. The drones could fly hundreds of miles and then loiter over a target area for hours, observing possible enemy activity through onboard cameras. Certain versions carried Hellfire missiles.[39]

The Taliban's written history of the period stresses the impact of the bombing and the fact it targeted many of their government buildings and military head-quarters.[40] After a few days, Afghan civilians in Kabul and other cities started fleeing to safer places in Afghanistan or Pakistan.[41] But the Taliban fighting forces held firm. During the first two weeks of the bombing, the history claims the morale of the Taliban soldiers ("holy warriors") stayed high. From Kandahar, Mullah Omar called his commanders and ministers over a satellite phone and directed them to preach patience, determination, and firmness to their soldiers and the people.[42]

The air campaign lasted two weeks, during which Bush grew more and more frustrated. It was taking time to put in place sufficient CIA and special forces teams for the Northern Alliance to launch its offensive.[43] Meanwhile, targets for air strikes were becoming harder and harder to find. The Taliban had few headquarters and little infrastructure to hit. Their military forces were suffi-ciently good at blending into the countryside to avoid being targeted—unless the Northern Alliance advanced and forced them to defend themselves, which was yet to happen.

Hank Crumpton, an innovative CIA officer, ran the war in northern and eastern Afghanistan. He worked in Washington but traveled back and forth to Afghanistan. From Islamabad, Robert Grenier ran the war in the south. The first ten-man CIA team arrived on September 26, 2001, in the Panjshir. Their most important duty was to hunt down and kill Osama bin Laden and al-Qaʻeda. In order to do so, they were to cooperate with Massoud's Tajik forces, now led by his lieutenant, Mohammed Fahim. Over the next weeks, two more teams arrived: one to work with Ismael Khan near Herat, another to work with Dostum and Mohammed Atta in the north.[44] The CIA team members were highly expe-rienced. The leaders had previous tours in Afghanistan or Pakistan and spoke Dari. Before 2001, the CIA had nurtured a close relationship with Massoud. Several team leaders already had friendships with their Afghan counterparts.

Special forces teams deployed weeks after the first CIA team, much to Bush's chagrin. The first arrived on October 19. Three 12-man teams initially went to Takhar, Panjshir, and Mazar-e-Sharif. Nearly a dozen more would arrive within a month and go to the Mazar-e-Sharif front, the Hazaras in the center of the country, Ismael Khan in Herat, Uruzgan, and Kandahar, and Tora Bora.[45] One of the first special forces troopers, Cliff Richardson, recalled, "When we first walked into the country, I mean, you had the weight of the nation on your shoulders. We were America's response to the most catastrophic terrorist attack on US soil ever. And for a lot of us, you know, we felt that we had a responsibility to the people who died to set the stage that you just don't do that to America and not pay the price. It was about, not retribution, but it was about justice."[46]

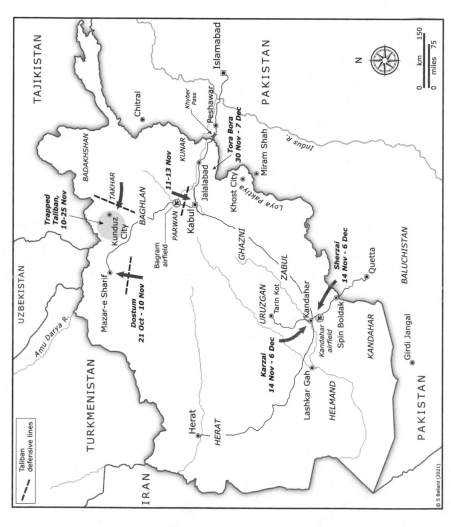

Map 5 US invasion of Afghanistan

Known as the Green Berets, US special forces are the subject of countless movies. Legend has it special forces were beloved by President John F. Kennedy. They were highly trained to accomplish a variety of missions, such as working with local militaries or militias (known as foreign internal defense), capturing enemy leaders (known as direct action), or running a guerrilla war (known as unconventional warfare). They were especially famous for advising local irregular units in Vietnam. Their 12-man teams included highly trained snipers, medics, intelligence experts, and forward air controllers. The latter could call in air strikes, one of the main reasons special forces could work in such small numbers. A captain commanded each team. Training included local languages and regional familiarization. With these skill sets, special forces teams were tailor-made to advise and fight alongside local armies, militias, or guerrillas.

The leaders of the Northern Alliance—Dostum, Ismael Khan, Atta, and Fahim—were eager to work with the United States. The CIA funded the Northern Alliance leaders. The Northern Alliance had 15,000 to 20,000 men, split between the four commanders, across five different locations: the Kabul front line, Badakhshan and Takhar, south of Mazar-e-Sharif, central Afghanistan, and Herat.

Throughout Afghanistan, the Taliban had around 45,000 men, plus 2,700 or so al-Qaʻeda and other foreign fighters.[47] The Taliban fighting forces were arrayed across the north. They were not regular armies but fronts made up of cadres of fighters under various commanders. These fronts faced the Northern Alliance forces near Kabul, Badakhshan, and Mazar-e-Sharif. The Taliban had other cadres in the south and east where there was no fighting. They were either organizing to go fight in the north or pulling local security. Once the air campaign began, Taliban reinforced their front line in Kabul with forces from the south. Additionally, volunteers rushed in from Pakistan, perhaps as many as 500 per day. According to some Taliban accounts, 10,000 volunteers from all over Pakistan entered Afghanistan during the first weeks of the war.[48]

Before the US intervention, the focal point of the Taliban and Northern Alliance campaigns had been Kabul. Mohammed Fahim, who had become leader of the Panjshiris after Massoud's death, had roughly 8,000 Tajiks immediately north of Kabul on the Shomali plain. Trenches and defensive positions defined the front line. The CIA team leader later wrote, "Taliban tanks, troops and artillery dug into trenches, command posts and ammo bunkers. . . . Without air power, General Fahim's commander in that sector, Bismullah Khan, wasn't going anywhere. He had at most 8,000 men, including regulars and reserves. He knew that the Taliban, on the other side, boasted at least 12,000."[49] Every day, machine guns shot back and forth at each other. Bismullah Khan, who had long been one of Massoud's best front line commanders, used Bagram airfield, the beat-up old Soviet airbase, as his front line headquarters.

Kabul would not be the main effort of the Northern Alliance offensive. The US national security council, heavily influenced by Secretary of State Powell, decided to hold the Tajiks back from Kabul in order to prevent discord with the other Northern Alliance factions. General Franks ordered that the main effort be Mazar-e-Sharif. Once captured, a supply line could be opened to the Northern Alliance via the Central Asian republics.

The Taliban had approximately 10,000 fighters in northern Afghanistan, centered on Mazar-e-Sharif. Mullah Fazl Mohammed commanded them, a thick mujahideen from Uruzgan rumored to have killed people with his own hands. Taliban fighters feared him.[50] He was the acting chief of the Taliban military but really the field commander in the north. The deeply religious Mazar-e-Sharif governor, Nooriullah Noori, supported him. Mullah Omar had deployed several hundred al-Qaʻeda and foreign fighters (especially from Pakistani militant groups), known as a "brigade," to bolster the defenses. The Taliban were also supported by hundreds of Pakistani advisors and trainers from the ISI, who had been trying to complete the Taliban defeat of the Northern Alliance.[51]

The Northern Alliance had roughly 7,000 fighters in the north, divided between the Tajiks of Mohammed Atta, the Hazaras of Mohammed Mohaqqeq, and the Uzbeks of Abdur Rashid Dostum. The key leader was the hard-drinking Dostum. He was based west of Mazar-e-Sharif in the Uzbek corner of Afghanistan. His 3,000 men had been fighting roughly 100 kilometers south of Mazar-e-Sharif for months, unable to take much ground.

After October 19, Franks was ready to launch a ground offensive and shift his air assets to support the Northern Alliance in combat. This, in the vernacular, is "close air support," to be differentiated from targeting economic infrastructure, logistics, or leaders often far from the battlefield. CIA and special forces teams were now in place with Dostum and Atta. On October 21, they attacked the Taliban front lines south of Mazar-e-Sharif.[52] The CIA and special forces teams called in precise close air support.

Dostum's Uzbek fighters were largely on horseback. The CIA operatives and special forces team famously rode horses alongside, their equipment strapped to donkeys. "We had greater maneuverability on horseback in that terrain than the Taliban or al-Qaʻeda did. They're in armored vehicles and pickup trucks. They're tied to their fuel depots," remembered Captain Mark Nutsch, the special forces team leader. "We were able to cut 'em off from reinforcement and cut 'em off from retreat. I probably rode three hundred miles or more."[53] They reduced Taliban sangar after sangar, dugout after dugout through rocky terrain up the main river valley toward Mazar-e-Sharif.[54] The special forces team coordinated air barrages ahead of the cavalry, including massive BLU-82 15,000-pound bombs (also known as "fuel-air explosives" for the pressure they exert when detonating just above the ground).[55]

The air strikes shocked the Taliban. A commander on the front line later told *Newsweek*, "The bombs cut down our men like a reaper harvesting wheat. Bodies were dismembered. Dazed fighters were bleeding from the ears and nose from the bombs' concussions. We couldn't bury the dead. Our reinforcements died in their trenches."[56] The air strikes decimated Taliban reserves moving to the front line. Political scientist Stephen Biddle wrote in a post-campaign study, "[US] officers who surveyed the scene afterward said it brought to mind the infamous 'Highway of Death' leading out of Kuwait City in the 1991 Persian Gulf War."[57]

On November 8, Dostum's forces came up against significant Taliban defenses at the Tangi gap, a narrow point in the valley, 20 kilometers south of Mazar-e-Sharif. The Taliban had concentrated hundreds of their fighters there. The CIA and special forces teams called in two days of air strikes on the Taliban positions and the surrounding area. On November 9, Dostum broke through. The Taliban retreated in disorder, unable to defend the critical approaches to Mazar-e-Sharif.[58] On horseback, Chief Warrant Officer Bob Pennington "looked back; looked south. And then I just realized it was—it was the most unbelievable shot I've ever seen. It was a thousand riders on horseback. It was peaceful yet magnificent."[59]

According to their own history, Taliban resistance across the north buckled under the weight of air and ground attacks. Upon hearing of the breakthrough south of Mazar-e-Sharif, Mullah Omar understood that his forces were in danger of destruction. He directed the commanders, Fazl and Noori, to have the Taliban around Mazar-e-Sharif retreat.[60] The next day, Atta and Dostum entered Mazar-e-Sharif, engaging in only scattered skirmishes. Omar seems to have hoped for an organized retreat back to Kabul, Kunduz, and Herat. Once he gave the order, however, the front collapsed across 12 northern provinces. Herat fell to Ismael Khan on November 12. The Taliban only held in Kunduz, with its largely Pashtun population. Fazl and Noori and thousands of fighters from surrounding provinces retreated there.

With Mazar-e-Sharif in hand, Franks turned to Kabul. Bush and his team hoped to defeat the Taliban yet restrain the Northern Alliance from entering the city until a political settlement on the future of the Afghan government could be reached. On November 11, US aircraft started pounding Taliban lines north of Kabul.

The Americans knocked on an open door. According to Mutawakil, the defeat in the north had given "an extremely fearful picture to all Taliban."[61] Mullah Omar radioed out general instructions to the whole force to reorganize a defense of Kabul and the south.[62] Yet, by recognizing the setbacks, he only spread fear. The collapse of the north unnerved the Taliban high council in Kabul. Escalating air strikes on the Kabul front line and on the city itself pushed them into a state of panic. Mullah Obaidullah, the Taliban minister of defense, was in charge.

On November 12, after conferring with Mullah Omar, who did not object, Obaidullah decided to withdraw from the city. The intention of Obaidullah and the Taliban commanders in the city was to fall back to Jalalabad and Kandahar to continue resistance.[63] Without coordinating well with Obaidullah and before commanders could formulate an organized plan, the deputy minister of the interior, Mullah Khaksar, sent out messages to Taliban units and fighters to evacuate the city, with no mention of further resistance. By the end of November 13, Taliban military forces in Kabul had dissipated.

Collapse fanned out from Kabul. Word spread south and undermined Taliban morale everywhere. Taliban fighters outside the city, in the eastern and southern regions, started laying down arms, blending into their villages, heading to Pakistan, or making for the mountains. In a few places, local Taliban leaders, speaking with village elders, decided it was better to spare the people bombing, a Northern Alliance assault, and the accompanying atrocities than stand and fight. The authority of the religious state crumbled. Other than the heart of the south in Kandahar, Taliban surrendered authority to tribal leaders.[64]

Seeing the writing on the wall, Mullah Omar ordered the Taliban to prepare to defend Kandahar and the surrounding provinces of Helmand, Uruzgan, and Zabul. He permitted his commanders to surrender the provincial capitals in other provinces. He told them that defense was impossible because US bombers would easily target emirate offices and buildings.[65]

On November 13, as the Taliban evacuated, Mohammed Fahim occupied Kabul with Massoud's Tajik troops, disregarding US entreaties to await a larger political settlement. Burnahuddin Rabbani, the former Tajik president and leader of Jamiat Islami (the mujahideen party in which the Tajik commanders of the Northern Alliance were members), installed himself as Afghanistan's new president. The international community and other Afghans rejected his claim. Fahim and other Tajik leaders recognized they would have to cede the position soon to avoid renewed civil war.

With the fall of Kabul, the only significant Taliban forces outside Kandahar were those in Kunduz. About 5,000 Taliban were surrounded there, along with Pakistani trainers, advisors, and ISI operatives.[66] Pakistani president Musharraf called Dostum and asked him to agree to let Taliban in Kunduz surrender. Fazl and Noori, the Taliban commanders in Kunduz, negotiated the surrender of their forces on November 25 with Dostum. The Pakistan Army supposedly airlifted out as many as 2,000 Pakistani military officers, Pakistani Taliban, and Afghan Taliban.[67] The remaining Taliban handed over their weapons in return for free passage to their homes in the south and east. Unfortunately, many of the Afghan Taliban never got home. The United States would eventually ship Fazl and Noori off to Guantanamo prison in US territory on the island of Cuba.[68] Worse,

Dostum inhumanely transported hundreds southward in shipping containers. Hundreds died of asphyxiation. Human rights meant little to Dostum.

Such amnesty did not extend to the remaining Arab and Central Asian foreign fighters with the Taliban. They were detained and shipped to Qala-e-Jangi prison. They started a prison riot, seized control of their compound, captured weapons, and killed a CIA officer. In a seven-day battle, US air strikes and Dostum's tanks crushed the insurrection.

By mid-November, the Taliban had lost most of Afghanistan. Omar still controlled the Taliban heartland in Kandahar and its surrounding provinces. The Northern Alliance moved little farther south than Kabul. Fahim had no interest in advancing into Pashtun regions. He was happy to have Kabul and declined US entreaties to send men with US teams to Jalalabad or toward Kandahar.[69] As Grenier and Tenet had argued, the United States needed Pashtun allies to overthrow the Taliban in southern Afghanistan. Fortunately for the United States, the CIA had been carefully nurturing Pashtun contacts for years.

One of those contacts was Abdul Haq, among the most capable Pashtun commanders of the Soviet-Afghan War. He attempted to go into Afghanistan and start a revolt. Against the advice of the CIA, on October 23, Abdul Haq entered Nangarhar with fewer than 20 followers and went to his home district to rally fighters. After a few days, the Taliban located, captured, and killed him. Without coordinated US support, he could not survive in Taliban country. The CIA worried the same fate might befall another contact: Hamid Karzai.

Hamid Karzai was a 44-year-old diplomat and Pashtun tribal leader. He had been part of the mujahideen throughout the Soviet-Afghan War, on the political side in Pakistan. Karzai's father, Abdul Ahad, had been the leading Popalzai tribal leader. His family descended from Ahmed Shah Durrani, founder of the modern Afghan state.

Karzai had attended college in India and spoke fluent English, as well as Dari and Pashto. He had served briefly as deputy foreign minister in Rabbani's government during the civil war. Americans would sometimes miscast him as Western in thinking because of his English and support for democracy. Karzai was Afghan, having lived his life in Afghanistan, Pakistan, and India. He was adept at tribal politics—patient and skilled at mediation, acceptant of patronage as a tool. He was oddly unwarlike, preferring diplomacy and disdaining violence. A role model was Ghaffer Khan, a colleague of Gandhi who had led peaceful Pashtun movements against the British and then the Pakistani state. Karzai's tribal skills and peaceful preferences would be both a blessing and a curse.

Karzai had joined the Taliban regime when they first seized Kandahar and even met Mullah Omar but soon changed his mind and returned to Pakistan, where he led a relaxed life. When the Taliban assassinated his father in 1999,

Karzai assumed the role of Popalzai tribal leader. His sights did not rest there, he later confided with Americans, "I had only been back to Afghanistan once since [1992], to bury my martyred father. From that day I was convinced that, mark my words, I would return, not at the head of a funeral train, but as the head of Afghanistan."[70] He befriended the CIA and aligned with Massoud and the Northern Alliance. He still moved slowly, until September 11 prompted him to take action. Karzai devised a plan to enter Afghanistan, lead a tribal uprising, and overthrow the Taliban. He would start with his Popalzai in Uruzgan, the dry and rugged province north of Kandahar, and then rally other tribes.

Karzai shared his plan with Grenier's CIA team, who liked it.[71] A Pashtun ally would be in the field fighting the Taliban. Journalists, foreign diplomats, many Afghans, and US military officers would later argue that the CIA and other US officials had decided at this early moment that Karzai should be the next leader of Afghanistan. CIA and other US officials certainly spotted Karzai's potential. Whether they planned anything more is unknown.

Karzai's tribesmen and his brother Ahmed Wali warned Karzai not to go. Undeterred, Karzai entered Afghanistan on October 9, right after the war started. Kabul and Mazar-e-Sharif were still a month from falling. Karzai crossed the Pakistani border near Spin Boldak with three other men. They rode two motorcycles, two men per bike, unarmed. Grenier's team had given Karzai satellite phones and money to communicate with tribal leaders and pay them. Karzai rumbled through the teeth of the Taliban in Kandahar City to rugged Uruzgan and his Popalzai tribesmen.[72]

In Tarin Kowt, the Uruzgan provincial capital, Karzai called together the Popalzai and other tribes. He raised a couple hundred men. Taliban got word of his activities. Karzai and his contingent trekked west into the hills and received a US air drop of weapons and ammunition. Shortly thereafter, somewhere between 50 and 500 Taliban attacked him. Karzai's men fended off the Taliban long enough to escape. After two days wandering in the hills, Karzai called the CIA for a rescue. A helicopter flew him back to Pakistan on November 3. He had escaped by the skin of his teeth.[73]

Karzai spent a few days in Pakistan reorganizing and then, on November 14, returned to Afghanistan, by which time the United States had sufficient forces deployed to help Karzai on a scale beyond what had been possible six weeks earlier. This time, a CIA officer and a special forces team accompanied him. Kabul had now fallen and Karzai's tribal allies in Uruzgan warned the Taliban provincial governor that he had best leave. The Taliban evacuated Tarin Kowt by the time Karzai and the special forces arrived. Karzai formed a tribal army and prepared to move south.[74]

The Taliban sent a column of 300 to 500 fighters up the road from Kandahar in pick-ups and jeeps to crush the uprising. After a panic when his tribesmen ran from the battlefield, Karzai steadied the defense. Three miles from Tarin Kowt, the special forces team was able to call in air strikes on the elongated Taliban column. "We kept bombing the convoy," recalled Captain Jason Amerine. "We worked the aircraft so the lead elements in the convoy were struck first. At this point it was maybe 7 or 8 in the morning. . . . With the adrenaline going you lose track of that. . . . We successfully destroyed or drove off the lead elements of the convoy . . . We just started working our way back, striking targets all along the main road."[75] In short order, the special forces team annihilated the Taliban column. Karzai advanced southward. US air strikes brushed aside occasional Taliban counter-attacks.[76]

Throughout his endeavors, Karzai displayed a sense of conciliation and mercy, traits he would continue to favor in the future, sometimes to the exclusion of practicalities. He focused on talking with tribal leaders and convincing them to leave the Taliban as much as on the military operations. Early on, he was wary that air strikes could kill innocents and turn people against him. When Taliban were captured, he granted them amnesty and let them return to their families, often with their weapons. He was known to shout at his men, "No killing!"[77] Higher-ranking leaders came to Karzai to ask to surrender, including the governor of Nangarhar and Mullah Dadullah Lang (who had commanded in Kunduz and would make his way to Quetta).[78] By then, Ramadan had started. Every day Karzai and his men fasted. He could have taken exception because he was traveling and at war; but he prioritized ideals over practicalities.

As Karzai advanced on Kandahar, the United Nations, United States, Pakistan, Iran, and Northern Alliance and other exiled Afghan political leaders discussed the future of Afghanistan. By 2001, Afghanistan had endured two decades of war. The Taliban had been the most stable government. With their fall, Bush and his team understood that establishing a new government would be difficult and risk of slipping back into civil war was great, hence the erstwhile attempt to keep Fahim and Rabbani out of Kabul. They also understood that Pashtuns had to be deeply involved in the process or they might continue to back the Taliban. Hence the support for Karzai's endeavors in the south.

In late September, Bush directed Powell to create a plan to establish a political settlement and transition the country to democracy.[79] Powell's diplomats worked with the United Nations. In order to bring the opposition groups together, the United Nations convened the Bonn conference, in Germany. The conference opened on November 27, 2001. Representatives of the Northern Alliance, the old Afghan monarchy, and smaller Pashtun groups were present, as were delegations from the United States, Pakistan, India, Russia, and Iran. The degree of international unity was notable. Adversaries worked together. Bearing no love for the Taliban, Russia and Iran cooperated with the United States and would continue to do so for years.

The Taliban were excluded. A conference for a political *settlement* without one of the most important parties seems to have struck no one as odd. Ambassador Jim Dobbins, the experienced diplomat who led the US delegation at Bonn, later described his own thinking at the time, indicative of the general mood: "Out of the question. They have been defeated. Why should they be included?"[80] It was another case of how the mood of the time overrode wiser diplomacy.

The highly respected diplomat Lakhdar Brahimi was UN envoy to Afghanistan and the moderator of the Bonn conference. Although Bush ultimately wanted to see democracy take root in Afghanistan, Ambassador Dobbins was given latitude to form any kind of broad-based representative government.[81] Dobbins's key subordinate was Zalmay Khalilzad. An Afghan-American of Pashtun descent, Khalilzad was the senior White House official for the Middle East and well-connected within the US administration, having ties to Rumsfeld and Wolfowitz. He had grown up in Kabul before the Soviet war and understood Afghanistan better than any other American official.

At the conference, the Afghans reached agreement on the political process, later known as the Bonn agreement. They received input from the United Nations and the other delegations but it was an Afghan product. The agreement stipulated a series of steps that would lead to democracy (the "Bonn process" for short). First, an interim administration, to be selected at the conference, was to stand up for six months. Then, a loya jirga was to meet and decide who would form a transitional government. That transitional government was to last 18 months. Its job was to draft a new constitution and organize national elections. The elections were to select the permanent government.

The most controversial issue was who would lead the interim government. The question had supreme weight for Afghans and for their neighbors, especially Pakistan, which deeply opposed any non-Pashtun leadership. On the Afghan side, the Northern Alliance was divided. The Tajik followers of Ahmed Shah Massoud—Dr. Abdullah, Yunis Qanooni, and Mohammed Fahim—wanted Afghanistan's next leader to be a Pashtun from outside the Northern Alliance. Massoud had believed that the Tajiks would have to share power with the Pashtuns if Afghanistan was to escape civil war. His belief rubbed off on his subordinates. Abdullah, Qanooni, and Fahim doubted a Tajik would be accepted by the majority of Afghans as their ruler. They did not want King Zahir Shah, the old king who had been living in Italy since his ouster in 1973. They wanted someone young and active who could actually lead the country. Rabbani, the official leader of Jamiat Islami, was still in Kabul, however, and considered himself president.

The Pashtuns were even more divided than the Northern Alliance. They had no natural leader. Various tribal leaders and representatives of old mujahideen parties represented them at the conference. The "Rome group" of King Zahir Shah was the strongest though lack of mujahideen credentials tarred its credibility.

Of the Pashtun field, Karzai stood out. Karzai's demeanor and background were well-known, and his revolt in the south was gaining notoriety. Before the Bonn conference, Dobbins had traveled to Afghanistan and visited Pakistan. He had spoken with Dr. Abdullah, Ahmed Shah Massoud's chief diplomat. Abdullah had told Dobbins, "We need more than a figurehead . . . We need someone who will be able to deal with the terrible challenges Afghanistan now faces . . . Hamid Karzai would be an acceptable choice."[82] In Pakistan, the ISI also proposed Karzai, who must have seemed less anti-Pakistan than the king's supporters or the Northern Alliance.[83] Iran was amenable to Karzai as well. At the opening of the Bonn conference, Brahimi allowed Karzai to give a brief speech via satellite phone from Uruzgan.

Weighing the competing interests, Khalilzad and Dobbins proposed an arrangement in which King Zahir Shah would play a ceremonial role, the Northern Alliance would step back from the presidency, and the Pashtuns would nominate a different interim president. They suspected that nominee would be Karzai. Brahimi supported the arrangement. Khalilzad skillfully negotiated with the Afghan parties until all sides concurred.[84]

As Dobbins and Khalilzad had expected, the Afghans settled on Karzai—though not without more back and forth. Brahimi gently pressured ambitious supporters of the king to step aside. According to Bette Dam, one of Karzai's foremost biographers, it was King Zahir Shah who settled the matter: "Choose Karzai," the king said, "He's like a son to me. He's the only one of you actually in Afghanistan."[85] Rabbani and the Northern Alliance were tougher. Rabbani did not want to surrender the presidency and the rest of the Northern Alliance leaders could not decide which of them would be nominated for cabinet positions. They felt they had fought the war and deserved to dominate the government. Pressure from Dobbins, Khalilzad, and other international leaders, including a press conference by Dobbins, a telephone call from the Russian foreign minister, and back-corner deal with the Iranians, convinced Rabbani and the other Northern Alliance leaders to let things move forward. The Northern Alliance won just over half the cabinet positions, including the three key ministries.[86] Mohammed Fahim became minister of defense. Yunis Qanooni became minister of interior. Dr. Abdullah became minister of foreign affairs. All Panjshiri Tajiks. All followers of Ahmed Shah Massoud.

Karzai was informed of his selection on December 5, in northern Kandahar. Minutes earlier a US bomb had mistakenly struck his position. Luckily, he escaped with minor facial lacerations from a piece of shrapnel. Ten members of his retinue and three US special forces troopers were less fortunate. Captain Amerine was among the wounded and had to be evacuated. Shaken physically, but now in a position of far greater authority, Karzai continued toward Kandahar City.

As Karzai advanced southward, more and more tribal leaders, their tribesmen, and defeated Taliban joined his ranks, which eventually swelled to 3,000. The most important was the great Alikozai tribal leader Mullah Naqib. The Alikozai and Popalzai shared a certain bond. Ahmed Shah Durrani, founder of the Afghan state, had been Popalzai. His mother, Zarghona Ana, had been Alikozai. Karzai was keeping in touch with Naqib via satellite phone. Naqib had aligned with the Taliban in 1994 and respected their devotion to Islam. But tribe came first. A peaceful transition from the Taliban to a new Popalzai regime was deeply in his interest. Since the beginning of the war, he had been encouraging the Taliban to lay down their arms.[87]

Meanwhile, the United States backed another Pashtun commander in the drive toward Kandahar City: Gul Agha Sherzai, a hulking Pashtun who had been a mujahideen commander during the Soviet-Afghan War. He was Barakzai, the tribe of King Zahir and 150 years' worth of Afghan kings. Common Durrani ancestry and centuries of rulership in the face of common enemies tied the Barakzai and Popalzai together. They were also political rivals for the throne itself.

On November 14, Sherzai and 350 Barakzai and Achekzai tribal militia advanced from Pakistan into Kandahar via the desolate Arghestan frontier.[88] A US special forces team accompanied them, coordinating supply and calling in air strikes. Three thousand Taliban defended Kandahar City, fewer than the combined forces of Karzai and Sherzai. Sherzai's force stepped forward slowly, letting US air strikes overcome Taliban resistance in a series of engagements along the road toward the city. At first the Taliban fighters, commanded by Hafiz Abdur Rahim, a religious scholar and veteran commander of the Soviet-Afghan War, resisted staunchly. A contingent of 300 al-Qaʿeda fought alongside them.[89] Concealing themselves in irrigation ditches and culverts, the Taliban and al-Qaʿeda fighters slowed Sherzai's advance in a series of rearguard actions. A Taliban history records that heavy air strikes wore them down: "Day after day, war supply and logistical shortages caused resistance to weaken."[90]

The Taliban were under great pressure. Convinced the battle had been lost, several of Mullah Omar's lieutenants pleaded with him to give up Kandahar and the emirate. On November 23, Mullah Omar met with the senior council of Taliban leaders. At that time, after heated debate, Omar demanded that they fight on. The council obeyed.[91]

Mullah Omar ordered his forces to steadily withdraw until they were closer to the city and better able to put up a concentrated defense. He was determined to defend Kandahar long enough for Arabs living there to escape and for the Taliban that had surrendered to Dostum to complete their fair passage home. After that, he was willing to surrender the city to tribal leaders in order to save the civilian population from US bombardment.[92] The Taliban fell back from village to village and culvert to culvert after initial bouts of resistance and then put up a stiffer defense of the airport, southeast of the city. Commander Hafiz Abdur Rahim was wounded in the fighting and unable to lead. Many of his fighters headed back to their villages.[93] Al-Qa'eda types were more determined. Some fought to the death. On December 3, after days of bombardment, Sherzai's forces began their assault on Kandahar airport, just south of the city. Determined Taliban and a few Arab fighters defended the airfield.[94]

When Sherzai's forces neared Kandahar airfield, to the southeast of the city, high-ranking Taliban leaders went to Mullah Naqib to arrange a meeting with Karzai. On December 5, the same day as the errant bomb strike, Mullah Obaidullah (Mullah Omar's deputy and minister of defense), Mullah Baradar (Mullah Omar's future deputy), Tayeb Agha (Mullah Omar's assistant and future head of the political commission), Raees Baghrani (powerful Alizai tribal leader), and other senior Taliban met with Karzai. They reported directly to Mullah Omar.[95] According to the research of several Western journalists, the Taliban delegation was willing to lay down arms in return for immunity. They gave Karzai a letter that may have offered a way for the Taliban to step down from power peacefully. Mullah Omar may have signed it.[96] In a second meeting on December 6, consensus was reached that the Taliban would depart Kandahar. Karzai agreed that Omar would go to northern Helmand and live with Raees Baghrani, who had sided with the Taliban since 1994.[97] Karzai trusted Baghrani as a respected tribal leader of long lineage who would not allow Omar to instigate violence against the new state. Baghrani was known as a man of his word. From Islamabad, Mullah Abdul Salam Zaeef, Taliban ambassador to Pakistan, announced a deal had been reached and the Taliban would hand over Kandahar and their weapons to Mullah Naqib.[98]

What happened after this is the subject of debate. According to certain interviews with Karzai's retinue and Taliban leaders of the time, Karzai and the delegation had reached a meaningful agreement and Mullah Omar was quite possibly ready to stand aside. Former Taliban foreign minister Mutawakil writes that the delegation had agreed to hand over Kandahar to Karzai, though they had not come to an overarching peace deal.[99] Some evidence exists that Mullah Omar had already been talking with Karzai on the satellite phone during his march south from Uruzgan, which would give credence to the idea that a comprehensive peace deal was in the offing.[100]

Two things overturned the deal. First, Sherzai and the accompanying US special forces team captured Kandahar airfield on December 6 and marched into Kandahar City on December 7 before the deal could be finalized.[101] Second, the United States pressured Karzai to ignore the Taliban overtures.[102] Karzai told Lieutenant Colonel David Fox, the commander of his special forces advisors, of the proposed deal. Fox was skeptical and passed it up the chain. In a press conference on December 6, US Secretary of Defense Donald Rumsfeld vetoed any peace with the Taliban. He also sent a private warning to Karzai that any deal would be against US interests.[103] In this and other discussions with the Northern Alliance and Karzai, Rumsfeld and US officials may have even threatened to pull US support if any deal went through. Right after Rumsfeld's news conference, a Northern Alliance spokesman said, "It has been communicated to us that if we arrange a peace plan that allows for the release of Mullah Omar, Karzai would lose support from America, and the Northern Alliance would lose the support of the coalition."[104] This version of events—that the Taliban and Mullah Omar were seriously ready to lay down arms and accept peace—is of profound importance for the history of Afghanistan. If true, the United States purposefully scuttled a chance for peace at its moment of peak bargaining power and set Afghanistan back down the road to war.

Other sources, also Taliban leaders of the time, tell a different story. In their accounts, Mullah Omar was not party to whatever agreement was reached with Karzai. Zaeef states in his history of the Taliban regime that Omar had no intention of surrendering to Karzai and that he gave no one authority to negotiate surrender on his behalf.[105] The members of the Taliban delegation were merely negotiating the peaceful turnover of Kandahar City and individual amnesty to return to their homes. A Taliban military commander present at the delegation's meeting with Mullah Omar before the December 5 meeting with Karzai backs up what Zaeef writes: "We were gathered in a house in Kandahar and everyone was making arguments about what to do . . . Mullah Omar just sat and listened to everyone quietly. Finally he told them, 'You should do what you like, you should protect yourself. But don't try to contact me anymore.' "[106] Likewise, Mullah Naqib and Raees Baghrani, both party to the negotiations, separately told journalists Sarah Chayes and Carlotta Gall that Mullah Omar decided to leave Kandahar on his own accord in order to continue the movement. Omar, they say, departed before his delegation came back from their second meeting with Karzai on December 6. Baghrani returned to Kandahar City that day to find Mullah Omar and most of the Taliban gone. In retrospect, he told Gall that Omar was right not to negotiate.[107] Naqib, who was also with the delegation, told Chayes a similar tale. He said that the Taliban delegation itself decided to renege on their agreement with Karzai: "When we reached Kandahar . . . the Taliban declared they were not going to wait two days to pull out, they were going to leave tomorrow."[108] This different version of events would suggest there never was a meaningful chance for a full-blown 2001 peace agreement. Even had the United States been willing, nothing would have come of the initiative; Mullah Omar wanted no deal.[109]

In either case, Mullah Omar disappeared. The Taliban history of the period states that on December 6 Mullah Omar ordered the cessation of all resistance and the evacuation of Kandahar airport and city: "From the direction of the Emir al-Momineen, Kandahar was evacuated."[110] The order allowed Sherzai to capture the airport. Mullah Omar then issued a message to the Taliban that announced the beginning of guerrilla war against the "crusader invaders."[111] One story is that Omar headed directly for Pakistan. Another is that he drove off to Zabul, his tribal homeland, in a lorry with a few close friends. Yet another is that he fled to northern Helmand and lived for months under the care of Raees Baghrani.[112]

The Taliban movement dispersed in different directions. Dadullah Lang, Jalaluddin Haqqani, and other high ranking Taliban leaders escaped to Pakistan. Thousands of fighters went with them. So did respected religious scholars. The mere idea of an infidel-backed government seems to have prompted many to go to Pakistan. They would often describe themselves as taking refuge (*hajrat*) in the manner the Prophet Mohammed had fled to Medina during the first days of Islam.

If Omar, Haqqani, and Dadullah may have been already committed to a long guerrilla war, the feelings of the majority of the Taliban are unclear. One well-known religious scholar and teacher, Maulawi Anayatullah, advised his followers, "Everywhere that infidels come, on that pure soil, they cannot stay. It is necessary that they face with defeat. Do not support or help them."[113] Other Taliban, however, tried to return to their homes. After the collapse of Kandahar, Karzai announced that all Taliban could live openly and freely with their families.[114] Those who took advantage of the offer included Baghrani, scores of front line commanders and scholars, hundreds of mullahs, and future Taliban leader Akhtar Mohammed Mansour. They may not, at that point, have been committed to a long guerrilla war—at least not yet. What the majority thought may always remain a mystery.

Regardless of Mullah Omar's willingness to talk, the United States can be faulted for shutting down talks. What was going on in the US government is murky. There is no national security council meeting on public record in which Karzai's negotiations were discussed. Other than Rumsfeld, no principal cabinet member is known to have been informed, although CIA officers in Afghanistan and Pakistan knew and it is hard to imagine that Tenet was left in the dark.[115] Both Dobbins and Khalilzad in Bonn were unaware of exactly what was transpiring on the ground.[116] Even if acting alone, Rumsfeld was consistent with Bush's overall attitude that the Taliban and al-Qa'eda were inseparable. Rumsfeld later boasted to Cheney that success in 2001 "required recognizing that defeating the Taliban regime had to be a goal, rather than preserving it to avoid chaos in Afghanistan or separating 'good' Taliban from bad ones."[117] Bush wrote in his own book, "By 9/11, Afghanistan was not only a state sponsor of terror, but a state sponsored by terror."[118] Washington was clearly cold to the idea of compromise.

Even without the benefit of hindsight, this narrow and inflexible approach contravened diplomatic wisdom to bring adversaries into a post-war political settlement. How Omar would have reacted to a conciliatory US approach is a mystery. New opportunities might have opened, even if Omar opposed peace. The US decision to reject any negotiations foreclosed the chance of such a future. In that regard, it must be regarded as one of the greatest mistakes of the Afghan War.

Since September 11, the CIA had been following clues to Osama bin Laden. Around November 10, several reports placed him moving through Jalalabad in a convoy of 200 pick-ups and sport utility vehicles (SUVs) with hundreds of his Arab and other foreign fighters. They were headed toward the Spin Ghar mountain range, along Nangarhar province's southern border with Pakistan. Whether these reports were accurate is unknown but by late November, bin Laden was at his training camp near Tora Bora mountain, well-fortified by a complex of caves and the natural cover of the mountains.[119]

The Spin Ghar ascend to peaks of 15,000 feet in height. Below the summits are forested mountainsides, valleys, and canyons, and hundreds of gullies and ravines filtering into Afghanistan and Pakistan. Bin Laden had chosen the Tora Bora site because he thought it a good defensive position. He insisted on locating most of his fighters and their families there in spite of the advice of other Arabs who believed the isolated spot would be a trap. He thought he could defeat the Americans in the mountains like he had defeated the Soviets at Jaji. Over the years, his fighters had dug trenches and cave complexes and stocked supplies. When the war started, bin Laden was determined to fight at Tora Bora. His key lieutenants and local Taliban commanders objected, citing the difficulty of resupply in the mountains and the power of US air strikes. They preferred guerrilla tactics in which the Americans would have difficulty finding him or his fighters. He disregarded their advice. Legend has it that he told his lieutenants that he openly used radio communications at Tora Bora because he wanted the Americans to "know where to come."[120]

The United States had known about the Tora Bora camp since the beginning of the war and had suspected al-Qa'eda elements to be hiding there.[121] The CIA lead in the Panjshir, Gary Berntsen, sent a detachment to catch up with Osama. His men cooperated with three tribal militias from Jalalabad that were opposed to the Taliban and aligned with the Northern Alliance. The leader of one of the militias was Haji Zahir, nephew of Abdul Haq.[122]

On November 30, the team and some of their Afghan allies came within sight of the training camp and started calling in air strikes. Bin Laden and a few hundred fighters were there.[123] Osama's voice could be heard on captured al-Qaʻeda radios encouraging his men, who also referred to his presence. With battle now underway, special operations forces arrived to reinforce the CIA team. Soon several special forces teams were calling in AC-130s, B-52 and B-1 bombers, and other types of aircraft for strikes on Tora Bora.[124]

The three tribal militias—totaling more than 1,000 men—slowly advanced as al-Qaʻeda steadily withdrew deeper into their camp. The militias fought in a tribal manner. They shied away from storming al-Qaʻeda positions, pursuing retreating al-Qaʻeda, rooting out caves, or fighting at night. Since it was Ramadan, they retired every evening to break the fast, some returning to their families off the mountain. Although the commanders themselves were open to fighting al-Qaʻeda, at least a few of the fighters were torn. Many had supported the Taliban. Others considered al-Qaʻeda fellow Muslims. Most were unaware of the events in New York City. Religious leaders, including the famous mujahideen commander Maulawi Mohammed Yunis Khalis, for whom many in the militias had fought in the past, told them to let bin Laden escape. There is even evidence that one of the three militia commanders gave al-Qaʻeda the option to retreat before attacking and later negotiated with them. For all these reasons, the militias were not inclined to fight aggressively and some probably purposefully ignored opportunities to stop bin Laden from escaping.[125]

On December 1, Berntsen requested that Franks send in a battalion of 800 Rangers, the elite light infantry unit within US special operations forces, to directly assault al-Qaʻeda and make up for the limitations of the Afghan tribal militias. The special forces teams were too few to get into regular combat. Franks never approved the request, which Berntsen and Crumpton made repeatedly. Besides the Rangers, there were also marines with plenty of helicopters at Kandahar airfield.[126] Their commander, Brigadier General James Mattis, was ready to deploy into Tora Bora. His requests too went nowhere. Franks believed things would move faster if he continued to rely on the Afghans.[127]

The battle of Tora Bora lasted 18 days, until December 17. Day after day, the CIA and special operations forces vectored air strikes onto al-Qaʻeda positions. As many as 100 per day pummeled the al-Qaʻeda fighters, who were continuing to slowly withdraw toward Pakistan. In all, the United States dropped more than 1,600 bombs and precision-guided munitions, including another BLU-82 fuel air explosive on December 9. Meanwhile, the al-Qaʻeda fighters were running out of food. On December 15, the remaining al-Qaʻeda fighters split into two groups and descended the southern slopes of the Spin Ghar toward Pakistan.

They bribed the tribes in this area and eluded Pakistani blocking forces until they were out of danger. At least 220 al-Qaʻeda fighters were killed and 52 were captured in the battle of Tora Bora. There were no US losses. Around 100 fighters probably escaped.[128]

Exactly when and how bin Laden escaped is another subject of debate. The conventional American viewpoint was that he directed and joined the December 15 withdrawal down the southern slopes of the Spin Ghar into Pakistan. Mustafa Hamid, Arab associate of bin Laden, claims bin Laden escaped much earlier, during the first week of December, and fled to Pakistan through Jalalabad. If true, the opportunity to capture bin Laden was slimmer than has generally been realized.[129]

Tora Bora was the United States' best chance to capture bin Laden in 2001. Since then, participants and observers have seen it as a lost opportunity.[130] Indeed, had bin Laden been captured, America's war on terror might have been curtailed. The foremost threat to the United States would have disappeared. The odds were never good. The terrain would have tried the best Rangers or marines. And it was winter. After 2001, the United States would conduct literally thousands of raids against precise targets in villages, cities, and farmland. In these more amenable locales, special operations forces would often miss their targets. Even a whole division of the best US troops, supported by 24-hour drone surveillance, would have had trouble sealing off the mountain range. The truth is that bin Laden probably always had a good chance of escape.

An addendum to Tora Bora is the battle of Shah-i-Kot in Paktiya in March 2002, better known as Operation Anaconda. Two US Army battalions and special operations forces attacked Taliban and al-Qaʻeda fighters located there. Another battle in rugged mountains, fighting was confused and lasted ten days. US forces suffered 80 casualties before taking the area and driving out al-Qaʻeda. It was the last major battle in Afghanistan for four years.

America's 2001 campaign in Afghanistan is a striking military success. With 110 CIA officers, 350 special operations forces, and roughly 5,000 marines and Rangers, backed by overwhelming air power, the United States toppled the Taliban. As many as 15,000 Taliban had been killed or taken prisoner.[131] Until March, only twelve Americans were killed. Popular resistance had been minimal. The tactical combination of special operations forces working with local forces and precision air strikes would be a model for future campaigns. It is the foundation for how the United States waged war in Afghanistan, Iraq, and Syria from 2014 onward. The campaign was also notable for the negotiation of a political settlement between long-feuding Afghan leaders. Whatever his future faults, in 2001 Hamid Karzai was an enlightened choice. He was conciliatory and personally brave, with political legitimacy unmatched by any of the contenders other than the aging king himself.

The victory altered the course of Afghan history. The religious direction of the Taliban was overturned. Afghanistan shifted back to a more secular direction under traditional state rule. Yet the brilliance of victory can overshadow the seeds of prolonged war. Al-Qaʻeda was severely hurt but bin Laden's dream of drawing the United States into Afghanistan came true. Bush and his team were under heavy pressure to secure the United States from additional terrorist attacks. They missed how their immediate course could trap them over the long term. Opportunities to avoid a long war eluded them.

Two opportunities stand above all others. First was the chance to convince the Taliban to hand over Osama bin Laden before the outbreak of war. Second was the opportunity to include the Taliban in the new political settlement. In both cases, the urgency of the moment overcame diplomacy. Omar was thinking rigidly in terms of what he had to do to lead his faith. His strength in forging a movement was his weakness in compromising for peace. Bush was also thinking from the heart—or the gut, as he was fond of saying. He felt America needed protection. The nuanced diplomacy required to reach out to an adversary amid a climate of fear and vengeance was not his forte, though he was a man of compassion. His strength in bringing the country to war was his weakness in seeing alternatives. Under the pressure of time and in a fog of bad information, Omar and Bush were on a collision course. One of the tragedies of 2001 is that Bush and his team could not find a way to give compassion a little more time.

5

The Karzai Regime

With the defeat of the Taliban and selection of Hamid Karzai as interim president, Afghanistan was at relative peace for the first time in 20 years. Little opposition existed to Karzai's interim government or the United States. Years of civil war and the shock of the US military victory discouraged Afghans from rising up as they had against the Soviet Union. People were tired. Mullah Omar and his colleagues were in disarray. Thousands of Taliban had returned to their homes. A mid-level Taliban commander told journalist Carlotta Gall, "In the early days, when there was a drought and poverty, and the foreigners were promising a lot, that was when we did not have support of the people."[1]

It was a time of opportunity. US and Afghan leaders had unique freedom to implement new policies and design a new government. Big questions confronted Bush and his team about future US presence and strategy in Afghanistan. Should the United States commit to creating a stable Afghan government over the long term—an expansive, interventionist form of foreign policy, or simply go after terrorists—a strict, restrained form of foreign policy? What kind of post-war political settlement should be established; how much of a victor's peace should it be? Should the United States seek to impose the writ of the new democratic government and build a national army, or leave the Afghans to manage affairs as they see fit? Bush, Cheney, Rumsfeld, Powell, and their generals were inattentive to the opportunity before them, largely thanks to overconfidence. Their decisions would lay the foundation of the new state and the US commitment. They would be most fateful for the outcome of the war.

When the initial military campaign ended, President George W. Bush and his administration had two goals. The first was to eliminate the remnants of al-Qa'eda and the Taliban. They repeatedly cited that as a US goal. The Taliban and al-Qa'eda had been defeated but Mullah Omar, Osama bin Laden, and key subordinates were at large. They were to be captured or killed.[2] The second was to help set up a new democracy that could prevent terrorists from coming back.[3] Bush and his team assumed that once these things had happened the

United States could withdraw. Significant investments in reconstruction, economic development, and institutions were not conceived, let alone a heavy footprint of US boots on the ground.

In early 2002, 8,000 US and 5,000 allied troops were in Afghanistan. Before the war had started, Bush, Powell, Rice, and Rumsfeld had assumed that the United States would have to leave thousands of troops to prevent terrorists from coming back. All agreed that the overriding lesson of the 1990s in Afghanistan was that the United States had created a vacuum by ignoring the country after the fall of the Soviet Union. Within that vacuum the conditions were generated for the rise of the Taliban and al-Qaʻeda.[4] Bush himself writes that after 1989, "the U.S. government no longer saw a national interest in Afghanistan, so it cut off support. America's noninvolvement helped create a vacuum . . . Ultimately, the Taliban, a group of Islamic fundamentalists, seized power."[5] An option of "attack, destroy the Taliban, destroy al-Qaʻeda as best we could and leave" was never appealing because "that would have created a vacuum into which . . . radicalism could become even stronger."[6]

Bush and his team also agreed that US troop presence could be light. Afghanistan was peaceful. Brigadier General Stanley McChrystal, a staff officer in Afghanistan and future commander of all forces in the country, writes, "It wasn't clear whether there was any war left. The hunt for al-Qaʻeda continued, but the Taliban seemed to have been decisively defeated; most had essentially melted away, and we weren't sure where they'd gone."[7]

Domestic factors shaped the mindset of Bush and his team. With the September 11 attack still fresh, the political atmosphere in the United States was charged with risk of another terrorist attack on the homeland and the need to capture or kill terrorists. Throughout 2002, various Gallup polls showed 50 to 85 percent of Americans worried a terrorist attack on the United States was likely or very likely.[8] The Taliban were widely thought to be one with al-Qaʻeda. Bush confronted pressure to eliminate al-Qaʻeda and their Taliban friends.

Thus the Bush administration decided almost inadvertently to stay rather than declare victory and go home. The idea of cutting and running was never even discussed. In later years, many Americans would say that was exactly what should have been done. It was not naturally apparent at the time.

Of Bush's principals, Secretary of Defense Donald Rumsfeld most opposed a US entanglement in Afghanistan.[9] He was wary of getting bogged down in nation-building—the practice of committing tens of thousands of US troops and hundreds of millions of dollars to stabilize conflict-ridden states. He writes in his memoirs, "Our . . . modest goal was to rid Afghanistan of al-Qaʻeda and replace their Taliban hosts with a government that would not harbor terrorists."[10] There is no greater villain in America's Afghan War than Donald Rumsfeld. He made many of the most-criticized decisions of the war, starting with his refusal to talk with the Taliban in 2001. Ironically, he had far-reaching foresight. He knew Afghanistan could become a quagmire. He was concerned about driving up US expenses. Respectful of Afghanistan's history, he was aware that US troops could upset the Afghan people and trigger an uprising. He wanted to outsource to Afghan partners and be done with the place as soon as possible. In hindsight, he was prescient. Yet his actual decisions cut off opportunities to avoid the future he so feared.

In White House meetings, Rumsfeld argued for a light US footprint. He was worried both about an Afghan backlash and diverting US troops from a possible war in Iraq. He sought to focus the small force on counterterrorism—killing and capturing al-Qa'eda fighters along the border with Pakistan.[11] General Tommy Franks, commander of central command, agreed. Franks and military planners inside Afghanistan thought the best plan was to underwrite the victorious Northern Alliance and mujahideen commanders. Rumsfeld convinced Bush and the rest of the national security council to leave a light footprint and rely on special operations forces.

The administration ended up deciding in early 2002 that the 8,000 US and 5,000 allied troops would stay in Afghanistan (the figure would creep up to 13,000 US troops by early 2004 to meet various operational requirements).[12] President Bush writes that in late 2002, "13,000 [US and allied] troops seemed like the right amount . . . it seemed like the enemy was on the run . . . We were all wary of repeating the experience of the Soviets and British who ended up looking like occupiers."[13]

Though Bush and Rumsfeld stated again and again that the troops would not stay in Afghanistan permanently, no timeline was placed on their presence. The assumption was that once al-Qa'eda and Taliban leaders had been ticked off and democracy had been established the United States could leave things in the hands of the new Afghan government. Besides this rudimentary set of goals and light footprint, the United States lacked much of a plan, which frustrated Rumsfeld. In April 2002, Rumsfeld remarked to senior officials in the Pentagon, "I can't believe that it takes that many months to figure it out. . . . We are never going to get the US military out of Afghanistan unless we take care to see that there is something going on that will provide the stability that will be necessary for us to leave. Help!"[14] Six months later there was still no plan.[15]

But such statements should not be misinterpreted to mean US troops in Afghanistan were sitting around doing nothing. There was a clear operational concept, reiterated repeatedly for over three years: counterterrorism, killing and capturing al-Qa'eda and Taliban senior leaders. With or without a well-constructed plan on how to reach victory, there was no question counterterrorism was the center of US military activity. US troops went about that task with a purpose.[16]

Completing the Bonn process was also a priority. But what to do beyond that—in terms of building new institutions, economics reconstruction, developing armed forces, and improving women's and human rights—was unsettled. Bush's thoughts on nation-building are ambiguous. Throughout the 2000 election campaign, Bush had criticized the concept.[17] In his memoirs, he would claim the attacks of September 11 shifted his perspective:

> At the time [2000 election campaign], I worried about overextending our military. . . . after 9/11, I changed my mind. Afghanistan was the ultimate nation-building mission. We had liberated the country from a primitive dictatorship, and we had a moral obligation to leave behind something better. We also had a strategic interest in helping the Afghan people build a free society. The terrorists took refuge in places of chaos, despair, and repression. A democratic Afghanistan would be a hopeful alternative to the vision of the extremists.[18]

In April 2002, quite out of the blue, Bush called for a "Marshall Plan" for Afghanistan in a speech at the Virginia Military Institute. The speech implied he wanted to rebuild Afghanistan like the United States had rebuilt Western Europe after the Second World War. Bush would later assert, "When you rout out a government like the Taliban you have a responsibility to replace it and to help a new government grow."[19] Oddly, he did not follow up on his speech. Rumsfeld disregarded it and forbade commanders from pursuing nation-building.[20] Though supportive of specific initiatives such as women's rights, roads, and an Afghan army, Bush never insisted on nation-building and cautioned Zalmay Khalilzad, his special representative to Afghanistan, against trying to build Afghan institutions.[21]

Yet to follow the strict policy debates alone is to miss the idealism of the intervention. That idealism existed in the strong American preference for a democracy, which was central to Bush's vision of counterterrorism but conceptually tied to nation-building. Deputy national security advisor Stephen Hadley explained the strategy involved as "a kinetic phase and then an ideological phase based on using the idea of freedom as an alternative vision to terrorism and to counter the appeal of al-Qa'eda."[22]

The idealism also existed in the strong American interest in improving the lives of Afghan women. Taliban treatment of women under the Taliban had horrified the United States and its allies. Americans perceived the Taliban's acceptance of terrorism as inherently linked to oppression of women. In the weeks after September 11, cable and television news highlighted the cruelty of the Taliban with images and documentaries. *The New York Times* editorial page celebrated "the reclaimed freedom of Afghan women" and the hope that "women's political participation will make Afghanistan a more democratic and less radical nation, as women prefer a more moderate form of Islam."[23] Though not an explicit strategic goal, Afghan women's rights were a moral cause for Americans, invoked by Bush in his 2002 State of the Union: "The last time we met in this chamber, the mothers and daughters of Afghanistan were captives in their own homes, forbidden from working or going to school. Today women are free, and are part of Afghanistan's new government."[24]

Powerful figures in both parties called for the protection of Afghan women almost immediately after September 11. First Lady Laura Bush delivered a radio address on the topic and Senator Hillary Clinton wrote in *Time* magazine, "There is an immoral link between the way women were treated by the oppressive Taliban in Afghanistan and the hateful actions of the al-Qa'eda terrorists."[25] The bipartisan consensus was visible when all 13 women senators co-sponsored the Afghan Women and Children Relief Act of 2001. Democrats in the House of Representatives and a coalition of US women's groups would successfully get $60 million allocated for women's programs in Afghanistan.[26] American and other Western advocates of women's rights, an influential network, became a constituency for intervention in Afghanistan. Helping Afghan women would be an informal reason that the United States would fight in Afghanistan for decades.

Emphasis on women's rights was associated with the broader international development community that also encouraged nation-building in Afghanistan. The Bonn Process corresponded with US and international economic assistance to build a new government. The United Nations Assistance Mission in Afghanistan (UNAMA) was founded to help facilitate the Bonn process and coordinate the international effort. The United States contributed to the development effort through the US Agency for International Development (USAID) funding.

The development community had set methods that encouraged the United States to increase its involvement in the construction of a new centralized government. Development methods focused on creating institutions—a ministry of justice to execute laws, a ministry of finance to manage a budget, a ministry of education to run schools, a ministry of public health to administer hospitals and clinics, a ministry of rural rehabilitation and development to spur development in the countryside. Such institution-building naturally called for international and American investment and against the opinion of Rumsfeld and others who wanted to let the Afghans do things their own way. The fact that European allies largely ascribed to the development community methods further nudged the Bush administration toward nation-building.

The Bonn Agreement of December 2001 had laid out the process for designing a new government. Karzai was the new interim president. Tajik leaders who worked with Ahmed Shah Massoud—Mohammed Fahim, Dr. Abdullah, and Yunis Qanooni—were now ministers. But there was not a lot more than that. There was no army other than the militias of the mujahideen commanders and tribal leaders. There was no legislative body, no constitution, and no formal legal system. The process for the confirmation of a provisional government, writing of a constitution, and election of a permanent government had to begin.

After Uruzgan and Bonn, Karzai was something of an international celebrity. Westerners thought that his conciliatory nature was just what war-torn Afghanistan needed. His image was enhanced by his kingly voice and regal trappings—gray lambskin hat, green and purple cloak, Western jacket, and Afghan blouse and pants. Karzai spent much of his first year consolidating his position and balancing the big northern alliance powerbrokers: Minister of Defense Mohammed Fahim, leader of Panjshir; Abdur Rashid Dostum, the Uzbek warlord who now dominated the north; and Ismael Khan, the Tajik governor of Herat. Karzai nurtured a close relationship with the United States and worked hand-in-glove with Khalilzad, who traveled back and forth from Washington as Bush's special representative for Afghanistan.

Khalilzad continued to play a leading role in the political process. The Afghan-American was highly energetic and knew all the Afghan players. He would shuttle back and forth between them and fluently broker deals. Khalilzad had an affinity for Karzai, remarking, "I was impressed by how deftly and emphatically he conducted business with people from all walks of life. I learned a great deal simply by observing him."[27] More than Bush or Rumsfeld, Khalilzad felt that the United States needed to commit more resources to Afghanistan:

> I was skeptical that we could prevent the reemergence of terrorist safe havens in Afghanistan without rebuilding the country's institutions. . . . Otherwise, Americans, rather than Afghan troops and police, would have to stand watch. In order to steer Afghan leaders in the right direction, we had to convince them that we would not abandon the country again and that we would make the necessary investments to create a functioning Afghan state.[28]

Khalilzad viewed the democratic process as something best negotiated by traditional Afghan elites: "The right formula . . . was to create a broad-based governing coalition of Afghan leaders."[29]

The loya jirga, meaning "large council" in Pashto, is an Afghan process for reaching consensus on national decisions. It had been used occasionally in the past, such as in the crowning of Ahmed Shah Durrani in 1747 and approval of Amanullah's reforms in the 1920s. Representatives of different tribes and provinces, as well as notable religious leaders, gathered for days to discuss the matter at hand. It was a way of involving the Afghan people in decisions and gaining public approval. The Afghan representatives at the Bonn Conference had agreed to use loya jirgas to create a provisional government and new constitution. The international community was amenable because the loya jirga's representative nature lent the flavor of democracy.

The first step in the constitutional process after Bonn was the June 2002 "Emergency Loya Jirga." It assembled in a large tent in Kabul. The purpose was to confirm a provisional government that would rule for two years while a new constitution was being written. Every district and province was allowed to send a set number of leaders as their representatives. Approximately 1,500 representatives from around the country attended. They were often respected tribal or religious leaders. One-hundred sixty seats were reserved for women. Several mujahideen commanders (warlords) were also given special dispensation to attend.

Taliban were not invited. Considering the movement defeated, Bush and his team had no intention of dealing with it. Conversations with Taliban representatives in the 1990s had convinced Khalilzad they were bent on a harsh Islamic regime divorced from Afghanistan's past. He was also sensitive that Taliban participation could harden Northern Alliance leaders to compromise. Years later, Khalilzad would argue that Taliban leaders would never have participated, invited or not: "Even in hindsight . . . the United Nations and the Afghans made the right call: they did not invite the Taliban to participate. . . . It is doubtful that the more committed Taliban would have been cooperative. The Taliban made decisions via a *shura* of Islamic scholars. The very concept of a *Loya Jirga* was anathema to them, representing the democratic and national values they despised."[30] He may have been right. The historical record, unfortunately, shows no attempt by the United States or United Nations to find out. It is rumored that a few senior Taliban leaders were corresponding with Karzai at the time. Something might have been possible.

The biggest issue at the Emergency Loya Jirga was who would be president of the provisional government. Karzai was strongly favored. The former king, Zahir Shah, who attended the jirga, was also a contender. A possibility arose that Zahir Shah would become "head of state," a ceremonial position akin to a constitutional monarch. The restoration of the old king would limit Karzai's authority and incite palace intrigue. The idea stirred controversy and threatened to split the Pashtuns until Khalilzad threw the weight of the United States behind Karzai. The old king backed down.[31] The Emergency Loya Jirga then confirmed Karzai.

The other controversial issue was the ministries. The Bonn conference had left the Tajiks most of them. The Pashtuns wanted more influence. The Tajiks, especially the Panjshiris, saw the security services as their right. For centuries, Tajiks had largely been bureaucrats and merchants, barred from being political leaders or soldiers within the Pashtun-dominated state. Now, they were the pillar of armed power. With Massoud as their standard-bearer, they had outfought the Soviets and then kept resistance alive against the Taliban. After Massoud's death, they had been central to the 2001 victory. Tajik leaders refused to forfeit the political power their sacrifices had bought.

Between the Tajik leaders, Minister of Defense Mohammed Fahim, Massoud's successor as leader of the Panjshiris, was first among equals.[32] If neither a military genius nor charismatic like Massoud, he was very good at helping people and responding quickly to requests, which built loyalty among his people. Karzai was often asked by Fahim to "appoint one, two of the people who brought the kingdom to you," a none-too-subtle demand that a ministry, governorship, or other position go to a Panjshiri.[33] Unsurprisingly, Fahim was said to be prodigiously amassing wealth through corruption.[34] Other Tajik leaders—Yunis Qanooni, Ismael Khan, Mohammed Atta, Dr. Abdullah—did not report to Fahim but all coordinated well.

In the end, the Emergency Loya Jirga did not change much. Fahim remained minister of defense. Dr. Abdullah remained minister of foreign affairs. A third Tajik, Mohammed Arif remained director of national intelligence. Under pressure from Khalilzad, the Tajiks gave up Yunis Qanooni's spot as minister of interior, which was then filled by a Pashtun, the well-educated Ali Jalali.

The Emergency Loya Jirga also laid out a provisional legal system. Islamic law (*sharia*) would guide the judiciary in combination with Afghanistan's old secular legal codes. Human rights, including those of women and minorities, were protected. The harsh punishments of the Taliban regime were prohibited.

In November 2003, Bush elevated Khalilzad to US ambassador to Afghanistan. He was impressed with Khalilzad's diplomatic skills and wanted him to shepherd through the rest of the constitutional process. The next big event was the December 2003 Constitutional Loya Jirga. Attended by 500 representatives from throughout the country, its purpose was to draft a new constitution.

Karzai and Khalilzad pressed for a system that gave a president nearly a monopoly on power. Leaders of the Northern Alliance preferred a federal system that delegated greater power to the regions. After two decades of war, they felt they had earned the right to run their own territory. Historically, Afghan rulers before 1979 had faced no legal checks on their power. The parliament that had existed after 1964 had been largely a consultative body. The real check on tyranny had always been extra-legal—the tribes, regional power-brokers, and religious leaders. Kings had always been forced to respect their space or face rebellion. The proposed presidential system followed the old model of no formal guarantees for the power of local actors. The system had the advantage of being more in line with tradition than a federal model. Afghanistan had never formally had the latter and Pashtuns generally opposed it, seeing themselves as the country's rightful rulers. At the jirga, Karzai and Khalilzad won out.

The approved constitution resembled the 1964 constitution. The main difference was that Afghanistan would have a president instead of a king. The president would be elected by popular vote and could rule for no more than two five-year terms. He would have power to appoint all the ministers, provincial governors, and provincial police chiefs. Local people would not select their provincial or district leaders. All taxes would go to the central government. The provinces were technically forbidden from collecting an independent budget. Their money would flow from the center. The constitution also set up a parliament that approved budgets and confirmed ministers. In addition to male representatives, two women from each province were allocated seats. In terms of law, the constitution reaffirmed Islam as one source, along with secular codes. At the same time, it ensured protections for minorities and equal rights for women. Karzai would always take pains to identify the new government as Islamic. The official name of the country would be the Islamic Republic of Afghanistan.

Presidential elections followed the approval of the constitution. Election day was October 9, 2004. Karzai was the main contender. Widespread popular enthusiasm buoyed the event. Eight million people turned out to vote. Fifty-five percent voted for Karzai. Seen as a unifying figure, he won votes across the ethnic groups.[35] His Popalzai heritage made it easier for Tajiks, Uzbeks, and Hazara to accept him. Afghans looked to the future with hope.

Parliamentary elections were the last event in the constitutional process. They took place in September 2005, with a lower turnout than the presidential election. The parliamentary elections empowered a variety of regional powerbrokers and other famous leaders, such as Abdur Raouf Sayyaf, Arif Khan Noorzai, and Yunis Qanooni. It also elevated newly elected women representatives to national prominence.

Three of these women were Shukria Barakzai, Fawzia Koofi, and Maulali Ishaqzai. The 35-year-old Shukria Barakzai was a journalist who hailed from the old Barakzai royalty of Kabul. You could see Ghazi Akbar Khan and Ayub Khan, princes of the 18th century who had fought the British, in her. She had run an underground girls' school during the Taliban regime and had been beaten by the Taliban for disobeying their rules. Before being elected to parliament, she had been one of the women who had helped draft the constitution. Gul Agha Sherzai, warlord of Kandahar, purposefully made space for her in Barakzai discussions. Karzai looked out for her.

Fawzia Koofi was a hard-nosed 30-year-old Tajik from Badakhshan, embedded in the Jamiat power networks of the province. Like Shukria Barakzai, she spoke English. When the first parliament convened, she won appointment as the second deputy speaker. She would push forward legislation that criminalized violence against women, create nearly 50 female police officers in Badakhshan, become a key leader in Jamiat Islami, and survive multiple assassination attempts.[36] Few women would succeed in Afghan politics as long.

Maulali Ishaqzai was a 35-year-old Kandahari *Pashtuna* of the underdog Ishaqzai. Tribal politics were in her blood. She had connections all over the Ishaqzai and Taliban. She hated how the Taliban treated women but delighted in the romance of fighting for tribal honor, including against Americans. Pashto was proudly her first language. Karzai's brother, Ahmed Wali, had backed her run.

The reforms for women in Afghanistan occurred because of the United States and its allies. UNAMA had as a task to "focus on combating violence against women and enable their participation in the public sphere."[37] A result of these efforts was the protection of seats for women in the loya jirgas and in parliament and of their rights in the law (a ministry of women's affairs was also created). The seats were one of the longest lasting reforms that Westerners advocated in support of women. They guaranteed women had a voice.

Karzai helped the cause. Shukria Barakzai, Fawzia Koofi, Maulali Ishaqzai, and other women faced abuse from their male colleagues but won the ear of US and Western commanders and ambassadors, who valued their insights and wanted to empower them. In turn, perceptive Afghan powerbrokers such as Sherzai and Ahmed Wali Karzai took care to respect women leaders. President Karzai picked this up from the beginning.

Afghanistan now had a popularly approved constitution, president, executive branch, and parliament. Karzai had garnered the sustained support of Pashtuns, Tajiks, and Hazaras, as well as the international community. The new government was overall in keeping with Afghan traditions, though with a new stress on elections, women's rights, and the role of parliament. The new system worked largely because of Karzai. Attuned to Afghanistan's political dynamics, he was careful to ensure the Tajiks, Hazaras, Uzbeks, and eastern Pashtuns were included in his government. Hence his acceptance of Fahim for years as minister of defense. Americans called it Karzai's "big tent" model of government. Problems with the new constitutional system would be muted as long as Karzai ruled.

Karzai enjoyed popular support. Nevertheless, the United States had been heavily involved in the constitutional process and had used its power at critical moments to help him. Khalilzad's assessment was that Karzai's "stature derived in large part from his relationship with the United States."[38] Karzai's obvious ties to the United States would come to haunt him, as would Taliban exclusion from the constitutional process.

While the political process advanced, the future military formed. After the fall of the Taliban, Afghanistan's military forces were the militias of the Northern Alliance and Pashtun tribal leaders and warlords. In 2002, the militias totaled somewhere around 100,000 men. The larger militias of Ismael Khan, Dostum, and Fahim fielded tanks, helicopters, and artillery. Under the Bonn Agreement, militias were subsumed into the ministry of defense, renamed "Afghan military forces" (AMF), and assigned division and brigade numbers. They answered to their warlord or tribal leader, not the government. An astounding 40 "divisions" were created (comparable in no way to a division in any other army). Twenty-four were in the north or around Kabul, tied to the Northern Alliance. Only four were in southern Afghanistan.[39]

Bush decided in early 2002 that the United States would build a new Afghan army.[40] The United States then agreed at an April 2002 meeting between donor countries in Geneva to oversee the development of the Afghan military.[41] Rumsfeld supported the initiative. He recognized a functioning military as essential for the United States to exit Afghanistan. He pressed the Pentagon for a plan and when one was not forthcoming, berated his subordinates.[42]

Yet Rumsfeld was oddly reluctant to expend resources, which prevented much from getting done. Upon learning Ambassador James Dobbins had committed the United States to pay 20 percent of the costs of training an Afghan army, Rumsfeld curtly told Powell and Rice, "The U.S. spent billions of dollars freeing Afghanistan and providing security. We are spending a fortune every day. There is no reason on earth for the US to commit to pay 20 percent for the Afghan army."[43] He said the United States should spend "zero" on the Afghan military.[44] Powell objected and argued that the United States should pay for a new army and police force. In his view, a strong centralized army was needed to prevent the state from fragmenting. His argument had little effect, other than to annoy Rumsfeld.[45]

For months, Rumsfeld preferred to leave the military in the hands of the Northern Alliance and other warlords, as did General Franks at Central Command.[46] Their primary concern was targeting al-Qa'eda and Taliban remnants. The Northern Alliance and warlords were allies in this task, especially the Panjshiri Tajiks. In addition to Fahim as minister of defense, Bismullah Khan, who had commanded the Panjshiri front outside Kabul, donned a uniform and became the "army" chief of staff. Rumsfeld told Bush, Powell, and Rice that the United States should simply let the militias be the army and no money should be spent.[47] He did not even want to supply any new equipment and instead sought to exploit existing stocks and used weapons in Afghanistan.[48]

Nor would Rumsfeld allow the US military to deter warlords from challenging Karzai. He told his subordinates and Rice that any such use of US forces concerned him. To US senators, he expounded, "How ought security to evolve in that country depends on really two things: one is what the interim government decides they think ought to happen, [the other is] what the warlord forces in the country decide they think ought to happen, and the interaction between those two."[49] During 2002, Karzai met with Rumsfeld and asked for several warlords to be disarmed. Rumsfeld refused, saying, "We don't do green on green," a military term for when two allies fight each other. [50]

Only over time was Rumsfeld worn down. A memo on building a diverse national Afghan army of 30,000 to 50,000 from former Speaker of the US House of Representatives Newt Gingrich convinced Rumsfeld to "put a major press on in Afghanistan and really train up the Army fast."[51] Penny-pinching got in the way again. Rumsfeld capped the size of the Afghan army at 50,000 in order to control costs and create something the Afghans could later fund on their own.[52] Karzai and Fahim argued for a higher number of 100,000 120,000 in negotiations with Khalilzad. According to Khalilzad, Rumsfeld "wouldn't start the process until they agreed to that 50,000."[53] Consequently, planning languished into the summer. Come September Rumsfeld was still pestering Franks, "When are we going to have a plan?"[54]

In August, Bush asked for greater urgency in getting money and assistance to Afghanistan for security and the army. Rumsfeld assured Bush that any security problem was a perception, not reality.[55] To allay concerns from this "perception," Rumsfeld appointed Brigadier General Karl Eikenberry (soon be promoted to major general) as chief of the office of military cooperation and security coordinator between the Afghan military, US military, and the international effort.[56] Eikenberry arrived in Kabul in October. Afghan leaders would eventually dub Eikenberry the "father of the Afghan National Army."

A thoughtful former defense attaché to China, Karl Eikenberry is one of the most important American figures of the war. He had been in the Pentagon on September 11. The plane struck below his office and killed several colleagues.[57] He would later rise to be the senior US commander in Afghanistan and finally US ambassador to Afghanistan. The top US generals in the Afghan War flash on and off the stage, one after another, on one- or two-year tours.[58] Naming all 15 in order is a bit like naming all the US presidents. Eikenberry would be in a leadership role in Afghanistan for five out of the first ten years of the war, touching on key issues and present at pivotal moments. He was the rare American commander with longevity.

Rumsfeld endowed Eikenberry with modest authority. His job was merely to link together US, Afghan, and international efforts to build an Afghan military. He was also to advise Washington on what it would take to help Karzai develop appropriate security institutions.[59] Eikenberry grabbed the ball and ran with it, using his position to argue that Afghanistan required a professional army.[60]

Even more than Khalilzad, Eikenberry cared about the establishment of a capable state. He was inclined to believe that the government should be accepted by the people and that it should have representative institutions, such as a ministry of defense and a national army. The government, Eikenberry thought, should be imbued with nationalism. Warlords and militias were the antithesis of a capable state. The sense that a capable state and national institutions mattered more than military operations or troop numbers would characterize Eikenberry's extensive work in Afghanistan.

Eikenberry, Khalilzad, and a well-informed scholar named Marin Strmecki lobbied Rumsfeld that the United States needed to commit to funding an army and stop relying on militias. Khalilzad was especially emphatic that the warlords needed to be sidelined.[61] A briefing by Strmecki that a modernizing and stable government had been historically feasible in Afghanistan had a big impact on Rumsfeld. Strmecki recommended that the United States build broad-based national institutions and constrain the Northern Alliance warlords.[62] Rumsfeld ordered that the recommendations be considered for action.[63] Finally, in December 2002, an entire year after the end of the invasion, the United States officially committed to build and largely fund a new army.

Eikenberry and technocrat-genius Ashraf Ghani, Afghan minister of finance, worked out roughly 70,000 as the right size for the army. They believed that number would be both sufficient and affordable enough for the Afghan government to eventually fund on its own.[64] Rumsfeld relented on a cap of 50,000. Khalilzad wanted an army of 120,000 but was overruled. The Taliban presumed defeated, the Bush administration deemed the insurgent threat too small to warrant anything larger than 70,000. Eikenberry later recalled, "The Taliban seemed at the time a spent force with only some small remnants to be mopped up."[65] Rumsfeld announced at a news conference in early 2003, "We clearly have moved from major combat activity to a period of stability and stabilization and reconstruction activities. . . . The bulk of the country today is permissive; it's secure."[66] The White House dismissed arguments by Karzai and Khalilzad that insurgent sanctuaries had formed in Pakistan.[67]

Eikenberry supervised the development of the new army. Karzai relayed that it had to be representative of all ethnicities, which accorded with Eikenberry's own belief in a national army.[68] "As I arrived, I was given as a first principle that [the army] would stay all-national and it would stay all-ethnic," Eikenberry told army historians.[69] Eikenberry's vision was for a volunteer, well-trained, and professional light infantry force—"The one fundamental that I wished to apply to the Afghan National Army was to make them a very rigorously trained and focused group."[70] US planners assumed this would suffice to allow the United States to withdraw from Afghanistan in the future.[71]

By early 2003, Eikenberry realized that light infantry units alone would not be enough. A well-managed ministry of defense, general staff, and supporting commands would also be needed. He and his office created a robust plan to build such an institution. Eikenberry prioritized the reform of the ministry of defense and general staff. After that came the development and deployment of the fighting forces themselves.[72]

In terms of reform, Eikenberry devoted significant energy to fixing the ethnic imbalance within the ministry of defense and realigning recruitment to represent the general population. Fahim had filled the ministry with Tajik appointments. Thirty of 33 directorates within the ministry were under a Panjshiri. To pressure Fahim, Eikenberry withheld investment into training and equipping new units. After Karzai, Khalilzad, and Eikenberry dueled with Fahim for the better part of 2003, the imbalance was reduced to 19 of the 33 directorates under a Tajik, the remainder divided between the other ethnicities. Eikenberry encountered similar challenges in realigning recruitment of the rank and file. He put a 10 percent cap on the portion of the army that could be from demobilized militias. Fahim reacted by easing the way for Tajik militias while throwing up administrative roadblocks against fighters from Pashtun militias. The rank and file ended up with a disproportionately large number of Tajiks.[73]

Meanwhile, recruitment and training moved forward. Solid training over rapid recruitment was the priority. With no threat seen on the horizon, there was no impetus to move fast. Eikenberry did not envision posting Afghan units outside Kabul until late 2004.[74] The full 70,000 was not to be fielded until 2009.[75] Eikenberry also restrained recruitment and training when battalions were not all-ethnic: "There were several times where we delayed the training of infantry battalions because the Afghan recruiting system wasn't able to deliver the necessary all-ethnic characteristics that we insisted upon."[76] Rumsfeld occasionally asked Eikenberry to "[move] along quicker."[77] Eikenberry pushed back and argued that expediency would result in a force that lacked the training and institutions to be effective. Quality over quantity was Eikenberry's goal.

Rumsfeld's stinginess got in the way again too. After December 2003 Rumsfeld complained from time to time about the slow growth of the army but devoted insufficient resources to speed it up. In 2004, after repeatedly criticizing the pace (the Afghan army then numbered about 16,000), he instructed that costs be minimized because there could be no increase in funding. He dictated that the size and infrastructure for the army be sustainable by Afghanistan's economy in the long run.[78] Funding was then inadequate to overcome unexpected shortfalls. Training personnel and facilities were too few to handle the number of recruits. Equipment, basing, and housing were insufficient. Pay was too low to attract good recruits. To stanch these problems, the overall production of the force had to be slowed. Throughput could not be increased until a new budget request was fulfilled at the end of 2004.[79]

Resource shortages damaged not just the quantity but the quality of the force. Each 1,000-man Afghan battalion was to receive 10 weeks of training, raised to 14 during 2005. Neither was enough to produce highly capable infantry. Trainers wanted 6 to 12 months. When resource limitations slowed the growth of the force, battalions started losing strength because new recruits were arriving too late to replace soldiers that retired or deserted. Training had to be curtailed to get replacements into their units.[80]

Building a professional officer corps was slow-going. Eikenberry established a board to vet officer candidates in order to ensure selection was based on merit.[81] Its effect was limited because Rumsfeld forbade US officers from directing officer selection. Whenever Fahim resisted recruiting or training or appointing a qualified candidate, the Americans could do little about it. Rumsfeld's order was rescinded in 2004 after a year had been lost.[82]

Part of the problem in building a high-quality force was that US trainers were switched about. The best were not in place. The US military's most effective force for training local military forces were its green beret special forces, the same who had performed so well partnering with the men of Karzai, Dostum, and Fahim in 2001. Special forces teams helped train the army's first units. Eikenberry removed them from that role in 2003 because special forces teams were designed to train elite light infantry units, not entire armies. Eikenberry decided that building a whole army would exceed the number of available special forces teams and that the complexities of training brigades, corps, and the general staff were outside their skill sets.

Regular infantry from the 10th Mountain Division briefly replaced special forces in the training mission. US teams, which became known as "embedded training teams" (ETTs), also started advising battalions in the field. Then, after a year, the Pentagon rotated out the regular infantry as the Iraq War got underway. The National Guard replaced them, with contractors and British and French troops assisting in much of the work.[83] Although motivated, the experience of the National Guard in training foreign forces was low. The National Guard would train the Afghan army until 2009.

Eikenberry strove to instill a sense of nationalism in the new Afghan army. "One of the big pleasant surprises," he said, "was discovering that the Afghans do have a very deep sense of national identity. . . . As I got on the ground, I developed quickly an appreciation for the Afghans. Despite great pride in their tribal identities and great pride in their ethnic identities, at the end of the day . . . there is a very firm consensus on their part that they are Afghans."[84]

It is thus all the more stunning that Eikenberry felt that neither the government nor the army symbolized that identity.[85] Soldiers joined the new Afghan army for a variety of reasons: the guidance of an elder, the orders of a militia commander, a salary, or just, in the words of one, "good uniforms, boots, and socks."[86] Nationalism did not figure highly. It was not flowing from the people into their army. National identity had long been a problem for the army. Since the 19th century, Abdur Rahman Khan and other Afghan rulers had always had

trouble breaking officers and soldiers from tribe and kinship and imposing obedience to the state.[87] Eikenberry was too smart to miss all this:

> What I have said is that the soul of that army can't be breathed into
> the army by a foreign military power or a foreign military force on the
> ground. Only the Afghans can give their army a soul and its identity.
> That is why it is absolutely imperative that if this is going to work ... the
> civilian leaders of Afghanistan and the tribal leaders of Afghanistan have
> to embrace that army as their own. That has proven to be the toughest
> challenge.[88]

Eikenberry could not help but underline how identity was problematic for both
the new army and the new regime.

The shortcomings in the resourcing of the army were neglected for years.
Rumsfeld occasionally asked for proposals to accelerate its growth but was
too busy on Iraq to force it to happen or to change policies that were stopping
things up.[89] His gaze would turn to Afghanistan every few months, usually after
a trip there, and then swing back to Iraq. Eikenberry's goal to build a quality
force did not transpire. If often brave, the army was moderately trained, unevenly
equipped, indifferently led, and small. At the end of 2003, just 6,000 Afghan
army soldiers had been trained. Two years later, at the end of 2005, the number
was only 26,000.[90] President Bush later admitted that "in an attempt to keep the
Afghan government from taking on an unsustainable expense, we had kept the
army too small."[91]

The Afghan police were more neglected than the army. Historically,
Afghanistan never had possessed robust police forces. Those that had existed
had been concentrated in the cities. In 2002, the size of the police was 50,000 to
70,000. Unlike the army, they stood up very quickly. Also unlike the army, they
were largely recruited from the province in which they served. Their ethnic mix
was more representative of the country as a whole. Because of their local roots,
they tended to be tied to local tribal leaders or power-brokers. It was the police
who were out in the districts and provinces.

For 2004 to 2007, the United States set aside $1.5 billion for the 50,000 to
70,000 police compared to $3 billion for the army. The weakness of the insti-
tution resulted in a poorly trained, supplied, and equipped force. Policemen
received paltry salaries irregularly. They were often issued less than half of
their assigned weapons, ammunition, and vehicles, leading to corruption and
desertion.[92] The Germans and later the US Embassy (through the contractor
DynCorp) set up training centers in Kabul that were inadequate to the scale of
the task. It was not until 2005 that the US military took responsibility for police
development and training.[93]

The Afghan security forces shared a structural problem. They were split between the ministry of interior, ministry of defense, and the national directorate of security (NDS). The police did not answer to the army. The army did not answer to the police. The NDS answered to neither and had authority over neither. The only person with authority to control all three was Karzai. The unity that had given the Taliban a comparative advantage in the 1990s was something the new government was structured to disrupt. In a nation already prone to infighting and tribal and ethnic competition, this broken chain of command would lead to much grief.

Karzai paid scant attention to the army and police. This was partly because the army was an American creation, run by northerners, not him. The army could not be a tool to reinforce his power, as it had his Durrani predecessors. Quite the opposite, it reinforced the power of potential northern rivals. More than that Karzai was a man of politics and persuasion, not war. He disdained guns, the military profession, and talk of war. Whereas his great ancestor Ahmed Shah had loved his soldiers and ordered his son to follow his example, Karzai took his soldiers' lives for granted. He once remarked, "I am not worried about army and police casualties. They are recruited for that. I am worried about the civilians and boys in the fields."

Between 2001 and 2006 too little was accomplished in building an army and police. The United States had stood up capable armies in less time in Korea and a variety of smaller cases. In Afghanistan, the United States lost the opportunity. US leaders, overrating the 2001 victory, did not appreciate how much an army would be needed. The oversight would open the door to the Taliban in years to come.

When the United States invaded Afghanistan in late 2001, there was little infrastructure to speak of. Most schools, hospitals, and government buildings had been damaged in the preceding 20 years of war. There were almost no paved roads. Few towns had electricity or running water. The country had no functioning civil administration—either in the capital or the provinces.

The United States and the international community tried to reconstruct the country and improve governance. Ambassador James Dobbins famously wrote that the international community gave nearly $2 billion to Afghanistan in 2002 and 2003, which amounted to $52 per capita, far less than the $1,390 per capita given to Bosnia, $814 per capita given to Kosovo, and $200 per capita given to Haiti in those interventions. The Bush administration eventually accepted that some reconstruction had to occur and that essential infrastructure and services, such as roads and schools, should be built.[94]

USAID ran much of the US reconstruction effort. The focus was on programs to improve education, health care, and community development. The most visible projects were the well-designed schools and government offices built throughout the districts and provinces, usually one-story, concrete, and painted white. In line with America's aversion to nation-building, USAID steered away from large-scale infrastructure projects. Yet the level of disrepair was so bad that a few national-level projects had to be undertaken—the Kajaki dam, Gardez-to-Khost road, and Jalalabad-to-Asadabad road. The most important was Highway One, or the "ring road," the key highway between Mazar-e-Sharif, Kabul, Kandahar, and Herat. It had been severely damaged over the years of war. The approximately 400-mile drive from Kabul to Kandahar could be days in duration. Karzai discussed the highway personally with Bush during his 2002 visit to the United States. Bush ordered his government to organize the international community to repave it. USAID began its share of the task in 2003 and completed the stretch between Kandahar and Kabul before the end of 2004. Work on the full ring would go for years.

A groundbreaking initiative in community development was the national solidarity program (NSP), designed by Minister of Finance Ashraf Ghani. Set up in 2003 and funded by the World Bank, the national solidarity program fell under the ministry of rural rehabilitation and development. Local communities received small grants to contract projects in their villages. Each community had to select a community development council to determine what kind of project should be implemented. The funding was enough for something helpful to the village, such as a few wells or culverts, a graveled path, or a couple diesel generators—nothing grander. The idea was that the process of choosing and implementing a project would bring local communities together, thus facilitating good governance, while at the same time connecting those communities directly to the central government. In each community, a non-governmental organization (NGO; such as Oxfam or Relief International) supervised the process. The number of projects per province ranged from 270 to 1,400, in certain cases amounting to $8 million to $10 million in spending. No province was excluded. According to local Afghan leaders, community-level governance indeed became stronger as new councils formed to partake in the program.[95]

The most famous step to address development and economic problems was the provincial reconstruction team (PRT). Provincial reconstruction teams were meant to jump-start reconstruction in the provinces. They were conceived as the vanguard of reconstruction efforts—an organization that could venture into areas too dangerous for civilian agencies. A combination of military personnel and civilian diplomats and development experts staffed them. US-led teams fielded 60 to 100 personnel, with a State department diplomat and USAID development officer. The US military provided security, a civil affairs detachment, and a few engineers. They would work daily with Afghan provincial governors and officials and implement a range of projects from wells and culverts to schools and roads. The idea caught the attention of National Security Advisor Condoleezza Rice and Defense Secretary Rumsfeld, who championed the effort.[96]

The first provincial reconstruction team opened in January 2003 in Paktiya province. Seven more were up by the end of the year, followed by 11 in 2004. Germany, Sweden, Great Britain, Canada, and several other countries staffed their own teams, each with its own structure and lines of funding. By 2008, there would be 26, 12 under the United States and 14 under another country.

In their early days, provincial reconstruction teams focused on small, quick-impact projects designed to win hearts and minds. As time went on, funding streams increased. In 2006, USAID had a budget of $500 million for the country and the military could spend $200 million from a specially designed fund known as the commander's emergency response program (CERP). With the increase, spending went up in the provinces. For instance, spending went from $2 million in Khost in 2005 to $22 million in 2007. The change was even more dramatic in Kunar, where spending went from $2 million in 2004 to $13 million in 2007 and finally $80 million in 2008. With greater funding came larger projects. The cost of a provincial reconstruction team project in Kunar, Khost, and Ghazni in 2007 ranged from $218,000 to $387,000 compared to $13,000 to $15,000 for the national solidarity program. Thirty to sixty percent of each provincial reconstruction team's spending was for provincial roads and bridges.[97]

Provincial reconstruction teams were controversial. USAID and non-governmental organizations (NGOs) tended to object to their military signature. Many civilian aid workers argued that the military should not do reconstruction at all. From their perspective, a military face on reconstruction ensured insurgent attacks on neutral aid workers. Others insisted that military personnel know little about development, reconstruction, or Afghan culture. And provincial reconstruction teams experienced problems in completing projects. Several structures were found to be unsound. The development community told stories of clinics without doctors, schools without teachers, bridges washed out by the next spring's floods, and generators beyond the upkeep most Afghans could provide. To some extent these problems would eventually be addressed by better contracting processes and quality control. But the controversy surrounding provincial reconstruction teams would never disappear.

Economic growth was most visible in Kabul. The city transformed from a cold, war-ravaged shell at the outset of 2002 into the bustling, traffic-jammed heart of the state. International funds flowing through Kabul fueled the renaissance. Non-governmental organizations, aid organizations, embassies, the United Nations, and other international organizations flooded in. As the government stood back up, ministries and bureaucracies hired thousands of Afghans.

Demand for services drew people to Kabul. Restaurants, guest houses, apartment complexes, hotels, and giant wedding halls materialized. New neighborhoods sprung up on the outskirts of the city. The city's population expanded from around 2 million in 2001 to 4 million in 2009.[98]

The Taliban in 2002 were broken. After fleeing Kandahar, Mullah Omar hid out in northern Helmand, Uruzgan, and Zabul.[99] A new direction for the movement had yet to coalesce. Various commanders were preparing to continue the war, a few in al-Qa'eda and militant camps in Pakistan. Others were resting in Pakistan or attempting to retire to community life inside Afghanistan. A number wanted to cooperate with the new Afghan government.

After the failed negotiation between Taliban leaders and Karzai in December 2001, senior Taliban delegations reached out to Karzai again between 2002 and 2004.[100] Mullah Omar may have authorized them or they may have been independent endeavors.

One occurred right after the fall of the Taliban. Former Taliban foreign minister Wakil Ahmed Mutawakil went to Kandahar in January 2002 to meet with Americans. He was arrested but then discussed a plan with a CIA official to create a Taliban group allied with Karzai. The idea was briefed in Washington to Vice President Dick Cheney. He immediately shut it down. According to a participant, Cheney's view was that all Taliban were bad.[101] Mutawakil was locked up in Bagram.[102]

Around the same time, senior Taliban leaders met with Abdul Hakim Mujahed, former Taliban ambassador to the United Nations. He had left the movement and was living in Kabul. They told Mujahed that they wanted peace. Mujahed relayed these conversations to Karzai.[103] Another delegation led by former minister of justice Nuraddin Turabi saw Kandahar governor Gul Agha Sherzai. Worried the Americans would detain them, Sherzai told them to return to Pakistan.[104]

In spring 2002, before the Emergency Loya Jirga, Mullah Omar's former aide Tayeb Agha sent Karzai a letter. According to certain sources, Mullah Omar himself had dictated it. The letter proposed the Taliban play a role in the formation of the new state.[105] Karzai apparently wanted to pursue the opportunity. Khalilzad and other US officials never discussed inviting the Taliban to the jirga and later claimed ignorance of the letter. Certain research says that the Bush administration actually told Karzai no.[106]

Karzai thought opportunities were being missed. He was frustrated with the Bush administration and US military officers for turning off the 2001 agreement in Shah Wali Kot. In his view, the Taliban should have been at Bonn and the Emergency Loya Jirga; they were Afghans and should have been represented in the new government. Karzai's submission is a sign of how he was unsure of himself and was growing into his role as a leader of Afghans. Five years later Karzai would never be so submissive to foreigners.

The Bush administration assessed that the Taliban were defeated and there was no need for negotiations, just as there had been no need for an Afghan army.[107] For years, policy documents treated the Taliban the same as al-Qaʿeda and called for the movement's elimination.[108] The US military reflexively targeted those who had been Taliban. Khalilzad, both as White House lead for Afghanistan and then as ambassador, seems to have opposed negotiations. He consistently thought the main Taliban leaders uninterested. It was Karzai who was fruitlessly asking Khalilzad to reach out to the Taliban, not the other way around.[109]

At least a few Taliban senior leaders wanted to keep trying. In November 2002, Taliban senior leaders met in Karachi. Mullah Omar was absent, although they may have met with his approval. The leaders apparently agreed to seek peace and abandon what was left of their resistance. They wanted amnesty and to join the political process then underway.[110]

The effort went nowhere. According to various accounts, anti-peace groups within the Taliban scuttled the agreement. Gul Agha, an influential Taliban leader heavily involved in finances, evidently refused to agree that any Taliban leader should talk with the government.[111] A senior participant in the meeting recalls similar trouble from other hard-liners:

> I was there at the meeting. Mullah Mohammed Omar wasn't there, but everyone else was there, all the high-ranking ministers and cabinet members of the Taliban. . . . We took a decision that, yes, we should go and join the [political] process. But later some other hands entered into the mix and sabotaged our decision on this matter. Some other Talibans—small Talibs—who were outside the inner circle started to turn people against us. . . . They would say things like, "These are not real Talibs! . . . Make sure not to join the political process with them." . . . So it came to nothing.[112]

Mullah Omar's absence from deliberations probably inhibited the movement from coalescing on a position. Other sources on this period do not refer to this meeting and contend that several Taliban were already set on war.[113]

After 2003, the Taliban put their energies into preparing to attack Afghanistan.[114] Even then, a few more delegations came to see Karzai.[115] Whether any had Mullah Omar's blessing and what exactly they proposed is unknown, at least other than to Karzai and the Taliban delegates.

When Karzai brought up the 2004 Taliban peace feelers, the Bush administration banned negotiations with the top Taliban leaders. The US National

Security Council wrote up a "blacklist" of 31 Taliban leaders (according to certain sources it was more than 80). The Afghan government was forbidden from talking with those on the list. Just about anyone who mattered in the Taliban was on it, including Mullah Baradar and Tayeb Agha, two leaders who had been instrumental in the December 2001 talks with Karzai and would play leading roles in future peace efforts. The blacklisted leaders were to be captured or killed. Karzai told his Taliban interlocutors that he could not protect them from the Americans.[116] He also sent a representative to Pakistan who told senior Taliban leaders that America did not want peace but would accept individual Taliban returning to live in Afghanistan. The Taliban interpreted the offer as no better than surrender and disregarded it.[117]

If the failure to build an army is one major US mistake in the war, the failure to include the Taliban in the political process is another. The United States purposefully excluded the Taliban from the political process from Bonn onward. In fairness, the Taliban hardly helped themselves. They did not renounce hosting groups that planned to attack the West. Nevertheless, Bush and his team could have done more. After October 2001, there are no known US attempts to talk with Taliban leaders until the Obama administration. The Taliban were a major party to the civil war. Excluding them almost ensured substantial numbers of Afghans would dislike the new state. What is truly damning is that there was no real obstacle to trying to talk to the Taliban. Few other policies for Afghanistan would be so low-cost.

From 2002 to 2005, the United States had the freedom of maneuver to implement new policies in Afghanistan before violence set in. Opportunities to avoid a resumption of war were lost. By their own admission, Bush and his team neglected to build a military quickly and excluded the Taliban from the political process because they believed the Taliban had been utterly defeated. Khalilzad later confessed that the United States had underestimated the Taliban's resilience. In retrospect, the administration's assessment appears to have been more than a simple underestimation. It was wishful thinking. Enough information was there. With the Taliban's leader free, residual violence in parts of Afghanistan, and known training camps in Pakistan, a Taliban resurgence was a serious possibility. Excluding a defeated adversary from peace discussions and then neglecting to build a military was a remarkable oversight.

How did Bush and his team and his generals succumb to wishful thinking so starkly at odds with their precautions of 2001? Overconfidence is the best answer. The ease of the 2001 success carried away sensibility. Hubris shocked and awed careful thought. Bush and his team glided forward heedlessly as if on autopilot, deciding to stay, exclude the Taliban from the political settlement, leave governance to militias, and build an army haphazardly without much deliberation. Even Rumsfeld, who alone foresaw the dangers of commitment, let confidence in victory lull himself into complacency toward both getting out—otherwise in line with his instincts—and enacting circumspect policies to circumvent a return to violence. We can discern among Bush and his team a certain disinterest in alternative interpretations and a widespread self-assuredness. That might have helped when confronted with adversity. It failed them when presented with opportunity.

The consequences would be immense. Policies and structures once set in place would prove difficult to change. Adversaries would close their minds to compromise. The return of violence would harden positions and remove a peaceful environment to build institutions. What once could have worked would no longer work. The dynamics of peace and war would evolve. Opportunity would narrow.

|| 6 ||

Disorder in Kandahar

From 2002 to 2005, Afghanistan was deceptively peaceful. As the political process progressed, the Taliban rebounded from the brink of total defeat. Troubles brewed in the provinces and the countryside, the heart of Afghanistan. Tribal rivalries and misguided US military operations generated a degree of popular support for the Taliban. At the same time, Taliban leaders were reorganizing in Pakistan, where the movement planned, recruited, trained, and raised funds. US leaders, overconfident and focused elsewhere, detected little of what was happening. These years set the stage for the tremendous violence that would follow. The center of the Taliban's reemergence, where grievance and rivalry converged, was where the movement had originated—Kandahar.

Without an army or militia of his own, Karzai's rule depended on his legitimacy as a Popalzai, on the backing of the United States, and on a patchwork support base of Pashtuns. He had to balance the different ethnic factions carefully. Christina Lamb, a British journalist who lived in the palace for a time with Karzai, observed:

> He spent so much of his time in gatherings . . . yet I could see that it was through such meetings that Karzai kept the country together. Balancing all of Afghanistan's competing tribes and ethnic groups was a tricky business that we foreigners couldn't begin to fathom. . . . Earlier in the day Karzai had received a delegation of Uzbek parliamentarians who had come to complain that there were not enough Uzbeks in the bureaucracy. "They're right," he told me afterwards. . . . "Then tomorrow the Barakzai are coming with the same complaint. . . . My job is to build this country with a stable future, to reverse the past which was inclusivity for one group, exclusivity for another. I want to make an Afghanistan for all Afghans, and that's what I've done."[1]

In any province, the governor, appointed by Karzai, oversaw government activities, including security, education, and reconstruction work, and had an important role in resolving disputes. The provincial police chief, separately appointed by Karzai or the ministry of interior in his stead, commanded the police. Every district in the provinces also had a district governor and a district police chief. Karzai held the power to appoint district governors and police chiefs, though he often delegated decision-making to either the minister of interior or the provincial governor.

Karzai allotted power to other ethnicities and let tribal leaders or warlords run their territory with little interference. No ministries or governorships went to his family. Few went to other southern Pashtuns. Karzai recognized he had to give top posts to Tajiks, Hazaras, and eastern Pashtuns.

Minister of defense Mohammed Fahim, as the pre-eminent Tajik leader and de facto leader of Panjshir, had input over governor appointments in Parwan, Panjshir, Kapisa, Takhar, and Badakhshan—Ahmed Shah Massoud's old territory. Ismael Khan was again governor of Herat. After his glorious victories in 2001, Abdur Rashid Dostum outright ruled much of the north, especially the Uzbek provinces of Faryab and Jowzjan. The prize of Mazar-e-Sharif was more complicated. Dostum and Mohammed Atta Noor, the Tajik commander from Jamiat, competed for control of the city, the nearby customs post with Uzbekistan, and the surrounding province of Balkh. Whoever ruled Mazar-e-Sharif would dominate the north. Fahim, for whom Tajik power in the north was a political priority, naturally supported Atta. To prevent fighting, Karzai temporarily permitted Dostum and Atta to split the province.[2]

At the same time, Karzai preempted these and other potential competitors from threatening his rule. When Ismael Khan refused to accept Kabul appointees and clashed with a Pashtun tribal leader, Karzai, with the help of Ambassador Khalilzad, promoted him minister of water and energy and transplanted him to Kabul. In 2004, as Dostum became increasingly obstreperous and refused to disarm his 10,000 to 20,000 militia, Karzai turned to Atta while Khalilzad threatened Dostum by flying a B-1 bomber over his house. The warlord backed down and consented when Karzai appointed Atta governor of Balkh.[3] Atta, who switched out his Kalashnikov for a suit and tie, would become by far the most effective governor and Mazar-e-Sharif the safest city in the Afghanistan.[4]

Kandahar was the birthplace of Ahmed Shah Durrani, the Afghan state, and the Taliban. It was where Karzai had staked his claim to power. It would be where Afghanistan slid back into civil war.

Like most of Afghanistan, Karzai and the United States secured Kandahar through warlords and armed tribal leaders.

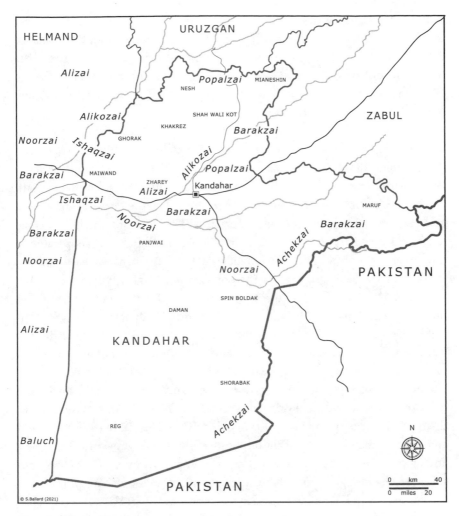

Map 6 Tribes of Kandahar

Large tribal militias formed the police and "Afghan military forces" (the temporary substitute for the army). Within the Afghan military forces, the militias retained autonomy, reported to their tribal leader, and controlled their own tribal territory. Afghan military forces "commanders" and the police chiefs were often the tribal leaders themselves.[5] Fighters commonly joined at the behest of their tribal leaders. They were a combination of old mujahideen and young new recruits. Very few had been with the Taliban. Half had been fighting since age 18. Less than 15 percent had gone to school.[6]

As is often the case with tribal systems, there was plenty of infighting as tribal leaders competed for power. These dynamics existed throughout the country but were most important among the assortment of tribes in the south, Karzai's power base. The majority tribes were from the Durrani tribal confederation that had ruled Afghanistan for 240 years. The Durrani included the Popalzai, Barakzai, Alikozai, Achekzai, Alizai, Noorzai, and Ishaqzai tribes. The other tribal confederation were the Ghilzai, traditional rivals of the Durrani. The big Ghilzai tribes in the south were the Hotak and Tokhi, concentrated in Zabul. Also in the south was the Kakar tribe, close to the Ghilzai.

The Popalzai, Barakzai, Alikozai, and Achekzai tribes constituted Karzai's base. The Popalzai and Barakzai were the ranking tribes. The Popalzai had been the first rulers of the modern state of Afghanistan. The Barakzai supplanted the Popalzai in the early 19th century and ruled almost without break until the death of Daoud Khan in 1978. The Barakzai were larger than the Popalzai and spread into Helmand and Herat. Gul Agha Sherzai, the governor of Kandahar, was the most influential Barakzai tribal leader. The Popalzai and Barakzai cooperated to monopolize rulership while simultaneously conspiring against each other.

The Alikozai were also close to the Popalzai and Barakzai while similarly in competition with them. Pashtuns tacitly understood that the other two tribes outranked the Alikozai. The Alikozai tended to fill military posts over political ones. The Alikozai leader, Mullah Naqib, was the most effective warlord in Kandahar. He controlled Arghandab, the strategic and prosperous valley that protected the northern flank of Kandahar City.

The Achekzai (pronounced "a-tsek-zai") were often treated as the lowliest of the Durranis. The tribe had originally been Barakzai until Ahmed Shah broke them off as part of his divide-and-rule policy. The Achekzai lived in the desert and drier farmland near the Pakistan border. They were known for smuggling and fighting. The Barakzai and Popalzai traditionally used the tribe as their foot soldiers.[7] Their toughness would make them a player in Kandahar's future.

The defense of Kandahar depended on these four tribes. Sherzai was not just governor; he had his own militia that went after possible Taliban (or his rivals) and defended the southern approaches to the city. Naqib's Alikozai controlled the police in the city itself. His militia controlled Arghandab. Lesser tribal leaders ran other districts. An Achekzai militia, under a 24-year-old named Abdul Razziq, served as the border police. It was based at Spin Boldak, the border crossing with Pakistan. In all, somewhere around 7,500 militia defended Kandahar in 2002.[8]

Karzai tried to divide the Kandahar tribes while building the power of his family. Centuries of competition within the ruling southern tribes ingrained a concern about coups from within as much as attacks from without.[9] Tribal rivalry was accentuated by the fact that the Americans had allowed Sherzai, Karzai's Barakzai rival, to proclaim himself governor in 2001. The villain of Sarah Chayes's classic, *The Punishment of Virtue*, Sherzai had blatantly flouted Karzai's instructions to wait outside the city. Karzai had wanted to give the job to Mullah Naqib. Popalzais had better relations with the Alikozai and Naqib had helped Karzai during his march south from Uruzgan. Karzai's agreement with the Taliban supposedly stipulated that Sherzai would be responsible for the airport and Naqib would be responsible for the city.

But when the Taliban abandoned Kandahar on December 6, Sherzai reached the governor's palace first. Karzai was furious. Worried about the possibility of shooting breaking out and distrustful of Naqib's Taliban past, Lieutenant Colonel David Fox, the special forces commander with Karzai, sat down with Karzai and counseled that he concede in order to avoid any violence.[10] Karzai backed down.

Karzai's younger brother, Ahmed Wali Karzai, served as the defender of his interests in Kandahar. With a thick black moustache, a stubbly black and grey beard, and a stocky build, his appearance resembled a strongman or bodyguard more than the tribal leader that he was. His brother's position, his family's tribal rank, and strong connections to both the Kabul elite and US forces made him Kandahar's predominant powerbroker.

Ahmed Wali spent 2002 and 2003 sparring with Sherzai over appointments, land, and poppy smuggling routes. He became head of the provincial shura and used it as a platform to influence the distribution of goods and services, much to Sherzai's chagrin.[11] Sherzai was also at odds with Naqib and tried to remove various Alikozai police and militia commanders. The capable Alikozai provincial police chief, Akrem Khakrezwal, was shipped north in 2003, stripping the Alikozai of their control of the Kandahar City police. The post was turned over to outsiders with less knowledge of the city. Ahmed Wali hardly helped Naqib, happy to watch Alikozai power erode.

The tendency of the Popalzai, Barakzai, Alikozai, and Achekzai to marginalize the other tribes in Kandahar further undermined political order. Instead of drawing the other tribes in, tribal dynamics naturally pushed them out. The tribes that had dominated during the first Taliban regime—Ishaqzai, Noorzai, and Ghilzai—were excluded from the new southern distribution of power.[12] The old Taliban leaders themselves were mainly from these tribes, which had profited under their rule. This reality complicated any reconciliation between the Ishaqzai, Noorzai, Ghilzai, and the government. The tendencies of Karzai and his tribal leaders made it worse.

To a degree, Karzai simply did not have room for them. Like land and water, political positions in Afghanistan were scarce. Deals with Alikozai, Barakzai, and Achekzai left few for the Ishaqzai, Noorzai, and Ghilzai. Karzai tried to bring the Noorzai into the fold, giving them several positions, including police chief of Helmand. He could never satisfy them. They were angry that the government had transferred their control of the lucrative Spin Boldak border crossing to the Achekzai (who kicked up proceeds to Sherzai and Ahmed Wali). They were essentially asking to retain the economic and political position they had enjoyed under the Taliban. It was as provocative as a Democrat Secretary of Defense demanding to stay in place following a Republican presidential victory. Tribal imbalance in the south was directly related to the national balance Karzai was able to maintain in Kabul. He had given choice positions to Tajiks, Hazaras, and eastern Pashtuns. He had to give his southern Pashtun supporters something as well. The only place he could do that was in the south. The Ishaqzai, Noorzai, and Ghilzai of southern Afghanistan were the losers in Karzai's big tent.

To a wider degree, however, Karzai could have done more to protect these tribes. He, Ahmed Wali, and Sherzai expanded their power and influence without regard for balance. The pro-government tribes had better access to government projects and kept these benefits away from the Noorzai, Ishaqzai, and Ghilzai, who had few jobs and needed the assistance.[13] The Ghilzai, among the poorer Kandaharis, often lost claim to their land. During their regime, the Taliban had given away government land to Ghilzai, as well as to other poorer tribesmen. The Karzai government reclaimed this land, invalidated titles issued by the Taliban, and sometimes evicted the erstwhile owners. Government officials told Haji Babay, a Kakar tribal leader, that his tribesmen had no right to the land the Taliban regime had given them. In the worst cases, landed, pro-government tribes moved into Kakar territory and tried to push them off their farms. Babay's tribesmen became angry with the government.[14]

Karzai rarely appointed Ishaqzai, Noorzai, and Ghilzai leaders governor or police chief of their own districts, even where they were the most populous tribe. Officials from other tribes were allowed to oversee their territory. In Noorzai districts minority tribes controlled the government and the police. The Noorzai feuded with these smaller tribes over land and power.[15] The Noorzai felt that they were being cut out. Their fears were solidified in 2003 when Sherzai divided the Noorzai stronghold of Zharey-Panjwai into two districts in order to fracture the Noorzai vis-à-vis other tribes.[16]

Poppy shaped the 2002 economy of Kandahar and southern Afghanistan. Farmers planted seeds in the autumn. Stalks grew waist-high and in March blossomed white, red, and purple. In April, hundreds of thousands of workers invaded the fields and drained the gooey sap from the flower bulb by hand. Farmers then sold the paste to smugglers. It garnered a high price because of international demand for heroin. The goo was refined into heroin in laboratories outside Afghanistan. Even amid Kandahar's renowned pomegranates and grapes, poppy flourished. It needs little water and thrives in drier cropland away from the rivers, where grapes, watermelon, and pomegranates perish. And it is easy to transport. The paste easily survives hours on bumpy dirt roads. Money and power flowered from poppy—its cultivation, its trade, and its taxation. Tribal leaders, smugglers, police chiefs, and governors eagerly competed to control it, the currency of Pashtun realpolitik.

Ahmed Wali and Sherzai interfered with Ishaqzai and Noorzai poppy smuggling. Noorzai and Ishaqzai fields in western Kandahar were covered with poppy. The government targeted them in their eradication efforts, punishing the two tribes in the process. Before long, Ishaqzai, Noorzai, and Ghilzai spoke of being oppressed. Many Noorzai and Ishaqzai smugglers and poppy farmers were detained and only released for a bribe. From the point of view of the tribal leaders, Sherzai and Ahmed Wali were taking their money.[17] To top it off, the US Drug Enforcement Agency lured Haji Basher, the famous Noorzai drug smuggler who had been one of the Taliban's first funders in the 1990s, to New York and then imprisoned him. Ahmed Wali benefited from his departure and may have helped arrange it.[18]

The United States never intervened in these tribal dealings. US military officers accepted Sherzai as governor. They viewed him as reasonably effective in providing security. Various officers and diplomats were aware of how marginalized groups were being treated but could not change policies. Sarah Chayes was living in Kandahar at the time. In the spring of 2003, she told Lieutenant General McNeill about Sherzai's abuse of power and the wider misbehavior of warlords throughout the country. McNeill explained that with the Iraq War just underway the White House did not want to rock the boat in Afghanistan, where things appeared peaceful. He appreciated Sherzai's efforts to suppress Taliban activity.[19]

In June 2002, Lieutenant General Dan McNeill, commander of the XVIII Airborne Corps, assumed responsibility for conventional combat operations in Afghanistan.[20] Of the 8,000 US military forces in Afghanistan, about half were at the main military headquarters at Bagram airbase, a 30-minute drive north of Kabul. Al-Qa'eda was known to be operating along the eastern border with Pakistan. Their senior leaders had dispersed throughout Pakistan but their subordinates had quickly established camps in Pakistan tribal regions, where the reach of the Pakistani state was limited. McNeill concentrated his effort on that border.[21]

McNeill assigned the other half of the troops to watch over southern Afghanistan—a brigade headquarters, two battalions, and logistics and aviation elements, in addition to special operations forces with their own chain of command. The total was just over 4,000 troops. The brigade headquarters and its battalions were at Kandahar airport, southeast of Kandahar City. The battalions were often sent into Uruzgan or Zabul to chase after possible al-Qa'eda leads or Taliban remnants. Three or so 12-man special forces teams were also in Kandahar, Helmand, and Zabul. They cooperated with local militias to hunt down Taliban and terrorist leaders.[22]

The primary focus of the US forces in southern and all of Afghanistan was counterterrorism: capturing or killing terrorist and insurgent leaders. Although they acknowledged building the Afghan army as a task, Secretary Rumsfeld and General Franks passed guidance to McNeill that counterterrorism was the mission—forget everything else. The foremost military objective was to kill and capture terrorists and get bin Laden.[23]

Approximately 4,000 US and allied special operations forces, plus CIA, were in Afghanistan.[24] Special operations forces came in different flavors. The special forces teams, or Green Berets, that had succeeded in the invasion were one kind. There were also forces that specialized in conducting raids to capture terrorist leaders, often known as "black" special operations forces. They included units such as Delta Force, SEALs, and the Rangers.[25]

In the first months of 2002, a string of bases was set up along Afghanistan's eastern frontier with Pakistan, at Jalalabad airfield in Nangarhar, Khost city in Khost, and Orgun-e and Shkin in Paktika. Special operations forces operated out of each, with their main hub at Kandahar airbase. Special forces teams partnered with Afghan militias to kill or capture Taliban leaders while other special operations forces and the CIA targeted Taliban leadership and al-Qa'eda through surveilling areas of interest with drones, raiding suspected homes and compounds, and calling in air strikes on possible Taliban or al-Qa'eda.[26] Operations were executed inside both Afghanistan and Pakistan.

Upon taking command, Lieutenant General McNeill developed an operational plan focused on counterterrorism. McNeill added his conventional battalions to raids and searches, in his words, "a rolling series of operations going on all the time."[27] The battalions flew out of Bagram and Kandahar to strike targets, often in the east. McNeill had US forces collect intelligence and conduct operations to prevent al-Qa'eda from establishing a sanctuary there.[28] McNeill set up additional bases, in Asadabad in Kunar and Salerno in Khost and in Helmand near Gereshk.[29]

Counterterrorism had a downside. US operators lumped Taliban leaders together with al-Qa'eda. A few Taliban leaders indeed supported al-Qa'eda, but the majority inside Afghanistan were doing nothing of the sort. US guidance was to engage, defeat, and destroy al-Qa'eda, and since they were presumably inseparable from the Taliban, the Taliban too. Units in country were told to capture or kill suspected terrorists regardless of the cost. Under this pressure, according to one official who was on the ground, US operators started attacking former Taliban simply because they were there rather than for any clear tie to al-Qa'eda.[30]

By their own admission, special operations forces at the time neglected careful intelligence. They were anxious to prosecute whatever leads came, no matter how questionable the source.[31] Analysts who warned that intelligence might be faulty were often overruled. In February 2002, for example, special forces based in Kandahar conducted a night raid on compounds in Uruzgan that local intelligence sources claimed were al-Qaʻeda locations. Fighting broke out. The special forces killed 16 and took 27 prisoners only to discover all the "targets" were allies of President Karzai and the "intelligence sources" had been their tribal rivals.[32] Operators were willing to follow such poor-quality intelligence in order to carry out raids, which is what senior leaders in Washington were demanding. Central Command (CENTCOM) ordered all detainees that might be al-Qaʻeda, Taliban leaders, or foreign fighters held for interrogation since they could pose a threat to US interests or have intelligence on terrorist activities.[33]

Missions often captured innocent civilians or came up empty-handed. The experience of one special forces team in Kandahar in 2003 and 2004 is indicative. Almost all of the team's missions turned out to be "dry holes." A few mistakenly targeted Afghan civilians. The team did not find a single insurgent leader and saw little fighting.[34] Another team in Kandahar had a similar experience. "A lot of [operations] ended with us capturing low-level leaders or people who were associated with the Taliban," said its master sergeant, "I don't think . . . we ever caught anybody who was a confirmed al-Qaʻeda member. Rather, they were low-level Taliban operatives."[35] Prison populations ballooned. Few detainees had good information on al-Qaʻeda or the Taliban.[36]

Worst was how raids and "targeted" air strikes accidentally killed civilians. Six special operations raids into Uruzgan in the summer of 2002 came up empty-handed but killed 80 Afghans in the process. Most famously, on July 1 of that year, an AC-130 gunship and B-52 bomber mistook a wedding party of more than 200 people for Taliban engaging them with anti-aircraft fire. A special forces mission was underway nearby and Mullah Omar was thought to be in the area. At Afghan weddings, men often fired guns into the air in celebration. The presence of rifles among 200 people at night and celebratory fire misled the Americans to think they had encountered an organized anti-aircraft defense system. They blasted four villages and killed 54 men, women, and children. "There was no trace of the Taliban," found one of the special forces teams on the ground.[37] When Americans were so unfamiliar with Afghanistan, aggressive operations had a high potential to cause harm. Accidental or not, such deaths angered Afghans.[38]

Violation of home and killing of innocent family members were deeply offensive to Afghans, especially Pashtuns. Honor demanded a man defend his home and protect the women of the family. A failure to do so signified weakness. Revenge was the only option to recover that honor. Raids became a symbol of occupation.

Just as pernicious, special operations forces detained Taliban who had stopped fighting. After 2001, many Taliban, including several of its founders, returned to their homes in the south. According to relatives, religious leaders, and even tribal warlords, these former Taliban wanted to live in peace under the new government.[39] Unfortunately, US forces, rival tribal leaders, and certain government leaders harassed or detained them.

For US special operations forces, these men were targets because of their past and presumed ties to al-Qa'eda. For tribal and government leaders, they were rivals and it could be useful to trick Americans into targeting them. Special operations forces relied on the militias, especially those of Sherzai and Ahmed Wali Karzai, to provide them fighters for strike forces. Sherzai and Ahmed Wali fed US officers information on personal rivals who may or may not have been actual Taliban, let alone tied to al-Qa'eda.[40] A special forces team member stationed in Kandahar in 2002 boasted that they worked with Sherzai's ally, the provincial intelligence chief, "more than anyone else. He was the source of a lot of solid actionable intelligence he'd earned the hard way—although he was later fired over human rights abuses."[41]

Journalists and scholars have detailed the accounts of scores of Taliban who had tried to live peacefully until US forces raided their homes, imprisoned them, or hurt a family member.[42] One example is Baz Mohammed, a Noorzai tribal leader who had been a Taliban commander in the 1990s. When Kandahar fell, he returned to his home in Farah, the province west of Helmand. US special operations forces targeted his Noorzai colleagues and old Barakzai rivals close to Karzai worked to marginalize him. In 2004, he went to Pakistan, intent on taking up arms. His tribesmen later said the oppression was so bad that he had been given no choice. This may have been a bit of an exaggeration but the government certainly could have done more to preserve his neutrality.[43] Baz Mohammed would become the most powerful Taliban leader in Farah.[44]

The most famous example of how counterterrorism drove people back to arms is Bergat Khan.[45] An elderly Ishaqzai tribal leader of stature, Bergat Khan had been one of Mullah Omar's first sponsors in 1994. In May 2002, US special operations forces raided his home in Maiwand, shot him, and detained him and 55 villagers. Bergat Khan died in custody. The tribe was furious and protested in Kandahar City. Both Sherzai and Ishaqzai tribal leaders later said that the attack caused much of the Ishaqzai tribe to turn against the government, creating widespread malaise in western Kandahar.[46]

These stories may oversimplify. Even had Bergat lived, the Taliban leadership had so many other ties into the Ishaqzai that it is hard to see how many tribesmen would have stayed neutral. Nonetheless, whatever may have passed otherwise, the killing catalyzed the tribe's opposition.[47] It did not help that after the raid US forces went on to kill or capture more Ishaqzai.[48] "If one's home is damaged, is it not oppression? . . . The whole tribe was oppressed. . . . The government and United States imprison innocent Ishaqzai," pleaded Haji Kaka, a foremost Ishaqzai tribal leader from Kandahar.[49] Kandahar police chief Akrem Khakrezwal said that the Ishaqzai "are thinking of when the Russians came and killed a lot of people, and they are thinking that the Americans and British are going to repeat that."[50] In the following years, Ishaqzai tribesmen frequently headed to Pakistan.[51]

It is possible that most former Taliban leaders living in Afghanistan left for Pakistan to rejoin the movement by 2004. The list includes former Defense Minister Obaidullah and future Taliban leader Akhtar Mohammed Mansour. US or government harassment was a major reason for the exodus. A Taliban biography of Mullah Omar by Abdul Hai Mutmain reads:

> Those average Taliban—who after Hamid Karzai's promise had returned to their own villages and homes were captured and followed at the hands of the Americans and their Afghan militia supporters— scattered in every direction. . . . As a result, it can be said that many peaceful people again prepared to resist because of the unfortunate behavior of the Americans, Northern Alliance, and local warlords. They thought, "If I am disrespected when I sit in my own home, then I am reconciled to prison and death."[52]

Journalist Anand Gopal identifies 11 leaders who left to rejoin the movement because of some kind of US or government harassment and went on to positions of influence.[53] The real number was probably higher. The total leadership of the Taliban was much larger, of course—70 to 80 is probably a good guess. Of these, in addition to those who had actually been mistreated, many others went to Pakistan out of fear of mistreatment by Afghan rivals or US forces.

If US forces targeted innocent people partly because of Washington's stress on counterterrorism, there was also a feeling among the military, special operations forces in particular, that any former Taliban were bad and deserved to be detained in order to prevent another September 11. "Most of us wanted retribution," writes Scott Mann, a special forces officer, "Even Green Berets, who normally thrive on an indigenous approach, didn't have much use of working by, with, and through the local population. Not this time. We were more interested in avenging the 9/11 attacks by putting bullets through al-Qa'eda and the Taliban."[54]

This mindset gets to a larger point. US military actions, like the Bush team's aversion to peace talks, derived from wider American fear of another September 11. The best way to protect innocent Afghans would have been to scale back counterterrorism operations, something that contradicted Bush administration policies, policies the American people widely supported in the early years of the intervention.[55]

Certain diplomats and generals noted the dangers of harming civilians. Major General Dave Barno succeeded McNeill as commander of US forces in October 2003.[56] He drafted a strategy that focused on reducing the use of force. But he did not have authority over special operations and completed his tour in May 2005 before his ideas could stick. Those ideas would not be implemented for half a decade.

One of the important questions of the Afghan War is whether the mistreatment of former Taliban caused the movement to reemerge. The question implies the United States could have avoided over a decade of war by calling off night raids and capture missions. It indicts Bush's entire American war against terror by showing it to be the very cause of instability in Afghanistan. The explanation leads to a counterfactual: if the United States had done nothing, or maybe focused solely on Osama bin Laden and his immediate colleagues, then it and thousands of innocents would have been safer.

The argument carries weight but needs to be considered in light of other conditions for the Taliban's return. Even without US counterterrorism operations, war may have returned. High-ranking Taliban leaders, including Mullah Omar, Jalaluddin Haqqani, and Dadullah Lang, never settled into a peaceful life. They probably would have re-formed the movement, regardless of US counterterrorism operations, especially after early peace feelers had been turned down. None of this is to condone US actions. The United States should have been much more careful. It also could have done much more to curb the poor behavior of certain government leaders. At the very least, the United States missed another opportunity to dampen Taliban momentum and sympathy among the local population. At the very least, the United States fell short of its own moral standards.

After the capture of Kandahar in 2001, Mullah Omar fled to northern Helmand. His life from that point on is cloudy. We know little about his plans, his decisions, what he told his subordinates, or where he lived.

There are two legends about Mullah Omar's post-2001 life. The first is that after hiding in northern Helmand, Omar made his way back to Pakistan sometime between the middle and the end of 2002.[57] He went to Quetta and received protection from the ISI. He then re-formed the Taliban movement. This legend emerged before 2009 and was promulgated by various Taliban leaders. It can be seen to serve a purpose. It conveys that Mullah Omar was directly involved in decision-making, implicitly legitimizing every decision and order coming out of Quetta.

The second legend also emerged before 2009 but became dominant after 2015. In this telling, Omar never left Afghanistan. He roamed northern Helmand, Uruzgan, and Zabul, taking refuge in remote villages. He refused to go to Pakistan because he did not trust Musharraf or the ISI.[58] He issued direction and approved decisions by courier or other clandestine means of communication. Only a few of the most trusted commanders met with him face to face. His wives and children never saw him. This legend serves a different purpose. It casts Omar as a traditional Afghan religious hero. He removes himself from society, subjects himself to hardship, stays close to Allah, shows unwavering resolve.[59] Equally important, by keeping the Emir al-Momineen in Afghanistan, the legend paints the Taliban movement as independent and Afghan, not Pakistani.

Where does the truth lie? The most compelling evidence was discovered by Dutch researcher Bette Dam and supports the latter; Omar spent years in Afghanistan living close to the front lines (a rather surprising revelation), though it also may be conceivable that he visited Pakistan at times.[60] Between the two legends, one thing is likely true. Mullah Omar was in charge of the movement but rarely seen and divorced from day-to-day management. He made strategic decisions and gave direction to the senior Taliban leaders. He was a charismatic figure, obeyed and revered. Even in hiding his commanders and fighters were loyal.

Omar guided the resurrection of the Taliban movement. It is unknown if he did this because he felt excluded from the new political settlement or because he was never serious about peace in the first place.[61] Shortly after leaving Kandahar, he may have begun laying the groundwork for an insurgency. Mutmain, his Taliban biographer, writes that Omar visited Helmand, Uruzgan, and Zabul with a few fighters. He assembled the important local commanders and advised them on how to start a guerrilla war. He then, Mutmain says, gave various commanders money to go to their villages and prepare for a guerrilla war.[62]

In February 2003, Omar published a letter that called on all Afghans to wage jihad against the United States in Afghanistan. He warned that anyone working with the United States or the government would be killed.[63] Around the same time, he sent an audio recording to all Taliban fighters and commanders. The recording named Mullah Abdul Ghani Baradar and Mullah Obaidullah (former defense minister) as his two principal deputies. They were to execute operations in his name. He called both his *nayeb*, meaning viceroy or regent. Doing so signified that he was purposefully handing operational authority to them. He would focus himself on guiding the vision and direction of the movement.[64]

Omar secluded himself and limited his contact with the Taliban senior leaders. He would issue most of his orders and decisions solely to Baradar and Obaidullah. With perhaps a few exceptions, other commanders no longer saw or heard directly from him. His instructions were usually issued via audio recording or letter.[65]

Mullah Baradar was close to Omar. He had a medium build, calm yet foxy eyes, a slightly pointed nose, and a fully black beard. Supposedly one of Mullah

Omar's childhood friends, Baradar had served in Omar's cadre during the Soviet war and joined the Taliban early on.[66] During the first Taliban regime, he was Omar's assistant in Kandahar, then the corps commander in western Afghanistan, and next commander of the Kabul garrison. It was later rumored that he married Omar's sister.

Baradar was Popalzai, which gave him a connection to Karzai. Karzai's repeated failure to reconcile with Taliban leaders disappointed Baradar. As far as he was concerned, Karzai was powerless, subservient to the Americans. Baradar believed Karzai had given up a true opportunity for peace in 2001 when they had met in Shah Wali Kot. According to many Taliban, Baradar picked up arms again after 2001 because Karzai failed to enforce an amnesty that would have allowed him to live peacefully in Afghanistan and subsequently failed to include the Taliban in the Emergency Loya Jirga.[67] "Hamid Karzai is the slave of two houses," Baradar once told an Afghan official. "First he is the slave of the Panjshiris and second he is the slave of America. Slavery cannot create peace."[68]

In Quetta, where hundreds of Taliban mingled on the streets, the top Taliban leaders met that March of 2003 for the first time since the fall of the regime. Obaidullah, Baradar, and Dadullah Lang were present. Despite the assertions of a few sources to the contrary, Omar was likely absent. At this meeting, the leaders agreed that they would reestablish their Islamic emirate through violence, as per Omar's message of a month earlier.[69]

In June 2003, Omar announced the formation of a new ten-member leadership council (it later grew to 18 and then 33 members), known colloquially as the "Quetta Shura."[70] He had sent a voice recording to the key Taliban leaders, directing them to form the council.[71] In addition to Baradar and Obaidullah, a few prominent members of the council were Jalaluddin Haqqani, Mullah Abdul Razzaq, Hafiz Majid, Mullah Akhtar Mohammed Mansour, Mullah Akhtar Mohammed Osmani, and Mullah Dadullah Lang.[72]

The voice recording included specific instructions for a future Taliban offensive. Omar directed the shura to prepare for an offensive against the United States and the new government in Afghanistan. He ordered his Taliban subordinates not to strike immediately but to wait years until a massed offensive could be organized. Immediate attacks, he warned, would be piecemeal and look like acts of personal vengeance by individuals that could be dismissed by the government as mere crimes. Omar did not want the jihad tarnished. He wanted the strength of the movement on full display.[73] The shura reorganized the movement and laid the groundwork in Afghanistan for the future offensive. The commander who would play the largest role in these endeavors would be Dadullah.[74]

Mullah Dadullah Lang was fearsome. The hardened veteran of the Soviet-Afghan and civil wars would command the Taliban in southern Afghanistan. His sobriquet "Lang" means lame. He had lost half a leg to a land mine during the civil war. The same name was given to the Tartar conqueror Timur Lang (or Tamerlane), who had ravaged Iran and Afghanistan in the 1300s. From the poorer Kakar tribe, Dadullah had been with the Taliban from the start. From 1997 to 1998, he had led the 6,000 fighters who had been surrounded in Kunduz for more than a year. Abdul Salam Zaeef, the former Taliban ambassador to Pakistan and early member of the Taliban, writes in his memoir that without Dadullah "the 6,000 *Taliban* would have faced certain death."[75] He praises Dadullah's bold yet cruel leadership: "The one-legged commander was always ready to lead each military operation himself, standing among his men on the front line and dashing into the offensive as the first person over the ridge. His style of command was so strict that no one dared to escape or failed to perform their duty."[76]

Dadullah was known for his serious demeanor, piety, and cruelty. According to a Helmandi student who was in Kabul during the 1990s and met Dadullah several times, "Dadullah put up with no issues that were not important. He made decisions summarily. If anyone strayed or said something stupid, he would throw his leg at them. . . . He was deeply religious and often spoke about how he was fighting for Islam."[77] Dadullah had once shot in the leg one of his men who was running away from battle. After that Zaeef says no one ever retreated without Dadullah's direct order.[78] Infamously cruel, Dadullah killed Hazara civilians in Bamiyan and Tajik civilians in Parwan. In the Helmandi student's words, "He was not merciful. He was not kind."[79]

When the United States invaded in 2001, Dadullah again fought in Kunduz. From there, he returned to Kandahar and ultimately escaped to Pakistan, where he stayed with much of the rest of the Taliban leadership. By then, Dadullah was in his mid-30s.[80] Unlike many other Taliban leaders, Dadullah supported al-Qa'eda. He liked their idea of global jihad and eventually endorsed the terrorist group openly.[81] After Mullah Omar's letter of February 2003, Dadullah started running operations, cruelty unabated. In March 2003, he personally ordered the execution of Ricardo Munguia, a Red Cross engineer who had been stopped at a Taliban checkpoint.[82]

After the formation of the Quetta Shura, Dadullah was appointed commander of the southern provinces.[83] Dadullah's authority was such that he could run Helmand, Kandahar, Zabul, Uruzgan, and Farah as one war. He was known to strictly obey Omar—and argue with other senior leaders.[84]

Dadullah's vision was for Omar's major offensive to capture most if not all of the south.[85] In preparation, Dadullah began re-forming insurgent cadres. Thousands of Taliban fighters and commanders had fled to Pakistan in late 2001 and early 2002. The Pakistani police and military had let them in and sometimes helped them. The Taliban returned to refugee camps or set themselves up in Peshawar, Quetta, or other towns. Some tried to settle into normal life. Others waited anxiously to rejoin the movement. A few had already rejoined cadres, trained, and initiated low-level attacks, usually along the border. The Haqqani network—the highly effective organization of Jalaluddin Haqqani based across the border from Khost—specifically started minor operations almost immediately after 2001.[86]

Over 2003, Dadullah and other ranking Taliban tracked down old cadre commanders all over Pakistan and told them to get their men back together. One Taliban commander described the effort:

> We went to a meeting at night near Peshawar, and I couldn't believe what I saw: my top commander . . . Mullah Dadullah! He was my ideal; his name meant victory for us. . . . After six or seven months I was called to Miram Shah. Dadullah was there; so were Akhtar Mohammed, Osmani . . . and our defense minister, Mullah Obaidullah. It was decided that each commander should go find his former soldiers and prepare to return to Afghanistan to fight.[87]

Dadullah set up training camps for new recruits. He contacted Iraqi insurgents too. In 2005, he brought experienced Iraqi insurgents to the Pakistani tribal areas to teach the latest tactics and technology. Compact discs, videos, and other materials showing tactics and techniques from the Iraq War were distributed among the fighters. They included films of improvised explosive device (IED) attacks and suicide bombings.

More than anyone else, Dadullah introduced suicide bombings to Afghanistan. Suicide attacks tended to come in two forms: an explosive vest strapped to a person who would blow him or herself up near a particular target, or explosives packed into a vehicle that the driver would detonate. The latter was particularly destructive. One car bomb could level a building. Dozens of civilian bystanders could perish.

Previously, Afghans had been unimpressed with the idea of killing themselves, let alone innocent lives along the way. The Soviet invasion spurred the idea of martyrdom, but not suicide bombing. That came with al-Qa'eda. Even then, the Taliban abstained from the tactic until after 2001. Dadullah presented writings from Arab religious leaders to justify suicide attacks. He put special effort into recruiting 100 volunteers.[88] Omar approved of Dadullah's extremism at this time, believing that jihad demanded hard action.[89] The suicide bombing campaign was officially launched in January 2004.

The Taliban relationship with al-Qa'eda strengthened during this time. In 2002, al-Qa'eda reorganized in Pakistan's Federally Administered Tribal Areas (FATA). Its commanders based themselves in the region because Pakistani counterterrorism raids frequented Islamabad, Peshawar, and Karachi. Al-Qa'eda's focus was on fighting in Afghanistan but they also executed international attacks such as the July 7, 2005, London subway bombings.[90] Al-Qa'eda operated a few training camps in the Pakistan tribal areas along the border in North and South Waziristan.[91] Al-Qa'eda, other Arabs, and Pakistani militants, as well as Taliban, trained in the camps, wherefrom they launched guerrilla raids into Afghanistan.[92] Dadullah, senior Taliban commanders, Jalaluddin Haqqani, and other commanders affiliated with the Taliban cooperated closely with al-Qa'eda and other militants.[93]

Dadullah and a significant faction of commanders and fighters believed in al-Qa'eda's cause. Taliban had sheltered Osama bin Laden in Pakistan as he escaped from Afghanistan in the last days of 2001. Certain founding members maintained their friendship. Later, bin Laden resumed giving the Taliban money. Not every senior Taliban leader was pro-bin Laden and Omar himself may have preferred distance. Yet reticence to jettison bin Laden and al-Qa'eda was palpable. When in 2005 Abdul Hai Mutmain, as a Taliban spokesman, publicly condemned the attacks of September 11 and stated that the Taliban had no intention to wage war outside Afghanistan's borders, a variety of Taliban commanders were outraged.[94]

The Taliban leaders and supportive religious leaders recruited rank and file. A network of mullahs spread the word. "We would meet every week with the mullah," remembered one fighter. "We would talk about the situation, especially about the government and the foreign forces. We had long discussions and the mullah would try to convince us to fight against these people."[95] The message could be compelling. "I was determined to bring back our Islamic regime and get rid of the Americans and the traitors allied with them," attested another fighter.[96] In remote places such as the mountains of Zabul, Paktiya, and Nangarhar, former Taliban, the Haqqanis, and other long-standing mujahideen groups such as the families of Latif Mansour and Yunis Khalis had never abandoned jihad.

Taliban recruits came from three sources: former Taliban fighters now living in Pakistan, former Taliban fighters and villagers living in Afghanistan, and refugees in camps or students at Pakistan madrasas. The majority were the latter.[97]

Large numbers of Afghan refugees lived in Peshawar, Miram Shah, and Quetta. Since 2001, Peshawar had expanded by half to 1.5 million people as a result of the refugee influx. The jihad against the Soviet Union followed by the Afghan civil war and then Taliban regime had turned the city into a hive of the black market and various militant groups, including the Taliban. Quetta had likewise ballooned, nearly doubling in size to 1 million people. The city and the surrounding refugee camps were recruiting centers for the entire movement. Pakistani Pashtuns from the border regions as well as Karachi were also inspired to volunteer for the Taliban, usually educated at madrasas.

Madrasas had multiplied along the Pakistani side of the border since 1979. Within Baluchistan and the tribal areas, they were the source of education for children and adolescents, especially Afghan refugees. Hundreds of madrasas were in and around Peshawar, including the famous Dar-ul-Ulum Haqqania and Chageriya madrasas, attended by a large percentage of Afghan students and the alma mater of many Taliban leaders.[98] In and around Quetta was the same, with madrasas interspersed with Afghan refugee settlements. In Karachi, where tens of thousands of Pashtuns had immigrated to work, the number of madrasas increased from 20 in 1971 to 1,800 in 2007.[99]

The wars in Afghanistan, the influence of extremist ideas, and Pakistani funding had caused madrasa education to emphasize jihad and support for the Taliban. The adolescents who joined the Taliban had been taught that the infidel Americans had occupied their home and jihad was an obligation. The orientation of madrasa education could be radical, endorsing improvised explosive devices and suicide attacks. The anthropologist David Edwards describes why madrasas were such fertile recruiting grounds:

> Given that madrasa students begin their classes at a young age, that they are never given access to any other way of viewing the world, and that they are separated from the potentially moderating views of parents and other family members who might hold contrary opinions or who might take their physical safety more seriously than the students do themselves, it seems hardly surprising that Taliban leaders would look to madrasas to provide the raw material for the exercise of regaining power of terrorizing the government and people to Afghanistan."[100]

Madrasas were a fundamental part of the Taliban network. Having attended the madrasas themselves, Taliban commanders down the ranks had deep ties to the religious scholars who ran them. After the Taliban defeat in 2001, many of the foremost religious scholars in the country fled to Pakistan. Three standouts are: Shaykh al-Hadith Maulawi Mohammed Naim Kalandi who had advised the Taliban leadership and delivered prestigious sermons in Kabul; Maulawi Abdul Ali Deobandi who had taught mujahideen during the Soviet-Afghan War and preached on the radio for the Taliban; and Maulawi Aynatullah (Ghbrguy Akhundzada Sahib) who had been a famous teacher at Afghan and Pakistani madrasas. In Pakistan, these scholars continued to teach at madrasas. Their networks of students and colleagues grew. They had wide influence, with scores of noteworthy students who became scholars themselves teaching hundreds of students.[101]

Omar asked the Pakistani and Afghan religious scholars at the madrasas to support war and condemn religious leaders who did not. Yousaf Qureshi, head of an influential madrasa in Peshawar, told journalist Elizabeth Rubin, "We are supporting them [al-Qaʻeda and Taliban] to give the Americans a tough time . . . All the administrators of madrasas know what our students are doing, but we won't tell them not to fight in Afghanistan."[102] The deputy of a major madrasa in Quetta was even more frank in an October 2003 meeting with Pakistani journalist Ahmed Rashid: "We are proud that the Taliban are made and helped here and we do everything we can to facilitate them. The Afghan government and Karzai are the stooges and puppets of America. . . . Only the Taliban can constitute the real government in Afghanistan."[103]

Many of the madrasas affiliated with Pakistani religious parties, such as Jamiat Ulema-e-Islam, were run by a powerful religious leader and longtime Taliban supporter, Maulana Fazel Rahman. The religious parties had supported Pakistan's backing of the Taliban in the 1990s. During late 2001, they protested Pakistan's abandonment of the Taliban and cooperation with the United States. In 2002, these parties won control of the North-West Frontier Province and Baluchistan. They also gained 68 seats in Pakistan's national assembly. Mullahs who took these seats had fought in the Taliban during the 1990s. The new political power of Jamiat Ulema-e-Islam and Pakistani religious parties made it easier for the Taliban to organize. Shortly after these elections, Musharraf allied with religious parties in order to balance the political power of his civilian political rivals, Nawaz Sharif and Benazir Bhutto.[104] Jamiat Ulema-e-Islam and the Pakistani religious parties were in a unique position to facilitate the return of the Taliban.

Because of Bush's pressure in 2001, Pakistani president Parvez Musharraf had officially cut off Pakistani support for the Taliban. He closed military and economic assistance programs and detained various Taliban leaders at the request of the United States. Unofficially, he turned a blind eye to the ISI (Pakistani military intelligence) and military officers who persisted in helping the Taliban. Musharraf minimized military operations in the tribal areas along the border against either the Taliban or al-Qaʻeda.[105] Security services abstained from targeting the Taliban, allowing the leadership to survive and reorganize in Pakistan.[106]

One reason for Musharraf's leniency was popular Pakistani opposition to the US invasion. As in Afghanistan, political rulers of Pakistan—whether military or civilian—did not have authority to say whether war was justified or unjustified. That fell to the religious leaders and many were calling for jihad.[107] Musharraf could not overrule them. Feeling was widespread in Pakistan that Taliban opposition to the United States was just. Numerous surveys and interviews document the opinion.[108] Musharraf faced serious opposition to suppressing the Taliban, especially within the military. Pakistani officers deeply opposed a crackdown. Many felt a tie as Muslims to the Taliban, supported their cause, and happily admitted as much in interviews with Westerners.[109] One officer told British scholar Anatol Lieven in 2002, "We are being ordered to launch a Pakistani civil war for the sake of America. Why on earth should we? Why should we commit suicide for you?"[110]

The more important reason for Musharraf's leniency was that rivalry with India dominated Pakistani strategic thinking. Musharraf and his generals feared that India would gain influence in Afghanistan and encircle Pakistan. Musharraf distrusted Karzai for allowing Tajiks to play a large role in his government (during the civil war Tajiks had received support from India) and for having good relations with India, which reopened its embassy in Kabul and consulates in Kandahar and Jalalabad, close to the Pakistan border. India was funding infrastructure, eventually including a dam, the national parliament building, and a trade corridor to Iran that would bypass Pakistan.[111] Musharraf increasingly wanted to reverse course.

In 2004, Musharraf decided to reopen assistance to the Taliban, a fact he later admitted in the press. Musharraf would say that Karzai "helped India stab Pakistan in the back."[112] Pakistani officials told Afghan officials that as long as Afghanistan remained friends with India, Pakistan would ally with the Taliban.[113]

The ISI intensified support to the Taliban, supposedly providing tens of millions of dollars and safe houses in Quetta and Karachi, where they could hide from US counterterrorism operations.[114] A member of the Haqqani network informed researcher Antonio Giustozzi, "They supported us financially and logistically . . . Pakistan promised us that any time we conducted operations in Afghanistan, they would provide us refuge in North Waziristan, South Waziristan, Quetta, Bajaur and Peshawar. After any operations we would cross back to those areas in Pakistan. This was the reason we could commence operations after Karzai came to power."[115]

According to Taliban living in Pakistan at the time, the ISI protected key Taliban leaders, specifically Mullah Dadullah, Mullah Baradar, and Mullah Akhtar Mohammed Mansour. Pressuring them to pursue Pakistan's interests. The ISI advised them on planning for war.[116] Taliban leaders interested in peace were discouraged from working with the Afghan government. Those no longer fighting were encouraged to take up arms. Training camps were built near the border, possibly run by active and retired ISI officers.[117]

The Bush administration bothered Pakistan little over its relationship with the Taliban. Bush, Powell, and Rumsfeld considered Musharraf a close ally. Because of the war on terror, the 1990s ban on aid to Pakistan over their nuclear tests and Musharraf's 1999 military coup were lifted. Over the course of its tenure, the Bush administration would provide Afghanistan with $5.3 billion in economic and military assistance and another $6.7 billion in reimbursement for military operations. The administration even sold Pakistan F-16s to compensate for the ones cancelled by the Pressler Amendment in 1990.[118]

Evidence was as yet scarce that Pakistan was working with the Taliban, which Bush and his team still considered defeated. Additionally, the administration highly valued Pakistan's role in counterterrorism. Pakistan was instrumental in the detention of a string of al-Qaʻeda leaders in 2002: Ibn al-Sheikh al-Libi, who ran a training camp; Abu Zubaydah, the head of al-Qaʻeda external operations; Khalid al-Attash, who had assisted in the bombing of the USS *Cole*; and Ramzi bin al-Shibh, one of the planners of the September 11 attacks. Then in March 2003, the Pakistanis captured Khalid Sheikh Mohammed, al-Qaʻeda's third-in-command, chief operational planner, and creator of the September 11 plot.[119] From the administration's point of view, Musharraf was a good partner.

In 2003, Taliban deputy leader Mullah Baradar instructed Mullah Dadullah to go to southern Afghanistan and prepare for the offensive. Baradar was the only leader other than Omar respected enough to issue instructions to Dadullah. Baradar gave Dadullah latitude to operate freely with minimal supervision.[120] Dadullah went to Panjwai in Kandahar and then to Zabul to organize resistance. After his visit, Taliban religious leaders and small teams of fighters filtered in.

Dadullah had widespread support in the barren foothills of Zabul, Uruzgan, and northern Helmand. The government had never really penetrated these areas. Zabul was almost entirely Ghilzai, the tribes of which felt a deep tie to Mullah Omar and to Dadullah. One of the stories about Mullah Omar's life has him commanding the Taliban in Zabul. He funded fighters with cash he had taken with him from Kandahar and from time to time picked up his Kalashnikov and personally took part in combat.[121] Even if the story is apocryphal, by 2004 Zabul was Taliban country once more.[122]

Meanwhile, Dadullah slowly gathered support in western Kandahar—the districts of Panjwai, Zharey, and Maiwand—where the Taliban movement had been founded.[123] Communities of Taliban-leaning Ishaqzai and Noorzai lived in the three districts. If Dadullah could restart the movement in western Kandahar, the Taliban offensive would have a base on the doorstep of Kandahar City.

At first, locals in western Kandahar were not ready to fight.[124] Dadullah sent in only a few commanders, organizers, and small cadres in 2003 and 2004. They went to sympathetic communities and began building networks and recruiting. Religious leaders—some coming from Pakistan, others long residents of the area—began encouraging people to wage jihad against the infidel Americans.[125]

Dadullah intimidated government allies in order to demonstrate the Taliban's growing power to the people. In April 2005, the Taliban media spokesman, Abdul Latif Hakimi, declared that government officials, aid workers, and international forces would be targeted. Over the year, district governors were assassinated and suicide car bombs and suicide bombers exploded. Night letters threatened those working with the government, labeling them collaborators or spies.[126] The Taliban also attacked schools and teachers. Infamously, the Taliban beheaded a teacher in Shah Wali Kot district before his own class. Twenty schools were destroyed in Kandahar in the last four months of 2005. Then, two hundred more shut down across the southern provinces.[127] The Taliban assassinated the head and 70 other members of the 100-member religious council that had formed in the province and openly aligned with the government. There was no blowback among religious leaders.[128]

Dadullah targeted tribal leaders as well. Mohammed Issa Samad Khan was a tall Noorzai landowner in Panjwai. He was one of the few Noorzai to have been a district governor. He lived in a large compound with his family. One evening, two Toyota Land Cruisers and two motorcycles pulled up. The Land Cruisers halted some 100 meters from the compound. The motorcycles rode in close. The riders stepped off and knocked on the front gate. When hailed, the two men responded "*Mooj melma yu*. We are guests." They were dressed in camouflage uniforms and claimed to be police. Samad Khan's guards noticed the men were wearing sandals, not boots. Something was amiss. Samad Khan called Hakim Angar, the deputy police chief, and asked if any police were in the area. Angar said no. Samad Khan and his guards then went up to the roof of their main building, with all of the Kalashnikovs in the house.

The "guests" demanded to be let in. Samad Khan shouted, "*Ma Radzay!* Stay away!" Dropping their ruse, the two guests asked if just one could enter— Mullah Baqi, one of Dadullah's commanders and a fellow Kakar tribesmen. Samad Khan shouted, "No. I have called the police. They are coming." Mullah Baqi and his men then opened fire. Samad Khan and his guards held them off, a guard wounded in the exchange. Baqi and his 20 or so men fell back and then bumped into Angar and his police. Samad Khan sent his guards to help in the gunfight. One of them shot and killed Baqi. Samad Khan had won but a sense of fear prevailed. After the attack, Samad Khan tended to stay in the city where it was safer.[129] He was one of many whom Dadullah intimidated.

The Taliban also exploited government mistreatment of the Ghilzai, Ishaqzai, and Noorzai.[130] The leaders of the Ishaqzai tribe, well-represented in the Quetta Shura and still seething over the death of Bergat Khan at the hands of US forces in 2002, continued to align themselves with the Taliban and keep the government at arm's length.[131] In the words of Haji Kaka, the Ishaqzai tribal leader from Maiwand, "The Taliban helped the Ishaqzai more than the government."[132] The Noorzai were more divided but were also tired of government harassment. A few Noorzai villages in Kandahar decided to invite the Taliban to return to Noorzai territory. They expected Taliban rule to be better than what they were experiencing under the government. These Noorzai brought Taliban into their homes and fed and cared for them.[133] The Taliban now had a firm base in their old homeland of Maiwand, Zharey, and Panjwai.

In late 2005, Dadullah deployed larger cadres into Kandahar. Musharraf's opening up of ISI support assisted his effort. The cadres moved up through the red desert south of Panjwai from Pakistan, or down from the Uruzgan and Helmand foothills of the Hindu Kush, or west from Zabul.[134] Because the Taliban were still in the process of reorganizing, Arabs sometimes led these teams.[135] In November and December 2005, cadres from Pakistan massed in Maiwand district, in western Kandahar. Low-level skirmishes and improvised explosive device (IED) attacks became frequent.[136] The police were too few to stop the Taliban. There were only 35 to 50 in Zharey, Panjwai, and Maiwand respectively. Their leaders were lethargic. Panjwai police chief Zahman Jan whiled away his days watching dog fights.[137]

The Karzai regime was not ready to face a Taliban offensive. In the south, competition within Karzai's power base—between Governor Gul Agha Sherzai, Ahmed Wali Karzai, Alikozai leader Mullah Naqib, and others—had worsened. In 2004, Ahmed Wali was elected chairman of the new provincial council, a better perch from where to expand his family's power. He broke up the Alizai that protected Zharey by pushing out their tribal leader. He promoted competition within the Alikozai to undercut Naqib. By weakening his opponents, Ahmed Wali weakened their influence over their tribes. Tribes in certain districts became too divided to withstand Taliban influence.[138]

Laid over this tribal infighting was an ill-timed decision to disarm militias, including the Afghan military forces. Conventional wisdom among diplomats and development experts was that these forces hindered the construction of a professional army and ran counter to sound state-building practices. The United Nations favored disarming militias before the creation of an army. They did not want militias to undermine the professionalization of an army. Rumsfeld had opposed the move in 2002 but had softened his position after lobbying by Major General Karl Eikenberry and Zalmay Khalilzad. He went further the next year. New evidence of the situation in Afghanistan and a May 2003 visit impressed upon him the dangers of militia misbehavior and the need to accelerate the creation of an army.[139] He endorsed a strategy to weaken the warlords written by Marin Strmecki, the scholar who had helped convince him of the merits of a professional army in 2002.[140] Demobilization of militias became US policy by the summer of 2003.[141]

Shortly thereafter, the United Nations and the United States and its allies formulated a demobilization plan. Realizing the process would weaken his political rivals, Karzai went along. That October, Khalilzad mediated an agreement between the government and the major warlords, including Mohammed

Fahim and Ismael Khan, to demobilize the militias. Later in the year, the United States reduced militia funding.[142] The United States, the United Nations, and Japan instituted the disarmament, demobilization, and reintegration program (known as "DDR") throughout the country. Over the next two years, militia numbers countrywide fell from 100,000 to 8,000. Many units were disarmed and demobilized. Others merged into the police and army. Still others became private security contractors, paid to protect convoys or reconstruction projects. Thousands of fighters went home.

Disarmament and demobilization occurred in the south in 2004 and 2005 while Dadullah was infiltrating into the countryside. The process became a tool for Ahmed Wali. One of his relatives ran the program in Kandahar. He focused on demobilizing the militias of Karzai rivals. Over 6,000 of the 7,500 militia in Kandahar stood down, including Sherzai's allies in Zharey and Naqib's forces in Arghandab. These forces were a bulwark of the defense of Kandahar City.[143] Ahmed Wali's militia survived. Sherzai fenced off 500 of his militia as a special "Governor's Reserve Police." Razziq's Achekzai border police were unaffected because they were part of the official security forces.[144] Although several hundred demobilized militia transferred into the police, the net result was that at the very moment Taliban were infiltrating back into the south, thousands of men who had been in position to fight were swept off the field.

Police and the meager army brigade that was arriving in Kandahar were too few to replace them.[145] Roughly 3,000 police—nearly half the force—in Kandahar had deserted since the 2003 removal of Akrem Khakrezwal, another casualty of tribal infighting, and had never been replaced. The succeeding police chiefs lacked the political power to draw in new recruits and Ahmed Wali and Sherzai were not invested in building the force. They had political maneuverings to attend to.[146]

In June 2005, Karzai finally transferred Governor Sherzai, who had been temporarily removed in 2003 and then sent back, out of Kandahar for good. Sherzai went to Nangarhar, to be governor. Asadullah Khalid, the capable 35-year-old former governor of Ghazni, replaced Sherzai. A Kabul insider with no Kandahar power base, Khalid did not stray from Ahmed Wali Karzai or the president. Karzai and his family had gained political dominance over Kandahar. "Divide and rule" had served them well.

As 2005 drew to a close, Dadullah was ready to launch Omar's offensive. Taliban fighters had infiltrated back into the countryside and reestablished old strongholds. Thousands of Afghans had decided to accept the Taliban. The United States, the new Afghan state, and tribal powerbrokers had mistreated former Taliban and tribes and poor communities that had formerly supported the Taliban, unleashing grievances that pushed them back into the arms of the movement. Until the end of 2005, the Taliban and their supporters had been too weak to overturn the government. That was about to change. Taliban cadres waited in Pakistan for the offensive that Dadullah had carefully prepared.

Little stood in their way. The average district had no more than 50 police, too little to do more than defend their own headquarters. A few districts had no government presence at all. The army was just beginning to deploy. US and allied forces were scarce. Large numbers of foreigners would probably have been counterproductive anyway. The tribes that the government had relied upon to fill the gap in army and police manpower were feuding with each other, their militias largely disarmed in the process. Competition within the tribes, the hallmark of tribal systems, had removed the government's defenses. The stage was set for the Taliban's return.

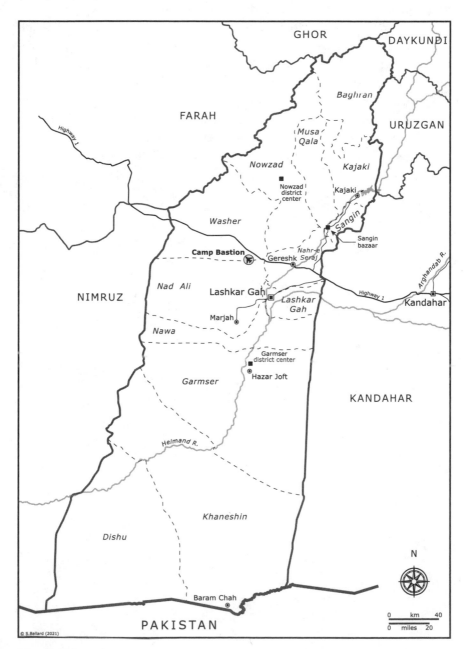

GHOR

DAYKUNDI

FARAH

Baghran

URUZGAN

Musa Qala

Nowzad

Kajaki

Kajaki

Nowzad district center

Sangin

Washer

Sangin bazaar

Camp Bastion

Nahr-e Seraj

Gereshk

Argandhab R.

NIMRUZ

Nad Ali

Lashkar Gah

Lashkar Gah

Highway 1

Kandahar

Marjah

Nawa

Garmser district center

KANDAHAR

Garmser

Hazar Joft

Highway 1

Helmand R.

Khaneshin

N

Dishu

Baram Chah

0   km   40

0   miles   20

© S.Ballard (2021)

PAKISTAN

Map 7 Helmand

The 2006 Taliban Offensive

Helmand, west of Kandahar province, was one of the great battlegrounds of America's Afghan War. Thousands of Afghans and hundreds of Americans and British would die in its villages and fields. The province covered more land than any other and had a substantial population of 1.5 million to 2.5 million. The Helmand River ran its length, pouring out of the depths of the Hindu Kush into the Kajaki reservoir (constructed by the United States in the 1950s), through its dam, and thence southward, irrigating a green band of farmland, flanked by desert on either side. American-built canals diverted water into cropland. Near the provincial capital of Lashkar Gah, the river merged with the Arghandab River flowing out of Kandahar before eventually bending westward toward Iran.

The wealth of Helmand was poppy. It was more abundant than in Kandahar, where richer irrigation nourished licit crops. In 2006, most farmers grew poppy, earning a better return than anything legal. Both the Taliban and government taxed poppy, providing a major source of revenue. Helmand was strategic.

From 2002 to 2005, Sher Mohammed Akhundzada was governor of Helmand. His uncle had been the province's most powerful warlord during the Soviet-Afghan War. It is this dead uncle—Nasim Akhundzada—who had introduced mass poppy cultivation to Helmand. In 2001, Sher Mohammed supported Karzai during his mission to Uruzgan. Karzai subsequently appointed Sher Mohammed governor of Helmand.[1]

Unfortunately, Sher Mohammed indulged in the same kind of tribal infighting that was wrecking Kandahar. As in Kandahar, powerful tribal leaders ran their own militias and smuggled poppy. Sher Mohammed tried to disarm their militias, encroach upon their territory, and eradicate their poppy, seeking to monopolize the poppy trade.[2] His policies wantonly stripped out the province's defenses.

Karl Eikenberry returned to Afghanistan in May 2005 as a lieutenant general. His work founding the Afghan army in 2002 and 2003 had impressed Defense

Secretary Rumsfeld. Eikenberry succeeded Major General Dave Barno as commander of US forces in Afghanistan, other than special operations forces which reported up a separate chain. For a former defense attaché to command US combat forces in a war zone was rare. Such jobs were usually reserved for officers with experience in brigade and division command. In this case, Rumsfeld wanted Eikenberry.[3]

Taliban unwillingness to break with al-Qa'eda had been the original reason that President Bush had invaded Afghanistan in 2001. Five years later, al-Qa'eda and the Taliban were still deemed linked. The mission as Lieutenant General Eikenberry stated to Congress in June 2006 was to "First, to defeat al-Qa'eda and their Taliban allies; and second . . . to help create the conditions where international terrorism could never again find witting support and sanctuary."[4] At this time and later, Eikenberry could point to tangible evidence that Taliban senior leaders such as Dadullah were collaborating with al-Qa'eda.[5]

Eikenberry faced a complicated situation. While Taliban momentum was accelerating, the Bush administration's attention was elsewhere. In the middle of 2005, Bush and his team still believed Afghanistan had been won. Before deploying, Eikenberry attended meetings at Central Command, the joint staff, and intelligence agencies and "with the exception of a minority of analysts, no one raised serious concerns about the potential for the insurgency to become lethal at the operational level."[6] After arriving in Kabul, Eikenberry visited his commanders in the field. At first he found them overly pessimistic: "Our commanders . . . at the brigade, battalion, and company levels consistently told me that the planned US force reductions would possibly bring a risk of Taliban resurgence. . . . Only recently having arrived in the theater, I discounted the advice being rendered."[7] Then Eikenberry traveled to more districts and villages. He made a point of getting out into the countryside, taking a minister with him whenever possible. He liked to talk to the average Afghans—the village elders, shop-owners, drivers. After a month or so in the country, "as I got around, I had growing doubts. . . . What I saw indicated we were in trouble."[8]

Throughout 2005, Washington focused on Iraq, where 140,000 US troops were deployed, not Afghanistan, with its 20,000. Looming problems eluded attention. In June 2005, Bush whisked Khalilzad off to Iraq to steer its political process. Once the October 2005 parliamentary elections were complete, Rumsfeld intended to reduce the number of US forces to between 10,000 to 12,000 and concentrate even more on counterterrorism operations along Afghanistan's eastern border. Eikenberry was instructed to prepare to do so.[9]

To make up for the shortfall, Rumsfeld looked to the North Atlantic Treaty Organization (NATO) and other US allies.[10] In 2004, he and Bush had encouraged them to play a larger role in Afghanistan. Members of the alliance had already been sending a few thousand troops to help secure Kabul and assist with counterterrorism operations. Agreement was reached for a new NATO headquarters to preside over military operations in Afghanistan. The arrangement included a much larger NATO as well as Australian troop contribution.

On December 8, 2005, NATO and allied foreign ministers finalized a plan to send British, Canadian, Dutch, and Australian forces to southern Afghanistan. The idea was to plant a robust footprint in the south. In late 2005 and early 2006, the Canadians sent 2,200 men to Kandahar, the British sent 3,150 to Helmand, and the Dutch and Australians respectively sent 1,300 and 700 to Uruzgan. Romania jumped on the bandwagon and sent roughly 500 soldiers to Zabul. These governments and their generals underestimated how badly the situation had deteriorated.[11] They expected a few skirmishes here and there, not prolonged combat.

The new NATO headquarters in Afghanistan was named the International Security Assistance Force, or ISAF for short. General David Richards, a polished British officer experienced in insurgencies, would command. Eikenberry would remain in charge of US forces until a US general could take over ISAF in 2007. For the better part of 2006, however, the ISAF headquarters was still organizing. So until August 2006, Combined Joint Task Force 76 (CJTF-76), the US divisional (10th Mountain Division) command in Afghanistan, under Major General Benjamin Freakley, was responsible for the British, Canadian, Australian, and Dutch forces fighting in southern Afghanistan. Freakley reported to Eikenberry.[12]

Washington and the other Western capitals disregarded indications of the Taliban offensive even though Eikenberry and US ambassador Ronald Neumann were calling out the danger. Neumann had been an infantry officer in Vietnam and was no rookie to fighting insurgencies. He explicitly warned of a Taliban offensive in a late 2005 cable. Neither the cable nor additional warnings from Eikenberry and Neumann registered in Washington. Rumsfeld visited Kabul in December 2005. In the course of the trip, he came to realize that the situation was indeed deteriorating but refused to do much about it. He blamed the downturn on poor governance and did nothing to invigorate the Afghan army. On the contrary, reverting to his 2002 skepticism of the Afghan army, he tried to pare it down. Penny-pinching once more got the better of Rumsfeld. When he met with defense minister Rahim Wardak, he criticized him for the long-standing plan to build an army of 70,000. He summarily reversed three years of US military planning and said Afghanistan needed an army of 45,000 to 52,000, suited for Afghanistan's limited revenues.[13] Rumsfeld's office had reassessed that Afghanistan could not sustain an army of 70,000 and that reductions were needed. Shortly after his trip, Rumsfeld decided to withdraw 3,000 US forces and cancel the planned deployment of one of two army brigades headed to

Afghanistan. Eikenberry managed to reduce the size of the cut but still lost the brigade.[14]

On March 1, 2006, President Bush visited Kabul to dedicate the new US embassy. During the visit, Eikenberry and Neumann told him that the coming summer would witness very heavy fighting and reinforcements were needed.[15] Bush listened intently but ordered no change in policy. He had scant time and fewer resources to spare for Afghanistan. Sectarian violence was now exploding in Iraq, where Bush would eventually "surge" reinforcements. Little would be left for Afghanistan. Later in 2006, Eikenberry and Neumann were ordered to draft plans for a US drawdown in Afghanistan and turnover of security responsibilities to the immature Afghan army, starting that very year. Events would soon overtake these plans.[16]

British advance elements arrived in Helmand in December 2005. They assessed prospects for success there, noting difficulties posed by Governor Sher Mohammed. The British government decided Sher Mohammed would have to go. London lobbied Karzai for his removal as a condition of the British deployment. Karzai begrudgingly complied and appointed Mohammed Daoud, an engineer respected by the West, in his place. The sacking is one of the deepest foreign intrusions into Afghan politics in the whole war. Rarely did the United States or an ally force Karzai to remove a governor. The cost was high. Karzai felt spurned. He later said, "I made the mistake of listening to [the British]. And when they came in, the Taliban came."[17] Sher Mohammed himself sought revenge.[18]

The British had chosen to go to Helmand because the Canadians wanted Kandahar and Britain was the lead country within the coalition for counternarcotics. In retrospect, Helmand was a poor choice. Even though Afghan resistance to British occupation in the 19th century was well known, the degree to which that hatred persisted escaped just about every US and British decision-maker. For Americans and British, those wars were generations in the past. For Pashtuns, the wars were timeless. A common rumor among Helmandis was that the British had come to avenge their defeat at Maiwand, 126 years earlier. Michael Martin, a Pashto-speaking British officer, describes how much his countrymen were disliked in his book, *An Intimate War*:

> A senior (well-educated) provincial official remembers sitting on his grandfather's knee as he was told stories about Maiwand where his grandfather had fought. "People rose up; some came with guns, some with knives, some with sticks; we went to defeat them." . . . He then recalled a meeting with British officers in early 2006. A young intelligence officer asked him what the Helmandis thought of the British

in light of their shared history. The provincial official replied that the Helmandis hated them.[19]

Resistance to the British would be a powerful rallying cry.

By the end of 2005, the offensive the Taliban had been preparing since 2003 on Mullah Omar's orders was nearly ready. In early 2006, Mullah Omar ordered his deputies, Mullah Baradar and Mullah Obaidullah, to kick off soon.[20] Mullah Dadullah Lang, Taliban commander for southern Afghanistan, went to northern Helmand. There, the Taliban influenced territory as big as many provinces, populated by at least 100,000 Afghans, divided into five districts—Baghran, Nowzad, Musa Qala, Kajaki, and Sangin. Dadullah stayed a few months in northern Helmand and organized the front. "His return was like the arrival of rain after five years of drought," said a local commander.[21] The main bazaars became Taliban supply points. Experienced commanders and their subordinates returned from Pakistan to their villages to rebuild their old cadres.[22] People in northern Helmand were willing to enlist. Dadullah mobilized hundreds.[23]

From Helmand, Dadullah returned to Pakistan for final preparations before going to his headquarters in Maiwand, where he would run the offensive, traveling to the various districts as necessary. The offensive would have three fronts. The first would be northern Helmand, specifically the districts of Musa Qala, Sangin, Nowzad, and Kajaki. The second would be southern Helmand—the districts of Garmser and Nawa. The third and most important would be western Kandahar—the districts of Maiwand, Zharey, and Panjwai. Dadullah would announce in a May 2006 Al Jazeera interview that his goal was to capture Kandahar City and Lashkar Gah. He considered the south an entry point to conquer the rest of Afghanistan.[24] Mullah Omar's goal is less clear. According to some research, he may have wanted to use the offensive to pressure the United States to question its role in Afghanistan and consider withdrawal.[25]

In early 2006, Dadullah could probably field around 4,000 fighters in Helmand and Kandahar out of a total of 7,000 to 10,000 across the country.[26] The Taliban rank and file were largely Afghans living in Pakistan, often attending a madrasa, whose families were originally from Helmand and Kandahar.[27] Local recruits filled out the cadres.[28] Of the fighters, only a small minority were Punjabis, Arabs, or other Muslims from the Middle East and Central Asia, usually with a tie to al-Qaʿeda or another terrorist group.

Taliban fighters were armed with Kalashnikovs, PK medium machine-guns, and rocket-propelled grenades (RPGs) to at least the same standard as the police. The Taliban later published poems by a few of these fighters and their biographies. These biographies and poems are part propaganda, part window into how the Taliban saw themselves. One of these "warrior-poets" was Abdur

Rahman Kamran. He had grown up in a refugee camp in Pakistan and had been schooled at various madrasas. At 16, he entered the Taliban and fought the Northern Alliance in Kabul and Kunduz. In 2006, he went to Kandahar. In the course of his campaigning, Kamran composed poems about his duty to defend Islam. "The Muslim's home with non-Muslims inside is shamed," he wrote. "Today, healing will come to all mad villages."[29] Another warrior poet was Maulawi Mohammed Rassoul Wotanmal. Like Kamran, he had been schooled in a madrasa in Pakistan. In 2004, at 25 years of age, he left the madrasa to campaign in the south. His poetry too shows a strong devotion to Islam:

> White Talib on white field has done what amazing deed
> In the place of this lawless world, he has rebelled
> His attack, in darkness, has gained strength
> This jihadi movement has how great an author
> Faithlessness has reason for contempt, contempt has a sore crown
> Then the Muslim community became determined in their intent.[30]

How much was propaganda and how much was real in these biographies and poems is hard to say. The theme of Islam and resistance to occupation runs strong. Captured Taliban often expressed similar feelings.[31]

Opposite the Taliban were the newly arrived Canadians, a few British (their main forces yet to arrive), a few Americans, and the Afghan army and police. The Canadian military contingent, Task Force Kandahar, arrived in February 2006. The US brigade of roughly 1,000 soldiers stationed at Kandahar airbase would depart in March before most of the upcoming battle.[32] A handful of US special forces teams and occasional raids by units from elsewhere in Afghanistan would be the major US contribution to the battle. The British would not be fully in place in Helmand until May, after the offensive was well underway.

The Afghan army was still too small to fight the Taliban on its own. Of the 70,000 planned, between 2002 and the beginning of 2006 only 26,000 soldiers had been recruited and retained. Upon returning to Afghanistan in 2005, Eikenberry found the army he had fathered two years earlier in a distressing state: "Their attrition rates were higher than reported, the number of losses exceeded the number of recruits, and the quality of leadership at the tactical level was very uneven."[33] The situation improved some by early 2006 as Eikenberry sent more recruits to training. The army would grow from 26,000 to 36,000 during the year. But fundamental issues remained.

One brigade of roughly 1,500 men was in the south. One battalion of at most 600 men was in Helmand (the authorized size of a battalion in 2006 was 613 men but they were usually understrength due to leave, desertion, and recruitment shortfalls). The other two battalions were in Kandahar, totaling about 200 soldiers on hand at any time.[34]

Lieutenant Colonel Mohammed Ishaq was a battalion commander, a Tajik who had joined with Massoud when he was 17. He "could barely walk from his injuries," said his advisor, a US marine. Ishaq owed his position to Fahim and Bismullah Khan and was angling with them for further promotion. His battalion was a combination of Pashtuns, Tajiks, and Hazaras, loosely disciplined former mujahideen and strictly disciplined former communists. "Some companies had a Hazara first sergeant or a Tajik first sergeant and the commanding officer was Pashtun, and those two guys hated each other." The Tajik soldiers, usually Panjshiris, were the fighters. In skirmishes in 2005, they would "stand and fight" while the Pashtun soldiers would "break and run." The entire battalion disliked being far from home and had little attachment to the south. Ishaq's advisor noted, "They don't do well being away from their families. If you're taking a battalion that's been mustered in Kabul from the outlying areas and you go down south . . . keeping in contact with their families is very difficult and very trying. . . . It's a very debilitating thing."[35]

The police were the front line. The thousands of militia that had enforced the will of the tribal power-brokers had been largely demobilized. Of 3,700 total, 1,900 police were in Helmand and 1,800 were in Kandahar.[36] Of these, at least 700 were tied down in the cities, unable to face the Taliban in the country-side.[37] The police were ill-trained, lightly armed, and poorly supplied. Less than a quarter had been through the eight-week training course, which left out weapons familiarization. Eikenberry's headquarters estimated that only 15 percent of police had a working Kalashnikov assault rifle.[38] For mobility, the police had blue Ford Ranger pickup trucks. Common tribal identity or any other source of esprit de corps was rare. Most patrolmen had enlisted for the salary rather than out of patriotism or tribal duty. That salary was $70 per month, when it came. It rarely covered a policeman's expenses. International trainers noted that morale was low.[39] Western journalists and soldiers often saw younger policemen in Helmand and Kandahar smoking hashish or opium. Lashkar Gah's police chief admitted that the police were not up to the high risk of their job.[40] A few police units that were tribal militia subsumed wholesale into the force, such as Abdul Razziq's border police in Spin Boldak and Mullah Naqib's Alikozai police in Arghandab, were tougher—exceptions to the rule.

At first glance, the Afghan government and the coalition outnumbered the Taliban. In all Helmand and Kandahar, roughly 5,700 soldiers, police, Canadians, and Americans confronted roughly 4,000 Taliban. The government's advantage, however, falls apart upon scrutiny. After subtracting forces committed to city policing and other security duties, the government and its allies could field something closer to 1,850 soldiers and police in the front-line districts, with

1,200 as reserves near Kandahar City and Lashkar Gah for reinforcements and counterattacks. The police in the countryside were in small posts of 15 to 50 at the district centers, spread out over dozens of kilometers apart. Provincial capitals were hours, if not days, away. Dadullah could concentrate his forces on a few districts and expect numerical superiority before reserves could arrive, which would rapidly exhaust themselves rushing about to parry the various Taliban thrusts.

Neither the allies nor the Afghan government had an equivalent of Dadullah—an aggressive commander with clear authority. There was not even someone in charge in each province. The British and Canadians technically fell under Major General Freakley but in reality answered directly to London and Ottawa. The Afghan government was equally divided. Leadership was a hodgepodge of governors, police chiefs, and tribal powerbrokers, each with constrained authority. Karzai appointed no single commander. Each province had its own police chief and its own governor, each independent. The Afghan army brigade commander in Kandahar had no official authority over the governors or police chiefs and too few troops to be a player anyway. When it came down to it, the only leader on the government or American side who could command authority throughout the south was Hamid Karzai himself.

The timing, scale, and length of the offensive would come as a tactical surprise to the US, Canadian, and British forces. By their own admission, Eikenberry and Neumann did not expect "the size of the forces employed."[41] Eikenberry and Freakley were receiving spotty and haphazard intelligence, partly because of an overreliance on signals intelligence and overhead surveillance. Afghans in Kandahar City and Lashkar Gah, on the other hand, knew from word of mouth and preaching at the mosques that something was coming. US special forces teams, operating closer to the people and the police, got word but their warnings went unheard at higher levels because other sources did not corroborate. An invidious assumption existed among American generals that signals intelligence and overhead surveillance would see Taliban massing in time for the allies to react.[42]

Dadullah's offensive kicked off on the night of February 3, a Friday, Islam's day of rest and prayer. The opening targets were three district centers in northern Helmand—Musa Qala, Sangin, and Nowzad.

A "district center" was the location of the government offices in a district, where the district governor and district police chief resided. Each had his own building. The district governor tended to work in a standard-model USAID-built one-story square building with a grass courtyard in the middle. The building was usually white, sometimes enclosed by a wall. The police chief tended to have his own less-appealing mud building, often within the same wall as the district governor's building. Later in the war a few hundred Afghan soldiers would also be headquartered within a kilometer of a district governor's building, but that was not the case in 2006. The district center was also usually the location of a bazaar—rows of stalls occupied by shopkeepers and business owners. Farmers brought their goods in for sale and purchased goods caravanned in from the provincial capital or over the border from Pakistan and Iran. Only a handful of people actually lived in the district center. The business owners and shopkeepers lived out in the villages. Control of the district center did not imply control of the people.

In Musa Qala, the district governor's building was on the eastern side of the main road, across from the bazaar. Fifty police defended the district, under hard-bitten Commander Abdul Wali Koka. They, Koka, and the district governor, Haji Abdul Quduz, were Sher Mohammed Akhundzada's men. On February 3, Taliban fighters overran the bazaar and fired RPGs into the police headquarters and the district governor's building. An RPG explosion killed Abdul Quduz, who was sitting in his office. Twenty-eight police were killed in the next two days of fighting. Koka and the remainder retreated to the Kajaki dam, which was Sher Mohammed's territory.[43] Reinforcements from Lashkar Gah under Sher Mohammed's brother, Deputy Governor Amir Mohammed, had to reoccupy the Musa Qala district center.

The Sangin attack was bigger. Dadullah massed 300 fighters around the district center. Sangin was the crossroads between the populous center of Helmand and the tribes in the five northern districts. The district center's large bazaar was a center for poppy trafficking. Taking Sangin would open a route for poppy from the north to go south to Maiwand and thence to Pakistan. It would also cut off the government garrisons at Nowzad, Musa Qala, and Kajaki Dam.

Sangin had its own little tribal drama. The district has two main tribes: the Alikozai and the Ishaqzai. The Sangin Alikozai were at odds with the local Ishaqzai, who like the rest of their tribe had aligned with the Taliban in the 1990s. Alikozai had enjoyed top jobs in the district since 2001, led by the warlord Dad Mohammed (known locally as "Amir Dado"). The Ishaqzai were mistreated by Dad Mohammed and his supporters. He had detained and whipped an Ishaqzai tribal leader and drug smuggler named Feda Mohammed.[44] The Ishaqzai naturally sided with the Taliban and formed Dadullah's attack force.

The Taliban had enough supporters to move freely through the bazaar. The district governor's office—a large mud compound—and the police headquarters, as well as a mosque, were located at the end of the bazaar, beside the Helmand River. The bazaar stood between them and the main road (and supply line) 500 meters away. It was easy to surround the district governor's office and police headquarters by moving through the bazaar's alleys and rows of stalls.

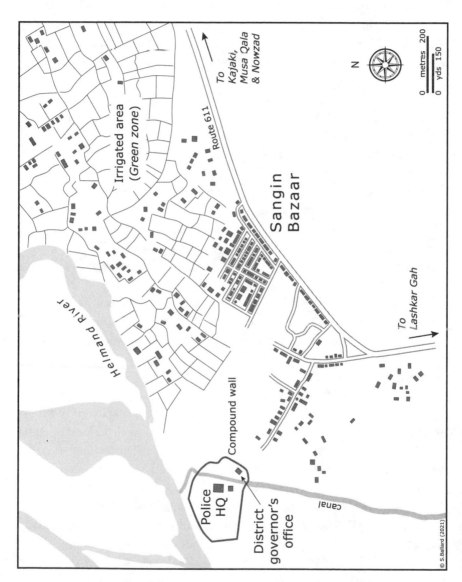

To Kajiaki,
Musa Qala
& Nowzad

Irrigated area
(Green zone)

Route 611

Sangin
Bazaar

Helmand River

Compound wall

Police
HQ

District
governor's
office

To
Lashkar Gah

canal

N

0   metres   200
0   yds   150

© S.Ballard (2021)

Map 8 Sangin Bazaar and district center

On February 3, Ishaqzai tribesmen with the Taliban ambushed a group of Alikozai police patrolling south of the district center. The patrol was cut off and called the district chief for assistance. Like Musa Qala, there were about 50 police in the whole district. Unaware he was severely outnumbered, the police chief dispatched reinforcements. The Taliban ambushed them too. Surprised, the police fell back to the bazaar and then to the government compound and police headquarters where Taliban fire pinned them down.[45] Mortar and RPG rounds splashed against the walls of the mud compound and police headquarters. Fighting lasted three days before a US special forces team arrived. That team engaged in a 12-hour firefight. Karzai got word of the battle and ordered the ministry of defense to send reinforcements. Air strikes drove back the attackers long enough for a green Afghan army battalion from Herat with US advisors to occupy the compound and police headquarters. Of the 50 or so defenders, five had been killed and 16 had been wounded.[46] The Americans judged the district center indefensible and repositioned to higher ground on the eastern side of the road, leaving the police on their own again.

On the higher ground, the Afghan army battalion and US advisors faced weeks of grueling firefights, mortars, and improvised explosive devices. Having received scant training, the Afghan soldiers were shocked by the combat and casualties. "We lost over forty Afghan Soldiers within a week," remembered the advisors' sergeant major, Wesley Schutt, "and many were selling their weapons or other equipment in order to get a taxi ride out of the Helmand Province."[47] The US special forces and advisors suffered casualties as well. To hold the base against continual attacks, fresh advisors and Afghan units had to be rotated through.

Nowzad, the northernmost of the three districts that Dadullah attacked, got off lucky with only one policeman killed. Taliban casualties for all the fighting are unknown. The government claimed 18 Taliban were killed, barely half of the 34 police and army deaths.

Over the next four months, Taliban attacks persisted in Helmand. Seven district police chiefs and three district governors were killed in the course of the fighting. Approximately 150 police were killed or wounded.[48] Morale plummeted. All but 75 of the governor's 500 auxiliary police deserted. Looking to the winner, more and more tribesmen joined the Taliban.[49] The police were trapped in their district centers, unable to influence their districts. The Taliban cut the road northward to Kajaki dam and its hydroelectric turbines.

During this opening round of Dadullah's offensive, the British were still flowing into Helmand. It was not until May that British forces—the 16th Air Assault Brigade, commanded by Brigadier Ed Butler—fully arrived, roughly 3,150 in all. Unfortunately, the "brigade" had only one battalion (3rd Battalion, the Parachute Regiment, known as "3 Para") and an assortment of other small combat detachments, for about 1,500 fighting men, instead of the three battalions standard for most brigades.[50] Third Brigade, 205th Afghan National Army Corps, reinforced Helmand along with the British. It had two battalions of roughly 250 to 350 soldiers each.[51]

Dadullah launched another wave of coordinated attacks on the northern district centers in mid-May.[52] Governor Mohammed Daoud insisted the district centers be secured. Butler went along. British soldiers flew into small fortified posts in the district centers of Nowzad, Musa Qala, and Kajaki (overlooking the strategic Kajaki Dam). All were on the verge of collapse.[53] Butler could only commit a platoon (30 men) to each. The platoons' fortified posts became known as "platoon houses." Alone and unafraid, the platoon houses were targets for the Taliban, who controlled everything around them.

Resupply and casualty evacuation had to be done by air. Unfortunately, the British had only seven CH-47 Chinook helicopters, which naturally limited the food and ammunition any unit could stock. They had to be careful not to lose any helicopters. Landing under fire risked damage or destruction, which in turn could mean too few helicopters to fulfill critical duties. Losing a single helicopter could imperil resupply and casualty evacuation for every platoon house. The British frequently delayed or canceled supply missions rather than risk one of their precious helicopters.

In mid-June, the Taliban captured Sangin, defeating the Alikozai of Dad Mohammed. They killed 33 members of his family, beginning with his brother, the former district governor.[54] Journalist Elizabeth Rubin, who spent time with the Taliban, recounted how one Taliban commander, Mullah Razayar Nurzai, described these attacks: "A few days earlier, Nurzai and his men had attacked Amir Dado's extended family. First, he told me, they shot dead his brother—a former district leader. Then the next day, as members of Dado's family were driving to the site of the first attack, Nurzai's men ambushed their convoy. Boys, cousins, uncles: all were killed."[55] The police chief survived the attacks. He frantically called Governor Daoud for help and then fled, leaving Dad Mohammed's family and a contingent of Alikozai police on their own.[56] One resident recounted, "The fight started after Amir Dad Mohammed Khan's brother was killed. The situation worsened with more than fifty supporters of Amir Dad Mohammed killed in one day. The district office was seized, ending government authority. Soon after there was general fighting and bombings."[57] Taliban in Quetta hosted celebrations for the victory. Fifty-two policemen perished in fighting around Sangin during the first six months of 2006.[58]

Distressed, Governor Daoud and Karzai pressured Butler, who had already been debating whether to commit forces, to retake Sangin. On June 21, Butler sent in 120 paratroopers in two Chinook helicopters. They landed in the early morning between the Helmand River and the governor's compound.

The Taliban at first put up no resistance. The paratroopers occupied the unde-fended compound with ease but then found themselves besieged as the Taliban reemerged. Butler left 90 paratroopers with 20 of the remaining police to de-fend the compound. A delegation of local elders, suspicious of the British, asked them to leave.[59] That night, Taliban hiding in the shops and alleys of the bazaar shot at the British in the compound with mortars, assault rifles, and RPGs. Skirmishing continued over the next week. On July 1, 30 or so fighters attempted a two-pronged assault supported by indirect rocket fire. The paratroopers' heavy machine guns mowed down the attackers and Apache gunships and A-10 at-tack aircraft shot them up as they fell back. The British suffered eight casualties, which could not be evacuated until nightfall because of the danger to helicopters from ground fire. Over the following week, an average of five attacks erupted per day. More air strikes and attack helicopters were required to beat them back.[60] The 20 police deserted.[61] The paratroopers were trapped in a never-ending battle to save the district governor's compound.

In June, Dadullah opened his second front, launching an offensive against the southern end of the province. Five hundred Taliban attacked the district of Garmser. The Taliban overran its district center and moved north. The gov-ernment and British eventually recaptured and outposted the Garmser district center, another unsupportable island in the sea of Taliban. The only part of Helmand that the government clearly controlled was the central core of Marjah, Nad Ali, and the two towns of Gereshk and Lashkar Gah.

Northern and southern Helmand were two of Dadullah's fronts for the offensive. The third was western Kandahar. From his headquarters in Maiwand, he often visited the front line villages in Kandahar to observe operations, issue directions, and confer with field commanders.[62]

Unlike the British, who had not arrived in force by the outbreak of the Helmand attacks, Canadian forces were largely in place when Dadullah struck Kandahar. The first Canadian element to arrive was their provincial recon-struction team (PRT) in August 2005. It got off to a rocky start. A suicide car bomb killed its director, Ambassador Glyn Berry, on January 15.[63] Task Force Kandahar, commanded by Brigadier-General David Fraser, arrived a few weeks later with 2,200 soldiers. Of these, only the 850 of 1st Battalion, Princess Patricia's Canadian Light Infantry plus their attachments, were meant for combat opera-tions. Permanent garrisons were set up in Kandahar City and at Spin Boldak on the border. Brigadier-General Fraser planned to conduct a "maneuverist ap-proach." With few soldiers and a large area to cover, he wanted to move around and disrupt the enemy, giving the government a chance to get the upper hand. Like Eikenberry and Freakley, Fraser and his battalion commander, Lieutenant-Colonel Ian Hope, had poor warning of the scale and intensity of Taliban attacks.

Dadullah hit Kandahar in mid-April. In the countryside, Taliban cadres attacked police posts, ambushed Canadian patrols, and laid improvised explosive devices on the major roads. In the city, where he was unable to mass, Dadullah sent in suicide bombers that terrorized police and civilians alike. The populous and fertile districts of Zharey and Panjwai, adjacent to Kandahar City, were Dadullah's main effort. Over the course of April and May, 500 to 1,000 Taliban moved into Zharey and Panjwai from Maiwand, filling in around the small cadres already in place.[64] Dadullah's front line commander was Mullah Abdul Manan, a 35-year-old Hotak (Mullah Omar's tribe) from Sangesar, the location of Mullah Omar's mosque. A tall, hefty man, he had joined the Taliban in 1994 as a fighter and had been captured during 2001 fighting for Kandahar and then released.[65]

The roughly 100 police in western Kandahar were severely outnumbered. For many villages, the government was simply absent.[66] The undermanned police confined themselves in the district centers and their handful of posts, rarely patrolling the surrounding countryside. Massoum Khan, an Alizai, was one of the police officers in Zharey. He had fought alongside Mullah Naqib against the Soviets and would later become the district police chief. He remembered, "I was here with ten men when the Taliban attacked. The people had no weapons to defend themselves. There were only 45 police in the district. No militia. No Afghan national army."[67]

In the villages and countryside, Canadian and American surveillance observed multiple Taliban cadres, 20 to 100 men in each.[68] They first ambushed police and Canadian patrols. Next, they overran villages such as Zangabad, Taloqan, and Sangesar. Then, they assaulted the district centers and police headquarters. Dadullah positioned himself in Zharey and moved around western Kandahar, organizing attacks. He and his security detachment sometimes got into firefights with police or Canadians. To keep the Taliban off balance, the Canadians sallied forth for missions into western Kandahar, and occasionally northern Kandahar and Helmand. They encountered heavy resistance, often facing more than 100 insurgents and suicide car bombs.[69] Canadian troops were in contact every day. A Canadian company commander, Major Nick Grimshaw, noted, "It was like somebody flicked a switch, and the insurgency was on. . . . It was off the scales for this area."[70]

Taliban determination impressed the Canadians. On May 17, in one of its first battles, half the Princess Patricia's Canadian Light Infantry battalion probed into Zharey and ran into around 50 Taliban. The Canadians used AH-64 attack helicopters to drive them back. When the Canadians pursued through the villages and narrow farm paths, the Taliban ambushed the lead elements with RPGs from two sides. Four RPGs destroyed one Canadian light armored vehicle. The battle ended only when a B-1 bomber flattened the Taliban firing positions. Ian Hope, commander of the Princess Patricia's battalion, concluded, "It is my assessment that there is . . . considerable enemy in the Zharey-Panjwayi area; they are confident in their ability to fight, and they do not want to give up this ground."[71]

Fraser, Hope, and US special forces teams in Kandahar realized that the Taliban could soon threaten Kandahar City itself. Major General Freakley disagreed. To his credit, Freakley had recognized the rising violence in Afghanistan before his deployment but was intent on executing a set of search and destroy missions in the mountains of Kandahar, Zabul, Uruzgan, and Helmand, crowned "Operation Mountain Thrust." He instructed, "By disrupting the Taliban's command chain and killing and capturing the core leaders and fighters we will [persuade] the less committed that there are better alternatives than supporting the insurgents."[72] Freakley had planned the operation before arriving in Afghanistan as a way creating "space" for the NATO allies to get set up.

The Canadians and US special forces wanted to focus on defending Kandahar City and not be diverted elsewhere. Hope, who spent his days in the field with his battalion, warned his boss, Fraser, and an incredulous Freakley that he was barely holding hundreds of fighters back. Eikenberry cautioned Freakley against chasing about the mountains but did not disapprove the operation.[73] Eikenberry's leadership style was to leave subordinates a wide berth to plan, not to force his wisdom upon them.

Mountain Thrust went on for six weeks in June and July. Canadians, British, and Americans participated.[74] Companies and battalions cleared remote districts and valleys and then pulled back, rarely getting into combat. Nowhere did forces stay. Freakley assessed that Mountain Thrust had no lasting effect.

As the Taliban offensive progressed, locals in western Kandahar, various Ishaqzai and Noorzai tribesmen, at least 800, rallied to the Taliban colors.[75] Hamidullah, a Popalzai leader from Zharey, remembered, "When the Taliban came in 2006 . . . the poor people rose up. They were not getting much help from the government."[76] Elizabeth Rubin learned from one of the Taliban propagandists that "the Taliban were exploiting the grievances of the Noorzai, a tribe that has felt persecuted and unfairly targeted for poppy eradication . . . The Taliban were paying poor, unemployed men to fight."[77]

The Taliban's call for jihad against infidel occupation was changing the entire atmosphere. Their offensive created a spirit absent before. The propagandist relayed, "Religious scholars were delivering the message that it was time for jihad because the Americans were no different from the Russians."[78] An Afghan engineer told Rubin, "Just like in Russian times they come and say, 'We are defending the country from the infidels.' They start asking for food. They ask the people for soldiers and say, 'We will give you weapons.' And that's how it starts. And the emotions are rising in the people now. They are saying, 'Kaffers [infidels] have invaded our land.' "[79] Abdul Wadood, an Achekzai tribal leader in Panjwai, recalled the same thing: "People helped the Taliban because they believed they were taking part in a jihad against infidels. They were fighting for the Koran."[80]

Suicide attacks, the weapon Dadullah was pioneering, became common. Throughout Afghanistan, 119 occurred in 2006, greater than half in Kandahar. Though the targets were usually police, Canadians, or Americans, their explosions killed large numbers of civilian bystanders. Approximately 420 civilians were killed or wounded over the year, often in shocking mass casualty events. One suicide car bomb in Spin Boldak in May killed and wounded 49 Afghans, most of whom were civilians. Another in July against a police post in Kandahar City killed or wounded 55. On August 3, a suicide bomber drove into the middle of Panjwai district center bazaar, filled with shoppers, and blew up his car and himself. The blast lit stalls afire. Twenty civilians died and fourteen were wounded, including children.[81] In the words of one Taliban fighter, "Against non-Muslims it [suicide bombing] is very good because they can stop any kind of attack but not these kinds of attacks."[82] Dadullah proved he could strike anywhere, at any time. The Americans, Canadians, and British had air strikes. He had suicide bombers.

By August, Dadullah had all but seized the western half of Kandahar province. Large numbers of Zharey and Panjwai police deserted under the strain. The district centers were teetering. On August 19, a Canadian platoon barely prevented 400 Taliban from overrunning 200 police and soldiers and the Panjwai district center—12 kilometers from Kandahar City. Brigadier-General Fraser outposted the Zharey and Panjwai district centers and contested Taliban activity on Highway One, the main thoroughfare of all Afghanistan.[83] Equally important, Mullah Naqib, the powerful Alikozai tribal leader, ensured his tribesmen and police kept the Taliban out of the strategic Arghandab Valley that guarded the northern entry into Kandahar City.

8/06

In August, Ambassador Neumann reported to Washington, "We are not winning in Afghanistan; although we are far from losing. We still can win."[84] He asked Washington to send more equipment for the Afghan army and police and to push Pakistan to restrict Taliban infiltration across the border. Over the next three months, he and Eikenberry convinced Washington to expand the police from 62,000 to 82,000 and Karzai to permit the recruitment of a few thousand "auxiliary police" on top of that.[85] With reports in the press and from the field of a Taliban "resurgence," Rumsfeld backed off his demand to draw down US forces. That did not mean reinforcements were coming. In the early autumn, Eikenberry submitted an official "request for forces" of 3,500 army and police trainers. It sat at Central Command for months, unapproved. The White House and the Pentagon agreed that the priority had to be Iraq, where violence and instability outstripped what was happening in Afghanistan.

Theoretically, with Karzai at their head, pro-government tribes—Alikozai, Popalzai, Barakzai, Achekzai, and Sher Mohammed's half of the Alizai—should have united and driven out the Taliban. Although the large militias had been demobilized, these tribes still had young men, weapons caches, and money. Out of self-interest, their leaders did little to bring them together. Most stayed in Kandahar City or Lashkar Gah.[86] Mullah Naqib was an exception. Agha Lalay Distegeeri, the distinguished Alikozai tribal leader of Panjwai and a rival of Naqib, exemplified the thinking of the majority: "The government was doing nothing to help. We had no weapons, no money, and no police. What was I to do? If I had fought, I would have sacrificed my villagers to the Taliban for nothing. If the government does not back a tribe, it is senseless for a tribe to fight on its behalf."[87] Most tribal leaders followed this model, absent an outside push, intent on saving their individual tribes or families rather than uniting for the greater good—Pashtun realpolitik at its worst.

President Karzai could have issued a call to arms but sat silent. He had a better sense of what was happening on the ground than anyone else in Kabul or Washington. Provincial governors and tribal delegations regularly visited him at the palace and described in detail the attacks in the districts and their conversations with the Taliban.[88] The violence worried Karzai. Yet he chose to lobby the Americans and the allies for help rather than to go down to Kandahar and rally the tribes to stand up and fight as he had in 2001. America and its allies' disregard for his wishes was coming home to roost. He was annoyed at the British for forcing out Sher Mohammed as governor of Helmand.[89] He was annoyed at the Americans for accidentally killing civilians. The deaths of children especially troubled him. He saw them as victims of Pakistani warmongering and American heavy-handedness.

Karzai spared time in May for a brief visit to Kandahar to see civilian casualties. He did not return until December, long after defeat was in doubt. According to an Afghan provincial advisor who served at the time, "Karzai told many Afghan leaders from the provinces between 2005 and 2009 . . . that he was not concerned with the war. He said it was America's war, not his war. He did not encourage or press mujahedin commanders to fight."[90] Eikenberry inferred the same, noting that "the Karzai Administration . . . did not seem deeply interested in the development of the ANSF (Afghan National Security Forces)."[91] Christina Lamb, a British journalist, spent a week with Karzai that autumn. He was unplugged: "Though I spent a lot of time with Karzai . . . I found it hard to pin him down on anything serious. All he wanted to do was reminisce about the past."[92]

Shukria Barakzai, the recently elected parliamentarian and Karzai friend, was learning of the battles in Helmand and Kandahar from refugees fleeing to Kabul. She worked to establish schools in Kabul for children from the war-ravaged south, an alternative to Pakistani madrasas. When she spoke with Karzai, she came away thinking, "The palace is like a jail. The walls are so high that he has become distant from his own nation."[93]

The military heavyweights of Kabul—the old Northern Alliance and the Panjshiris in particular—were similarly disinterested. In contrast to Karzai, Bismullah Khan, Yunis Qanooni, and other leaders had a harsh view of the Taliban, bred from years of ethnic war. "The Afghan security forces must know their opponents are terrorists," Qanooni, minister of interior and then education, would say.[94] The Pashtun provinces that had created the Taliban were not high on their list of priorities. Tajik leaders had never liked the idea of venturing into them. Although Rahim Wardak had replaced Mohammed Fahim as minister of defense in 2004, Bismullah Khan remained chief of the general staff, ensuring a Panjshiri grip over the army. His political concerns were around Kabul and in the north, the power base of the Northern Alliance. In a sign of how little Kandahar mattered to him, Bismullah allowed the Kandahar corps to be commanded by an old Pashtun communist, Major General Rahmatullah Raoufi.[95]

Frustrated with Canadian and American setbacks, Ahmed Wali Karzai and Governor Asadullah Khalid tried to defeat the Taliban cadres their own way. Khalid was frequently out on operations with his Afghan special police unit. In his opinion, there were enough troops to defeat the Taliban but the Canadians were being too cautious; they should have been doing more operations.[96] For his part, Brigadier-General Fraser rated Khalid as "a rebel and difficult to work with. . . . He had numerous cell phones that he would answer any time they rang (even in meetings), and he would often run off because of what he'd been told in the call. When I first met him, it was not uncommon for him to charge out of the office, jump into his SUV and head straight into some firefight with his AK-47. That was simply how he did business."[97]

In August, Ahmed Wali and Khalid turned to one of the most controversial figures of the Afghan War—Abdul Razziq, the Achekzai border police commander in Spin Boldak. His father and uncle had been famous mujahideen from Spin Boldak and leaders of the Achekzai tribe. Rival Noorzai, who were Taliban, killed them both shortly after the movement captured Spin Boldak in 1994, hanging Razziq's uncle from a tank barrel.[98] Thenceforth Razziq sought vengeance upon the Taliban and the Noorzai.[99]

Raised amid war and bereft of much schooling, Razziq knew the long border's desert tracks like the back of his hand. With the barest beard, boyish looks, and thin frame, Razziq was 22 in 2001 when he jumped in with the Achekzai militia for Gul Agha Sherzai's attack on Kandahar. Shortly thereafter, he took charge of the Spin Boldak border police and the Achekzai militia. For the next eight years he gripped Spin Boldak, eventually as the border police commander for Kandahar, making money from the customs post at the crossing point into

Pakistan. US special forces worked with him side by side. He was a legend on the border, raiding in Land Rovers from the high desert mountains of Maruf to the red dunes of Registan, 200 miles to the south. US special forces marveled at how he would fearlessly plunge his truck into the middle of a firefight. His Achekzai adored him.

Razziq and the Noorzai fought out a bloody tribal vendetta around Spin Boldak. In 2004, the Noorzai killed Razziq's brother. In March 2006, Razziq allegedly caught the Noorzai assassin and summarily executed him and 15 fellow Noorzai tribesmen.[100] Once Dadullah's offensive was underway, large numbers of Spin Boldak Noorzai aligned with the Taliban.[101]

Because of Razziq's loyalty and military skill, Khalid and Ahmed Wali decided to send him into western Kandahar. In August, at the height of the blazing summer, he drove into Panjwai—Noorzai territory. The foray went poorly. A local Noorzai eyewitness told journalist Anand Gopal, "People began to say he was here to kill every Noorzai he could find."[102] A rumor spread that Razziq's men were abducting Noorzai women. Noorzai young men came in droves, from all over the province, to fight.[103] Another Noorzai elder exclaimed, "In our area, the Taliban went from 40 people to 400 in just days."[104]

Concerned, General Mir Wais, brother of the great Noorzai tribal leader and Karzai ally Arif Khan, sped into Panjwai ahead of Razziq. He went to the Noorzai region of Sperwan, midway through the district. When Razziq arrived at Sperwan, Mir Wais was waiting on the road. He ordered, "Stop. Do not enter Sperwan. Go on." While they talked, a mob of armed Noorzai tribesmen approached, armed and ready to fight. Mir Wais turned to them and ordered, "Stand down. Razziq is not entering Sperwan. He is passing through to Taloqan and Zangabad." They replied, "Razziq is coming to oppress us." Mir Wais reassured, "That is all propaganda. Go home. I guarantee Razziq will not come." To Razziq, he claimed that there were no Taliban in Sperwan.[105] Razziq drove on to the western end of the district, got into a few firefights, suffered a few casualties, and then withdrew back to Spin Boldak. The expedition was a defeat for the government. Mir Wais had averted a Noorzai uprising but a story gained credence that the entire tribe had united with the Taliban against the heartless oppression of Razziq.[106]

West of Kandahar City, craggy ridges, like backs of giant whales, breach every few miles along the length of Zharey and Panjwai, plunging into the desert sands. One, near the center of both districts, stands perhaps 1,000 feet above ground, overlooking the village of Pashmul below. The village and its surroundings would be the center of the biggest battle of 2006. After Razziq's defeat, Dadullah staged his forces in Pashmul and surrounding villages, possibly in preparation for an assault on Kandahar City. He visited Pashmul in person and brought in as many as 1,500 well-armed men. They walked openly in the

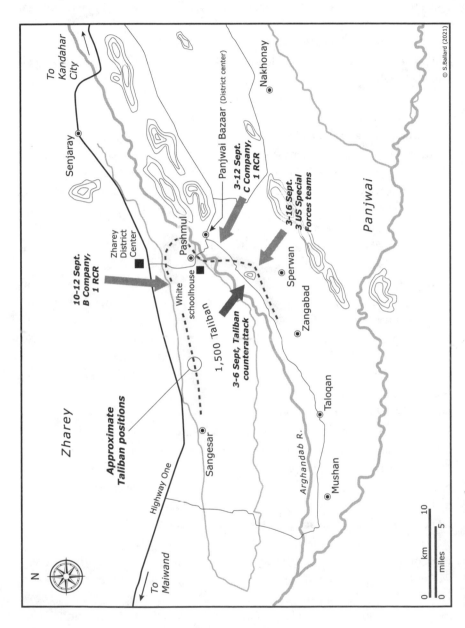

Map 9 Operation Medusa

villages with their Kalashnikovs and RPGs, waiting to attack.[107] Mullah Manan would run the battle. He rotated men in from Zangabad and Taloqan, which he frequented, farther west.[108]

Locals got wind that an assault on the city could be pending. Fear spread. The United Nations prepared to close its office. Frightened city dwellers braced themselves for a Taliban return. Many packed their belongings and left in anticipation of an urban battle.[109] Some reached out to the Taliban for guarantee of safe treatment.[110]

Eikenberry and Brigadier-General Fraser learned in August that Taliban were massing. Fraser planned a robust operation with heavy preliminary artillery and air strikes for mid-September, named Operation Medusa.[111] Then in mid-August, Governor Khalid and Ahmed Wali Karzai summoned Ian Hope and Fraser's other subordinates to the governor's office for a meeting with Panjwai and Zharey tribal leaders. The Canadians were informed that tribal leaders were facing no choice but to make deals with the Taliban for their own security. Khalid, Ahmed Wali, and the tribal leaders demanded Operation Medusa start as soon as possible.[112]

General David Richards was now commander of ISAF. Freakley had relinquished command of the south on July 31. Informed of the situation by Fraser, Richards ordered an attack. Operation Medusa was put into action. Eikenberry, as commander of US forces, concurred and lent US forces to assist. Freakley reassigned strike aircraft and his Predator unmanned surveillance assets to Fraser. First Battalion, the Royal Canadian Regiment (which had replaced the Princess Patricia's days earlier), a US infantry company, three US special forces teams, and five Afghan National Army companies (roughly 30 men each) took part—2,200 personnel in all. Medusa would be Canada's largest combat operation since the Korean War.[113]

The plan was to surround Pashmul and the villages in central Zharey and Panjwai and move in. Afghan army soldiers and their US trainers would close in from the north, while US special forces, their Afghan commandos, and the Canadian battle group would close in from the south and then clear out the villages.

Governor Khalid announced the operation over the radio on August 30 and leaflets were air-dropped on the villages. The Taliban too told the locals that there would be fighting. Thousands of civilians—mostly old men, women, and children—fled. Thousands of others hid in their homes.

Manan and Dadullah's men prepared to defend Zharey and Panjwai. They stockpiled weapons, mined roads and footpaths, and concealed themselves among marijuana stalks, grape vineyards, and trees lining the fields. Mud compounds and grape storehouses were natural bunkers. Americans and Canadians would mistake their two- to three-feet-thick sundried mud walls, with slits for ventilation, for purpose-built fortifications. Manan planned to use improvised explosive devices, mortars, and ambushes to slow up the Americans and Canadians and then hit them with direct assaults.[114]

Operation Medusa began on September 2. Artillery and air strikes crashed onto the villages, ahead of the Canadians, Americans, and Afghans. Charles Company, 1st Battalion, the Royal Canadian Regiment, spearheaded the assault in eight-wheeled light armored vehicles, known as LAVs. These freshly arrived Canadian soldiers were professionals but green to combat and unaccustomed to the summer heat that cooks well into October and turned their armored vehicles into ovens. The first day, they seized two high points overlooking Panjwai. The next morning, they rolled through the Panjwai bazaar and over the Arghandab River—at that time of year a shallow stony wash—on their way into the Taliban stronghold. They bumped across the fields and irrigation ditches. Air strikes had been arranged to soften up the Taliban on the north side of the river but Fraser called them off because civilians might be present.[115]

A few hundred meters away at a standard USAID-built white schoolhouse, 100 Taliban lay in wait. The Taliban had predicted that the Canadians would pass the schoolhouse on their way to the villages. They had killed four Canadian soldiers a month earlier at the same spot. The fighters had large stocks of ammunition and were well-concealed, some in mud compounds and the school, others behind trees. They watched as the convoy splashed through the shallow Arghandab.

When the convoy halted about 30 meters from the schoolhouse, the Taliban unleashed a barrage of RPGs from three different directions, followed by a hail of small arms fire. Though inaccurate, the sheer magnitude of the fire, coming from multiple different angles, suppressed the Canadians. The initial volley disabled three of the convoy's six vehicles, killed one soldier, and wounded two. The Canadians were too confined within their armored vehicles to easily identify the Taliban firing points. They fell back a hundred meters or so to treat the wounded. Taliban fighters crept forward, firing more RPGs, killing another soldier and wounding several more. In more than seven hours of heavy fighting, the Canadians were forced to withdraw across the Arghandab River.[116] A second attempt the next day was aborted when a US A-10 attack aircraft strafed the Canadians forming up on the south bank of the river, inflicting 34 casualties. Fraser paused the Canadian advance until his countrymen could reorganize.[117]

Meanwhile, three US special forces teams (30 men in all) together with 60 new Afghan army commandos moved up from the south. They encountered heavy resistance around a ridge overlooking villages southwest of Pashmul. A group of Taliban on top watched the special forces and commandos approach. When they got within a few hundred meters, the Taliban opened fire from three sides with RPGs and small arms. The special forces teams and commandos fought for 20 minutes until they nearly ran out of ammunition. They then broke contact and moved back to the south to await resupply by helicopter.

Two days later, on September 5, the special forces teams and Afghan commandos assaulted the ridge a second time, having since organized close air support. This time as they neared the summit the Taliban retreated and the position was secured during the late afternoon. That night, the Taliban counterattacked. Four of their number were killed and they retreated. The next day they tried again. US firepower was too much. From their vantage point, the special forces teams, covered in sweat and dust, called down artillery and air strikes on homes and compounds below, where the Taliban were moving to and fro, firing from windows and over walls. At one point, 20 aircraft were on station within two and a half hours. After four or five hours the Taliban disengaged. For the next ten days, air and artillery blasted suspected Taliban positions in the villages.[118]

Fraser, Richards, and Afghan army chief of staff Bismullah Khan worked out how to fulfill the push through Pashmul. After inspecting the battlefield from a Blackhawk helicopter, Freakley contributed a US infantry company from Zabul. Fraser arranged for Charles Company to resume their attack on the schoolhouse while Bravo Company of Royal Canadian Regiment company and the new US infantry company would sweep in from the north. Bismullah Khan arrived from Kabul to direct the Afghan soldiers in the field. Fraser requested Leopard main battle tanks from Ottawa for the armor and direct firepower to punch through mud compounds. A squadron of ten was sent that arrived too late for the battle.

From September 7 to 10, Canadian, US, and Afghan soldiers resumed their advance, moving in slowly from three sides. The Taliban fought back from mud compounds and irrigation ditches.[119] In the words of one Taliban fighter, "It was very strong fighting for seventeen days. It shook the whole world. This shows that the Canadians are strong fighters and that we fought strongly against them."[120] By September 17 the battle was over. Surviving Taliban fighters retreated or went to ground. Some fled to Pakistan, others to nearby districts of Kandahar and Helmand. Many hid in Zharey and Panjwai. Mullah Manan and Dadullah survived the battle. The former would die fighting Americans in Sangesar in 2007.[121]

Six Canadians were killed during Operation Medusa. Over 50 Canadians, Americans, and Afghans were injured. Estimates of Taliban casualties vary. A reasonable one is probably 300 killed, 80 captured, and an unknown number of wounded that probably ranges into the hundreds.[122] Regarding civilian casualties, media reported at least 40 civilians killed and 24 wounded— likely an underestimate..[123] Men, women, and children hiding in compounds had been blown up during the bombing rampage. The rules for the use of close air support had been fast and loose. Once the Taliban engaged, a US or Canadian unit could carry out air strikes against their attackers and other possible enemy locations as they deemed fit. In the palace in Kabul, Karzai received Panjwai and Zharey villagers who spoke of lost brothers, wives, and infants. One lamented to the president, "I came out [of the mosque] and saw my home destroyed and all the bodies. There were no Taliban in our area, the place where Taliban were was . . . kilometers away. A lot of civilians were killed and I don't think the bombs killed a single Taliban. I will never . . . forgive the foreign troops."[124]

Success proved short-lived. The Canadians left a patrol base to hold what had been cleared. The Canadians and Americans lacked the forces for anything more. In October, 800 Taliban returned and attacks resumed.[125] Ismatullah, an Alizai tribesmen, recalled that at the beginning of 2007, "There were many Taliban. IEDs were everywhere. All of Zharey was under the Taliban. Only the district center was in government hands. IEDs were on Highway One. There were posts on the highway but still IEDs. At that time all the people supported the Taliban."[126]

As Operation Medusa played out in Kandahar, fighting waxed in Helmand. Beleaguered platoon houses fought hard for three months. In Sangin, 100 paratroopers fought off 44 attacks in 25 days; in Kajaki, eight advisors and 24 Afghan soldiers fought off 30 attacks in 10 days; in Nowzad, 40 Gurkhas fought off 28 attacks in 14 days—pithy yet telling statistics.[127]

The worst was Musa Qala. Brigadier Butler, the British commander in Helmand, could only commit 60 men (two platoons) to secure the district center and its bazaar. In one attack, 150 Taliban fell upon the district governor's compound. In another, they knocked out one of the compound's two .50 caliber machine guns. To beat back attackers, the British called in air strikes within 30 meters of their own position.[128] Ammunition and rations often ran short. Helicopters could not land without serious risk of being shot down. Relief columns twice had to fight their way in. In late August, a full-scale battalion-level operation—replete with a Canadian light armored vehicle detachment—was required just to rotate the garrison.

The turning point was September 6. Three casualty incidents occurred simultaneously. Two soldiers died and two more were injured while waiting for evacuation. In the process, two helicopters came very close to being destroyed by mines and RPGs.[129] Theo Farrell writes in his history of the British war in Afghanistan, "Butler had been told in no uncertain terms by the new Chief of the Defense Staff . . . not to lose a Chinook . . . For Butler it was a matter of when and not if a Chinook would be lost in Musa Qala. He saw no choice: the British had to pull out."[130] British senior generals in London agreed; staying on was prohibitively costly in men and materiel. In Kabul, Richards was reluctant. He thought that withdrawal would be a public relations disaster. London ordered him to move forward.[131]

Before a decision was taken, local Alizai tribal elders stepped forward. If the British withdrew, the elders promised to keep out the Taliban. Governor Daoud conveyed the proposal to the British on September 12. Butler agreed to a tentative cease-fire and negotiations ensued the next day. US military officers and Ambassador Neumann opposed the cease-fire. Butler saw it as a means of empowering the tribal elders against the Taliban. Backed by Richards, he demanded 30 days of peace before his forces would withdraw. Governor Daoud spoke to the elders and they agreed. They were as good as their word. For 30 days, no attacks occurred.[132]

Because British military vehicles could not reach Musa Qala, local "jingle" trucks ferried out the British garrison on October 17. The cease-fire survived until February 2007 when Taliban fighters marched into Musa Qala and drove out the elders. The town became a Taliban sanctuary with armed fighters walking the streets. The Musa Qala deal would live in infamy as a symbol of defeat.[133]

The Musa Qala withdrawal was an ominous end to a grueling year. British Minister of Defense Des Browne called Musa Qala "iconic."[134] All the fighting of 2006 could be described in those terms, dwarfing in scale anything seen in Afghanistan since 2001. Kandahar and Helmand's 3,700 police suffered 27 percent losses—nearly 500 casualties and at least another 500 desertions.[135] Taliban successes extended beyond Helmand and Kandahar. By the end of the year, Taliban had also taken most of Zabul, Farah, Uruzgan, and Ghazni. They controlled so much territory that, with Kandahar City almost surrounded, they could foreseeably threaten the survival of the Afghan government. The offensive was one of the most decisive events in America's war in Afghanistan. The era of hope and opportunity relapsed into civil war, the new definition of Afghanistan. In spite of America's best efforts, the verdict of 2006 would not be repealed.

How the Taliban returned and the government was defeated in 2006 is a central question of the whole Afghan War. The traditional answers have been that the government and the United States aggrieved the people and Pakistan gave the Taliban safe haven. Available evidence supports these explanations. Tribal and government leaders anxious to reestablish their power and honor-bound to avenge past defeats marginalized, hurt, and killed former Taliban, religious leaders, and their tribal allies, pushing them toward violence. Pakistan provided Taliban leaders and fighters a refuge to recuperate after 2001 and then plan and organize.

Something else may have been happening too. What I have tried to expose is a separate way of thinking about the return of war to Afghanistan, focused on the military failings of the government and the tie to tribalism. Pakistan and grievances definitely bolstered the Taliban but they do not explain why the government and its local allies were so ineffective at military operations—it was on the battlefield that they lost, after all. War is a competition between two sides that plays out in the execution of violence. The government was poor at executing violence. It had not ordered itself for war. When the Taliban attacked, the problem was not that the government was defeated after a hard fight; the problem was that barely any defenses existed in the first place. This was a major failing in and of itself rather than something incidental to the other explanations. On every occasion, a few hundred Taliban trapped a few dozen police in a district center. Musa Qala, Nowzad, Sangin, Kajaki, Garmser, Maiwand, Zharey, Panjwai: the story is the same. On their own, other explanations—Pakistani safe havens and grievances—lose sight of the fact that few armed men were actually fighting for the Karzai regime in 2006. Addressing Pakistani safe havens and grievances would have been fruitless as long as the government could field little—whether in the form of tribal militias, police, or soldiers—to defend itself. A simple and cruel way to put it is: if a state faces a hostile safe haven on its border and mistreats various segments of its population, it had best have capable military forces of one form or another.

The absence of order—order necessary for military effectiveness—within the government and its allies was the fundamental problem. The past few chapters have described how the government and the tribal leaders did not unite against the common threat. Together, they should have been strong enough to defeat the Taliban. Each had bodies of armed men, which together outnumbered the Taliban. Yet the government and their tribal allies were divided, riven by feuds and competition. Staunch opponents of the Taliban had their armed men stripped away by other opponents of the Taliban. So when the Taliban attacked, a few tribes fought, but others either switched sides or sat things out. Thus the Taliban overwhelmed them. These divisions derived from the nature of the tribal system. It had no single authority and was based on what was essentially an anarchic competition for power. It tended toward fragmentation. That situation was fine—indeed it could have a natural balance—when the state only had to deal with isolated rebellious tribes. It was deadly when facing a widespread movement such as the Taliban.

Ideally, Karzai would have held these disparate factions together. The Karzai of 2001 would have hastened south, united the great Pashtun lords, reconciled with the Taliban, and reached out to the oppressed. The Karzai of 2006 fretted in Kabul, annoyed at British meddling in Helmand and preoccupied with his personal power base in Kandahar. Indeed, rather than unite he tried to divide up tribes lest they become a political threat. Karzai was diverging from America. In the course of five years, Karzai had soured to Western advice. He would continue to sour on it.

The tragedy is that the 2006 defeat was probably avoidable. The United States could have stemmed the tide. The drift back to war might have been overcome if not for a series of regrettable mistakes.

Most obvious among them is that the United States invaded Iraq, redirecting scarce resources and limiting its own options to help Afghanistan. At the very time the Taliban were attacking, the United States was facing its direst moment in Iraq as that civil war was spinning out of control. Bush and his team had to devote most of their time to the unfolding disaster. Reinforcements sorely needed for Afghanistan in 2006 were unavailable as the US military surged into Iraq.

Before this crisis and of greater importance, from December 2001 onward, the United States rejected out of hand the idea of talking to the Taliban or allowing them into the political process. Had Bush and Rumsfeld been open to compromise, a large number of key leaders and their supporters may have never returned to the movement. Dadullah himself would still have been bent on war but could have been denied the manpower necessary to attain the sweeping success of 2006.

Having given its adversary cause to fight, the United States then decided to build a small army slowly. Not only did the United States fail to build a large army, it failed to build a small capable one. Had the Afghan government possessed an army in 2006, it would have been less dependent on the tribes and able to confront the Taliban. We cannot say for certain that the army and police would have defeated the Taliban but they surely would have put up a better fight. Instead, before the offensive even began the stage had been set for defeat.

These mistakes bore fruit in 2006. Avoiding any one of them may have set history on a different course. No correction is likely to have averted war altogether—Dadullah and others were too determined and the tribal system too anarchic. But the war may have been far different. The Taliban offensive would have encountered widespread setbacks. The Taliban movement may have regressed into a marginal insurgency against an up-and-coming government. A war would have occurred, but without the peril to the government and its cities.

The one thing I have not named as a causal factor is an Islamic or national reaction to foreign occupation. Existing evidence is weighted toward explanations based on Pakistani safe havens, grievances, and tribal anarchy, coupled with US mistakes. There is just not the same weight of evidence that people were choosing to support the Taliban out of hatred of the foreigner—the United States and its coalition partners. It does not appear to explain the mass and scale of the Taliban resurgence. Still, I wonder if our data collection has been biased to date, if those of us who study and love Afghanistan have inadvertently neglected questions that might lead to an unwanted discovery. Rejection of foreign occupation runs deep in Afghan history.

What I can say is that the 2006 offensive catalyzed resistance to foreign occupation and in so doing revolutionized the war. The reemergence of the Taliban drew the dynamic of resistance versus occupation to the fore. A religious-based call to fight infidel occupation spread. As it turned from a defeated movement into a battlefield victor, more Afghans could see the Taliban as fighting a foreign invader and puppet government. At the same time, intensified American air strikes and operations in reaction to the Taliban heightened the sense of oppression and an obligation to resist. A series of US surveys showed favorable views among all Afghans toward the United States steadily fell from 88 percent in 2006 to 52 percent in 2010. After that it never recovered. The war reaffirmed an ideal rooted in Afghanistan's beliefs and history. It would be a source of strength for the movement, a source of weakness for the government. There would be no going back.

After 2006, opportunities to end the conflict would narrow. The Taliban became larger and ensconced across the south and east. With vast ground under their control, the Taliban could mobilize fighters and raise revenues at an impressive rate. The United States and the government would no longer be able to suppress them with a few advisors and a token Afghan army. Whereas a properly trained police force and army of 150,000 (as per the plan) should have defeated the 10,000 or so Taliban of 2006, a much larger number, supported by a more substantial US presence, would be required to defeat the expansive Taliban of 2007 onward. With military success, Taliban peace feelers would also fall by the wayside. That is what makes the mistakes of 2001 to 2006 so tragic. They set the United States and Afghanistan on course for 14 years of war.

8

Taliban Rule, 2007–2010

After the 2006 offensive, the Taliban ruled an impressive amount of territory. They established a degree of stability in their areas that was at least as resilient as what Karzai had provided. Though the front lines were violent, villages within Taliban territory were fairly peaceful, other than the random air strike or special operations raid. Taliban rule had enduring strengths. Justice and income growth via poppy cultivation provided the people tangible goods. A deep belief in unity as a religious imperative buffered the movement from the anarchy endemic in the tribal system and the government itself. And their dedication to Islam and resistance to occupation resonated with what it meant to be Afghan.

Information on Mullah Omar's activities between 2007 and 2010 is murkier than that in any other period of his life. Very few Taliban saw him. Very few knew anyone who recently had.[1] Abdul Hai Mutmain, his Taliban biographer, insists that Mullah Omar was in Zabul hiding, running a network of guerrilla cadres, and sometimes joining in battle. In Mutmain's telling, Omar had been so far forward between 2003 and 2006 that at some point his men had to dissuade him from exposing himself to danger. Supposedly they pulled him aside and counseled, "Your presence and survival is a vital issue for the whole movement. Your military operations are not so important as your leadership."[2] Mutmain says that Omar heeded their advice:

> Mullah Mohammed Omar, from the emphasis and advice of his friends, separated himself, and with a militia of a few devoted followers in a mountainous area set up a home. At first, his followers chose one house, then some time later another. In that house, they set up a small simple room for him. In that room, they also built a place for ablutions for him. . . . Mullah Mohammed Omar Mujahed lived in that house until his last breath.[3]

[margin note: what B.S.]

Dutch journalist Bette Dam discovered several sources who swore Mullah Omar was in the desolate Shinkai district, between Highway One and the Pakistani border. It was Hotak territory, the original homeland of his father's family. The dominant rumor across Afghans and Taliban alike before 2015 was that he was hiding in Pakistan. Various Taliban claimed to have seen him in Quetta or Karachi. So widespread was the rumor that US intelligence often picked it up and accepted it as true.[4]

What is more certain is that in either Zabul or Pakistan, Omar was secluding himself. He left operations in the hands of his two deputies, Mullah Baradar and Mullah Obaidullah, who communicated with him via courier as had probably been the case since 2003. Major issues such as appointments, removals, policy announcements, and codes of conduct occupied Omar's time. Policy tended to be announced in messages for the yearly religious holidays of Kuchinay Eid and Loya Eid, as well as in a message for Nowruz (New Year). Baradar, Obaidullah, or a spokesman would draft these and then send them to Omar. Possibly with the help of an assistant, Omar would review the drafts and approve them, presumably with revisions. The same process applied for the codes of conduct.[5]

Communication with Omar became problematic. War stressed the courier system. It took weeks simply to retrieve a message. Months could pass between asking Omar a question and receiving an answer. Reacting to an emergency or unexpected event was very difficult.[6] Baradar and Obaidullah managed things well, if overshadowed by Mullah Dadullah Lang, who was rapidly gaining power from his battlefield victories.

Taliban strength rose dramatically from the mid-2006 onward. At that time, the movement was fielding from 7,000 to as many as 12,000 combatants (if you believe Dadullah). By early 2009, the range was from 25,000 to 46,000.[7] Estimates of insurgent numbers are always sketchy. In this case, they correspond with other measures that suggest a significant increase in the Taliban ability to cause harm: US and allied deaths climbed from 191 in 2006 to 296 in 2008; Afghan army and police deaths from roughly 1,000 to 1,600; and the number of attacks from almost 5,000 to more than 11,000.[8]

Territorial conquest allowed the Taliban to recruit Afghans from villages now under their control. As Afghan recruits swelled, the number of true "foreign fighters"—non-Pashtun Pakistanis, Arabs, and Central Asians—decreased.

Throughout the war, Taliban fighters received modest formal training. Many received bits of instruction in weapons, improvised explosive devices (IEDs), and tactics in camps or at madrasas near the Afghan border in Baluchistan and Waziristan.[9] Short training sessions also convened in villages and compounds under Taliban control in Afghanistan itself. The ISI (Pakistan military intelligence), Pakistan army, or former Pakistani soldiers supposedly ran at least some of the training. The percentage of trained fighters is unknown, but, as time went on, growing proficiency in improvised explosive device techniques suggests more and more attended some kind of course.[10]

The improvised explosive device or IED, the scourge of Iraq, became the Taliban weapon of choice: less destructive than a car bomb and easier to execute, without the time-consuming process of indoctrinating a suicide bomber. Taliban had used improvised explosive devices in 2006 but had preferred more traditional tactics, such as ambushes, raids, and, when possible, assaults. Between 2006 and 2008, attacks involving improvised explosive devices increased 400 percent.[11] They were easy to hide under or next to a dirt road or footpath. The explosive within an improvised explosive device was sometimes an old land mine or artillery shell but most often a homemade mixture of nitrogen and sulfur. A nearby fighter could trigger it by a remote-control device or a command wire running directly to the explosive. Or it could be detonated by a pressure plate depressed by the weight of a vehicle or inadvertent foot. The great advantage of improvised explosive devices was that they allowed fighters to stay out of harm's way. A fighter in a ditch or a mud compound could trigger a device and then run away or blend into the population.

Until 2009, the Quetta Shura (the Taliban leadership council) armed and supplied its cadres to the same standard as the police and army. Cadre commanders were responsible for providing their fighters with weapons, ammunition, and food. The Quetta Shura, provincial governors, and regional commanders tried to acquire these resources and funnel them down but cadre commanders had to scrounge for guns and ammunition.

Pay was not guaranteed. Fighters received wages as their commanders saw fit and funds were available. By some accounts, wages averaged out to $50 to $300 per month, which falls in roughly the same range as the salaries of policemen and soldiers ($70 and $200 per month, respectively).[12] At least a few fighters received so little money they had to farm on the side (or participate in the poppy harvest) to raise an income.[13] A Taliban commander in Kandahar in 2006 and 2007 informed journalist Anand Gopal, "We sometimes got money from our leaders, but it was usually for weapons and it was very intermittent. . . . We would raise money from the village. . . . Once in a while a rich person from the village would come and give us money. They believed that this was a holy jihad and is just for God."[14]

Young men joined the Taliban for many reasons: some because they were aggrieved by government policies, others to avenge the dishonor of a US night raid on their home or a family member killed or detained by the United States or the government, and yet others to fight ethnic or tribal rivals, sometimes along with the rest of their tribe.[15]

The role of Islam and resistance to occupation in motivating men to fight should not be underestimated. Both were part of Afghan identity. Jihad was now in full swing. The Taliban's Islamic credentials and the fact they were fighting occupiers made for a powerful recruitment device. When asked why they had decided to fight, former Taliban frequently told US officers and officials things like, "We were young. We decided to fight. We wanted to take up jihad and fight the infidel." Village elders often encouraged sons and nephews to pursue jihad against the foreign occupier as a religious obligation.[16] One elder told a BBC reporter, "The Taliban come and ask each house for their sons. Not forcing them, but telling them, asking them, 'How Muslim are you? Why are you not doing jihad?'"[17]

Islam and resistance to occupation are unavoidable themes in how Taliban described why they fought, starting with Canadian journalist Graeme Smith's seminal 2007 study of 42 Taliban fighters. Smith writes that the most important thing he learned from his set of interviews is that the Taliban were nationalists, to a large extent fighting for Afghan identity.[18]

Another set of interviews, run by Andrew Garfield and Alicia Boyd between 2009 and 2012, found that "among the 78 interviewees in this study, many more assert that they wage jihad in defense of the Islamic umma and the people of Afghanistan than the number . . . who indicated that they fight to right wrongs done to them personally or due to a lack of employment." The report continued, "No interviewee had anything positive to say about NATO or the United States; meanwhile almost all argue that the U.S. presence results in the killing . . . of Afghans, the . . . subservience of the Afghan government to foreign interests, and in the imposition of extraneous secular, non-Islamic values."[19]

That is not to say that other factors such as grievances did not also matter— Smith notes that most of his interviewees were from specific tribes that had issues with the government, and one third of the interviewees in the Garfield and Boyd study said a close family member had been killed or injured by violence involving foreign military forces.[20] But Islam and resistance to occupation was overarching.

Nationwide surveys similarly suggest that Islam and resistance to occupation inspired the Taliban. The Asia Foundation 2009 annual survey, widely considered the most authoritative survey of Afghanistan, found that a stunning 56 percent of Afghans admitted sympathy for the Taliban.[21] Although the figure fell to 40 percent the next year, it was still disturbingly high, breaking 50 percent in the south and parts of the east. Of the respondents who strongly supported the Taliban, almost half said they did so because the Taliban were Afghans or Muslims. Pashtuns and Afghans living in the countryside generally had much higher sympathy for the Taliban than those living in the cities, where education, jobs, and government bureaucracy had nurtured a more progressive class.[22]

Mullah Omar's 2008 Kuchinay Eid message is a good example of how he and his lieutenants spoke in terms of Islam and resistance to occupation: "All Afghans and the region's Muslim peoples need to understand this truth: the enemy upon our soil and our beliefs will not be content as long as we do not completely accept being their slaves. Freedom from their slavery is the only path that the Koran has shown. Armed jihad and resistance in defense of one's own country and religion is a command."[23]

Islam and resistance to occupation coursed through poetry written by Taliban fighters and poets. Too often, Westerners dismissed Taliban poetry as propaganda. Such accusations overlooked poetry's popularity and the extent to which Taliban, and Afghans in general, read it, passed it to each other on cell phones, composed it, and shed tears over it.[24] Maulawi Abdul Rahman Akhundzada, one of Dadullah's cadre commanders, told *Newsweek*, "There are famous Taliban poems about how mujahedin come to free villages from occupiers at the point of a bayonet. I began living that poem."[25]

Poems frequently mentioned Afghanistan's history of resistance, citing Maiwand and Afghan heroes such as Akbar Khan (who defeated the British in the First Anglo-Afghan War), Ayub Khan (who won the Battle of Maiwand), and Mir Wais Nika (who freed Kandahar from the Iranian Safavid Empire). The poetry of Mohammed Hussein Mustasad, a Taliban poet who died in a firefight in Zabul in 2007, is one example of many:

> When will Mir Wais reconcile? When will Ahmed Shah return?
> Akbar Khan is not lost from me. Ayub Khan has not left me.
> No din in Maiwand and humming does not return to Kabul
> No tribe exists that will call for the award of Maulali
> God, do not bring the bad time that will make happiness foreign
> God, what happened to my flower buds, ghazi culture lost?
> Buds always will flower, when do flowers bud?[26]

The government could not claim the same dedication to Islam as the Taliban.[27] The state was named the "Islamic Republic of Afghanistan" but lacked the Taliban's credentials. If accepted by the majority of Afghans, democracy had secular overtones that disadvantaged the government in religious authority. In the 2007 Asia Foundation survey, 30 to 45 percent of respondents in the south and east felt that democracy challenged Islam.[28] Still more offensive, the government's very existence depended on the open support of foreign non-Muslim powers. It was ensnared in historical analogies to defeated Afghan rulers who had been installed by the British and Soviets.[29]

With characteristic incisiveness, Karzai explained the government's weakness to Lieutenant General Eikenberry (and later many others):

If we have an insurgency in Afghanistan, it means there are some Afghans who question the legitimacy of my government. And because we have foreign troops here fighting for my government, then I must lead a "puppet government." And since Afghanistan is a pious Islamic country, those fighting this "puppet government" propped up by infidels could reasonably declare jihad against you and me. So there is no insurgency in Afghanistan.[30]

In his description of what could not happen, Karzai no doubt knew he was capturing exactly what was actually happening.

Unity continued be a Taliban virtue. Compared to the tribes and the government, the Taliban were cohesive. There was a hierarchy, even if it worked imperfectly. Cadre commanders answered to their district governor, he to a provincial governor or regional commander such as Dadullah Lang, and thence to Mullah Baradar, Mullah Obaidullah, and Mullah Omar. Dadullah's influence caused friction but the system worked. Mullah Omar and his deputies could generally appoint and remove leaders as necessary. There were few instances of Taliban fighting each other.[31]

How did this drive for unity endure while the tribes and government leaders undercut one another? To start, a hierarchical system was a natural form of command and control for the Taliban, a movement founded by mullahs and religious scholars. Whereas a tribesman always had a fundamental right to reject the authority of any other man, a religious leader was expected to obey his teacher, and his students, him.[32] As Amir Khan Motaqi, member of the Quetta Shura, lectured me some years later: "The Taliban follow an emir. Our system is of obedience. We must do what he says. We are not like other Afghans."

Omar's personal role also matters. He had prioritized unity from his first day as military commander of the movement. Just as important, the Taliban's formative experience—the civil war after the jihad—reinforced their cohesion. In 2006, the memory of anarchy was still fresh. Taliban leaders recalled how cohesion had been one of their great strengths. Jalaluddin Haqqani, leader of the powerful Taliban-affiliated Haqqani network, said, in an interview in 2008, "We, during the jihad against the Russians, we saw the unity and alliance of the mujahideen leaders come to an end. The leaders were disunited and buried the pride of winning the jihad in dirt. Afghans will never again allow that experience to be repeated. We are united and we will be united."[33]

Beneath it all, however, were deeper Islamic roots based on the existence of one God and Prophet Mohammed's victories against fractious Arab tribes. To be one was to be Muslim. Mullah Omar's pronouncements drew on Islam to encourage unity: "In following our religion (Islam), we have harshly prohibited every type . . . of tribal prejudice. Our only truth is Islam. Every Muslim is our brother and friend and we respect every Muslim because Islam considers all Muslims one body. Islam's great prophet Mohammed, may peace be upon him, in a Hadith that Abu Daoud narrates, orders: 'He who fights on behalf of tribal prejudice is not part of our group (Islam).'"[34]

The Taliban reestablished their role in the areas under their control. Provincial governors and district governors were appointed. They created their own district centers, usually in outlying bazaars that became trade hubs. Strategically located mud compounds became Taliban headquarters, staging points, and sometimes prisons. In their strongest centers of power, administrative offices, courts, and madrassas went up.

Justice under Islamic law was a centerpiece of Taliban rule. In a 2010 interview, Mohammed Issa, then the Taliban governor of Kandahar, described the Taliban justice system:

In those areas the Islamic Emirate authority completely exists. . . . An independent commission of judges is active. . . . We review petitions and resolve cases in courts from rural areas that otherwise have to send petitions and issues of rights to the provincial center. . . . In Kandahar City, the government courts stand empty and its judges that have been appointed in Kabul do not have the boldness to work here. After that experience again and again, people now understand that to solve their problems the only recourse is the Islamic Emirate Court because their obstacles are solved very quickly through Islamic law.[35]

The Taliban generally ran a two-tiered justice system. As in their first regime, the village mullahs were empowered to settle disputes in their villages. Above them were senior judges who roamed a given district to handle cases the mullahs could not resolve on their own. They were sometimes referred to as "mobile courts." In districts or parts of districts firmly under their control, the Taliban set up standing courts where locals often took cases, especially land disputes.[36] Like the cadre leaders, judges reported to the district governor, another facet of Taliban hierarchy. Every province also had an assigned judge to adjudicate cases that could not be decided at a lower level. That judge fell under the provincial governor.

As in the 1990s, punishments were harsh. Those found guilty could be sentenced to death. Taliban justice seems to have been well-received. By several accounts, the people appreciated the relative security and order.[37]

The Taliban used land to reinforce support. Upon regaining power in many districts, Taliban governors restored to poor farmers the land that they had received during the first regime. The restoration pleased poor tribes. Under the Karzai regime and the tribal leaders, their land deeds had been invalidated. They had been forced to live under the threat of eviction. With the Taliban back, they were fully recognized citizens again. The Taliban did not stop there. In many districts they brought in new Ghilzai immigrants and gave them government land. Private land was sometimes sequestered as well. This was especially the case in Helmand where the land of pro-government tribes was given over to the Ishaqzai, Alizai, and small Ghilzai families.

The Taliban collected revenue from several sources. Villagers often gave *zakat* or other religious donations to the Taliban, sometimes voluntarily, sometimes not. Taliban in southern Afghanistan in 2007 reported to Graeme Smith that a single family might donate $2 to $600 per year.[38] Taliban cadres also sold captured vehicles and weapons. A larger source of income came from extortion: forcing businesses and contractors working with the government and international community to pay a cut in return for being left alone.[39] The Taliban taxed trucks carrying all manner of goods. In certain areas, they taxed land and the wheat crop. More cruelly, they sometimes kidnapped people for ransom. A greater source of revenue was foreign donations from Islamic charities and individuals and foreign aid from Pakistan.[40]

The most important source of revenue was poppy. The old ban was never reimposed. On the contrary, the Taliban encouraged cultivation. Throughout Afghanistan, cultivation rose from 100,000 hectares at the end of 2005 to 165,000 in 2006, to almost 200,000 in 2008. The increase was even more marked in Helmand, where the Taliban had captured so much ground. The roughly 30,000 hectares under cultivation at the end of 2005 soared to almost 80,000 in 2006 and leveled off at just over 100,000 in 2007 and 2008.[41]

Taliban officials managed the shipping and the all-important taxation of the crop. The Taliban taxed a percentage of farmers' poppy crop and a cash percentage from smugglers. The taxes were passed from the districts up to the province and thence to the Quetta Shura. The specifics of how much a provincial governor could keep and the mechanisms for budgeting are not clear. Estimates of Taliban poppy revenue range from $90 million to $160 million per year prior to 2009. Even the low end is four times as high as a rough estimate of revenue from local donations (*zakat*) and roughly equal to financial assistance from Pakistan.[42]

Taliban governance was effective but should not be romanticized. The Taliban were far from perfect. Their rule contained the barest elements of due process and what the West considered acceptable. If often admired as fast and impartial, justice could be brutal. Taliban courts sometimes tortured people. They searched out spies and informants and often executed them. Not all suspects saw a court. In Ghazni, Taliban pulled buses to the side of the road, dragged out suspected spies, and shot them on the spot.[43]

In spring 2006, the Quetta Shura had issued a code of conduct, the *layeha*, approved by Mullah Omar for the whole movement. It contained 30 clauses, with rules for recruitment, administration, prisoners, funds, accountability, and personal behavior. The code was rather harsh. Converts who betrayed the movement were to get "no second chance." Secular education was banned. Aid organizations were to be attacked regardless of whether their projects helped the people.[44] The code did contain certain provisions to protect civilians. Taliban who repeatedly mistreated innocent people were to be thrown out of the movement. Confiscating money and personal possessions was forbidden.

Yet even these sensible provisions were unevenly enforced. Dadullah was vicious. He beheaded Afghans suspected of working with the government and displayed pictures of decapitated bodies in bazaars and the victims' communities. Other Taliban doubted such acts were permitted under the Koran. The Quetta Shura later officially stated that Dadullah had operated "outside of control and punishment," perhaps as a way of divorcing themselves from acts gone too far.[45]

Taliban delivery of goods and services also left much to be desired, most notably for education. Mullah Omar ordered all secular schools closed or burned. Government teachers were to be beaten and, if they did not quit their job, killed. The reason, as stated in the code of conduct, was that secular schools and teachers strengthened the "system of the infidels" and were "destroying Islam."[46] The code allowed only mullahs and religious scholars to teach. In certain districts, large madrasas replaced secular schools. In most villages, children simply attended their local mosque where their mullah taught basic reading, writing, math, and religion. In Panjwai, for example, only one school—the last school in government hands—was open from 2005 to 2010. The Taliban closed the rest. Children could study in mosques but few had classes. Overall, education fell short of what it had been during the first Taliban regime.

In the 1990s, the West had condemned the first Taliban regime for its treatment of women: the forced imposition of full veil (burka), barring of civic freedoms, and barbaric stonings. Under their restored order, the lot of women improved only slightly. Executions and corporal punishment did not return but girls were still banned from school, forced to be fully veiled, and effectively trapped inside the home. As they had during their regime, the Taliban justified themselves by saying that they were protecting women in accordance with Islamic law. They criticized the government for letting women go outside and exposing them to mistreatment, a sentiment many Afghan men, even in Kabul, shared.[47] Akbar Agha, one of the Taliban's founders, exemplified this view: "We protect women by keeping them in the home. Men are stronger, more capable, than women."

Yet it would be wrong to say that all women despised the Taliban. The Taliban cause was too tied to feelings of what it meant to be Afghan, especially for the women of marginalized tribes such as the Ishaqzai. Many Pashtun mothers and wives, even those who benefited from Western programs, praised Taliban fighters. "The Taliban are not bad people. These young men are the sons of Ahmed Shah and Mir Wais Nika. They are heroes," Maulali Ishaqzai, the female member of parliament from Kandahar, exclaimed to me.[48]

Such words fit a traditional role of women in Pashtun society: enforcing honor upon men. One woman from the countryside spelled out to researchers, "Even though women have very little role in decision making, they can still motivate and provoke men to do ... things. For example, if a mother tells her son or a wife tells her husband to take revenge from someone or to do jihad, then there is nothing that can stop the son or husband. It becomes an issue of honor."[49] Taliban conceptualized women in line with that tradition. Maulali at Maiwand, driving Afghans to fight the British or face dishonor, appears again and again in their announcements and poems. There may have been a few women who wrote poems for the Taliban. Two examples are Hanifa Zahid and Belinda Badari. The stories of their lives and their poems are as interesting as whether they themselves are fact or fiction.

Hanifa Zahid was supposedly a girls' school teacher from a religious family in Zabul. Her father and father-in-law, both religious scholars, educated her, a background that would have legitimized her poems and differentiated her from the progressive women of Kabul and the cities. Her name appears in Taliban publications beginning in the 1990s.[50] Poems under her name, such as "The Art of My Village," touched on traditional values of Pashtun life:

> The loyalty of its youth, the modesty of its girls
> Courage and bravery like ornaments, in my village
> In fire, in rain, in thorns, in flower
> You cannot comprehend, the art of my village.[51]

In sanctifying village life, the poem invokes the values of home and family that tradition levies upon young men to protect.

Belinda Badari was supposedly from Paktiya but lived in Pakistan all her life. She went to school through the fifth grade and then studied religion and memorized the Koran under various religious scholars. Her poem, "The Corpse of a Maiden from Bala Baluk," tells of a night raid on a home in Farah from the perspective of a young woman:

> The first line of the book
> The helicopter's roar

My father quickly silenced the radio
I held my little brothers quiet . . .
But in a moment like electricity . . .
The room was all lost
A high report, every wall
From every direction turned upside down . . .
I am a corpse under the fallen wall
A Muslim maiden
Pashtuna of Bala Baluk
We were farmers, we were poor
We were no one's murderers . . .
The inheritance of those who live is
To ask from our murderers
What was our sin?[52]

Through Badari's eyes, the poem indicts the violation of Afghan home, family, and honor by foreigners—all forms of oppression that justify war.

Zahid and Badari may have been fiction, fabrications of male Taliban propaganda. But at the very least, their stories and poems show how the Taliban perceived of the role of women—paragons of Islam and Afghan identity, inspiration for keeping foreigners out of Afghanistan. The message appealed to more than a few Afghan women.

Pakistani support for the Taliban continued after 2006. The extent that Dadullah or Baradar had direct contact with the ISI (Pakistan military intelligence) is unclear. Nevertheless, the existence of a relationship is uncontested. President Parvez Musharraf gave broad guidance to the ISI on how to support the Taliban, who then executed their own plans or further delegated to retired ISI personnel.[53]

The United States had been conducting counterterrorism operations within Pakistan since 2001, in close coordination with the ISI and Pakistan military. Those operations concentrated on al-Qa'eda rather than the Taliban. At the behest of Musharraf, the Bush administration refrained from striking Pakistan soil without first informing them and committed to striking no targets around Quetta and Baluchistan where the Taliban were operating.

Bush, Powell, and Rumsfeld appreciated Musharraf's assistance in detaining al-Qa'eda leaders after 2001 and had disdained intelligence he was helping the Taliban. The 2006 offensive was a wake-up call. Intelligence and other information confirmed that Taliban leaders were in Pakistan and that the Pakistani state had connections with them. At the end of the year, the administration finally decided that Pakistan was not doing enough.

Vice President Dick Cheney went to Islamabad in February 2007 to tell Musharraf to act or US assistance could be in jeopardy. To placate the United States, Musharraf detained Mullah Obaidullah, one of the movement's two deputies, a day before Cheney's arrival. Baradar became Omar's sole deputy. Obaidullah would die in captivity in 2010.[54]

The gesture did not alter Pakistan's overall policy. General Ashfaq Parvez Kayani, the director general of the ISI, told US ambassador to Pakistan Ryan Crocker in early 2007, "If you think we are going to turn the Taliban and Haqqanis and others into mortal enemies of ours and watch you walk out the door, you are completely crazy. Are we hedging our bets? You bet we are."[55]

From 2004 onward, the Taliban movement's importance to Pakistan's internal security increased. The reason is that Pakistani Pashtun tribes and militant groups were clashing with the Pakistan government, marked by the formation that year of the Pakistani Taliban, or Tehrik-e-Taliban Pakistan (TTP), out of several militant groups in Pakistan's tribal region. In 2007, the Pakistani Taliban advanced into the Swat Valley and then occupied the Red Mosque in Islamabad in a weeklong confrontation. Over the next two years, Pakistan was immersed in a civil war that frequently touched the heart of the country. Musharraf and the Pakistani leadership needed a neutral Afghan Taliban lest the insurgency become overpowering. All the more reason to help the movement.

The ISI let the Quetta Shura and Taliban commanders in Quetta and Peshawar roam relatively freely inside Pakistan. The ISI also provided money, safe houses, and intelligence. Pakistani military assets may have transported Taliban fighters to the border. Wounded fighters were allowed to go to Pakistani hospitals. The ISI may have set up clinics specifically for them in Baluchistan. US officers widely suspected the ISI was tipping off Taliban leaders ahead of US operations.[56] Pakistani advisors occasionally traveled into Afghanistan to gather information or deliver discrete advice or training. One Taliban commander in northern Helmand admitted to researcher Antonio Giustozzi, "Our Punjabi trainers work very hard and always find a solution when the enemies use new tactics against us."[57] Scant evidence, though much rumor, exists that Pakistani advisors were fighting alongside the Taliban.

Pakistan support to the Taliban would outlast Musharraf. His time as military dictator expired as his rule precipitated domestic opposition. In 2007, former president Benazir Bhutto returned to Pakistan from exile and challenged Musharraf for the presidency. A suicide bomber assassinated Bhutto that December. An extended political crisis forced Musharraf to step down in August 2008. Asif Ali Zardari, Bhutto's husband, was elected president. The real power, though, still rested in the hands of the military. General Kayani, recently promoted to army chief of staff, took over military and defense policy. He maintained Musharraf's policies toward the Taliban and the Afghan government.

A good deal of Pakistani support for the Taliban was probably more spontaneous than organized. Various Pakistani generals, intelligence officers, government officials, smugglers, religious leaders, and average people helped the Taliban of their own volition. They shared the tie of Islam and in many cases tribe and ethnicity.

A 2010 survey in the Federally Administered Tribal Areas (FATA) found that 28 percent of respondents, a sufficient minority to sustain an insurgent movement, supported Taliban presence in Pakistan. Just as Islam and resistance to Western intervention inspired Afghans, so too did they inspire Pakistanis. Seventy-five percent of respondents believed that the United States was in Afghanistan to wage war on Islam; 77 percent believed the United States should withdraw from Afghanistan.[58]

Garfield and Boyd, from their interviews with Taliban fighters and commanders, wrote that "there is an affinity between the Afghan and Pakistani people as Muslims" and that the Pakistani people are more supportive of the Taliban than the Afghan people.[59] One Taliban from Kandahar told them, "As infidels help each other so do Muslims."[60]

The Quetta Shura never openly admitted to friendship with Pakistan. They only admitted to accepting support from any Islamic country willing to donate. The shura sometimes issued official condemnations of accusations that they received support from Pakistan.[61] Omar himself wanted to preserve the movement's independence and disdained subservience to Pakistan. He even sent emissaries to nearby countries to ask for support so he could lessen the movement's dependence on Pakistan.[62]

A major sub-group within the Taliban movement was the Haqqani network founded by Jalaluddin Haqqani. The network was a branch of one of the original mujahideen parties from the war against the Soviets (Hezb Islami Khalis). Their headquarters was in Miram Shah, across the border from Khost. They were more organized than any other insurgent group in Afghanistan and specialized in complex and high-profile terrorist attacks in Kabul.

The venerable Jalaluddin Haqqani was a Zadran tribesmen from Khost. He had completed religious studies at the prestigious Dar-ul-Ulum Haqqania madrasa near Peshawar. He then earned fame in the war against the Soviets as a commander with extensive battlefield experience. His group was highly effective in Khost and Paktiya. When the Taliban attacked Kabul in 1995, Jalaluddin joined them. Mullah Omar appointed him minister of border and tribal affairs. In 2001, a US air strike wounded Jalaluddin. He and his sons fell back to Pakistan and in short order initiated guerrilla operations against the Americans and the new Afghan government.[63] He became one of the founding members of the Quetta Shura. According to a few sources, he was especially upset that the United States had arrested his brother and other relatives.[64] His son, Sirajuddin, assumed most leadership responsibilities after 2007 as Jalaluddin's health declined.[65]

The Haqqani network formally fell under Mullah Omar. Jalaluddin spelled out the relationship in a December 2008 interview:

> Praise Allah, the Islamic Emirate wages jihad against America and its slaves, entirely in one heart and one voice under the authority of Emir Leader of the Faithful Mullah Mohammed Omar Mujahed. In the Islamic Emirate mujahedin there is no such thing as extremists and moderates. All mujahedin . . . are under their emir. . . . I myself am part of the Islamic Emirate organization and a member of the leadership [Quetta] shura and have responsibility for operations.[66]

In practice, the Haqqanis ran their own operations and Baradar did not stand in the way.

The network's sphere of operations was Khost, Paktiya, Paktika, and into Kabul. The Haqqanis were ruthlessly effective. Like Dadullah, Jalaluddin glorified suicide attacks. He told an interviewer in 2008, "That I could become a martyr for Allah is my whole's life's great longing. The longing is that I hope my own spirit with sacrifice is taken into his hands. But as of yet that great longing has not arrived."[67] The network mastered suicide bombings. Escalating dramatically in 2006, high-profile explosions rocked Kabul and killed and wounded hundreds. They tended to be Haqqani operations and would increase in sophistication over the next five years. The Haqqanis also specialized in kidnapping Westerners and ransoming them off. The *New York Times* journalist David Rohde, US soldier Bowe Bergdahl, the Coleman family, and many others were their guests.

The Haqqani network was closer to Pakistan than the rest of the Taliban. Jalaluddin had been friends with the ISI since before the Soviet invasion. Pakistan funded the network, trained fighters, and provided intelligence.[68] In 2006, the Pakistani military and the ISI arranged a deal with Jalaluddin in which the military would not attack his network and in return he would focus operations against the Karzai government.[69] When chairman of the joint chiefs of staff, Admiral Mike Mullen, asked that the Pakistan military move against the Haqqani network in July 2008, army chief Kayani replied that it was a bad time; he did not want to turn a friend into an enemy while fighting the Pakistani Taliban.[70]

The other significant insurgent organization was old Hezb Islami Gulbuddin, Hezb Islami, for short, the party that had been one of the two largest mujahideen organizations in the war against the Soviets. Gulbuddin Hekmatyar, aged but no less obstinate, still led Hezb Islami. The Taliban and Hezb Islami had established a relationship before 2005 after Mullah Omar had sent emissaries to Hekmatyar.[71] Hekmatyar allowed his cadres to fight but refused Mullah Omar's overall leadership. Hezb Islami cadres therefore operated independently.

The organization was fractured. Hezb Islami leaders had been university students, not mullahs and religious scholars used to a form of hierarchy. Hekmatyar's authority was tenuous. His own ambition and widespread allegations of atrocities weakened it. His commanders decided for themselves whether to fight, work with the government, or sit at home. Many went to work with the government. A number fought, but in select regions such as Kunar, Laghman, and Wardak. Hezb Islami cadres clashed with Taliban cadres from time to time over territory, money, and influence. For most of the war, the clashes were small and inconsequential.

Mullah Dadullah Lang had masterminded the 2006 Taliban offensive. By year's end, he had become a military commander of immense power, unmatched on the battlefield. His infamy was growing. He put out videos of himself selecting suicide bombers, executing spies, and meeting with al-Qaʿeda. The videos spread through the Kandahar bazaars. Al Jazeera television interviewed him twice—dour, calm, surrounded by armed men, openly showing his face in a display of fearlessness.

Dadullah was ever a brazen al-Qaʿeda partisan. In Al Jazeera interviews, he spoke of his opposition to US occupation of Afghanistan and the possibility of launching attacks on the United States or Europe. In 2006, he calmly told the Al Jazeera interviewer that the Taliban have "close links" to al-Qaʿeda and that "our cooperation is ideal."[72] In 2007, he repeated the sentiment, "We thank God that [Osama bin Laden] is still alive; we know that he is. He puts [together] the plans for both Iraq and Afghanistan."[73] Dadullah's elder brother, Mansour, also met with al-Qaʿeda leaders. A 2007 meeting was publicized in a film entitled "A Meeting between Brothers."[74]

Some Americans nicknamed Dadullah the "Afghan Zarqawi," in reference to terrorist Musab al-Zarqawi who had founded al-Qaʿeda in Iraq and catalyzed the insurgency there. The comparison is fitting. Dadullah was the most brutal senior commander in the history of the Taliban. His tactics generated controversy, just as Zarqawi's had with bin Laden and Zawahiri. Not all Taliban approved. Mullah Baradar argued with Dadullah. Omar was reportedly unhappy.[75]

In May 2007, Dadullah met with his Helmand commanders in Garmser district to prepare for the summer fighting season. That night, British Special Boat Service (SBS) commandos smashed into the meeting. The British shot and killed Dadullah and wounded the Taliban commander in southern Helmand, Mullah Naim Barech.[76] There are numerous conspiracy stories that members of the Quetta Shura, upset with Dadullah, had tipped off the United States and Britain. His brother, Mansour Dadullah, accused members of the Quetta Shura of betrayal, and threatened revenge. He detained and beat two Taliban he suspected of giving away his brother's location.

Concerned with Mansour Dadullah's behavior, Omar stepped in. He issued an audio recording that praised Dadullah as a true mujahideen and honored his martyrdom and then coldly proceeded to excommunicate his brother, Mansour. He told Mullah Baradar to sit with Dadullah's men and impress upon them that the Taliban have but one leader.[77] Baradar took the reins and the Taliban provincial governors, cadre commanders, and fighters fell in line. The Pakistanis detained Mansour in February 2008, less than a year after his brother's death. It was an impressive demonstration of Omar's authority. The truth of how Dadullah was located in the first place is unknown.[78]

Dadullah had made his mark. His legacy was military victories, a resurgent movement and suicide bombings. The Taliban issued an elegy in the name of Mullah Omar: "May Allah have mercy on his soul and on the souls of all those who carried weapons in jihad for his cause. He was not killed before he raised a generation and trained brigades on sacrifice, heroism, and zeal. His strict words are still resonating in their ears, feeding their hearts and encouraging them, and his brave positions will remain a strong jihadist lesson raising heroes and reviving men."[79]

With Dadullah's death and Obaidullah's detention, the 40-year-old Baradar was now the predominant Taliban leader. Taliban field commanders respected him for his military service both during the Soviet-Afghan War and operations during the Taliban regime. His peaceful demeanor conveyed a closeness to God and an ability to weather the toughest situations.[80] Trust between Omar and Baradar was undimmed.[81]

Baradar ran the movement while Omar guided from hiding. He had permission to chair the Quetta Shura, control Taliban funds, and appoint and fire Taliban governors. Unlike Dadullah, Baradar never traveled to Afghanistan. For the most part, he worked in Karachi and Quetta and the surrounding Pashtun refugee camps where he was safe from US operations.[82]

Baradar was more moderate than Dadullah. Within the Quetta Shura he tried to build consensus and hear different opinions. Baradar in many ways set the Taliban on the course they would follow for years. He was the force behind a series of Taliban reforms from 2007 to 2010, emplacing strategies that largely carried on until 2014.[83] Omar allowed Baradar to pursue these reforms, which curbed the worst excesses of Dadullah while preserving suicide car bombs, improvised explosive devices , assassinations, and other proven tactics.

Baradar streamlined the Taliban's official hierarchy so that district governors reported to provincial governors and provincial governors up to him, removing regional commanders (sometimes termed front, or "mahaz," commanders). He wanted to prevent the rise of a second Dadullah. Mullah Omar enshrined this hierarchy in his 2009 code of conduct, probably drafted by Baradar. The new code specified the chain of command from the lowliest fighter to Mullah Omar himself:

> On mujahedin, their own cadre commander; on cadre commanders, their own district governor; on district governors, their own governor; on the governor, the tanzimi director; on the tanzimi director, the religious leader and the deputy religious leader [Mullah Omar and Mullah Baradar]. Subordination is a religious duty. That condition is legitimate in Islamic law."[84]

Separate fronts outside this chain of command were expressly forbidden, though in practice they had residual influence and the chain of command never operated as perfectly as officially articulated.[85]

The new code of conduct reined in the 2006 code's harsher strictures. Government schools and teachers, as well as aid organizations, were no longer targeted. The ban on secular teachers was lifted. Executing a captive required Mullah Omar's permission, unless a foreign soldier, a contractor working for the United States, or a government official. Suicide attacks were to avoid civilian casualties and had to be approved by the provincial governor. The code forbade cutting noses or ears (a common punishment for spies), forcing people to donate money, and conducting house searches other than when essential and approved by the district or provincial governor. Any executions had to be simple, humane, and unglorified. Public beheadings were frowned upon.[86] The message was reiterated by Taliban spokesmen and in Mullah Omar's later Eid messages.[87]

On the ground, Mullah Omar's dictums made some difference. The worst of the brutality seemed to abate, although schools never really opened—lifting a ban is not ordering them to open—and intensifying combat prevented a reduction in civilian casualties. The United Nations reported that civilian casualties inflicted by insurgents rose from 700 in 2007 to 1,160 in 2008 and then steadily up to 2,080 in 2010. American and government forces caused fewer civilian casualties than the Taliban over this time.[88] Nevertheless, surveys showed that harm caused by the Taliban, fighting for Islam and resistance to foreign presence, was less disliked than that caused by the Americans and their allies.[89] The Taliban rarely faced the widespread outcry triggered by American-inflicted civilian casualties.

After Dadullah's death, Baradar stepped back from al-Qa'eda. This probably had to do with his moderate views and Omar's reticence to engage in international terrorism. Afghanistan had always been Omar's foremost priority, not an international war. An additional factor was that, during 2007 and 2008, bin Laden escalated operations against the Pakistani state and backed the Pakistani Taliban in their anti-government insurgency. Omar and Baradar were unwilling to antagonize the Pakistani military. In 2009, the Quetta Shura officially announced that, if foreign forces would leave Afghanistan, Afghans would have no intentions against other countries and no one would be allowed to use Afghan soil as a base of operations against other countries.[90] In June 2010, Tayeb Agha (Mullah Omar's assistant and head of the political commission) delivered a letter to bin Laden written by either Mullah Omar or the Quetta Shura. It expressed discomfort with a large-scale al-Qaʿeda presence in Afghanistan once the Taliban returned to power.

Al-Qaʿeda training of Taliban fighters and operating alongside Taliban decreased. Around 2010, Osama bin Laden wrote to a colleague, "We are participating in the work in Afghanistan, and we have to do that, but praise be to God, Taliban almost does not need us. We are providing only moral and symbolic support, but in spite of that, our participation is good and important."[91] Although some amount of low-level cooperation and mutual facilitation occurred, bin Laden's words indicate that al-Qaʿeda's role in the war had diminished.

But due to internal resistance Omar and Baradar would never sever ties with al-Qaʿeda. Omar's biographer Abdul Hai Mutmain says that several Taliban commanders questioned the 2009 Quetta Shura announcement's implication that the objective of the war was to push out the United States and not to support al-Qaʿeda in its struggle. A few argued with Baradar over similar statements made in Mullah Omar's yearly Eid announcements.[92] So Omar and Baradar protected the movement's long-standing relationship with al-Qaʿeda while rejecting a shared goal of international terrorism. The same year as the Quetta Shura announcement, Baradar said in a public interview, "In Afghanistan, the ongoing jihad is the authority and choice of the leadership [Quetta] shura of the Islamic Emirate. The international talk of division of al-Qaʿeda from the Taliban has no agreement. Indeed, that is a deception."[93]

The Haqqani network had its own relationship with al-Qaʿeda. Like Jalaluddin Haqqani's relationship with ISI, it had originated in the Soviet war. For years, Jalaluddin had housed al-Qaʿeda training camps on his territory. One of his wives was Arab and liaised with al-Qaʿeda. After 2001, he sheltered al-Qaʿeda and other militant groups fleeing from Tora Bora and eastern Afghanistan.[94]

When war resumed, al-Qaʿeda provided training, funding and supply arrangements, and suicide bombers for various Haqqani attacks. According to Western interviews with Jalaluddin's son Sirajuddin, the Haqqani network and al-Qaʿeda pursued different goals: the former's was to liberate Afghanistan, the latter's to launch attacks throughout the world. "This does not interest us,"

Sirajuddin told two French journalists in 2009.[95] Nevertheless, he and his father refused to break ties with al-Qaʿeda and many of their fighters approved of international terrorism.[96]

The ambiguity in the Taliban-al-Qaʿeda relationship would help fracture US policymaking consensus around the mission in Afghanistan. After 2006, decreasing evidence that Taliban commanders were pursuing terrorist aims would cause American policymakers to ask why the United States needed to defeat the Taliban. At the same time, the Taliban leadership's refusal to actually renounce al-Qaʿeda would deter them from getting out. Whether intentional or not, the movement's attachment to al-Qaʿeda would perpetuate the war, just as it had started it.

In late 2008, Mullah Omar's Loya Eid message congratulated the Taliban on the successes of the past two years:

> In the blessing of your life filled with nightly and daily challenges, the enemy has been defeated and because of your tough resistance, today the Muslim umma feels the merit of vengeance within itself. This is very proud and honored talk since today elsewhere in the Islamic world people put on new and colored clothes, but you make yourselves beautiful in your sangars with bullets and a heavy load in your vest. For the Muslim umma, in the ongoing situation it is correct that one free believer wears clothing more beautiful and respectful than all others. That is the clothing you wear today.[97]

The message was of military success, of selfless fulfilment of duty to resist occupation.

This second Taliban regime proved it could rule effectively. Unity overcame squabbles and rivalries. Justice, land redistribution, and poppy cultivation appeased the villages. Amid change and imbalance, the Taliban offered a form of order. There is beauty in how that order grew out of Islam and its message of oneness and justice. There is tragedy in how it bound women, razed schools, and shredded bodies.

Taliban rule from 2006 onward proved that they were more than a passing religious movement. They had permanence. They were not a late 1990s flash in the pan. Historically, longevity distinguishes them. Afghanistan had previously witnessed fleeting religious movements, never in control of much territory. The combination of repeated superpower intervention and years of civil war, on top of the anarchy of Afghanistan's tribal system, had created the circumstances for a religious movement to become a permanent political body, more successful than the communists or the mujahideen parties, more successful than Karzai's new democratic government.

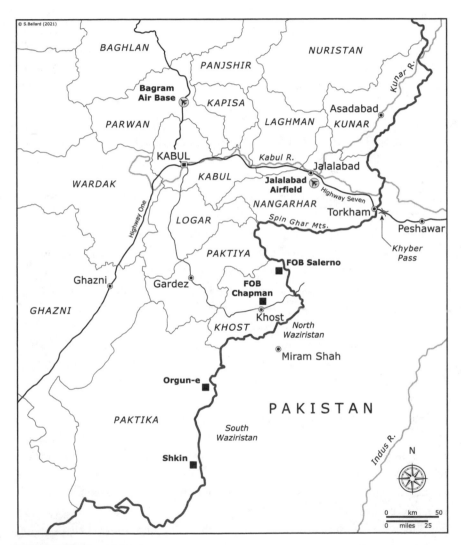

Map 10 Eastern Afghanistan

‖ 9 ‖

War in the East

While the south was under unrelenting Taliban attack, American generals fixed their attention upon the east. From 2002 onward, they concentrated forces in eastern Afghanistan in order to fight al-Qa'eda and other terrorists that operated on either side of the Pakistan border. Until 2010, the east was the main effort of the US military in Afghanistan.[1]

The war in the south had a centricity to it. Kandahar City was the metropole. Helmand, Zabul, and Uruzgan radiated from it. The east on the other hand contained many smaller provinces traversed by inaccessible mountain ranges with no single metropole. The only true city was Jalalabad in prosperous Nangarhar, the largest province in the east, with a population of 1.4 million people, circa 2006.[2] The neighboring provinces of Nuristan, Kunar, and Laghman gravitated to Jalalabad but it was geographically isolated from other eastern provinces. Forested mountain ranges and the meandering Pakistani border partitioned the provinces of Paktiya, Paktika, and Khost—together known as Loya Paktiya. Khost "city" was a fairly large town and a kind of minor metropole. Ghazni, one of Afghanistan's more populous provinces, was almost a region unto itself, strategically located along the main highway from Kabul to Kandahar. Logar, Wardak, and Kapisa—the other eastern provinces—surrounded Kabul.

All this meant that many different campaigns were being fought out in the east in different valleys and mountain ranges and along the border with no common objective in contrast to the more coordinated campaign in the south. Even the enemy varied across the east. A hodgepodge of Hezb Islami, al-Qa'eda, Pakistani Taliban, and Afghan Taliban were the enemy in Nangarhar, Kunar, Laghman, and Nuristan. The Haqqani network was the main enemy in Khost, Paktiya, and Paktika. The Afghan Taliban were the main enemy in Ghazni.

US forces were disposed in the set of forward operating bases along the Pakistan border. The southernmost, Orgun-e and Shkin, were in the mountains of Paktika, opposite the unruly Pakistani provinces of North and South Waziristan. Tribes here were known to exert unparalleled authority over their territory. US special forces teams worked with an energetic militia commander named Commander Aziz to combat al-Qaʿeda, Haqqani, and Taliban elements. The next bases, Salerno and Chapman, were to the north, in Khost province. The United States conducted extensive operations there, centered on Khost city. Skipping north over the Spin Ghar mountains to Nangarhar province, US forces were headquartered near Jalalabad. The government ruled the green city and the lush surrounding farmland. The last bases, Asadabad and Blessing, were north of Jalalabad in Kunar and near Nuristan, the location of Afghanistan's highest and most forested mountains.

When Lieutenant General Karl Eikenberry took over in May 2005, General John Abizaid at Central Command tasked him to create conditions for success in the east while the British and Canadians occupied the south. The de facto meaning of success for the Bush administration was the annihilation of al-Qaʿeda and defeat of the Taliban and other insurgent groups. Eikenberry's inclination was for judicious military operations combined with economic reconstruction and development of the Afghan army. Eikenberry later said that he had "tried to apply our limited resources in RC East [regional command east] with an eye on the long haul."[3]

At that time, the United States had two brigades in Afghanistan—one (that was understrength) at Kandahar airbase and one at forward operating base Salerno in Khost. After the Kandahar brigade departed in February 2006, there was only the single brigade in the east, spread out through Paktika, Paktiya, Khost, Nangarhar, and Kunar.[4] As the Taliban massed in the south, Eikenberry and other US generals focused on this eastern line, especially the high mountains of Kunar and Nuristan. For US soldiers and generals, the most significant battles of 2006 to 2009 would be in these two provinces.

Focus on Kunar and Nuristan intensified in June 2005 when insurgents ambushed a SEAL team in Kunar and shot down a CH-47 helicopter descending to help. Nineteen Americans died. Only one escaped. The incident happened near the Korengal Valley, where al-Qaʿeda and other terrorists were thought to hide and train. Later that year reports came in that Ayman al-Zawahiri, the al-Qaʿeda number two, was operating just a few miles from the Kunar border in Pakistan.[5]

Because of the possibility of al-Qaʿeda activity, Eikenberry saw Kunar and Nuristan as the specific place in the east where his scarce resources should be applied: "We had a limited number of forces and could not try to be strong everywhere. Based on the suspected presence of foreign fighters in the Kunar, Nuristan, and eastern Nangarhar Provinces, and the tenacity with which the enemy fought in these areas that extended across the Durand Line into Bajaur Agency in Pakistan, it seemed al-Qaʿeda or their affiliates had a presence in the area."[6]

Kunar and Nuristan are treacherously beautiful. Snow-capped mountains, expansive pine forests, rushing streams, and pastoral lowland farms paint a dramatic scene. Mountains cut by narrow river valleys define the terrain. It was common to see men praying on boulders beside a thrashing river. The two main rivers are the Kunar and the Pech. The Kunar runs north to south through a wide valley and into the plains north of Jalalabad, where it joins the Kabul River. The Pech runs west to east through a narrower valley, villages clinging to the sides of hillsides and the river itself, until it meets the Kunar River. Numerous mountainous tributary valleys intersect both valleys, their waters feeding the two rivers. Farmland was sparse, most concentrated along the two rivers and then in patches in the lusher lower portions of the mountain valleys. Nuristan was so high that it was mostly pasture. Scenery masked danger. The stunning mountains, narrow valleys, and forests offered insurgents cover, concealment, and high ground to kill from a distance.

Map 11 Kunar and Nuristan

Kunar's population numbered roughly 380,000, Nuristan's roughly 126,000.[7] Both populations were distributed in small villages throughout the various valleys. The largest concentrations of people in the two provinces, like the farmland, were along the Kunar and Pech Rivers. At their confluence was Asadabad, Kunar's provincial capital and biggest town. People also lived in the tributary valleys, farming on small plots, grazing goats and sheep, or logging timber. Villages were often ensconced on mountainsides, with homes laid of stones terraced above each other. Tribesmen cleared patches of farmland, similarly terraced for irrigation flow. The layered terraces of stone homes and farm plots created an architecture all their own that blended into the natural scenery.

The people of Kunar and Nuristan differed from the Pashtuns of southern Afghanistan. Scarce farmland made for less poppy and a poorer livelihood. Life in the mountains, with fewer roads and harsher winters, was tough. A mere 20 kilometers on dirt roads could take two hours. People were thin, sinewy, and fit. Old men could bound up mountains at breathtaking speed. Women could be seen working shrouded in the fields. Unlike in the south, farmers in Kunar and Nuristan were too poor to cloister women indoors. Clothing was plainer and less decorative. Because of cooler temperatures, men preferred beret-shaped woolen pakols to turbans, and vests or sweaters to loose, embroidered, Kandahari blouses.

Kunar's largest tribe was the Safi. Afghan lore has it that the Safi immigrated to Kunar 200 to 300 years ago and then allied themselves with Emir Abdur Rahman Khan at the turn of the century to supplant the Nuristani people in the Pech and Kunar Valleys. In 1979, they were one of the first tribes to revolt against the communist regime. Their territory spanned the Pech River Valley, much of the Kunar River Valley, and a few other tributary valleys. With most of the fertile lower land under their control, the Safis were better off than the tribes living in the mountain valleys.

Safi tribal structure was fractious. A few tribal leaders were particularly powerful but none could influence the whole tribe. Councils, or shuras, of tribal elders of a valley or district took on special weight as the only commonly accepted way to reach decisions or resolve disputes. Different Safi sub-tribes incessantly feuded with each other, especially in the Pech.[8] It was a known trait. A Safi district governor lamented before a tribal shura in Chapahara district, the ancient heart of Safi territory:

> I do not like the Safis being divided. I do not like us identifying ourselves as separate [sub-] tribes. I want just Safi. Safi is a big nation in three districts. We must stand together as one tribe. We must defend ourselves against the insurgents . . . Last night clans were fighting with

each other. How long has there been fighting? Stop killing each other. Who is the enemy?[9]

Pashtunwali notions of tribal honor ran thick among the tribe. For centuries, skirmishes, reciprocal hostage-taking, and honor killings had prevailed between clans, families, and cousins, usually carefully bounded so that violence could not get out of control. It was a more discreet form of violence than the insurgency.[10]

The Nuristani people were a separate ethnic group from the Pashtuns and spoke their own language, Nuristani, of which each valley had its own dialect. Pashtuns and Tajiks sometimes claimed Nuristanis to be descendants of Alexander the Great's army that moved through southern Kunar because of their lighter skin tone and occasional blue eyes.[11] Until 1896 and conquest at the hand of Abdur Rahman, the Nuristanis had followed their own religion, distinct from Islam. In 2006, although Nuristanis had converted to Islam and individuals filled important roles in the government, the Nuristani people fortified themselves in the 20,000-foot-high mountains of Nuristan and northern Kunar. They disliked the Safis in the richer valleys and were deeply skeptical of outsiders.

In terms of religion, Kunar and Nuristan were the only places in Afghanistan with significant Salafist strands of Islam.[12] Salafism calls for a strict practice of Islam on the basis of the Koran and sayings of the Prophet Mohammed (Hadith). It is an interpretation of Islam followed by al-Qaʻeda rather than the Taliban. In Kunar and Nuristan, Salafism translated into a more intense opposition to the United States among religious leaders than elsewhere. The opposition could be detected in four madrasas in Kunar affiliated with Arab benefactors that included jihad in their course of instruction.[13] Salafist connections allowed al-Qaʻeda inroads into Kunar and Nuristan. It should not be construed, however, that the populations of the two provinces naturally supported al-Qaʻeda. Plenty of people and religious leaders—probably the majority—were not Salafist at all. Hezb-Islami was influential in both provinces and not Salafist. Furthermore, many average people who were Salafists worked in the government and opposed terrorism.[14] The United States famously detained the chief Salafist religious leader, Rohullah, before 2005 and sent him to Guantanamo. He was released when it was discovered that he had no ties al-Qaʻeda. He went to live peacefully in Jalalabad.

Resistance to US presence was strong in Kunar and Nuristan. Unlike elsewhere in Afghanistan, the Taliban movement did not command the insurgency. The Quetta Shura had a few commanders, cadres, and a nominal provincial governor but they were mixed in with other insurgent groups. Hezb-Islami controlled certain valleys, which they fortified as veritable strongholds, conducting attacks as suited their interests. Pakistani Taliban also spread into Kunar, especially along the border where skirmishing was constant. The Pakistani Taliban had good

relations with al-Qa'eda. Finally, a great many insurgents were just locals determined to keep Americans and the government out of their valleys and villages.
There was no overall commander of the insurgent forces, although there were
influential names, such as revered Hezb-Islami commander Kashmir Khan,
Korengali leader Haji Matin, Pakistan Taliban commander Faqir Mohammed,
and al-Qa'eda commander Abu Ikhlas. Strategically, they were each their own.
Tactically, they cooperated.

A few al-Qa'eda cells worked with various insurgent groups throughout
Kunar and Nuristan. They moved around the provinces, taking refuge in the
mountains and providing local insurgents with specialized skills and equipment for their attacks. They set up training camps in parts of the remotest
mountain valleys. Abu Ikhlas was their commander. He was an Egyptian Arab
who had lived in Afghanistan and Pakistan for years, reputedly marrying into
the local tribes.[15] His focus was supporting the insurgency rather than plotting attacks against the United States, although the latter may have been a
long-term goal.

In February 2006, Major General Ben Freakley, commander of the 10th
Mountain Division, was in charge of the east as well as the south. Because of al-
Qa'eda's presence and Eikenberry's intent, he decided to outpost the mountain
valleys of Kunar and Nuristan. The offensive-minded Freakley had free reign to
create his campaign plan, with little higher supervision, which he embraced. He
wanted to hunt down the insurgents involved in the ambush of the SEALs and
go after terrorists out of Pakistan thought to be creating safe havens in those
valleys.[16] Freakley reckoned going into the mountains would exploit the US
military's strengths—the mobility of helicopters and the firepower of aircraft
and artillery—against the enemy's weaknesses.

Freakley had graduated from the School of Advanced Military Studies
(SAMS), the US Army's premier school for planning. Planning mattered to
him. In fact, like Mountain Thrust in the south, he had planned his main operation for the east before arriving in Afghanistan. It was named "Operation
Mountain Lion."

Freakley's subordinate, Colonel John "Mick" Nicholson, commander of the
7,000-strong 3rd Brigade, 10th Mountain Division ("Task Force Spartan"),
ran operations in the east. Headquartered at forward operating base Salerno in
Khost province, Nicholson had three battalions, plus supporting units, to cover
11 provinces of eastern Afghanistan. Nicholson was energetic and intellectual.
Ironically, one of his ancestors had been a British officer during the first Anglo-
Afghan War (1839–1842). He himself had been a paratrooper and Ranger for
ten years. He would become one of the US army's most experienced officers
in Afghanistan, rising to command all US and allied forces in Afghanistan in
2016–2018.

In preparation for the deployment, Nicholson studied tactics for fighting insurgents and assigned key texts to his officers.[17] He believed in protecting the population and living close to them, operating out of small bases with small patrols in order to better draw insurgents into a fight.[18]

Freakley and Nicholson labeled Mountain Lion a "clear, hold, build, and engage" operation. The notion was to go where Americans had not gone before in strength, establish combat outposts and partner with the Afghan military, stay there, and initiate reconstruction. Previous units had focused on raids and temporary clearing operations within their areas of operations, going out for a period of time and then returning to a central base.[19] Nicholson believed it essential to go into "ungoverned spaces" so that the government could influence the people living in them.[20] Through them, the Americans could deny insurgents sanctuary—a high bar in Afghanistan.

When briefed on the plan, Eikenberry, who tended to take the long view, was unimpressed. Kunar and Nuristan were familiar to him. He had flown to Nuristan and spoken with contractors working on projects at the provincial capital in the middle of the mountains. He had spent time in Asadabad and forged a friendship with the leading religious scholar, a white-bearded old mujahideen who liked fried potatoes and warned of the perils of American presence. Helping develop the population centers and respected leaders was a sensible way forward from Eikenberry's point of view. He saw a theme of his command as helping "the central government of Afghanistan to try to connect to their own people . . . helping to build the foundations of the state."[21] Presented with Freakley's plan, Eikenberry preferred a step-by-step clearance of the river valleys coordinated with provincial reconstruction team projects to getting drawn deep into the mountains. Freakley nevertheless liked his plan and stuck with it. Eikenberry did not stand in the way.

In April 2006, in consultation with Freakley, Nicholson planted two of his three battalions—1st Battalion, 32nd Infantry Regiment (700 men) and 1st Squadron, 35th Cavalry Regiment (300 men)—in Kunar and Nuristan.[22] Both dispersed into company- and platoon-size detachments along the rivers and into the remote Korengal Valley in Kunar, and the Waygul and Kamdesh Valleys in Nuristan.[23] In the high mountains, away from the rivers, posts were surrounded by peaks and could only be resupplied via helicopter. Operations commenced to destroy insurgents. Perhaps the toughest fighting the US army had experienced since Vietnam followed.

The United States sent some of its finest infantry to the Korengal, Waygul, and Kamdesh Valleys of Kunar and Nuristan. They operated in larger units—the 900-person traditional battalion of three "line" companies plus a heavy weapons company—than the special operations forces and were composed of younger men. In the words of embedded journalist Sebastian Junger, "They fought on foot and carried everything they needed on their backs. Theoretically, they could walk for days without resupply," as their predecessors had in the Second World War, Korea, and Vietnam.[24] They were the heart of the US Army. First in was 1st Battalion, 32nd Infantry Regiment of the 10th Mountain Division, under Lieutenant Colonel Chris Cavoli. His soldiers specialized in mountain warfare. Second Battalion, 503rd Infantry Regiment, under Lieutenant Colonel Bill Ostlund, would replace them in May 2007. Another highly trained unit, it had deployed to Kandahar a year earlier and plenty of its soldiers had also seen combat in Iraq.

Of the mountain valleys, Korengal would become the most infamous. Steep mountain ridges rise up to 8,000 feet on either side. The heights were forested with conifers, the lower reaches with oaks twisted by weather and foraging. A wide stream flowed at the bottom of the valley into the Pech River that runs perpendicular toward Asadabad. The people of the Korengal were the Korengalis. They dwelled in scattered villages up and down the valley. Hard life made men appear wizened with age, their piety signified by beards dyed red with henna. They followed Islam strictly and were said to be Salafists.[25] The Korengalis survived on chopping down timber and selling it in Asadabad to lumber companies and smugglers who ran it into Pakistan. Portions of ridgelines had been stripped bare. The Korengalis spoke their own dialect and numbered at least 10,000.[26] Anthropologists assessed them to be a branch of the Nuristanis or of the Pasha'i of Nangarhar.[27] Whatever the case, they had a long-running feud with the Safis. They claimed the Safis had pushed them out of richer lands near the Pech River and now oppressed them. Indeed, the Safis regularly taxed the Korengalis or cut off their roads and access to the outside world. The Safis had never dared invade the valley itself. The Russians had attempted an incursion once—and had been defeated.[28]

In April 2006, Nicholson staked an outpost 6 kilometers into the middle of the Korengal Valley. One of Cavoli's companies, reinforced to around 300 US soldiers, accompanied by an Afghan company of at best 100, manned it. The soldiers patrolled from that central outpost and a set of peripheral posts beyond. They sought to protect the population and root out the insurgents.

Heavy fighting erupted shortly after their arrival. The Korengalis wanted to be left alone. They epitomized anthropologist David Kilcullen's concept of the "accidental guerrilla"—people who fight for their own local way of life, not for a wider cause or at the behest of a terrorist movement, "fighting us because we are in his space, not because *he* wishes to invade ours."[29] The Korengalis fought because Americans had intruded upon their valley, not to overthrow the Afghan government nor to support al-Qa'eda.

Cavoli and Nicholson had purposefully built the central outpost on the mill of a timber smuggler named Haji Matin who was no friend of the government and

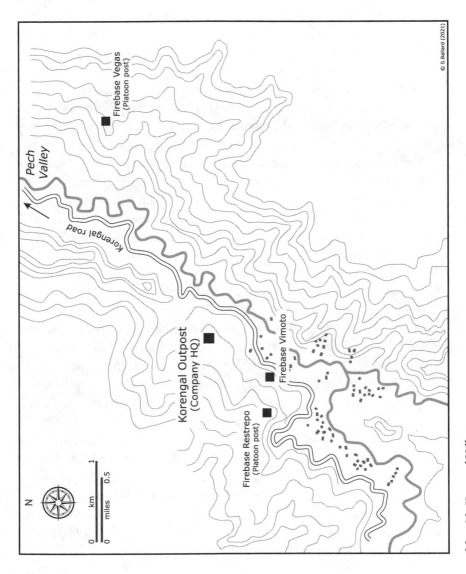

Map 12 Korengal Valley

the Americans. In an earlier foray into the valley, a marine battalion had called in an air strike—presumably inadvertently—on his home. Incensed, Matin vowed to kill every American in the valley. Matin was in his 30s and a man of action. He had ties to the Taliban from the timber trade during their regime and was in touch with their provincial leaders.[30] He was also an inveterate rival of Matiullah Khan, one of the more powerful Safi tribal leaders. Matin led attacks against the Americans for the next five years. During the course of the fighting, US soldiers dropped another bomb on Matin's house, then being used as an insurgent firing position, which only inflamed his spite.

Resistance to the idea of occupation in Kunar and Nuristan was not limited to the Korengalis, although their anger was particularly sharp. US bases in other Kunar and Nuristan Valleys also triggered a local reaction. A July 2007 survey by the US command showed that only 19 percent of people across Kunar and 24 percent across Nuristan thought that they would be worse off if the Americans left their provinces.[31]

Locals mobilized to defend the Korengal in Kilcullen's accidental guerrilla phenomenon. The commander of the Afghan army company in the Korengal said to the US company commander, "Everyone we see [in the villages] is old. All the young men have gone to fight."[32] Zahwar Khan, a leading Korengali elder, told the Kunar governor the same thing: "There are no brave men willing to do anything [with the government]. There are only insurgents."[33] US officers assessed 75 percent of tactical commanders in the Korengal to be locals.[34]

They were reinforced by outside fighters who came to join the battle. Most were Afghans from Jalalabad or elsewhere in Kunar. Others were Pashtuns from tribes in Pakistan.[35] A few were actual al-Qa'eda, specialists to help with certain weapon systems and instruct on sophisticated tactics. Abu Ikhlas was known to visit in order to improve coordination with his al-Qa'eda operations and facilitate the flow of money, fighters, arms, and supplies from Pakistan. Al-Qa'eda, the Pakistani Taliban, and the Quetta Shura sent money, arms, supplies, and ammunition to support the local fighters, usually from across the border via the numerous unguarded tracks on donkey or slipped through checkpoints via road on trucks. Haji Matin received much of the incoming money and supplies and distributed it to the cadres. Additional funds came from the timber trade, which the Americans and Afghan government only cut off periodically.[36] Matin presided over all insurgents operating in the valley.

Soon the Korengal was the hot spot of eastern Afghanistan. Insurgent attacks and ambushes were well organized, often combining heavy machine guns and mortars with ground maneuver. Insurgents fought in small teams of two to three men, armed with Kalashnikov assault rifles, RPGs, and a medium machine-gun. They preferred to fire at distances of at least 500 meters. Certain teams would have heavier weapons, such as a DShK heavy machine gun or a recoilless rifle.

Multiple teams took part in most attacks.[37] Sometimes 100 insurgents or more joined in firefights that lasted hours. Timber bunkers, dug-in fighting positions, and dirt-filled HESCO barriers fortified the US outposts. The insurgents shot at the outposts from hidden positions among trees on ridges above or across the valley itself, which was less than a kilometer wide, within range of RPGs, DShK heavy machine guns, and recoilless rifles.

Soldiers were most vulnerable on patrol. Hiking up and down the steep ridges was exhausting and open to ambush when bounding through uncovered and exposed patches of mountainside. In 2007, every patrol that traveled beyond a kilometer south of the main US outpost was attacked. One lieutenant was in 75 firefights during his first five months. Every few months, insurgents pulled off an ambush that killed several US soldiers.[38]

When an attack or ambush occurred, the US company commander would call in air or artillery fire as quickly as possible. Artillery rounds would career over the mountains from guns emplaced in bases in the Kunar and Pech River Valleys. Apache and, later on, Kiowa attack helicopters out of Jalalabad airfield flew regular routes through the Kunar and Pech Valleys, on call for battles in the Korengal. They could be vectored in to buzz up the valley and walk in rockets, missiles, and guns on insurgents. For a bigger blast, an F-15E, F-16, or F-18C/D fighter would drop sticks of GPS-guided 1,000- or 2,000-pound bombs from 1,000 feet above. Or an A-10 ground attack aircraft would lazily hang over the valley, circling again and again, dropping bomb after bomb, or strafing with its cannon that abruptly ripped through the sky, thundering for dozens of miles.

As much as the insurgents were outgunned, the terrain often shielded them. Trees concealed their positions, even with muzzle flashes, the crack of rifle-fire, and tracers to cue the defender. If not precisely targeted, bombs could fall in a gully or behind a slight rise that would shield the blast. And once insurgents heard an aircraft, they could quickly disassemble their heavy weapons and bolt up or down a mountain to safety. In larger, coordinated attacks, Matin's cadre commanders learned to set up enough firing positions across the mountainsides to hinder aircraft from targeting them all at once. It was not uncommon for aircraft to expend their bombs and missiles without breaking up an insurgent attack. The Korengal was less like the counterinsurgency of Iraq or southern Afghanistan than the front line of the Korean War.

There were never enough US soldiers to clear and hold the valley. The Americans could not expand into villages in its upper reaches. The steep terrain complicated freeing just the villages around the outposts from attack. As months passed, Korengali ardor endured. Zahwar Khan, the Korengali elder, warned the Kunar governor, "Still the Americans and Afghan army in Korengal are trying to bring security. Allah does not want security."[39] The Afghan army company's first sergeant was more blunt in his advice to US soldiers: "In Korengal, everyone is enemy. There are no friends."[40]

In 2007 and 2008, the battalions in Kunar and Nuristan were on extended 15-month deployments, which made the fighting all the more grueling. The standard US army deployment was 12 months. First Battalion, 32nd Infantry Regiment, the first battalion posted to Kunar, took 120 casualties in firefights during its deployment from January 2006 to May 2007, more than a tenth its strength. Second Battalion, 503rd Infantry Regiment, the second battalion posted to Kunar, took more—169 casualties.

Journalist Sebastian Junger and photojournalist Tim Hetherington depict US soldiers fighting in the Korengal in their documentary film, *Restrepo*, and follow-up book *War*. They capture the hardships the soldiers endured—posts subject daily to sniper and machine-gun fire, frequent heavier attack with RPGs and DShKs, devastating ambushes on platoons outside the wire. "They were staggering under their loads and still strung along the road when the first burst came in. That was followed by a massive barrage from virtually every enemy position in the southern valley, and O'Byrne watched the rock wall he was hiding behind start to disintegrate from the impacts. . . . 'This is the day I'm going to die,' he thought."[41] Captain Dan Kearney attests, "I was blown away by the insurgents' ability to continue fighting despite everything America had to throw at them. From that point on I knew it was—number one—a different enemy than I fought in Iraq and that—number two—the terrain offered some kind of advantage that I'd never seen or read or heard about in my entire life."[42]

The Korengal and the other mountain valleys became the main effort of the whole US war. In January 2007, 4th Brigade, 82nd Airborne Division ("Task Force Fury"), under Colonel Marty Schweitzer, was assigned to the east. The brigade went to Khost to cover the southeastern provinces. Nicholson and his brigade displaced to Jalalabad where he could focus on the fighting in Kunar and Nuristan. A new brigade—the 173rd Airborne Brigade—would replace them in May.[43] The majority of attacks on US forces throughout Afghanistan were now in Kunar.[44] Pech had the most attacks out of any district in the entire country. Ostlund's 2nd Battalion, 503rd Infantry Regiment, in the course of its 15-month deployment would expend 36,225 mortar or artillery rounds and 3,789 bombs and missiles. The sum represented the majority of aircraft and artillery ordnance expenditure for all Afghanistan.[45]

A sense pervaded the various generals, colonels, battalion, and PRT commanders that they were being innovative. There was something to this. Cavoli and then Ostlund embraced the principle that Nicholson had seized upon to set up in an area and stay, not simply come and go. Their soldiers lived in austere conditions on small posts, away from large comfortable air bases. For Cavoli and Ostlund, the intensity of fighting was expected given their battalions were in the middle of an enemy sanctuary. They took pride in it. "I saw that you had a choice between sitting on FOBs (forward operating bases) and making forays forward, sorties out into the wilds, and having almost zero effect or planting yourself out there among the population," Cavoli explained, "in which case the enemy was going to come after you with everything he had. . . . We had a tough fight and we did extremely well in it. That is how I like to think about it."[46]

While heavy fighting went on in the mountains, stability increased in the river valleys. As part of the effort to stabilize Kunar, Nicholson stressed governance and economic development. Kunar's provincial reconstruction team (PRT)— made up of two civil affairs units, a State Department political officer, a USAID development officer, and a US Navy commander and staff—implemented a set of ambitious projects.[47] The idea was to enable better governance, improve people's lives, bring them closer to the government, and thus reduce violence.

The provincial reconstruction team's effort centered on road construction in the major river valleys. In 2006, all Kunar's roads were dirt or gravel. The 100 kilometers from Kunar's provincial capital of Asadabad to Jalalabad, the regional center of commerce, was at least six hours on a dirt road. The 31 curving dirt kilometers from Asadabad to Nangalam, the district center at the heart of the Pech Valley, went only a little quicker. The idea of Lieutenant Colonel Cavoli and the provincial reconstruction team commander, Commander "Doc" Scholl, was to pave the roads in order to ease government movement, help villagers get to markets and services, and hopefully confound insurgent efforts to lay improvised explosive devices. The plan fit Eikenberry's overall reconstruction strategy. Road construction was something Eikenberry prioritized for his limited reconstruction funds. Like Cavoli and Scholl, Eikenberry assessed that roads could help the military campaign by improving access and allowing the Afghan government to expand its own reach and ease trade and commerce. He coined the phrase "Where the road ends, the Taliban begin."[48]

The roads would be built in the heart of Safi territory. The Safi tribe distrusted Americans and viewed their presence as unjust occupation. Armed tribesmen got into firefights with US forces up and down the Pech. A Safi tribal leader living in the mountainous Shuryak tributary valley off the Pech River warned the provincial reconstruction team, "If you place a base in the valley, tribes and groups will gather. They will attack the base. The tribal shura will not be able to stop them."[49] When it came to the government, however, the Safis were less intransigent than the Korengalis and Nuristanis. Safis were district governors, police chiefs, and policemen. Insurgent attacks on the police, who also tended to be local Safis, bore the hallmarks of tribal warfare—limited, meant to signal honor as much as enact destruction. Safi "insurgents" from one village attacked the Safi police post of another Safi village. The high point was when the opposing commanders slurred each other's wives and mothers over handheld radios. Few police were ever killed or injured.[50] As long as it did not intrude from the provincial capital, district centers, and main roads onto village life, the Safis were willing to deal with the government as part of their ecosystem.

The Jalalabad to Asadabad road through the Kunar River Valley was the first road to be paved. It was completed in November 2006. USAID funded the road but the provincial reconstruction team ended up managing its execution— resolving disputes over land and labor, conducting quality control, and convening shuras to raise community support. The road went a long way toward improving governance by opening an avenue for the delivery of goods and services. Provincial line directors, such as the director of education, director of irrigation, and director of agriculture, could now send workers to rural districts to interact with local communities and observe projects. As the road neared completion, the national solidarity program, Afghanistan's main organization for rural development, directed project funding into Asadabad. No national solidarity program projects had ever before been committed to Asadabad. From then until the end of 2007, the town received about $1 million of $2.5 million in funding for Kunar. Violence decreased as the road was paved. Improvised explosive device incidents fell from a high of 17 in 2006 to seven in 2007 following the completion of the road.

The next road was built in the Pech River Valley, funded entirely by the provincial reconstruction team.[51] It cost $7.5 million to pave 31 kilometers. The Pech River Valley cut through three districts—Watapur, Pech, and Chapa Dara. Roughly 100,000 people lived in numerous small villages (Korengal is a tributary valley within Pech district). As a means of undercutting the insurgency, Lieutenant Colonel Cavoli advocated paving the dirt road through the valley. He had posted soldiers along the valley in order to protect the people and keep the road open. From his perspective, paving the road would increase trade and economic activity, providing the people with an alternative to violence. At the same time, pavement would obstruct laying of improvised explosive devices.[52] Paving started in earnest in early 2007, under the guidance of the provincial reconstruction team, now led by Commander Larry LeGree.

LeGree's provincial reconstruction team completed the road in March 2008. Americans and Afghans alike said that the scale of violence on the valley floor decreased. As hoped, improvised explosive device incidents fell off, going from a high of 21 in the first six months of 2006 to 2 during the first six months of 2008. Insurgents labored to dig a hole through the pavement to lay a device, especially considering that the necessary tools are hard to find in rural Afghanistan. Locals were happy that they could get to bazaars and the hospital in the provincial capital quicker. What had been a four- to six-hour drive dropped to an hour.[53] Like the road from Jalalabad to Asadabad, the Pech road brought goods and services.

The national solidarity program initiated projects in the Pech Valley. Out of $2.5 million total for Kunar, roughly $1 million was committed to projects in Pech district.[54]

The Pech and Kunar roads would be open to traffic through the next 12 years. The provincial reconstruction team also executed a variety of school, higher education, and bridge projects. LeGree found a competent partner in Governor Faizullah Wahidi, the former head of a non-governmental organization (NGO) from Jalalabad with a strict sense of how to conduct development. He steered away from corruption and was one of Afghanistan's finest governors. He would govern until 2013. The progress on river valley floors had no effect on the battles of attrition in the higher mountains. It was almost as if two separate wars were being fought. Other roads would be constructed up into the tributary mountain valleys; a few were successes, a few were abject failures. A bold venture to pave the dirt road into the Korengal advanced a few kilometers from the Pech River and no further. The hopes of a handful of Korengalis who wanted a road for the economic benefits were dashed by Haji Matin and others who opposed it as an avenue for US and government power projection. "You have no hope for the road," Matin decreed, "Do not pretend to start it. It will not start."[55]

The battles in the Korengal and other mountain valleys of Kunar and Nuristan dragged on. At the end of their tours in early 2007, Nicholson and Freakley assessed that the strategy was succeeding. They had nearly doubled the number of outposts in the east from 19 to 35, primarily in Kunar and Nuristan. They insisted that the outposts in the Korengal and other mountain valleys were bringing insurgents to battle, preventing them from threatening other areas, and disrupting infiltration lines from Pakistan.[56]

With time, the casualties and sacrifice became apparent to Nicholson's and Freakley's successors—Colonel Chip Preysler (commander of the 173rd Airborne Brigade) and Major General David Rodriguez (commander of the 82nd Airborne Division). Preysler, who was deployed from May 2007 to July 2008, believed the decision to outpost the mountain valleys had been a mistake that tied down too many forces in unwinnable battles. Hesitant to get drawn in deeper, he sought to hold onto the positions under his control and not extend his men any further. His thought was to disrupt insurgent activities rather than deny sanctuary comprehensively. Forces were too few to do anything more.[57] Rodriguez gradually leaned toward closing the mountain posts but never acted. Preysler and Rodriguez were reluctant to actually withdraw out of concern that the Taliban and other insurgents would pursue them into the Pech River Valley and down to Asadabad. So the battles dragged on.

Journalist after journalist traveled to Kunar and wrote articles, photographed soldiers, and filmed combat. The casualties and horrific battles in those dangerous valleys helped sap US domestic support for the war. The Korengal became known as the "Valley of Death." Combat writer Bing West observed, "The writing in the *New York Times* and other national papers was so vivid that the Korengal became a symbol of the war. . . . The generals were oblivious that the Korengal illustrated the war's strategic drift."[58]

For insurgents too, the battles in Kunar and Nuristan acquired their own mythology. Zahwar Khan, the Korengali elder, embellished, "Young boys and old men joined the fight; even women at times would pick up weapons to attack the Americans."[59] If a bit of an exaggeration, there was more than a grain of truth to his words. US soldiers found children's drawings of insurgents fighting American soldiers in village homes.[60] The Taliban published their own poetry of Kunar and Nuristan. One, entitled "Rebels," by Maneer Ahmed Nafeez, painted a picture of locals fighting a technologically superior yet outwitted enemy:

> Above, with the high Kunar
> Under, on the ground also, is the fountain of blood . . .
> Above, jets and helicopters
> Below the drunken foreign army walks
> Our sleep, our calm has gone
> The happiness of my tribe has gone . . .
> In Bar Kalay, it was quiet
> They martyred a few young men.[61]

The roots of the insurgents as local come across clearly in the poem, with its references to tribe and small villages.

Another poem was by Samiullah Tarun, a 20-something-year-old poet from Kunar who had studied at Nangarhar University and then decided to fight the Americans in Kunar.[62] His poem is entitled, "I touch my forehead in Islamic affection for the Talib":

> Now I have knocked my rival down, now do not seek peace
> Now I take vengeance, I go on the path of war . . .
> Now our country is not the foreigners' caravan
> Now, but we cannot walk in our own free country . . .
> With the kalima tied on my head, I go to the battlefield
> I touch my forehead in affection for the Talib . . .
> Now, the mosque and the church will clash
> Now, then in rights and in null God will come.[63]

The two poems highlight different reasons that Afghans fought. The local reasons for fighting given by Nafeez contrast with the role of Islam and resistance to occupation given by Tarun. If tribe and independence created local accidental guerrillas, notions of resistance against an infidel occupier may have attracted others, both locals and outsiders.

Elsewhere in the east, the situation was difficult but in a few places improving. In Nangarhar, flat farmland and heavy government presence around Jalalabad inhibited insurgent movement outside the province's mountainous southern border. Jalalabad city itself had a large, active, and organized police, with a quick reaction force and the country's first provincial coordination center—to coordinate police, army, and NDS intelligence operations. Karzai had transferred Gul Agha Sherzai from Kandahar to be governor in 2005. Sherzai proved more adept at balancing the great eastern powerbrokers—Haji Zahir of the Ahmedzai (nephew of the late Abdul Haq), Hazrat Ali of the Pasha'i, Haji Zaman of the Khogiyani, the distinguished khans of the Mohmand, and the contentious tribal leaders of the Shinwari—than their counterparts in Kandahar where his personal interests had been at stake. Sherzai tightly controlled the highway going to Pakistan and Kabul. He reaped profits from the customs post at Torkham Gate on the Khyber Pass, redistributed them among tribal leaders, and bought off possible rivals.

The eastern powerbrokers tended to oppose the Taliban, who as in Kunar and Nuristan were one of several insurgent factions. Hazrat Ali and Haji Zahir bore long-standing grudges against the Taliban while the Mohmands held sway over their tribal territory. "*Qawmi joraysht*—tribal structure—helps create stability," explained Mohammed Durrani, a Mohmand leader. "It is what stabilized places without US presence in 2009–2011. It is more important than US forces or the government."[64] The numerous Hezb Islami leaders of the province also flirted with the government.

The calm security environment permitted widespread development projects. "There was no problem going to the districts. All of them . . . anyone could go back and forth. Bati Kot, Ghani Khel. In 2009, projects were going on everywhere," said provincial council member Abdul Basir Ghulab.[65] Six hundred kilometers of road were paved from 2008 to 2010, including the reconstruction of the main highway from Kabul to Pakistan through Torkham Gate and the Khyber Pass. Not only the provincial reconstruction team but the United Nations, non-government organizations, and Afghan government ministries worked freely in Jalalabad and the surrounding districts. With reconstruction came employment and ease of access of goods to market.

Sherzai transformed himself into a champion of reconstruction, civil liberties, and women's rights, acquiring the nickname "the Bulldozer." He made a point of inviting women to high-profile meetings, convening women's conferences in which participants could be unveiled, and insisting that women vote in elections in person instead of via a male relative. Love of music, dancing, and freedoms had always accompanied Sherzai's excesses and he had always been wise to how to please his American friends.[66]

Sherzai even suppressed poppy cultivation for a few years. Nangarhar had been a top poppy producer in the 1990s. Poppy was grown in the foothills of the Spin Ghar mountains along the province's southern edge. Sherzai paid tribal elders money and development assistance to tell their people to forego poppy while threatening eradication and arrests upon those who continued. Sherzai mounted security operations into the hinterlands to put muscle behind his threats. US special operations activities and the presence of the forces of Nicholson and his successors increased credibility, even though their role was purely counterterrorist and counterinsurgent. Sherzai threatened Shinwari villages in southern Nangarhar: "You should not grow poppy! I don't have the power to protect you and your land from US forces."[67] Ismatullah Shinwari, a Shinwari leader recalled, "There was no poppy. The government was too strong. The government came and eradicated. . . . Sherzai was very strong."[68] Shinwari tribal leaders agreed to give up poppy as long as US forces were not permanently posted in their region.

Luck also favored Sherzai. The price of wheat, grains, and other licit crops—which were easy to grow and get to market in Jalalabad and thence to Kabul, Peshawar, and Islamabad—was high due to insecurity in Pakistan while the price of poppy was low due to the massive increase in cultivation in southern Afghanistan. Hectares under cultivation in Nangarhar fell from roughly 20,000 in 2007 to under 5,000 between 2008 and 2013. Farmers in the fertile and accessible cropland around Jalalabad diversified into a variety of profitable crops. Farmers in the foothill regions, however, eventually returned to poppy in search of a source of income as wheat prices inevitably fell. Sherzai had nevertheless overseen a reduction of remarkable duration and scale.[69]

Farther south, the small province of Khost was also progressing. Khost was roughly the size of Rhode Island, with around 500,000 people. Forested mountains ringed agricultural lowland and Khost city, the provincial capital. In 2005 and early 2006, insurgent violence in Khost was relatively light but attacks did occur, improvised explosive devices in particular. Insurgent activity increased in 2006 and spiked in February 2007 with large numbers of improvised explosive devices and suicide car bombs going off. Unlike Helmand, Kunar, or Nuristan, however, violence escalated no further for the next couple of years.

The Haqqani network was the primary insurgent threat. Jalaluddin Haqqani had been born in neighboring Paktiya and his tribe, the Zadran, were powerful in both Paktiya and Khost. Haqqani's headquarters in Miram Shah was less than a 30-minute drive across Khost's long border with Pakistan. Jalaluddin and his son Sirajuddin exploited their ties to recruit, infiltrate, and conduct operations in Paktiya and Khost. "Haqqani had good influence ... because of organization, good relations with tribal leaders ... and they gave money to the tribal leaders," said a Zadran religious leader.[70]

Colonel Marty Schweitzer (commander of 4th Brigade, 82nd Airborne Division) and the Khost provincial reconstruction team, enjoying the guidance of State Department diplomat Kael Weston, played an active and innovative role. They oil-spotted their effort out from the large US base (FOB Salerno) near the provincial capital to multiple smaller district centers. Fortified, these district centers housed 20 to 30 soldiers, the district governor, 50 to 100 police, and sometimes an Afghan army detachment. The provincial reconstruction team projects executed $22 million for 50 schools, 30 small dams, and 50 kilometers of road.[71] A high-profile project initiated in 2003 paved the road over the mountain pass to Gardez and thence Kabul. The paving was cursed with problems and stumbled along for ten years before completion but trade and travel to and from the capital gradually improved. Weston, who had years of experience in Iraq, writes that in Khost he "saw the U.S. government and the U.S. military getting things done. Building things. Making friends. Developing ties. That 'better face' that contrasted so much with the stereotypical 'ugly American' image. And the PRT was full of good soldiers and leaders, some with multiple tours."[72]

Just as important in checking violence were Khost's geography, history, and people. The conditions were better than those in Kunar and Nuristan. Khost's small size eased protection of the population without heavy fighting or casualties. Khost city had long been known as a government bastion and had effectively defended itself against the mujahideen until 1991. It boasted an active media, a university with 5,000 students, poetry and law societies, and a relatively high literacy rate (40 percent of the male population). Girls' education was more successful than in other provinces. Weston's Afghan advisor reported, "Trend is up. ... In previous times, parents would only allow their younger girls to go to primary school or a mosque-conducted village class. Parents used to remove them from class before the age of ten, but that concept is vanishing. Many parents hope to see their daughters" become "doctors ..., lawyers," or qualified teachers ... in close-by districts, including downtown Khost, the ratio between girls and boys is close to 50/50."[73]

Governor Arsala Jamal, a former NGO worker who had lived in Canada, was experienced, intelligent, active, and trusted by both the people and US forces.[74] He visited the villages, fostered development programs with US assistance, and tried to sensitize Americans to the dangers of civilian casualties. One American civilian at the provincial reconstruction team observed, "Governor Jamal has the capabilities of a senior executive in the Defense Department." Jamal survived repeated Haqqani assassination attempts, including one Toyota pickup car bomb that blew up next to his convoy.

More so than in Nangarhar, strong tribes in the countryside—the Mangal, Tanai, and Zadran—were a bulwark against Haqqani influence. Haqqani could by no mean order the tribes, even the Zadran, around. The tribes of Khost, as well as neighboring Paktika and Paktiya, governed themselves and closely followed traditional Pashtun codes of rule by jirga. A Zadran religious leader stated, "The tribe controls all areas of Zadran, not the government. The government is too weak."[75] The tribes fielded militia, known as arbakai, to defend themselves. The United States backed an assortment of these militia to guard the border against Haqqani intrusion, which they did rigorously. A government official complimented, "The arbakai on the border are the best of all" the military forces in the province.[76]

For the next decade Khost would experience ups and downs—civilian casualties in US operations and the 2009 suicide bombing of Forward Operating Base Chapman in Khost city stand out—but security would overall hold. With some hyperbole, the Khost Provincial Council chairman claimed in 2007, "The Taliban have lost; they have been unable to separate the people from the government."[77] Other than Badakhshan in Afghanistan's far northeast, Khost was the safest province on the Pakistan border. Jamal's successors could travel on road to every district center. Eventually the province would have nearly 300 schools and judges across 12 districts.

Khost was hailed as a counterinsurgency success story. Secretary of Defense Robert Gates called it "a model of a concerted counterinsurgency effort."[78] Rodriguez and other US leaders would look at how to export this "Khost model" to other parts of Afghanistan. It never really worked, partly because terrain, tribe, and culture made Khost unique, partly because US commanders in Kunar and Nuristan were committed to their own course.

Korengal was only one of the remote mountain valleys in Kunar and Nuristan where Americans were enduring a battle of attrition. A northerly tributary to the Pech River runs down Nuristan's Waygul Valley, almost opposite the Korengal. American soldiers were posted into the uppermost reaches of that valley. Like the Korengalis, the Nuristani people of the Waygul cared little for American interlopers. And they probably received even more assistance from al-Qaʻeda. The Americans were overextended and tactically vulnerable. The outposts were so deep in the mountains that prompt artillery or air support was unavailable, granting insurgents a temporary advantage in the opening minutes of an attack. In the high mountains, those insurgents could almost always overlook US outposts and see what was going on. The forests afforded cover to stage large numbers of fighters and then sneak up close to the US perimeter or a patrol. Soldiers in the Korengal had escaped these vulnerabilities through their proximity to US artillery in the Pech River Valley and Asadabad and the careful siting of multiple mutually supporting posts by Lieutenant Colonel Cavoli and then Lieutenant Colonel Ostlund.

Slowly, insurgents in the Waygul pushed the Americans back. First, in August 2007, the insurgents nearly overran the "Ranchhouse," the outermost platoon position at 7,000 feet in the northern Waygul Valley. Soldiers had to call in B-52 strikes on their own positions to drive off the attackers, like some bad Arc Light dream from Vietnam. Eleven of the 25 American defenders were killed; all but five of the remaining were wounded. Ranchhouse was abandoned. It was only the beginning. The soldiers fell back to Bella, the outpost to the south, still high in the mountains. In November, insurgents ambushed a 28-man patrol returning from a shura. The mountains were too high and steep for helicopters and aircraft to arrive quickly or to accurately hit the insurgents. Fourteen men were killed. Everyone else was wounded. Ostlund held out at Bella for another five months but in spring 2008 decided the situation was untenable. In July, he pulled his men southward to the Waygul district center at Wanat.

Then on July 13, 2008, came the most famous firefight of the Afghan War. Roughly 200 well-trained insurgents—many of whom were local Nuristanis— attacked the 49 American and 24 Afghan soldiers at the new outpost at Wanat. The attackers loosed volleys of RPGs and barrages of DShK heavy machine gun fire into the main outpost. "Things just started exploding inside our fighting positions," described Sergeant Ryan Pitts, the post's forward observer. "Multiple RPGs were shot at us, along with hand grenades. . . . I was shell-shocked for a couple of seconds and I had been hit immediately."[79] Creeping up against the perimeter, attackers blew into one of the observation posts. Private First Class Stenoski, who manned the mortars, recalled:

> We were surrounded. They were popping up behind HESCOs and shooting RPGs at us. Sergeant Phillips and I hung four 120 millimeter rounds. It was all we could get off before an RPG round came in from the south side and hit inside our mortar pit, so we stopped firing the 120. . . . There were trees behind the HESCOs and most of them were trying to climb the trees to shoot over the HESCOs. One guy actually side-stepped and shot an RPG through the crack of the HESCO in the corner. It went right between the middle of Sergeant Phillips and me and right over the 120 tube. It hit the bazaar and missed us.[80]

Insurgents benefited from the high ground before the Americans could call in enough air strikes and artillery to gain the advantage. Sergeant Brian Hissong recounted the tense moments as the fighting turned:

1st platoon returned with a massive amount of fire from their machine guns. It seemed like they drove the enemy out . . . but the OP [observation post] was still taking fire. The CO [commanding officer] had already told the Apaches to level several enemy occupied buildings in the area and they were doing a pretty good job with that, but it still seemed like I was hearing about a new casualty at the OP every few minutes.[81]

Four hours had passed by the time the insurgents finally retreated. Nine Americans were killed. Twenty-seven more plus five Afghan soldiers were wounded.[82]

The battle attracted international news coverage. Two days later, Americans withdrew from the Waygul entirely. The battle of Wanat occurred at the end of Colonel Preysler's tour. He would resign his commission because of it, guilt-stricken at the sacrifice for a strategy he did not believe in.

Two years after the start of Operation Mountain Lion, the battles of the Korengal, the Waygul, and other mountain valleys of Kunar and Nuristan were going in the wrong direction. Disrupting sanctuaries had turned into endless attrition. Successes on the river valley floors could not compensate for the costs of the war in the mountains.

The wisdom of the campaign is questionable. Successive US generals and their subordinates devoted their attention to it. By 2008, the United States was deploying more than 20,000 troops to eastern Afghanistan. Once in, it was hard to get out. Lives had been sacrificed. The insurgents might claim victory and possibly expand into the river valleys. Withdrawal admitted defeat. That is a hard thing for an officer to swallow. The decisions to go to Kunar and Nuristan and then stick it out for round after round distracted from deadlier threats. Instead of removing insurgent sanctuaries or disrupting attacks elsewhere, the campaign wasted valuable US resources and thereby helped the Taliban advance in far more important parts of the country. As US commanders battled it out in the mountains, the Taliban were encircling Kandahar City and closing on Kabul.

For the American soldier, the battles became legend. A generation of the US Army witnessed the war in the eastern mountains, either as commanders overseeing it or soldiers on the ground in the middle of it. The soldiers were pitted against the toughest terrain and a hard enemy. The conventional nature of the firefights and ambushes lent a real war reality only matched in the post-2001 wars by the street battles of Fallujah and Baghdad. For the American people, the battles also left an impression. The foremost image of war in Afghanistan was of grunts toiling up and down the mountains through harrowing firefights. The well-publicized war in the mountains stretched American patience with the war, belying the old sense of a good war going well.

10

Taliban Advances

The intensity of the 2006 fighting forced President Bush and his team to accept that the Taliban had upset progress in Afghanistan. Bush steadily increased forces over the next two years. For all the distraction of Iraq, Bush cared deeply about Afghanistan. He had never foreseen leaving the country in a state of violence and did not plan to do so now. He spoke every other week with Karzai, believing a personal relationship the best way to give advice. He avoided lecturing, even when Karzai publicly criticized the United States. In 2001 and 2002, a vague unstated assumption for Bush and his team had been that once al-Qaʻeda and the Taliban were completely eliminated and democracy had its feet under it that US troops could, at least theoretically, leave. Bush now came to the opinion that the United States would have to stay in Afghanistan as long as it had been in Korea. Unlike Rumsfeld, Bush felt obligated to help Afghanistan indefinitely.[1]

Bush relieved Rumsfeld at the end of 2006, largely over the running of the Iraq War. Robert Gates, a highly respected former CIA director, became the new Secretary of Defense. On his first trip to Afghanistan in January 2007, Gates recognized things were going sideways, an impression that deepened over the following months: "It became clear to me that our efforts in Afghanistan . . . were being significantly hampered not only by muddled and overly ambitious objectives but also by confusion in the military command structure, confusion in economic and civilian efforts, and confusion over how the war was actually going."[2]

While in Afghanistan, Gates discussed Eikenberry's request for an additional 3,500 troops that had been sitting at Central Command.[3] Gates extended the single brigade under Colonel John Nicholson then in Afghanistan. Shortly thereafter Bush and Gates decided to send a new additional brigade (Colonel Marty Schweitzer's brigade that served in Khost and Loya Paktiya) so that there would be two brigades at all times. The total number of US troops in the country increased from 20,000 at the end of 2006 to 25,000 at the end of 2007. Numbers bumped up again to 32,000 by the middle of 2008 when the 24th

Marine Expeditionary Unit temporarily deployed. Of these reinforcements, the majority went to the east and around Kabul and Bagram. Because of the surge of forces to Iraq, more could not be spared.[4]

Shocked by the intensity of the fighting, the Canadian and British governments dispatched their own reinforcements. Midway through 2007, 2,500 Canadians (up from 2,200) were in Kandahar, including a squadron of Leopard main battle tanks. British numbers in the south rose to nearly 6,000, almost double their May 2006 contingent. The reinforcements had a minor effect and Britain, Canada, the Netherlands, and Australia bid in yet more troops. By the end of 2008, 8,100 British, 2,750 Canadians, 1,700 Dutch, and 1,000 Australians were in the south, 6,200 more than the initial deployment of 7,350.

Lieutenant General Karl Eikenberry's tour as commander of US forces in Afghanistan ended in February 2007. He had grasped Afghanistan better than almost any other American. He had forecast the 2006 Taliban offensive and cautioned his commanders against unneeded operations. Too often his wisdom had been brushed aside, both by Washington and his subordinates. By his departure, Eikenberry was one of the very few Americans to see that the war was at an impasse. The setbacks in the south and interminable battles in the east convinced him the military could not solve Afghanistan.

A few months before his departure, Eikenberry drafted a memorandum to General Abizaid (commander of Central Command) and Secretary Rumsfeld that went all the way to President Bush. Eikenberry wrote that corruption, Pakistan, and growing Afghan distaste for US presence were hindering progress. He warned of the dangers of committing additional forces and sketched out an option of building up the Afghan army and police to handle the insurgency while drawing down US forces over time.[5] The memorandum bounced off thinking at the top. President Bush was determined to stick it out. Doubt would continue to weigh on Eikenberry. His memorandum is an early example of a new development in American thinking on Afghanistan: a recognition that the United States could not stabilize the country and therefore should narrow its efforts to enabling the Afghan government to carry on the war on its own. Over time, Eikenberry's line of thinking would gather momentum.

With Eikenberry's departure, General Dan McNeill returned to Afghanistan to succeed General David Richards as commander of the International Security Assistance Force (ISAF) and Eikenberry as the senior US general.[6] Although he first focused on the south and occasionally sent forces there for temporary operations, McNeill left the east the main effort.

Since 2001, the United States, Britain, and other allied countries had been targeting al-Qa'eda and Taliban leaders. For the United States, the CIA and special operations forces conducted this work. During the first years of the war, they concentrated on al-Qaʻeda but also hit Taliban and other targets as appropriate. Units experimented with different techniques and operations proceeded at a relatively low tempo.

Meanwhile, Lieutenant General Stanley McChrystal was pioneering a new method of counterterrorist operations in Iraq. McChrystal was in charge of counterterrorist special operations in both Iraq and Afghanistan. He was headquartered in Iraq at the time. There, he brought surveillance, human and signals intelligence collection, analysis, and the different special operations units into a single network, which allowed him to find and strike targets rapidly. A specific process matured: gathering intelligence on a target; using surveillance assets such as drones to locate the target; striking the target with a raid or missile from a drone or an aircraft; collecting new evidence, either from interrogation of a detainee or exploitation of materials such as computers left on site; analyzing that evidence; and then starting the process over again. McChrystal demanded a high operational tempo. He aimed to disrupt terrorist and insurgent networks and gather evidence to go after high level leaders through conducting as many strikes as possible. Single units often executed several raids per night.

McChrystal was extraordinarily effective. His operations disrupted al-Qaʻeda in Iraq and killed their leader, Abu Musab al-Zarqawi. Success and his innovative drive would make McChrystal one of the most respected generals in the US Armed Forces, the quintessential special operator.

In 2006, McChrystal directed his forces in Afghanistan to apportion greater effort to striking Taliban. McNeill thought that counterterrorist strikes could severely damage them. He sought to capture or kill the Taliban's "hardline leaders" in order to disrupt their organization.[7] Echoing his inclination toward counterterrorism back in 2002, McNeill wanted to "deliberately go after the command and control, to target those people who had the ability to go into a village and incite fence sitters to take up a Kalashnikov to attack the internationals." He recalled, "So, I put a lot of effort into going after the value targets, high, medium, or whatever we could get our hooks in."[8] The idea was that leadership might only be removed temporarily but in the meantime the organization would operate less effectively. As McNeill's spokesperson mentioned, "If you take out the head, often the body doesn't know what to do."[9]

McChrystal implemented his Iraq methods in Afghanistan. With fewer resources, tempo was lower than in Iraq but several missions per night were common. Southern Afghanistan was a focal point. The US special operations forces were assisted in the effort in the south by British special operations forces. In 2007 and 2008, hundreds of targets were hit and several Taliban commanders were captured or killed. Dadullah Lang was the most important. Besides him, special operations forces killed several district governors and Mullah Akhtar Mohammad Osmani (the same who had talked with Robert Grenier in 2001).[10]

McNeill hoped Dadullah's death would cripple Taliban command and control.[11] That never happened. Other experienced leaders, such as Mullah Baradar, stepped in and carried on. Capturing and killing Taliban leaders thus inflicted marginal damage on the movement writ large. No direct correlation exists between Taliban leadership losses (including captures) and the number of insurgent attacks. In the year following the deaths of both Osmani and Dadullah, the number of overall attacks in the south actually increased.[12]

From 2006 onward, the main Taliban theater was southern Afghanistan. Following Dadullah's death in May 2007, Taliban deputy leader Mullah Baradar ordered cadres to push closer to the provincial capitals, including Kandahar and Kabul.[13] He announced to the movement, "We will seek the besieging of the cities and the provincial centers and will launch raids against them," and "We will implement this plan with Allah's permission in a number of southern, eastern and central provinces."[14]

At the same time, Baradar adjusted Taliban tactics. The prior year had been a bloody one. Baradar wished to avoid repeating the experience.[15] Consequently, Taliban were to continue attacking police posts, British platoon houses, and Canadian patrols but reserve massed assaults for decisive opportunities.[16] "We . . . will particularly focus on martyrdom operations, the detonation of explosives and the planting of mines," said Baradar. "At the level of urban warfare, we will focus on mine explosions and guerrilla warfare against the enemies' military and diplomatic posts."[17] Tactical adaptation occurred naturally on the ground as well. Realizing that the British, Canadians, and Americans had the advantage of air power, Taliban cadre commanders eschewed sustained combat. According to one Taliban fighter from Kandahar, "When fighting starts, airplanes arrive and begin to fire on insurgents so they cannot engage with ISAF forces for more than 15 minutes."[18]

During 2007 and much of 2008, fighting persisted around the fronts of the end of 2006. The British defended and reinforced their platoon houses. The Canadians pulled their forces out of northern and southeastern Kandahar and concentrated on maintaining a foothold in Panjwai, which they had identified as critical terrain.[19] Taliban operated out of their strongholds of northern Helmand and western Kandahar, taking advantage of newly captured territory around Musa Qala, Sangin, Zharey, and Panjwai.[20] While the battle lines temporarily settled, Taliban consolidated their influence. As Baradar intended, the provincial capitals would soon be in danger.

The defeats of 2006 and 2007, especially Musa Qala, shocked Karzai. Helmand tribal leaders called him incessantly. Karzai never took to the business of war. US Ambassador Bill Wood reported, "Karzai did not want to hear, or at least did not want to hear from the foreigners, about military developments."[21]

He distanced himself from his own army. General McNeill would try to brief him only to be frustrated by his disinterest and unfamiliarity with the basics of military planning. Karzai rarely spoke in front of his army or praised their sacrifice.[22] He once even told an audience of US generals and diplomats, "I am surrounded by generals right now. I do not like generals and armies. If I was in charge of the world, I would get rid of the Afghan army . . . first the Pakistani army, then the Afghan army, then the US army!"[23]

Karzai, a man who loved peace, a man who cared for the innocent above defeating terrorists, had different ideas about what it would take to win the war than Eikenberry, McNeill, or Bush. As we can see, he had little faith in the Afghan army. Nor was he eager for more American boots on Afghan soil, let alone the accompanying American air strikes and night raids. He was painfully aware of how the state's dependence on US support could be a crippling vulnerability. His devotion to Islam and Afghan identity dissuaded him from dubbing the Taliban an enemy lest he tar himself as a foreign-backed puppet facing a legitimate jihad.

In August 2007, Karzai and his cabinet met with President Bush and the principals of the national security council at Camp David to reaffirm the strategic partnership. During a series of warm meetings, Bush, out of curiosity, queried: "Do you want to have the areas beyond the Durand Line again?" He was referring to the land in Pakistan that had been part of Afghanistan before the 1893 drawing of the Durand Line. Karzai responded "No Afghan can ever give up his land." Conversation then shifted to other matters, but Bush's query convinced Karzai that "the Americans were ready to help Afghanistan" with regard to Pakistan, a misinterpretation that in the view of his Minister of Foreign Affairs, Rangin Dadfar Spanta, "shaped Karzai's analysis of US goals and policies in our region" for the rest of his tenure.[24]

What was Karzai's strategy—if we can call it that? To watch how things played out and react rather than act; to truculently refuse to be America's puppet; to condemn harm to Afghan civilians, whether at the hands of the Taliban, the Americans, or his own forces; to treat Pakistan as the enemy rather than indict himself by declaring war on the Taliban, fellow Afghans. "We will win if we turn the war inside out," Karzai once told his cabinet, "We do not need to fight the Taliban on the inside. The enemy is Pakistan."[25] Because the Afghan state lacked the power to pressure Pakistan to end the Taliban's war, Karzai, looked to the United States, initially thinking that Bush would act on his own accord, and in later years bringing up the possibility himself. Harbored within were heroic assumptions that the United States actually wanted to pressure Pakistan and had enough leverage to succeed.

Karzai's laissez faire approach to the war in his own countryside was part and parcel of his strategy. Karzai continued to focus on weakening political rivals over defeating the Taliban. Karzai's brother, Ahmed Wali Karzai, after seven years of politicking and outmaneuvering potential rivals, was kingpin of Kandahar, more powerful than the governor or police chief.[26] He had a clear-eyed sense of the American relationships and corruption that would be necessary for his brother to rule. His advice steadied the president like none other. Governor Asadullah Khalid was too astute to get in the way. His job was to manage the government apparatus in accord with Ahmed Wali, not cross him.

Ahmed Wali ran Kandahar through his chairmanship of the provincial council. He was tirelessly interested in the politics of the wider Kandahar region, known as *Loy Kandahar*. Tribal leaders from Kandahar, Zabul, Helmand, and Uruzgan met with him all the time to solve major disputes. Ahmed Wali exploited his family position and nurtured ties with ministers to direct aid to his supporters. He could pick up the phone and issue orders to ministers to get things done. Even rivals admitted that Ahmed Wali quickly fixed problems. His name was famous throughout Afghanistan and in Pakistan and Iran.[27]

Ahmed Wali grew richer and richer. In addition to funding from Karzai, he used his good relations with the United States and control over the provincial council to win contracts. He lobbied for the provincial council to oversee reconstruction activities and succeeded in getting the lauded national solidarity program to go through it. Afghans widely claimed that Ahmed Wali ran the drug trade in Kandahar. He supposedly levied a tax on all drug smugglers. On top of this, the *New York Times* uncovered evidence that US military and intelligence agencies funded him.[28] Ahmed Wali's militia may have enforced his business deals, killed his political opponents, and tortured prisoners. He had a secret prison west of the city run by a Popalzai district police chief. Suspicion was widespread that he framed his opponents as terrorists and had US special forces detain them. Hard evidence of such crimes never surfaced.[29]

Ahmed Wali ruthlessly divided and ruled. Together, he and the president made sure no other tribe or powerbroker could threaten their dominance, as they had been doing since 2002. "You are with me or you are against me," Ahmed Wali was known to tell tribal leaders.[30] In the words of a Karzai family ally, "Karzai does not encourage tribes to unite. He will stop any tribe from uniting."[31] Another Kandahar tribal leader said, "Karzai tries to break up all tribes in order to keep them weak. . . . It is the policy of Karzai and his appointees."[32] A district governor close to the Karzais once spelled out the logic for me: "I do not want to build an alliance of tribal leaders because they will be more powerful than me and tell me what to do. If they are broken up, I can do things. If they are not, I cannot. . . . I can solve the [tribal] split in one day but I do not because my position would be weaker."[33]

Ahmed Wali rewarded those loyal to him and punished those who were not.[34] Parliamentarian Maulali Ishaqzai, whose 2005 election bid he had supported, is a good example. Her love of tribe ran afoul of Ahmed Wali. After a few years Maulali grew disillusioned with how "Ahmed Wali Karzai oppressed the Ishaqzai, took away our land, stole our money." A true Pashtun, she shifted political allegiances and campaigned for Dr. Abdullah, Karzai's rival in the upcoming 2009 presidential election. In retaliation Ahmed Wali cut her off. "Ahmed Wali called me and threatened me," she vengefully recalled.[35] She would get no support in the 2010 parliamentary elections and lose her seat.

Similar maneuvers pertained to poppy eradication. Ahmed Wali and Governor Khalid ignored the fields of allies and plowed under those of rivals. The United Nations Office on Drugs and Crime (UNODC) found that 91 percent of the poppy fields targeted for eradication in 2008 fell outside approved eradication zones, which were usually the lands of the established, powerful tribal leaders, implying that Khalid and Ahmed Wali were purposefully ignoring the fields of their allies.[36] It was the poorer tribes that usually lived outside the zones.

President Karzai and Ahmed Wali particularly conspired against the Alikozai and Barakzai, whom they viewed as threats to their power, regardless of the fact that these two tribes opposed the Taliban. Karzai removed powerful Alikozai police commanders and had them posted elsewhere in the country. Ahmed Wali supposedly knocked off the famous Alikozai mujahideen commander, Gran Agha. Shot and mortally wounded, in his dying breaths Gran Agha whispered he had been attacked by Ahmed Wali's men.[37] Similarly, President Karzai forbade Barakzai from forming a tribal council.[38] In Kandahar, Barakzai leaders received few government positions. To further fragment the tribe, Karzai and Ahmed Wali drew certain capable Barakzai leaders to their camp.[39]

Barakzai, Alikozai, and other tribes cursed the Popalzai. They saw divisiveness as a uniquely Popalzai trait, sometimes calling them "the people who blind each other," a reference to the bloody succession struggle between Ahmed Shah Durrani's grandsons in the early 1800s.[40] By 2007, tribal feuding was open and virulent, unmatched since the 1990s.[41]

Through an opening between two jagged ridges—looming like a gate on the northern edge of Kandahar City—glowed the deep green of Arghandab. Here, for 50 kilometers, the Arghandab River, flowing southerly out of the Hindu Kush, irrigated a rich valley. Square plots of purple-pink pomegranate orchards garrisoned the vale, broken by football-field-size grape vineyards. Sarah Chayes the Pashto-speaking journalist who lived in Kandahar City memorably wrote, "Arghandab is shade and water, and mud-walled orchards, and mulberries and apricots, and pomegranates the size of grapefruits hanging from the willowy branches."[42] The United States dug irrigation canals on the eastern side of the river in the 1960s at the same time the Dahla Dam was being built to the north. Few places in Afghanistan matched Arghandab's prosperity. Close to the markets of the city, Arghandab fruit could compete with poppy. The people of Arghandab did not need the forbidden flower to live a good life.[43]

Arghandab was known as "the gateway to Kandahar." Through the ridges that overlook Kandahar City to the north, the valley was the only viable northern route for commerce or invaders. If Arghandab was held, an invader could not enter the city from the north. In 2007, the Alikozai tribe ruled Arghandab, led by the mujahideen commander, Mullah Naqib. He and his Alikozai had safeguarded the city since 2001. The Arghandab Alikozai had a certain *esprit de corps*. They were proud of their green district and its pomegranates and grapes. They were even prouder of their warrior history and Mullah Naqib. They saw themselves as one group. If asked his home, a young tribesman would shout back, "Arghandab!" That pride was a powerful check on a Taliban advance on Kandahar—whether in 1994 or 2007.

Even after Ahmed Wali had disarmed his militia in 2004 and 2005, Naqib used his influence to convince his tribesmen to turn away the Taliban. Sarah Chayes, witness to all things Arghandab, writes, "As the Taliban gained strength and insolence . . . they would contact the mullah from time to time, trying to strike a deal . . . just to pass through Arghandab. . . . He would get on the radio and vow by God that if they dared set foot inside his Arghandab, the whole population would rise up. And thus he held his fractious, disgruntled tribesmen firm against them."[44] In March 2007, an improvised explosive device wounded Naqib. He survived until October when, in weakened condition, he succumbed to a heart attack. He passed sorrowed by the tribal infighting in Kandahar and worried about the future of his tribe.[45]

It was a critical moment for the balance of the tribes against the Taliban. The Alikozai had to select a new leader. At such a time, even a united tribe was at risk of fracture. A weak leader might be unable to hold the tribe together, meaning the Taliban could capture Alikozai lands.

A great Alikozai shura convened in Kandahar in late October. Such was its importance that President Karzai himself chaired. Afghan rulers did not usually choose the head of a tribe. The right of each tribesmen was to follow whoever suits him. For this reason, Afghan tribes rarely chose an official leader. But sovereign intervention was not unprecedented, especially when the ruler felt his influence was warranted. Ahmed Shah Durrani had split tribes in two in order to strengthen his own power. In this case, the Karzai family was consolidating power in Kandahar and the 2009 presidential elections were around the corner. Key Alikozai leaders, including Naqib, had long been part of Jamiat Islami, the Tajik-dominated party of Dr. Abdullah who was set to run against Karzai in the elections. Naqib had always put his tribal relationship with Karzai above party politics. Karzai was less confident other Alikozai leaders would do the same. Karzai thus had great interest in the outcome of the Alikozai shura.

The favored contender was Khan Mohammed, an experienced police chief, former mujahideen, Taliban foe, and Jamiat Islami supporter. Instead, Karzai chose Kalimullah, Mullah Naqib's 26-year-old son. Kalimullah, Karzai judged, would be less able to hold the Alikozai behind Jamiat Islami than Khan Mohammed. Additionally, a weakened Alikozai tribe would help Ahmed Wali dominate politics in the south.[46] One of Karzai's Alikozai confidantes said that Karzai was not interested in holding the Alikozai together: "For a broken tribe to come together, the government must encourage and help the tribe. Karzai will not do this."[47] It would be one of Karzai's worst decisions.

Within two weeks of Naqib's death, Taliban cadres were infiltrating into Arghandab. One Taliban commander brashly called the Alikozai police chief and threatened, "You're alone now that Mullah Naqib is gone. . . . We're coming to Arghandab, no matter what."[48] Facing greater Taliban pressure, the district governor of Khakrez (the district to the north of Arghandab) relinquished his district to the Taliban. From there, the Taliban pushed south into Arghandab. Taliban cadres converged from the other adjacent districts—Zharey and Shah Wali Kot—as well. There was no overall commander. They moved in spontaneously. Taliban entered Naqib's own village on the western side of the river, occupied his home, and met in his mosque. Rumors spread that they danced on his roof.[49] Villagers fled toward the district center. A Canadian and Afghan counteroffensive temporarily pushed the Taliban out but the Alikozai were severely shaken.[50]

Kalimullah was unable to hold the Alikozai together. He was too young to win the loyalty of the tribal elders. Large factions of the tribe did not respect him and believed that a council of tribal leaders rather than Karzai should have selected their new leader. Various tribal leaders went their own way. Authority split between Kalimullah, Khan Mohammed, the district governor, and other tribal leaders—all were Alikozai, few cooperated. Khan Mohammed, the snubbed favorite, refused to work with Kalimullah or act to protect Arghandab. Nor would other tribal leaders. More than a few were content to watch Kalimullah fail. They turned to their personal business and let Taliban pass through their villages. Kalimullah was too timid and inexperienced to take charge in war. Karzai left him hanging. Kalimullah soon retreated to his homes in Kandahar City and Kabul.[51] A kind and thoughtful young man, a few years later he tacitly admitted his own shortcomings: "Karzai divided the Alikozai and every tribe. . . . He put in weak and immature leaders over the more experienced. . . . [E]xperienced elders then refused to cooperate or help the new young leaders. . . . The Taliban took advantage of the situation to expand their power and push tribes aside."[52]

The Taliban solidified their access into Arghandab via the minority Ghilzai population. A smattering of villages in western Arghandab on the border with Khakrez were Ghilzai. Their elders had been active in the Taliban's first regime and sympathized with them. Mullah Naqib had managed to convince the Ghilzai to work with him. After his death, the Ghilzai waved the Taliban in. Taliban moved freely in these villages. Elders allowed their villagers to join them. Hundreds filled the Taliban ranks. The Taliban even set up a district court that was known to hang captured police officers from trees.

One of these elders was Haji Amir Mohammed Agha. His village, Jalawar, was strongly Taliban. Widely respected, Amir Mohammed Agha had been in charge in Arghandab during the first Taliban regime. At the time, he had commanded 300 fighters. He knew Mullah Omar well and cared for him deeply. When the Taliban came back to Arghandab, he helped them once more. Scores of his villagers enlisted as fighters from 2007 onward. Amir Mohammed Agha's son became a commander and was later killed by Americans. Over the next years, 165 of Amir Mohammed Agha's villagers would die fighting, either as Taliban soldiers or as innocents killed accidentally by bombs and stray rounds.[53]

Bereft of strong leadership, large numbers of Alikozai villages were left to fend for themselves. Taliban deputy leader Baradar played the situation beautifully. He had a close handle on Kandahar because he had sent his fellow Popalzai tribesman, Mohammed Issa, to be Taliban governor of Kandahar. Issa, under Baradar's mentorship, appointed an Alikozai, Mullah Shafiqullah, to be his district governor in order to reach out to these villages. Many Alikozai tribesmen started working with the Taliban. A few did so out of intimidation or for pay. Others because it was to their private benefit—they could get land, raise their social position, or edge out a rival. The leadership that had deterred these tribesmen from putting their personal interests over tribe was now gone.[54]

The only government force was the 150 police, roughly half Alikozai. These police prevented the Taliban from capturing the entire district but were confined to seven posts, surrounded by Taliban cadres in the villages. There were no Canadian or US posts. Any Canadian or US force coming into Arghandab endured firefights that could last 30 minutes or more.[55]

Between their advances in Arghandab and Zharey and Panjwai, the Taliban now had easy access to Kandahar City. Suicide attacks went on unabated. In February 2008, a suicide car bomb on the outskirts of the city killed or wounded 154.[56] Other suicide attacks within the city caused another 130 casualties over the course of the year, out of a total of more than 420 casualties from suicide attacks throughout the province (approximately the same number as in 2006).[57] On top of the suicide attacks came ground assaults.

On June 13, 30 to 50 Taliban specially trained in Pakistan sneaked into the city, intent on breaking open the Sarposa prison, which housed hundreds of detainees. During the early evening, the Taliban instructed locals to clear out.

The police heard nothing, a sign of the gulf between them and the people. The operation started with attacks on police posts near the prison, effectively pinning them down. A suicide fuel truck bomb then drove into the main gate. For unknown reasons, the truck did not explode. The Taliban improvised and ignited its fuel tank with an RPG. The explosion stunned the prison guards and breached the main gate. Taliban fighters then stormed the prison on foot, overcoming the stunned guards and freeing the prisoners. The Taliban guided the escape of over 1,000, splitting them up into small groups to move through Kandahar and into the safer rural areas. Neither the police nor the Canadians could get to the prison in time to stop them.[58]

The Taliban were not done yet. Three days later, 300 to 400 fighters swept into the remaining pro-government villages in Arghandab, causing more than 10,000 civilians to flee. General David McKiernan, the new ISAF commander, was deeply concerned. He flew in two Afghan battalions as temporary reinforcements. On June 18, Canadian and 700 Afghan soldiers counterattacked and, after fierce fighting, drove back the Taliban—and then left once more. The Taliban returned within days.

The Sarposa prison break and its aftermath in Arghandab was a humiliating defeat for the Afghan government and the Canadians. Karzai lashed out with threats to send Afghan troops into Pakistan to strike Taliban leaders.[59] The attacks brought down Asadullah Khalid. Karzai removed him and the provincial police chief. Toorayalai Wesa, an educated agricultural expert and a Barakzai with close ties to the Karzai family, was ultimately installed as the new governor. Still worried, General McKiernan re-routed a US battalion (2nd Battalion, 2nd Infantry Regiment) to western Kandahar to shore up the defense.

Inside the city, Taliban provincial governor Mohammed Issa started a guerrilla campaign, trying to break down government control. Taliban infiltrated from their bases in Zharey, Panjwai, and Arghandab into the city. They moved in ones and twos, planning attacks and setting up hiding places.[60] They laid improvised explosive devices, sprung ambushes, and assassinated government officials and police. A policeman could not walk the streets, even in civilian clothes. Taliban would find and shoot him. Attacks were almost daily, nearly 300 in 2009. Violence caused a few schools to close. Attendance dropped at the rest.[61] Many parents refused to let their children go out on the streets. "Women felt they had no right to go outside," recalled Zarghona Baluch, the daughter of a provincial councilwoman. "There was no education for them. It was too dangerous even to go to the bazaar."[62] Breadwinners walked straight from work to home, making a detour for the bazaar or pharmacy if necessary.[63] A few years later an old shopowner remembered that during those days, "I stayed in my shop. I went home at night and then back to the shop during the day. I did not see what else was happening."[64]

As 2008 came to an end, Kandahar City was being strangled. Taliban were rife in the city's outer neighborhoods. Other than besieged district centers and a few villages, Taliban controlled Panjwai, Zharey, and Arghandab—the key districts next to Kandahar City. Highway One was drivable, but thick with improvised explosive devices.[65] Surviving government strongholds were in danger: the Barakzai and Popalzai neighborhoods to the south and west where Sherzai and Ahmed Wali still ran militias, and Spin Boldak, where Abdul Razziq and his Achekzai border police fought on.

A similar dynamic unfolded in Helmand. The British had been enduring a battle of attrition in district centers throughout the province since 2006. On the bright side, in December 2007 a British and American operation recaptured Musa Qala, after a year as the Taliban's open hub.[66] Then, in April 2008, McNeill ordered the 24th Marine Expeditionary Unit (which Central Command had sent forward from its reserve as a temporary reinforcement) to clear and hold the northern, most densely populated, part of the district of Garmser.[67]

Taliban nevertheless advanced to the doorstep of Lashkar Gah, the provincial capital. Abdul Qayum Zakir led the Taliban offensive. An Alizai from northern Helmand, Zakir had been detained in 2001 in northern Afghanistan and sent to Guantanamo. The United States transferred him to Afghanistan in 2007. The government released him in 2008. He immediately returned to the Taliban. Zakir was a grim leader who enforced discipline. His serious demeanor sometimes reminded Afghans and Taliban fighters of Dadullah Lang, though he lacked Dadullah's taste for atrocity.[68]

Zakir first attacked the nearby communities of Marjah and Nad Ali, the western approaches to Lashkar Gah in September. They were defended by the militia of Abdur Rahman Jan, former Helmand police chief. Both communities fell, opening the path to the provincial capital.[69]

Zakir massed roughly 400 Taliban around the outskirts of Lashkar Gah on the night of October 10. Their target was the NDS headquarters and the governor's compound. Zakir led a three-pronged attack supported by mortars and rockets, an uncommon event in Afghanistan. Firefights erupted between the Taliban and the police and soldiers around the town limits. Mortars and rockets fell on the governor's compound and the British brigade headquarters. People inside the town were frightened. Some panicked. A group of 150 Taliban reached the Bolan bridge over the Helmand River, across from central Lashkar Gah. The British headquarters vectored in Apache helicopter gunships, drones, and a B-1B bomber to save the capital. Air strikes killed 50, enabling the police to repel the attack on the bridge.[70]

Fighting surrounded Lashkar Gah for the next ten days. As many as 1,000 Taliban joined the battle. In response, the Afghan army and police poured in

2,300 reinforcements.[71] Finally, on October 22, Zakir backed off. Lashkar Gah had been saved but was still in a precarious position.

As the Taliban advanced in the south, the outpost war hammered on in the east. Following the July 2008 defeat at Wanat, the focus of US generals in Afghanistan remained the mountain provinces of Kunar and Nuristan, with their outposts in the Korengal and other distant mountain valleys near the Pakistan border. In the middle of 2008, 35 of regional command east's 125 posts were in far mountain valleys and reaches.[72]

Major General Rodriguez's successor at regional command east, Major General Jeffrey Schloesser, thought the mountain posts were indefensible and should be closed. He and others doubted the outposts served much purpose. "Rodriguez talked to me about this," reported Brigadier General Mark Milley, Schloesser's deputy and future chairman of the joint chiefs of staff, "the situation up in the various valleys, not just the Waigal, but several of the valleys that were up there, had very limited value added with respect to a population centric counterinsurgency. If the purpose is to secure the population . . . there wasn't much population to secure."[73]

Schloesser initiated a plan to consolidate outposts. He only got so far. Afghan army chief of staff Bismullah Khan and Minister of Defense Rahim Wardak argued strenuously against any closures. Schloesser's brigade combat team commander in the area, Colonel John Spiszer, believed the outposts were necessary to obstruct insurgents from attacking the main river valleys. What really deterred Schloesser, though, was the likely perception that such a withdrawal would constitute strategic defeat and reluctance among his peers and superiors to close bases. McKiernan, as the senior US commander, appears to have lent little urgency. Although he ostensibly concurred with Schloesser, he fundamentally believed outposts in the mountain valleys were needed to interdict insurgent sanctuaries and lines of communication.

So instead of writing off a failing effort McKiernan and Schloesser ended up reinforcing it. In January 2009, Schloesser, with McKiernan's approval, assigned an additional battalion—1st Battalion, 32nd Infantry Regiment, the same that had spearheaded the initial 2006 operation—to Kunar. Part of the battalion later went into an eight-week battle in Barge Matal, far into the mountains of Nuristan.

As reverses in Kunar and Nuristan stacked up, the Taliban advanced in Ghazni and Wardak, approaching Kabul. Roughly five times the size of Khost with three times the population (931,000 people), Ghazni sits south of Kabul on Afghanistan's ring road, Highway One. From 2006 to 2008, insurgent activity was greater than in Khost, Paktika, or Paktiya but less than in Kunar. Ambushes and improvised explosive devices occurred along Highway One daily. Taliban surrounded Ghazni city, the provincial capital, and established a thriving shadow government in the countryside. US patrols could not eliminate them. A single overstretched US battalion had been assigned to Ghazni, Wardak, and parts of Paktika since 2006. A Polish battalion, soon reinforced to a brigade, deployed to Ghazni city in 2008 but Taliban still roamed the surrounding countryside freely.[74]

From Ghazni, the Taliban expanded into Wardak and Logar, just south of Kabul itself. Major General Schloesser assessed that the Haqqani network, with intent to conduct terrorist attacks in the capital, was infiltrating along with other Taliban into the two provinces. Minister of Defense Rahim Wardak and other Afghan leaders insisted Schloesser and McKiernan do something about the enemy at the "gates of Kabul." Haqqani suicide attacks on the Serena Hotel and the Indian Embassy heightened concern that Kabul was in danger. McKiernan and Schloesser decided they needed more forces to fight the Taliban and Haqqani in Wardak and Logar.

In Washington, the realization that the war was going poorly sunk in. The defeats in Kandahar and Helmand featured in Western newspapers. The *New York Times, Washington Post,* and *Economist* all ran stories.[75] In August, the *New York Times* editorial board declared:

> The news out of Afghanistan is truly alarming. . . . Kabul, the seat of Afghanistan's pro-Western government, is increasingly besieged. . . . Taliban and foreign Qaeda fighters are consolidating territory. . . . And the more territory the Taliban controls, the more freedom al-Qaʻeda will have to mount new terrorist operations against this country and others. There is no more time to waste. Unless the United States, NATO, and its central Asian allies move quickly, they could lose this war.[76]

Things looked much worse than a year and a half earlier when Defense Secretary Gates and President Bush had taken a few steps to buttress the country. Gates told Pentagon officials that in Washington's view of the situation Afghanistan had "gone from twilight to dark in six to eight weeks."[77] During the summer, Bush received a memo from his national security council staff that Afghanistan could fall apart within six months.[78] On September 10, 2008, chairman of the joint chiefs of staff Mike Mullen admitted to Congress, "I'm not sure we're winning."[79]

That September, McKiernan asked for 20,000 reinforcements. He requested two battalions specifically for the east, which the Pentagon upgraded to an entire brigade combat team. By this time, violence had fallen in Iraq. More forces could be freed up for Afghanistan. President Bush was well-apprised of the state of affairs. He was having video teleconferences with McKiernan every other week, in addition to his video teleconferences with Karzai. Bush ordered his national security council staff to review the war effort in Afghanistan. The review concluded reinforcements and counterinsurgency tactics were required. Bush approved the one brigade for the east—3rd Brigade, 10th Mountain Division (Brigadier General John Nicholson's old brigade)—and a marine battalion but no more at that time. Bush withheld because he was at the end of his term and did not want to dictate policy to his successor.[80]

When the 3,500-strong 3rd Brigade, 10th Mountain Division returned in 2009, Schloesser arrayed two battalions in Wardak and Logar. The third battalion was the aforementioned 1st Battalion, 32nd Infantry Regiment that returned to Kunar.

By this time support for the Korengal and other mountain valley campaigns was at last running out of steam. Colonel Randy George, the new brigade commander for Kunar and Nuristan, assessed the outposts were too far from the population and too costly. Before even arriving in Afghanistan he proposed closing them down to Major General Mike Scaparotti, Schloesser's successor as commander over eastern Afghanistan. Scaparotti was amenable. Once in Afghanistan, planning stumbled forward with the usual delays and obstructions.

Defeat followed defeat. In May, insurgents attacked an outpost in rugged Ghaziabad along the northern Kunar River and killed three Americans, two Latvians, and five Afghans, and captured twelve Afghan soldiers. In September, on the Pakistan border, insurgents ambushed 13 marine advisors and 80 Afghan soldiers and police in Ganjigal. Over 30 were killed or wounded. The battle became famous for the heroism of Corporal Dakota Meyer, United States Marine Corps, who was later awarded the Congressional Medal of Honor for his valor that day pulling out the wounded under heavy fire.[81] Then, in October, 400 Nuristanis attacked Combat Outpost Keating, which was holding Nuristan's Kamdesh Valley. Again, the attackers nearly overran the position. Again, US forces withdrew shortly after the battle. US forces had now withdrawn from almost all of Nuristan.

By late 2009, Brigadier General Kurt Fuller, Scaparotti's deputy, had had enough. The string of defeats in Nuristan had convinced him and Scaparotti that the mountain valley outposts would have to be ruthlessly shut down, regardless of the opposition of Afghan leaders or anyone else. Brigadier General John Nicholson objected. After leaving Afghanistan as colonel in 2007, he had been promoted to brigadier general and was now in the Pentagon running of the joint staff's Afghanistan and Pakistan desk. He let his opinion be known that the Korengal should not be abandoned. He said US soldiers should stay in place because of all the American blood and treasure sacrificed in that steep and treacherous valley. He insisted that the valley's use as a sanctuary be denied.[82] Fuller pressed ahead anyways.

In addition to Major General Scaparotti, Fuller had the backing of General McChrystal, the new ISAF commander who replaced McKiernan in 2009, and Lieutenant General David Rodriguez, who had returned to manage operations countrywide for McChrystal. It was a new era. McChrystal's main effort was the south. In the east the Haqqani network was deemed more dangerous than insurgents in the Kunar and Nuristan high country. For his part, Rodriguez remembered commanding the 82nd Airborne Division in 2007 and 2008 and the casualties and pain that Colonel Chip Preysler and Lieutenant Colonel Bill Ostlund had experienced in the mountain valleys. He believed time had shown the cost to outweigh the gain.

In April 2010, the last American company posted to the Korengal evacuated its men and equipment. Haji Matin, the Korengali insurgent commander, agreed to let the Americans withdraw unmolested. He enforced a two-week ceasefire, as helicopters ferried out US soldiers and equipment. On April 14, 2010, Lieutenant Colonel Brian Pearl, the last battalion commander over the Korengal, handed over the intact buildings and fuel stores of the Korengal outpost to the Korengali elders. After almost exactly four years, US generals gave up on denying the insurgents sanctuary in the mountains of Kunar and Nuristan.

One hundred and twenty Americans died fighting in the Korengal and other mountain valleys. At least another hundred were wounded. Fourteen soldiers and one marine would receive the Congressional Medal of Honor for their valor in these areas, out of the 18 total awarded in the war. US commanders stuck it out largely out of fear withdrawal might embolden the Taliban. Their fears were partly substantiated. The Quetta Shura exuberantly publicized the withdrawal, seeming to reflect a rise in insurgent confidence.[83] Insurgent cadres pressed closer against the populated Kunar and Pech Valleys. Yet insurgents got no farther than that. They conquered only small and distant portions of the Kunar or Pech Valleys. Down among the villages the government reigned year after year. Even after US soldiers withdrew from them altogether in 2012 and 2013, the government was able to handle the violence. In a variety of places, soldiers and police pushed insurgents out of the lower valleys and back into the mountain valleys on their own. According to local leaders, for many insurgents, US departure stripped fighting of its raison d'etre. They made deals with the army and police to live and let live. Hezb-Islami stopped fighting the government entirely. For their part, the Korengalis had little interest in getting in a fight with the Safis and feared the government might simply blockade the path up the valley, cutting off timber profits.[84] Consequently, insurgents could not amass the strength to overwhelm the army and police in the Pech and Kunar Valleys, let alone the provincial capital. The two paved roads gave the army and police freedom of movement. For all the disappointments of the war in the east, the roads were an investment that lasted.

On the counterterrorism front, US special operations forces intensified their raids and targeted air strikes after 2010. The results exceeded those of battles in mountain valleys. US special operations forces finally captured al-Qaʻeda commander Abu Ikhlas in December 2010. A drone killed Haji Matin in the Korengal in 2013.[85] A series of other leaders would be captured or killed over the following years.[86] Raids and targeted air strikes probably would have been a better strategy to have pursued in Kunar and Nuristan in the first place. Such means would unlikely have defeated the insurgency but, over time, could have eliminated the largest threats to the United States without the large number of boots on the ground and accompanying casualties.

In retrospect, the Kunar and Nuristan campaign was an unneeded diversion of US resources. It neither eliminated terrorists nor protected the populous lower valleys. At least a portion of the battalions posted there would have been better used to free up reinforcements for more important battles elsewhere, such as Kandahar, Afghanistan's second city. In war, things can be sticky. Once invested it can be hard to get out. In Kunar and Nuristan, US commanders had not helped. They had been perhaps too dedicated to winning, too prideful to accept losing, at the cost of flexibility. Instead of cutting a bad investment, they toughed it out. A little more entrepreneurship would have been good for the whole strategy.

Since the 2006 Taliban offensive, the Afghan government had grown weaker and weaker while the Taliban had grown stronger and stronger. The wave of defeats across the country set the stage for the 2009 surge that would dispatch tens of thousands of reinforcements and cost hundreds of billions of dollars and greater than 1,000 lives. A major driver behind the decision to surge would be a belief among Americans that the Afghan government was about to fail. The threat to the gates of Kabul, the assault on Lashkar Gah, and above all the attacks in Kandahar City brought about that belief. They pressured Washington to up its commitment to Afghanistan.

Bush's presidency ended in January 2009. The initial intervention had been impressive. His administration had swiftly overthrown the Taliban and overseen the creation of a new Afghan state. In Karzai, they had found a legitimate ruler and delayed a spontaneous Afghan backlash to foreign occupation. Neglect marked the intervening years. For too long, Bush and his team stuck to their initial biases. They consistently overrated the 2001 victory and resisted sensible courses of action, such as peace talks, building a competent military, and reducing civilian casualties. The threat of another terrorist attack and closeness of September 11 hardened thinking. A good deal of blame rests on Rumsfeld's shoulders. His dislike of a long-term US commitment set course to the very quagmire he so feared. Gates and Bush—as well as Secretary of State Condoleezza Rice and National

Map 13 Taliban territory, 2009

Taliban areas of
influence in 2009

TAJIKISTAN

UZBEKISTAN

TURKMENISTAN

IRAN

PAKISTAN

BADAKHSHAN

Chitral

NURISTAN

KUNAR

Peshawar

Islamabad

Khyber
Pass

Miram Shah

Khost City

Loya Paktiya

Kunduz
City

BAGHLAN

PARWAN

Panjshir Valley

Bagram
airfield

Kabul

Jalalabad

GHAZNI

ZABUL

Quetta

BALUCHISTAN

URUZGAN

Mazar-e Sharif

Tarin Kowt

Kandahar

Kandahar
airfield

Spin Boldak

Girdi Jangal

KANDAHAR

Gereshk

Maiwand

Lashkar Gah

HELMAND

Herat

Indus R.

N

km   150

miles   75

0

0

© S Ballard (2021)

Security Advisor Stephen Hadley—were more attentive. They never gave up on Afghanistan. They belatedly tried to do more after the 2006 offensive but were hamstrung by the Iraq War, which mercilessly diverted resources. By the time Iraq had finally been righted and resources were available, the administration's time had run out.

The era of British and Canadian leadership in the south was also coming to a close. Citing public war weariness, Canadian Prime Minister Steven Harper decided in September 2008 that he would withdraw Canadian forces from Kandahar before the end of 2011. The British soldiered on in Helmand but lobbied for US reinforcements. Within months, a new US strategy under a new president would push both the British and the Canadians into a supporting role. The era ended on a note of defeat. British and Canadian forces had saved the Afghan government, preventing the Taliban from completing the victory they had won in early 2006. Nevertheless, the Taliban had only grown in power. British Ambassador Sir Sherard Cowper-Coles reported, "The current situation is bad; the security situation is getting worse; so is corruption and the Government has lost all trust. . . . The foreign forces are ensuring the survival of a regime which would collapse without them."[87]

The Obama Administration and the Decision to Surge

Now we come to the heart of America's war in Afghanistan, when combat and casualties dwarf what had come before and what would come later. The United States had been in Afghanistan since 2001. Thrilling successes had been washed away by years of defeat. The dire military situation brought the United States to the most controversial decision of the war: the surge of 2009, a new strategy with an ambitious timeline. The decision has been scrutinized ever since, most notably in Bob Woodward's *Obama's Wars*. The surge marks America's largest attempt to fix Afghanistan, an immense military, political, and economic undertaking. The best minds, accomplished generals, and a careful president led the way.

Barack Obama, a Democrat, succeeded George W. Bush as president of the United States on January 20, 2009. Momentum to reinforce Afghanistan had accelerated. Obama campaigned on an assertion that Afghanistan was a war of necessity. He criticized the Bush administration for focusing on Iraq.[1] At one point, he famously referred to Afghanistan as the "good war," a well-accepted position. Three years of *New York Times* editorials clamored for the United States to send more troops.

Obama's embrace of Afghanistan contrasted with his worldview. He was wary of pouring US troops and dollars into military interventions and deeply disapproved of Bush's foreign policy. As a senator, he had opposed the war in Iraq and had voted against the 2007 Iraq surge. Getting out of Iraq was another campaign pledge, as important as tending to Afghanistan. Obama stated in his inaugural address, "Our power alone cannot protect us, nor does it entitle us to do as we please. . . . Our power grows through its prudent use; our security emanates from the justness of our cause, the force of our example, the tempering qualities of humility and restraint."[2]

Obama was a man of cool deliberation. He tried to keep things in perspective, with the big picture in mind. On a trip to Iraq shortly before the election, he told General David Petraeus that it is "the job of the president to think broadly, not narrowly, and to weigh the costs and benefits of military action against everything else that went into making the country strong."[3] In the big picture, foreign policy was secondary to domestic policy. The great recession was at hand. The US economy was falling apart; banks were crashing and the entire financial system was in danger. The top priority was fixing the economy. Health care came close behind.[4] Later on he would have to worry about increasing federal budget deficits. "The state of our economy calls for action, bold and swift," Obama declared in his inaugural address, "And we will act, not only to create new jobs, but to lay a new foundation for growth."[5] Reinforcing Afghanistan clashed with the rest of the agenda.

From 2006 to 2009, the US military implemented counterinsurgency in Iraq. Under the guidance of General David Petraeus, reformist military officers bonded with liberal intellectuals to write the famous counterinsurgency field manual (FM 3-24). The manual called for protecting the population over killing insurgents. Tactically, this meant patrolling and outposting where the people lived rather than striking insurgent leadership or sweeping through insurgent sanctuaries. The manual also called for training and advising the local army and police with small teams of embedded advisers. Other well-known principles were limiting civilian casualties, winning over the population, and building a good and fair government. The manual stated, "The primary objective of any COIN [counterinsurgency] operation is to foster development of effective governance by a legitimate government."[6] Effective governance was defined ambitiously: a government in which leaders are supported by the majority of the population, corruption is low, rule of law has been established, and economic and social development is progressing.[7]

Petraeus succeeded in using counterinsurgency methods to turn around the war in Iraq in 2007 and 2008. In Afghanistan, on the other hand, US strategy was an ad hoc combination of counterterrorism, counterinsurgency, and conventional-style operations. Where referenced, counterinsurgency was hazily executed. Success in Iraq encouraged Petraeus and many others that a strategy based on counterinsurgency could yield improvement in Afghanistan. Petraeus wanted to repeat the Iraq model in Afghanistan and expected that Obama would be as enthusiastic a supporter as Bush had been.

Obama was concerned about Afghanistan and before inauguration had asked Vice President Joe Biden to help him determine how many forces were immediately needed.[8] Upon inauguration, US forces in Afghanistan totaled 32,000, alongside 31,000 NATO and other foreign troops.[9] One of first decisions Obama faced was ISAF commander General David McKiernan's request for reinforcements. President Bush had approved part of his initial request for 20,000, deferring the remainder to the new administration. The request now went forward, topped off with 10,000 additional troops McKiernan calculated necessary. Obama directed that former CIA official Bruce Riedel oversee a 60-day review of the strategy. Riedel favored counterinsurgency. His review, ongoing while Obama decided what to do about McKiernan's request, would argue that the insurgency in Afghanistan had to be thwarted in order to prevent al-Qaʻeda from regaining sanctuary and attacking the United States. Pakistan was central to his analysis; efforts in Afghanistan would fail if Pakistan did not stop sheltering the Taliban.[10]

Al-Qaʻeda still seemed a real threat. Osama bin Laden remained at large. The group had conducted the July 2005 London subway bombings. The following year, the United States and United Kingdom uncovered an operation to detonate explosives on 10 to 15 airliners out of Heathrow. Both plots originated from the Afghan-Pakistan border area. Intelligence analysts briefed Obama that al-Qaʻeda was more dangerous than it had been in years.[11] So close to these events, no US president could discount al-Qaʻeda.

Obama was cautious about over-committing to Afghanistan but willing to make a reasonable investment. McKiernan's request was approved on February 16, after the Pentagon had pared it down to 17,000. Obama doubted the reinforcements would bring victory. Rather, he hoped to stave off further setbacks, stanch the bleeding, and pivot to his bigger priorities. Obama later told Bob Woodward that he had decided to send in 17,000 troops because of assessments that without them Afghanistan's upcoming presidential elections would fail and the country would splinter.[12] He writes in his own memoirs: "I didn't like the deal. But in what was becoming a pattern, the alternatives were worse. The stakes involved—the risks of a possible collapse of the Afghan government or the Taliban gaining footholds in major cities—were simply too high for us not to act."[13]

A month later, Obama approved another 4,000 troops for training and advising the Afghan army and police—mildly displeased with the Pentagon for putting forward a second request on the heels of the first. When announcing the 4,000 reinforcements on March 27, he outlined the strategy for Afghanistan: military operations in the south and east, advising and expanding the Afghan security forces, building governance and economic development, and countering narcotics.[14] The goal was to "disrupt, dismantle, and defeat al-Qaʻeda in Pakistan and Afghanistan, and to prevent their return to either country in the future."[15] The 21,000 reinforcements (17,000 approved in February plus 4,000 in March) would arrive over the spring and summer.[16] In May, Defense Secretary Gates, whom Obama had asked to stay on from the Bush administration, dismissed McKiernan and appointed the highly regarded Stanley McChrystal, former commander of special operations in Iraq and Afghanistan, as commander of US and allied forces in Afghanistan (Commander, International Security Assistance Force—ISAF).

General Stanley McChrystal was renowned for his successes in Iraq from 2003–2008 and for revolutionizing the way special operations forces targeted terrorists. He had worked closely with Petraeus and was impressed with the effectiveness of counterinsurgency in conjunction with special operations. Secretary Gates, General Petraeus, and several senators had great confidence in him.

McChrystal was an athletic figure with spartan habits. Legend has it that his daily routine was to run six to eight miles, eat one meal, and sleep for four hours. He was driven to succeed. He accepted the Bush-era conceit that the United States could defeat the Taliban. Years later McChrystal's optimism would seem folly. At the time, many generals and civilian officials, myself included, shared his outlook. The turnaround in Iraq encouraged them to see the impossible as possible. In 2006 the United States looked to be on the verge of defeat in Iraq. Then by the end of 2007 the surge had turned the tide. Aware of the value of time, experience, and continuity, McChrystal planned to stay in Afghanistan for years, until the war was all but finished, as he had in Iraq. One of McChrystal's exceptional traits was his willingness to enforce change, even in the face of US military tradition or protocol. Because of his role as the general of the surge, McChrystal would have greater impact upon the Afghan War than any predecessor or successor.

Petraeus, victor of the Iraq surge, was now commander of Central Command (CENTCOM) and McChrystal's immediate superior. Like McChrystal, he supposed the Taliban could be defeated. Unlike McChrystal, he reckoned their defeat would reverse itself if the US military did not stay in Afghanistan for decades. Woodward quotes Petraeus as saying in 2009 or 2010, "You have to recognize also that I don't think you can win this war. I think you keep fighting . . . This is the kind of fight we're in for the rest of our lives and probably our kids' lives."[17] Although he never said so to Obama, Petraeus sought a near-indefinite commitment.

Both McChrystal and Petraeus had believed that the terrorist threat to the United States warranted escalation. Both had witnessed unswerving resolve and personal self-sacrifice turn the tide in Iraq. As the 2001 success had swept Bush and his team into overconfidence during their early years in Afghanistan, so the successes of the Iraq surge swept Petraeus and McChrystal into overconfidence in 2009.

On the civilian side, Obama appointed a special representative for Afghanistan and Pakistan, the irrepressible Richard Holbrooke, who had negotiated the 1995 Dayton Accords that brought an uneasy peace to the Bosnia conflict. His job was to oversee economic development and diplomacy, looking at both Afghanistan and Pakistan.

Obama also appointed a new ambassador—Karl Eikenberry, recently retired from the army. Inside Afghanistan, US civilian activities (other than intelligence) were under his authority. Having started the US program to train the Afghan army in 2002 and 2003 and having commanded all US forces from 2005 to 2007, Eikenberry had more experience in Afghanistan than any other US senior official. He was skeptical that counterinsurgency lessons coming out of Iraq applied. Time had eroded his earlier confidence that Americans could win. During his last deployment (2005–2007), the ineffectiveness of the Karzai government had troubled him. He suspected its misdeeds had opened the door to the insurgency.

Upon returning to Afghanistan, Eikenberry resumed his old habit of talking to average Afghans. Their opinions were a check for him on what American and Afghan officials and officers were saying. I remember well his visit to Garmser, Helmand, where I was stationed. In his tour of the bazaar, he diverted from the formal agenda of greetings with local officials to crawl down eye to eye with truck drivers resting under their "jingle truck," then barter with shop-owners outside their busy shops, and finally huddle with village elders in the district center courtyard. He would later say: "I've traveled a lot in this country. I've been to all 34 provinces. I've walked in a lot of bazaars. When I drive through the streets of Kabul, about 50 percent of the people will look up and recognize me and give me a thumbs-up—that matters a lot to me. I think it matters a lot to the American people."[18]

Eikenberry was convinced that change needed to come from the inside, not from US military forces. Morally, he disliked the idea of sending US troops into danger to prop up the Karzai regime. Nevertheless, he hoped an approach that forced the government to improve could eventually yield stability.

Gates asked McChrystal to provide an assessment of the situation for the White House and the Pentagon within 60 days.[19] Once in Kabul, McChrystal started the assessment, bringing in a team of outside scholars. Work proceeded through the summer.

As had been the case in 2001–2002, the policy debates alone obscure the idealism of the US intervention. Obama and his team favored a self-described "realist" foreign policy, stripped of the moralistic rhetoric of Bush that had justified wars and destruction. Biden once shouted at Holbrooke for supporting Afghan women's rights in the context of US soldiers at war with their lives on the line: "It just won't work, that's not what they're there for."[20] Although fighting terrorism was the primary justification for surging, morality nevertheless played a role. As Holbrooke's opinions revealed, good governance, women's rights, and countering corruption were often deemed critical to any progress. On top of that, American leaders understood that, in addition to a terrorist threat, defeat meant anarchy and a human rights disaster.

Women's rights remained important for US policy, even though Obama never embraced Afghan women's rights to the extent that Bush had. For him, women's rights were a responsibility, not a justification for a war. They were included in his policy, stripped of soaring rhetoric, as highlighted in his March 27 announcement on the first tranche of the surge: "For the Afghan people, a return to Taliban rule would condemn their country to brutal governance, international isolation, a paralyzed economy, and the denial of basic human rights to the Afghan people—especially women and girls."[21]

After that speech Obama continued to face pressure to protect Afghan women. Human rights groups lobbied him. Bipartisan amendments required the administration to work on protections for women. Congressional delegations visiting Afghanistan regularly met with Afghan women and stressed women's rights when meeting with Karzai, McChrystal, and Eikenberry. Key Democrats were leading advocates. Secretary of State Hillary Clinton, Senator Dianne Feinstein, and other lawmakers worried women could again face Taliban oppression. They therefore supported McChrystal's recommendations.[22] Other Democrats skeptical of the war conditioned their support on progress on women's rights. Speaker of the House Nancy Pelosi, a critic of a surge, stated: "We are not there to promote women's rights per say. We are there to say that women's rights are central to security, and that is essential to our national security."[23]

In his 60-day review for President Obama, Riedel had argued that Pakistan was the key to ending the terrorist threat to the United States and violence in Afghanistan. Since 2006, US suspicions of Pakistan's relationship with the Taliban had increased but the degree of support directed at the highest levels was unknown.

Obama and Biden rebuffed entreaties by Karzai to pressure Pakistan as the source of the violence in Afghanistan. "For us, Pakistan is fifty times more important than you," Biden scolded Karzai in a confrontational dinner in January 2009.[24]

Rather, Obama and his team attempted a new policy toward Pakistan based on the belief that the two states shared a common enemy in extremism. The Pakistani Taliban, allied with al-Qa'eda, were clearly a real threat to the Pakistani state and its nuclear weapons.

Obama decided to increase support for the Pakistani government for the fight against al-Qa'eda and the Pakistani Taliban while trying to dissuade the Pakistani military from supporting the Afghan Taliban and Haqqani network. He hoped to persuade Pakistan to pursue a set of mutual strategic objectives, including stability in Afghanistan. The administration's carrots were significant.

US drone strikes and counterterrorism operations that targeted the Pakistani Taliban intensified. The Pakistan Counterinsurgency Capability Fund and other programs allotted $3 billion over five years to the Pakistani military. In October 2009, Senator John Kerry, head of the Senate Foreign Relations Committee, pushed through the Kerry-Lugar-Berman Act that gave Pakistan an additional $1.5 billion per year for five years to reduce the drivers of militancy. In all, Pakistan was to receive greater than twice as much per year as they had from the Bush administration.

Despite the assassination of Benazir Bhutto in December 2007 and the resignation of Musharraf in 2008, the Pakistani military under General Ashfaq Parvez Kayani still controlled Pakistan's foreign and defense policy. Kayani had run the ISI from 2004 to 2007, the time of Musharraf's Taliban retrenchment. Admiral Mike Mullen (chairman of the joint chiefs of staff), Richard Holbrooke, Senator John Kerry, and other US officials tried to work with Kayani to find common strategic ground.

 In conversations, Kayani tacitly admitted that the military was supporting the Haqqani network and the Taliban. When Kerry visited Pakistan in October 2009, Kayani said that Mullah Omar was in Karachi but "we do not arrest him for the sake of peace talks."[25] Since Mullah Omar's actual whereabouts at the time may well have been in Zabul, there is a strong chance that Kayani was embellishing Pakistan's knowledge and power in order to impress Kerry that Pakistan should have a large say in Afghanistan's future. Kayani nevertheless had surprisingly few qualms about confirming a Taliban-Pakistani military relationship.

Mullen, Holbrooke, Kerry, and others could never convince Kayani to change policy. For Kayani and the Pakistani military, the Afghan Taliban and the Haqqani network remained an invaluable check on the influence of India in Afghanistan and the influence of the Pakistani Taliban within Pakistan. Attacking either could drive them to the Pakistani Taliban and create an even bigger threat to the Pakistani state. The Pakistan military left the Haqqani network alone in Miram Shah and the Quetta Shura alone in Quetta.

Upon arriving in Afghanistan in June 2009, McChrystal began implementing counterinsurgency and its precepts of limiting civilian casualties, improving governance, and protecting the population. Over his first month, he visited all the regional commands, in what he called a "listening tour." Wanting to understand the situation on the ground, he spoke with every brigade and battalion commander. What he found concerned him. His commanders betrayed a haphazard understanding of counterinsurgency. He assessed they were under-resourced and that the fight was going poorly.

One of McChrystal's first moves was to try to reduce the number of Afghans killed by US and allied operations. Distinct from most every other US general,

McChrystal grasped how civilian casualties were a strategic problems *and did something* to solve the problem. For years, air strikes, night raids, and other activities had been killing innocent Afghans collaterally. A watershed event was in May 2006 when a US military convoy killed five Afghans in a traffic accident and triggered a riot in Kabul. Incidents worsened as Taliban attacks escalated throughout the country and US and allied military operations intensified in response. In August 2008, an air strike in Herat killed at least 78 civilians—mostly women and children—and infuriated President Karzai. He refused to see US diplomats for 15 days.[26] Of a reported 2,118 civilian casualties throughout Afghanistan in 2008, 828 were killed or wounded by the United States or its partners.[27] A few weeks before McChrystal's arrival, air strikes in Farah on May 4, 2009, killed roughly 90 civilians and lit off more riots in Kabul.

Civilian deaths and night raids were at the root of the growing feud between Karzai and the United States, a feud that deepened in 2009. Karzai saw it as his duty to protect Afghan civilians from the American and Afghan militaries as much as the Taliban. Repeated incidents of civilian casualties and unfulfilled promises to stop them damaged Karzai's trust in the United States. As early as 2006, he had cried on television over NATO and US air strikes killing civilians. The next year, after air and artillery strikes allegedly killed 100 civilians in one week, he called a press conference at the palace and denounced "careless" US and allied military operations: "Afghan life is not cheap and should not be treated as such.... The extreme use of force, the disproportionate use of force to a situation, and the lack of coordination with the Afghan government is causing these casualties."[28]

When little changed, anger over civilian deaths consumed Karzai. He told journalist Carlotta Gall, "I want an end to civilian casualties. As much as one may argue it's difficult, I don't accept that argument.... the war against terrorism is not in Afghan villages."[29] Protecting Afghan civilians was more important than carrying out the surge. He cared not if a military operation failed as long as civilians were unharmed.

Too many Americans dismissed Afghan outrage at civilian casualties as a Taliban ruse or Karzai-manufactured complaint. It was neither. Karzai personified widespread Afghan distaste for civilian casualties and night raids. The most hard-bitten rivals of the Taliban shared it.

Polls showed that Afghans strongly opposed American raids and arrests.[30] Seventy-seven percent of respondents to an ABC/BBC poll said that air strikes were unacceptable because they endangered too many civilians.[31]

Afghans generally considered bombing people and also night raids (specifically entering homes at night) oppressive. Certain leading Afghans, including elected members of parliament, criticized US presence because of them. A common question posed to US diplomats and officers was, "The United States kills a family to get one Taliban. Is that just?"[32] Maulawi Mohudin Baluch, a member of the national ulema council and one of the most respected scholars in the country, put it best: "Mullahs in Afghanistan are upset at American bombardments and raids. To get one Taliban, you will destroy an entire village. This goes against the Koran."[33] Even Gul Agha Sherzai, one of the most pro-American warlords, said, "People do not trust the government and do not trust the United States. They are upset with the United States for killing innocent people and detaining innocent people."[34]

McChrystal judged that civilian casualties could cost the United States the war.[35] In order to reduce them, on July 2, 2009, he issued a tactical directive that restrained the use of air strikes against homes except in self-defense or other prescribed conditions. He also forbade US and allied forces from entering mosques (except in self-defense), and recommended that only Afghan forces conduct searches of homes.[36] McChrystal wrote in his memoir:

> I would ask soldiers and marines to demonstrate what we soon termed "courageous restraint"—forgoing fires, particularly artillery and air strikes, when civilian casualties were likely. . . . I was emphatic that fires could and should be used if the survival of our forces was directly threatened, but in cases where the only purpose was to kill insurgents, the protection of civilian lives and property took precedence.[37]

Plenty of soldiers and officers cringed, believing the directive put their lives in danger by denying the full force of air and artillery strikes in battle. The directive did not actually change the legal rules of engagement, which always guaranteed the right of soldiers to defend themselves by all means necessary. Nevertheless, comrades and men would sometimes die, especially when commanders misinterpreted McChrystal's intent and banned all artillery and air strikes.

The media publicized their criticisms, often sharp and poignant after a unit had suffered avoidable losses. "I wish we had generals who remembered what it was like when they were down in a platoon. . . . Either they never have been in real fighting, or they forgot what it's like," protested one army sergeant in the south.[38] Other officers, right-wing commentators, and veterans accused McChrystal of hanging young Americans out to die. Many journalists and liberal groups and politicians, often originally supportive of the changes, went silent—or even joined the critics. Other than support from Petraeus, McChrystal was on his own. Only McChrystal's standing as the foremost terrorist hunter licensed him to see the directive through.

The directive would make a difference. In 2008, American and coalition troops had killed 828 civilians. The number would fall to 449 in 2010 and then 369 in 2011. It would decline further over the following years. Karzai appreciated

McChrystal's effort. According to British ambassador Sherard Cowper-Coles, McChrystal forged the best relationship with Karzai of any US or allied commander of the time.[39]

In addition to reducing civilian casualties, McChrystal tried to clean up the Afghan government. Major progress in governance and development became part of the US plan on the ground. McChrystal later wrote, "Afghanistan's inherent weakness in governance was at the core of the problem. . . . [A]bsent legitimate governance, real progress was impossible."[40] Indeed, experts deemed such improvements vital to attaining even minimalist goals. The argument went that the government could never stand on its own if corruption, weak delivery of goods and services, and unfair policies drove people to the Taliban.

The White House and State Department also wanted corruption and governance problems remedied.[41] Obama was critical of Karzai for the corruption of his government.[42] At their first meeting, on a trip to Afghanistan in July 2008 as a senator and presidential candidate, Obama had warned Karzai: "I want to stress that whoever becomes president, the United States will continue to support Afghanistan, but the government of Afghanistan also must counter corruption and narcotics."[43]

McChrystal's staff and Eikenberry's embassy composed an ambitious "integrated civil-military campaign plan." It addressed justice, accountable and transparent governance, sustainable jobs, agricultural opportunity and market access, and corruption and narcotics.

McChrystal sought to counter corruption systematically, including by trying to remove corrupt leaders.[44] He set up an anti-corruption task force and retained Sarah Chayes as an advisor. The US and UK embassies convinced the independent directorate for local governance (IDLG), which managed the district and provincial governors on behalf of Karzai, to subject every provincial and district governor to a written exam in order to make selection more meritocratic. From 2010 to 2012, the directorate would try to replace unqualified governors and district governors.[45] These efforts would garner some successes but politics and money would continue to dominate appointments. Afghans were adept at circumventing exams and other meritocratic processes.

Improving governance followed the conventional wisdom of the time. Western military officers, human rights advocates, development experts, and intellectuals prioritized fixing Afghanistan's government.[46] Counterinsurgency evolved into a broad effort to build the Afghan nation-state instead of a focused one to protect the people from insurgent attacks. Reforming government is a formidable goal that historically consumes decades.

In support of the military surge, the US State Department launched its own "civilian surge." Nearly 900 additional civilians were sent to Afghanistan to work in provincial reconstruction teams and district support teams. The latter were a new innovation, consisting of two to five civilians, placed in a district under the provincial reconstruction team. The US embassy and State Department wanted to bring greater assistance to the countryside and villagers than was possible via a provincial reconstruction team alone. Civilians at both the provincial reconstruction teams and new district support teams mentored government officials, implemented small projects, and tried to improve the delivery of goods and services from the government to the people. One of their main duties was to help the Afghan government elect community councils in order to improve representation of aggrieved groups.

On the security front, counterterrorism operations intensified. Years of innovations, technological advances, and increased funding had improved effectiveness. Drones were more lethal. Intelligence analysis was more refined. Tempo was higher. From 2003 to 2008, McChrystal had instituted many innovations himself as commander of special operations. Intelligence fusion centers, onsite exploitation of evidence, intelligence sharing, and rapid prosecution of actionable intelligence fueled hundreds of raids per month.

In June 2009, McChrystal requested a larger portion of the US military's special operations forces and drones for Afghanistan. He wanted an aggressive campaign of precision strikes. General Petraeus and Vice Admiral Bill McRaven, the commander of joint special operations command, fulfilled McChrystal's request.[47] Starting in the autumn, the number of special operations teams in Afghanistan tripled.[48] McRaven made Bagram his primary command post. He would supervise counterterrorist targeting from there.

From August 2009 onward, McRaven's special operations forces expanded their target set to include low-level Taliban, the idea being to work up the food chain to senior leaders. Strike forces raided a target every night. The number of night raids rose five-fold between February 2009 and December 2010.[49] Because of the demand for action, often on sketchy intelligence, more raids came up empty-handed than not. But the tempo was impressive. Special operations forces killed or captured scores of Taliban per month.

The United States also struck terrorist leadership in Pakistan. Drones had been hitting targets in Pakistan since 2004. Obama stepped up their use. Strikes into Pakistan went from 36 in 2008, to 54 in 2009, and then to 122 in 2010.[50] A variety of terrorists, especially al-Qaʻeda and Pakistani Taliban, were killed, including several al-Qaʻeda leaders and Baitullah Mehsud, leader of the Pakistani Taliban.[51]

The White House did not authorize drone strikes against the Afghan Taliban inside Pakistan, other than select strikes against the Haqqani network. Obama and Biden deigned military requests for strikes on the Afghan Taliban in Pakistan as irresponsible attempts to expand the war. Kayani wanted neither the Afghan

Taliban nor their Haqqani subset struck. He continued Musharraf's restriction against US drone and air strikes in Baluchistan, the province where Quetta was located and Taliban leadership was prevalent. Special operations forces themselves were not allowed to raid into Pakistan. In September 2008, US special operations forces had raided a supposed al-Qaʻeda location in the tribal areas and accidentally killed civilians. The Pakistani press strongly criticized the raid. President Bush had also been upset and had banned future raids into Pakistan. Concerned about US relations, Obama left the ban in place. Taliban in Pakistan could operate relatively unhindered by US counterterrorism operations.[52]

Since 2006, Eikenberry and then McNeill and McKiernan had improved the Afghan army and police. US funding for the Afghan security forces had increased from $1.9 billion in 2006 to $7.4 billion in 2007.[53] The army had grown from 26,000 in 2006 to 68,000 in 2008.[54] It now had five "corps": the 201st for the eastern region around Nangarhar, the 203rd for the southeast around Loya Paktiya and Ghazni, the 205th for the south around Kandahar, the 207th for the west around Herat, and the 209th for the north around Mazar-e-Sharif. The standalone 111th Capital Division defended Kabul. Each corps contained three brigades. Each brigade contained three infantry battalions ("kandaks") and an artillery battery. Each infantry battalion officially numbered 650 men. Actual strength of a battalion in the field at any one time varied between 250 and 350.

In spite of these efforts, the army and police were still too small. At the end of 2008, after seven years, there were just 148,000 soldiers and police in a country of 33 million fighting off a raging insurgency. At the turn of the 20th century Emir Abdur Rahman Khan had possessed only slightly fewer—130,000 (70,000 tribal levies plus a 60,000-man army) for a population of just 5 million.

McChrystal wanted to raise the planned total strength of the army and police. He and Washington settled upon a combined army and police of 352,000 (195,000 for the army and 157,000 for the police). Under McChrystal's direction, the army shifted from a smaller, slower-built to a larger, faster-built force that could quickly go into action. McChrystal accepted the risk that quality might suffer in the process.[55] Even with the stress on size and speed, soldiers and police would be better equipped and trained than before—a low bar, to be sure. The standard army recruit would be trained for six months. Officers would go to an academy. For the police, a painstaking process began to train new recruits and the majority of the existing force, who had never received any formal training in the first place. McChrystal's command set police training at three weeks minimum.[56]

McChrystal emphasized advising. Ten to fifteen advisors were already assigned to every Afghan battalion, brigade, and corps headquarters. Besides the advisors, US battalions partnered with Afghan army battalions and operated with them. Every US battalion generally had at least one Afghan counterpart.[57] A smattering of units advised the police: US civilian contractors, provincial reconstruction teams, military police detachments, and platoons on the ground picking it up as an ad hoc responsibility.[58]

McChrystal expected advisors to try to live in the same headquarters as the Afghans or right next to it. Americans used the Dari phrase *shona ba shona* (shoulder by shoulder) to characterize the spirit of cooperation, saying it over and over again. Over the next two years, nearly every US battalion would run one or two advisory teams of as many as 30 men each that worked with the Afghan army and police as closely as possible.

The Afghan army was diversified between Tajiks, Hazaras, Uzbeks, and Pashtuns but the Tajik bias persisted. Minister of Defense Rahim Wardak was a Pashtun with a technocratic bent who nurtured very close relations with the Americans. The Tajiks preserved extensive power within the army through the extant network of former defense minister Mohammed Fahim and Bismullah Khan, still chief of the general staff. Bismullah Khan had influence over appointments and carefully placed Tajiks in key billets. Wardak lacked the power to overrule him. The majority of brigade commanders and a good number of the battalion commanders were loyal to Bismullah.[59] A large picture of a pensive Ahmed Shah Massoud often overlooked their desks, next to the official one of Karzai. Eastern Pashtuns from Jalalabad were a minority in the army. Southern Pashtuns were rarest of all.

The big event of 2009 was the presidential election. Dr. Abdullah—Massoud's diplomat and Karzai's former foreign minister—was Karzai's primary challenger. Because of his time as foreign minister and visibility working national issues, Dr. Abdullah had risen as a Tajik political figurehead among the coterie of other Tajik powerbrokers. Former defense minister Mohammed Fahim was still the most powerful Tajik while Bismullah Khan oversaw military affairs and Mohammed Atta accumulated power in Mazar-e-Sharif. The brilliant Amarullah Saleh was the up and coming director of the NDS (Afghanistan's intelligence directorate). The Tajiks had good relations with Karzai. Fahim was on Karzai's ticket as his selection for first vice president (in Afghanistan, the president has a first and second vice president). Abdullah's candidacy was as much about posturing as winning. Even if Dr. Abdullah might concede to Karzai in the end, running a Tajik candidate was a way of asserting Tajik power in Afghan politics.

In the run-up to the election, America's relationship with Karzai frayed. Karzai disregarded entreaties by Ambassador Eikenberry and other US officials to do something about corruption within his government, professing that the war in Afghanistan was because of Pakistan, not poor governance. Rangin Dadfar Spanta, who was now Karzai's national security advisor, would channel Karzai's complaints that US officials "repeated the unrealistic analysis of American and English experts and the media of the two countries that the main cause of the Afghan crisis is bad governance" and that "there were cases when US and British officials took over responsibility for Afghan prosecutors and police and effectively deprived us of our sovereignty."[60]

Bush had always been partial to Karzai and had made time for him, videoconferencing every other week, even while politely disregarding his concerns about civilian casualties or Pakistan. Obama and his team thought Bush had been pandering to Karzai. Obama suspended the videoconferences until March 2010; the recession and other pressing matters deserved his attention. Armed with judgment instead of compassion, Vice President Biden and Special Representative Holbrooke had a series of frustrating meetings with Karzai that on occasion escalated to insult. Rumors spread through Washington and the US headquarters in Kabul that Karzai was a manic-depressive, on medication, and smoking marijuana.[61] Vague "intelligence" reports were cited as evidence. In retrospect it looks like the worst kind of gossip, a sign of where things were headed.

During the election campaign, Eikenberry and Holbrooke encouraged candidates to run against Karzai. On Holbrooke's wishes, Eikenberry even appeared at a press conference with Dr. Abdullah. Holbrooke claimed to be fostering a competitive environment, healthy for any democracy. Karzai inferred that the United States wanted him out.[62] McChrystal writes in his memoir, "President Karzai frequently raised with me his frustration at what he interpreted as Western efforts to find and support other candidates to supplant him."[63]

Eikenberry's role in this escapade can be attributed to a belief in helping the average Afghan and a belief in competitive elections, akin to his belief in an Afghan army driven by nationalism. Democracy outweighed his own relationship with Karzai. "My goal is not to have a perfect relationship," he would say, "Perfect relationships exist in heaven."[64]

Holbrooke's role can be chalked up to hubris. According to Defense Secretary Gates and certain others, Holbrooke wanted rid of Karzai, seeing him as undermining the legitimacy of the state.[65] Gates recalls, "Holbrooke was doing his best to bring about the defeat of Karzai. . . . What he really wanted was to have enough credible candidates running to deny Karzai a majority in the election, thus forcing a runoff in which he could be defeated."[66] If Holbrooke truly sought to oust Karzai, he both failed to remove him and through open campaigning embittered him toward the United States.

At the end of election day on August 20, Karzai claimed victory by majority. It was evident to Holbrooke and Eikenberry, however, that his supporters had perpetrated massive fraud. In the east and south, ballot boxes of entire districts had been stuffed with votes in his favor. Certain polling centers had existed on paper that never existed on the ground. Ballot boxes from these "ghost polling centers" were then stuffed in provincial capitals by Karzai supporters.[67]

The day after the election, Holbrooke went directly to Karzai, denounced the results, and called for a runoff. According to the head of the UN mission in Afghanistan, Kai Eide, "Holbrooke's first objective was to get rid of Karzai, which I thought was completely unacceptable interference in Afghanistan's internal affairs."[68] Under the Afghan system, a runoff was required if no candidate received more than 50 percent of the vote. Karzai hated that possibility. It would mar his legitimacy.

On October 20, a review process found that Karzai had not received a majority, which meant there would be a runoff between him and Abdullah. Senator John Kerry, a defeated presidential candidate himself, came in to convince Karzai to go along. In the end, the second round never happened. After a few weeks of argument and negotiation with Karzai, Abdullah stepped aside for the good of the country. Karzai was the reelected president. The fraudulent election caused many US officials to see Karzai as illegitimate.[69] For Obama, the fraud confirmed that Karzai was a poor partner.

In early November, after the elections had been decided, Eikenberry sent a cable to Washington that raised his concerns about Karzai. He wrote, "President Karzai is not an adequate strategic partner. . . . Counterinsurgency strategy assumes an Afghan political leadership [that is] . . . able to take responsibility . . . in furtherance of . . . a secure, peaceful, minimally self-sufficient Afghanistan hardened against transnational terrorist groups. Yet Karzai continues to shun responsibility. . . ."[70] The cable leaked to the New York Times, further damaging relations.

Distrust would poison relations between the United States and Karzai for the next five years. Spanta, the national security advisor, observed that for Karzai, "after 2009, everything became a US conspiracy . . . and absolute sovereignty became the single monologue."[71] Obama would lose because Karzai would obstruct US strategy. Karzai would lose because his distrust-fueled vitriol would turn off the White House to his insights.

Ironically, the idea that had most caused Holbrooke to look for alternatives to Karzai—that his reelection would undermine popular support for the government—never came to pass.[72] The 2010 Asia Foundation survey found that positive assessments of the national government were at their highest levels since 2007. Satisfaction with the national government rose from 67 percent in 2008 to 71 percent in 2009 to 73 percent in 2010. Seventy-four percent of respondents believed that elections had improved the country. Fifty-four percent considered the 2009 elections free and fair. In the south, where US policymakers most feared Karzai's reelection, satisfaction with the government rose from 59 percent in 2009 to 69 percent in 2010.[73] I was in Helmand at the time. I recall no Afghans complaining about Hamid Karzai, Popalzai descendent of

Ahmed Shah Durrani, founder of the Afghan state. Karzai's legitimacy rested on much more than a fraudulent election.

Over the summer, Washington's attitude toward the war changed. The election debacle caused Obama to question whether governance, already identified as the key problem in the country, could be fixed. More importantly, concern over the US economy deepened. The consensus of late 2008 that Afghanistan was a good war dissolved by autumn 2009. Counterinsurgency doctrine (sometimes abbreviated as "COIN") had been written in 2005 and 2006, before the economic downturn. The banking crash of 2008 and the beginning of the great recession dampened America's enthusiasm for foreign wars. Following his confirmation, congressmen and senators warned McChrystal that he had a year to turn things around or public support would dry up.[74]

A September 2009 CBS poll found that 41 percent of Americans thought the number of US forces should be reduced rather than increased. Only 26 percent had held that same view at the beginning of the year.[75] According to a December Gallup poll, 73 percent of Americans worried that the war in Afghanistan would distract from more pressing economic matters at home.[76]

Obama opposed sending further reinforcements to Afghanistan. In June, Gates informed Obama of McChrystal's ongoing assessment of the situation and that more troops might be necessary. Unaware that Gates had asked for an assessment in the first place, Obama reacted angrily. He said there was no political support in Congress for another troop increase. He felt the generals were trying to force escalation upon him.[77]

On August 30, 2009, McChrystal delivered his formal assessment of the situation in Afghanistan to the White House and the Pentagon. In it, he wrote, "The key take away from this assessment is the urgent need for a significant change to our strategy. . . . [The] new strategy must . . . be properly resourced and executed through an integrated civilian-military counterinsurgency campaign that earns the support of the Afghan people and provides them with a secure environment."[78] If no change were to occur, McChrystal warned that the war would likely end in failure because the insurgency could gain such momentum that within a few years the government might be defeated.[79]

The assessment called for a robust implementation of counterinsurgency. It bluntly stated, "ISAF is not adequately executing the basics of COIN doctrine." The goal was to protect the population: "Our strategy cannot be focused on seizing terrain or destroying insurgent forces; our objective must be the population." The interpretation of "protecting the population" was expansive: "Protecting the population is more than preventing insurgent violence and intimidation. It also means that ISAF can no longer ignore or tacitly accept abuse of power, corruption, or marginalization."[80]

The effect on the policy debate was subtle yet important. US officers in Iraq had usually interpreted "protecting the population" in the strict sense of protecting the people against insurgent violence through years of patrolling and outposting the places where large numbers of people lived—towns, important villages, and the immediately surrounding countryside. It was a guideline against operations that ignored the population, ventured into peripheral regions, or swept through but did not stay. McChrystal's expansive interpretation called for much more: "'Protecting the people means shielding them from *all* threats.' Those threats were not just from insurgent and collateral violence. Those threats were also from the corruption and predation of the Afghans' own government."[81] The underlying theme was that all the problems of Afghanistan had to be tackled urgently in a dramatic fashion—rather than managed over time.

To support this strategy, a few days after submitting his assessment, McChrystal asked for 40,000 additional reinforcements.[82] He presented options for 11,000 or 85,000 as alternatives, but 40,000 was the number he strongly supported. His staff's analysis had convinced him fewer could not get the job done. No timeline was placed on the surge but McChrystal was thinking out to around 2013.

The 40,000 request sparked a long debate between the White House and Pentagon. McChrystal's counterinsurgency strategy and his request for more forces contradicted Obama's desire to limit his commitment. Obama, and especially Biden, challenged the necessity of a counterinsurgency strategy and 40,000 reinforcements. Obama questioned how such a surge would help defeat al-Qaʻeda, the true threat to the United States. He initiated a long series of national security council discussions on Afghanistan and Pakistan. The entire policy underwent a full review.

In its latter years, Bush and his team had followed an unwritten conviction that the Taliban had to be defeated before the United States could leave Afghanistan. It had been Eikenberry in 2007 who had first proposed that the United States might instead build up the Afghan army and police and then turn over the war at least in part to them. The idea of enabling the Afghan government to stand on its own instead of winning the war now gained currency.

Vice President Biden argued a long-term surge would be politically and economically unsustainable. He championed counterterrorism, dubbed "counterterrorism-plus," as an alternative. In his heart, disappointed with the Afghan government, he wanted to go down to a few thousand special operations forces in a few bases but thought it politically infeasible. The possible fall of Kabul would be too much. Counterterrorism-plus was the best he felt he could do. Special operations forces would hunt down al-Qaʻeda and terrorist leaders while advisors would train the Afghan army and police. The idea resembled

Eikenberry's 2007 suggestion. Eikenberry sided with Biden and opposed McChrystal's surge recommendation.

Counterterrorism-plus captured the imagination of the media. Journalist David Ignatius wrote, "By using ISR sensors, U.S. forces can see what's coming at them across Afghanistan's porous borders. And with new surveillance tools, they may be able to identify the networks and individuals that pose the biggest threat—and then call in Special Forces teams to capture or kill insurgent leaders."[83]

At first, Biden did not specify exact numbers. He then shifted from no reinforcements (perhaps even removing 4,000 to 10,000) to his final proposal in November of 20,000 reinforcements (84,000 troops in country).[84]

McChrystal and Petraeus stuck to their guns on counterinsurgency and 40,000. Confident of success, they composed no additional options for the president. They believed the United States could commit such numbers to Afghanistan for years without popular or political repercussions—and that Obama would go along. The success of Iraq was narrowing their forethought.

McChrystal's claim that the entire war effort would fail without reinforcements tainted the debate by raising the specter of political catastrophe if reinforcements were denied. In retrospect the risk was exaggerated. The danger to the centers of government power, namely Kabul, Kandahar City, and Jalalabad, was manageable. The two battalions McKiernan had sent to Wardak and Logar were obstructing the Taliban threat to Kabul that had been so concerning in 2008. McChrystal himself knew there was time but nevertheless highlighted the risk of failure. He admits in his memoir, "While Kandahar's security was a serious concern as the districts around the city were inflamed, it wasn't besieged or in imminent danger of falling."[85]

A longer-term strategy of building up the Afghan forces and holding back the Taliban should have been feasible under the conditions of mid-2009, without any reinforcements beyond the first 21,000. McChrystal's warning of failure crowded out serious consideration of such an alternative. Impressed with McChrystal's assessment, Gates dismissed a longer-term, no-surge strategy outright, arguing that "standing pat, middling options, [and] muddling through are not the right path forward and put our kids at risk for no good purpose."[86] Biden's counterterrorism-plus came closer but in the end even he called for 20,000 reinforcements.

The only advocates of a long commitment without further reinforcements were US diplomat Kael Weston, veteran of Fallujah and Khost now stationed in Helmand, who often advised US generals and the US embassy to "go low to stay long," and former British diplomat Rory Stewart, who testified to Congress that with "a very long-term presence" and "a much lighter and more limited presence . . . we can, over 30 years encourage the more positive trends in Afghan society and help to contain the more negative. . . . In the long-term, less will be more."[87]

The debate over troop numbers and counterinsurgency versus counterterrorism bled into the media. The public role of the military affected President Obama's choices. McChrystal's assessment leaked to the *Washington Post* in late September. During the autumn, Petraeus, Mullen, and McChrystal made a series of ill-advised comments in speeches, testimony, and interviews in the press that advocated for counterinsurgency and 40,000 troops. Most famously, at a talk in London on October 1, McChrystal dismissed Biden's counterterrorism-plus.

Obama viewed these actions as insubordinate. The military's open lobbying, he reprimanded Gates and Mullen, had "boxed him in."[88] If Obama chose an opposing course of action, political rivals would accuse him of disregarding military advice, a dangerous allegation for any Democrat president. CIA director Leon Panetta, a former senator and chief of staff to President Bill Clinton, was attuned to this reality: "Obama was a new president, a Democrat without military experience. For him to defy his military advisers on a matter so central to the success of his foreign policy and so early in his presidency would have represented an almost impossible risk."[89] Every public comment by a general was essentially an ultimatum that Obama would pay a political price to debate. Against this backdrop, Obama came to distrust the military. Speaking out in public, Petraeus and McChrystal ceased to be military advisors and became political actors in their own right. In Obama's view, the military was overly committed to winning the war and unable to see that broader US interests, especially at home, could be more important.[90]

The sense of being boxed in appears to have driven Obama toward a surge he otherwise would have avoided. In addition to the pressure from the military, he was concerned that Gates, who was widely respected, might resign if no new reinforcements were deployed. Obama had asked Gates to stay on from the Bush administration because of his reputation as a professional and to strengthen his administration's defense credentials. Gates's resignation could do the opposite. For months, Gates had expressed frustration that Americans were being left in harm's way without proper support. When the debate started in September, White House anger at the troop request caused Gates to privately ponder resignation. Obama detected his frustration.[91]

With unappealing options before him, Obama searched for ways to avoid getting stuck in Afghanistan. He assessed that completely defeating the Taliban would take too long and be too costly, untenable from both a domestic political and a strategic standpoint.[92] In March, he had told the national security council, "I think I have two years with the public on this. . . . They'll stand by us for two years. That's my window."[93] The expense of the surge especially troubled him. He learned that with 40,000 additional troops the cost of the Afghan War would be

$889 billion over 10 years. His fiscal stimulus package to get the United States out of the recession that had passed in February was roughly $800 billion over the same period.[94] Afghanistan was going to cost the same as fixing the economy, perhaps the country's greatest interest. Obama told his staff, "This is not what I'm looking for. . . . I'm not doing 10 years. I'm not doing a long-term nation-building effort. I'm not spending a trillion dollars."[95] Such expenditures would divert political resources from other pressing domestic issues within the United States as well. The war, Obama warned, could suck the oxygen out of everything else.[96] With this wider matter at hand, Obama firmly opposed any open-ended commitment as incommensurate with limited US goals in Afghanistan. He refused to let Afghanistan become a war without end.[97]

In discussions through October and November with his team, Obama decided the goal of the surge would be to break Taliban momentum in Afghanistan and enable the Afghan government to stand on its own so that the United States could pull back the surge reinforcements. Al-Qaʻeda was his overarching concern. If the Afghan government collapsed, al-Qaʻeda was expected to return to Afghanistan and make it into a safe haven. That had to be prevented. Obama's idea was to "transition" to the Afghan government, reducing the US footprint in Afghanistan at the end of five years. The exact meaning of transition was left slightly ambiguous. Obama did not say explicitly that the United States would pull out entirely from Afghanistan once Taliban momentum was broken. What is important is that his goal raised the possibility.[98]

Fed up with Petraeus and Mullen, Obama composed the final surge plan on his own after conferring with Gates. Obama decided to send 30,000 additional reinforcements. He wrote the goals as: deny al-Qaʻeda a safe haven, reverse Taliban momentum against the government, and strengthen the Afghan armed forces and government so they could secure Afghanistan on their own.[99] He foreswore "fully resourced counterinsurgency." He gave Gates an option to send 3,000 more for emerging needs, which was eventually taken, for a total of nearly 100,000 US troops in country. Because he rejected a long-term commitment of so many troops, Obama decided the drawdown would begin in July 2011—a tight timeline for success. He believed a timeline was necessary to win the support of the American people and would impose urgency on the military and the Afghan government. He did not fix the pace of the drawdown at this point. A review was set for December 2010 to inform that decision. For his part, McChrystal disagreed with 30,000 and the timeline but, determined to try, told Obama he could live with it.

Obama announced the decision on December 2, 2009, in a speech at West Point: "Our overarching goal remains the same . . . to disrupt, dismantle, and defeat al-Qaʻeda. . . . We will pursue a military strategy that will break the Taliban's momentum and increase Afghanistan's capacity over the next 18 months."[100]

He stressed the strategic shift to handing over to the Afghans: "It must be clear that Afghans will have to take responsibility for their security, and that America has no interest in fighting an endless war in Afghanistan."[101] The big picture featured highly: "I refuse to set goals that go beyond our responsibility, our means, or our interests. And I must weigh all of the challenges that our nation faces. I don't have the luxury of committing to just one."[102] The surge was subordinate to economic growth: "Our troop commitment in Afghanistan cannot be open-ended—because the nation that I am most interested in building is our own."[103]

Obama's July 2011 timeline drew fire. Senators John McCain and Lindsey Graham, and a variety of experts, argued that the timeline gave the Taliban reason to wait out the surge and partners reason to hedge. Determining the actual effect of the timeline on perceptions is shaky business. Changes in perceptions are very difficult to prove. The best historian has trouble getting into people's heads, especially the heads of hundreds of Taliban cadre leaders scattered across the deserts and mountains of Afghanistan and Pakistan, or the heads of senior leaders, such as Mullah Omar and Mullah Baradar, hidden away in Zabul and Quetta.

In this case, some evidence suggests that the Taliban senior leaders might have decided to wait things out. For example, in 2010, Mullah Naim Barech, Taliban governor of Helmand (living in Pakistan), told a group of Helmand village elders that the United States would leave in 2011 and that the Taliban would return.[104] Watching from Pakistan, Osama bin Laden encouraged the Taliban to think this way. He wrote to Mullah Omar in November 2010, "America's wise men are telling the government it must reduce the size of the Pentagon budget . . . and interest on their (national) debt. . . . The situation requires a bit of patience from the mujahedin . . . Even Obama believes they need to withdraw in the coming months, as he said publicly."[105]

The Quetta Shura and Taliban cultural commission put out official commentary in their publications. On December 7, they issued a response to Obama's announcement that implied that Taliban took heart from the timeline: "Now Afghans, international observers and some parts of the American people know the truth very well. Obama's cleverness cannot pass."[106] Similarly, an article in the Taliban magazine *Shah Mat* in 2010 derided the idea that the United States could succeed within a year as a foolish and childish claim and stated that "if America had an expectation for victory, then they would never raise talk of the withdrawal of their forces."[107] Altogether the evidence is persuasive that the Taliban expected the United States to leave but far too scant to prove they would have caved had there been no timeline.

From General Kayani and his colleagues in the Pakistani army, little changed. In December, Kayani "was openly skeptical that we would succeed," recounted McChrystal. "He stated . . . that while we had the correct approach . . . we lacked the time to accomplish all that was necessary before support for our effort would fade. He particularly doubted our ability to create effective Afghan security forces to which we could later transfer control."[108] Kayani and Pakistani generals repeated such comments to many other Americans.[109] They continued to help the Taliban to the degree they felt necessary to secure Pakistan's long-term interests.

The surge marks a major milestone in the Afghan War. It ushered in tens of thousands of US troops and ensured the war would intensify. It also shifted US goals. The goal of defeating the Taliban gave way to reversing Taliban momentum within two years and then handing over to the Afghan government.

The fact that Obama set a timeline on his own strategy raises the question of why he did not consider all-out withdrawal in 2009 and save himself the costs of years of war. Reviewing the history, it seems that full withdrawal was never on the table, even within Obama's close White House staff. At the outset of the autumn strategy review, Obama had said that the United States would not abandon Afghanistan, a point he later repeated to his national security council and congressional leaders.[110] And in September, Obama and his full national security council unanimously agreed to the same point. During the meeting, even Biden denied an alternative to the surge was to leave Afghanistan. He merely opposed additional reinforcements. According to the available evidence, at no point during the surge discussions, from early 2009 to the final decision, did any participant advocate a full US withdrawal from Afghanistan or much of a reduction from 64,000 (the number of US troops present after the March decision to deploy 21,000 reinforcements).[111]

In terms of domestic politics, withdrawal would have opened the Democrat administration to intense criticism, possibly disturbing Obama's larger domestic agenda, including saving the economy. For the public, although increasing troops came under question in the course of the surge debate, complete withdrawal was not favored. A Gallup poll in early December found that 55 percent of respondents feared withdrawing troops from Afghanistan would make the United States vulnerable to terrorist attacks.[112]

During these discussions and later, journalists, analysts, and commentators often claimed that Obama's campaign pledge to turn around the Afghan War prevented him from withdrawing. Indeed, Obama told the national security council on September 13 that he "owned" the war.[113] Yet there is no good evidence that Obama personally wanted to withdraw but held back purely out of fear of political criticism.[114] On the face of his known remarks, he seems to have also concluded that the cost of failure in Afghanistan for US strategic interests was too high. Jonathan Alter, in his inside account of Obama's first year, writes, "Liberals who assumed that in his heart Obama was for withdrawal were mistaken. The president genuinely believed that national security interests—namely, preventing another attack on U.S. soil, were at stake."[115]

Looking backward it is hard to see how in 2009 the United States could have done anything other than stay in the war, whether at 43,000, 64,000, or 100,000 troops. Withdrawal would have raised the threat of attacks in the United States, a concern that had dominated US foreign policy since 2001. The United States was *stuck*. Obama had to make tough decisions to manage the problem. He could not cut America's losses and get out.

Bush had enjoyed freedom to maneuver for half his presidency. Obama never enjoyed such freedom. The Afghan government had been formed, violence had returned, old spirits had arisen in the Afghan people, defeats had been suffered, and greater ones loomed. In a time of freedom, Bush and his team made large, obvious mistakes. In a time of constraint, Obama played the cards he had been dealt. He minded the big picture, balancing the shifting terrorist threat against economic recession and geostrategic interests. His errors derived less from willful refusal of clear opportunities than oversights and miscalculations under the pressure of a tough situation. They could have big implications but they were not obvious.

The Surge in Helmand

The surge campaign spanned Afghanistan. The main effort was the south, where the threat was most dire. McChrystal's scheme of maneuver was to clear and hold Helmand and Kandahar, and then turn to the east. McChrystal originally wanted the 21,000 troops of the first tranche of the surge to go to Kandahar, the larger population, second in political importance only to Kabul. Earlier decisions stymied him.[1] Before McChrystal's appointment, McKiernan had decided to parse out the first tranche between different provinces. That first tranche was a Stryker brigade, a marine expeditionary brigade, and an 82nd Airborne brigade retooled as advisors. The marine expeditionary brigade (nearly 12,000 marines) went to Helmand. The Stryker brigade (roughly 5,000 soldiers) went to Kandahar.[2] The 4,000 advisors were parceled about Helmand, Kandahar, and several other provinces.

McChrystal grudgingly went along with McKiernan's decisions.[3] The marines had gone to Helmand for two reasons. First, the British were willing to work with the marines whereas the Canadians in Kandahar did not want to be overshadowed. Second, a separate Marine battalion was already in Helmand and the Marine Corps leadership wanted all the marine units operating in one area. Success in Helmand, McChrystal hoped, could be the first step in breaking the perception of Taliban strength.[4] The provincial capital of Lashkar Gah was barely afloat. If the Taliban captured the province, pressure against Kandahar would swell. But he was unhappy the decision had been forced upon him. He let marine generals coming through Kabul know, "I did not agree to the dispositions here!"[5]

In early 2009, the Taliban controlled most of Helmand, following three years of war that had begun with their 2006 offensive. The hilly north was in their hands, other than a few government buildings and police headquarters. Southern Helmand from the Pakistan border all the way up to Lashkar Gah was theirs too, other than the chunk of Garmser that the 24th Marine Expeditionary Unit had recaptured in 2008. Most importantly, roughly 1,000 to 2,500 Taliban operated in Marjah and Nad Ali, the two large farming communities adjacent to Lashkar Gah.[6] That put the provincial capital in danger.

Marjah served as a major logistics and command and control node. Special operations forces encountered severe resistance during incursions in March and May 2009. The target of the May incursion, known as "Operation Siege Engine," was Marjah's main bazaar. For two days, dozens of Taliban came at them from all directions. The fighting was so intense that the elite troops had almost exhausted their ammunition before they finally withdrew.

The marine formation that deployed with the first tranche of the surge was the 2nd Marine Expeditionary Brigade. Its elements began arriving in Helmand in May 2009: two infantry battalions (roughly 1,000 men each), a light armored reconnaissance (LAR) battalion, and an air element of CH-53 transport helicopters, new V-22 tilt-rotor aircraft, and AH-1 Cobra attack helicopters. Together with the marine battalion already operating in northern Helmand, the brigade was 10,700 strong.

Brigadier General Larry Nicholson was in command. Nicholson had been seriously wounded near Fallujah in 2004 and recovered to lead a regiment in the same city in 2006. Now in Helmand he was determined to make a difference. He wrote in his operational order that his method was to "partner with our Afghan Security Force brothers and the local population to vigorously pursue the enemy and destroy his ability and will to fight."[7] He and his marines had absorbed the lessons of Iraq and were adept at the tactics of small-unit patrolling, calling in air strikes, and advising local forces. "We're not going to drive to work. We're going to walk to work," he instructed marines going into the field. "Get to know the people. That's the reason why we're here."[8] Nicholson had witnessed the value of Iraqi soldiers and police in Fallujah and believed strong Afghan soldiers and police to be the key to long-term success. His concept of operations was based on holding key areas around Lashkar Gah and "ink-spotting" outward. "Clear, hold, and build" was an explicit principle of his operational concept. Above all, Nicholson demanded speed and was willing to take risks in order to break Taliban momentum as fast as possible.

As important as Nicholson's plan was the marine style of fighting. "Lieutenant Sean Connor . . . gave a patrol brief to his platoon," describes Major Gus Biggio of 1st Battalion, 5th Marine Regiment early in the campaign, "The assembled group were mostly white, but with a sizeable number of blacks and Hispanics too. They chose to serve for a variety . . . of reasons: patriotism, adventurousness, economic necessity, and family tradition. But . . . they now found themselves part of the tight-knit cadre of warriors."[9] "Every marine is a rifleman" was the saying. Lieutenants and captains, corporals and sergeants were taught to take initiative and close with the enemy. Marines were also thoroughly trained in the science of calling in close air support. Marine pilots, forward air controllers (who were pilots attached to infantry battalions), and infantry perfected the combination of ground maneuver and air strikes.

On this foundation, the marines had refined sophisticated tactics in Iraq. Experience in places such as Ramadi and al-Qa'im had demonstrated that lots of little outposts could watch lots of corners and city blocks round the clock and impede groups of insurgents from moving about. The risk of spreading marines out tended to be worth the effect. At the same time, marine units had reaffirmed that the best way to keep insurgents out of an area was to patrol on foot, in as few numbers as wise, as frequently as possible. Patrols could get into areas too tight for Humvees or mine resistant vehicles, chase insurgents, and, if lucky, ambush them. Marine technique mattered here. It was not a soft walking-the-beat patrol, but a combat-ready, trained-to-shoot-the-enemy patrol. Bing West, author of the classic Vietnam book, *The Village*, who accompanied the marines in many Helmand battles, writes, "There is only one way for American troops to clear insurgents from a district: patrol alongside Afghan soldiers until they're exhausted, and then patrol some more."[10]

Building again on their Vietnam and Iraq experiences, marines placed a premium on advising the police and army, living close to them and joining them in combat in order to mentor as closely as possible. They expected that policemen and soldiers could identify insurgents better than Americans.

Nicholson wanted the Afghan armed forces to play a large role in combat operations. Approximately 4,000 Afghan soldiers and 2,400 police were in Helmand.[11] Brigadier General Mohaiuddin Ghori, a hardened officer of the old communist army who fought because it was his profession, commanded the soldiers. Helmand fell under the 205th Corps, headquartered in Kandahar. Over the year, more Afghan army units would arrive. In the middle of 2010, the Afghan government would establish the 215th Corps, an entire new corps for Helmand. The police had their own set of unsavory problems. Tribal leaders looked down on them as the dregs of society.[12] Nicholson hoped to improve the police through the establishment of a Helmand police training center that would put recruits through an extended eight-week course, five weeks longer than McChrystal's standard.

The marines worked alongside 9,000 British of "Task Force Helmand." At the time, the commander was Brigadier Tim Radford. All told, 20,000 marines and British were in Helmand by mid-2009, working with roughly 4,000 Afghan soldiers and 2,400 Afghan police.[13]

The British had seen three years of hard combat in Helmand and had suffered significant casualties. Before 2006, British soldiers had prided themselves on being skilled counterinsurgents. Musa Qala and Taliban advances toward Lashkar Gah bruised their reputation. By 2009, Task Force Helmand was realigning its forces to get the upper hand and inkblotting out from Lashkar Gah into the surrounding districts of Nad Ali and Gereshk.

Besides Task Force Helmand, the British ran a provincial reconstruction team (PRT). Since 2005, the British had turned the provincial reconstruction team into the most skilled development organization in Afghanistan, with a staff of nearly 150 and a budget of about $45 million for programs and projects.[14] The leadership included top civil servants, diplomats, and development experts. The head of mission, Hugh Powell, outranked Radford. Different offices handled specific aspects of counterinsurgency: governance, rule of law, counter-narcotics, and politics, each with a well-prepared program. The British boldly sent "stabilization advisors," former British officers or experienced civilian experts, to the districts to implement programs directly and work with the district governors.[15] The civilians of the US surge came into Helmand from mid-July onward and joined the British provincial reconstruction team. In the districts, US civilians worked with the British stabilization advisors and formed district support teams.[16]

The most decisive British action to improve governance was Ghulab Mangal. In March 2008, Karzai appointed Mangal to replace Asadullah Wafa as governor of Helmand. Mangal was from Paktiya, in his mid-40s, with a stubble-short, graying beard. His preferred dress was a collarless suit with baggy pants and European-style eye-glasses—a combination of Afghan tradition and Western professionalism. He was educated and had extensive experience as a provincial governor in Paktika and Laghman and before that as an official in the government of communist leader Najibullah. He had no relationship with Helmand's warlords. The British backed Mangal to the hilt. They underwrote a large staff, transported him to events throughout the province, funded a counter-narcotics program, and created a public affairs team that televised him daily.

In backing Mangal, the British went against the grain. Karzai had no natural tie to Mangal and had never forgiven the British for forcing him to remove his ally, Sher Mohammed Akhundzada, back in 2005.[17] Sher Mohammed poisoned Karzai's ear with incessant criticism of Mangal. High-ranking British, and later US, officials repeatedly had to weigh in to prevent Karzai from firing him.[18] In 2008, on one of the first occasions, Prime Minister Gordon Brown personally told Karzai that the British had confidence in Mangal and Sher Mohammed could not return as governor. Karzai backed off for the time being.[19] The continual effort to protect Mangal absorbed British political capital and time. Such was the cost of good government.

In Quetta, the Taliban leadership monitored the US preparations for a surge. By 2009, Mullah Omar was increasingly sick, some say with diabetes, others tuberculosis.[20] Abdul Hai Mutmain, Mullah Omar's biographer, heard one of his last audio recordings, done in 2009: "His voice was weak and his speech sounded sickly. With great difficulty, he spoke."[21]

Sometime during the year, Omar withdrew himself even further from guiding the movement. Bette Dam, the most knowledgeable scholar on Omar, attests that "the people of Kandahar and Quetta had a fairly good idea where he was . . . then, in 2009, it stopped."[22] It was rumored he had gone into hiding in Karachi. Much more likely is that he was in Zabul, in desolate Shinkai district. The Taliban biography of Omar makes this case. A handful of Taliban were aware of his whereabouts and able to pass messages to him. His family may have been able to see him, or he may have been secluding himself completely, living only with the family of his bodyguard. In several stories, he spent his days reading the Koran and the Hadiths, and meditating. Omar had not foresworn issuing spiritual and strategic directions but his activity significantly diminished.[23]

In early 2009, partly in reaction to the surge, Omar's deputy, Mullah Baradar, reformed Taliban tactics. Baradar's guidance for the spring fighting season stressed guerrilla-style tactics rather than 2006-style offensives to seize new ground: "In this operation will be ambushes, swarming attacks, . . . and surprise attacks. Targets will be occupation forces, diplomatic centers, rival convoys, puppet administration high-ranking officials, members of parliament, NDS, defense, and interior ministry members."[24] In July 2009, as marines entered Helmand, Baradar gathered top Taliban commanders together near Quetta. In order to reduce casualties, he ordered them to avoid prolonged firefights with US soldiers and marines. Instead, they were to favor improvised explosive devices and small ambushes. Baradar was willing to surrender ground rather than suffer heavy losses. He said he wanted to minimize Taliban losses while maximizing those of the enemy.[25] Taliban leaders would later admit that because of the surge they had to stop fighting in large groups of 500 or more.[26]

Two Taliban leaders handled operations in Helmand: Mohammed Naim Barech and Abdul Qayum Zakir. Mohammed Naim was the Taliban provincial governor for Helmand. He had been wounded in 2007 in the special operations raid that killed Dadullah Lang. Naim now operated out of Girdi Jangal, Pakistan, entering Afghanistan from time to time.[27] Abdul Qayum Zakir was the leader of the Taliban's 2008 assault on Lashkar Gah. In early 2009, Zakir became head of the Taliban military commission, falling under Baradar.[28] The military commission's job was planning and oversight but it actually had no command authority. Zakir nevertheless took special interest in northern and central Helmand. His power base was northern Helmand. Stories of his fearlessness abounded.[29]

When he stepped on deck in Helmand, Nicholson's intention was to clear out Marjah immediately. McChrystal denied it. He wanted to focus on the election.[30] Nicholson and Radford turned to the Taliban-controlled areas near Lashkar Gah city: Nad Ali to the north and west, across the Helmand River; Nawa to the south; and southern Garmser to the south of Nawa, along the Helmand River. Control of these areas plus Marjah is what positioned the Taliban to threaten Lashkar Gah.

British operations kicked off first. Radford expanded his foothold in Nad Ali, which the British had been clearing since December.[31] On June 19, 3,000 Afghan, Danish, and British troops went into the community of Babaji (actually split across Nad Ali, Lashkar Gah, and Gereshk) from three directions. In five weeks of very tough fighting, Radford cleared villages of insurgents and improvised explosive devices. Casualties were heavy. Over one hundred British were killed and wounded, including one of Radford's battalion commanders.[32]

Two weeks later, on July 2, Nicholson advanced into Nawa and southern Garmser. Lieutenant Colonel Bill McCollough's 1st Battalion, 5th Marine Regiment, helicoptered into the Nawa countryside, fanned out, and set up outposts.[33] In less than a month, the Taliban pulled back into Marjah. Lieutenant Colonel Christian Cabaniss's 2nd Battalion, 8th Marine Regiment advanced into southern Garmser. Marines would clear farther and farther south over the next year, eventually forcing the Taliban entirely out.[34] Both Nawa and Garmser were characterized by very aggressive marine tactics. They set up as many posts as possible and patrolled as much as possible. There were 22 posts in Nawa by autumn 2009. The average number of patrols per day was 64 in Helmand compared to 22 in other provinces.[35]

In Nad Ali, Nawa, and Garmser, the provincial reconstruction team and its district support teams implemented governance and development programs.[36] The district support teams started with repair of the bazaars and government compounds. Health care and education projects followed, reopening the main clinics and schools. In late 2009, USAID brought in "AVIPA," a huge $310 million set of cash-for-work projects, seed and sapling distributions, and training programs for Helmand and Kandahar.[37] The USAID office of transition initiatives had another $160 million for quick impact projects in Helmand, Uruzgan, Zabul, and Kandahar.[38]

Once marines and British soldiers had instilled a measure of calm in the districts, the provincial reconstruction team and provincial government ran elections for community councils. Community councils were an initiative of the independent directorate for local governance (IDLG), the Afghan government agency that helped Karzai manage the district and provincial governors. The initiative established councils of 35 to 45 representatives in select districts and provinces. British governance experts Jon Moss and Derek Griffiths specially designed the Helmand program, which would be funded by the provincial re-construction team.

The role of the community councils was to resolve disputes, bring issues to the government, and identify projects. They resembled the tribal councils that had traditionally functioned in every district. Each community council would receive a budget. Moss and Griffiths hoped that the community councils would link the people to their government. With an outlet to voice their views and present their grievances, and access to projects, otherwise neglected villages might become less marginalized and therefore less likely to support the Taliban. The United States managed the initiative in other provinces. The US program flopped. The United States outsourced creation of the councils to non-governmental organizations (NGOs) that haphazardly appointed councils, distributed salaries, and then left them to their own devices. Most of those councils existed in name only. The Helmand councils were plugged into the government system and thrived for years.

Mangal's flagship program was the "food zone," designed to eliminate poppy in Helmand. The provincial reconstruction team and Mangal had crafted the program in 2008. It combined crop substitution with eradication. In order to reduce the cost to farmers' livelihoods, in the autumn, before planting season, Mangal distributed wheat seed to farmers as a substitute for poppy. In the spring, government tractors plowed under poppy in the areas where wheat had been distributed. That way, those farmers subject to eradication received a degree of compensation for their lost income. In order to further reduce discontent, the program was phased. Seeds were be handed out and poppy was only to be plowed under in secure areas. Violent areas were to be left alone.

In autumn 2009, the food zone program was implemented in the secure areas of Nawa, Garmser, Gereshk, and Nad Ali.[39] It generally succeeded. Within the area of the program, poppy cultivation fell from 33,000 hectares in 2008 to 20,000 in 2010.[40] Farmers and elders complied for a variety of reasons. Coupled with the threat of eradication, the tremendous number of projects provided Afghans, especially tribal leaders, an alternate source of income beyond wheat seed. The fact Islam considered the production of drugs forbidden (*haram*) mattered too. Afghans tended to feel a certain obligation to attempt alternatives to poppy, at least for a time. Plenty had a secret stash of harvested opium paste to ride out a rainy day.

The dark side of the food zone program was that only landowners could receive wheat seed; the government did not recognize land titles issued by the Taliban or communists. Consequently, numerous farmers were denied seed. If living within a secure area, they had to shift to a licit crop on their own or be eradicated. The policy pressured landless farmers to move out of government-controlled areas into areas under outright Taliban control.

By the end of 2009, Nicholson and Radford had cleared and held several areas of Helmand but not Marjah. So for the first year of the surge no crushing success occurred. Once Obama announced the second tranche of the surge in December 2009, McChrystal approved a Marjah offensive for February. Marjah would be the big event of 2010.

Marjah and adjoining Nad Ali were artificial communities. From the 1940s until the 1970s, the United States helped fund a massive modernization program to irrigate Helmand and Kandahar. This program is what dammed the Helmand River far to the north at Kajaki and dug new irrigation systems along both it and the Arghandab River in Kandahar.[41] The project divined Marjah and Nad Ali out of the desert. US engineers dug a canal that that diverted water from the Helmand River near Gereshk westward for 50 kilometers. Smaller canals, all parallel, dispensed water southward from the main canal, irrigating what would become Nad Ali. After 50 kilometers the main canal bent southward. New parallel canals dispensed water eastward into the community that became Marjah. They intersected lateral canals that drained water from the fields, turning the topography of Marjah (and Nad Ali) into 90 degree grids. Villages were placed in these grids, known as "blocks." The roads followed the canals, giving Marjah a remarkably American-looking road network.

In the 1950s and 1960s, the government distributed the land of Marjah and Nad Ali to "immigrants" from southern and eastern Afghanistan. Roughly 150,000 Afghans lived in the two communities, with the official district center in the latter. Different tribal groups of 20 to 100 households (roughly seven people per household) were allotted different blocks.[42] No tribe was dominant. Marjah and Nad Ali were diverse, hodgepodge, yet symmetrical.

After the Taliban captured Marjah and Nad Ali in 2008, the local tribal leaders largely submitted to Taliban rule. They let them enter their homes and fed them.[43] Few tribal leaders or farmers opposed the Taliban's policy of poppy cultivation. Various Marjah locals would later tell the marines that they feared the government would eradicate poppy and bring back wheat.[44]

Nicholson began planning for the Marjah offensive in summer 2009. McChrystal paid attention to the Marjah preparations, Karzai less so. Unwilling to proceed without the president of Afghanistan, McChrystal pulled Karzai in, briefed him and secured his final approval on February 12, a day later than the planned start of the operation.[45] The offensive was named Operation Moshtarak, Dari for "together."

Part of the plan was to get the government up and running in Marjah as soon as possible. Nicholson hoped to bring in a district governor and start the flow of goods and services as the military operation was ongoing. Nicholson and the provincial reconstruction team (now under Lindy Cameron) worked to ready a district support team, identify a district governor, prepare development packages, and help the provincial government prepare to restart education and health services. McChrystal promised rapid reconstruction and reestablishment of the government, saying that an Afghan "government in a box" would follow the assault. British and American civilians in the provincial reconstruction team were skeptical that a bright shiny new government could appear out of thin air.

Somewhere between 400 and 2,000 Taliban defended Marjah. Their ranks included as many as 200 fighters from Pakistan and Arab countries.[46] Baradar and Zakir knew an assault was pending. The Taliban tactical concept followed the course Baradar had laid in 2009 of surrendering ground rather than suffering heavy losses and relying on improvised explosive devices, small ambushes, and assassinations. At the end of 2009, Baradar affirmed that the new strategy was a success: "Praise be to Allah, with great determination, this year's jihadi strategy was filled with success. In an individual way, improvised explosive devices in roads, guerrilla attacks in Kabul and other areas, and massed attacks on government and foreign centers, and ambushes on foreign invaders and interior hired workers were very effective. It should be that such tactics can continue."[47] Zakir visited Marjah in February, shortly before the marine assault, to review defensive preparations. He and the Taliban Marjah commanders planned to use large numbers of improvised explosive devices, snipers, and hit and run attacks to wear down the marines.[48]

Nicholson and McChrystal "shaped" the Marjah battlefield for months ahead of the assault. "Shaped" was a military term used to describe actions to weaken the enemy before a main assault. Ground forces blocked enemy lines of communications. Air strikes hit Taliban leaders, command and control targets, and troop concentrations. British and US special operations forces raided into Marjah to go after specific commanders. They killed at least 50 Taliban. Before the final assault, marines dropped leaflets to warn civilians of what was coming and to give them a chance to escape. As the day of the assault approached, marine and allied forces isolated Marjah from outside assistance and the British cleaned out Taliban hotspots in Nad Ali. On the day of the assault itself, British units would clear the last parts of Nad Ali with major Taliban presence.

Marine forces in Helmand had now grown from 12,000 to almost 20,000 (British forces were at 9,500). Nicholson arrayed 2,250 marines for the assault, based on Regimental Combat Team-7, under Colonel Randy Newman. The main assault force was composed of 1st Battalion, 6th Marine Regiment (under Lieutenant Colonel Cal Worth) and 3rd Battalion, 6th Marine Regiment (under Lieutenant Colonel Brian Christmas). These were two of the most experienced battalions in the Marine Corps. The former was said to have turned the tide in Ramadi in Iraq in 2006 and 2007 through relentless patrolling, outposting, and cooperating with the Iraqi police and army. After Iraq, it had been the battalion that had cleared out northern Garmser in 2008, inflicting upon the Taliban their worst defeat in Helmand to date. Equally notable, 3rd Battalion, 6th Marine Regiment had cleared out al-Qaʻeda in Iraq's desert stronghold of al-Qaʻim in 2005. Its system of constant patrols, multiple outposts, and close partnership with Iraqi soldiers and police had become a model for the rest of the marines in Anbar.

Approximately 940 Afghan soldiers took part in the operation—three battalions from a green new brigade formed specially for Helmand. The Afghans were broken into contingents to work with the US units.[49]

Nicholson's scheme of maneuver was to load three companies of the two infantry battalions (each had three line companies plus a heavy weapons company) and their partnered Afghans on helicopters, hop over Taliban improvised explosive devices, and offload near the central bazaars and a key intersection, getting behind the front line Taliban fighters and dislocating their defense.

In the small hours of February 13, more than 60 helicopters flew 900 marines and Afghan soldiers into the middle of Marjah. Two companies of 1st Battalion, 6th Marines and their partnered Afghan soldiers landed near Marjah's two central bazaars. To the north, a company of 3rd Battalion, 6th Marines landed upon the key road intersection in northern Marjah and held it against Taliban attacks from several directions. Meanwhile, the marine companies that did not fly in attacked Marjah from the outside. Even though it was the tail end of the very mild Helmand winter, the night was cold. The landscape was brown and open, with wheat and poppy just popping up, allowing clear fields of fire between the mud compounds and tree-lined canals.

Over the next days, the marines and Afghan soldiers in the middle of Marjah pushed out from their initial entry points. In southern Marjah, 1st Battalion, 6th Marines advanced into the central bazaars. One by one, the marines rooted out improvised explosive devices from the shops and buildings of the bazaar and adjacent mud-walled homes and buildings. Firefights erupted with the surprised Taliban that unsuccessfully tried to bottle the marines up. Taliban cadres of anywhere between four and 20 fighters laid improvised explosive devices, skirmished with marine posts, and ambushed marine patrols. A few of their better shots were painfully frustrating to deal with. In spite of plenty of warning that the marine assault was coming, much of Marjah's civilian population was around. Marines had to be careful with air strikes, cognizant of McChrystal's tactical directive. For the average rifleman, firefights were longer and tougher. "I knew what it was going to sound like and feel like," reflected Thomas Gibbons-Neff, veteran scout sniper team leader, "but I wasn't expecting the intensity on such a regular basis."[50] While persistent, the Taliban defense was nevertheless porous because of Baradar's decision to forego the kind of in-depth defense based on compounds and irrigation ditches that Dadullah had put up in Operation Medusa. By February 16, the marines advancing from outside Marjah linked up with the companies that had assaulted via helicopter.[51]

With the key bazaars and main road in hand, Nicholson and Lindy Cameron launched the "government in a box." The new district support team arrived, the

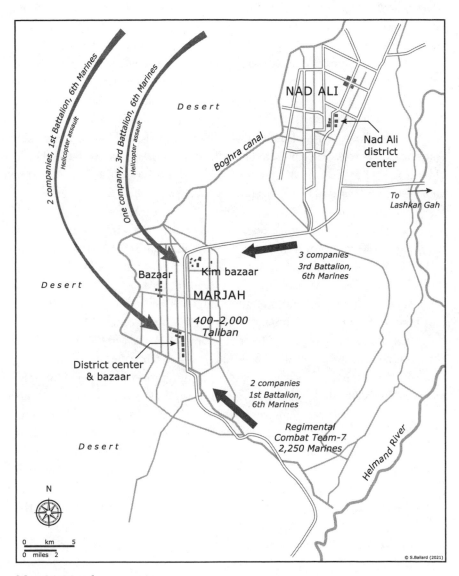

Map 14 Marjah

central bazaars reopened, and a temporary district governor named Haji Zahir took office. One of the central bazaars was designated the new district center. A makeshift district governor's building stood up in a building next to Lieutenant Colonel Worth's headquarters. On February 28, Governor Mangal visited Marjah, along with Ambassador Eikenberry. A stream of provincial directors and representatives from the ministries of education, agriculture, health, and rural development filed through over the following days. They tried to deliver services and programs as quickly as possible. The provincial reconstruction team and marines supplied them with funds and programs while starting projects of their own as well. In the course of three weeks, the marines expended $60,000 in cash-for-work projects.

On March 7, McChrystal and Karzai came to Marjah, with Sher Mohammed Akhundzada in tow. Three hundred people attended a large shura. Several local elders openly berated Sher Mohammed.[52] "Do you trust me?," Karzai asked the shura. "Yes, we trust you," random elders replied, "but you do not have authority. What you promise, you cannot do."[53] Stung, Karzai promised to make Marjah a district, which he followed through on a few days later. The act ensured the district governor position would become permanent and that Marjah would receive its own police force and allocation of government services (for education, health care, rural development, etc.).

Despite all this movement, the government-in-a-box disappointed. Goods and services from the government did not arrive for months. Marines found Zahir a weak district governor.[54] For the people of Marjah, the biggest bone of contention was not the speed of government support but poppy. It was March. The local farmers had planted poppy in the late autumn. Poppies were blooming and would be cultivated in April. Eradication would destroy a farmer's income. Farmers shared their fears with the marines and Zahir. Mangal—whom Kabul rated partly on his counter-narcotics effectiveness—decided poppy should be eradicated in places where security was permissible. Nicholson and Newman were unenthusiastic. They wanted to placate the farmers. It seemed obvious that eradication would drive farmers to pick up arms.

In the end, eradication was deemed too contentious and waited until the following year. Instead, Mangal asked farmers to destroy their poppy crop on their own in return for seeds for summer crops and a cash payment from the marines. About 8,000 farmers eventually enrolled in the program.[55] Many Afghans assumed government control meant no poppy. It is unclear how many people helped the Taliban because of the government's counter-narcotics policy.

Meanwhile, the battle heated up. Marines had taken the main roads, main bazaars, and nearby villages. The marines steadily patrolled outward—expanding their oil spot—to clear out the rest of the canal zone. The landscape was now green. Waist-high wheat shafts and poppy stalks filled the fields, better to hide

Taliban. The weather was hot. Temperatures were climbing toward the 115-degrees Fahrenheit of the summer. Small Taliban teams ambushed foot patrols, using as many directions and cover as they could find. Journalists C.J. Chivers vividly recounts one ambush in a May *New York Times* article:

> The opening skirmish was like many small-unit engagements in Helmand. . . . Watching from hiding the Taliban waited until several marines were exposed between canals that restricted their movements. Then they fired. The marines dropped onto their stomachs or leapt into irrigation ditches . . . found their bearings and returned fire. The Taliban stopped shooting, either to pull back or take another position. Then fire came from the south. The marines maneuvered, pouring sweat and trying to flank. The second Taliban group ceased shooting, too. The marines were now spread out and ready, but without targets to shoot. Had the Taliban pulled back? Or were they waiting for the marines to expose themselves again?[56]

The exhausting process could go on for hours during a single patrol.

In May, 1st Battalion, 6th Marines in the center of Marjah was facing 12 attacks per day.[57] Marine casualties in late spring and early summer exceeded those of the initial assault. The situation prompted McChrystal to call Marjah "a bleeding ulcer" during a May trip to Helmand. The comment lit up the press and added to domestic unease about the war effort. Henceforth in the minds of the American public that phrase signified the battle of Marjah. It was unfair. Under pressure from Washington on the heels of the surge debate, McChrystal was frustrated. He thought violence would have been suppressed much faster.[58]

Colonel Newman pressed outward—expanding the oil spot to clear out the rest of the canal zone. As in Nawa and Garmser, his marines set up as many posts as possible, 13 to 30 marines and a smaller number of Afghan soldiers in each.[59] Foot patrols were constant. One or two dozen marines ventured kilometers into the farmland, off the roads, jumping over ditches, wading in canals, flushing through tree lines, navigating the maze of walled Pashtun village compounds. "When we spread out," said Sergeant Jeffrey Benson, "they have a hard time determining where all the marines are, and where we're going to pop out. . . . They might have eyes on four or five of us at one time, but they don't know where the other four or five are."[60] Corporal Kyle Carpenter, a squad machine-gunner, writes, "There really is no way to prepare yourself to get shot at every day, battling for your life in a firefight, having to constantly scan the ground so you don't step on an explosive but seeing it happen anyway, watching your buddies and your leaders bleed out."[61] Carpenter won the medal of honor for jumping on a grenade to save a fellow Marine's life. "It's still a very tough fight," reported Captain

Chuck Anklam, one of the marine company commanders. "We're in firefights all over, every day . . . there's no area void of marines and (Afghan forces). . . . It's a constant presence both sides are trying to exert."[62]

At this point, Taliban fighters could operate among the people of Marjah. Supporters helped handfuls of fighters who survived under the noses of the marines and Afghan soldiers. Taliban blasted around on motorcycles, into the bazaars, intimidating those working with the marines. The marines and Afghan soldiers had trouble getting the villages outside the main bazaars to quiet down.[63] Villagers and tribal elders were in a poor position to help. Mohammed Asif was a 32 year-old Wardak immigrant who lived in northern Marjah, far from a bazaar, on the edge of the desert. Taliban patrols came through his village. Sometimes they set up checkpoints.[64] His family and tribesmen in his "block" were lying low. They were already tied to the government—Asif's nephew was a district governor in Garmser. Asif quietly encouraged his tribesmen to move against the Taliban but they thought it too dangerous.[65] They had had no rifles. No marines were posted nearby. Asif could not risk doing anything.

The marines faced a classic insurgency identification problem. They could not distinguish a villager from an insurgent. The locals would not tell them. Marjah tribal leaders generally feared cooperating against the Taliban.[66] Afghan soldiers were somewhat better informed but as a mix of Tajiks, eastern Pashtuns, and a few Hazaras they too were treated as outsiders by the locals. Pictures of Ahmed Shah Massoud often adorned the windshields of their pickups.[67]

Nicholson tried to recruit a police force to address the problem. The government provided 265 police spots to Marjah. The normal policy was to assign recruits to anywhere throughout a province. Nicholson arranged for the recruits to serve in Marjah. Things still went poorly. The Taliban tried to intimidate, kidnap, beat, or kill anyone working with the government or marines. Individual assassins and bombers could evade marine patrols to exact retribution on cooperative villagers. An equal obstacle was that locals did not want to leave their homes to go to police training in Lashkar Gah. They feared the Taliban would target their families during their absence and distrusted the government to uphold its promise to send them back to their villages for service after training. As of the end of June, 91 of the 265 spots were filled. Of those, only 8 or 9 were from Marjah and on duty; another 30 were still in training. The rest had been either recruited from elsewhere or assigned from the provincial force to Marjah.

The solution came from a few good marines, guided by local Afghan leaders. In these kind of wars a first principle is always to work through a local partner. Lieutenant Colonel Brian Christmas commanding 3rd Battalion, 6th Marine Regiment, in northern Marjah had previously served in Afghanistan in 2004 in the middle of Uruzgan and had later fought in Iraq. Prior experience taught him that only the learned eyes of local tribesmen could discern Taliban from villager. By May he was exploring how to create "local community watches"—village militias under a more democratic name. Christmas knew marines were pursuing similar initiatives on a subdued scale elsewhere in Helmand.[68]

Kim bazaar, off the main road, was one of the first blocks Christmas had secured. Gul Mullah was the 40-year-old leader of the cluster of villages around the bazaar. His younger brother, Omar Jan, was the Garmser and later Nad Ali police chief.[69] Gul Mullah and Omar Jan were from the Andar tribe, part of the Ghilzai tribal confederation, outside the privileged Durrani. Their parents had died years before, after coming to Marjah from Ghazni. The two took care of their younger brothers and their own growing families. They sought independence from Helmand warlords such as Sher Mohammed Akhundzada. Gul Mullah later told me, "We are free people. We have heard their orders. We do not want to listen."[70]

Gul Mullah had Sufi training. With shoulder-length black hair and a slightly red-dyed beard, he was a combination of tribal and religious leader. His people affectionately dubbed him "Gully Mullah Malang"—a malang is a mystic who could heal the sick and cared for a shrine—even though Gul Mullah performed no such duties. Other Sufi leaders in Marjah, particularly the influential Bohuiddin Jan Agha, a Sufi pir, and his halting tribal protector, Gul Mohammed were tied to Gul Mullah. They too cared neither for the old warlords nor the Taliban. "I stand for my own village. I do not stand for the government, or for the Taliban," stated Gul Mohammed.[71]

Gul Mullah and Omar Jan shared the view of many tribal leaders that Afghanistan was a broken country. They fiercely valued independence. They wanted American troops out of the villages, cities, and countryside as soon as possible. But they also believed American assistance was needed for the sake of stability and the survival of their families.

Once the marines arrived, Gul Mullah and Gul Mohammed started to organize in secret. They spread propaganda against the Taliban and told their people to oppose them.[72] Their Sufi background gave their calls legitimacy. In May, Gul Mullah and Gul Mohammed decided it was time to contact the marines. They met with Lieutenant Colonel Christmas, who recognized the opportunity. The meeting marked the beginning of their effort to raise militias.[73]

A marine lieutenant colonel had leeway to exploit an opportunity like this. Nicholson and Newman lived by delegating. No other service would have allowed a battalion commander to experiment so boldly. US-backed militias were a sensitive topic that McChrystal, Eikenberry, and Karzai had yet to endorse. Not only did the marine leadership allow the initiative to move forward, they encouraged it.

Marines were already authorized to pay salaries for small forces to defend villages and in June Christmas was permitted to assist Gul Mullah and Gul Mohammed. At this point, Gul Mullah fielded six men, enough to defend him and his home, enough to make him a hard target, enough to free him to rally more fighters. Over the summer and autumn, his numbers would surpass 50, enough to cover Kim bazaar.

Around the same time, Baz Gul from southern Marjah also agreed to form a militia. He was another Ghilzai tribal leader and had fought the Soviets in the 1980s. His large village in central Marjah was tribally cohesive. Baz Gul had stayed in Marjah after the Taliban seized the area in 2008. A few weeks after the marines arrived in February 2010, he started talking with Lieutenant Colonel Cal Worth, commander of 1st Battalion, 6th Marine Regiment. Baz Gul said he could keep the Taliban out of his village but asked that a few of his tribesmen be allowed to carry weapons. Worth agreed. For the next months, Taliban were unable to operate in Baz Gul's village. In June, Baz Gul and Worth agreed to try to mobilize a militia. Baz Gul recruited 59 men before the end of the month.[74]

Colonel Newman wanted to spread the village militia to the rest of Marjah. A large shura of Marjah tribal elders convened in June. Baz Gul joined Gul Mullah and Gul Mohammed in endorsing village militias.[75] On June 23, the deputy provincial governor appointed a group of 25 tribal leaders from the area around the central bazaar as Marjah's new temporary community council with Baz Gul as the chairman.

Meanwhile, marine patrols had been pushing outward. Estimates of Taliban strength fell to the low hundreds. Newman set up a new line of posts on the periphery of Marjah, deep in Taliban territory. The posts drew Taliban attacks away from the roads and bazaars.[76] Villages close to bazaars were now much safer.

The militias of Baz Gul, Gul Mohammed, and Gul Mullah accompanied marines on patrol. The marines valued them for their knowledge of the area and élan in a firefight, carelessly chasing after Taliban. As his militia grew, Gul Mullah assigned detachments to outpost villages and help the marines. Sometimes he went out with the marines himself. Once, shrapnel from an improvised explosive device scratched him. The story is that he wept for the marine who died in the same blast.[77] Gul Mohammed remembered, "We lost many men. Without our efforts, the marines could not succeed in Marjah. It was only together."[78]

In August, Taliban were conducting 80 attacks per week in northern Marjah. At the end of October, as the heat lost its edge and the summer corn crop was harvested, the number was 30.[79] The marines were now into the edges of Marjah. Taliban had nowhere left to hide.[80]

As the Taliban ebbed, the militias multiplied. Tribal leader after tribal leader asked to have his own militia.[81] Forty different leaders would be approved, each allowed retinues of 12 to 45 men.[82] Between October and the end of the year, the total number of tribesmen in militia doubled from roughly 400 to 850.[83] Tribesmen wore civilian garb with marine-issued yellow armbands for identification. Mangal blessed the program as long as the militia were eventually transitioned into the police. The tribal leaders told the marines that the promise that their young men could protect their own villages and not have to leave first for training was key in their newfound eagerness to serve.[84] Marine riflemen probably had something to do with it as well.

One new militia commander was Mohammed Asif, the 32-year-old Wardak immigrant living in northern Marjah. Asif had been waiting to stand up as Taliban patrolled his village. In August, marines briefly passed through the village. Then they emplaced a post a kilometer or so from the village. And then another. Soon his village was on the front line between Taliban and marine control. Finally, with the Taliban falling back, Asif and his tribesmen promised to defend their village against the Taliban. The marines were now close by and they felt comfortable preventing Taliban from laying improvised explosive devices or ambushes.[85]

By far the most interesting new militia commander was Bibi Firoza, also known as Haji Yani Abeda. From dry northwestern Marjah, *she* was 47 years old and had never been to school, but had commanded mujahideen against the Russians. Local legend has it that she decided to fight the Taliban and form a militia after they killed her son. Because of her age, she could walk outside with only a head scarf, face uncovered, without causing a scandal. Because of her experience, the male tribal leaders tolerated her in meetings. The Taliban tried to claim that she was on their side; that was a lie. She brought her family into the war against them, including her teenage grandsons. Living on the edge of the desert, she would face frequent fighting for the next six years, eventually receiving the "Maulali Medal," the government's highest award for a woman.[86]

By November, the marines, Afghan army, and tribal leaders had quelled Marjah. Improvised explosive devices still dogged marine patrols but at a much lower level. Taliban continued to threaten anyone working with the government but without much success. The militias hindered their night letters, kidnappings, and assassinations.[87] Villagers knew that fellow tribesmen with a few rifles were close by. The tribal leaders themselves were always under protection—hard targets. On December 7, 2010, Operation Moshtarak officially ended. Confident, Major General Richard Mills, the new marine commander for Helmand, removed one battalion from Marjah, halving the forces in the district. Fifty-eight Americans and British died in the battle of Marjah.[88] At least 200 more were wounded. Taliban losses are unknown. Marjah and the other districts cleared by the marines in 2009, would be among the most stable in Afghanistan. McChrystal simply had not realized that success would take months, not weeks.

With time came governance and development. Before the end of spring, 25 government officials were working in the district. Marjah's bazaars had reopened with 75 percent of shops back in business. Over the summer, USAID's AVIPA cash for work and distribution program employed 1,500 laborers clearing canals.[89] In retrospect, the government-in-a-box was less a failure as over-hyped.

By autumn 2010, 18 months into the surge, the Taliban in central and southern Helmand had gone back to their homes or been pushed into outlying areas. Northern Helmand, on the other hand, was well in Taliban hands.

In October 2010, the last British units turned over responsibility for northern Helmand to the marines.[90] The British government was under domestic political criticism because of losses, especially in Sangin, where 106 British soldiers had been killed, roughly a quarter of the total British killed in Afghanistan from 2001 to 2014.[91] The British pulled their forces southward and concentrated on Gereshk, Nad Ali, and Babaji. Northern Helmand was now a marine problem.

The Kajaki dam had been built to power Helmand and Kandahar. In 2010, only one of the dam's three turbines functioned, leaving Kandahar City with only four hours of electricity per day. The British had famously mounted a battalion-size operation in September 2008 to deliver a new second turbine in order get more electricity flowing to Lashkar Gah and Kandahar City. The turbine was never installed. Taliban presence prevented heavy equipment and material from being transported up from the ring road. General Petraeus believed that long-term stability in Kandahar depended on adequate electricity to fuel economic development. He decided the Kajaki dam had to be repaired. At Camp Bastion, Major General Mills set in motion a series of operations to open the road to Kajaki.

The marines would advance into the teeth of Taliban opposition. The Ishaqzai and Alizai tribes of northern Helmand had been with the Taliban since before 2005. At least 200,000 people lived along the Helmand and its tributaries. The far upper reaches of northern Helmand—foothills of the Hindu Kush—had never really seen any government presence after 2001. Zemindawar, a set of five fertile Alizai valleys north of Kajaki, was a rich source of poppy and the home of a bustling Taliban bazaar.

Between Kajaki and the rest of Helmand was Sangin, the strategic crossroads between Lashkar Gah, Kajaki, and Musa Qala. Six to eight hundred Taliban operated there. The British had defended a bastion around the district center bazaar and nearby villages. The Ishaqzai that before 2006 had been mistreated by the pro-government Alikozai made for a tenacious insurgency. Whereas the tribal leaders of Marjah, Nawa, and Garmser had been pro-government or mixed, in Sangin, a solid block opposed the government.

In September 2010, 3rd Battalion, 5th Marine Regiment, started clearing Sangin.[92] Marines who had previously served in Marjah found Sangin was a much harder fight.[93] Carefully placed improvised explosive devices littered the bazaar, villages, and footpaths. Small Taliban teams timed firefights to when marines neared an improvised explosive device. Sergeant Clint Thoman, a squad leader, observed, "The platoon felt everyone would be blown up eventually. Made no difference if you were a boot on your first tour or an experienced NCO. You'd walk and walk until an IED got you. It was a matter of time. Not if, but when. That didn't stop us from patrolling, but everyone thought about it. You were going to get blown up."[94]

In three weeks, the battalion engaged in 100 firefights and suffered 62 casualties. The marines called in an impressive amount of firepower: by Christmas, at least 177 artillery and air strikes, including 44 five-hundred-pound bombs—more than any other marine battalion.[95]

Over late autumn and early winter, Mills reinforced Sangin with more than 600 additional marines. By several accounts, marine aggressiveness stunned the Taliban fighters. A local elder told researchers Theo Farrell and Antonio Giustozzi, "When the American marines arrived in Sangin, they did a miracle fighting; they were fighting more dangerously than Taliban fighters. They pushed back the Taliban in one month, very far away of Sangin district center."[96] Taliban commanders told the researchers that the heavy fighting forced them to change tactics and reduce contact with the marines.[97]

By the end of December, the marines had taken control of the bazaar and the road toward Kajaki. In the surrounding villages, they were driving the Taliban out of the belt of farmland running between the road and the river northward.

At the same time, Governor Mangal had been reaching out to the Alikozai of Sangin. Mangal knew the clan were inveterate rivals of the Ishaqzai.[98] In the first week of January 2011, after months of back and forth, Mangal reached a "peace agreement" with the Alikozai tribal leaders. They promised to keep the Taliban out of their villages in northern Sangin. In Mangal's view, the deal opened the way to secure the road to Kajaki.[99] In the spring, the first Alikozai "community watch," or militia, were recruited, following the model of Marjah. Numbers were few at first. Three hundred would eventually join the new Afghan local police program.

The government gained control of most of Sangin during 2011. A community council formed, schools opened, and roads were paved, as had occurred in districts to the south. The cost was high. Third Battalion, 5th Marine Regiment, and the companies that reinforced it suffered 29 killed and 200 wounded. In total, from 2006 to 2013, 150 British soldiers and US marines died fighting in Sangin.[100]

From Sangin, the marines pressed northward over 2011 and 2012 until the road was open to Kajaki dam. The main Taliban cadres fell back to sanctuary in the furthest northern reaches. They could easily survive in the fertile valleys of Zemindawar. Marines occasionally forayed there but did not stay long. Pockets of Ishaqzai between Gereshk and Sangin continued to fight with the government as well. On the bright side, the Taliban had been cleared from the strategic terrain at Sangin and Kajaki.

Between 2011 and 2013, the provincial reconstruction team repaired the road from Lashkar Gah to Kajaki to allow movement of heavy equipment to the Kajaki dam. USAID funded repair work on the dam. There was always some problem with the project—security on the road, contractor issues, technical delays. In spite of the Herculean effort, the two new turbines were never installed.

With the support of the marines and provincial reconstruction team, Mangal reformed government in Helmand. He reduced the warlordism of the past. He championed the district community council program. He forced the officials for education, health care, rural development, and agriculture to visit the districts and get goods and services flowing. He did not tolerate shortfalls in teachers or doctors. He held the district governors to task.

The results were noteworthy. In the central and southern districts, the objects of extensive development programs, the percentage of children going to school rose from 30 percent in September 2010 to 55 percent in July 2011.[101] Over 126,000 would eventually enroll. Fifty-seven health facilities would eventually open. Community councils were elected in eight districts. Perhaps most dramatic was the curtailment of the power of the warlords.[102] The percentage of survey respondents who believed district government acted on behalf of the people in southern and central Helmand rose from 44 percent in mid-2010 to 72 percent at the end of 2011.[103]

Underneath the surface something else was happening. Nicholson, Newman, Christmas, Worth, and other marine commanders were changing the balance of power in Marjah, Nad Ali, Garmser, Nawa, and Sangin. Marines were empowering tribal leaders who were living in their villages and on the front line, inadvertently disempowering the old warlords, especially Sher Mohammed. A whole new set of independent Helmand leaders rose up.

The police improved dramatically. As their political role expanded, tribal leaders volunteered their sons and tribesmen. They went to the academy, graduated, and returned to their districts to oversee security. The militias became a stepping stone to join the police. As villages stabilized, parts of the tribal militias were trained and converted into police. Nicholson's nearby training center in Lashkar Gah paid dividends. Marjah, Nad Ali, Nawa, Garmser, Gereshk, and Sangin each eventually had 200 to 300 police, in contrast to the 15 to 50 of 2006. A new police chief—Hakim Angar, a taciturn and experienced Alikozai from Kandahar—enforced training, reporting standards, and uniforms and boots. According to surveys, the percentage of the population in central and southern Helmand that believed the police acted with impunity fell from 60 to

30 percent between December 2010 and October 2011.[104] Captain Matthew Lesnowicz, a marine advisor in Marjah in 2011, commented:

> Considering the conditions, the police weren't bad. Police weapons and ammunition were clean and uniforms were kept in surprisingly good condition. In fact, in some areas, the Afghans were superior to coalition forces. At the platoon level, Afghans were far faster than marines. The Afghans were lightly armed and equipped, producing short response times.... The police could rally and deploy a platoon-sized outfit within 20 minutes or less. In another few minutes, they could surge and completely saturate an area, which was a formidable capability from the enemy's perspective.[105]

Helmand represents the most ambitious and forceful British and American attempt to reform Afghan government. Even with such effort, important things could not be accomplished. Creating good government pushed up against Afghan culture and politics to an insurmountable degree. Land reform was too hard, as was fully eliminating corruption. Mangal's administration was less corrupt than those in other provinces. Still, poppy taxation, bribery, and payoffs to escape prosecution went on. Politics was based on patronage. Corruption could not be sucked out without revolutionary intervention, something far beyond the means of the British and American effort in Helmand, which was already by far the most interventionist, nigh-colonial, endeavor of the war.

Against poppy, substantial effort—five years (2008–2013) of crop substitution and eradication—produced temporary success. Poppy cultivation in the regions under government control fell from 33,000 in 2009 to 6,000 hectares in 2013. In Helmand as a whole, however, including the regions not under government control, poppy cultivation dipped from 2009 to 2011 but then in 2012 bounced back to 2008 levels, with 100,000 hectares under cultivation. Cultivation had been pressed into regions beyond the government's reach.[106] In 2014, after the food zone program ended, poppy cultivation resumed in full. The centers of government power such as Marjah, Nad Ali, Gereshk, and Garmser that had been poppy-free in 2011 and 2012 returned to cultivation.

And the fields of poppy were where the Helmand surge had its most ominous demographic impact. Government authority in central Helmand ended at the edge of the canal zone, where the vast desert started. Upon this space, desert settlements multiplied as poor landless families immigrated in droves. These were families that the Taliban had allowed to squat within the canal zone. The government denied their claim to land and banned poppy. In the desert, the poor families dropped deep wells to farm on parched soil, good enough for poppy.[107] By 2013, 90,000 people would live across the desert settlements, more people than in Marjah alone. Eighty-eight percent grew poppy.[108]

The Taliban controlled most of the settlements. Approximately 30 percent of the settlers wanted to see the Taliban rule Afghanistan, in contrast to only 5 percent who held that opinion in the canal zones. In the words of one elder, "the Taliban keep the area secure, protect people's poppy cultivation by not allowing government force to destroy it and claim that they fight for the interests of Islam— these are the factors that can persuade many people, young men in particular, to join Taliban."[109] Support for violence lived on. Hauntingly, one elder betrayed to a survey team, "If security . . . worsens in the districts [the canal zones] it allows people to grow poppy there in the districts, so many people would move there and cultivate poppy where there is enough water and fertile land."[110]

Mangal survived as governor until September 2012. The British fended off attempt after attempt to remove him. Finally, after four years, they let Mangal go. Karzai replaced him with a closer ally, Mohammed Naim Baluch (not to be confused with the Taliban governor, Mohammed Naim Barech). Comfortingly, Mangal's reforms endured. The British supported Baluch, though less robustly than they had Mangal. Schools and community councils kept functioning, as long as security remained. Baluch was a kind man, but older. Helmandis tended to remember Mangal as a wise and energetic governor.

Obama wanted the surge to reverse Taliban momentum. In Helmand, the surge succeeded in that goal. The center and south were secure and the marines were edging into the north long before Obama's July 2011 deadline. Three army brigades of the new 215th Afghan army corps defended Helmand. A full battalion garrisoned nearly every district, in addition to trained police. Seven hundred thousand Afghans now lived under government rule, compared to roughly 350,000 before the surge. The Taliban were on their back foot. Researcher Antonio Giustozzi surveyed 28 Taliban commanders across seven districts in 2011 and 2012. From their responses, an average of 20 percent of their cadres had been killed over the previous two years. In spring 2011, Taliban leadership ordered their cadres to stick to improvised explosive devices, assassinations, and other indirect tactics in order to conserve their forces.[111] Helmand was the Taliban's worst defeat since the end of 2001.

The cost had not been insignificant. Over a third of the surge had gone to a province of secondary strategic importance. Success had depended on a long, expensive, and casualty-ridden British and American intervention. Kael Weston, Nicholson's political advisor, writes at the height of the campaign, "Larry and I visited the wounded . . . almost nightly, the double, triple, quadruple amputees. Corporals, captains. One . . . had survived quadruple amputation. He had a tube in the side of his rib cage, what was left of him under green blanket with some blood on it—and 'Fi' from a 'Semper Fi' tattoo inked above, on his pale chest."[112] Only time would tell if the successes would last. No time was needed to tell that they were unlikely to equal the cost.

Uzbek fighters of Abdur Rashid Dostum with US special forces on horseback, in 2001, during operations near Mazar-e-Sharif against the Taliban. Photo by Maj. Melody Faulkenberry

President Hamid Karzai speaking with Secretary of Defense Donald Rumsfeld and Minister of Defense Mohammed Fahim in Kabul in 2002. The United States at this time was working with warlords such as Fahim. Photo by Robert D. Ward.

Afghan tribesman from the Taliban-dominated northern Helmand district of Baghran covers his face in accordance with Islamic tradition upon being photographed by a US soldier in 2005. Photograph by Private First Class Leslie Angulo.

Canadians and Afghan police on patrol in Kandahar, 2007, after Taliban attacks had increased dramatically. ISAF photo.

Taliban fighters in Nangarhar. Voice of America photo.

US soldiers fire a mortar in the mountains of Kunar, where the United States military engaged in some of its heaviest fighting of the war. Photo by Staff Sergeant Mark Burrell.

Afghan soldier in combat in Kandahar in 2008. ISAF photo.

Afghan women and girls in Kunar receiving humanitarian assistance. Rarely would US troops see so many women as in this photograph. Photo by Capt. Tony Wickman.

President Barack Obama speaking with General Stanley McChrystal, commander of US forces in Afghanistan, during his 2010 visit to Afghanistan. ISAF photo.

US soldiers from the 173rd Airborne Brigade and Afghan soldiers receive fire while escorting detainees in Wardak in 2010. Photo by Sergeant Russell Gilchrest.

Marines from 3rd Battalion, 6th Marine Regiment on patrol in Marjah, scene of one of the main battles of the surge, in February 2010. US Department of Defense photo.

Afghan army soldier on break on a patrol, 2010. US Department of Defense photo.

US soldiers on a night raid into an Afghan compound in 2012. Afghans disliked night raids and the invasion of their privacy. Photo by Private First Class Travis Jones, Combat Camera Afghanistan

Abdul Razziq with Afghan border police in 2010, before he became Kandahar police chief from 2011 to 2018. ISAF photo.

US infantry patrolling a village in Andar district, Ghazni province in 2012 at the time of uprising against the Taliban in the district. The soldiers are talking with Afghans outside the village mosque, distinguished by the speakers used for the call to prayer. Regional Command East photo.

General Joseph Dunford, commander of US forces in Afghanistan from 2013 to 2014 and chairman of the joint chiefs of staff from 2015 to 2019. ISAF photo.

Secretary of State John Kerry declaring the 2014 unity government deal between soon-to-be President Ashraf Ghani and Chief Executive Dr Abdullah. US Department of State photo.

Taliban fighters in the center of Kunduz in September 2015.

Taliban fighters in Nangarhar during the 2018 Eid ceasefire. Photo by Voice of America.

Ambassador Zalmay Khalilzad (US special representative for Afghanistan reconciliation) and Mullah Abdul Ghani Baradar (Taliban deputy for political affairs) signing the US-Taliban agreement on 29 February 2020. US Department of State photo (state.gov).

13

The Surge in Kandahar

By the middle of 2009, the Taliban had ruled most of Kandahar for three years. The government held Kandahar City but little of the countryside, save a few district centers, villages, and the Spin Boldak border crossing to Pakistan. Taliban territory edged right up against the city. Assassinations and suicide bombings terrorized the people. Violence was four times higher in spring 2009 than the year before.[1] The risk that the Taliban might reclaim their former seat of power and press the Karzai government to the brink of collapse had been a justification for the surge. Until Kandahar province was secure, Taliban momentum would not be broken.

At the beginning of 2009, around 5,000 Americans and Canadians were in Kandahar, largely at Kandahar airbase. Roughly 2,000 were combat troops, far too few to push back the Taliban. After General Stanley McChrystal allowed Helmand to go forward, 5,000 reinforcements from the first tranche of the surge arrived in Kandahar halfway through 2009.[2] Even then, operations in Kandahar would not begin in earnest until the middle of 2010, six months into the battle of Marjah and 16 months after Obama had approved the first tranche of the surge.

Kandahar's allotment of the first tranche of the surge was 5th Stryker Brigade, 2nd US Infantry Division. "Stryker" was the name of the US Army's lightly armored wheeled vehicle. The brigade operated in them. They were unsuited for the foot patrolling necessary in Kandahar's fields and villages. Colonel Harry Tunnell, the brigade commander, disdained counterinsurgency tactics as "musings from amateurs, contractors, plagiarized journal articles, etc." and disparaged "the prioritization of the protection of civilians above that required by the law of war."[3] He tried to disrupt the Taliban by striking out into the countryside. His battalions were too widely dispersed and too mobile to make a difference in any one place.[4] McChrystal did not overrule Tunnell. One battalion suffered 21 killed. The brigade is most infamous for harming Afghans. Five of the brigade's soldiers would be tried for murdering unarmed Afghans for sport and keeping body parts as war trophies.[5]

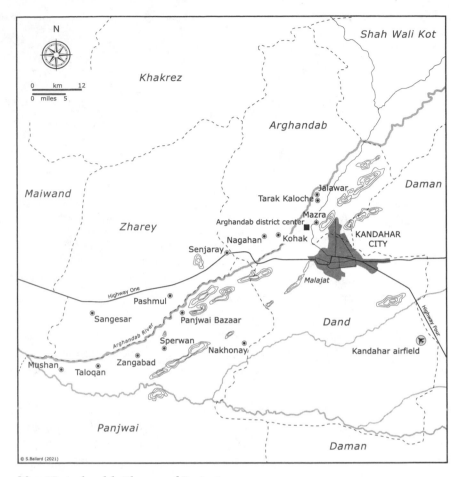

Map 15 Arghandab, Zharey, and Panjwai

In November 2009, British Major-General Nick Carter took over regional command south and Canadian and US forces in Kandahar, including Tunnell's brigade.[6] Carter was an irrepressible man of ideas with previous experience in Iraq and Afghanistan. Unafraid to speak his mind, he often rubbed Americans the wrong way—perhaps he shared too many of our own characteristics. He enforced counterinsurgency, reassigned Tunnell's brigade to road security, and drafted a new plan to secure Kandahar, named Operation Hamkary (the Pashto and Dari word for cooperation).

The idea of Operation Hamkary was to secure Kandahar City and the surrounding districts with a "clear, hold, and build" approach that minimized damage to civilians. The centerpiece was Kandahar City. It would be fortified with lines of posts. Citizens would be enrolled in biometric databases. Everyone entering the city would be searched and registered. To prevent the kind of exodus that had occurred in Marjah, there would be no massive operation with air strikes and artillery bombardments. Outside the city, counterinsurgency would focus on clearing and holding Arghandab to the north and Panjwai and Zharey to the west. Because of their agricultural fertility, high population, and proximity to the city, clearing out these districts was crucial to freeing the city from a state of siege.

To build support for the plan, Carter traveled back and forth to Kabul to speak with ministers and generals at McChrystal's headquarters. Operation Hamkary was set to kick off in June 2010, after the second tranche of the surge had started to arrive in Kandahar. Eight thousand US troops would reinforce the 7,000 already in Kandahar. There were also nearly 4,000 Canadian troops in the province, for a total of about 19,000 US and Canadian troops.

A key part of Hamkary was reforming the government and fostering long-term economic development. Major-General Carter designed Hamkary to connect the Afghan population in the province of Kandahar to its governor, and by extension, to the government in Kabul. McChrystal's headquarters and the Obama administration considered poor government policies, corruption, and poppy smuggling—associated with Karzai's brother Ahmed Wali Karzai and border police commander Abdul Razziq—a major reason the Taliban had returned to Kandahar from 2005 onward. In 2009, Ahmed Wali and Razziq masterminded the presidential election fraud in Kandahar. In Razziq's home district of Spin Boldak, every vote was for Karzai. Early on, Richard Holbrooke told the national security council that Ahmed Wali must be the poster child for the US anti-corruption campaign. Throughout 2009, McChrystal had resisted working with Ahmed Wali and Razziq because of their history of warlordism and drug smuggling. US officials in Washington and officers in McChrystal's headquarters saw Ahmed Wali as the drug kingpin of Kandahar, whose smuggling was destabilizing the entire country.

Carter and the US State Department tried to strengthen the government administration and weaken Ahmed Wali and Razziq by establishing community councils, funneling projects through the governor, and getting the provincial civil administration to send goods and services to the districts. Regarding economic development, Carter worked with Governor Tooryalai Wesa to design projects that would build institutions and develop the economy.[7] The US military and USAID allocated more than $400 million for Kandahar, much of which would eventually go to large-scale infrastructure projects and agricultural cash-for-work programs. The US military would spend an additional $225 million on diesel generators to power Kandahar City until new generators were in place at Kajaki dam.

McChrystal's command itself went about planning how to remove Ahmed Wali and Razziq. Major General Michael Flynn, McChrystal's intelligence chief, told the *New York Times*, "If we are going to conduct a population-centric strategy in Afghanistan, and we are perceived as backing thugs, then we are just undermining ourselves." Of Ahmed Wali, he said, "The only way to clean up Chicago is to get rid of Capone."[8] The attitude in the command was to detain him and let the Drug Enforcement Administration (DEA) arrest him or banish him to an overseas ambassadorship.

McChrystal's staff spent months hunting for proof of Ahmed Wali's wrong-doing and came up empty-handed. Nor did President Karzai want him removed. Deciding Ahmed Wali and Razziq were too strong to be circumvented or removed, during March 2010 McChrystal and Carter started to work with them.[9] Carter explained to *New York Times* reporter Carlotta Gall, "By this stage of the insurgency you cannot afford not to get the help of everybody . . . some of these guys have probably got the clout to be able to encourage elders to be braver, and we need to do that."[10] Indeed, it is hard to see how McChrystal and Carter could ever have won Karzai's support for Operation Hamkary if one of their objectives had been to wreck his Kandahar political base.

Improving governance was a hallmark of the surge strategy. It was not turning out as expected. In Helmand the United States and Britain tried to change the political system. They made progress but at great exertion and still could not solve key problems. In Kandahar they went with the grain. The old political and tribal system prevailed. The irony is that the failure to introduce a professional, meritocratic, Western government may not have mattered.

By March, the plan for Operation Hamkary was nearly set. On April 4, 2010, Karzai, who since 2006 had shunned the role of war leader, traveled to Kandahar. He was skeptical of the surge and rationed his support for kinetic operations. McChrystal came with him; as had been the case in Marjah, he genuinely wanted Karzai involved and was committed to heeding his guidance. Karzai had concerns. He worried about civilian casualties. He also objected to search and biometric enrollment of people entering the city. Karzai spoke to 2,000 tribal leaders and other notables. Donning a dark turban that made him look especially Kandahari, he asked "You don't want an offensive, do you?" The crowd cheered in affirmation—few humans want a big battle around their home. Karzai replied, "There will be no operation until you are happy," and postponed Hamkary indefinitely.[11] Ahmed Wali had to speak to him in private to convince him to let preparations continue, minus the biometric scanning and searching.

On the flight back to Kabul, Karzai complained to McChrystal about the chaotic situation in Kandahar and said, "I think there is an invisible hand in Kandahar that wants to make the situation worse." According to Rangin Dadfar Spanta, Karzai's national security advisor, the remark was intended to convey displeasure to McChrystal for "lack of attention to Kandahar's security."[12]

McChrystal's toil did have an upside. The trip convinced Karzai to adjust his laissez faire approach to the war and involve himself in fixing Kandahar.

From May 10–14, 2010, Karzai visited the United States and met with President Obama. The White House conceived of the visit as a way to mend relations after the election imbroglio. Kandahar was a major topic of discussion. Karzai asked that the United States forego a destructive urban battle with air and artillery strikes. Obama agreed. On his return to Kabul, Karzai directed that military force only be used in Kandahar City as a last resort. McChrystal and Carter modified Operation Hamkary for a more methodical clearing of districts with fewer artillery and air strikes.[13]

His concerns met, Karzai let Operation Hamkary go forward. On June 13, along with McChrystal, he returned to Kandahar. Ahmed Wali had been laying the groundwork for the visit, bringing tribal leaders together and encouraging them to oppose the Taliban.[14] He made sure there were 300 to 400 elders, food and transportation, and anything else needed for a successful political event. During the visit, Karzai again stood before the gathering. He told the tribal leaders that the operation would begin soon—minus the biometric scanning and ring of posts walling off the city. He recalled how Ahmed Shah, the founder of modern Afghanistan, had once wanted to wall Kandahar but his mother, Zarghona Ana, had warned him against it: "Son! . . . a Pashtun never takes shelter behind a wall and leaves the soil and never makes himself comfortable from his enemies with a moat. A Pashtun protects himself and his country through the help of God and his own dry fist."[15]

Karzai asked the tribal leaders to help him bring peace to the province: "Stand for our homes! Doubtful men, doubtful behavior, everyone that helps indirectly— sit with them. Sit with the formal and informal Taliban! Confront the Taliban and informal Taliban and challenge their orders and commands!"[16] Shamed into action, nearly to a man they promised to help.[17] McChrystal and Ahmed Wali had chalked up a notable success in coaxing Karzai to once more involve himself in leading the people of Kandahar during war.

McChrystal never got to see Operation Hamkary. On June 22, 2010, a *Rolling Stone* article revealed his staff had been criticizing the White House.[18] Since the surge debate, they had taken to complaining about Obama and Biden, possibly even ridiculing the latter. They did it in front of Michael Hastings, an embedded *Rolling Stone* reporter. McChrystal abided his staff's offenses and hinted at his own distaste for the administration. It was a sign of disrespect for the office of the president. Realizing the gravity of his error, McChrystal resigned. Had he not, Obama would have fired him. The behavior confirmed for Obama an "air of impunity" among the generals to the principle that politicians have a duty to interfere in the running of a war.[19]

McChrystal had commanded for almost exactly one year. Other commanders served longer, none with so great an impact. He authored the surge that brought the United States back into the war. He changed the nature of US operations through his wholehearted endorsement of counterinsurgency. With his care for improving the Afghan government and reducing civilian casualties, he endowed operations with a moral compass. He would have stayed in Afghanistan for years. Ironically, his enthusiasm for counterinsurgency and determination to win contributed to his demise. He let devotion to the cause supersede the trust of his civilian leaders.

Obama dispatched General David Petraeus, founder of American counterinsurgency, to replace McChrystal. Petraeus executed McChrystal's plans with alacrity. The discipline and organization learned from his experience in Iraq and at Central Command was instilled upon the headquarters. Petraeus wanted to rack up successes. In his calculus, successes could convince Obama to extend the July 2011 deadline to start withdrawing troops. "Put time back on the clock" was a favorite saying. A little time in 2011, he thought, might allow US forces to win more success in 2012, and then gain yet more time. In theory, the rate of the drawdown could be slowed sufficiently to defeat the Taliban. Petraeus had seen something like this happen in Iraq when US political opposition to that surge declined after successes in Baghdad and Anbar.

Anxious to accomplish as much as possible before mid-2011, Petraeus accelerated a range of military activities while retaining McChrystal's strategy. He issued counterinsurgency guidance to his forces to secure the population, live among the people, hold what was cleared, foot patrol, and partner with the army and police. At the same time, he demanded action. "Pursue the enemy relentlessly," he instructed, "Together with our Afghan partners, get your teeth into the insurgents and don't let go. When the extremists fight, make them pay. Seek out and eliminate those who threaten the population. Don't let them intimidate the innocent. Target the whole network, not just individuals."[20] Petraeus increased air strikes to more than 500 per month, breaking 1,000 in October, an average of 80 percent higher than the year before he took command.[21] He streamlined the restrictions of McChrystal's tactical directive and forbade subordinates from piling on additional restrictions.

Petraeus also encouraged special operations forces to intensify their tempo as a means of racking up successes before the 2011 deadline. The special operations forces were then undergoing their own "surge." On top of McChrystal's 2009 buildup, the number of teams dedicated to raids increased by another fifth. During summer 2010, nearly 4,000 raids were conducted, triple the number of 2009. In the last three months of 2010, special operations forces claimed to have killed 1,000 insurgents and captured 3,000 more.[22]

Petraeus hyped up the strategy to the Afghan government and regularly briefed Karzai on the tally. Petraeus elaborated to national security advisor Spanta: "If we can kill Taliban shadow district governors within three days of their appointment and shadow governors within a week, they [the Taliban] will not be able to replace those losses and will collapse."[23]

Petraeus's tour in Afghanistan would be just a year, the great captain's final campaign. He had been running hard since 2003; as commanding general of the 101st Airborne Division, head of the training command in Iraq, mastermind of the counterinsurgency manual, commander of all US and coalition forces in Iraq during the surge, and lastly commander of Central Command. The new job somewhat displeased Petraeus. Leaving Central Command was technically a de-motion and a return to the deprivations of life in a war zone. He had also recently recovered from prostate cancer. His staff sometimes found him tired and prone to treat Iraq as a model of success for Afghanistan when the two countries were quite different. The high expectations of the time may have overshadowed the leadership, tactical execution, and innovation that Petraeus brought to the table.

Shortly before McChrystal's resignation, Taliban leadership changed too. After further secluding himself in 2009, Mullah Omar's health continued to deteri-orate. Since at least 2007, Omar had relied on Mullah Baradar, his deputy, to manage the movement. Baradar had done a fine job on the tactical preparations for the surge and improving the Taliban's public image.

In February 2010, Pakistan detained Mullah Baradar in Karachi. The CIA tipped off the Pakistanis, who had no idea they had captured Baradar until the CIA told them. Under American eyes, the ISI had no choice but to detain him.[24] To cover up how they had been used, the ISI and Pakistani security officials then told the *New York Times* that they had detained Baradar in order to cut off Taliban peace feelers to Kabul.[25] One official claimed, "We picked up Baradar and the others because they were trying to make a deal without us . . . We protect the Taliban. They are dependent on us. We are not going to allow them to make a deal with Karzai and the Indians."[26] The ISI reportedly summoned at least ten other high-level Taliban leaders in a show of power, including military commis-sion head Abdul Qayum Zakir, Sirajuddin Haqqani, and political representa-tive Tayeb Agha.[27] A rumor emerged that Baradar had been corresponding with Hamid and Ahmed Wali Karzai, his Popalzai tribesmen.[28] Years later Baradar himself would deny he had any contact with Karzai, his brother, or anyone else about peace at this time.[29]

Baradar would be in Pakistani prison for three years.[30] Mullah Akhtar Mohammed Mansour succeeded him as Mullah Omar's deputy. Mansour was 45 years old, from the Maiwand district of Kandahar, and Ishaqzai. Perhaps a third of the tribe was in Pakistan. That portion of the tribe and at least another

20 percent in Afghanistan fell under his influence.[31] Mansour had attended the famous Chageriya madrasa in Peshawar. Many Taliban had also taught or attended there, meaning Mansour had a wide network of contacts. Like other Taliban leaders, he had been too young to fight against the Soviets. Because of his ties to the movement's founders, he was appointed minister of civil aviation during the Taliban first regime. He set up the networks and organization to transport poppy out of Kandahar to Iran and Pakistan, a lucrative business that would last the rest of his life.[32]

Mansour fought in the north and, when the Taliban lost Mazar-e-Sharif in 1997, the Uzbeks captured him. Legend has it that he was tortured and thrown down a well before the Taliban recaptured the city and freed him in 1998.[33] After the Taliban regime fell in 2001, Mansour retired to Maiwand. US special forces raids against other former Taliban leaders and a search of his own home prompted him to flee to Pakistan in 2002 or 2003. He complained to friends that "this government won't let me live in peace."[34] From Pakistan, he continued to smuggle poppy out of Kandahar, specifically Maiwand. The funds he generated translated into influence within the movement as it re-formed. He briefly served as Taliban governor of Kandahar, but was overshadowed by the more charismatic Dadullah Lang. After Dadullah was killed and former defense minister Obaidullah was captured by Pakistan in 2007, the Quetta Shura appointed Mansour as Baradar's assistant, paving the way for him to take Baradar's spot in 2010.[35]

Mullah Omar's role in Mansour's ascent is opaque. Once deputy, Mansour presumably passed messages to Omar, living in seclusion. Pakistan's role is similarly shrouded. Its operatives are not known to have engineered Massoud's selection, though Baradar's imprisonment must have sent an unintentional signal. Although he distrusted them, Mansour maintained close ties with the ISI to bolster his position within the Taliban. They gave him a Pakistani passport and permitted him to travel frequently to Dubai and Iran.[36]

Whereas Dadullah Lang had been a fearsome warrior, Mansour was a behind-the-scenes political operator. Whereas Baradar had been a reformer, Mansour was a businessman. Mansour spent his time in Quetta and Karachi, Dubai and Iran, shoring up his political power. Poppy wealth enhanced his influence across the movement.[37] Although he had rivals, he could bend the military commanders to his will.[38] Especially while Mullah Omar was alive, Mansour's orders were obeyed.[39]

Mansour took great interest in Kandahar. With McChrystal's preparations all over the press, Mansour and the Quetta Shura were well-informed of Operation Hamkary. Mansour sent reinforcements, especially to Maiwand, his home and heart of Taliban operations in southern Afghanistan.[40] Fighters also went to

Kandahar city's southern outskirts and Arghandab. More than 4,000 Taliban fighters, not including people who supported them, were in Kandahar in 2010.

In terms of tactics, Mansour retained Baradar's doctrine of guerrilla war and planned on carrying it out as long as possible in Kandahar. Operation Hamkary did not worry Mansour or Mohammed Issa, the Taliban governor for Kandahar, who was responsible for tactical matters. Their goal was to turn Kandahar into a quagmire. In the countryside, Issa believed the Taliban could evade search missions and months of improvised explosive devices, ambushes, and guerrilla attacks could inflict heavy casualties on the Americans and choke their supply lines so that long-term presence in the villages would be impossible. They would be trapped in their bases. Within Kandahar City, Issa wanted to "intensify our operations . . . and with bomb explosions also start aggressive attacks face-to-face on the enemy."[41] Issa planned for "commando" raids and suicide bombers to assassinate government officials and hit government and US facilities. He sent specially formed teams into the city for this purpose. He also strengthened cadres on Kandahar city's southern outskirts and in Arghandab so those areas could serve as conduits for operations in the city.

For the first seven months of 2010, Issa's campaign in Kandahar City progressed. He used a sprawling set of mixed-tribal villages known as Malajat on the city's southern outskirts as a base for missions. Fighters walked openly with weapons and set up checkpoints. The police got into firefights. US air strikes blasted compounds.[42] As Operation Hamkary began, in August 2010, Taliban raids into Kandahar City killed Karzai supporters. Karzai ordered Malajat cleared.[43] Governor Wesa asked him to get US forces to help. Karzai replied, "Shame on you. . . . Go after them. Do not wait for NATO."[44] The army and police tried but took casualties from improvised explosive devices and pulled back. Border police chief Abdul Razziq then volunteered.

Since 2006 and his disastrous foray into Panjwai, Razziq had grown from a brash militia captain into an astute general. While the rest of Kandahar was crumbling, Razziq and his disheveled border police in their light-gray camouflage fought their corner around the vital Spin Boldak border crossing. Razziq collected the customs proceeds and sent them to Governor Wesa and Ahmed Wali. President Karzai allowed Razziq to take a cut for himself. Over time his border police expanded to roughly 3,000. A succession of US special forces teams in Spin Boldak mentored Razziq. He steadily improved his reading and writing and picked up a good ear for English. With access to customs proceeds and the US military, Razziq strengthened his hold of the border.

The border police were more tribal militia than disciplined military unit. They were entirely local and largely Razziq's Achekzai tribesmen. The Achekzai tribe straddled the border with Pakistan. The tribesmen knew the mountains, desert tracks, smuggling routes, nomad camps, and who was Taliban and who was not. Tribesmen on the Pakistani side of the border tipped off Razziq on Taliban activities before they struck inside Afghanistan. The Achekzai militia-turned-border police were far better at running the border than the professional army soldiers or regular policemen.[45] The Taliban governor of Kandahar, Mohammed Issa, openly admitted that the Taliban faced "problems" in Spin Boldak and along the border.[46]

Razziq ran the border with an iron fist. Rumors of his ruthlessness—secret prisons and summary executions—ran rampant. Some were false. Some were true. The Noorzai particularly despised him for pushing them out of power in Spin Boldak.[47] Razziq put his family knowledge of smuggling and the border to good use. In addition to his share of the customs proceeds, Razziq ran his own taxation schemes at the border crossing and allegedly smuggled opium from Kandahar into Pakistan and Iran. Rather than hoard his profits for himself, Razziq used them to finance his border police.[48]

Razziq went into Malajat with 100 border police and no Americans. His one request was US air support. He cleared the village in five days and detained most of the Taliban.[49] His methods were harsh. He paid children to point out improvised explosive devices. He imprisoned all the men and then interviewed them and enough other villagers to determine who might be Taliban. It worked. The Taliban were driven out. According to one of the policemen, "Razziq's greatest success was fiercely clearing out Malajat. He killed all kinds of Taliban."[50] It was not the end. Issa's terror campaign in Kandahar City continued. Malajat was only the first step in Operation Hamkary.

With the start of Hamkary, Major-General Carter launched major operations in Arghandab, Panjwai, and Zharey—the districts surrounding Kandahar City. Fertile Arghandab, guarding the northern approach to Kandahar City, was the most important. Little had changed from when the Taliban had taken the district in 2008. The mighty Alikozai tribe had fallen apart. Many Alikozai families had fled to Kandahar City. The last police foothold was in the south of the district, at the district center and a handful of nearby villages. Their chief had been severely wounded a few months earlier and evacuated. The police tended to stay on the eastern side of the Arghandab River that ran roughly down the center of the district. The main road was on this side. Taliban operated on both sides of the river but were thicker to the northwest, where they were headquartered out of a cluster of poor Ghilzai villages.

In December 2009, Carter had sent 2nd Battalion, 508th Parachute Infantry Regiment from the 82nd Airborne Division (roughly 900 men) into Arghandab to fight alongside the 300 Afghan soldiers and 150 or so rudderless police. The airborne battalion had been originally deployed as advisors to the Afghan army (part of the 4,000 advisors within the first tranche of the surge). Carter reassigned them to combat operations. A district support team, including a State Department political officer and USAID development officer, came too. The paratroopers moved into two outposts. They primarily foot patrolled the villages, district center, and road on the eastern side of the Arghandab River. In April, they started constructing new outposts on the western side, multiplying the total number of outposts to 11. In June and July 2010, two US battalions (1st Battalion, 320th Field Artillery Regiment and 1st Battalion, 66th Armored Regiment) replaced the airborne battalion, raising the number of US troops in the district to roughly 1,300. Additionally, an Afghan civil order police battalion and an experienced army battalion (1st Battalion, 1st Brigade, 205th Corps) arrived, for another 700 soldiers.[51] These would be the forces that would conduct Operation Hamkary in Arghandab.

On July 25, at the height of the summer, American and Afghan soldiers attacked into the farmland along the river. The Americans expanded the number of combat outposts from 11 to more than 17. In these outposts, US soldiers worked side by side with Afghan soldiers.[52]

Clearing was slow-going. In the first week of the operation, 1st Battalion, 320th Field Artillery Regiment suffered 30 casualties capturing a key canal crossing known as "Objective Bakersfield" in western Arghandab. Taliban laid hundreds of improvised explosive devices. First Lieutenant Scott Hendrickson, a platoon leader in 1st Battalion, 66th Armored Regiment, remembered, "Basically, people moving from the west side of the river would cross, put in an IED, wait for us . . . to move through and detonate on us. They would also use . . . RPGs." They would, he added, "draw attention one way, and then attack us or fire from a different direction."[53] The orchards, low mud walls that Afghans use for grape trestles, and thick-walled homes made for Taliban fieldworks. The two US battalions suffered greater than 100 casualties during their year. Certain platoons endured 50 percent losses, as well as often bloody amputations from improvised explosive devices.

US offensive operations gained ground but did not end improvised explosive devices and small arms engagements. As per Taliban shadow governor Issa's plan, the Taliban avoided face-to-face battles and ran a guerrilla war. The same problem existed in Arghandab that had existed in Marjah: it was difficult to identify insurgents without locally recruited police or militia. US soldiers, Afghan army soldiers, and non-local police, no matter how well trained, had an awful time telling who was an insurgent and who was not.

Lieutenant Gul Agha Haqsar commanded an Afghan army company partnered with the US soldiers. He was a 30-year-old Tajik from Takhar who remembered fighting the Taliban attacks in Takhar in the late 1990s. Of his 40 men, only two were Pashtuns. Like many Afghan army units, he and his men tried to respect the locals. A Tajik soldier professed "We are the same people. We are all from Afghanistan." Good intentions were not enough. "We can be here in the Pashtun area for 1,000 years, but they will never be our friends," Gul Agha predicted.[54]

The police in Arghandab were better off than the soldiers but also faced challenges. About half were local Alikozai. The rest were from elsewhere in the province, especially Kandahar City, sent to Arghandab without training. The city boys did not know the area, could not find insurgents, and had shoddy discipline. Most stayed until payday and then deserted.[55]

Unlike Marjah, an initiative was already underway to recruit local militia. The US special operations component commander in Afghanistan, Brigadier General Ed Reeder, had realized that local tribal militia could help turn Arghandab against the Taliban. In late 2009, two special forces teams had come to Arghandab and looked into how to recruit a tribal militia. Arghandab was especially ripe for such an initiative because of its large numbers of formerly anti-Taliban Alikozai. The special forces teams funded 150 Alikozai fighters in a cluster of villages in southwestern Arghandab, known as Nagahan. "When we . . . conducted Village Stability in Nagahan back in 2009," recounted one of the special forces sergeants, "it was bottom-up. The community was completely involved in the process. We were invited to live among the people and there was almost no conflict between the villagers and us. We worked together to help the village stand up against the insurgents."[56]

The militia was effective. An official Taliban announcement on the situation in Arghandab confessed, "The Nagahan region in Arghandab is the only region that the mujahedin do not have influence. . . . The region is situated very close to a foreign post and also police, government workers, and base workers are in very great numbers."[57]

Over the first half of 2010, the prowess of the special forces emboldened a few more Alikozai to fight.[58] In turn, Taliban tried to intimidate them. They executed tribesmen and killed the district governor, Haji Jabar. To add insult to injury, they confiscated cell phones and confined villagers to their homes. The most dramatic event happened in southwestern Arghandab in June. A Taliban suicide bomber killed 40 people and wounded 87 at a wedding party attended by special forces, members of the Alikozai tribal militia, and several influential Alikozai tribal leaders. The Alikozai saw it as Taliban oppression.[59] Tribal leaders went to Governor Wesa and demanded retribution. Karzai appointed a new district governor (Shah Mahmud) and police chief (Nyaz Mohammed) who were Alikozai and very active. They knew their job was to get Arghandab under control. Major-General Carter tried to ensure they received due assistance from the government.[60]

While the Alikozai stirred, heated debate was playing out in Kabul over whether the United States should build tribal militias. The marines in Helmand had created their tribal militias ad hoc. Something more official would be needed if a program were to be implemented countrywide. Since 2007, US commanders in various provinces had thought about tribal militias. Poor supervision, piecemeal implementation, and opposition by generals and ambassadors who saw militias as undemocratic had stunted action. In early 2010, Brigadier General Scott Miller, Reeder's successor as US special operations component commander in Afghanistan, carefully crafted a new program, known as "Afghan local police."[61] Afghan local police would be village militias, but paid and armed by the government and under the supervision of the district police chief. To check warlordism, volunteers would be approved by a tribal council, the district governor, and the ministry of interior. They would be trained by special forces, or, in Helmand, marines.

McChrystal liked the idea. Ambassador Eikenberry did not. He, along with many human rights groups, thought it would undermine the government and harm civilians. Eikenberry forbade any diplomat from working on local police initiatives. McChrystal and Eikenberry could not come to agreement. Eventually, McChrystal stopped discussing the matter with Eikenberry. Karzai agreed with Eikenberry that the militias might harm civilians and also simply doubted local police would achieve much. Politically, he worried that the initiative would empower certain tribes and disturb his own influence. McChrystal never brought the matter to him.[62]

There things sat until Petraeus replaced McChrystal. Petraeus championed the Afghan local police program. He hoped to repeat Iraq's Sunni Awakening, when Sunni tribes and their militias had rapidly turned against al-Qa'eda in Iraq and helped defeat them. In Iraq, the United States had bankrolled the Sunni tribes and their militias, in most places paying little heed to the wishes of the Iraqi government. The downside was that the Iraqi government divorced itself from the Sunni militias once the United States had left Iraq. In Afghanistan, Petraeus wanted Afghan government endorsement of any local police program so that history would not repeat itself.[63]

Petraeus went straight to Karzai. Local police was the very first item in their very first meeting. Petraeus waxed on the Sunni Awakening in Iraq and the potential for something similar in Afghanistan. Karzai, who knew Afghan tribes better than anyone, thought the notion that Iraq's grand tribal movement could be repeated in his country preposterous and was annoyed at the lecture. "But Petraeus was very insistent. He believed this was the only way," writes Spanta, who was present at the meetings. After ten days of contentious meetings, Karzai approved the program. "After going round and round in small circles in the national security council and cabinet," complains Spanta, "we finally had to accept a modified version of Petraeus's plan, reluctantly."[64]

Karzai issued a formal decree, implementing the Afghan local police program on August 16, 2010, barely a month after Petraeus had taken command. The Afghan local police (ALP) would fall under the ministry of interior. The United States eventually decided to fund 30,000 for all Afghanistan. By March 2011, 5,900 special forces and SEALs would be assigned to the mission.[65]

Once the program was approved, Afghan local police recruitment proceeded in Arghandab. The first official Afghan local police unit formed in the village of Kohak, in southern Arghandab. A special forces team set up a base (known as a "village stability platform") on a lone brown and black speckled hill overlooking western Arghandab, the highest point for kilometers around. The Taliban had surrounded the village and tried to enforce their writ inside it. They did not let children go to school.[66] A few villagers helped the Taliban.

A special forces team approached Haji Khaliq Dod, the 45-year-old robust yet worn village elder. Khaliq Dod agreed to cooperate because "the Taliban were abusing and oppressing people."[67] He and the other village elders encouraged their sons and relatives to join the local police. The fact that the village could arm itself and would be able to employ its young men appears to have been a powerful inducement. From the point of view of its elders, the village would rise in power within the Alikozai. To help bring the village together, the special forces team built a new white and light blue school and refurbished the shrine of Zarghona Ana, Ahmed Shah Durrani's mother, who lay in the village.

The first recruit was Mirza, a former Alikozai policeman in his late 20s. According to Mirza, "The Taliban were close around the village. . . . It was the special forces' arrival that got the local police started. They motivated people to stand. They cared."[68] Mirza joined because he wanted to "protect the village and stop Taliban oppression" and also because he "wanted a weapon, ammunition, and [a] uniform."[69]

After about a month, 20 local police had been recruited and started patrolling. Khaliq Dod's eldest son became their commander, another son a patrolman. Groups of five or six Taliban—one or two locals and four or five from outside the district—tried to stop them with ambushes and improvised explosive devices. The local fighters helped the outsiders with terrain and contacts. Within a few months, Khaliq Dod convinced families of local Taliban to have their sons live peacefully at home.[70] Once that happened, the Taliban from outside the village were on their own. Bereft of local eyes, they had trouble operating. Khaliq Dod, Mirza, and the special forces had the upper hand.

Elsewhere in Arghandab, momentum accelerated but things did not transform overnight. On September 13, 2010, Taliban fighters emptied a whole magazine into a young Alikozai man whom they suspected of working with the government. The next day, 100 or so Alikozai elders called on Governor Wesa, Ahmed Wali Karzai, and Razziq. They told Wesa and Ahmed Wali that they were all mujahideen commanders and that it was shameful to be oppressed by the Taliban.[71] Ahmed Wali Karzai was at the meeting and announced that the Afghan security forces would assault Arghandab. Razziq stood up and asked who would go with him. The next day, Razziq charged into Arghandab with a retinue of Alikozai tribal leaders, a detachment of his Achekzai border police, and Lieutenant Colonel Chris Riga, the US special forces commander in Kandahar. With the tribal leaders' help, Razziq cleared out part of the district and in one day found at least 100 improvised explosive devices and captured 30 Taliban. The operation stunned the Taliban and knocked them out of many villages. The confidence of the Alikozai living in the district rose.[72]

Less than a month later, Karzai came to Kandahar and went directly to Arghandab, accompanied by Petraeus and Eikenberry. On the shrine on the hill that overlooks the Arghandab River, Karzai convened a shura with hundreds of Alikozai tribesmen and their leaders. Karzai berated tribal leaders for fleeing their villages to live in the city. He told them that if they returned to their villages, and cooperated with the police and army, no enemy would walk openly in Arghandab. Military posts could not create security, he said; only the cooperation and leadership of the tribal leaders could keep out the Taliban. He asked them to protect their district and to build local police. He promised the government would give them what they needed to defend their villages on their own.[73]

Through this speech, Karzai paused his divide-and-rule politics in order to save Arghandab. Shortly after the shura, he appointed Khan Mohammed, the Alikozai favorite that Karzai had passed over in 2009 for leadership of the tribe, to the coveted position of Kandahar police chief. The presence of the ruler of Afghanistan standing near the front line, speaking to a tribe in the tradition of Afghan heroes, was a powerful symbol. It was a reminder of Karzai's inspirational power. The tribal leaders declared they were willing to join the police and army and fight the Taliban.[74] Alikozai tribal leaders later said that the combination of Karzai, Razziq, and US operations (especially special forces activities) had turned the tide.

Still, the Alikozai did not fill the local police at once; tribal words had to be turned into action. The special forces teams and police chief Nyaz Mohammed and his deputy for local police traveled from village to village and urged tribal leaders to provide recruits.[75] Over the autumn, more and more villages decided to join. As had happened in Kohaq, Alikozai tribal leaders negotiated with local Taliban and convinced them to lay down their arms. As the movement grew, more and more Alikozai Taliban stopped fighting. By the end of the year, almost the whole tribe had mobilized against the Taliban.

US clearing operations continued alongside local police mobilization. The Ghilzai villages on the northwestern side of the river proved hardest to crack. Families from the Taraki tribe (a Ghilzai tribe) lived in Tarak Kolache and three nearby villages. They let the Taliban use their villages as a stronghold. Dense thickets of improvised explosive devices thwarted several clearing attempts by 1st Battalion, 320th Field Artillery Regiment.

Rather than risk heavy casualties, Lieutenant Colonel David Flynn, the battalion commander, resorted to carpet bombing. Petraeus personally approved the strikes. US intelligence reported that most civilians had fled. On October 6, 2010, twenty-five 2,000-pound bombs and fifty 500-pound bombs destroyed the villages. The US brigade commander responsible for Arghandab, Colonel Jeffrey Martindale (1st Brigade, 4th Infantry Division), reported, "We obliterated those towns. They're not there at all . . . These are just parking lots right now."[76]

Flynn tried to rebuild Tarak Kolache as quickly as he could, constructing a new bazaar and new concrete homes. Supposedly, the people were not upset.[77] Few ever returned. They had fled to Kandahar City. The strange concrete homes built with American dollars sat empty.[78] Such was the lot of the Ghilzai. Hundreds of Ghilzai from these villages died during the battle for Arghandab, either as Taliban fighters or as civilians killed accidentally by bombs and stray rounds.[79]

Mansour and Issa were displeased at the situation in Helmand and Kandahar. They ordered commanders to fight through the winter. Many refused and went

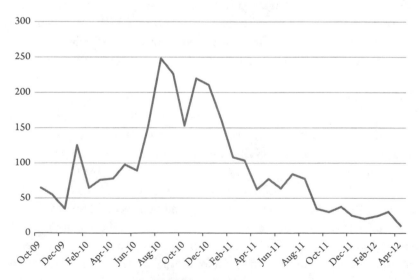

Figure 1 Attacks in Arghandab, 2009–2012 Mike Simmering and Leo Qyszynski, "Enabling the Afghans to Take the Lead: Transition at the Tactical Level," *Small Wars Journal*, website, September 24, 2012.

to Pakistan for rest. Violence eased over January and February. Mansour, Issa, and the Quetta Shura debated over what to do. In early spring, Mansour and Issa sent reinforcements to Arghandab and elsewhere with orders to target, in addition to US forces, government officials, the police and army, and civilians working with the United States.[80]

Fighting in Arghandab gasped through the spring and early summer before Issa finally called it quits. The Taliban cadre commanders pulled out of Arghandab and went to Panjwai. A few unlucky fighters were left behind.[81] By June, a total of 350 local police had taken the field, trained and advised by the US special forces teams. By the end of the year, all 72 villages in the district were under government control, in contrast to just the district center and a handful of villages in 2009.[82] First Lieutenant David Burgio, another platoon leader in 1st Battalion, 66th Armored Regiment, described the turnaround:

> It is night and day, you know. We went from a string of independent villages with leadership scared off by the Taliban under a strict Taliban control, people that wanted nothing to do with the government or nothing to do with ANSF or coalition forces, to, by the time we left, every single village was either strongly connected or I would say connected to the government. . . . People were always receptive to us; people were nice, and actually the biggest thing—I would say, the biggest indicator of success that we had was . . . when we [were] starting to get into the spring, [that was] the time when the Taliban [would] typically come-back and inflow into the area and they just never came back.[83]

As the battle for Arghandab came to a close, the battle for Kandahar City continued. On April 14, 2011, a suicide bomber killed provincial police chief Khan Mohammed after barely six months in office. A week later 476 prisoners escaped from Sarposa prison through a cleverly dug tunnel. Then, in early May, the Taliban carried out a string of suicide bombings and firefights for 30 hours against the police headquarters, governor's office, and other government buildings. Attackers even got past guards and shot down the hallway into Governor Wesa's office. US advisors and Wesa's guards gunned down the intruders in the ensuing room-to-room shootout.

On July 12, 2011, Karzai suffered a much bigger blow. Ahmed Wali, his brother and loyal executor, was killed, shot in the chest by one of his own guards over a personal dispute. In spite of his grief, Karzai moved quickly to protect his political base in Kandahar. He put his other brother, Shah Wali Karzai, in charge of political affairs. He sent Asadullah Khalid, former governor of Kandahar and

Ghazni and a trusted fixer, to Kandahar for six months to watch over security and supervise the army, police, and governor. And he turned to Razziq.

Karzai had appointed Razziq as provincial police chief in April, after Khan Mohammed had been killed. He had done so over the objection of Minister of Interior Bismullah Khan, signaling that Razziq's authority flowed directly from him. Razziq proved himself, losing none of the courage that had marked him as the border police commander. When the Taliban attacked the police headquarters with a car bomb and an assault squad in May, Razziq was firing out of the windows and rallying his men. Khalid trusted Razziq. Soon Karzai did too. Every week, Razziq reported to Karzai on the phone. Every few months, he traveled to Kabul and saw the president in person. Like Karzai and Khalid, Razziq was a nationalist. He believed Americans should stay out of Afghan internal business. He assiduously separated his many American friends, whom he treated like brothers, from Afghan political matters. He believed that eventually the foreigners had to leave.[84]

Razziq cared deeply for his police. After battles, he handsomely rewarded policemen and even army soldiers outside his command. US advisors were accustomed to seeing him pull out a wad of cash in front of police formations and hand a few 1,000 Afghani ($20) bills to each man. He was following the model of Ahmed Shah Durrani, the founder of the Afghan state, who had been renowned 250 years earlier for his generosity to his soldiers. Casualties left Razziq visibly upset, further endearing him to front-line police. In 2013, at the site of an improvised explosive device explosion, he met an Afghan engineer who had been trained to locate and defuse them. Impressed, Razziq ordered, "Go out and recruit 140 more smart young men and train them to do exactly the same thing." The engineer responded, "The Ministry of Interior will only pay for three engineers per province." Razziq's answer was, "Do not worry about that." He would eventually pay for 145 technicians out of his own pocket (or coffers). The technicians found 7,000 improvised explosive devices in nine months. Razziq's willingness to lead from the front, and his love for his men quickly earned the respect of the best American officers.

To the surprise of many, Razziq professionalized the police. Despite his scant education and militia roots, he improved discipline. He demanded that men wear their uniforms and carry their weapons correctly. He rotated police through the academy until eventually the vast majority of the force had been trained. One police sergeant commented, "Before Razziq sent men to the academy, the police were walking blind. The academy opened their eyes."[85] Even policemen loyal to the previous Alikozai police chiefs admitted that Razziq brought professionalism.

Razziq kept the police on a tight leash. Upon becoming chief, Razziq cleaned out senior officers who had failed to support policemen on the front line. He would later fire several district chiefs for poor performance: one for failing to secure a district, another for skimming police pay, a third for neglecting his wounded.[86] Other provincial police chiefs could not control their deputies and district chiefs because patrons in the parliament, palace, and ministry would raise a fuss. Razziq did not have that problem: "If my police chiefs are bad, I put them in jail. If the ministry orders me to put in a bad leader, I refuse. In other provinces, senators try to get their favorite police a district. If they try that here, I reject them."[87] Karzai's support meant Razziq could do as he pleased. Kandahar soon suffered fewer police leadership woes than other provinces.

For all his strengths as a military commander, brutality continued to darken Razziq's reputation. The United Nations dubbed him "brutally efficient."[88] Stories of secret prisons, torture, and executions trailed him. Without a doubt, policemen close to him summarily executed some number of Taliban who had been captured in battle. In December 2010, in a moment of indiscretion, Razziq told journalist Michael Hastings, "General Petraeus and I have very similar opinions . . . I want to kill the Taliban, he wants to kill the Taliban. . . . We don't take prisoners—if they are trying to kill me, I will try to kill them. That's how I order my men."[89] Worse, he allegedly kidnapped suspected Taliban at night and executed them without trial. Some may have been active Taliban. Others may have been former Taliban trying to live peacefully.[90] From time to time, US officials and generals counseled Karzai about Razziq's human rights record. Karzai refused to do anything. The White House considered cutting Razziq off from US assistance, but never forced the issue with Karzai.

For Razziq, life was short. The possibility that the international community might punish him for taking customs proceeds, smuggling poppy, or executing a Taliban was irrelevant. He doubted he would live that long. From his point of view, the security that his actions produced was needed immediately. He cared less about the future than the present. Before becoming police chief, the Taliban had tried to assassinate him numerous times. They got his brother across the border in Pakistan in 2005. They had killed his father and uncle long before in 1994. Once he was police chief, the Taliban sent suicide bomber after suicide bomber to kill him, over 20 in all. He was wounded twice. "Will we ever become old men?" he once morosely asked his advisor. "We may not live that long."[91] What did an iron fist matter if he might die tomorrow in a bomb or ambush that was coming anyway?

Razziq and the US Army locked down Kandahar City. The number of Afghan police in Kandahar City increased fivefold after 2009.[92] Razziq demanded every precinct run six patrols per day. Almost nightly, special operations forces raided insurgent locations.[93] Razziq also imposed a curfew. Attacks slowly decreased. The ambushes and occasional assaults stopped. Taliban reverted to improvised explosive devices and assassinations, with car bombs from time to time. From the 300 or so attacks in the city in 2009, there would be 150 in 2011 and then only 60 in 2012. With the drop in violence, schools and shops reopened. Parents no longer kept their children locked up at home, off the streets.[94]

Razziq's actions, the Taliban threat, Karzai's speeches, and the calls of other local leaders motivated Kandaharis. Shafi Afghan, a friend of Sarah Chayes, networked across reform-minded leaders to reduce tribal friction. Zarghona Baluch, daughter of a provincial councilwoman, drove to nearby district centers and spoke with women about discouraging their sons from joining the Taliban.[95] Maryam Durrani, a provincial councilwoman of education and daughter of a progressive father, ran a radio program and used it to call for Afghans to volunteer for the police and army. She had "defied Taliban rules" during their regime and she was going to resist them now.[96]

Little better exemplifies how the United States went with the grain in Kandahar than Razziq's rise to power. Razziq was both respected and a source of discontent. Many Afghans, from politician to street vendor, acknowledged that he had improved security, even if they believed he detained innocents, ran secret prisons, and executed people. Others were outraged and wanted him gone.[97] Americans were also divided. Generals and colonels tended to note Razziq's courage and self-sacrifice; diplomats and journalists, his iron fist. Razziq was a moral dilemma, to put it charitably. The prevaricating comments of a well-educated, progressive Kandahari capture the two sides of thought on Razziq: "Razziq is oppressive. More oppressive than Gul Agha [Sherzai] was. But life is better for most average people. But he oppresses those who live in traditional Taliban areas. If there is any evidence of Taliban activity, or just an accusation, he imprisons people. But security is still far better than before."[98] The question of whether the United States was right to empower Razziq, whether the military gains were worth human rights, troubled US officials and generals but none dared remove him. Civil war refuses moral clarity.

Arghandab and Kandahar City were two of three targets of Operation Hamkary. The third was western Kandahar, immediately to the west of the city. Three districts made up western Kandahar: Zharey, Panjwai, and Maiwand. The region was the Taliban homeland, where the movement had started, where Taliban leaders had relatives and tribesmen. Mullah Omar's mosque was in Zharey. Large numbers of pro-Taliban Noorzai and Ishaqzai lived in these districts. Since 2006, the Taliban had run a shadow government that covered the whole area. Taliban commanders there had often been serving since 2006 or 2007. They were both experienced and committed to their homeland.[99] As long Zharey and Panjwai were unsecure, Kandahar City would be in danger.

Five US battalions, one Canadian battalion, and seven Afghan battalions— roughly 10,000 troops—flooded western Kandahar in August 2010, an unprecedented concentration of forces.[100] To pacify an area, the counterinsurgency rule of thumb is 20 soldiers or police for every 1,000 people. In general, clearing and holding a district in Afghanistan required the rule of thumb or greater. US and Afghan security forces had roughly hit the rule in Garmser, Nawa, Arghandab, and Sangin, and doubled it in Marjah. The combined western Kandahar population was roughly 150,000, computing to 3,000 soldiers and police by the rule of thumb. Without even counting police forces, US, Canadian, and Afghan soldiers tripled that number and then some.

Of the 10,000 US and allied troops, 9,000 went into Zharey and Panjwai. They deployed throughout the districts, including deep into Taliban strongholds. The US battalions were under 2nd Brigade, 101st Airborne Division, commanded by Colonel Art Kandarian. Petraeus took personal interest in the operation and visited the brigade repeatedly to monitor progress.[101]

Kandarian posted units throughout Zharey and Panjwai but his immediate focus was clearing the Taliban away from Highway One, which his men referred to as a Taliban "free-fire zone." Kandarian preferred heliborne insertions—31 in 82 days—because road movement was too slow to get to certain locations. The US, Canadian, and Afghan troops met staunch resistance. One of Kandarian's battalions—2nd Battalion, 502nd Infantry Regiment—fought for three days just to advance a half mile south of the highway.[102] "We were south in the green zone," recalled a soldier on his first deployment. "The Taliban had driven out the families that lived there.... It was a den of IEDs. This was our first mission: to go down there and push them out. So naturally it was a big mission." His platoon's patrol that day was in 130-degree heat. "All of a sudden, there was a huge explosion." A buddy had "hopped over the wall, landed on the pressure plate, and immediately had a double amputation. Immediately we hear, 'Medic! Medic!' Someone is hysterically screaming, 'Get doc! Get doc!' ... We had two docs on him.... Everyone was like, 'What do you want me to do?' ... He was like, 'Just open bandages. Just open bandages.'"[103]

A company from another battalion—1st Battalion, 502nd Infantry Regiment—suffered 23 casualties from improvised explosive devices in a village in a night filled with shouts of "IED! IED!," "Who's hit?," and "Don't move!" "I think I used six tourniquets," said Lieutenant Nicholas Williams. The soldiers razed the village in response.[104]

Kandarian purposefully withheld from seizing ground further south around the river. He explained to querulous Kandahar and Kabul staff officers, "I don't have to go to the river. I could go to the river, but then that's a fist in the bucket of water. So we clear the river, and now what? We can't hold it, unless we have enough police, which we don't have. Or Afghan local police willing to come."[105]

Positions far west of Kandahar City where Noorzai and Ishaqzai were most numerous were frequently attacked and could control little ground. Clearing operations in Zharey near Mullah Omar's old mosque were especially onerous.[106] In one air assault in late September, 2nd Battalion, 502nd Infantry's scout platoon fought off 12 attacks in 48 hours. "We had to expend a lot of ammo. . . . We didn't see where they were coming from," recalled Specialist Marvin Speckhaus.[107] Staff Sergeant Spear, one of the squad leaders, reported to the platoon leader, Captain William Faucher, "These people are getting close. . . . You know this is getting bad," before a second US company closed on the Taliban from another direction and ended the firefight.[108] Attacks in Zharey and Panjwai doubled from 1,000 in 2009 to roughly 2,000 in 2010 as the Taliban battled the new American units.

In November 2010, Major General James Terry and the 10th Mountain Division arrived in Kandahar. Major-General Carter went home to Britain, his tour complete. As Arghandab calmed, Terry devoted greater effort to western Kandahar.

The Taliban did the same. Concerned about Operation Hamkary, Mansour and Issa dispatched reinforcements to Zharey and Panjwai early in 2011 (this was the same time they were sending reinforcements to Arghandab). Mansour and Issa held to their guerrilla tactics. "Proven military tactics that counter the use of modern air and ground weapons will be focused on," ordered the Quetta Shura's 2011 spring offensive announcement, such as "aggressive hit and run attacks," improvised explosive devices, and "martyrdom attacks," aka suicide bombings.[109] Mansour and Issa intended these tactics to prevent the Afghan and US forces from moving freely and actually controlling the districts. As in Arghandab, commanders were directed to especially target the police, army, and government officials.[110]

As they pushed the Taliban back from Highway One, Kandarian's soldiers tried to secure the eastern parts of Zharey and Panjwai, closest to the city and farthest from the Taliban strongholds in the west. Almost every patrol encountered an improvised explosive devices or gunfight. Kandarian built stretches of wall parallel to Highway One to obstruct Taliban movement. Months passed before pockets formed where Taliban could no longer move freely.[111] By the middle of 2011, the main highway, district centers, and the biggest villages near the city were secure but elsewhere was still contested, including Pashmul, the populous cluster of villages and old Taliban stronghold of 2006. Improvised explosive devices in the villages hindered US soldiers on foot and vehicle movement on roads. A US Army captain who completed a year-long tour in Panjwai in July 2011 remembered, "When I left, the situation was bad. We could not hold ground."[112]

The problem was that western Kandahar was the Taliban homeland. It was much harder to get locals to support the government or provide intelligence than in Arghandab.[113] This was the very reason Taliban fighters and commanders fled from Arghandab to Panjwai. According to one of these Arghandab fighters,

Taliban sought refuge in Panjwai "because here all of the people are Taliban. The Americans cannot put everyone in prison."[114] An internationally funded survey in 2012 found that the majority of the people of Kandahar viewed the Taliban as "good Muslims" and opposed the long-term presence of US boots in their province.[115] Tribalism, kinship, Afghan identity, and Islam combined to stiffen the Taliban in western Kandahar.

In the wake of clearing operations, Terry's commanders tried to recruit local police. It was slow going. US State Department civilians on the district support teams found locals reluctant to work with the United States or the government.[116] Tribal leaders refused to help, somewhat out of fear of Taliban retaliation, somewhat out of sympathy.[117] Frustrated, Colonel Patrick Frank, the US commander in Zharey (Kandarian had redeployed), opened recruitment to men from Kandahar City, where labor was abundant, violating the local police program's carefully crafted procedures for recruiting only locals approved by their communities. They were posted all along Highway One and the main roads instead of in the villages. The special forces team in Zharey disagreed with Frank's approach and pulled out of the district rather than go along. Frank recruited 400 local police in a few months. Most could not identify insurgents or relate to the villagers.[118] Without much care for the villagers, their behavior strayed. They extorted money, killed a detainee by dragging him behind a car, and sometimes participated in Taliban activity. One local policeman shot a US soldier.[119]

In early 2012, two additional US battalions reinforced Zharey and Panjwai, for a total of seven US battalions (the Canadians had departed in July 2011).[120] In Zharey, 4th Brigade, 82nd Airborne Division rotated in for a short six-month deployment. The brigade commander, Colonel Brian Mennes, intended to make the most of it and clear out Pashmul and other Taliban strongholds throughout Zharey and Panjwai. He put an entire battalion onto Pashmul alone. Mennes ordered every platoon to conduct four patrols per day, equaling 152 patrols per day across the brigade or one patrol per day per every 600 of Zharey's 90,000 inhabitants.[121] He explained:

> To get into those strong points, you had to walk. To touch the people . . . you had to go live with them. . . . Half of our FOBs were expeditionary, our guys living with Afghans, ALP, ANA, and ANP, living out with the people. . . . Pick a company, Bravo, 2Fury—they took a place called Kotizai, which is southeast of Sangesar . . . a huge difficult area for us initially. The troopers lived in a qalat and the first sergeant would go out every day . . . and he would bring back three or four guys to recover. Every ten days, they would come back to get a shower. So after nine days living in the rough, they would come back and use the Internet,

phone, shower, chill out, day off. That was how [we] lived, probably
40 percent of our guys out there living with the Afghans and sleeping
with them.[122]

"Aerostat" balloons (the size of a small blimp), tethered to outposts, armed with
video cameras, went up throughout both districts. Command centers vectored
patrols against suspicious behavior or, especially in Panjwai, called in air strikes.
Over the summer of 2012, one battalion alone called in 202 air strikes that killed
178 Taliban, of the estimated 600 to 900 in the district, a significant loss.[123] The
Taliban could no longer move openly with weapons or explosives without running into an American or Afghan soldier or being seen and targeted.

Mennes's troopers empowered new local elders to form new local police
militias. He created 20 new police posts within the villages, all sited by the local
community. Three special forces teams were also directed to Zharey to re-vet and
retrain the local police.[124] They traded out a good number of the Kandahar City
boys for actual tribesmen from Zharey. As US security operations intensified,
Taliban intimidation faded. Massoum Khan, the long-time police chief, found
that now "the people give their family members to become local police because the army and police brought security to the villages."[125] At the end of the
summer, 500 local police were in Zharey, with a better mix of actual locals.[126]
They joined for different reasons: the orders of their elders, money, revenge
against Taliban who had killed family members, "to help my village and to stop
improvised explosive devices from being laid," and "to serve my village."[127]
Additionally, the number of uniformed police grew to 420. In Panjwai, district
governor Feda Mohammed, tribal leader Agha Lalay, Razziq, and the Karzais
also rallied tribesmen to provide local police recruits. Razziq's policy in Panjwai
and elsewhere was to try to recruit a core of local police from families that the
Taliban had hurt, families that wanted revenge. That way, he would not have to
worry about local police turning to work with the Taliban.[128] One hundred and
fifty local police were in Panjwai by the end of the year.[129]

The sheer weight of US and government numbers finally bore down on the
Taliban. In 2007, the Taliban had been able to move freely throughout almost all
of Zharey, Maiwand, Sangin, and Panjwai.[130] Now only Maiwand was left. Many
villagers still sympathized with the Taliban but for the time being had been subdued.[131] Helping the Taliban equaled improvised explosive devices, air strikes,
and night raids. They had seen six years of war and were tired. Even within the
Noorzai and Ishaqzai, fewer men picked up arms than had done so in 2006.

The tougher types did not turn. Their fellow tribesmen may have called it
quits but they were too dedicated. They got up and left, determined to fight
on elsewhere. The Taliban command structure pulled out of most of Zharey
and Panjwai. The influential Taliban leaders, with their long-standing ties to

the communities, headed for Maiwand or Pakistan. Mullah Zayid and Mullah Numan for example, two commanders who had been fighting in Panjwai for six years, stuck to the Maiwand border and carried on operations where US forces were sparse. Mullahs and religious scholars fled back to Pakistan too. They rejected the government's secular foundations. A few village mullahs stayed around but without much influence. "Respected mullahs six years ago called for us to fight jihad against the Americans," said Rahmatullah, a local police commander in Zharey. "Now they have all fled to Pakistan. Just the village mullahs are here."[132] Thousands of villagers who had supported the Taliban also decamped to Pakistan over the next few years, unwilling to live under the government or risk imprisonment by Razziq.[133] The surge in Zharey and Panjwai had forced out a whole part of society.[134] With the Talban and religious leadership gone, fighting abated. Roughly 200 Americans had died in western Kandahar.[135]

In the autumn of 2012, Kandahar province was largely secure. Over 600 American and Afghan outposts had been emplaced. Fifteen thousand army and police—including 1,800 local police—patrolled the streets and villages. The city was safe. The main highways were open. Education had returned. The province had at least 450 schools and 200,000 students, compared to 80 schools and 60,000 students in 2009.[136] The Taliban had been driven out of the districts that mattered. Those who had not laid down their arms had retreated all the way back to Pakistan, to the mountainous northern districts, or to Maiwand, their last stronghold, besieged by US operations. Nazr Mohammed Mutmain, a former Taliban official who was affiliated with the movement, admitted, "From the year 2009 until 2012, in many areas that had been under Taliban control, the Taliban were pushed out of the villages because of the creation and expansion of arbakai [Afghan local police] by General Petraeus."[137] Lost territory crippled poppy revenues. A Taliban commander from Zharey recalled, "We were lacking money. We did not have money for weapons, logistics, or anything else."[138]

With the losses in territory and poppy to tax, the movement as a whole went through 2012 and 2013 short on funds, which restricted operations. One estimate is that Taliban tax revenue in 2013 was 40 percent of what it had been in 2009.[139] In all, the Quetta Shura estimated the movement had suffered 26,000 killed from 2009 to 2011, peaking at 12,000 in 2010 out of a force variously estimated at 30,000 to 70,000 total combatants.[140]

Hamid Karzai played an active, helpful role. Under the pressure of looming Taliban victory, he unified instead of divided. A political adversary and re-nowned former NDS director Amarullah Saleh—someone hardly prone to flattery—noted, "One of Karzai's greatest accomplishments is reenergizing the tribal system in the south."[141] Karzai's post-2008 interventions in Kandahar selected the right leaders, instilled the right amount of caution, and mobilized people at the right times. If Karzai had intervened like this in 2006, the surge may never have been needed.

Obama had wanted the surge to break Taliban momentum. With Kandahar, it was broken. Credit goes foremost to the lieutenant colonels, captains, sergeants, and privates in the field who by and large adopted aggressive small-unit tactics, learned to work through Afghan partners to root out the Taliban, and suffered injury and death in the process. The surge was above all a soldier's war. Petraeus had guided tactical success by giving soldiers and marines the right tools, programs, and support. Tactically, his last campaign was a success. Progress toward the other goal of the surge—to strengthen the Afghan armed forces and government so that they could stand on their own—had also occurred. Whether they would survive without the Americans was an open question.

Yet what matters more than whether the surge met its goals is the cost in time, money, and lives. Kandahar had taken a long time: three and a half years to suppress an insurgency in a single province. When Obama reviewed the surge in spring 2011, Kandahar had just improved. The whole affair was tremendously expensive: thousands of US troops, an airbase the size of a small city, and when all was said and done greater than $650 million in aid. All to protect 2 million people and enable the government to reestablish its authority. In America, the surge looked like a failure, a rotten investment, regardless of the damage the Taliban had suffered on the ground.

14

End of the Surge

When the surge began, al-Qa'eda was operating out of North and South Waziristan. They ran training camps and facilitated international attacks. Obama's drone strikes disrupted their North and South Waziristan safe havens. The organization's key operational leadership was all but wiped out. By one estimate, drones killed roughly 75 percent of al-Qa'eda leaders in Pakistan.[1] Osama bin Laden wrote to a subordinate from his hideaway, "Over the last two years, the problem of the spying war and spying aircraft benefited the enemy greatly and led to the killing of many jihadi cadres, leaders, and others. This is something that is concerning us and exhausting us."[2] In October 2010, bin Laden advised his subordinates to relocate from Waziristan to Kunar, where al-Qa'eda cells had been operating under Abu Ikhlas. Bin Laden thought they would be able to hide from US drones in Kunar's mountains and forests.

The CIA had been tracking bin Laden for years. He had disappeared from sight after 2002. As he hid from capture, his control over his organization loosened. In 2010, the CIA found his hideaway, a walled home in plain sight in Abbottabad, Pakistan, 35 miles north of Islamabad. The town housed the Pakistani military academy. Obama approved a daring helicopter raid by elite SEALs onto bin Laden's compound. On May 1, 2011, the SEALs killed bin Laden. Nearly a decade from the attacks of September 11, 2001, America's number-one enemy was dead.

After bin Laden's death, al-Qa'eda was a shambles. Ayman al-Zawahiri, the old number two, was now leader. He lacked bin Laden's charisma. Though planning to strike the United States persisted, the remnants of the organization hid in the mountainous border regions. In 2012, the main group of al-Qa'eda fighters, under Farouq al-Qahtani, followed the late bin Laden's advice and relocated from Waziristan into Kunar and Nuristan. The group would survive in the mountains for years, slowly whittled down, under frequent US air strikes and special operations raids.[3] Qahtani would be killed in October 2016.[4]

The debate over the drawdown began in late 2010. Petraeus played his gambit to turn back the clock, hoping successes might convince Obama to leave most of the surge forces. If the clock could not be turned back, Petraeus feared that the gains of the surge would wash away. He had doubted the surge could enable the Afghan government to stand on its own and had expected that a long-term US military presence would be needed. "Even with the commencement of the drawdown," he optimistically told his biographer in April 2011, "enough troops and civilians will remain in Afghanistan to pursue all the campaign plan's lines of operation—protecting the people, dismantling insurgent networks, building Afghan forces, aiding local government, fostering development, attacking corruption. Progress still needs to be made in all of those areas before transition is possible in additional areas."[5]

Petraeus especially wanted to delay withdrawal in order to turn to the east. Clearing the south had taken so long that McChrystal's original plan to shift parts of the surge to eastern Afghanistan had never happened. Military plans forecast the east would take years to pacify. Petraeus's intent was to try to divert resources there from the south at the end of 2012.

Obama was in a very different place. Lieutenant General Douglas Lute, who managed Afghanistan and Pakistan policy on the national security council staff, had warned Petraeus that Obama would not change his position. He counseled that the play to turn back the clock was a dramatic misreading of the president.[6] Indeed, Obama was set on drawing down. A few months after the surge announcement, Defense Secretary Robert Gates inferred from a conversation with Obama that he believed the surge would fail.[7] Then during the June 2010 *Rolling Stone* debacle, Obama told Gates, "I don't have a sense it's going well in Afghanistan. . . . [McChrystal] doesn't seem to be making progress. Maybe his strategy is not really working."[8] Describing the moment, Gates writes, "Hearing the president express doubt about the strategy he had approved six months earlier . . . and his lack of confidence in his commander and the strategy floored me. These feelings did not spring from a magazine article but had been there all along."[9]

Through 2010 and early 2011, Obama and the White House staff carefully monitored the surge. The results confirmed his low expectations. He was unsure Taliban momentum had been reversed and the government looked unable to survive on its own. Unlike Iraq and its "awakening," there had been no tipping point. Progress in Kandahar was at that point pending. Helmand was an expensive success. The number of attacks in Afghanistan in 2011 was slightly lower than 2010 or 2009 but still higher than 2006. The same was true for casualties; 418 Americans would be killed in 2011, compared to 499 in 2010 and 312 in 2009.[10] In all, the United States suffered 1,230 killed and more than 12,500 wounded from 2009–2011, the majority of its casualties for the whole war to

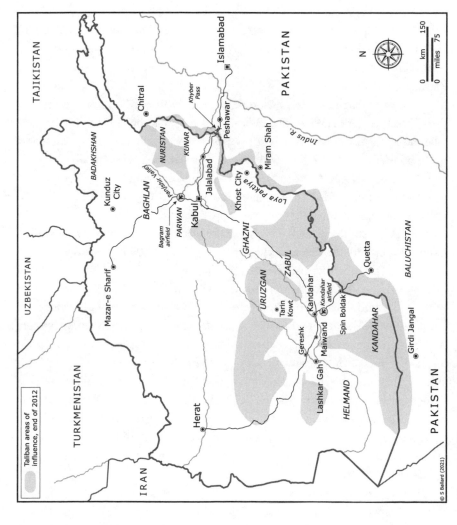

Map 16 Taliban territory, 2012

the end of 2019. The Afghan army and police were assessed as dependent on the United States and taking responsibility too slowly on their own.

US efforts to improve the government also disappointed. Obama had reminded Karzai in March 2010 during their first videoconference that "Good governance must be implemented and corruption must be fought" only to have Karzai brush fault back onto the United States and other donors for mismanaging their aid.[11] Come early 2011, the few bright spots in the efforts to improve the Afghan government were the August 2010 parliamentary elections and an increased number of qualified governors, district governors, judges, and community councils. Corruption still prevailed. In September 2010, the Kabul Bank collapsed after nearly $1 billion in loans disappeared. The US Embassy discovered that Afghan elites, including Karzai's brother Mahmoud and one of First Vice President Mohammed Fahim's brothers, had been using the bank to take out loans, invest the money for personal gain, and never repay it. Obama spoke about the matter in May with Karzai, who claimed "US officials in Kabul" had prevented his government from intervening, implying the scandal was due to American ineptitude.[12] The White House viewed Karzai as a damning obstacle: erratic and complicit.[13]

Besides the surge's results, the big picture was very much on Obama's mind. Domestic support for the surge was thin. In January 2009, a Gallup poll had found that 66 percent of Americans agreed with the decision to send military forces to Afghanistan. By March 2011, that number had dropped to 53 percent. In the middle of 2010, Democrats in Congress were already calling for steep reductions in US forces. For most Americans and their congressmen, Afghanistan was an unneeded expense during the slow recovery from the great recession. Tens of thousands of boots on the ground no longer seemed affordable. At the same time, the death of bin Laden removed the primary threat to the United States. According to a May 2011 Gallup poll taken days after bin Laden's death, 59 percent of Americans believed that the US mission in Afghanistan had been accomplished.[14] In late May, a motion in the House of Representatives by Speaker Nancy Pelosi to accelerate the withdrawal was narrowly defeated by 215 to 204 votes.

Obama's priority was economic recovery. At the height of the surge, the United States was spending approximately $110 billion per year in Afghanistan, double US federal spending on education. The White House was preparing a deficit reduction plan of $1 trillion over ten years. Reducing the number of forces in Iraq and Afghanistan (roughly $1 million per man per year) was a significant component of the expected savings.[15] Obama and the Republican Congress were in the middle of a debate over raising the debt ceiling in order to pay for government spending that had risen during the great recession. Obama would ultimately negotiate a budget control act (August 2011) with Congress that allowed the debt ceiling to be raised but emplaced stringent spending caps (including on defense) and automatic across-the-board cuts (sequestration) on any budget in excess of them. Afghanistan was in the way.

There was a personal component to Obama's views as well. The president and the first lady visited the wounded and attended the funerals. They saw the amputees, mangled parts, wounded chests; the grieving girlfriends, wives, fathers, and mothers; the human cost of the war under their watch. "Almost all were male and working-class: whites from small rural towns to fading manufacturing hubs, Blacks and Hispanics from cities like Houston or Trenton, Asian Americans and Pacific Islanders from California," writes Obama. The experience anchored his perspective: "I was never more clear-eyed than on the flights back from Walter Reed and Bethesda. Clear about the true costs of war, and who bore those costs. Clear about war's folly . . . Clear that by virtue of my office, I could not avoid responsibility for lives lost or shattered, even if I somehow justified my decisions by what I perceived to be some larger good."[16] First Lady Michelle Obama confided to one wounded officer lying in Walter Reed hospital, "If I had my way, I would end this war right now."

Under these circumstances, Obama's thinking moved beyond zeroing out the surge to drastically reducing the entire US presence to as low as possible. Weighing priorities and assessing progress convinced him Afghanistan was a poor use of resources and going nowhere. Not only the surge but much of the US commitment was not paying dividends.

Ahead of the official drawdown decision, Obama announced in December 2010 that US forces would transition responsibility for security to the Afghan government and end their combat mission by December 2014, four years away. Obama left enough time for the process to be gradual. He was also careful not to specify how many US forces would stay after 2014, leaving himself flexibility to adjust. Obama's strategic goal was ending the US war in Afghanistan, not carrying on the surge. It is doubtful there was ever a chance to turn back the clock.

The end of the drawdown debate occurred on June 21. Since Obama had already resolved to hand over responsibility to the Afghan government, the timing of the drawdown was the last thing to decide. Petraeus argued that 90,000 of the 100,000 US troops should stay until the end of 2012. Obama disagreed. After some discussion with Defense Secretary Gates, Secretary of State Clinton, and General Petraeus, Obama decided all 33,000 surge troops would leave by September 2012, with large cuts to follow in 2013 and 2014. Journalist Rajiv Chandrasekaran recounts that after hearing Obama's decision Petraeus protested, "That invalidates my campaign plan, Mr. President." To which Obama replied, "You shouldn't have assumed I wouldn't do what I told the American people I would."[17]

Obama announced the drawdown on June 23, 2011. Ten thousand troops were to depart by the end of 2011, followed by 23,000 in 2012. The remaining

67,000 would continue to draw down until 2014 when the government was to take the lead in security. That, however, did not mean that all US military forces were to leave by then. Obama promised to continue supporting the Afghan army and police without specifying how many men that would entail. It was nevertheless clear that those numbers would be few. Obama ended with "America, it is time to focus on nation-building here at home."[18]

Americans broadly supported the president's decision. A Gallup poll found that 55 percent of respondents were not worried that withdrawing from Afghanistan would risk terrorist attacks on the United States, compared to the 43 percent that had not been worried in 2009.[19]

As had been the case in 2009 when Obama had tied the surge to an end-date, critics in the United States claimed the new drawdown timeline encouraged the Taliban to keep fighting. The charge was logical. Evidence is again unclear as to how much the Taliban thought this way. Shortly after the speech, the Quetta Shura declared that the withdrawal was a ruse. They claimed that the United States was building permanent bases in Afghanistan and forcing Kabul to sign a strategic treaty: "Obama . . . in truth . . . has no intention to end the Afghanistan war and occupation and has no determination to keep his word."[20] Nor did the drawdown seem to have mattered much to Akhtar Mohammed Mansour, Mullah Omar's deputy. According to tribesmen who knew him, Mansour foresaw years and years of war ahead, whether or not Americans were present. Even if the Americans were gone, he did not expect the government to fall quickly. He was undeterred. He remembered how the Taliban had taken years to recuperate after 2001 and expected they could do so again after the defeats of the surge.[21]

US allies and partners in Afghanistan also began drawing down. NATO had already decided in November 2010 to withdraw combat troops by the end of 2014. For a few countries, withdrawal was already underway or complete. Canada completed their withdrawal by the end of July 2011. The Netherlands, amid public opposition to the war, had announced in February 2010 that their 2,000 troops would leave Uruzgan by the end of the year. Other allies and partners executed steadier drawdowns in line with the United States.

Thus the surge, the height of America's Afghan War, came to an end. It was a tactical success but a strategic failure. Brilliant minds and great generals, brave soldiers, marines, Green Berets, and SEALs could only get so far. The resolve of the Taliban fighter was difficult to overcome. The costs had been too great. They signaled to Obama not only the unsustainability of the surge but the unsustainability of the whole Afghan endeavor. The strategic discourse reoriented to withdrawal. That shift in direction is the true strategic significance of the surge. It was the opposite of Petraeus's hope to turn back the clock. The surge turned the clock forward.

Petraeus relinquished command in Afghanistan to General John Allen on July 18, 2011, less than a month after Obama's June 2011 drawdown announcement and six weeks earlier than expected. Obama promoted Petraeus to Director of Central Intelligence, a job that fascinated him. The unhealthy lifestyle of little sleep, air pollution, and limited exercise of Kabul had worn on him. He was ready to go.

Kabul had worn on Eikenberry as well. He stepped down as ambassador on July 24, six days after Petraeus's change of command. Thinner, a tad pale, and mildly saddened, Eikenberry departed Kabul with love for the Afghan people and skepticism about the future. The damaged relationship with Karzai had been difficult to handle, if necessary from Eikenberry's point of view to help the Afghan people and democracy. Since 2002, Washington and other generals had too often disregarded Eikenberry's wisdom on the impossibility of winning, but in the end the administration was following the policy he had pioneered—to turn over the war to the Afghan government and army to stand on their own. Upon leaving, he told reporters he was most proud that "I'll leave here with the moniker of being the father of the Afghan Army" and "having led the civilian surge."[22]

In the wake of the surge, counterinsurgency fell into disgrace. New chairman of the joint chiefs of staff, General Martin Dempsey lectured General Allen against thinking in counterinsurgency terms. Counterinsurgency became a dirty word, synonymous with expensive deployment of ground troops, written out of US strategic debates. As Afghanistan wound down, the Obama administration restrained its involvement in Libya and Syria's civil war. US policymakers strongly endorsed counterterrorism operations as the preferred means of waging irregular war. The final blow came in autumn 2012 when Petraeus's affair with a younger officer leaked and he resigned his new job as director of the Central Intelligence Agency. Counterinsurgency lost its champion.

Where counterinsurgency lived on was among disparate marines, soldiers, advisors, and Green Berets. For many of them, counterinsurgency was less a grand theory of strategic victory or an idealistic hope of winning hearts and minds than a practical way of going about business day to day. Living near the people was better than coming and going in a big operation or venturing into the mountains. Patrolling on foot was better than being locked in an armored vehicle. Mentoring Afghan soldiers and police was better than sitting on a base. It had nothing to do with whether the surge was a good or bad idea. These common sense lessons had become ingrained in American tactics, where they had always belonged.

Relations between the United States and Pakistan were on the rocks in early 2011. Despite the administration's generous aid packages and campaign against the Pakistani Taliban, the Pakistan military helped the Taliban. In a variety of places along the mountainous eastern border, US and Pakistani soldiers were waging an unannounced border war. Pakistani army and frontier force posts supported Taliban attacks on Afghan and US positions with mortars and small arms fire. US forces retaliated with artillery. Dozens of Pakistani soldiers were killed. Outrage over an October 2010 border skirmish and a shooting involving a US contractor caused Kayani to temporarily shut down US supply lines through Pakistan.

The bin Laden raid threw relations over the brink. Pakistani military chief General Ashfaq Kayani was furious, humiliated that the United States had so easily penetrated the heart of his country, brazenly violating its sovereignty. Pakistanis demonstrated on the streets. A Gallup poll found that 64 percent of Pakistanis disapproved of the raid.[23]

Kayani, who was in charge of Pakistan defense policy, expelled US special operations forces and trainers and paused US drone strikes over the summer. The United States responded by holding back $800 million in military aid. Because of a November border skirmish in which US attack helicopters killed 24 Pakistani soldiers, Kayani then closed land supply routes through Pakistan indefinitely (they ended up being shut for seven months, at cost to the US taxpayer since supplies now had to be flown in). Pakistani ire was the price of killing bin Laden. For the next two years, the Pakistanis would be more recalcitrant than ever.

Afghanistan's relationship with Pakistan went south too. Karzai repeatedly asked Obama and Clinton about "the need to pressure Pakistan and dismantle the safe havens," his single-minded strategy to defeat the Taliban.[24] The response was always cautious. Frustrated, Karzai acted on his own. He annoyed Kayani by signing a strategic partnership agreement with India in 2011. India would assist in training and building the Afghan army and police.[25] Meanwhile, Asadullah Khalid and Abdul Razziq in Kandahar had been secretly supporting Baluch separatists in Pakistan and arranging for them to set up training camps inside Afghanistan. Those Baluch separatists regularly attacked the Pakistani military in Quetta and Baluchistan. The Pakistani military had evidence that the separatists received significant support from India. They believed the Afghan government was in cahoots with India and their Baluch proxies.[26]

Of far greater threat, Karzai permitted the NDS, Afghanistan's intelligence agency, to reach out to the Pakistani Taliban. Under the principle of "the enemy of my enemy is my friend," he partnered with them against the Pakistan military. Karzai explained a few years later to US generals, "Pakistan is interfering in Afghanistan. When Pakistan stops interfering in Afghanistan, then Afghanistan will stop interfering in Pakistan." The NDS allowed Pakistani Taliban sanctuary. Cover was blown in 2013 when Karzai invited Latif Mehsud, the Pakistani Taliban third-in-command, to Kabul for secret talks. The US military found out when they inadvertently detained him on Highway One in Logar under NDS escort. The story leaked to the *New York Times*. Karzai was furious.[27]

Kayani learned of it all. It confirmed conspiracy theories that Afghanistan was fueling extremism in Pakistan. He and his successors regularly demanded that the United States force the Afghan government to clamp down on Pakistani Taliban activity in Afghanistan. Whenever US diplomats brought up ISI support of the Taliban or Haqqani network, the Pakistani leadership blamed extremism on Afghanistan instead of their own policies.

Peace talks, first championed by Ambassador Richard Holbrooke (special representative for Afghanistan and Pakistan) and Barnett Rubin (an eminent New York University professor on Holbrooke's staff), had been an afterthought in the surge strategy. Holbrooke and Clinton briefly had brought up the idea of a negotiated settlement during the surge debate. The idea went nowhere.[28] General Petraeus and Admiral Mullen (chairman of the joint chiefs of staff) doubted the time was ripe for negotiations, assuming that security had to be in place first. It was unfortunate. Obama could have used the threat of the incoming reinforcements as a bargaining chip to bring the Taliban to the table. Instead, at the moment that the United States had the greatest military leverage, there would be no negotiations.

It was only in 2010 that the idea entered into Obama's Afghanistan strategy. Even then Petraeus preferred to wait till the surge produced a favorable military situation. Over the course of the surge the White House became interested in peace talks as a way of ending the conflict. Clinton brought up talks at length with Karzai at a meeting in February. During Karzai's May 2010 Karzai visit to Washington, he discussed peace talks with Holbrooke, Clinton, and Obama. The two sides agreed contact with the Taliban would proceed after Karzai convened a loya jirga to affirm Afghan support for peace talks, which happened a month later. Around the same time, the White House lifted the Bush administration's ban on talking to the Taliban leadership.

Mullah Omar's former secretary, Tayeb Agha, had become head of the Taliban political commission in 2009. He was a younger leader fond of neither al-Qaʻeda nor Pakistan. The following year he convinced Mullah Omar to grant the commission responsibility to negotiate. Omar permitted Tayeb Agha to report directly to him and circumvent the Quetta Shura because the latter was consumed by military operations. He may have also wanted the direct line because the topic was so sensitive.[29]

Omar's exact reason for pursuing peace talks is hazy. He certainly sought to secure the complete removal of US troops. Tayeb Agha later wrote to him that only "when, in the year 2014, foreign forces leave from Afghanistan" should "our forces . . . make no more attacks."[30] In his analysis, the withdrawal of US forces would remove the obligation to wage jihad and allow negotiations between Afghans to begin.[31]

Omar never ruled on what the Taliban should demand beyond US withdrawal, specifically what to demand in talks with the Afghan government. The question was fundamental if a real political settlement was to be reached to Afghanistan's long civil war. The default position of most of the Quetta shura was restoration of their emirate and a monopoly on power. Their position amounted to a negotiated return to power, not a political settlement. Tayeb Agha thought the this "would be a problem," and that "war will continue" because the old northern allies would "rise up" like before.[32] He preferred a path of compromise. His advice to Mullah Omar was to order that "government authorities be entrusted to the people whom through a loya jirga or other worthy means are chosen" and assures "the return of an Islamic order."[33] The idea offered a way for Afghans to come together. The meaning of Islamic order was undefined and could be interpreted as something akin to the emirate or as an elected government with a strict adherence to Islamic law. Members of the political commission would eventually find that ambiguity constructive for the purposes of diplomacy and internal buy-in. One thing was clear. The Taliban opposed the 2004 constitution and sharing power with the Karzai regime or any elected successor. "We would be greatly disgraced," wrote Tayeb Agha.[34]

The core of the Quetta Shura, including deputy leader Akhtar Mohammed Mansour, military commission chief Abdul Qayum Zakir, and confidantes of Mullah Omar, were willing to consider talking directly to the United States if the result were complete US withdrawal. The Afghan government was a different matter. They condemned it as the illegitimate creation of the foreign-hosted Bonn conference and were reluctant to meet. Mansour, who must have also been receiving guidance from Omar, was pragmatic. He was open to a peace that attained Taliban interests but adhered to a demanding bargaining position because he was confident the government could eventually be defeated. From time to time reports came out that he favored negotiations even though he publicly opposed them.[35]

Omar, Mansour, and the Quetta Shura had their own audience in peace talks. Their decisions needed to be accepted by the body of fighters and younger commanders. Otherwise, the whole process would fall apart and they would lose credibility. From 2010 to 2012, no such consensus existed. "Young Taliban want to fight," explained Raees Baghrani, the respected Alizai tribal leader and former Taliban. "They want to shoot and kill. They get enjoyment out of it. . . . The older Taliban can control the younger Taliban if they try: if they produce a good peace; if they are united; if they act together; if Pakistan can be prevented from interfering too much. . . . When I was young, I enjoyed fighting and killing. Now I am old and want peace. Constant war is not worth it."[36]

The White House encouraged Lakhdar Brahimi, former top UN official in Kabul, and Tom Pickering, former undersecretary of state, to examine the possibility of a negotiated peace in Afghanistan. They headed an international team that visited Afghanistan and Pakistan, where they spoke with former and active Taliban representatives. The group reported back to Washington that the Taliban were open to talks with the United States. In November 2010, the first meeting between US diplomats and the Taliban, represented by Tayeb Agha, occurred in Germany.[37] Holbrooke died of a heart attack the next month, depriving the US peace effort of its great, if flawed, diplomat. He had been so self-centered that he had ostracized Obama. The peace effort suffered as a result.

In March 2011 Secretary of State Hillary Clinton announced that the United States was ready for peace negotiations. Although she imposed no preconditions, Clinton insisted that under a settlement the Taliban would need to lay down their arms, accept the Afghan constitution, and break all ties with al-Qaʿeda. Obama was open to removing all military forces if a real peace was in place. Petraeus was skeptical a meaningful peace was possible and thought a long-term military presence of some kind would be necessary.

American and Taliban representatives conducted further "talks about talks" from mid-2011 through the early months of 2012. At a May 2011 meeting, Tayeb Agha presented a letter purportedly from Mullah Omar, addressed to President Obama. The letter expressed a willingness to engage in negotiations that would lead to complete US withdrawal. It called for confidence-building measures in the form of prisoner releases and the opening of a political office in Qatar as steps ahead of official negotiations.[38]

Near the end of 2011, Mansour convened a council of Taliban military commanders and political leaders in Quetta. Supposedly most of the important figures were present. The military commanders conceded to a proposal for a political effort that would lead to negotiations, possibly with the Afghan government as well as the United States. According to some information, Omar had ruled that negotiations with the Afghan government could occur in the event of a full US withdrawal.[39] Clinton's conditions of laying down arms and accepting the constitution as a product of talks were not discussed and were certainly unacceptable. The Quetta Shura was more willing to bend on al-Qaʿeda, hoping a verbal guarantee of their opposition to attacks on other countries would be sufficient. They were not ready to actually turn on al-Qaʿeda. They also wanted several former Taliban leaders released from Guantanamo.

On the basis of these discussions, Tayeb Agha carried forth negotiations with US diplomats, now under Ambassador Marc Grossman. The two sides agreed to a sequence of reciprocal steps. The United States would allow the Taliban to open a political office. In return, the Taliban would publicly affirm their support for peace and opposition to terrorism. Next, the United States would delist

Taliban leaders from United Nations terrorism lists and conduct a prisoner swap that would include five former Taliban leaders from Guantanamo. Then the Taliban would enter into peace talks with the United States and the Afghan government. Tayeb Agha would not consider negotiations until those Taliban leaders had been released.[40] He left out the condition that all US forces depart Afghanistan, presumably because Mullah Omar's letter had specified it as a goal of peace talks.

The reciprocal steps are notable in the history of the Afghan War. Taliban demands were less than they would be later on. At this point, they were willing to publicly oppose terrorism and meet with the Afghan government before a full US withdrawal or timeline to zero. How far and specific they were willing to go—vague assurances versus measurable actions—is unknown. Nevertheless, years later, the Taliban would demand a timeline to zero before distancing themselves from al-Qa'eda or talking with the Afghan government, if at all. An opportunity may have existed in 2011 and 2012 to end the war on relatively favorable terms, a significant historical counterfactual. As we shall see, the outcome of events obscures what potential actually existed.

US response to Taliban requests for prisoner releases was hindered by interagency wrangling. The Defense Department differed over timing and substance with the State Department. General Allen was skeptical of negotiations and wanted Karzai and the internationally recognized Afghan government in the lead.[41] Many defense officials strongly opposed prison releases, even in exchange for Bowe Bergdahl, an American soldier being held by the Taliban. Any transfers from Guantanamo required congressional certification. Attuned to the political perils, Defense Secretary Leon Panetta (Gates had retired) refused to sign any request to Congress without the Taliban first agreeing that the five prisoners would stay in Doha, Qatar, under observation. The Taliban demurred.

Ambassador Grossman was unable to rally principal decisionmakers to his cause. Secretary Panetta did not see talks going anywhere. Secretary Clinton, who had already stepped out to support talks, was wary of getting on the wrong side of a politically sensitive prisoner exchange—sure to draw heavy criticism from Republicans—for the sake of an uncertain and poorly defined peace process.[42] President Obama himself was not ready to force the issue.

For his part, President Karzai did his best to obstruct a process that he feared would marginalize him. He demanded the Taliban speak directly with his government before any political office could be opened.

Former Northern Alliance leaders, Kabul civil society, and other Afghans worried about a peace process as well. Compromises in the constitution and women's rights were particular concerns. Fawzia Koofi and Shukria Barakzai, both reelected in the 2010 parliamentarian elections, worried peace talks could reverse fragile improvements in women's rights. "The worst would be for us women and the young generation of this country," said Fawzia Koofi. "Things could go worse in terms of our rights . . . but also our security. Because most of us are now public figures. We've taken so much risk just to make reforms."[43]

Eventually Grossman decided to try to bring the Afghan government directly into negotiations. The United States had spent years building the Afghan government. Cutting them out of negotiations would paint the government as a US puppet. At a meeting in January 2012, the US delegation requested the Taliban talk to the Kabul government before the opening of a political office.[44] In March 2012 Tayeb Agha broke off further contact, enraged that the Americans would press such a thing.

Negotiations were at a standstill. Tayeb Agha sent Mullah Omar a letter asking what to do and tendered his own resignation. Ignoring the resignation, Omar replied, "It is a wartime situation. Right now answers to your questions are not easy. We are busy in a great war. Be patient. This situation will straighten with the passage of time."[45]

Things sat quiet for a year, until early 2013. Mansour's interest in finding a way to peace was rising. He disliked the Taliban's dependency on Pakistan. As Omar's deputy, he was reaching out to Iran as one alternative. A peace agreement could sever the dependency and allow the Taliban leadership to return to Afghanistan, out from under the ISI's thumb.[46] According to a variety of Taliban sources Mullah Omar blessed the initiative as long as the end result would be full withdrawal of US and other foreign troops.[47] If true, unlikely given his illness, it is his last known decision.

Mansour signaled to Washington via several third parties that the Taliban were now willing to enter peace talks with the United States and eventually with the Kabul government if an official Taliban political office could be opened. The Taliban political commission and fellow tribesmen later claimed that Mansour was genuinely willing to talk with the Karzai government as long as an office was set up.[48] The political commission told Abdul Hakim Mujahed, former Taliban representative to the United Nations, their goal was not to monopolize power over Afghanistan. Some number of Taliban leaders were concerned that Afghanistan could fall back into the anarchic civil war of the 1990s without a political settlement. "Not one percent of Taliban want the country divided," said Mujahed.[49]

Holbrooke's old team and much of the White House favored opening a Taliban political office. They saw the military campaign as failing. The better course for the United States, they thought, was to draw the Taliban back to the table, secure their commitment to break from al-Qaʻeda, and withdraw the remainder of US troops before things got worse. For these reasons, they were willing to circumvent Karzai and talk directly to the Taliban. Pentagon officials disagreed with the State Department's appraisal of the military campaign and Taliban intentions. Though supportive of a process that resulted in actual peace talks, they argued that the Taliban would not easily come to terms and that excluding Karzai was unwise.[50]

Obama supported the State Department plan to allow the Taliban to open a political office, in return for repudiation of terrorism and resumption of negotiations.[51] Beyond that, he was willing to guarantee full withdrawal of US forces, the Taliban's number one concern, in return for a peace agreement that prevented al-Qaʻeda from reemerging. To build trust with the Taliban leadership, Obama stated in a May 23 speech that America had no intention of keeping troops permanently in Afghanistan.

Working through Qatari intermediaries, US diplomats arranged for the Taliban to open a political office in Doha for the purpose of starting discussions. The initiative foundered at the last moment on a misunderstanding over how the Taliban office was to describe itself. The Taliban recognized that American and Afghan officials would only address them as representatives of the Taliban movement, not of the Islamic Emirate of Afghanistan, which is what they still called themselves. Both the Taliban and Qatari officials believed, however, it would be acceptable for Taliban to use the Islamic Emirate title when addressing others, including the media. The Quetta Shura was loath to calling the movement anything else. In contrast, American and Afghan officials believed, on the basis of oral and written assurances exchanged with and through the government of Qatar, that the new office in Doha would describe itself only as that of the Taliban movement.

On opening day, June 18, the world saw the Taliban office on television. Contrary to expectations, it did not look like an "office." The standalone white and tan compound with a high security wall unmistakably resembled an embassy. Worse, overhead the Taliban flew their flag and on the outside emplaced a sign with the title of the Islamic Emirate. Karzai was irate. The United States asked Qatar to take down the flag and the sign, which it did. In response, the Taliban "closed" the office and refused all contact with either American or Afghan officials. After a few days of trying to get a meeting with the Taliban, Secretary of State John Kerry assessed Afghanistan was not ripe for negotiations. Without tangible indications of Taliban good faith, he and Obama thought better of investing further time into peace talks.

The irony is that for all intents and purposes the Taliban gained their political office in Doha. Although the office was officially "closed," a steady stream of foreign diplomats, UN dignitaries, and non-governmental organizations made the pilgrimage to Doha to liaise with Tayeb Agha and the political commission. There were lots of conversations and little movement toward peace.

Throughout, Obama had refrained from steps that would have maximized the chances of success but distracted from his overarching policy goals. Nothing shows this clearer than the compartmentalization of the drawdown from negotiations. The drawdown was by far the biggest US bargaining chip. No known record exists of Obama considering to trade it for Taliban concessions. Instead, the drawdown proceeded on its timeline, a de facto if unintended unilateral concession. The Taliban had to do nothing in return. The big picture of getting out superseded the tactics of an uncertain negotiation with the Taliban.

Obama may or may not have squandered an opportunity. To the American diplomats talking with Tayeb Agha, the contacts and offers of 2010 to 2013 were tantalizing openings; in their view the United States should have taken what it could have gotten from 2011 to 2013 because the Taliban would be less accommodating in the future. To defense leaders, they looked unripe. CIA director, and then Secretary of Defense, Leon Panetta, judged:

> I kind of was operating in a different ballgame in terms of whether or not we could ultimately cut a deal with the Taliban. . . . I'm not sure they understand the opportunity to kind of resolve these issues politically. Because in the end for them to resolve it politically would mean that they had to recognize Karzai, had to recognize the changes, and they had to participate in the political process. And they were going, "Bullshit, we don't have to do that, that's not our game." So I felt that sometimes it was a little naïve to kind of think that the Taliban were going to be anxious to cut a deal.[52]

Whether peace talks could have actually started and led to a political settlement remains a mystery. Had the new office stayed officially open, when and how the Taliban would have met with the government is foggy at best. Who knows if Omar was really interested in a political settlement? Perhaps he simply sought unilateral US withdrawal. Most important, Mullah Omar would be dead by the time the office should have opened. Even if negotiations had started earlier, say in early 2012, a bare year would have stood before Omar's demise—precious little time for progress through uncharted territory. It is extremely hard to see how negotiations could have moved forward in Omar's absence, let alone amid a succession struggle. Indeed, it would be news of his death that would torpedo a later attempt at peace in 2015.

In 2019, I broached the 2013 peace initiative with two members of the Taliban political commission in Doha. I asked if they thought a real peace had been possible. They were certain peace could have happened had the United States allowed an office to open and guaranteed troop withdrawal. Unfortunately, they complained, Obama had not been committed to the process and had caved to Karzai. I asked "What about Mullah Omar? He had died but no one knew it." They at first hand-waved any problem, reminding me how the Taliban movement obeys its emir, whoever he may be. When I questioned them more strongly, however, about how peace talks might require guidance from the emir and how a succession struggle might disrupt negotiations, they admitted, "Well, yes. It would have been difficult to carry on peace talks without Mullah Omar. Once the movement learned of Mullah Omar's death, we would have had to discuss succession, not peace. The process would have taken months."

15

Ghazni and the Andar Awakening

Ghazni was one of the most strategic provinces in Afghanistan, a great block sitting between Kabul and Kandahar, bisected by the Highway One ring road. Without Ghazni, any Afghan state was split in two, Kabul sundered from Kandahar. The province was half high plain, half mountain. The plain is 6,500 feet in altitude, 50 kilometers in width. The mountains, the snow-capped Hindu Kush, run along the plain's western edge and stretch hundreds of kilometers westward, the highest peaks topping 15,000 feet. In the north the provincial capital of Ghazni City was a throw rug of one-story mud-walled buildings, shunted against a once-formidable citadel, the site of the ancient capital of the Ghaznavid Empire. The town had about 200,000 people. Most of the remainder of the province's 1 million people lived in the surrounding countryside. Ancient underground tunnels, known as *karezes,* stretched for miles and diverted water to the fields from mountain aquafers. Ghazni's altitude was too high for poppy. Farmers grew wheat and other legal crops during the summer. It was here on Ghazni's plateau that the Taliban suffered their most unexpected setback of the war.

In the course of the surge, the insurgency in eastern Afghanistan was contained, though less damaged than McChrystal and Petraeus had planned if a "turn to the east" had happened. Certain regions, such as Ghazni, could not be addressed. US soldiers were familiar with the east after multiple tours. On its second tour, the 82nd Airborne Division, under Major General Mike Scaparrotti, was responsible for the east during the first half of the surge, from mid-2009 to mid-2010.

McChrystal's guidance to Major General Scaparrotti in 2009 was to protect the people and partner with the Afghans. As he withdrew from the war in the mountains of Kunar and Nuristan during 2009 and 2010, Scaparrotti turned to protecting the more populated villages and valleys and to partnering with the Afghan army, living with them, training with them, and fighting alongside them.

Map 17 Ghazni

McChrystal also raised the priority of operations against the Haqqani network, given the threat the group's suicide attacks posed to Kabul and their known association with al-Qaʻeda. Jalaluddin Haqqani's son, Sirajuddin was considered more dangerous as leader of the network than his father had been. Scaparrotti employed McChrystal's methods of targeting a network through integrating intelligence, special operations forces, and his own regular forces. In his assessment, given the number of commanders killed or detained, the method damaged Haqqani and also assisted the effort to protect the population.

The surge had begun in 2009 with widespread concerns that Taliban were about to breach the "gates of Kabul" in Wardak, north of Ghazni. Taliban, Haqqani (which was a branch of the Taliban), and Hezb Islami cadres operated in the province. The two battalions from the 10th Mountain Division that General McKiernan had sent to Wardak stymied the threat through experimenting with local militia recruitment, attempting to protect the population, and targeting insurgent leadership.

Wardak and neighboring Logar nevertheless remained quite dangerous, with high numbers of "sigacts," the military's statistic for enemy attacks. Wardak was where a CH-47 Chinook helicopter on a night raid was shot down by an RPG in August 2011 with the loss of 20 SEALs and 10 other Americans.[1] The provinces' mountain valleys were never friendly to government forces. "Anyone who works for the government can't live in these districts," a government official stated. "They either live in Maidan Shar in the provincial center or they live in Kabul. In Jaghatu, Chak, Sayidabad, the Taliban has full control. The district center is like a checkpoint, nothing more. Most people don't go to the district center to solve their problems; instead they go to the Taliban."[2] Logistics convoys on Highway One through Wardak ran constant ambushes at a chokepoint at Sayidabad. Burned out tanker and supply trucks lined the highway.

Further east, Nangarhar, still under Gul Agha Sherzai, and Khost continued to progress. The Haqqani network hammered Khost with ten suicide attacks in 2009, including a coordinated attack by 11 suicide bombers on the governor's office and nearby government buildings in May and the heavily publicized attack on US Forward Operating Base Chapman in the center of the provincial capital in December. It was to little avail. Government institutions, US presence, and tribal unity thwarted the Haqqanis from disturbing government control. In both Nangarhar and Khost, US forces enabled Afghan army units and police to extend themselves into districts far from the provincial capitals. A Khost district governor reported: "I see Americans very little. Security is good in the district . . . Many projects have been completed in Khost. We have lots of paved roads."[3]

Establishing security in key rural villages was a theme of the latter half of the surge in the east. Also on its second tour, the 101st Airborne Division, under Major General John Campbell, was responsible for the east from mid-2010 to mid-2011. At this time, the Afghan local police program was coming on line. Afghan local police were recruited in 13 districts in the east, often in valleys and locations where the government lacked a presence and a special forces team would be on their own. Afghan local police were especially effective in Paktiya and Paktika, east of Ghazni. Special forces teams worked with the eastern Pashtun tribes that had a long-standing tradition of fielding tribal militia (arbakai). In Paktika, the aggressive Commander Aziz defended the mountainous border well against Haqqani and the Pakistan military.

Though safe from any direct threat of Taliban assault, Kabul continued to suffer suicide bombings, usually at the hands of the Haqqani network. As had been the case since 2006, the number of bombings in Kabul fluctuated from 10 to 20 per year. During 2009, for example, 14 attacks in Kabul caused 482 civilian, Afghan security force, and US and foreign casualties. Though the numbers were greater in Kandahar and sometimes in Helmand and Khost, attacks in the national capital attracted media attention and sent a message that even the heart of the government was unsafe.

One of the worst Haqqani attacks was on the cold winter morning of January 18, 2010. Five suicide bombers and 15 fighters, some disguised in police uniforms, struck the central bank, the ministry of education, ministry of finance, the five-star Serena Hotel, and other government buildings on the perimeter of the palace grounds. Fighters seized a multistory shopping center and fired down into the streets. Smoke billowed over Kabul as buildings caught on fire from the explosions. One suicide car bomb that arrived three hours into the firefight was an ambulance, designed to fool the police who were busy reacting to the insurgents and the civilian casualties. A shop-owner watched: "I had never seen the face of the war before, but I could see it all from there . . . The soldiers were running and they were shooting at the ambulance and then it made a very big explosion."[4] After five hours, Amarullah Saleh's NDS officers defeated the Haqqani attackers. Six Afghan security personal and civilians were killed and 71 were wounded.

Under these kind of attacks, Kabul gradually fortified itself. Concrete checkpoints arose in front of government buildings. A two-by-one kilometer square around the palace and including several embassies, and the US and coalition headquarters, known as the "green zone," was enclosed in a wall and entry points were strictly controlled. To reinforce the "Kabul security bubble," Petraeus circumferenced the city with layers of 25 police checkpoints, called "rings of steel."[5]

Fighting Haqqani was a continuous battle. When US targeting removed Haqqani leaders from the field, high-profile suicide bombings would wane for a few months. Then Haqqani would recover and sophisticated attacks would resume until they were disrupted again. During late 2010, President Obama, who had hitherto restrained targeting of the Haqqani network inside Pakistan, permitted intensified drone strikes against Haqqani there. Scores of Haqqani members may have been killed in the wave of strikes.[6] Strikes were dialed back again in 2011 as the relationship between the United States and Pakistan frayed. After that, drones struck Haqqani leaders and commanders in Pakistan selectively once or twice per year. At least five were killed between 2011 and 2015, including one of Sirajuddin's brothers. Targets often had a connection to al-Qaʻeda.[7] Inside Afghanistan, US conventional and special operations forces targeted the Haqqani network intensively throughout the surge and then until the end of the US combat mission in 2014.

General John Allen, General Petraeus's successor in Afghanistan, was a marine with a stentorian voice and a reputation for deep thinking. Petraeus had initially planned for Ghazni to be a target of the surge, once a "turn to the east" became feasible.[8] Scaparrotti had in 2009 calculated that a brigade task force was needed south of Kabul in Ghazni. Although the turn never happened, General Allen decided that Ghazni had to be firmly under government control. Highway One was passable but often cut by insurgents or laced with improvised explosive devices. It would be a vulnerability for the government once drawdown neared completion. Scaparrotti was also now back in Afghanistan as Allen's operational commander and worked to place forces in the province.

Ghazni had thus far been an economy of force. A Polish brigade of 1,500 or so troops operated around Ghazni City. An additional US battalion of roughly 700 troops was in the countryside.[9] Allen committed his only spare brigade—1st Brigade, 82nd Airborne Division, numbering 2,400 soldiers—in an attempt to clear Ghazni in a short deployment from May to September 2012. The Americans and the Poles would have three months to make some kind of difference before the additional brigade would be pulled out. The paratroopers pressed into the south of the province and strong-pointed Highway One. The deployment positioned the Americans to support an even bigger event in northern Ghazni, in Andar district.

Ghilzai Pashtuns ruled Ghazni. The Ali Khel, Kharoti, Taraki, and Andar tribes farmed the wide plateau. Nomadic branches spent their summers in the Hindu Kush foothills, before Ghazni's frozen windswept winter forced them south to Helmand and east to Jalalabad. The Hindu Kush themselves were the stronghold of the Hazaras, the other major people of Ghazni. The Hazaras often clashed with nomads pushing into their fastness.

The Taliban had captured nearly all of the fertile plateau following their 2006 offensive. For roughly six years, they controlled this ground. Most locals willingly cooperated. Hezb Islami cadres, under their own party structure rather than the Quetta Shura, were also in Ghazni but Taliban were the majority of the insurgency. While the Taliban were largely local tribesmen, Arabs and Pakistanis appear to have been in Ghazni in greater numbers than elsewhere, often waiting to infiltrate into Kabul.[10] Police and US and Polish troops were few so the Taliban roamed freely in the countryside. Groups of fighters drove around with their Kalashnikovs and RPGs. The Taliban established courts where locals often took cases, especially land disputes. The Taliban governor even issued Taliban identification cards.[11] Taliban commanders invited Western journalists to come and visit. In 2009, Paul Watson from the *Los Angeles Times* observed, "In Ghazni . . . the Taliban militants are not frightened fighters skulking in caves, sneaking out to ambush and then scurrying off to another mountain hide-out. They live comfortably in the farming villages where many of them were born, holding territory, recruiting and training new troops, reveling in what they see as God's gift of inevitable victory against heathen foreign occupiers."[12]

A 2011 independent study found that "a considerable portion of the population" supported the Taliban: "Typical responses were that the mujahedin were the 'saviors' of Afghanistan and that they implemented law according to the rules of Islam. In the view of the majority interviewed, any criticism demonstrated disrespect for the 'holy war.'"[13] In 2011, a woman from the Ghazni countryside told the research team, "We do not accept this government because they only have control over cities. The Taliban has control here and we accept that because they are solving all our problems and they are fighting against the infidels."[14]

The Andar tribe was perhaps the largest in Ghazni. They lived in the northeast quarter of the province, centered in their expansive, self-named district of 160,000 people. More than other tribes, they had a reputation for rebellion.[15] In 1879, during the Second Anglo-Afghan War, their famous religious scholar, Mullah Mushk-e-Alam, called Afghans to arms against the British: "Our people! Our land has been seized by infidels. It is our duty to God and his Prophet to fight against the enemy of our faith and country. If we kill them, we will be heroes, and if we die, we will be martyrs."[16] Andar tribesmen honored Mullah Mushk-e-Alam.[17] After the war, the mullah raised the Ghilzai and the Andar in rebellion against the heavy-handed King Abdur Rahman, "The Iron Emir." Only after a year of fighting and numerous setbacks did Abdur Rahman quash the rebellion. He then punished the Andar. In his words, "When they [the Andar] have no money left with them, [they] will not again raise disturbances," a tribute to the tribe's rebelliousness.[18] One hundred years later, the Andar became mujahideen and fought the Soviets, some with Hezb Islami, others with Harakat Islami (a party later affiliated with the Taliban). After that, the tribe aligned with the Taliban.

Sufism ran strong in the Andar tribe. The famous Sufi Mojalas madrasa, also known as Nur ul-Madares al-Faruqi, was in Andar, attended by hundreds of students.[19] Many future Taliban commanders trained there in the 1980s and 1990s. Compared to the Wahhabism of Saudi Arabia, Sufism in Andar was a freer form of Islam that cherished religious saints, shrines, and music. Andar tribesmen wore colorful patterns: sparkling beaded red prayer caps; yellow, orange, purple, and light blue turbans and patoos (a thin sheet wrapped around a man's shoulders). Music was a feature of Andar tribal life. At any celebration, tribal leaders would gather drummers and flute players. Tribesmen would lightly skip around the two or three musicians, hands outstretched in traditional dance. How so many Andar coming out of this culture were also so fervently Taliban is a mystery to me.

A large number of the Taliban leaders in Ghazni in 2012 were Andar. The most important was Mullah Ismael, who commanded the district for years and went on to become a prominent member of the Quetta Shura (not to be con-fused with a like-named cadre commander in Helmand). Zabiullah Mujahed, the Taliban spokesman, was also Andar, as was Abdul Latif Mansour, one of the main Taliban commanders who fought in the battle of Shah-i-Kot (Operation Anaconda) in 2002. Most Andar commanders had been religiously educated and joined the Taliban from 2003 to 2006, when they were in their early to mid-20s. They felt obliged to take up jihad against foreign presence and retaliate for US raids and air strikes on their villages. They saw themselves following in the footsteps of their ancestor Mullah Mushk-e-Alam.[20] A few knew Mullah Omar from the days of the Taliban regime. Many had spent years in Pakistan refugee camps after 2001.[21]

As elsewhere, the Taliban in Andar banned music and closed schools (the madrasas stayed open). Mobile phones had to be off from dusk to dawn, out of fear of American eavesdropping.[22] But the Taliban in Andar went beyond these standard practices. More than their counterparts in Helmand or Kandahar, Ghazni's Taliban commanders, even those who were Andar, were brutal. From 2006 to 2009, story after story of news-breaking Taliban acts of cruelty came out of Ghazni. Instead of humbly accepting offerings, cadre commanders demanded locals provide food, shelter, and fuel. Instead of asking for volunteers, they press-ganged young men.[23] Instead of punishing people in Islamic courts, they dispensed justice themselves. Kidnapping took on frightful popularity—aid workers, government judges, teachers, and girls attending school, sometimes followed by execution.[24] Over 60 people were kidnapped in 2007 alone.[25]

According to some, Mullah Ismael and the other Taliban commanders believed that they had to be oppressive in order to control their free-spirited tribe. Ismael was an antagonistic character whose unyielding behavior and taxation of major roads angered other influential Taliban leaders. He evaded punishment because he was close to Mullah Mansour.[26] Another story is that the ISI (Pakistan military intelligence) encouraged Taliban commanders in Andar to adopt harsh measures.[27] Seeking Pakistani money, these commanders disregarded their own tribal traditions.[28] Whatever the truth, senior Taliban leaders did little to rein in anyone in Ghazni.

Taliban harshness encountered resistance from certain fellow Andar commanders, most notably two named Noorullah and Rahmatullah. Both valued education. They ran a school that taught children English and Arabic. In 2006, Mullah Ismael accused them of disregarding their religious duties. Shortly after that, a US night raid killed Noorullah. A follow-on mission captured Rahmatullah. He spent two years in Bagram prison. Upon release in 2009, he returned to Andar, rearmed his cadre, and reopened the school.[29] Rahmatullah was not the only libertarian Andar tribesman. A few Andar commanders liked to listen to music and leave schools alone within their territory, drawing criticism upon themselves. Arguments and even fighting sometimes broke out between pro- and anti-school groups.[30]

The situation came to a head in March 2012. That month, in response to a government ban on motorcycles, Mullah Ismael reenforced the ban on schools and confiscated villagers' cell phones. The decision upset the pro-school groups. Rahmatullah was hell-bent on disobeying the ban. Many Andar commanders were also annoyed that Taliban from different tribes from Pakistan hung around the district.[31]

The Hezb Islami faction that operated in Ghazni alongside the Taliban was particularly confrontational. Because of their roots in universities, Hezb Islami also valued learning. Hezb Islami had long been competing with the Quetta Shura for political power. One branch of the party had become an important part of the government. Taliban commanders criticized Hezb Islami for this. Mullah Ismael had ordered the Hezb Islami commanders in Andar to swear allegiance to Mullah Omar. They refused to listen. Hezb Islami cadres fell outside the Quetta Shura command structure and had no obligation to follow its orders.[32] Rahmatullah knew Hezb Islami commanders and conspired with them against the school ban.[33]

Angry at Rahmatullah's growing influence, Mullah Ismael forbade him from arming his men and running a school. He called Rahmatullah to Quetta to account. In Quetta, Rahmatullah refused to recant, so Ismael had his brother kidnapped. Rahmatullah then escaped from Quetta and returned to Andar. Agitating among his fellow tribesmen, he cursed the Quetta Shura's "arrogance" in unyieldingly pressing their dictates. He was a mullah, he told them. He had spent years in Bagram. Yet they disrespected him and offered no compromise. Local elders tried to mediate the dispute to no avail. Ismael was intent on enforcing his orders. He killed Rahmatullah's brother and sent an assault force to wipe out Rahmatullah and his men. On a late afternoon in early April, 50 Taliban attacked Rahmatullah and his cadre of 25 fighters in their village. Rahmatullah was shot in the arm. Seven of his men, the younger ones, dropped their Kalashnikovs and ran. The remainder holed up with Rahmatullah in an empty compound and fought so fiercely that their assailants backed off.[34]

After the battle, both emboldened by the victory and bracing for Taliban retribution, Hezb Islami commanders, a few other aggravated Taliban cadre commanders, and village elders came together behind Rahmatullah and called for *patsoon*, an uprising.[35] These new rebels kicked the Taliban out of a salient in the middle of Andar district and then raided into Taliban territory. In early May, they even ambushed and captured 15 Taliban from Pakistan who bumbled into one of their villages.[36]

Uprising fighters looked like Taliban: 25 to 30 years old, fit, with long black beards, occasional long hair, loose-wrapped yellow or orange or light blue turbans. Many, particularly commanders, were educated. One was a teacher who had graduated from Ghazni University. Another was Engineer Lutfullah Kamran, an energetic Kabul University graduate whose father was a respected judge. He returned to Andar to join the uprising as it gained momentum. Lutfullah told Al Jazeera television, "Schools, our clinics, our roads, our hospitals, our markets— everything was closed. We feel like we are slaves. . . . The only choice we had was to start an uprising."[37]

Members of the uprising justified their actions in terms of resistance to Taliban oppression. In the words of one, "The Taliban damage the country. We cannot be against Islam or our own people."[38] Uprising commanders regaled the press and US officers with stories of the horrendous behavior of the Taliban, their former brethren.[39] While containing more than a grain of truth, these stories were paralleled by long-running rivalries, both with Hezb Islami and be- tween different Taliban commanders, as in Rahmatullah's case. Mullah Ismael and his deputy, Mullah Idris, had various other disputes with various families in the Andar tribe.[40] It is hard to tell whether the tales of grievance were a symptom of underlying competition, or the cause of that competition. In any event, there was an uncharacteristic breakdown in Taliban authority. Unlike elsewhere in Afghanistan, the Quetta Shura had been unable to resolve these disputes, partly because Ismael was a party to them, partly because Hezb Islami muddied lines of authority.

Andar caught the attention of President Karzai and General Allen. Karzai wor- ried that the uprisings could not be controlled and potential political opponents might gain power.[41] He also thought that the uprisings might have been instigated by Americans as a means of increasing foreign control of the provinces. Karzai sent Asadullah Khalid, recently promoted to minister of border and tribal affairs, to Ghazni to investigate. For this work, he only trusted Khalid, who had served him loyally as governor of Ghazni and then Kandahar, and was from Ghazni himself. Khalid was now in his late 30s, said to have the wisdom of an old man and the drive of a young one. A capable paramilitary tactician, Khalid traveled to Andar and immediately grasped the uprising's potential. He supported it with money and guns, encouraged young men to volunteer, and pressured the Ministry of Education to open up schools.[42]

Allen too saw the uprising as an opportunity. In 2007 and 2008, Allen had served in Iraq and had helped build the "Anbar Awakening," the tribal move- ment that pushed al-Qa'eda in Iraq out of their stronghold in al-Anbar province. Allen realized that if the Andar uprising spread, tribes throughout Afghanistan might turn, changing the nature of the war. His staff members even dubbed it the "Andar Awakening," in reference to Anbar. Allen was cautious, however. His first priority was keeping the uprising alive. He sent two special forces teams and one of the 82nd brigade's three battalions to the district to form local police out of the fighters, which would ensure pay, weapons, and ammunition. They also rebuilt several schools. Thanks to their efforts and those of Khalid, by 2013, 2,500 students were attending school in Andar, including a few girls.[43]

The Afghan army deployed a full battalion to Andar to back up the uprising. At first, uprising leaders refused to support the government, which led to angst among US generals and diplomats as to whether to distance themselves from the new movement. Uprising fighters said they were fighting for their tribe and villages and disliked the government and its policies, especially night raids, as much as the Taliban. Within a few months, however, the uprising drew closer to Khalid and the government. The enemy of my enemy is my friend.

Taliban deputy emir Akhtar Mohammed Mansour and the Quetta Shura attempted to crush the uprising. They ordered an immediate offensive. Rarely before had locals, let alone their own fighters, risen up against them. Governor Arsala Jamal of Logar, where a sympathetic smaller uprising broke out, observed, "I think the Taliban do not fear the ANA [army] or ANP [police]. Taliban fear the local police and the uprisings. It questions their legitimacy. The local police and uprising are whole communities. They are not just a few police and soldiers alone."[44]

From May onward, hundreds of Taliban attacked. The uprising, with increasing American and government support, survived. The Taliban suffered roughly 150 casualties in the first several weeks. Mansour sent in reinforcements from Pakistan.[45] The uprising captured 22 Pashtuns from Pakistan.[46] Over the summer, the uprising grew to 400 fighters. Fighting was dirty. Homes were burned. Civilians were killed. Some members of uprising cadres were infiltrators who let the Taliban into their posts to poison, shoot, or slit the throats of sleeping friends. Whole cadres were decimated in this fashion. Over 70 members of the uprising were killed by early 2013, several uprising commanders among them. New men stepped forward to replace the fallen. Posts that had been overrun with devastating losses were re-garrisoned, ranks replenished with new recruits.

The Andar tribe split in two. Roughly half rebelled. Roughly half stayed with the Taliban.[47] Most of the local religious leaders, key to conferring legitimacy on any movement or rebellion, remained with the Taliban. Only a single religious leader issued a fatwa in support of the uprising—and he was quickly dismissed by the rest of the religious leaders in Andar.[48] According to one of the uprising leaders, Andar commanders with the Taliban were not going to abandon jihad for the sake of schools or freedoms: "Andar Taliban commanders believe in jihad. Their thoughts are not right. They have been brainwashed."[49] This was a rough way of saying that the idea of fighting foreign resistance in defense of Islam was powerful enough to keep half the Andar tribe and most of the all-important religious leaders with the Taliban. For them, tribalism and freedoms mattered less than Islam and resistance.

Sometime between April and November, Mansour pulled Mullah Ismael out of supervision of Ghazni. He had failed to quell the uprising, and faced a variety of other charges related to his aggressive tax collection.[50] Mullah Idris, another Andar tribesman, replaced him. Idris had been fighting in Andar since 2006 or 2007. He headquartered himself near the famous Mojalas madrasa (which was still with the Taliban). Though not a religious scholar, Idris had a strong religious background and a bloody determination about him. He would combat the uprising in Andar for years, long after Rahmatullah. Annoyed at political squabbles within the uprising, Rahmatullah decamped for Kabul in mid-2012, leaving Lutfullah and others in charge.[51]

Asadullah Khalid convinced Karzai, who was still hesitant, to let him spread the uprising to other districts in Ghazni. With Khalid's help, at the end of July, new uprisings broke out in the strategic bazaar of Muqor to the south, near Highway One, and in Qara Bagh and Deh Yak districts next to Andar. In Muqor, the Ali Khel tribe knocked the Taliban out of most of the district. Even women gave information on Taliban activity.[52] In August, Khalid visited Muqor to wave the tribe on. He was looking like one of Afghanistan's most dynamic leaders. In September 2012, Karzai promoted him to the powerful position of director of the NDS, head of Afghan intelligence. His tenure might have been hard-hitting. But on December 6 Khalid met in a guesthouse in Kabul with various questionable characters. Friends had warned him be careful, that as NDS director he had to be wary of whom he met. He cheerfully shrugged off their counsel. The meeting went forward. Following custom, he hugged the entering guests. One guest wore a suicide vest, hidden under his clothes. When Khalid embraced him, the guest detonated the vest. The explosion gouged out Khalid's stomach. Allen rushed him to the United States for multiple surgeries. Khalid survived, his mind intact, his body broken. He would not return to Kabul until 2014, even then without the strength to lead.

With Khalid's injury, Karzai put the brakes on uprisings. He believed that large-scale tribal uprisings could threaten his own power as tribes gained strength, unity, and independence. The possibility that Hezb Islami, a political party as well as military organization, could gain control over territory particularly concerned him. Karzai let the existing uprisings persist but discouraged the NDS and other Afghan leaders from supporting new ones.[53] Allen might have been able to spread them on his own but he did not want to interfere in internal Afghan affairs. Tensions with Karzai were already high because of civilian casualties and other issues. A few small tribal uprisings broke out in Wardak, Logar, Kunar, and Nangarhar. They were isolated and short-lived.

The "surge" to the east ended as fast as it had begun. US forces began withdrawing from Ghazni in September 2012. The conventional battalions were the first to go. The special forces teams stayed into 2014.

During 2013 Mullah Idris dictated a steady drumbeat of attacks. Large Taliban units of 20 to 100 men regularly assaulted army and police positions, especially the local police and uprising fighters in the villages. Idris's men were emboldened by the US drawdown and were receiving better equipment from Quetta. He launched a sophisticated attack involving suicide trucks and assault squads on the main US and Polish base in Ghazni City. He breached the main wall before helicopter gunships and superior Western firepower gained the upper hand. One Andar leader admitted that "the Taliban fight the uprising extraordinarily hard."[54] Afghan soldiers often found that Taliban morale was higher than their own.[55] Jami Jami, the chairman of the Ghazni provincial council lamented, "The Taliban have excellent discipline. They have taken thousands of casualties but keep fighting for little money."[56]

As family and friends were killed, the Taliban and uprising fighters sought each other out for bloody vengeance. Neither side took prisoners. One uprising commander, scarred by wounds fighting the Taliban, coldly told me, "We capture Taliban. We gather evidence. If they are guilty, we kill them. . . . We cannot trust the government to keep them in prison." A compatriot explained, "We are forced to fight. The Taliban will kill us. There is no choice."[57] In 2013 and 2014, the Andar uprising captured at least 100 Taliban. Many of these prisoners were killed; some in the burning after-seconds of an emotional firefight, others long after being disarmed. The executions had begun in early 2014 after Karzai had released a Taliban commander from jail who then returned to Andar and started going after members of the uprising. It was all a bloody cycle. "We cannot remember how many we have killed," stated a local police commander.[58] When the US special forces (the last of the US forces) departed in late summer 2014, police chief engineer Lutfullah, uprising commanders, and local police commanders went after family members of Taliban commanders who were in Pakistan or elsewhere in Afghanistan. They allegedly harassed, beat, and sometimes killed them.[59]

The cycle of vengeance accelerated. Frustration bled over onto innocent people, whom some number of uprising fighters beat and robbed. In the words of Fayz Mohammed Zaland, an Andar professor at Kabul University, "The uprising has lost its heart and its cause. It is now focused on vengeance."[60] Indeed, Lutfullah's brother thought that "Ghazni can only be fixed with oppression. Oppression is what the Afghan people respond to."[61] The tribal obligation for revenge in the context of civil war had pushed the uprising to extremes. The local police and uprising fighters were now only fighting for their own sub-clans within the Andar tribe. They stood for little more.[62]

Harshness pushed the villagers away from the uprising. Instead of freedom, the uprising came to represent tribal anarchy. The local police and uprising fighters were behaving no better than the Taliban had at the beginning of 2012. It was a lesson in how civil war causes violence to spin out of control. In this environment, the Taliban, with their ties to Islam, their resistance to occupation, and their focus on unity, had an edge. Even at their most oppressive the Taliban could count on a degree of popular support. Controlling the Mojalas madrasa, Idris and his men appeared more authentic than local police and uprising fighters. Militarily, they were at least as effective. The Taliban could be brutal and still be legitimate and militarily effective. The uprising upstarts could not. After 2014, Idris would gradually suppress the uprising.

The 2012 Ghazni uprising was one of the rare occasions when Afghans started their own guerrilla war against the Taliban. In Andar, the Taliban's cohesion had broken down. The reasons were unique: overly harsh policies, the presence of Hezb Islami, and Andar individualism. It is a tribute to the Taliban's wider cohesion that the uprisings were a blip. The Taliban contained them, even after government and American reinforcements had arrived. The uprising is a powerful explanation of why the Taliban was such a strong insurgent movement.

16

Intervention and Identity

The Ghazni uprisings were the low point for the Taliban. At the beginning of 2013, the Karzai regime was at its zenith. More ground fell under its writ than at any time since 2005: Kabul, the heart of Afghanistan, the 17 provinces in the north and west with their cities of Herat and Mazar-e-Sharif, and most of the 16 largely Pashtun provinces in the east and south. The government could move freely through provincial capitals, populated and fertile districts, and main roads.

The Afghan army and police had grown substantially in both numbers and quality. At the end of 2008, their combined strength was 148,000. By the middle of 2011, the number had risen to 260,000. Recruitment quotas were easily being met. A larger number of young men in good health, with elementary school educations, and even from respected families, were volunteering.[1] Two years later, in 2013, the army and police reached their respective targets of 195,000 and 157,000, for a combined strength of 352,000. Almost 30,000 local police were also recruited. The proportion of Pashtuns to Tajiks had improved but the latter were still drastically overrepresented, especially in the officer corps.[2] Three of the six corps commanders were Tajik.

Tajiks continued to view influence over the army, police, and NDS intelligence agency as their right, as they had since 2001. The feeling was even more ingrained after a decade of fighting the Taliban. "Panjshiris are now throughout the security services. We can't be removed from it," said one Tajik deputy minister from Panjshir.[3] Bismullah Khan was promoted to minister of interior in 2010 and then minister of defense in 2012. Karzai granted him berth he denied to any Pashtun. First Vice President Mohammed Fahim remained in the background. His network, which included Bismullah Khan, persisted throughout the army and police. Other Tajiks, such as Amarullah Saleh and Mohammed Atta, also had influence. The Tajiks were not unified under Dr. Abdullah, Mohammed Fahim, or Mohammed Atta. "Tajiks aren't together like other groups," reported Amarullah Saleh.[4] But their leaders followed common interests. When it came to the Taliban, "Panjshiris will stay together," asserted the Tajik deputy minister. "We are always against the Taliban."[5]

The cost of the army and police was more than $11 billion in 2011.[6] The figure dropped to $5.4 billion per year by 2013, after the investments to recruit, train, and equip hundreds of thousands of men had been completed. In 2012, the international community agreed to give Afghanistan $4.1 billion per year for its armed forces from 2015 to 2017, with $2.3 billion from the United States.

With the addition of the 215th in Helmand, six corps operated in Afghanistan. Each fielded about 15,000 soldiers. Soldiers and police were better trained and equipped, with uniforms, boots, plenty of trucks, and sufficient weapons. Soldiers had gone through six months of training. The various corps fielded artillery, Humvees, and armored vehicles. "Now they look much more like real soldiers," complimented a British advisor in Helmand.[7] By early 2013, all but 20,000 police had been to three to eight weeks of training. Besides formal training, police and army units in the south and east had worked with US advisors for years on end.

The United States was also building an 8,000-person air force that would be centered on 80 Mi-17 Russian-designed transport helicopters, three C-130 transport aircraft, and 20 propeller-driven Super Tucano light attack aircraft. The air force would not have all its aircraft until 2017, at which time three Mi-35 and seventeen MD-530 attack helicopters would also be in the fleet.[8] US leaders considered the air force necessary so that US aircraft in Afghanistan could be drawn down.

Training and advising improved the quality of the army and police but significant gaps remained. "The Afghan National Army still has logistics problems," assessed a marine colonel. "Logistics needs are not met quickly. . . . The units are not stockpiling supplies and Kabul pushes things too slowly."[9] Advisors in the ministry of defense and ministry of interior in Kabul fruitlessly attempted to teach the Afghans. In the field, keeping units manned and supplied was a headache. "It's hard for me at the *kandak* [battalion] level to teach logistics to them when the system all the way up to the Ministry of Defense is broken," one advisor criticized. "The *kandak* logistics officer or S4 stops having any confidence in his logistical system after he's submitted that MOD-14 form for the tenth time. He's just going to blow you off because he knows he's . . . wasting his time."[10]

Army and police leadership displayed uneven competence. Bismullah Khan was committed and personally brave. He frequently visited troops in the field. When six Haqqani operatives infiltrated an unoccupied 15-story building on September 13, 2011, and lobbed RPGs into the US Embassy and ISAF headquarters, Bismullah Khan appeared a few dozen meters away and directed Afghan commandos in a clearing operation. The amiable General Sher Mohammed

Karimi had succeeded Bismullah Khan as chief of the general staff in 2010. American advisors considered him untainted by corruption.

A coterie of army corps commanders and provincial police chiefs were also capable: taciturn Hakim Angar (Helmand provincial police chief); English-speaking Abdul Hamidi (Kandahar 205th corps commander); martinet Mohaiddun Ghori, (now Herat deputy 207th corps commander); glowering General Waziri (Nangarhar 201st corps commander); and universally respected General Yaftali (Paktiya 203rd corps commander). All were former communists—with a bias for the methodical—and served out of dedication to their profession. Beneath them, brigade, battalion, and company commanders were more of the old mujahideen, often Panjshiris. Here too, officers could have dedication such as Brigadier General Razziq Safi, a pious Northern Alliance hero. "He is an old mujahedin commander who fights," said a US colonel, "even if he can be heavy handed, and will fire his D-30 artillery when necessary."[11]

Yet too many generals, colonels, and police chiefs were lethargic or old. They did not press their men to fight, or lead from the front themselves. They neglected to organize proper supply. They often took cuts of pay, fuel, and equipment for themselves, or for their own patrons, over investing those resources into the battle. These traits were far from universal but were widespread enough to be a problem.

The United States and its Western allies tried to institute merit-based promotion systems for the army and police. Few officers were selected that way. It was especially bad in the police. Many provincial police chiefs were chosen by Karzai or other officials in the palace on the basis of political loyalty. Senators, members of parliament, and Kabul and provincial powerbrokers could lobby or pay for a supporter to be promoted.[12] Powerbrokers would try to remove good police chiefs and pay off Ministry of Interior officials in order to get their own man into a job. That police chief could then tax people or smuggle for the powerbroker. Ashraf Ghani, the government's master organizer who oversaw police reform, referred to the police as "feudalizing" and threatened, "If MOI [Ministry of Interior] stays on course stealing from people without change, I won't back them. I will tell the donors to stop helping.[13]

A continuing problem was the absence of a centralized command-and-control structure. In any given province, no one was truly in charge. The army, police, NDS, and governor all had their own chains of command. Too often, they pursued counterproductive personal feuds. Kandahar police chief Abdul Razziq explained, "The government has no loyalty to a single leader. There are thirty-four provinces, each with its own leaders: a governor, army commander, police chief, NDS director. The Taliban do not have these different organizations. Taliban are just Taliban."[14] US generals uniformly tried to resolve the command structure issue through creating provincial and district coordination centers, where army, police, and NDS representatives received reports on attacks and met to coordinate operations. The coordination centers reduced friction, especially while the Americans or other allied officers were around to push all sides together, but could not stop the competition.

Despite their losses, through the years of the surge and the beginning of the drawdown the Taliban endured. What the Taliban still held were parts of desert and mountains next to Pakistan and within Afghanistan itself, most notably the vast arc spanning northern Helmand, eastern Farah, northern Uruzgan, and northern Zabul. In Pakistan, the Taliban and Haqqani leaders lived in relative safety, and could recruit, train, organize, and recuperate from the losses of the surge. The wide stretches of Afghanistan under their control meant that by definition the Taliban could return. Remnants in the more populated districts tied down government and international forces in suppression of low-level guerrilla activity. Estimated Taliban strength was between 25,000 and 60,000.[15]

Taliban endurance was not merely a result of safe havens in Pakistan and Afghanistan. The Taliban could do more with less. The government needed thousands of troops and hundreds of Americans plus air support to hold a district. In the victorious battlefields of the surge—Marjah, Arghandab, Zharey, Panjwai, Sangin—thousands of troops had to stay in place to prevent the Taliban's return. In contrast, the Taliban could hold a district with hundreds of poorly trained and poorly armed fighters (see Figure 2).

The government and international forces had to suppress guerrilla activity—the low-level improvised explosive devices, assassinations, and intimidation—in every district whereas the Taliban did not. Helmand police chief Baqizoi described this situation: "People are willing to help the Taliban. Any village without local police is with the Taliban. Elders tell me, 'We have no answer to the Taliban. If you do not defend us, we cannot be with you.'"[16] The reverse was not true. Outside Andar and a few other districts, there was no pro-government guerrilla war tying down Taliban cadres. Aoliya Atrafi, an Afghan BBC journalist who entered Taliban territory in northern Helmand, reported, "The thing about the Taliban is you can travel here for miles without seeing an armed person. It is more the idea of the Taliban that dominates here rather than their presence."[17]

Taliban fighters were willing to run a guerrilla war in places such as Kandahar City and Kabul, where the people generally disliked them; operations were likely to miss their target, medical care was paltry, and the risk of capture or death was high. In the countryside, they hung on for years in districts against local opposition, superior numbers, and US air power. Pro-government groups that did anything similar were markedly fewer—the Panjshiris of Ahmed Shah Massoud, the Achekzai of Abdul Razziq, the Andar rebels, Afghan army commandos[18]—singular tribes or units versus an entire movement.

District	Taliban forces when under their control	Government and international forces when under their control
Garmser, Helmand	600–1,000	1,800
Marjah, Helmand	400–2,000*	2,000
Nad Ali, Helmand	500	1,100
Sangin, Helmand	600–800	2,000
Zharey, Kandahar	600–1,500	3,000
Panjwai, Kandahar	600–1,000	3,000
Arghandab, Kandahar	800–1,000	1,200
Dai Chopan, Zabul	500	Never under government control
Andar, Ghazni	800	1,200

*This figure is the number of Taliban defending Marjah in 2010 against the Marine assault. Taliban numbers were probably fewer in 2009, when they were not preparing for the assault, which was well-publicized ahead of time.

Figure 2 Taliban control versus government control, 2007–2013

This leads to perhaps the greatest puzzle of the war: how could the outnumbered Taliban outperform the better manned, better equipped, and better trained army and police? There is no simple answer. Tribal disunity, unfair government policies, confused chains of command, and the nature of modern guerilla warfare are factors. Here, though, I would like to talk about what is too often overlooked: that the Taliban could touch on what it meant to be Afghan better than the government. The Taliban stood for Islam and resistance to foreign occupation, values deeply rooted in Afghan identity. The Taliban had an ability to inspire that the Western-installed government could never match. This capacity should not be discounted as a condition that drove the outcome of the war.

According to polling, throughout the surge and after, Islam and resistance to foreigners motivated Taliban fighters, as had been the case from 2007 to 2009. The 2014 Asia Foundation survey found that of the 32 percent of Afghans who had some sympathy for the Taliban (down from the 56 percent of 2009), 40 percent of respondents (the plurality) said the Taliban were fighting because of the presence of foreign troops, to gain power, to support Islam, or a similar reason strongly tied to Islam and Afghan identity.[19] In the 2012 survey, of the Afghans who strongly sympathized with the Taliban, 77 percent said they sympathized because the Taliban were Afghans, Muslims, and waging jihad.[20]

Islam, intertwined with Afghanistan's history of resistance to foreign intervention, enabled the Taliban to inspire their fighters—better than tribalism or democracy helped a government tinged by Western sponsors to inspire its soldiers and police. It was easy to hear of the inspirational role of Islam and resistance to occupation from Taliban leaders. During 2014, I oversaw interviews of 45 Taliban commanders and religious leaders. Just over half cited Islam or Afghan identity as integral to their morale. Take this contrast of Taliban versus police and army morale by a Taliban religious leader from Paktiya:

> I hear every day of an incident where police or army soldiers are killed. This means they are fighting, but it does not mean they are good at fighting. They seem well equipped. I see so many [police and military] trucks in the city roaming around, going out and into the city, but I do not know if they are committed to fighting the Taliban or not. Many of the police and soldiers are there only for dollars. They are paid good salaries but they do not have the motivation to defend the government. . . . Taliban are committed to the cause of jihad. This is the biggest victory for them.[21]

Another Taliban religious leader, from Laghman, elaborated: "Taliban are more committed because of the cause of jihad. They are supported by Almighty Allah. They are fighting foreigners who were defeated every time in the history of Afghanistan. The government is not an actual government. It is a servant of others, so people have no trust in them."[22] A cadre commander from Zabul put that perspective in blunter terms: "We are not ready to share power with those who are supported by non-Muslims. Therefore, we will continue jihad until we have defeated the government, as we defeated the Americans and their allies."[23] And to quote from one of Mullah Omar's messages, "For us life is not so dear that we will not spend it for our religion. Indeed, our death and life is all for Allah and for the path of Allah we are happy to sacrifice and leave our pride aside."[24]

My own discussions with Taliban reveal similar views. Former Taliban ambassador to the United Nations Abdul Hakim Mujahed told me, "The insurgency is strong now. There are two things that make them strong. First, the government fails to defend Islam. Second, the government fails to defend Afghan sovereignty. The United States keeps doing night raids and killing civilians, even though, time after time, President Karzai orders them to stop."[25]

Maulawi Mohammed Noor was a Taliban religious scholar who lived in Kandahar. He had gone to madrasa with the top leaders of the Taliban and then had run a madrasa during their first regime that trained fighters. Noor provided me with one of the most comprehensive explanations of Taliban morale. "The Taliban fight for belief," he argued, "for *janat* (heaven) and *ghazi* (killing infidels). The army and police hide in their tanks. The army and police fight for money." Islam inspired the Taliban to go to great lengths: "Every commander is

willing to die. They expect to die. . . . The madrasas prepare them for this." This
was their advantage: "The Taliban are willing to lose their head to fight. For the
Taliban, life has already passed. How can the army and police compete with the
Taliban? They cannot."[26]

It is no surprise that Taliban leaders believed that their men were inspired
by Islam and resistance to foreign occupation. What is surprising—and more
convincing—is how many pro-government leaders shared the Taliban view.
Mohammed Atta, the powerful Tajik governor of Balkh and Mazar-e-Sharif,
scorned claims that the Taliban fought for money and said "Taliban fight because of belief, not money."[27] Abdul Bari Barakzai, chairman of the Helmand
provincial council, complained to me in 2014: "Taliban fighters are better than
army soldiers or police. The Taliban fight without much in the way of equipment,
weapons, and ammunition. They fight well because they are inspired by mullahs
and by jihad. Anyone working with the government is known as an infidel who
deserves to die. The government has few mullahs to inspire the army and police
in the same way."[28] Shafi Afghan, a former Alikozai policeman, educated professional, and friend of Sarah Chayes, agreed with him: "The Taliban are surviving
because of their ideology. They are determined. That is why the Afghan army
and police, with 352,000 men, cannot defeat 10,000 Taliban."[29] And Kandahar's
dreaded police chief, Abdul Razziq, something of an authority on these matters,
ruled, "Taliban morale is better than government morale. Taliban morale is very
high. Look at their suicide bombers. The Taliban motivate people to do incred-
ible things."[30]

Additional surveys of Taliban fighters and commanders provide a wider
sample. The set of interviews with 78 Taliban fighters and commanders
conducted by Andrew Garfield and Alicia Boyd between 2009 and 2012 suggests
identity was indeed inspiring them to put their lives at risk:

> Interviewees have spent between five and six years, on average, involved
> in insurgent activity, with little variation by province. Some have fought
> for much longer. Only a few reported having elected to join the insur-
> gency recently (less than two years ago). . . . Despite such a lengthy
> commitment, most interviewees say that they have not grown tired of
> fighting. In fact, just three acknowledged a sense of fatigue. However, as
> most interviewees consider their fight a moral and religious obligation,
> it is not surprising that so few admit feeling worn out. A few also state
> that, since jihad continues perpetually, there can simply be no fatigue.[31]

A separate study by Theo Farrell and Antonio Giustozzi that interviewed 102
Taliban in 2011 and 2012 found that "when asked why they were fighting, most
Taliban interviewees presented the conflict primarily in terms of resistance

to foreign occupation. A number expressed it in terms of an 'Islamic duty to fight against the *kafirs* [infidels].'"[32] Islam and identity was an unavoidable theme: "Waging jihad on occupying foreigners is clearly a powerful strategic narrative for the Taliban, providing a crucial social resource for the purposes of motivating fighters and mobilizing resources."[33] And according to certain Afghan researchers, captured Taliban suicide bombers and fighters displayed an unwavering commitment to fighting on behalf of Allah and against the infidel occupier.[34]

A survey of 50 Taliban much later in the war by Ashley Jackson was more definitive. She discovered that Taliban members described their decision to join the movement "in terms of religious devotion and jihad—a sense of personal and public duty. In their view, jihad against foreign occupation was a religious obligation, undertaken to defend their values. . . . Religious and political motives were mixed, with religious obligations intertwined with narratives of collective honor, sovereignty, and nationalism."[35] Jihad was about identity, she concluded.[36]

In contrast, the government had trouble inspiring. It could never claim as strong a tie to what it meant to be Afghan as the Taliban. For this reason, Afghans were unwilling to go to the same lengths for the government as they were for the Taliban. As identity inspired Taliban fighters to take risk, distance from identity demoralized the army and police. The observation that soldiers are less inspired than mujahideen is nothing new. In the Middle East and South Asia, populations often looked down upon soldiers. The famous French social scientist Olivier Roy wrote of the Soviet-Afghan War, "In the resistance we encounter a regular feature of Islamic wars: the professional soldier (*askar*) is devalued with respect to the *mujahedin*, who is a volunteer and a believer, but also with respect to the warrior and the merchant and artisan. The *askar* is perceived as a simple mercenary (*mazdur*, the salaried odd-job man), as a victim of forced enrollment, or as too stupid to have plied any other trade."[37]

From Eikenberry onward, American officers tried to build the Afghan army into a force inspired by nationalism, in which different ethnicities would work together for the defense of the Afghan nation. By many accounts, soldiers and police struggled because they had nothing universally inspiring to fight for. Journalist Luke Mogelson spent a week with an Afghan army battalion and its commander, Dawood, in the wilds of Wardak. He observed, "My sense was that Dawood was genuinely conflicted: a committed soldier who spent 10 years of his life in the service of government he was profoundly disenchanted with. And he wasn't alone. Most soldiers I spoke to conspicuously avoided expressing any fondness for—much less allegiance to—their government."[38] Afghan army generals admitted the same absence of inspiration. One general confessed, "The enemies are ideological people; their slogan is Jihad and Heaven but our army doesn't have that motive and slogan."[39] A damning comment comes from

Bismullah Khan, given his experience as Panjshiri mujahideen commander, chief of staff of the Afghan army, and ultimately minister of defense. In 2011, he told an Afghan news show, "Undoubtedly, the police and the army do not have motivation—motivation that we had during jihad. We defended [our country] and we had very strong motivation. Regrettably, they [police and army] do not have it."[40]

Once more, the most convincing evidence comes from surveys. In 2010, the US military asked social scientists to run a survey of the Kandahar population. Forty-nine percent of respondents thought that their fellow Afghans joined the army for a job or for pay. Fifty-three percent thought the same reason pertained to the police. Only 10 percent thought Afghans joined the army or the police in order to defend their country. Sixty percent believed that the danger deterred Afghans from joining the police, 44 percent for the army. The survey hardly painted a picture of a recruit base eager to fight.[41]

In 2015, the Afghan Institute for Strategic Studies surveyed 1,657 police in 11 provinces throughout Afghanistan and asked them about their beliefs. Respondents were deeply conflicted about why they were fighting. An element of nationalism was there; 65 percent said they had joined the police out of love of country. A little more than half (57 percent) believed that the president was legitimate. Yet nationalism did not inspire the whole force; 19 percent of respondents said they had joined the police force, not out of love of country, but for a salary. More importantly, conflicted motivations did not translate into will to fight. *Only 11 percent of respondents had joined the police to fight the Taliban.*[42] This finding suggests that perhaps a small minority of the police actually wanted to fight at all. Certainly, a far larger percentage of Taliban had joined to fight the government.

The survey underlined the weakness of the government as a source of inspiration. Many interviewees claimed that police "rank and file are not convinced that they are fighting for a just cause."[43] The image of a puppet government was a key factor. Seventy percent of respondents said the government was overly influenced by the West (slightly fewer said the same thing regarding corruption). Another factor was an underlying reluctance to challenge Islam. Nearly a third of respondents believed that Taliban authority was legitimate. On top of this, 83 percent believed that violence was justified against a government that criticized Islam, which Western influence presumably encourages. These figures make clear that the government did not always live up to notions of Afghan identity that respondents valued. Consequently, the legitimacy of violence on its behalf was troubled.

Astute Afghan politicians, generals, and officials turned to an outside source for inspiration: Pakistan. President Karzai, General Abdul Razziq, and later Ashraf Ghani used Pakistan as an outside threat to unite Afghans behind

them. They refused to characterize the Taliban as anything but a Pakistani creation. Razziq relentlessly claimed to be fighting a foreign Pakistani invasion. He
skewered Pakistan in dozens of interviews and speeches, and face to face with
Pakistani generals on the border. Although Razziq had some success spreading
the accusation, Pakistan could never fully out-inspire occupation. A popular tale
illuminates the reality:

> An Afghan army officer and a Taliban commander were insulting each
> other over their radios while shooting back and forth. The Taliban
> commander taunted, "You are puppets of America!" The army officer
> shouted back, "You are puppets of Pakistan!" The Taliban commander
> replied, "Americans are infidels. Pakistanis are Muslims." The Afghan
> officer had no response.[44]

Or in the shorter Afghan proverb form: "Over an infidel, be happy with a weak
Muslim."[45]

It was not only in fighting the Taliban that identity affected the army and police.
The tension between foreign presence and what it means to be Afghan also affected their relations with US and allied soldiers—the non-Muslims with whom
they worked, shoulder by shoulder, every day. In 2012 it did so in ways that
questioned the fundamentals of America's partnership with the Afghan government and its army and police.

On February 20, 2012, US security personnel at the prison in Bagram tossed
several Korans into a burn pit, along with 2,000 other books thought to be extremist from the prison library. Afghan workers saw the Korans smoldering
in the dump. They were incensed and protested outside the base. Soon, the
burnings were all over the press.

Afghans were taught at the youngest age to treat the Koran with the greatest
care. Even by accident, burning or damaging a Koran was an act of sacrilege.
The Koran burning at Bagram was easily misinterpreted as a sign that Americans
sought to destroy Islam. Karzai was outraged that Americans could be so in-
sensitive a decade into the war. He condemned the accident and demanded
Bagram prison be turned over to his government. Parliament seconded his con-
demnation and requested the perpetrators be punished in Afghan court. The
Taliban spokesperson called for police and soldiers to attack American soldiers.
Violent protests erupted in Kabul and other major cities and towns throughout
Afghanistan, their fury bent on US bases. For the better part of a week, tens of
thousands of people took to the streets.

Discontent swept into the army and police. As the riots spread, an Afghan
soldier killed two Americans on a base near Jalalabad. Then, on February 24, a

police intelligence officer named Abdul Saboor shot and killed two American advisors working in the Ministry of Interior, the heart of the government's security apparatus. Saboor escaped and called the Taliban. He said he had killed the two advisors in retaliation for the Koran burnings. None of the US military had expected such an attack could take place at such a high echelon among partners so deeply trusted. Concerned more attacks might be on the way, General John Allen, commander of US and allied forces, pulled out his advisors across the country. He kept them back until Karzai at last calmed his people.

The rage over the Koran burning faded but something stayed in the body of the police and army. A steady drumbeat of killings followed, which the US military dubbed "insider" or "green-on-blue" attacks. Several times per month, an Afghan soldier or policeman tried to kill his American advisors or counterparts. The Taliban supposedly endorsed the tactic and mullahs encouraged Afghan soldiers and police to shoot Americans. In 2012, 142 American and allied soldiers would be killed or wounded in 44 insider attacks.[46] The attacks accounted for nearly 20 percent of their forces killed in action that year.

Insider attacks had always been a problem in Afghanistan. In the early 1900s, British officers serving in Pashtun tribal levies on the frontier had faced the same danger. They had already happened in America's Afghan War as well. Sixty-nine American and allied soldiers had been killed or wounded in such attacks in 2011 alone.[47] On January 20, 2012, a month before the Koran protests, an Afghan soldier had killed four French soldiers and wounded another 15 in one of the worst insider attacks of the war. The attack catalyzed French withdrawal from Afghanistan, which would occur at the end of the year.

Casualties from insider attacks were widely publicized and further undermined the American war effort. The repercussions distracted so much from operations that Allen dubbed the attacks a "meteor strike." President Obama considered insider attacks a huge problem. It looked as though average Afghans hated Americans and that not even the army that the United States funded was friendly. He read insider attacks as another sign that the US effort was bound to fail. When a series of attacks in August and September killed or wounded 44 US and allied troops, Obama suspended all operations with Afghans.[48] It took Allen a week to get the order rescinded.

American advisors and staff officers tended to argue that the attacks were either Taliban conspiracies or the result of personal misunderstandings between Americans and specific soldiers or police. Obama was closer to the truth. Research conducted on Allen's orders found conspiracy to be an overly simplified way of interpreting what was happening and that personal misunderstandings could only explain a few incidents. The source of most of the tension probably ran deeper. Occupation did not just undermine the morale of the army and police. Being dubbed a *ghazi*, the title of one who has killed an infidel, was a great honor, borne by some of Afghanistan's greatest heroes. The possibility that accepting occupation could be translated as un-Afghan tore at young police and soldiers. It drove a few, such as Saboor, to gun down their counterparts and also their own Afghan colleagues. Indicatively, the 2015 Afghan Institute for Strategic Studies survey of police found that 5 percent of respondents considered suicide attacks to be justified in the name of Islam—more than enough for a few insider attacks.[49] The *New York Times* reported, "Despite their public insistence that they employ vast ranks of infiltrators within the Afghan Army and the police, they [the Taliban] acknowledged that many of the insider attacks they take credit for start as offers by angry young men."[50]

Within the police and army there was a certain sympathy for insider attackers. After a failed insider attack on a base in Maiwand, for example, Afghan soldiers forever derided their American partners as infidels. In July 2013, an Afghan soldier killed a group of Slovakian soldiers at Kandahar Air Force Base. The Afghan was captured and put in a holding cell. He was from Jalalabad and said he was upset about US raids on his village. An Afghan lieutenant freed him. Both escaped and joined the Taliban. The soldier told his uncle that he wished he had died in the attack and wanted to become a suicide bomber. The lieutenant announced on a Taliban video, "I didn't want this ghazi to be turned over to the Americans. . . . These infidels who have come to Afghanistan do not want sharia [Islamic law] in our country. They want to spread their Christianity."[51] Such a sense of Afghan identity even touched women. On December 24, 2012, again inside the Ministry of Interior, an Afghan policewoman killed an American civilian advisor for reasons that have never been entirely clear. She was not found to be a Taliban agent. Nor was she found to have had a cultural dispute with the American.[52]

Thankfully, the majority of Afghans were not about to shoot Americans or their allies. New force protection measures, help from strong Afghan commanders, and the drawdown eventually reduced the number of insider attacks. The old "shoulder by shoulder" advising went away. Bases now had checkpoints or even walls dividing the Americans from the Afghans. An armed escort, known as a "guardian angel," usually accompanied advisors talking with Afghans. A few Afghan soldiers and police saw Americans as distant and disinterested in helping them.

Although the Afghan government never systematically forced its commanders to clamp down on insider attacks, stronger commanders did so on their own. They looked after their advisors and watched their own men carefully. Most notable was Kandahar police chief Abdul Razziq. After a policeman killed a soldier in Spin Boldak in August 2012, Razziq put an end to police insider attacks in Kandahar. To make an example, he fired the Spin Boldak police chief. He then ordered all his officers and police to stop any insider attacks before they happened. Americans were not to be killed. He put the responsibility on their shoulders and threatened to punish failure summarily.[53] After that, there was not one insider attack in Kandahar on the part of the police, local police, or border police.[54] Elsewhere, other police chiefs and army officers who trusted Americans did the same thing, enforcing their will.

Notwithstanding Razziq, the most important reason that the number of attacks declined was the drawdown. There were fewer and fewer targets. The desire to kill foreigners never disappeared. There were at least seven attacks in 2014, including one on international civilian doctors at a Kabul hospital and another on two journalists in Khost. On August 5, 2014, Rafiqullah, an Afghan soldier at the officer academy in Kabul, opened fire on a visiting US delegation, killing Major General Harold Greene and wounding 11 other Americans, British, and Germans. Greene was the highest ranking US officer to die in Afghanistan. Return fire killed Rafiqullah, who was a Pashtun from Paktiya. A US investigation found he had no ties to the Taliban and had taken advantage of a target of opportunity.[55] The Taliban did not claim responsibility. One of the Afghan scholars of the Asia Foundation in Kabul saw enough to assume what happened: "Questions within the Afghan army about Allah and the infidel is why there are insider attacks. It is why General Greene was killed at Qara Bagh."[56]

The United States had worked to improve women's rights in Afghanistan since 2001. President Obama himself, wary of wading into nation-building, was less vocal than Bush had been but recognized their importance. Secretary of State Hillary Clinton was the administration's main advocate. A variety of Democrats, Republicans, and prominent figures pressured the administration to demand reforms. Constituencies existed on both sides of the aisle in the Senate and the House of Representatives.[57] The media generally helped the effort with editorials, pieces on women's rights, and even criticism of skeptics. The famous journalist Christiane Amanpour grilled Speaker of the House Nancy Pelosi on national television in 2010 for being unwilling to support the Afghanistan mission and help Afghan women. Many of these same groups and leaders called on Obama to keep troops in Afghanistan rather than let human rights advances slip. Women's rights remained a reason to stay in Afghanistan.

Since 2001, significant reforms for women had been implemented. The most dramatic had been over the following four years when women were affirmed the right to vote and guaranteed seats in parliament and provincial councils. The 2005 parliamentary elections elevated a variety of women to a national political role. Additionally, over the next eight years, several women became ministers and one a provincial governor—Habiba Sarabi in Bamiyan.[58]

After 2005, other advances improved the daily lives of women, particularly in medical care, employment, and education. Health care is one of the great successes of the Western intervention in Afghanistan. The international community funded clinics and hospitals throughout the country under the Ministry of Public Health. Government clinics and doctors appeared in the farthest bazaars and villages of most districts. Seventy percent of the population gained access to medical care. The benefits to women were substantial. Maternal mortality fell by 80 percent between 2001 and 2013.[59] Clinics and hospitals were also two of the few fields women could be seen with a job in the countryside.

Economic opportunities in general varied and grew quickest in Herat and Kabul. Although the percentage of women countrywide who reported being employed was well under 10 percent, the percentage of households countrywide that reported women contributed to household income increased from 14 percent in 2009 to 22 percent in 2014.[60] Female income per capita doubled between 2000 and 2013.[61]

Education was a path of least resistance for women's rights. The Koran clearly states that women have a right to education. Afghan men were less recalcitrant in approving of women, especially young girls, going to school than in accepting other reforms. Throughout the war, at least three-quarters of Afghans, according to the Asia Foundation surveys, believed in gender equality in education.[62] The United States and the international community were able to build a number of girls' schools and fund successful programs for girls' education. A common reason that Afghans gave for why the country was moving in the right direction was the opening of girl's schools. Between 2001 and 2013, girls' enrollment in primary and secondary schools increased to 3.2 million. The 2013 Asia Foundation survey found that 29 percent of female respondents between the ages of 18 and 30 indicated that they had at least some formal education. These were the women who would have been exposed to the increased educational opportunities of the previous 12 years. In contrast, only 12 percent of female respondents between the ages of 31 and 50—those who would have grown up through the Soviet war, the civil war, and the Taliban regime—indicated some formal education.[63]

Advances were clustered in Kabul and the cities, where a minority of women lived. Educational and job opportunities bloomed in Kabul as new universities opened (including the Western-staffed American University in Afghanistan) and embassies, contractors, non-governmental organizations (NGOs), and ministries posted jobs for women. Advances were far more modest in the countryside. Provincial reconstruction teams and military units built girls' schools or larger schools for segregated classes of girls and boys. The US marines and army fielded female engagement teams, women with the cultural training and permission to interact with Afghan women in the villages and arrange for small projects.

The reforms did not change the traditional Afghan segregation and mistreatment of women. Surveys showed the majority of men in the east and south did not believe women should work outside the home.[64] Especially in the countryside, domestic violence, limited employment opportunities, and general lack of freedom prevailed. The repression was tied to traditional tribal life and Pashtunwali. Afghan men often claimed it to be guided by Islam. With a healthy awareness of the backlash to the interventions of Amanullah and then the communists in the past, the West and liberal-minded Afghans refrained from interfering in tribal life.

The Taliban naturally opposed reforms for women. They cast themselves as defenders of women's dignity. A Taliban website, al-Emera, argued in 2012, "In this dark period of American occupation and in complete disagreement of our Islamic and national customs and culture, women are intentionally being pushed towards ignorance, are having to face inhumane conditions under the name of democracy."[65]

A foremost reform to further advance the rights of women was the law on the elimination of violence against women. With the support of non-governmental organizations, the United Nations, and the US Embassy, Afghan women's leaders drafted the law from 2005 to 2009. Parliamentarian Fawzia Koofi was part of the effort. The draft criminalized and mandated punishments for rape, honor killings, beatings, and other oppression of Afghan women. Religious leaders, including the dean of the Islamic Law school of Kabul University, vocally objected to the proposal. To avert controversy, women's groups and Koofi maneuvered to have Karzai sign the bill into law by decree instead of through a vote in parliament.

The United States was exerting a good deal of pressure at the time over mistreatment of women. Secretary of State Clinton and President Obama, as well as German Chancellor Angela Merkel, had weighed in against a separate measure that treated Shi'a women as property of their husbands and permitted to be raped. Obama called it "abhorrent." Koofi leveraged Western support to drive home reform: "I don't ask that the international community come and make laws for us, but they have to make the government of Afghanistan accountable for their commitment to women and children."[66] Karzai signed the law on the elimination of violence against women on July 19, 2009.

After the signing, Fawzia Koofi worried that a future president might reverse the law. She and other lawmakers introduced the law to parliament for confirmation.[67] The move was probably not the tough Tajik's wisest. Former mujahideen commanders, religious leaders, and other conservative parliamentarians saw the law as a threat to their power, tribal traditions, and religion. An opposing parliamentarian declared, "This law is anyway for the women of the street. Good women living under the protection of Islam have no need for this law."[68] Discussions in committees revolved around whether the law was Islamic. Knowledge of Islam determined whose voice was credible. Western support turned into a liability. The opposing parliamentarians viewed Western support as undue foreign interference. One legal scholar tarred the law as "a gift from the foreigners."[69]

The law was mired in parliament until May 18, 2013, when Koofi brought it to a plenary session ahead of a vote. Rancorous debate ensued. "God says you can marry up to four wives. What should we do—change God's law?," bullied one parliamentarian.[70] Another with a religious background exclaimed, "Mr. Speaker, This law is in contradiction with several aspects of the verses of the Koran. Article 3 of the Constitution explicitly states that those laws that are contrary to sharia and the sacred religion of Islam have no validity whatsoever."[71] After 15 minutes, Speaker of the Wolesi Jirga Abdul Raouf Ibrahimi cut off debate and called for a special commission to determine whether the law was in accordance with Islam, where the matter languished. The law on the elimination of violence against women was never confirmed. Women leaders and groups criticized Koofi for introducing the law to parliament at all instead of simply treating it as official after Karzai's signature. Rivals accused her of playing for the media spotlight.

Yet because Karzai had signed it, the law was still in effect. Execution was mixed. A few thousand cases were logged and a few hundred men were convicted of crimes. Judges, even in Kabul, were hesitant to convict because of the controversy around the law.[72] In the broad scheme of Afghan history, the law on the elimination of violence against women has to be considered significant progress. It is also another example of the deep-seated adherence to tradition and resistance to foreign influence.

The same kind of reaction generally obstructed improvements in women's rights. After Obama announced the drawdown and end of the combat mission, northern members of parliament threatened Fawzia Koofi, who had by then represented Badakhshan for eight years: "Your friends are leaving anyways in 2014. We know what to do with you."[73]

Resistance to reforms was present on the streets of Kabul itself, the center of progress in the country, bustling with civil society groups, women leaders, educational institutes, and endless conferences. I well remember a Kabul bookseller telling me, in the center of the book bazaar, with bespectacled men poring through stacks upon stacks of Pashto and Dari books, that Western ways were the utmost sign of disrespect to women, that respect meant segregating women from the outside world. Women's rights were fairly controversial among the Kabul youth as well. Hearing comments from young men angered by educated, employed, or less than fully shrouded women was commonplace. Kabul University was known to be a source of young male discontent. Nor was dissatisfaction confined to men. *New York Times* journalists Azam Ahmed and Habib Zahori witnessed a group of 200 young women protest the law for the elimination of violence against women. They had a poster that read, "I am not a Self-Aware Woman, I Will Not Be Deceived by the Empty Slogans of the West."[74]

Horrifying proof of latent Kabul sentiments occurred two years later in 2015. That February, Farkhunda Malikzada, a 27-year-old from an educated family, visited the blue and yellow, faintly baroque-looking, Shah-Do Shamshira shrine on the banks of the foul Kabul River.[75] Inside the shrine, she saw a fortune-teller selling amulets and other items that were not properly Islamic. She got into an argument with the fortune-teller and the shrine's *malang*—keeper. A month later, on the afternoon of March 19, Farkhunda returned and told women not to buy the amulets. The malang rushed out amid the pigeons that flock the shrine and shouted to the throngs of people along the shops and road, "A woman burned the Koran!"[76] Reaction was frighteningly rapid. Men swarmed Farkhunda. They shouted, "The Americans sent you" and "Kill her."[77] Then the mob beat Farkhunda with fists, feet, and poles and planks of wood. Onlookers filmed the rage on their cell phones. A few policemen futilely tried to pull Farkhunda away. Others stood aside as the mob pummeled her, drove a car over her, thrashed her dead body, and set it on fire.[78]

The gruesome murder enraged thousands of Afghans in Kabul as well as Westerners. Hundreds attended Farkhunda's funeral. Farkhunda became a symbol of the oppression of women, a bitter judgment on years of reform efforts. She is also a sign of what Afghans deemed worth fighting for. I am hard-pressed to find incidents when the menfolk of Kabul spontaneously beat a suspected Taliban to death.

The tension between foreign presence and what it means to be Afghan affected the Taliban, affected the army and police, affected women, and affected the highest levels of government leadership. It affected no single person more than Hamid Karzai.

Karzai had been president of Afghanistan since the end of 2001. He had matured from the intrepid tribal leader of 2001, to the skillful politician of the big tent, and finally into his own leader. The 2009 elections had turned him spiteful and recalcitrant, even hurtful, toward the United States, but he also better claimed to represent Afghans. What Karzai valued—for he never really had goals—differed from America's objectives. Karzai had to value being an Afghan ruler, not a puppet, both for the sake of his own self-worth and for the sake of the legitimacy and survival of his government. He did not define the Taliban as his enemy. His enemies were outsiders who harmed Afghan people, whether terrorists in Pakistan, Pakistan itself, or the United States. Karzai had always been idealistic, caring about peace and disliking violence. The idealism contributed to his weakness as a war leader. He pinned his hopes for peace on the United States pressuring Pakistan to change its policies—hardly the aim of a realist. As the American stay lengthened and forces increased and bombings continued, being an Afghan ruler became tougher and tougher. Karzai pressed more and more to demonstrate that he was no puppet, regardless of the damage to the war effort and his relations with the United States.

President Obama's June 2011 speech had set December 31, 2014, as the end of the US combat mission in Afghanistan. After that date, the mission would change to training and counterterrorism. In order to legalize any residual US presence in the country from the end of 2014 onward, Obama wanted a set of formal agreements with Afghanistan. He signed a strategic partnership agreement with Karzai in May 2012 that established a ten-year relationship and named Afghanistan a major non-NATO ally of the United States. Obama next wanted a bilateral security agreement that would permit US military presence, define what kind of operations the military could undertake without Afghan permission, and determine whether Americans who committed a crime in Afghanistan would be charged under the Afghan or American legal system. The United States had bilateral security agreements with most countries where its troops were stationed.

Karzai and his national security adviser, Rangin Dadfar Spanta, visited Washington from January 8 to 11, 2013, for discussions with President Obama and his team on the US-Afghan relationship after 2014 and the bilateral security agreement. They first met with US national security advisor Tom Donilon at the White House. Donilon told Karzai that after 2014 US forces would focus on fighting al-Qaʻeda and training and advising the army, rather than fighting the Taliban, even if Afghan civilians were under attack. Nor would the United States pressure Pakistan. As Karzai's strategy had revolved around the United States pressuring Pakistan, Donilon's message was unwelcome.

The next day Obama reiterated Donilon's points: "We do not want to fight the Taliban. We do not want to intervene in the conflict between Afghans."[79] Karzai asked: "The presence of safe havens on the soil of Pakistan is a source of the threat to Afghanistan. Do you consider this an internal matter of Afghanistan or do you want to do something about it?" Refusing to be the instrument of Karzai's preferred strategy, Obama answered: "On this matter, we will act in cooperation with your forces . . . But we will not attack Pakistan. We do not want to destabilize Pakistan."[80] He also advised Karzai to temper Afghanistan's relations with India, a country which Karzai admired, to avoid friction with Pakistan. "We will never give Pakistan any right of veto over Afghan foreign policy," Karzai pointedly replied. "We, in the struggle with the Soviet Union, sacrificed countless numbers in defense of our independence and our people will not give up their independence."[81]

Karzai walked away from the meeting miffed. Months later, he confided to Spanta: "That same day that Obama told me that Afghanistan's relations with India should be tempered so as not to provoke Pakistan, as I was leaving the White House, I decided not to sign a security contract with America."[82]

In February 2013, General John Allen turned over command of ISAF and all US and allied forces in Afghanistan to another Marine—General Joseph Dunford, the twelfth commander of US forces and seventh commander of ISAF. Known for his cool head, perceptiveness, and organizational skill, Dunford would play a pivotal role in America's strategy in Afghanistan, first in Kabul and later in Washington.

The United States put great effort went into the negotiation of the bilateral security agreement. Until Afghan presidential elections approached in early 2014, the bilateral security agreement was the top issue for the White House, Ambassador James Cunningham, and General Joseph Dunford. It drowned out other priorities. The United States used its leverage to pressure Karzai to meet its demands on the bilateral security agreement rather than on army and police reforms, peace talks, or preparing for elections.

In a video teleconference on June 22, Obama informed Karzai that "it would be to our advantage if the bilateral security agreement could be signed by October, no later than October" and implied that otherwise the United States would pull all its forces from Afghanistan.[83] The threat was credible. Obama had pulled out all US forces from Iraq in 2011 after negotiations for a bilateral security agreement had fallen through.

The United States had two controversial demands. First, under very select circumstances, night raids and other missions to detain Afghans would continue. Obama saw no reason to leave troops in Afghanistan without freedom to conduct counterterrorism operations. Second, US troops would have immunity from prosecution in an Afghan court for any crimes committed on Afghan soil.

Even if they wondered why a bilateral security agreement was necessary, Afghans aligned with the government generally favored a relationship with the United States, though the civilian casualties and night raids from counterterrorism operations were a sore spot.

Tajiks, Hazaras, and Uzbeks of the old Northern Alliance supported a strong relationship. Concerned about security matters and Pakistan, Bismullah Khan and Atta wanted the United States to continue to support the Afghan army, especially with better equipment.[84] First Vice President Mohammed Fahim, most powerful of the Tajik leaders, was rumored to want to punch Karzai in the face for his obstinance.[85] Karim Khalili, Hazara leader and second vice president, assured US officials, "I asked the president [Karzai]: 'What country has the resources to take the place of the United States?' I told him, 'All the Islamic countries together cannot help Afghanistan like the United States, even the European Union cannot. You must protect the connection with the United States.' "[86]

Women leaders especially wanted the United States around. Shukria Barakzai and Fawzia Koofi lobbied Dunford and Cunningham. Shukria was already concerned that a peace process could undermine women's rights (the bilateral security agreement was playing out at the same time as the negotiations around the opening of a Taliban political office). As deputy of its defense committee, she called for parliament to push Karzai to support the bilateral security agreement and used her direct access to the US military to drive other women to act. At a meeting with General Dunford and female leaders, she stated, "Women's progress to now is not meaningful. It is just for show. . . . Members of parliament must push the government [to sign the bilateral security agreement] or we will be victims."[87] For her part, Fawzia Koofi organized enough signatures in parliament for the bilateral security agreement to be brought up for discussion and possible approval, only to be stymied by Speaker of the Wolesi Jirga Ibrahimi on the instruction of Karzai.[88]

Karzai dug in his heels. He assumed that the United States would stay with or without a bilateral security agreement. Obama's intent solely to counter terrorism, not help Afghanistan or provide security guarantees against Pakistan, annoyed him. Under these conditions, Karzai was uninterested in conceding, particularly on night raids, which he detested for harming innocent Afghans. Karzai's ministers badgered him. They feared losing US military and financial support. Karzai would not budge. Although he allowed a draft agreement to be drawn up with the US demands intact, he refused to sign.

The issue was much deeper than night raids or immunity or Pakistan. Karzai was loath to be the ruler who sold out Afghanistan. Signing the bilateral security agreement meant allowing an occupying power to stay on Afghan soil in return for little. Afghan history vilified Afghan rulers who were party to such agreements, especially if they got a bad deal. From Karzai's point of view, he was being asked to surrender his identity as an Afghan for the sake of a paper agreement when a handshake would have done the trick.

Karzai's disregard for the October deadline for a signature upset Obama. Relations between Karzai and Washington deteriorated to the point that they resembled feuding Pashtuns more than allies. Although McChrystal had temporarily smoothed things over, Karzai had never forgiven Americans for US interference in the 2009 elections. Karzai referred to the United States as "his enemy" in meetings with Afghans.[89] He berated Afghan officials who worked closely with the United States. At one tense moment, he poured invective upon his NDS director, Rahmatullah Nabil, in front the entire cabinet, ordering him to go "report back to your American masters!"[90] It was personal. Karzai's confidantes insulted

Obama and asked their US interlocutors when the United States would elect a new president. US officials amused each other with stories of how Obama hated Karzai. Obama's national security advisor, Susan Rice (who changed over with Donilon in July 2013), writes in her memoirs, "Karzai plainly hated the US, and increasingly many of us (myself included) reviled his vitriolic nationalism, incorrigibly corrupt governance, and pompous leadership style."[91]

Angry at Karzai's intransigence, the White House leaked plans for a "zero option" to the press in which all US forces would pull out at the end of 2014, the training and counterterrorism missions would be scuttled, and funds for the Afghan military would possibly be cut off.

To settle the issue, Karzai convened a loya jirga from November 21 to 24, 2013. Two thousand notable Afghans attended—members of parliament, famous religious scholars, and powerful tribal leaders. They had been selected by governors, tribal councils, the national religious council, and the palace itself. Sibghatullah Mojaddedi, the former president and renowned religious scholar, chaired the jirga. Their task was to decide whether or not the agreement should be signed. The jirga was "consultative," meaning its decisions were nonbinding.

On November 24, the jirga came out of deliberation. Mojaddedi stepped to the podium before the assembled participants. Karzai and his ministers sat in the front row. Television cameras were rolling. Mojaddedi announced the consensus decision: the bilateral security agreement should be signed as soon as possible. With his nation watching, Karzai seized the podium from the elderly Mojaddedi and rejected the decision. He refused to sign the bilateral security agreement unless the United States stopped raiding homes and also took steps toward bringing peace, which was code for pressuring Pakistan to stop the war. Mojaddedi implored Karzai to sign. He threatened to exile himself to Turkey if there was no signature. Karzai was adamant: "From now on the United States will not enter homes! There will be peace! The United States must guarantee it will not kill civilians!"

Americans watching the speech saw folly. Afghans saw a national hero. Karzai's words rang true. It did not matter that plenty of Afghans, perhaps the majority, wanted the agreement signed. Karzai's embodiment of Afghan values of independence and mercy mattered more than his policies. Afghan political leaders groused at Karzai's obstinacy but acceded to him. To cross Karzai was to cross what it meant to be an Afghan. At a cabinet meeting in February 2014, Karzai's ministers tried to convince him to reverse his decision and sign the agreement. Karzai refused. He said he was being pressured like Abdur Rahman Khan had been pressured to draw the Durand Line. He vowed that he would not succumb.[92]

Pashtuns in the countryside hailed Karzai for holding his ground and defending Afghan sovereignty. In their words, he was *pacha*—not president but king. As pacha, Karzai's status rose above that of a tribal leader or a president. While a tribal leader has an obligation to heed consensus, an Afghan king does not. A king is judged by a different standard, expected to stand against adversity, judged partly by the power of his enemies. The United States was the most powerful enemy of all.[93] One of Karzai's Kandahar political rivals informed me, "Karzai has become very strong. Before, he was America's slave. Now he oppresses America, so he is strong."[94] Karzai's Loya Jirga speech even impressed the famously obstinate Gulbuddin Hekmatyar, who sent envoys to Karzai in approbation.[95]

The upside was that the Loya Jirga consensus countered an impression in the White House that the Afghan people hated Americans. Obama eventually decided to wait for a bilateral security agreement until the election of a new president in 2014. Karzai never signed. At the new president's swearing in on September 29 of that year, Karzai offered Spanta a fitting summary of his instincts on the affair: "Spanta, thank God we are pulling our feet out of this battle. If not, many of America's future subversions would have fallen entirely upon our names."[96] An Afghan signature was not imprinted upon the bilateral security agreement until September 30, 2014, and then it was that of Hanif Atmar, the national security advisor of the new president. That new president and his ministers supported the agreement but refused to sign it themselves.

Islam and Afghan history flowed across the war, from Taliban morale and endurance, to insider attacks, to women's rights, and finally to Karzai's unwillingness to sign the bilateral security agreement. Themes of Islam and resistance to foreign intervention were deeply rooted in what it meant to be Afghan. Islam and Afghan identity offered the Taliban an edge—a point of sympathy, morale, and discipline that the government could not match—and served as a point of friction between Westerners and the Afghan people. It would affect the ability of the Afghan government and its police and army to stand on their own after the US drawdown and in turn the very ability of the United States to extricate itself from Afghanistan.

17

The 2014 Elections

American generals and diplomats had long known that 2014 would be a pivotal year for Afghanistan. It was the year of presidential elections and the year President Obama had designated to end the US "combat mission." The elections would conclude Karzai's tenure and, if successful, be another step in solidifying democracy in Afghanistan—the transfer of power from one leader to another. If something went wrong, this single event could precipitate an existential crisis for the Afghan state. There was reason to worry. Past transfers had been marked by violence, bloodshed, and regicide.

It fell to General Joseph Dunford to oversee the drawdown and the security of the election. Unlike Allen, Petraeus, and McChrystal, Dunford was indifferent about Afghanistan. He had visited marines in Helmand many times but this was his first command in the country. He was free of the romance for Afghanistan that many of us had acquired after a few tours. He had served in Iraq for nearly two years straight from 2003 to 2005. In his experience, expecting things to improve was naïve; the United States was unlikely to change countries as war-torn as Iraq or Afghanistan.

For Dunford, Afghanistan was solely about stopping terrorists from harming the United States. A heavy presence and nation-building were uncalled for. He often told his generals "go deep, not wide" and "keep the main thing, the main thing." He was especially strict when it came to force protection. He believed it morally irresponsible to put American lives in harm's way in a drawdown. Troops continued to advise and conduct missions, often seeing combat, but on a selective basis. Dunford instructed his generals, "We're risking lives for strategic and operational reasons. Not tactical."[1]

The United States and NATO planned to withdraw from combat operations in Afghanistan by the end of 2014 in accordance with the plan President Obama had outlined in June 2011. The 68,000 US troops were to draw down to a much smaller number by December 31, 2014, and combat operations were to end. At the beginning of 2013, those 68,000 US troops were in more than 800 posts and bases in Afghanistan. Eighteen months later, 30,000 troops would remain in 58 posts and bases.

During 2013 and 2014 another lengthy Washington debate over Afghanistan played out, this time over how many troops would stay after 2014 in advisory, training, and counterterrorism roles. Obama wanted a very small number of a few thousand, if any at all. He doubted that a longer military presence to assist the government was worthwhile. He had no interest in confronting the Taliban. What Obama did think important was disrupting any terrorist plots against the United States. A large military presence, let alone arguing with President Obama, was not Dunford's priority. Nevertheless, he calculated that, if Obama sought to continue counterterrorism operations, more than a few thousand troops would be advised. The debate occurred alongside the negotiations with an obstinate Karzai for a bilateral security agreement.

It was in this context that Obama put complete withdrawal, "the zero option," on the table. The *New York Times* endorsed the zero option in a series of articles and editorials.[2] Various administration officials have since claimed that Obama deeply wanted out. In 2009 and 2011, Obama had been unwilling to consider all-out withdrawal as an option. Why had he changed his mind? For one, the 2009–2011 surge had dispelled any notion that US military forces could improve the trajectory of the country. Of equal importance, the terrorist threat appeared manageable. If terrorists returned to Afghanistan, the United States might handle them with out-of-country counterterrorism operations. In the course of the debate, his national security council staffers told military officers that Afghanistan was no bigger an interest than Somalia, Yemen, or any other country with terrorists. Additionally, Obama judged the Afghans questionable partners at best. The Kabul Bank scandal, insider attacks of 2012, and Karzai's bilateral security agreement stubbornness strained Obama's patience.

Discussion between White House and Pentagon officials could be caustic. The old wounds from the surge had not fully healed. Obama viewed generals and the Department of Defense with some suspicion. Dunford tried to avoid lobbying and simply present the minimum capabilities that would be needed to meet Obama's intent. The debate would span 16 months.

By 2012, the vast majority of Taliban leaders had not heard Mullah Omar's voice for years. Rumors had surfaced from time to time of his demise. They had been false but his health was deteriorating. Conventional wisdom was that Omar was living in Karachi under the protection of the ISI (Pakistan military intelligence). After 2015, increasing evidence came out that Omar had been living in a simple house in seclusion in Zabul. He evidently refused medical treatment.[3]

One story among the Taliban is that during his last days, all but alone in Zabul, ill and contemplative, Omar reconsidered his 2001 refusal to turn bin Laden over to the United States. Supposedly the years of sacrifice and the loss of his emirate caused him to regret the decision. He realized the emirate could have stayed in power and Afghanistan would have dodged years of war. Or so the story goes. It would be ironic if Omar had come to see 2001 as a missed opportunity for peace, as had many Americans.[4]

Omar never appointed a successor, possibly because doing so could divide loyalties while he remained alive. Bin Laden advised the stricken Omar as much in a 2011 letter. Seemingly aware of Omar's illness, bin Laden wrote, "For the opposition in Afghanistan to appear before the world as united, I ask you not to appoint a future leader in the country."[5]

In 2012 Omar's condition worsened significantly. He never recovered. In April 2013, Mullah Mohammed Omar, Emir al-Momineen, passed away.[6]

Mullah Omar's brother and son met with ranking Taliban religious scholars, including head of the religious council Maulawi Haybatullah, and then notified Mansour. The group decided to cover up Mullah Omar's death. Omar's family wanted it so and the religious scholars worried the news and process of selecting a new leader could disturb the movement. They argued it was a complex time. The movement was still recovering from the surge. The United States was in the process of drawing down. The news could affect the US decision, raise army and police morale, or weaken Taliban morale.[7] Only Abdul Qayum Zakir, Jalaluddin Haqqani, and a few others were in the loop. Supposedly, Haybatullah and the religious council issued a fatwa that sanctioned the secret until the movement grew powerful and "enemy" morale had weakened.[8] Then, a new leader would be openly selected. In the meantime, Mansour was permitted to lead.

The Taliban rank and file, cadre leaders, and governors were in the dark. They obeyed Mansour as Omar's appointed deputy. Mansour and the inner circle drafted annual Eid messages from Mullah Omar and fabricated instructions. Taliban unity was such that there was little dissent for some time. Mansour and the Quetta Shura managed to run the Taliban fairly effectively for two more years—until new challenges outed the secret.

Mullah Omar's silent passing befits a leader whose role had become spiritual. Omar ended his life as a symbol for the Taliban of faithful determination and unity. He had never wavered in his lifelong struggle against occupation. Under his rule, the Taliban had formed, run a state, survived defeat, and reemerged. He forged unity by stressing obedience and structuring the movement to have a clear chain of command. The movement's ideal, however, was Afghanistan's bane. That same faithful determination had been closed to chances for peace and loyal to al-Qa'eda. His penultimate act—secluding himself—blessed violence by withdrawing from a place where he best could curb excesses or call for peace. Omar's unstoppable determination fueled two decades of war and destruction. The implications would carry beyond his death.

The Taliban summer offensive of 2013 was a prelude for 2014. The number of "enemy initiated attacks"—the US military's metric for violence in the country—was roughly the same as 2011 and 2012. The size of insurgent assaults increased, however. The Taliban occasionally gathered in groups of 50 to as many as 600 and tried to capture Afghan posts—a rare event in 2011 or 2012. Meanwhile, as part of the drawdown, the United States and its allies cut combat support for the Afghan army and police. US air strikes rarely came in to help. US soldiers and marines joined soldiers and police in battle even less.

The northern Helmand district of Sangin was especially hard hit. A battle of attrition dragged on all summer long, inflicting 500 casualties upon the police and army. Raees Baghrani, the great tribal leader of northern Helmand, explained how the Taliban fought against the government: "In the Sangin battle, Taliban came from all over northern Helmand. From Kajaki, Nowzad, Musa Qala, and Baghran, they came to fight. They would attack, go home, and then come back for another battle."[9] The brunt of the fighting fell upon the police and local police (the Afghan local police, or ALP, program that had been started in 2010 to recruit tribal militia and place them under the police) that garrisoned the villages. The army commanders preferred to stay in their well-fortified bases along the main road and closer to the district center.[10] The Alikozai police and local police (the Sangin Alikozai had been siding with the government since 2010) fought hard. Alikozai women even helped find improvised explosive devices and cooked for the police and army. But week after week on the front line, doing the job of the army proved too much for many tribesmen. In the course of the summer, half the Alikozai local police, invaluable because of their local knowledge, deserted.[11]

Finally, in September, provincial police chief Hakim Angar (himself Alikozai) quarterbacked a counteroffensive.[12] He sent 300 police north and convinced General Sayid Malouk, the army corps commander, to send 300 soldiers too. Angar called up his most combat-effective police chiefs—Hekmatullah from Gereshk (son of the stout Barakzai warlord, Malim Mir Wali) and Omar Jan from Nad Ali (the brother of Gul Mullah from Marjah)—along with a detachment of their best men. Omar Jan was almost 40 years old with a short, full black beard, a perpetual scowl, and prayer beads hanging from his wrist. He had been in charge of Nad Ali for two years and had established a robust force of 600 police and local police. He took great pains to supply his men, both through the official system and out of his own pocket. He went north with men who had served with him for years.

Angar put Hekmatullah and Omar Jan at the forefront of a counterattack against Taliban-captured villages. The only support from the army was artillery fire. The soldiers laid their cannons to fire directly onto targets from their bases overlooking the villages. The police stormed the villages and over five days pushed out the Taliban. Marine advisors commended the aggressiveness of Hekmatullah and Omar Jan in leading their men forward. Their squads often outflanked the Taliban or cut off their escape routes. At one point, Taliban retreated onto their own improvised explosive devices and blew themselves up. Eight police were wounded in the assault. None were killed. Taliban were reported to have suffered more than 100 casualties.[13] Malim Mir Wali, Hekmatullah's father, received reports that wounded Taliban in a Quetta hospital were crying "Hekmatullah wounded us!"[14]

Elsewhere in the country, the army and police sometimes stood up better, sometimes worse, sometimes losing ground, and in a few provinces—Kunar, Kandahar, and Logar—gaining it. Stalemate came at a cost. Casualties were higher than ever before. Fourteen thousand Afghan soldiers and police were killed or wounded, roughly half by improvised explosive devices, roughly half in firefights. Afghan casualties are not surprising. Few armies in the world shared the low casualty rate of the US armed forces afforded by body armor, lavish close air support, specially designed armored vehicles, and expensive medical care. Replacements over the year made up for the casualties, although in several districts generals and police chiefs failed to rebuild damaged units. The Taliban attacks and problems in the army and police foreshadowed things to come.

As 2013 progressed, Afghan attention shifted to the upcoming elections. As in 2009, elections in Afghanistan could have two rounds. The first included every candidate. Anyone who won more than 50 percent of the vote would become president. If no one did, the election would go to a second round between the top two vote-winners. The winner of that second round would be president. The independent election commission, a body of technocrats trained by the United Nations and non-governmental organizations (NGOs), would conduct the elections. The international community had stopped supervising Afghan elections after the 2005 parliamentary elections.

The big difference between the two previous Afghan presidential elections and 2014 was that Karzai was forbidden by law to run. In 2004 and 2009, he had won votes from all ethnicities. In both years he had avoided a second-round, fairly in 2004, fraudulently in 2009. In 2014, the Pashtuns lacked a unifying figure, let alone someone who could reach across to the Tajiks. In August 2013, 17 Afghans declared their candidacy. The number eventually whittled down to 11. Ten were Pashtun. Only Dr. Abdullah, who had run and lost in 2009, was Tajik.[15] Several of the Pashtun candidates were well known: Ashraf Ghani, brilliant scholar, World Bank expert, and creator of the Afghan Ministry of Finance; Abdul Raouf Sayyaf, snowy-bearded mujahideen warlord; Gul Agha Sherzai, rich from years in Jalalabad; Zalmay Rassoul, Karzai's foreign minister; and Qayum Karzai, Karzai's brother. The large number of Pashtun candidates split the Pashtun vote. Early on, various Pashtun leaders, including Ashraf Ghani, had tried to build a consensus ticket so as to collect enough votes to avoid a second round. Those efforts came to naught. The main Pashtun candidates hung on.

Karzai's backroom politics before the first round are a mystery. Openly, Karzai supported no one. Privately, he convinced Zalmay Rassoul to run. At the same time, he promised Ghani his support and suggested Uzbek warlord Abdur Rashid Dostum as vice presidential running mate. Karzai's allies and friends thought he was shifting between candidates, backing one and then another. Late in the race, he ordered his brother Qayum to pull out, shrewdly realizing that the international community would accuse him of rigging and might intervene if his own brother ran. On a deeper level, Karzai seemed to understand that Afghanistan's democracy would be damaged if the brother of its first president won the first democratic transition. He told his cousin, "I cannot support my brother. . . . I am the first Afghan president. If I was the 15th or 16th president, it would be different. But I was basically appointed."[16] In terms of restraint, Karzai's neutrality was laudable. The downside was that his maneuvering left Pashtuns unsure whom to support.

Abdullah was soon running strongly ahead. With their important role in the affairs of Afghanistan over three decades, Tajik leaders felt the time had come when a Tajik might be president. They interpreted comments from Pashtuns or Westerners to the contrary, in the words of Amarullah Saleh, as a kind of "prejudice against them."[17] A danger emerged that the Tajiks would rally around Abdullah and drive an ethnic divide with the Pashtuns.

The danger increased on March 9, 2014, when First Vice President Mohammed Fahim unexpectedly died of a heart attack. Fahim had been the Pashtuns' best ally among the Tajiks. During Karzai's tenure, he had mediated between the two ethnic groups.[18] Through him, Karzai had maintained an effective alliance with the powerful Panjshiri bloc. The alliance had prevented the Tajiks from uniting behind Abdullah in 2009, and the Pashtuns and Tajiks from polarizing into two camps. With Fahim's passing, the vast majority of Tajiks rallied around Abdullah.[19] The chances of a second round ethnic stand-off were growing.

Singed by the Afghan backlash to US interference in the 2009 elections, in 2014, US leaders scrupulously stayed out of election politics. The White House, Secretary of State John Kerry, Ambassador James Cunningham, and General Dunford thought the dangers of blowback far outweighed the benefits of backing any particular candidate. None were confident America could select the best candidate anyway. Just about every candidate asked for American support at one time or another. They were always informed that the United States would respect the vote of the Afghan people and the outcome of the election and support no one.

The Taliban had their own plans for 2014. The 2013 fighting season had been a warm-up. Mansour and Zakir would not sit out 2014 and wait for the United States and its allies to withdraw. They planned to disrupt the elections. Taliban provincial governors went to their provinces from winter refuge in Pakistan to organize and plan. More Taliban governors were now working out of their provinces than had been the case in 2011 or 2012.

A series of attacks started in January against foreigners in Kabul—marked by massacres by gunmen at the Lebanese restaurant and the Serena hotel—and accelerated in the weeks before elections into almost daily strikes on high profile targets, such as the headquarters of the international election commission.

The first round nevertheless occurred on time on April 5. The Taliban launched approximately 400 attacks, roughly the same number as election day 2009. They shot at polling stations, attacked police posts, and fired off rockets. Voters were surprisingly defiant. In spite of attacks, 6.6 million voted, far more than the 4 million who had voted in 2009, fewer than the 8 million who had voted in 2004. In Ghazni, people voted within sight of Taliban attacks on police posts. In Kunar, men and women repeatedly took cover when Taliban shot at their polling station and then repeatedly lined back up once shooting had ceased. In the southern provinces of Kandahar and Helmand, many tribal leaders convinced Taliban kin to stand down so that tribal candidates for provincial council seats could win. In the words of a prominent religious leader from Jalalabad, "the election was a success for the government. The Taliban put out propaganda and threatened people, but many, many people participated."[20]

In terms of results, Abdullah nearly won, with 45 percent of the vote, just under the 50 percent needed to avert a second round. Ghani came in second with 33 percent. The other Pashtun candidates trailed 20 or more points behind. Given the number of Pashtun candidates and the fact the Pashtuns were not united behind any of them, it was no surprise that Abdullah came in first or that there would be a second round.

According to a variety of Afghan government officials, turnout for the first round of elections disconcerted the Quetta Shura. In the round's aftermath, Mansour, tarnished, relieved military commission chief Abdul Qayum Zakir, a clutch of district governors, and the provincial governors of Herat, Helmand, and Kandahar. The election defeat may have given Mansour justification to move against his rival Zakir. Sardar Ibrahim, a leader from the first Taliban regime, replaced Zakir as chief of the military commission. New field commanders were assigned and new orders were issued for upcoming operations. Low-level commanders had to return to Quetta to be switched out or to meet with new superiors. Over half the Taliban fighters in Helmand returned to Pakistan or northern Helmand to receive orders and account for their weapons and equipment.[21] Angry at being dismissed, Zakir criticized Mansour for appointing new leaders from his own Ishaqzai tribe.[22] Mansour earned a reputation for favoring the Ishaqzai. Calls came forth for Mullah Omar to step forward and put things in order. Amazingly, Mansour managed to hide Omar's death.

Discord within the leadership proved temporary. Over the weeks after the first round of the elections, Mansour was able to assert his authority. One of Zakir's Alizai tribesmen put it, "Zakir's removal means little. The Taliban are not tribal like the government. They agree with each other. They are disciplined."[23] Zakir grudgingly obeyed orders and took a seat on the Quetta Shura.

The most important effect of the first round of elections was on US policymaking. In spring 2014, General Dunford laid out options to President Obama for US presence after 2014. Obama had signaled in a variety of Washington meetings that he wanted out. Dunford's options included going to zero but he recommended around 8,000 to 12,000 in order to continue to strike terrorists and prevent the defeat of the Kabul government. Dunford's logic was that Obama had told him that the main goal was to prevent terrorist attacks on the United States. To do that, he assessed the United States would need to maintain counterterrorism pressure—drone strikes and special operations raids—on terrorist groups. For those operations to continue effectively, the Afghan government had to survive. Dunford assessed that if any of the key cities fell, Kabul itself would be in danger. Therefore, he proposed placing advisors at the corps headquarters near each of the key cities: Kabul, Mazar-e-Sharif, Herat, Kandahar, and Jalalabad.

Dunford did not get hung up over the numbers or lobby for his recommendation or argue about how long US forces should stay after 2014. He told Obama what he thought would be needed to suppress the terrorist threat at that very moment. He did not sweeten the pot with predictions that these forces could stabilize the country and the United States could then complete the drawdown. He harbored no illusion that the Afghan government could someday somehow handle things on its own. The military presence could only suppress the terrorist threat as long as it was there. Once removed, the government would regress and the threat would return. "This is term life insurance," Dunford said. "It's only good as long as you pay." His thoughts diverged from the idea that Eikenberry had first proposed that the United States could hand off the war to the Afghan government. Dunford was articulating a new strategic concept, one of simply preventing failure and suppressing terrorists with as few forces as possible. Nothing more. It would become the de facto US strategy.

Dunford wisely stayed out of the press and avoided any action that could be perceived as boxing in the president. He closely guarded his recommendation in order to prevent debate from becoming politicized. He did not want anyone pressuring the president. While debate over US troops presence in Afghanistan could be heated, the divide of 2009 did not reopen.

After further discussions and a face-to-face meeting with Dunford, Obama accepted the basics of the recommendation. Obama was willing to leave a select number of troops in Afghanistan temporarily. He recognized that the fall of the government could allow al-Qaʻeda or other terrorist groups greater freedom to strike the United States. Forces were to stay for two years until the end of the Obama administration.

The success of the first round of elections had something to do with the decision. It signaled to Obama and his national security council staff that people in Afghanistan believed in their political system and that the Afghan army and police could resist the Taliban. Afghanistan looked less like an investment bound to fail. The 2013 Loya Jirga where Afghans voiced their support for a long-term US presence also helped—in spite of Karzai's obstinacy. Upon visiting Afghanistan right after the jirga, National Security Advisor Susan Rice had looked at everything going on and realized "we can't just pull the plug on all this."

Obama was still ostensibly withdrawing, just not immediately. By the end of his term, US military forces in Afghanistan were to be gone. The exit was underway. For the first time, a US president had decided to leave Afghanistan.

On May 27, 2014, Obama announced that 9,800 US troops would stay through 2015, drawing down to 5,500 in 2016, and just an embassy by the beginning of 2017. They would be based in five locations: Kabul, Bagram (north of Kabul), Jalalabad (the airfield and the army corps headquarters), Kandahar, and Khost. The Italians and Germans would keep advisors in Herat and Mazar-e-Sharif respectively. Most of the 9,800 Americans would advise and train the Afghan army and, to a lesser extent, the police. They would not go into combat. Obama did not consider the Taliban a threat and did not want to be dragged back into fighting them. A special operations contingent would continue to target al-Qaʻeda. In addition, it was planned that the United States and the international community would spend $3.6 billion per year from 2015 to 2017 on the police and army. As had been the case for much of its history, Afghanistan was too poor to pay for its own army and police.

Obama's words underlined his feelings: "The bottom line is, it's time to turn the page on more than a decade in which so much of our foreign policy was focused on the wars in Afghanistan and Iraq . . . I think Americans have learned that it's harder to end wars than it is to begin them."[24]

The advance of Ghani and Abdullah to the second round, scheduled for June, was a milestone in Afghanistan's political history. Instead of a Durrani Pashtun, widely accepted as the country's ruling class, the presidency would fall to a Ghilzai Pashtun or a Tajik. If elected, either candidate would have to overcome the baggage of Afghanistan's tribal and ethnic history.

Ashraf Ghani had been working for the Afghan government since 2002, with one break between 2005 and 2009. Absent from the country after 1977, the jihad and civil war had left him untainted. His doctorate from Columbia University and World Bank experience endowed him with extensive connections in the West. Upon returning to Afghanistan, he had become Karzai's master planner, redesigning the ministry of finance and ministry of rural reconstruction and development, and then moved on to become chancellor of Kabul University. He ran for president in 2009 and after a rather poor showing returned to work under Karzai. He believed deeply in institutional reform. "Dysfunctionality of civil institutions is our biggest problem," he told a gathering of Western ambassadors in 2013. "Segments of the ministry of interior function but not all. Few line ministries work."[25] Karzai's cabinet was treated to stern lectures on how "eighty percent of terrorism is caused by bad governance."[26] Ghani was short-tempered with those who got in his way, especially the old warlords, and warm toward the younger generation of eastern Pashtuns in Kabul who shared his reforming zeal. He vowed to General Dunford, "The time of Amanullah Khan has an unfinished chapter," referring to Afghanistan's liberalizing king of the 1920s.[27]

The dapper Abdullah also had extensive experience. Between his days with Massoud and then as Karzai's foreign minister, Tajiks widely viewed Abdullah as their most prominent leader. Abdullah was more moderate than Ghani and often compromised for the greater good, exemplified by how he stepped aside for Karzai in the 2009 presidential election crisis.

In the two months between the first and second round, Afghanistan's ethnic divides suddenly reappeared. For 12 years, Karzai had been able to bridge the rift. Ghani and Abdullah lacked Karzai's legitimacy. They could not reach beyond their own ethnic and tribal groups. Ghani's camp attracted Pashtuns. Abdullah's camp attracted Tajiks and Hazaras as well as a coterie of Pashtun warlords such as Abdul Raouf Sayyaf, Gul Agha Sherzai, and Sher Mohammed Akhundzada. Many Pashtuns railed against the idea that a Tajik could be president. Dr. Ayubi, a Pashtun member of parliament, exclaimed to me, "If Abdullah wins, there will be a great crisis. . . . Pashtuns will be cut out. . . . al-Qa'eda is not my enemy. Abdullah is my enemy!"[28] Eastern Pashtuns flocked to Ghani and embraced ethnic rhetoric. Southern Pashtuns were less hard line, preferring Ghani but unenthusiastic about an election without a Durrani candidate.[29]

Shukria Barakzai, still a member of parliament for Kabul, was one of the southern Pashtuns who went over to Ghani. She had hoped to run for president herself but had never committed. Sherzai had asked her to be his vice presidential running mate. She had declined that too. She doubted Afghanistan was ready for a woman. Once part of Ghani's team, she became a critic of Tajik leaders in the government. On the other side, Fawzia Koofi, also still a member of parliament (for Badakhshan), was part of Dr. Abdullah's leadership "board." Like

Shukria, she had explored a run for president but narrowly missed the age re-quirement. Maulali Ishaqzai, who had been their colleague in parliament until she had crossed Ahmed Wali Karzai, sat things out. Ever the player, she thought Karzai, her erstwhile patron then adversary, should reign. Echoing Machiavelli, she remarked, "In politics, there is no truth."[30]

The eastern Pashtuns, especially the pro-reform young generation, campaigned relentlessly for Ghani. They eschewed the big tent politics of Karzai in favor of exclusion of the Tajiks and warlords (minus Dostum whom they saw as a necessary evil). In order to win, eastern Pashtun government officials and members of the independent election commission prepared large-scale fraud. No evidence exists that Ghani or Karzai ordered the fraud. Supporters, in-cluding members of Karzai's staff, did it on their own initiative, including, most egregiously, the chief executive officer of the independent election commission, Zia Amir Khel. Many of the commission's young Pashtun technocrats favored Ghani and did not let their Western educations get in the way. High-ranking election commission officials reputedly told members of the Abdullah campaign that they could not abide a non-Pashtun as president. The fact that Ghani trailed Abdullah in the first round by 13 percentage points encouraged fraud. Ghani supporters thought they could lose without it.[31]

The second round of the elections took place on June 14. Total attacks were around 300 compared to 400 for the first round. Again, few materialized in the south. Attacks in the east were lighter than the first round, partly because eastern Pashtuns (Ghilzais) wanted to vote for Ghani. Rumors that the Taliban sided with Ghani and ordered people to vote were partially true. Certain members of the Quetta Shura were complicit in election day truces. Right before elec-tion day, Ghani had flown to Dubai and deceived Taliban representatives that he would delay signing the bilateral security agreement and press for US with-drawal from Afghanistan if the Taliban encouraged people to vote for him and reduced violence in parts of the country.[32] Elsewhere, especially in Paktiya and Khost, tribal leaders convinced many, if far from all, local Taliban commanders to hold back.[33] A few Taliban commanders later admitted to allowing people to vote in certain areas. They had not wanted Abdullah and their old Northern Alliance enemies to win.

Turnout was low, probably between 4 and 6 million people. International observers and journalists, district governors and police chiefs, tribal and reli-gious leaders reported that fewer people voted than in the first round. Lines at polling stations were short and streets were empty. Pashtun district governors and police chiefs readily admitted that voting closed early in the day and that few people had shown up. In their official reports, district governors throughout the country gave a low turnout figure, tallied from the exact number of voters from all the polling stations in their district. Voting was particularly sparse in

Kandahar and Helmand, where the average Durrani Pashtun cared little for either candidate. Yet, at the end of the day, to the disbelief of the international community and just about every Afghan I have ever met, the independent election commission claimed more than 7 million had voted.

Fraud was rampant. Tribal leaders, government officials, and even election officials stuffed ballots for Ghani. Independent election commission chief executive officer Amir Khel directed part of the effort. It was particularly bad in the east and the south. The commission claimed that 1,100,000 people had voted in Paktika, Paktiya, and Khost, and 250,000 in Kunar. These numbers begged credulity, either approaching or exceeding the estimated voting population of these provinces. Ghani's campaign was well organized and may have won more clean votes than Abdullah's. That could not change the fact that fraud was quite obvious. Abdullah's campaign stuffed too—but without the gusto of their rival.

The Abdullah camp was furious and complained to the election commission. Their complaints went unanswered. They then petitioned the United Nations and US Embassy but were told to "follow the process," which they interpreted to mean "concede to Ghani." Ghani's prolific social media and publicity campaign broadcast his supposed lead, which further panicked the Abdullah camp. They could see popular opinion running away from them.[34] "Even if I do not win, Ghani should not win," Abdullah told his leadership team. On June 21, a week after elections, in order to show his objection, Abdullah launched demonstrations in Kabul. They lasted off and on until July 4 and were almost entirely peaceful. The Abdullah team also released evidence of fraud on the part of election commission chief executive officer Amir Khel, who resigned. Still, the Afghan government and election commission did little to address their concerns. The United States, United Nations, and other embassies deliberated over what to do, letting the counting process drive on.

Sectarian rhetoric on Facebook and social media exploded. Ghani supporters cursed Tajiks and claimed only a Pashtun had the right to rule Afghanistan. Abdullah supporters accused Ghani of being a communist.

The political crisis brought the Abdullah camp—the old Northern Alliance—to the brink of secession.[35] As the vote count progressed and the independent election commission ignored their complaints, they grew more and more frustrated. In early July, the independent election commission was ready to announce preliminary results that heavily favored Ghani. The old mujahideen commanders backing Abdullah felt that Karzai, Ghani, and even the international community were spitting in their faces. Convinced that the commission was rigging the count against them, the Abdullah camp concocted a scheme for the northern and western provinces to secede. They also considered seizing power in Kabul by force. They felt they had no alternative. In their minds, it was shameful to bow to what they saw as a Pashtun attempt to hold onto power illegally. The consequences of violence for Afghanistan were secondary. As one Abdullah supporter explained, "War is better than accepting a corrupt vote. We have had 40 years of war. We do not mind it. We are ready to go back to war in an instant."[36] Tajiks could not forget the blood they had shed for Afghanistan, in the jihad, against the Taliban regime, and since 2001, epitomized by the memory of Massoud. "Why are Tajiks denied the right to be president?" asked Mirdab al-Haj Njrabi, a thoughtful Tajik member of parliament. "Tajiks are most of the army and do the fighting and suffer casualties. But the Tajiks get no privileges. They have stolen our rights. They have stolen our democracy."[37]

Abdullah's most powerful supporters—Balkh governor Mohammed Atta, Hazara leader Mohammed Mohaqqeq, and former NDS director Amarullah Saleh—began distributing weapons and mobilizing. A plan was considered to rush the palace itself.[38] Fawzia Koofi, on Abdullah's leadership board, searched for paths to a settlement and conferred with the United Nations. Since long before 2014, she had been worried elections could set the stage for civil violence. But she too promised the US military she would "vote for a new government if I have to."[39]

Karzai probably could have mediated the crisis. His stature in Afghanistan was unrivaled. He stood back. Rumor spread that he wanted the crisis to worsen in order to extend his presidency. He conveyed to certain close friends that it was not his job to fix the crisis and that, as president, he was obliged to stay out of it.

Unfortunately, Karzai and the independent election commission disregarded the Abdullah camp's warnings. On July 7, over the objections of the United States and the United Nations, the independent election commission released the election results, with Ghani at 56 percent and Abdullah at 43 percent of the vote. Karzai evidently had ordered the independent election commission chairman to do it. The announcement drove the Abdullah camp mad. That night, Ghani and Abdullah supporters got into fistfights, shouting matches, and a few shoot-outs in the streets of Kabul. Tajik neighborhoods set up community defenses, usually manned by Tajik police. Young men from youth movements associated with the campaign darted about the city distributing weapons.[40] Police in Ranger pickups joined pro-Abdullah demonstrations, chanting, "Death to fraudsters!"[41]

The morning of July 8, Abdullah gathered all his supporters together in the Loya Jirga tent. The plan was to secede from the government of Afghanistan. A relative of Ahmed Shah Massoud explained their mood to me:

> The Abdullah camp is very angry. They are not thinking. They feel the election was stolen from them in 2009, . . . So now if they do not win or the process is perceived as unfair, they are willing to fight. They have lived in hardship for years. They are willing to experience more. If you have nothing, in war, there is nothing to lose.[42]

At this moment, the United States intervened. President Obama called Abdullah and walked him down, promising that Secretary of State John Kerry would come to Afghanistan to mediate the crisis. Key leaders within Abdullah's camp later said it was only Obama's call that had dissuaded Abdullah from declaring a parallel government. The meeting in the Loya Jirga tent that followed was a spectacle. Abdullah's supporters tore down pictures of President Karzai. During Abdullah's speech, the crowd chanted for secession. Abdullah asked them to wait until Kerry had a chance to mediate. The enraged crowd chanted on. They declared Abdullah their new president and adorned him with ceremonial headgear and cloaks, even as he told them he needed more time.

Afghan leaders and officials feared that an official announcement of election results could spark demonstrations and then violence in Kabul, which could trigger revolt in the provinces. In mixed provinces, Pashtun and Tajik communities could take up arms against each other. A Ghani campaign leader worried: "Badakhshan, Mazar-e-Sharif, Panjshir, and Parwan could go over entirely to Abdullah. Other northern provinces are divided. There are many Pashtuns. War could break out between different communities."[43] Dai al Haq, a Tajik religious leader and deputy minister with Abdullah, said, "Everyone is going to their own ethnic group: Tajiks and Farsiwans versus Pashtuns. Education doesn't matter. Policies don't matter. Just ethnicity matters."[44]

The crisis affected the Afghan army. Dunford received widespread reports that if Abdullah seceded the army's Tajiks would follow. Tajik soldiers watched Abdullah's speech about secession on July 8 with tears in their eyes. After the speech, several Tajik brigade commanders flew to Kabul to receive instructions from the Abdullah camp. Officers in the north called Fawzia Koofi and stated, "We must defend our vote or we will defend ourselves."[45] Bismullah Khan pledged to Dunford as well as Abdullah that he was a "soldier" and neutral. He did nothing out of line but his very history as a Panjshiri mujahideen questioned where his loyalties ultimately lay. Dunford judged that soldiers from the north and west could not be expected to fight and die in the east and south for a country that would no longer be their own. Without the army, the south and east would be in peril.

Under these circumstances, Dunford and Ambassador Cunningham decided that Ghani and Abdullah were driving themselves off a cliff. They might be willing to face off in dueling parallel governments. Obama would not be, and could call it quits. Kerry saw the same thing and was worried congressional support would break, many members being "ready to wash their hands of Afghanistan."[46]

Kerry arrived on July 11. After two days of mediating between Abdullah and Ghani, he worked out an agreement for votes to be audited and for a political power-sharing framework. He broke through by turning to Ghani and ruling, "Ashraf, you're going to be president. Abdullah will help you implement a common agenda. But you have to be willing to transfer real power to him and give the opportunity to share in governance."[47] Abdullah would occupy a new job of "chief executive officer." The new position would be extra-constitutional and a source of confusion. Abdullah left with the impression he would have power of appointment over half of government positions. Ghani left with the impression that Abdullah's powers would be more limited. Both candidates wanted an audit process, which they saw as necessary to justify their respective demands. Although upset at the slight to Afghan sovereignty, Karzai endorsed the intervention, calling it a "bitter pill."

The recount process dragged on for another two months as the two teams bickered over the details of power-sharing. US ambassador James Cunningham and UN representative Jan Kubis met with the candidates and the international election commission almost daily to coax agreement. Secretary Kerry returned in August to push talks along.

In September, Karzai finally mediated in a more forceful fashion. He called together the major mujahideen commanders and the two candidates in a council that he personally chaired. At the same time, Obama and Kerry phoned both candidates again and again and pressed them to compromise. On September 21 the two sides came to an agreement. Under the leadership of the president, the chief executive officer would oversee the activities of the ministries yet ultimate authority and power of appointment would continue to rest with the president. A constitutional loya jirga would be held before September 2016 in order to revisit the structure of the unity government. A few hours later, the independent election commission announced Ashraf Ghani had won the recount. In order to prevent controversy, neither Ghani's margin of victory nor the number of invalidated ballots was disclosed. On September 29, Ghani was inaugurated.

Taliban relished the political discord surrounding the elections. One Taliban cadre commander from Ghazni who was interviewed during the election crisis boasted, "You can imagine our influence from the election: after 13 years, still the whole world and the Afghan puppet government is not able to hold an election."[48] Another, from Paktiya, echoed him: "You can now see that the [election result] is not accepted by either puppet candidate. Election is not the solution for Afghanistan's war. The only way to solve the problem is to join jihad and topple down the government and re-establish the Islamic Emirate."[49] Friends of the Taliban often quoted a Pashtun proverb, "Other peoples' quarrels are free entertainment." For its part, the Quetta Shura considered the election crisis a demonstration of how democracy had failed in Afghanistan and that Islam was the sole effective form of government.[50]

Karzai had tried to unite Afghans under one big tent—even as he divided and conquered the Pashtuns. He had subdued ethnic and political divisions, helped by his Popalzai heritage. The election crisis had reawakened those divisions. It had also damaged the credibility of elections in the eyes of the people. Democracy had been unable to elect a new government and instead had split the government into mutually suspicious camps. People were disappointed. Afghanistan's democracy was more fractured than at any time since 2001. Maulali Ishaqzai commented, "Democracy has been shamed in Afghanistan."[51]

The unity government was an experiment with an uncertain future. US leaders had hoped that the transfer of power would strengthen Afghan democracy. It turned out to be a strategic setback. The new unity government would have difficulty running itself effectively. Instead of producing a government that could stand on its own, the elections produced a government born of US mediation and dependent on further US mediation to survive.

After the second round of the elections, the Taliban intensified attacks on the government. Mansour believed that there were so few Americans that a larger-scale offensive could be risked. Pakistani ISI officers may have encouraged him. He and the Quetta Shura might also have been emboldened by the sweeping success of the Islamic State of Iraq and Syria (ISIS), which had captured Mosul and northern Iraq in June 2014.[52]

By this time, roughly 25,000 US and 14,000 allied troops were left in Afghanistan, posted in one or two bases per province in the south and east and almost absent from the north and west. No longer were US or allied soldiers in the districts ready to help the Afghan soldiers and police. Like Mansour, Taliban fighters and the lower ranking commanders had noticed the drawdown and were ready to test the army and police. As one Taliban religious leader from Ghazni explained, "Here in Ghazni, Taliban are quite safe now, because Americans are now less active or even not active at all. Their air force is used from time to time but on a daily basis Taliban operate openly in all districts and even in the city."[53] Because of their experience in the 2013 fighting season, Taliban fighters and commanders expected that the United States would drop few bombs in support of the Afghan police and army.

During January and February, Taliban units of 3 to 10 men—sized for improvised explosive devices and hit and run attacks—had grouped into larger cadres of 15 to 50—sized for firefights. Teenagers had been taken out of madrasas on the Pakistani frontier and trained in border towns such as Baram Chah in Helmand. Training centered on how to fight the army and police face to face.

Taliban numbers increased over the winter and spring as Karzai released more and more prisoners. In 2013, the United States had turned over the thousands of Afghans its forces had imprisoned over the previous 12 years to the Afghan government. Many were hardened insurgents. Others were innocents. Karzai had a team of prosecutors review their cases. They were unable to tell who was innocent and who was guilty. Determined to defend innocent Afghans, Karzai released 5,000 by June 2014. Many replenished the Taliban's withered ranks.

This would not be an all-out Tet offensive to overthrow the government. Mansour's goal in 2014 was to capture certain key districts in Helmand and Kandahar and then use those districts to extend Taliban authority. From these new havens, Taliban operations could expand against the provincial capitals in 2015. Secondary offensives were planned with the same idea for Kunduz and Ghazni.

Mansour's offensive started in northern Helmand, the battleground of 2013. Mansour intended to overwhelm the government positions in the districts of Nowzad, Musa Qala, Kajaki, and Sangin. It was easy to mass fighters since the depths of northern Helmand had been in Taliban hands since 2006.

The commander for the offensive was the new Taliban provincial governor of Helmand, Mullah Abdur Rahim Manan. An Ishaqzai from Nowzad in his mid-30s, Manan had a long frayed black beard and the tall broad-shouldered physique and tanned face of a hardened warrior. As a boy, he had attended the same madrasa in Peshawar as Mansour and been taught by the well-regarded Taliban religious scholar, Maulawi Shahabaddin Dilawar.[54] Disliking Pakistan, Manan had been fighting in northern Helmand for years. He had been quite a headache for the British back in 2008 and 2009. Being on the front line earned him loyalty among the rank and file. As in 2006, the idea was to overrun out-lying government posts in the villages and along the roads and then eventually surround the district centers. The district centers would be starved out or left isolated, granting the Taliban control over the population and freedom to do as they pleased.[55]

Mullah Manan planned the attack well. He coerced the cell phone companies to turn off service, befuddling police and army communications, since they pre-ferred cell phones over military radios. He laid improvised explosive devices and ambushes on the road leading from Lashkar Gah, the provincial capital, to northern Helmand in order to delay reinforcements. Sangin—the crossroads to all northern Helmand and northern Kandahar—was Manan's *schwerpunkt*. If Sangin fell, most of northern Helmand would go too, cut off from Lashkar Gah and Kandahar. Additionally, the 2013 fighting had turned Sangin into a symbol. Manan and his local fighters wanted vengeance for their defeat at the hands of Angar and the Alikozai tribe.

The fighters and commanders for the offensive were Alizai and Ishaqzai tribesmen from northern Helmand. This was not an offensive run by the Pakistanis. Nor was it a revolt of aggrieved villagers inside government territory. Over 200,000 people lived outside government control in northern Helmand; a few thousand recruits could be found easily enough. The Taliban had clinics, arms bazaars, courts, and other shades of government. Young men had grown up schooled in madrasas. The Americans, British, and government had rarely broken into this heart of the Taliban domain. Manan mobilized his Ishaqzai tribesmen. The Sangin front was under Mullah Abdul Raouf Khadim, a tough and respected Alizai commander from northern Helmand who had been imprisoned in Guantanamo and later released. He mobilized the Alizai. The fighters were adequately equipped with ammunition, rifles, and rockets. Their commanders massed them into large cadres of 30 to 50.

The 215th army corps commander, General Sayid Malouk, and other Helmand leaders had suspected for months that the Taliban would strike Sangin and northern Helmand.[56] Unfortunately, little had been done about it. Karzai fired veteran police chief Hakim Angar for allowing Abdullah and Ghani to campaign in Lashkar Gah. Angar's replacement, General Baqizoi, an imperious former communist with an iron handlebar moustache, did not prepare for the foreseeable battle. The police, battered in 2013, were left under-strength, including the Alikozai local police, with their valuable knowledge of the villages and people. Ammunition expenditure in 2013 had been severe, estimated at more than 1 million rounds.[57] The shortfall had not been refilled since that summer. No senior officers checked that police were even manning their posts. Several had just five police or local police with a handful of magazines for their Kalashnikovs.[58] There were few RPGs or medium machine guns, and no heavy machine guns.

The army, on the other hand, had ample weapons and ammunition and equipment—RPGs, heavy machine guns, armored Humvees, artillery. The problem was that morale was questionable. In Sangin, the long fighting of 2013 had rendered the army battalion in Sangin combat ineffective, a fact well known to US officers and the Afghan army's general staff. *New York Times* reporter Azam Ahmed had gone to Sangin in 2013 and found that the Afghan army battalion refused to leave its bases or go on missions. The soldiers said it was "too dangerous." Marines noted them to be "addicted to bases." The soldiers let Taliban lay improvised explosive devices right up to their front gate.[59]

Morale had hardly improved by summer 2014. A new brigade commander (2nd Brigade, 215th Corps) had been appointed but he avoided spending time in Helmand. The many Tajik enlisted were not fighting for homes or loved ones. They did not want to die for Sangin.[60] General Malouk recognized morale was a problem and asked for more supplies and recruits from the ministry.[61] The Tajik minister of defense, Bismullah Khan, otherwise a fierce adversary of the Taliban, was disinterested and preferred to berate the Helmand governor and police for losing posts.[62] The marines had left northern Helmand and were all on Camp Bastion, the main base, roughly 80 kilometers away in the desert. They could not inspect the northern Helmand defenses.

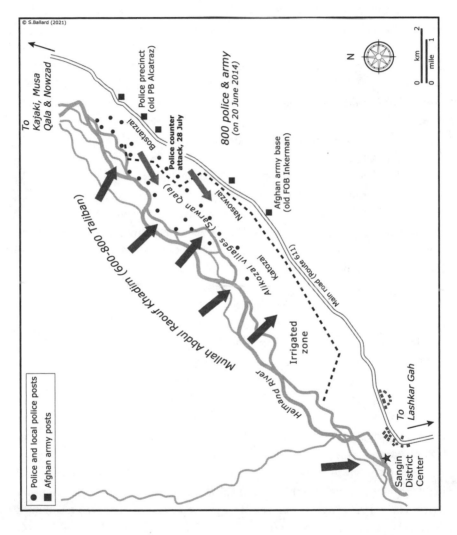

© S.Ballard (2021)

To
Kajaki, Musa
Qala & Nowzad

Police precinct
(old PB Alcatraz)

Bostanzai

Police counter
attack, 28 July

800 police & army
(on 20 June 2014)

Mullah Abdul Raouf Khadim (600-800 Taliban)

Nasowzai

A(l)kozai villages (Sarwan Qala)

Katozai

Afghan army base
(old FOB Inkerman)

Main road (Route 611)

Irrigated
zone

Helmand River

To
Lashkar Gah

Sangin
District
Center

• Police and local police posts
■ Afghan army posts

N

0 ____ km ____ 2
0 ____ mile ____ 1

Map 18 Sangin

On June 20, nearly 1,200 Taliban, backed by another 500 in reserve, attacked. Two thousand soldiers and police opposed them across northern Helmand. In Sangin, the center of the battle, the defensive scheme placed the lightly armed police and Alikozai local police on the front line in the villages while the better armed and supplied army sat in posts farther back on the main road and near the district center, outside the population. Cadres of 30 to 50 Taliban attacked posts—usually a single-story mud building surrounded by a 10-foot mud wall—defended by 5 to 15 police or Alikozai local police. Taliban cadres had medium machine guns, RPGs, and three to six magazines per man. The official police were only sometimes comparably armed and the Alikozai local police who manned much of the front line had only their Kalashnikovs and one to three magazines per man.[63] RPGs and medium machine guns outranged Kalashnikovs and had greater destructive power, putting the Alikozai local police at a distinct disadvantage.

The Alikozai fought. Taliban even praised their valor.[64] In many places, they eventually ran out of ammunition. One NDS intelligence officer commented, "Last year, the Taliban were fighting for two hours and shot maybe one RPG. Now they shoot them all the time."[65] Taliban themselves noted that the police and local police were poorly supplied.[66] According to government commanders, the Taliban fighters were aggressive.[67] Dead police and Taliban bodies lay in the fields because the fighting was too heated for a truce to bury them quickly as the Koran dictates.

Feda Mohammed, a self-confident 25-year-old Alikozai, son of one of the tribal leaders, commanded a local police post. He had 15 tribesmen, all armed with Kalashnikovs. They held off 32 Taliban. His conservative report was that the Taliban shot 20 RPGs in one day. His post and his men had none. He said, "The Taliban had more ammunition than the police and local police. Not a lot more ammunition, but more. Enough for them to outlast the local police."[68] He was not intimidated but respected Taliban aggressiveness: "The Taliban fought very hard and were determined. They had strong morale."[69]

The army, better armed and supplied, was arrayed too far back to immediately reinforce the police and local police. Precious time was lost trying to call the army for help. Without cell phone service, the police had to use military radios. Since few police posts had a radio, attacks were long underway before the army could determine what was going on. Even then, the army did little. Taliban improvised explosive devices deterred army officers from rushing headlong into the villages. The local army brigade commander chose to preserve his forces in their bases and on the road rather than risk them trying to save the police in the villages. Since the police and army had separate chains of command, no police commander could force an army commander to help. Within the army itself, different political loyalties undermined centralized command and control. The corps commander, General Malouk, in Camp Bastion, instructed the brigade commander to act. The brigade commander refused. Bismullah Khan had appointed him, not Malouk, who was a Pashtun from the east. He felt free to shirk Malouk and keep himself and his men out of danger. As Taliban hoisted their white flags over captured posts, the brigade commander did nothing. After five years of service in far off Helmand, Malouk had neither the energy nor the political connections to fix the situation. An experienced Taliban cadre leader in Helmand during the battle noticed the discord and commented, "As long as there is not mutual understanding among government military entities, we will become stronger and stronger."[70]

The marines at Camp Bastion, now reduced to around 1,000, pressed the army, police, and district and provincial officials to work together against the Taliban offensive. Because no Americans were in Sangin, the full scale of the offensive and number of casualties went unappreciated. The marines did not carry out air strikes for weeks. The Afghan army fired its own artillery liberally, 40 to 50 rounds per day. It was too inaccurate to fill the gap. When a number of civilians were killed and wounded, Karzai ordered Malouk to stop. Eventually, the marines were able to get a straight picture. Brigadier General Daniel Yoo, the marine commanding general, reported to Dunford, "Layered security doesn't work in northern Helmand. The ANA have no local guys to know what is going on."[71] A marine special operations detachment arrived with Afghan commandos to steady the defenders. Dunford had instructed US commanders not to win battles for the Afghans but, at the same time, not to let them fail. Since the marines believed the police and army could succeed, they called in air strikes sparingly.

By the time Malouk and Baqizoi got to Sangin to enforce cooperation in person, the Taliban had already captured the bulk of the villages. A few were seized in battle. Others after the police and local police, low on ammunition, had withdrawn. Feda Mohammed found himself alone. The posts around him had been abandoned after their defenders had run out of bullets. The Taliban torched the empty compounds and then beat local Alikozai tribesmen and looted their homes, partly in vengeance against villagers who had helped the government in 2013, partly out of the long-standing Alikozai-Ishaqzai tribal feud. They killed as many as 20 women, children, and old men. Another 20 were killed by improvised explosive devices.[72] Several male relatives of Alikozai local police were shot in the head. Fifteen captured Alikozai local police were executed.[73] Afghan commandos found their charred bodies, eyes gouged out. In the course of a week, nearly 400 policemen and soldiers in northern Helmand had been killed or wounded, compared to 500 killed or wounded over the entire 2013 fighting season. The government estimated that 3,200 civilians fled northern Helmand.[74]

Fighting persisted in northern Helmand through the summer.[75] A front line divided government from Taliban ground. One experienced Taliban cadre commander in northern Helmand boasted, "We are fighting against the army and police.... We regret killing them in every battle. You can see how much we are fighting them in Sangin.... They are very well equipped but still they cannot face us."[76] Sucked into the fighting himself, Baqizoi rated Taliban morale as better than that of the army and equal to that of the Alikozai local police.[77] To keep their fighters fresh, the Taliban rotated cadres out of the fight and into rest areas in far northern Helmand, where they had complete control. The government left the same Afghan soldiers and policemen on the front line week after week. An improvised explosive device lightly wounded Malouk. Treatment in Kabul and India removed him from the fight. Losses weakened units, forcing the government to send in new reinforcements. Morale stretched thinner.

The long tribal vendetta with the Taliban motivated the Alikozai local police, although they too were tiring. Fewer than 150 were left. Those remaining had seen friends and family killed and wounded or had been wounded themselves. Taliban execution and beating of villagers caused the government to respond in kind, especially the Alikozai local police. Feda Mohammed said, "We want revenge. We fight to the death. We kill Taliban. They never surrender. We take no prisoners."[78] Indeed, the government captured very few Taliban. One policeman explained, "The prosecutor in Lashkar Gah would release anyone whom we might capture."[79]

The scale of the Taliban offensive shook civilian confidence in the army and police throughout Afghanistan. Civilians in Helmand, Kandahar, and Kabul questioned how long the army and police could endure heavy casualties. They feared defeat in Sangin could demoralize the police and army elsewhere in Helmand. The Taliban cut the power lines from Kajaki, leaving Lashkar Gah and Kandahar with sporadic electricity and a deepening sense of gloom.

Karzai blamed the United States. He wondered why the United States was allowing the Taliban and by default Pakistan to capture parts of Helmand, suspecting a play to undercut his power after the travails of the bilateral security agreement. His suspicions deterred him from going to Sangin and fixing things, like he had done in Kandahar in 2010. Chief of the General Staff Sher Mohammed Karimi, Deputy Minister of Interior Ayub Selangi, and Minister of Defense Bismullah Khan each visited Sangin to inspect the situation. They decided to deploy additional reinforcements, fund more local police, and fire police chief Baqizoi.

The new police chief, Juma Gul Popalzai, went to Sangin straightaway to launch a counterattack. He took a page from Angar's book and called up the district police chiefs from elsewhere in the province along with 80 men picked from each of their districts. He again assigned Hekmatullah from Gereshk and Omar

Jan from Nad Ali to lead the assault. The Afghan army supported the police with armored vehicles, artillery, and commandos but did not fulfill their role as the front line infantry. The police did that.

Juma Gul launched his counteroffensive on July 28, the last day of the Ramadan fast. Roughly 600 police and local police and 200 Afghan soldiers attacked the 600 to 800 Taliban. The Taliban defended the mud villages, manning compound walls and shooting through loopholes. The audacity of Hekmatullah and Omar Jan impressed Feda Mohammed and the local Alikozai tribal leaders.[80] It was hard going. Improvised explosive devices seeded along the roads further slowed the advance. After ten days of heavy fighting, Hekmatullah and Omar Jan had recaptured two-thirds of the lost ground.

The victory came at a cost of 120 more casualties, a figure in line with historical casualty rates for forces operating with insufficient artillery or air support. Experienced and talented junior officers were among the fallen. Because of those casualties, Juma Gul had to stop the offensive before all the ground had been recaptured.[81] The Taliban suffered similar losses. Combat tired them too, though they were far from exhausted. Mullah Raouf, the Taliban front line commander, reorganized his cadres and prepared to rotate new ones forward.[82]

After the counteroffensive, Omar Jan, Hekmatullah, and the other police commanders filed back down the road to their districts. They stopped overnight in Gereshk, Hekmatullah's district, for a long dinner at the table of district governor Mohammed Fahim, to reflect on the fallen and ponder the future. With their departure, the police were again left undermanned. Juma Gul tried to hire new Alikozai local police but it took time to enlist and train new recruits. Meanwhile, there were no soldiers or police to bridge the gap. Sangin and northern Helmand had become a battle of attrition. It had bled the government.

In the middle of September, Raouf and Manan attacked for the last time. Four hundred Taliban struck Sangin. The front line collapsed. The local police abandoned the villages. Years of fighting had finally broken the Sangin Alikozai. Raouf captured almost the entire district. Only the district center and the main road remained in government hands. The Taliban controlled 500 meters to the north of the district center and 300 meters to the south. Farther north, Musa Qala and Nowzad had all but fallen; their district centers were besieged. In 2015, Manan would capture both and sit literally at the gates of the Sangin district government building. Helmand was divided. The north was Taliban country. The center and south were with the government, under pressure from Taliban coming out of Pakistan as well as from the north.

The final defeat was as much a failure of spirit as a lack of ammunition or manpower. It had been a three-month contest of wills. Taliban fighters fought for months, and rebounded from a counterattack, until the police and Alikozai tribesmen collapsed. If police and army morale had been higher, the police might have endured the Taliban blows, the army might have hurried to counterattack, and a stalemate might have sunk in. What was needed was a little more grit.

Helmand was the first wave of the Taliban offensive. Mansour launched a second wave in Kandahar. On July 9, 30 Taliban attacked the governor's palace and the police headquarters simultaneously. The attackers were from Pakistan and highly trained. Twenty-two of them were killed. Then, on July 26, roughly 200 Taliban hit Afghan desert border posts and police chief Abdul Razziq's family home in Spin Boldak. Six suicide bombers knocked on his home (he was in Kandahar City). At the same time, another 500 to 800 Taliban attacked Zharey, one of the surge's success stories. Mansour wanted to reestablish Zharey as a center of Taliban activity, and then threaten Kandahar City, which could destabilize the government. It would be a strategic blow.

The attack on Zharey was a surprise. The vast majority of the Taliban fighters converged on the district from Pakistan and Maiwand. They received some assistance from locals.[83] The fighters were largely Ishaqzai, Noorzai, Ghilzai, and Baluch. Many were originally from Zharey and had family there but were living in Pakistan, forced out by the surge. A few had years of combat experience. It was a bold move to attack Zharey, well-fortified with police, army, and one of the last US battalions (3rd Squadron, 61st Cavalry Regiment) in the field.

Taliban cadre commanders were confident, emboldened by Sangin and the elections debacle, as well as their cause. In the words of one cadre commander from Kandahar, "We will fight until we defeat anyone standing against us. Election is an imported idea of running the government. We have been practicing an Islamic emirate, which is a very successful way of getting rid of corruption and infighting. So how can we accept democracy where fraud and foreigner decides who should govern?"[84] Another cadre commander, who was in his mid-30s and had been fighting since 2001, said the attacking cadres were committed to "get rid of the foreigners and rebuild the Islamic Emirate."[85] "Foreigners are not liked by Afghans," he commented. "Look at the history. They are hated and defeated by Afghans."[86] Years of war had not tired him: "[Our achievement] is fighting the Americans for a very long war. We are not tired but we made our enemy tired. We are as powerful as ever but our enemy is getting weaker and weaker, day by day."[87]

Roughly 800 police, local police, and soldiers defended the portion of the district under attack. The local police were the same militia of farmers and city youth that had been recruited in 2012 and were fighting for their village, elder, or money. They were not the united tribal force of the Alikozai of Sangin. Behind them were 1,200 more Afghan soldiers and police and 500 American soldiers, including a special forces team.

From July 26 to 28, groups of 20 to 50 Taliban assisted by suicide bombers ambushed Afghan patrols and attacked posts. Again, the police and local police ran low on ammunition. Again, the army was slow to help. Again, some of the local police cracked. Eight posts fell.[88] Taliban attackers pressed all the way to the old 2006 battlefields in Pashmul. Hundreds of civilians fled to Kandahar City. Women and children choked Highway One.[89] People in the city itself feared the days of 2006 were returning.

Razziq learned about Zharey when he was sorting out the Taliban attacks on the border and his home in Spin Boldak. He headed straight for the battle. En route, he called his American advisor, Colonel Pat Crosby, for air strikes. Crosby's superior, Major General Bills, was initially reluctant but changed his mind as the battle intensified. Sangin was very much in his thoughts. Over 50 air strikes blasted concentrations of Taliban. Under their cover, Razziq personally led the counterattack. "*Razziq zmoong serra die!* Razziq is with us! He is honest!," Zharey police and local police shouted.[90] The US special forces team went out with the Afghan soldiers and police. When the Afghans encountered Taliban shooting at them from trench-like grape vineyard or compounds, the special forces team called in air strikes. After an air strike, police or army units assaulted the Taliban positions and cleared them out. "In Zharey district . . . 173 Taliban were martyred in one day," reported a Taliban commander in Spin Boldak.[91]

Razziq's presence restored morale.[92] He had authority from Karzai to control the entire government effort. Afghan army colonels frustrated him with lengthy planning and methodical operations. One army unit showed up five hours late to a movement. "The army does no work," Razziq cursed to Crosby. So he summarily issued orders and overruled the colonels' plans. In contrast to northern Helmand, Razziq pushed army soldiers to the sharp end. Right after the battle, one Taliban religious leader in Kandahar noted, "The police and army have improved. They are fighting strongly. In the recent battles . . . they fought very hard."[93]

By the first week of August, a week after the first attack, the Taliban had retreated out of Zharey and back to farther-off districts or Pakistan. US military advisors reported well over 200 Taliban casualties, compared to 75 Afghan army and police casualties. The casualties did not much damage police and army morale. They pale in comparison to what they had suffered from 2006 to 2009.[94] In Kandahar City, popular fear of defeat changed to elation over victory. It was a tactical victory with strategic consequences. Mansour was deterred from conducting any more major offensives in Kandahar. The Taliban would refrain from another attempt at the prize of Kandahar for six years. When compared to northern Helmand, air strikes and an Afghan commander with authority made a difference. Unfortunately for the Afghan government, both were in short supply.

By the end of the year, the army and police had suffered at least 5,000 killed and 9,000 wounded. Taliban confidence had risen. In addition to Helmand, the Taliban gained ground in Ghazni, Wardak, Nangarhar, and Kunduz. A set of interviews with 45 Taliban religious leaders and commanders paints a picture of resolve. One of the Taliban commanders from Helmand responded, "We are openly commuting all over the province. We have fought the government in many districts at once—we have thousands of mujahedin around the province. . . . We fought simultaneously in Sangin, Garmser, Musa Qala, and Kajaki."[95] Or as a Taliban religious leader from Jalalabad summarized, "Taliban are always fresh to the fight. They fight and rest while the government and Americans seem very tired. . . . The Taliban's biggest success may be their nonstop fighting, their untired mood of fighting, and their vast control in many rural areas which is increasing day by day."[96] All but one of the interviewees believed Taliban influence had increased since 2008 and all but one believed that the Taliban should reject peace until a total US withdrawal had occurred.

Dunford was aware of the battlefield setbacks. What was obscure was the scale of the problem. With far fewer Americans in the field, details on battlefield events came incompletely to Kabul. Afghan commanders hid the severity of defeats. It was often unclear whether posts had fallen or district centers had been surrounded. It was also difficult to predict the damage of losing the places under attack. Various US officers argued with some justification that Taliban successes in northern Helmand had no bearing on the rest of the country and could be left well enough alone. Above all, Obama's guidance had been clear: the US military would not fight the Afghan government's battles for it. Defeats were to be expected. Efforts to defend anything but the most vital terrain could be subject to criticism.

As the fighting intensified, the war got dirtier. For years, watchful US commanders and advisors had restrained the Afghan police and army from exacting vengeance on the Taliban and their supporters. Similarly, US numbers and firepower had prevented the Taliban from driving the police and soldiers to the point of desperation. That tidal wall was eroding.

Over 10,000 civilians were killed or wounded in 2014, the highest number since 2009 and 2,000 more than 2013. The largest portion of civilian casualties originated from ground combat, nearly twice as many as 2013.[97] Battles with larger insurgent groups in villages and substitution of US air strikes with inaccurate artillery and rockets were to blame.

Following improvised explosive devices, suicide car bombs were the third leading cause of casualties, 1,582 killed and injured. Deaths from suicide attacks rose from 255 in 2013 to 371 in 2014.[98] One suicide car bomb struck Shukria Barakzai in November while driving in Kabul in her armored sport utility vehicle. The explosion singed her hands and she spent months in recovery, but she survived. Ghani appointed her ambassador to Norway, where her family could live in peace. She had seen a lot over the years, between assassination attempts and abuse from male colleagues, exposing herself to danger again and again just by being an active woman. The war had a way of wearing people down.

A darker trend accompanied the civilian casualties: summary executions. Police and soldiers knew that the Karzai government would often release captured prisoners. This had always been the case but was particularly apparent in 2014 as Karzai personally released thousands. Many returned to the Taliban and went after the soldiers and police who had captured them. Police and soldiers feared for their lives and those of their families if they detained an insurgent. A few Afghan police chiefs and army officers admitted that they preferred simply to kill the insurgent on the spot—whether armed or not. During the Zharey operation, police executed at least six Taliban.[99] Dead Taliban bodies were left on the side of Highway One after the police had killed them. In a security meeting at the end of the operation in August, Razziq allegedly stated, "No matter where the operations are, I have ordered my soldiers not to let Taliban live from now on."[100] In Panjwai too, rumors abounded that the police chief executed captured Taliban.[101] The police chief in Baghlan and a district governor in the embattled district of Hisarak in Nangarhar made similar comments as Razziq.

The exact number of summary executions is unknown and there is scant evidence that civilians were targeted on purpose. Karzai and Ghani personally disapproved of such tactics but many others in the government, progressive Afghans with high educations, did not. They empathized with the policemen and soldiers who might see themselves or their family killed if a guilty Taliban were set free. These were not bloodthirsty murderers. These were people twisted by civil war.

By the end of 2014, Afghanistan had witnessed dramatic changes. The situation was discouraging. The country had a new divided government. The Taliban had put the police and army to the test in the provinces. US forces had drawn down to 9,800 and were to leave within two years. Since 2009, US strategy had been predicated upon building up the Afghan government so it could stand on its own and the United States could leave. Had the United States succeeded? As 2015 dawned, the answer would soon be known.

The Taliban Offensives of 2015 and 2016

After 2006, the key battles in the American war in Afghanistan occurred in 2015 and 2016. The government faced some of the biggest Taliban offensives of the war largely on their own. The result brought about a verdict on the whole US war effort.

The unity government of Ghani and Abdullah was seated on September 29, 2014. Officially, President Ghani retained the full authority of the presidency. In practice, he had to share power with Chief Executive Abdullah. The unity deal negotiated by Secretary of State John Kerry endowed the chief executive with vague powers to convene the cabinet and choose some number of ministers. Compared to Karzai, Ghani would have much less control over the government. Karzai had enjoyed sole authority to appoint and remove ministers, provincial governors, and senior generals. He had never had the equivalent of Abdullah—an electorally mandated chief executive officer who could challenge every decision if it so suited him.

With his intellectual demeanor, Ghani contrasted starkly with Karzai. He kept long hours, read voluminously, and delved into details. Centralized reform, in Ghani's vision, was the strategy both to defeat the Taliban and to raise Afghanistan into modernity. Building institutions his forte, he penned memoranda late into the night. Ministers had to prepare their own 100-day action plans. He called his 2009 book, *Fixing Failed States*, co-authored with Clare Lockhart, "a road map for where do you begin, when you arrive, and what you do as a leader."[1] The book states, "In the twentieth century, illegitimate networks will not be conquered except through hierarchical organizations that have legitimacy . . . Solutions to our current problems of insecurity, poverty, and lack of growth all converge on the need for a state-building project."[2]

The war was a priority. Whereas Karzai disregarded his own soldiers and police, Ghani believed with proper reforms that the army could defeat the Taliban.

Ghani praised the army, commemorated their sacrifices, and designed well-meaning reform programs. Corps commanders had to report to weekly, and sometimes daily, videoconferences. Ghani's guidance ranged from personal accountability to tactical operations. He shared none of Karzai's laissez faire approach to managing the war.

The biggest difference in strategy with Karzai was that Ghani terminated criticism of the United States and vocally supported US intervention. His World Bank experience instructed him that the Afghan state could not survive without external economic and military assistance.

From the day of the inauguration, Abdullah and Ghani were in a state of perpetual bargaining. The main issue was the appointment of ministers, deputy ministers, and other senior officials. The 2014 election deal had not defined how many jobs would go to each side. Believing the deal was that appointments would be divided equally, Abdullah bargained over every position, not only ministers, but deputy ministers, directors, governors, provincial police chiefs, and corps commanders. Believing the deal was for only a few ministers and governors to go to Abdullah, Ghani disagreed. Key jobs went unfilled for months as bargaining dragged on. For all 2015, Afghanistan had no official defense minister. Bismullah Khan was gone and Ghani shoved in high peace council chairman Massoum Stanekzai as acting, against Abdullah's wishes.

The situation was hardly optimal. Besides the delay in appointments, an appointee layer cake gridlocked the government. Within each ministry, if the minister was a Ghani supporter, Abdullah would insist the deputy be an Abdullah supporter, and vice versa. Competing loyalty at every layer stopped up the works. Too often, deputies would ignore instructions from ministers and ministers would ignore requests from subordinates.

Other government processes stalled as well. The unity deal had stipulated that both parliamentary elections and a constitutional loya jirga to revisit the structure of the unity government were to occur by September 2016. Parliamentary elections were deferred until October 2018 because Abdullah and Ghani differed over the composition of election commissions. Mutual animosity similarly shelved the constitutional loya jirga. The unity government stayed in place, angering Abdullah, that the constitution was not changed to institutionalize power-sharing, and Ghani, that he had to share power.

At various points, relations between Abdullah and Ghani were so bad that the unity government seemed about to dissolve. From time to time, Ghani tried to use his presidential power to override Abdullah. In reaction, Abdullah would threaten to leave the government. In each case, the two eventually reached an agreement and the unity government trundled on until the next crisis. Abdullah and Ghani grew to despise each other.

Politicking distracted Ghani and Abdullah from the war. Political drama detained Ghani in Kabul and delayed his reform program. For his part, Abdullah spent more time worrying about his share of appointments than winning the war. In one telling instance, Abdullah publicly accused Ghani of being "unfit to govern" in the middle of the 2016 fighting season. His comments brought the government to a two-month crisis at a time when the battlefield was very much in doubt.

Disorder in Kabul undermined the war effort in other ways as well. Decisions on purchase and distribution of vital ammunition and other supplies were delayed, putting combat units in a dangerous position.[3] The fractures of the unity government also worsened corruption within the army and police. Because competing networks of Abdullah, Ghani, and their unsupervised supporters each controlled various jobs in the police and army, there was no firm chain of command. All could pocket money with less fear of repercussion.

Under these conditions, the credibility of the government among the people and among its own soldiers and police nose-dived. Even though American soldiers were fewer than ever before, the government could not shake the image of being a puppet. John Kerry standing next to Ghani and Abdullah in July 2014 and pronouncing the form of the new government on television stuck in the minds of many. Karzai, with his relentless defiance of the West, looked like the true Afghan ruler.

Economic slowdown worsened things. With the reduction of US economic assistance and the loss of jobs supporting the large US troop presence, economic growth decreased from 14 percent in 2012 to 0.8 percent in 2015 (the average growth rate between 2003 and 2012 was 9 percent). Tens of thousands of Afghans, especially those with educations, emigrated to the Gulf States, Europe, the United States, and India.[4]

Surveys recorded the extent of damage to public confidence. The Asia Foundation Survey for 2016 found that 66 percent of respondents believed that the country was going in the wrong direction, the highest percentage since the survey had started in 2006, up from 40 percent in 2014. Satisfaction in national government performance fell from 75 percent in 2014 to 49 percent in 2016. From 2009 to 2014, more than 70 percent of respondents had reported satisfaction with the national government. Perhaps most depressing for Americans, satisfaction with democracy dropped from 73 to 56 percent.[5]

While the Afghan government struggled, the Taliban underwent their own growing pains. In 2013 and 2014, a new terrorist movement formed in the Middle East, known as the Islamic State. It had grown out of Musab al-Zarqawi's al-Qa'eda in Iraq, which had been severely defeated in 2007 during the US surge in Iraq. When the United States withdrew from Iraq in 2011, the organization regained strength under the new name. In June 2014, the Islamic State swept through northern Iraq and captured the city of Mosul and almost everything south to Baghdad. It was a stunning sign of their power. Their leader, Abu Bakr al-Baghdadi, declared a new Islamic caliphate, with himself as the new caliph. The Islamic State's battlefield successes and declaration of a caliphate electrified the Islamic world. The group drew supporters far outside of Iraq and Syria.

Unlike the Taliban, the Islamic State encouraged attacks on the United States and Europe. The movement exploited social media to try to inspire Muslims in the United States and Europe to carry out terrorist attacks.

The advent of smart phones offered the Islamic State worldwide reach. In 2014 and 2015, Afghans and Pakistanis were acquiring smart phones, especially in the cities, if less so in the villages where cell coverage could be spotty. The Islamic State broadcast high-quality videos and well-produced messages over social media into Pakistan and Afghanistan. Their products glorified execution and beheadings of captives and civilians. The propaganda attracted Afghan and Pakistani recruits.

In December 2014, Baghdadi issued a statement harshly criticizing the Taliban. He called Mullah Omar uneducated (his death was still a secret) and said he had no right to the title of emir al-momineen (leader of the faithful) over all Muslims. Islamic State propaganda spread the message and accused the Taliban of being tools of Pakistan. Baghdadi's criticism was a little unfair—Omar had only claimed to be emir al-momineen over Afghanistan, not the entire Islamic world. That did not lessen the threat posed by Baghdadi's words. The Islamic State's claim to a caliphate questioned the legitimacy of a separate Taliban movement.

In early 2015, Taliban commanders asked why Mullah Omar was not speaking against Baghdadi and also why he was not leading more aggressive operations against the government. Small cells of hard-line Salafist religious leaders and their students in Kabul and Jalalabad became activists.[6] In the countryside, a few Taliban commanders and Pakistani Taliban commanders went over to the Islamic State. Abu Rashid, a Taliban commander in Kunar, switched because "God says when there is a caliphate, you must join the caliphate. There is a caliphate now, so we've left the Taliban. We're fighting a holy war under the caliph's leadership . . . We want an Islamic system all over the world, and we will fight for it."[7]

In January 2015, Baghdadi officially recognized a group of adherents as the Islamic State in the province of Khorasan, the name for Afghanistan from the time of the Umayyad caliphate. Hafez Sayid Khan, a former Pakistani Taliban commander, became its leader. Abdul Raouf Khadim, the Taliban commander in Sangin in 2014, joined them as the deputy, bringing along 300 of his men. The new group received funding from donors in Arabian Peninsula and directly from the caliphate in Iraq and Syria.[8] Salaries from $500 to $700 per month, anywhere from two to ten times higher than the varying compensation that the Taliban offered, tempted some Afghan Taliban fighters to change flags.[9]

Akhtar Mohammed Mansour, leading the Taliban in Mullah Omar's name, ordered Taliban commanders throughout Afghanistan to contain the Islamic State. Soon after, clashes broke out in Helmand, Farah, Zabul, and Nangarhar. The Islamic State in Khorasan followed the Iraqi and Syrian model and ventured into far greater brutality than the Taliban. Copying the larger movement in Iraq and Syria, they published videos of beheadings and mass executions of tribal leaders, tribal militiamen, police, soldiers, and Taliban captives.[10]

The Islamic State lodged a foothold in the foothills and mountains of southern Nangarhar—the same area that traditionally had been a problem for poppy eradication and the same range (the Spin Ghar) where Osama bin Laden had fought his famous battle at the cave complex of Tora Bora. Pakistani Taliban groups had long hidden in the province and competed with Afghan Taliban. From 2013, Afghan officials noted an increase in foreign fighters from Pakistan and that local Taliban were supporting them in some places.[11] Through NDS intelligence officers, Kabul allowed the Pakistani Taliban haven since they were enemies of Pakistan. Governor Attaullah Ludin, Sherzai's successor and a noted Islamic judge, thought otherwise. "They shouldn't be here. They don't belong here . . . It is not right to breed extremism in Afghanistan," he warned US officials, foreshadowing what was coming.[12]

In 2014, several of the Pakistani Taliban cadres pledged themselves to the Islamic State, which Afghans sometimes referred to as "Daesh", in reference to its Arabic acronym. "We never thought that Daesh would suddenly operate in our district because we hadn't seen any sign of them before," remarked a village elder, "There were Afghan and Pakistani Taliban operating in our area. One day we received news that Pakistani Taliban in Shinwar district had decided to join Daesh . . . It happened like that, after some days we witnessed those Pakistani Taliban . . . change their flag from white to black, change their uniform and announce their support for Daesh, under the leadership of Abu Bakr al-Baghdadi."[13] Cadres such as these were then joined by new cadres of Pakistani Taliban fleeing the 2014 Pakistani offensive into Waziristan. A number of al-Qaʻeda also defected to the Islamic State.

The Islamic State cadres seized control of several valleys in the foothills in southern Nangarhar. They brought villagers to heel by the barrel of the gun, repeatedly executing elders in front of whole villages and then propagating videos of the atrocities as propaganda. They infamously filmed ten village elders on a hillside being forced at gunpoint to kneel on explosives and kill themselves. A local farmer who fled his home said, "You can't stand up to them. If you try, they come in the night and kill you with your children. Your children will be made to watch as you are beheaded."[14]

The Islamic State expanded from the foothills and mountains. In May 2015, heavy fighting broke out in the countryside around Jalalabad. Former Pakistani Taliban flying the black flag of the Islamic States marched into Bati Kot near the main highway while other cadres entered Chapahara and Rodat south of the provincial capital. The Islamic State fielded 1,000 to 3,000 fighters in the province, out of approximately 4,000 throughout Afghanistan.[15] The government was caught in the middle. Ghani permitted Nangarhar powerbroker Haji Zahir to deploy his tribal militia to help the embattled police and army.

In June 2015, the Islamic State in Afghanistan put out a video that said there cannot be two caliphs, a swipe at Mullah Omar: "In the presence of one, the other needs to be eliminated." Mansour responded on June 16 with an open letter warning the Islamic State and Baghdadi that if their interference in Afghanistan did not stop, the Taliban would be forced to defend their successes. The Islamic State replied in turn that to oppose them was a "religious crime." Their spokesperson, Abu Mohammed al-Adnani, instructed Islamic State fighters to show no mercy.[16]

The Islamic State had difficulty challenging the Taliban on the ground. Whatever its grand visions, the Islamic State had foreign origins whereas the Taliban were rooted in Afghan village life. Mansour created special quick reaction forces, known as *keetaq muntazaree*, to fight the Islamic State. During the first half of 2015, the quick reaction forces battered the Islamic State in Helmand, Farah, and Zabul. Over the summer, the Quetta Shura deployed reinforcements to Nangarhar. In a series of hard-fought battles between July 2015 and January 2016, uncoordinated Taliban and Afghan government counteroffensives then pushed the Islamic State back from the countryside around Jalalabad into the foothills and mountains.[17] An Islamic State fighter remarked at the time, "In Nangarhar Province most of the people stood against us, including Haji Zahir, the Taliban, and the Afghan government, and at the same time there were more drone attacks against us and we incurred many casualties."[18]

US drone strikes did their part. Early on, in February 2015, one strike killed Abdur Raouf Khadim, the Islamic State's deputy and commander in Helmand. In October 2015, Obama authorized US special operations forces and drones to go after the Islamic State at a higher intensity. US strikes and a series of US-advised Afghan military offensives pounded the Islamic State stronghold in the mountains south of Jalalabad during 2016. Conservatively, 100 Islamic State fighters were killed. A drone terminated their leader, Hafez Sayid Khan, in July 2016. The group was so disorganized that until September it could not find a replacement—Maulawi Abdul Hasib—and get him approved by Baghdadi.

Taliban attacks, drone strikes, and army and police offensives reduced Islamic State numbers from 4,000 in 2015 to 2,500 by early 2016, largely confined to a few mountain valleys in southern Nangarhar.[19] . Though they would recover in a more virulent form, the Islamic State was thwarted for the time being.[20] As Mansour confronted the Islamic State ideological challenge, a second, graver challenge surfaced.

During the first half of 2015, Afghanistan and Pakistan unexpectedly experienced a brief détente. For a moment, peace talks with the Taliban were in the offing. Ghani and the new Pakistani army chief, General Raheel Sharif, found common ground. Early in his term, Ghani was more sensitive to Pakistani interests than Karzai had been and distanced Afghanistan from India. Sharif then pressured Mansour to come to the negotiating table. Mansour did not want to work through Pakistan but believed in negotiation as a means of securing Taliban interests, as he had since 2011. He was even willing to consider talking with the Ghani government.[21] It had been shortly before his death in 2013 that Mullah Omar had given the political committee permission to pursue peace talks as long as the end result was full withdrawal of US and other foreign troops.[22] Under the cover of this guidance, Mansour entertained peace talks—first with unofficial meetings with government representatives in Qatar, Dubai, and China, and then an official one in Muree, Pakistan. As this happened, hard-line Taliban questioned the move toward peace and demanded to see Mullah Omar.[23]

Abdul Qayum Zakir, the well-known former head of the military commission, angry at his removal after the first round of the 2014 elections, leaked Mullah Omar's death to a few other leaders. The secret slowly spread and eventually prompted Mansour, and Mullah Omar's son, Yakub, to reveal the truth at a leadership meeting in late July.[24] It is unclear if the information came out because Mansour thought it might solidify his position as leader or because he now had no choice.[25]

Peace talks fell by the wayside as a succession struggle engulfed the Taliban. The Quetta Shura convened on July 30. As many as 150 Taliban leaders may have attended, few from the front in Afghanistan. Mansour was voted in as the new emir. Zakir, Yakub, and Mullah Omar's brother opposed his appointment. They claimed that the vote had been without a full shura of all Taliban leaders. They called for a new shura with wider Taliban representation. The political commission, living in Qatar, also chafed. Its chief, Tayeb Agha, resigned. Other Taliban questioned why the shura had happened in Pakistan and not in Afghanistan where the Taliban had been founded. In Zabul, Mansour Dadullah, the brother of Mullah Dadullah Lang and a rival of Mansour, swore allegiance to Omar's son and picked up arms.[26]

The succession struggle was the greatest test yet of the old Taliban norm of unity against political and tribal fissures. Mansour was a controversial figure, deeply involved in organizing poppy smuggling, with all its profits and free-market competition, and known to favor his Ishaqzai tribe.

Nevertheless, many Taliban leaders sided with Mansour in order to prevent the movement from descending into chaos. From Kabul, Maulawi Mutawakil, the former Taliban Minister of Foreign Affairs, spoke out that the strength of the Taliban was their unity and they must stay clenched like a fist. Mansour himself, in a message to the movement, announced, "If we and you are united, then the enemy cannot have influence, nor can anyone else. We must be together. Separation pleases the enemy."[27] In mid-August, hundreds of religious scholars and mullahs assembled in Pakistan to solve the disagreement. They deliberated for weeks. The old norm ultimately prevailed. On September 15, Mullah Omar's son, Yakub, and brother, Abdul Manan, swore allegiance to Mansour. The Quetta Shura declared that the disagreement had been solved.[28] Zakir eventually dropped his opposition to Mansour as well.[29]

Mansour contained the remaining discontents. In November, Mansour Dadullah, Mullah Mohammed Rassoul, and powerful Noorzai commander Baz Mohammed formed a splinter group. They declared themselves Taliban but opposed to Mansour. Mansour's response was swift. He dispatched one of his special quick reaction forces (*keetaq muntazaree*) to Zabul under a ruthless commander named Pir Agha.[30] Pir Agha crushed Mansour Dadullah, who perished in the battle.[31] The splinter group struggled on into 2016 and 2017, isolated in Farah, without much impact.

For all the political drama, far more decisive events were about to play out on the battlefield. At the beginning of the 2015 fighting season, US military presence was down to 9,800 troops located in six main bases: Bagram, Herat, Mazar-e-Sharif, Kandahar, Jalalabad, and the headquarters in Kabul. General Dunford had chosen those bases to cover the strategic points of the country. There were five lesser supporting bases. Members of the coalition contributed around 4,000 troops. Italy and Germany had roughly 1,000 soldiers each at Herat and Mazar-e-Sharif. The British had left Helmand and had 450 soldiers focused on special operations and training the Afghan officer corps. Dunford returned to the United States at the end of August 2014 and would soon become chairman of the joint chiefs of staff, the top position in the US military. General John Campbell assumed command of US and allied forces in Afghanistan.

As per President Obama's May 2014 decision to stay out of direct combat with the Taliban, US forces were dedicated to training, advising, and counter-terrorism. Only special operations forces were permitted to go on missions and only as advisors, other than in certain exceptions against al-Qaʻeda or the Islamic State.

Obama similarly restricted air strikes against the Taliban to situations of *in extremis*. If a strategic point or major Afghan formation was in danger of imminent annihilation, US commanders could call in air strikes to save them. The policy ensured a conservative use of air strikes. It denied the Afghan army and police the very advantage that had enabled the Northern Alliance, Karzai, and a small number of US special operations forces and CIA operatives to defeat the Taliban in the first place in 2001.

Obama's White House staff favored *in extremis* out of an expectation that the Afghan government had the numerical and material superiority to succeed on its own. They often asked Pentagon officials why the Afghan army needed air support when the Taliban so clearly did not. It would be a small misjudgment that would have a big impact.

For the first half of the 2015 fighting season, Taliban advances generally resembled those of 2014—mostly in remote districts and provinces. That changed after August, when Mansour coordinated a series of well-planned offensives across northern, eastern, and southern Afghanistan that harkened back to 2006, except over a much larger area. The offensives targeted provincial capitals and their surrounding districts, a dramatic escalation from the previous four years. Mansour's goal was not to conquer provinces but to compel the government, northerners, and other pro-government groups to accept a subordinate position to the Taliban in a new political arrangement in Kabul. Sher Mohammed Abbas Stanekzai, head of the Taliban political office, told an unofficial government delegation, "We do not want Helmand or Zabul. We can take Helmand or Zabul whenever we want. We want Kabul. If we cannot get Kabul, then we will fight. There will be civil war and civilians will die."[32]

One of Mansour's principal targets was Kunduz, the northern province that borders Tajikistan. The capital of Kunduz was Kunduz City, the sixth biggest town in Afghanistan. Pashtuns were the largest ethnic group in Kunduz, an island amid the Tajiks and Uzbeks of the north. The Pashtuns of Kunduz had supported the Taliban in the 1990s. After 2001, they never really cared for the government.[33] For years, surveys found that at least 40 percent of the province sympathized with the Taliban.[34] According to several research studies, the Pashtuns felt oppressed by Uzbek and Tajik warlords who influenced much of the province. Competing warlord militias extorted, robbed, overtaxed, and sometimes brutalized Pashtuns.[35] After 2010, Tajiks and Uzbeks also filled in the Afghan local police. The local police demanded money from the Pashtuns and seized land. Additionally galvanizing was the government's alignment with infidels, as one Uzbek from the Kunduz countryside put it, "The majority thinks that the current state is corrupt and non-Islamic, a sufficient reason that provokes many to fight against it."[36] During 2014, masses of Pashtuns in Kunduz resumed helping the Taliban.[37]

Over the winter of 2014, Mansour planned to move against Kunduz City. Mullah Abdul Salam, the Taliban's governor of Kunduz, who had fought in the province since 2001, organized the operation, along with experienced leaders and cadres. They helped pay and arm the local Pashtuns. They also recruited some number of Tajiks, Uzbeks, and Hazaras. A Hazara Taliban commander said, "We are all fighting side by side under one banner, which is Islam. We are struggling for Islam, not for any particular ethnic group."[38] In April, Mullah Salam attacked the six districts around Kunduz City. He captured nearly every one and reached the outskirts of the capital. Two thousand reinforcements from Kabul, including a large number of commandos and a US special forces team, were required to fend off Mullah Salam and his forces.

In the autumn, having solidified his position as the Taliban's new emir, Mansour facilitated an assault on Kunduz City. Mullah Salam carefully planned the attack. It would take place over the Eid holiday when many army and police commanders would be on leave in Kabul and elsewhere. Salam marshaled Taliban cadres around the town and prepared to attack from four different directions. Meanwhile, he infiltrated teams into the town itself. Sympathetic locals hid them in their homes. In all, roughly 500 Taliban prepared to take part.[39] Salam led the attack personally.

Three thousand police, army, and other militias defended the town. They were in a parlous state. The local police and militias were exhausted and demoralized from months of fighting. According to a 2014 survey, about half the police had joined in order to get a salary rather than to serve the country. They were reluctant to lay down their lives. Scores were resigning. The majority cited the risk of death or injury from the Taliban.[40] They had been willing to be police only when the risk had been low. Now that the time had come to fight, they were out. The army commander of 209th corps responsible for the north was General Abdul Hamid, who had distinguished himself in Kandahar. Hamid and police and army commanders in Kunduz informed Kabul about the issues in Kunduz. No response came. Ghani and his top leaders were aware but did nothing.[41]

The attack kicked off at 3:00 a.m. on September 28. The exhausted local police and militia outside the city surrendered or ran. As the Taliban cadres entered the town, the hidden teams struck, sowing confusion among the defenders. The will to fight almost completely broke down. A few scattered police posts and army patrols stood their ground. Garrisons of well-fortified police stations retreated pell-mell to the army headquarters at the Kunduz airfield, outside town. Two full army battalions, roughly 1,000 men, ran away, leaving Humvees, weapons,

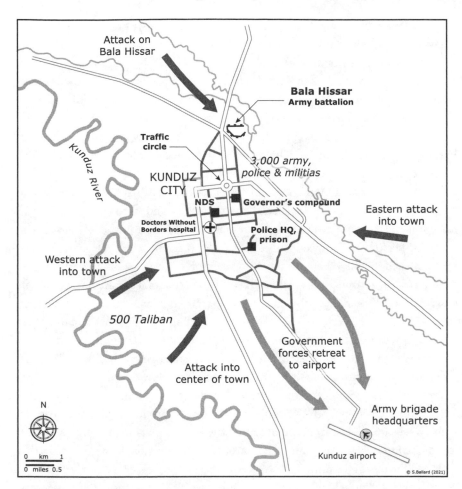

Attack on
Bala Hissar

Bala Hissar
Army battalion

Traffic
circle

3,000 army,
police & militias

KUNDUZ
CITY

NDS

Governor's compound

Eastern attack
into town

Doctors Without
Borders hospital

Police HQ,
prison

Western attack
into town

500 Taliban

Government
forces retreat
to airport

Attack into
center of town

Army brigade
headquarters

N

Kunduz airport

0 km 1
0 miles 0.5

© S.Ballard (2021)

Kunduz River

Map 19 Kunduz

and ammunition behind. The police provincial headquarters tolerated light skirmishes until 3:00 p.m. and then headed to the airfield too. No one tried to lead. Meanwhile Mullah Salam moved about the town, seeing things for himself and issuing orders. It was a complete rout. The army and police outnumbered the attackers and suffered fewer than 20 casualties but had disintegrated.

Blame must fall on Kabul's lethargy and the corruption that had often left soldiers and police without their full complement of arms and ammunition. Morale was also at play. A post-battle evaluation found that nowhere had soldiers or police left their posts because of a shortage of ammunition. Rather, the culprit was a shortage of determination.[42]

Throughout the day, General Hamid was trying to get a grip on the situation from his headquarters in Mazar-e-Sharif. He received bits and pieces of information. At 1:00 a.m. on September 29, he called Kabul and informed them that forces were retreating to the airfield and reinforcements were needed. He then flew to the airfield to take over command.[43]

Only US air strikes stopped Mullah Salam from reaching the airfield. Within two days of the onset of the attack, Taliban were occupying the town. It was the first time a provincial capital had fallen. Locals who were not hiding in their homes or fleeing snapped photos with incoming Taliban, which were televised all over the world. Cushy city-boys posed incongruously with sinewy fighters from the villages. Photos of Taliban cruising about in captured army and police Ford Ranger pickups proliferated across the internet.

Ghani scrambled Afghan commandos and army battalions from Kabul to counterattack. Two US special forces teams and their command team accompanied them.[44] The Afghan commandos were part of the Afghan special operations forces. They were far more capable than the regular Afghan soldiers. Established in 2007, they had received years of dedicated training and advising from US special operations forces. The army had ten total commando battalions of roughly 700 men each, organized into separate companies of roughly 100 men and smaller special forces detachments—17,000 in all.[45] For that size force, the US instructors and advisors could instill a standard of tactical proficiency unattainable with larger numbers of trainees. US special operations forces designed the program to attract the fittest and most dedicated Afghans. Entry standards were rigorous. US officers were involved in officer selection. Reviewing officer performance with the senior Afghan special operations leadership, they tried to make selection meritocratic. Consequently, leadership was of a high standard and the individual commandos had a sense of professionalism and pride that eluded the rest of the army.

General Campbell videoconferenced with Hamid, the special forces teams, and other Afghan leaders on September 30. He asked pointed questions about what was being done to recapture the town. The special forces commander was ordered to "Go save Kunduz."[46] Campbell's intervention spurred action.[47]

The Afghan commandos counterattacked on the night of October 1. With the help of a handful of US air strikes, they got into the town center, where one of the few urban battles of the entire war went on for days. Taliban cadres maneuvered up narrow streets to dislodge and ambush the commandos and special forces. A special forces team member later wrote: "I had been in a lot of effective firefights but this was on a completely different level than even the experienced special operators on any of the detachments had seen—particularly over such a sustained period of time. How no one was killed, or even wounded, is an absolute miracle."[48] During the counterattack, an American AC-130 gunship annihilated a Doctors Without Borders hospital in the middle of the night on October 3, incinerating 42 doctors and patients, and wounding at least another 40. The event shocked the world and would permanently weigh on US soldiers and officials working Afghanistan. The strikes destroyed other buildings as well. By October 5, the provincial capital was back in government hands. The police and army proceeded to try to retake the surrounding countryside without much success.

In all, 38 Afghan soldiers and police were killed in the battle of Kunduz. No Americans died. Taliban casualties in the fighting are unknown but probably larger. Civilians suffered the heaviest: 848 were killed or wounded, in addition to 13,000 families that were displaced.[49]

The Kunduz offensive was a Taliban strategic victory. The Taliban had demonstrated that they could capture a province. Popular confidence in the army dropped.[50] According to one civil activist, "The people are disappointed in the government. . . . [One reason is that] the security situation got worse, day by day. Kunduz scared people. They are not sure the country can be defended."[51]

Kunduz sparked sympathetic attacks throughout northern Afghanistan. The relative calm that had long ruled broke. Hundreds of Pashtuns joined or rejoined the Taliban in the provinces of Faryab, Sari Pul, Baghlan, and Takhar. In the winter, Taliban attacked the Baghlan provincial capital (Pul-e-Khumri) and cut power lines to Kabul. By the end of the year, parts of six northern provinces were in Taliban hands, something unimaginable two years prior. Violence escalated in the east as well. The Taliban overturned the government's successes in Ghazni. Mullah Idris, the steadfast Taliban commander, extinguished the Andar uprising and then surrounded Ghazni city.[52]

With northern Helmand largely under Taliban control, Mansour turned to central Helmand.[53] This was key terrain, the location of the province's most fertile districts, Highway One, and the capital of Lashkar Gah.

Central Helmand, with Lashkar Gah in the middle, had prospered under the government since late 2010. Lashkar Gah was protected by a layer of districts: Nad Ali, Gereshk, Marjah, Nawa, and Garmser. Roughly 4,500 soldiers, police, and local police, not counting reserves in the capital, were arrayed in a belt of mud posts along the perimeter of the districts' farmland and the desert. Since 2013, this framework had repelled attacks of 30 to 100 Taliban.

The constellation of tribal leaders who had aligned with the marines in 2010 were a cornerstone of Helmand's defenses. In Marjah, the family of Gul Mullah was among the staunchest government supporters. Since being one of the first tribal leaders to work with the marines to form local militias in 2010, Gul Mullah had been instrumental in mobilizing the small tribal leaders of central Helmand. He prided himself on building an Islamic and egalitarian Helmand, devoid of Sher Mohammed Akhundzada and the old warlords. The whole family had supported Ashraf Ghani in the 2014 elections because of his anti-warlord views. Gul Mullah's brother, Omar Jan, was still police chief of Nad Ali, right next to Marjah. After spearheading the counterattacks in Sangin in 2013 and 2014, he was known as Helmand's most effective police chief. He had defeated Taliban assaults coming out of desert settlements for two years. Unlike many other police and army commanders, he had maintained his police and local police at full strength, 600 total. He used funds from various extracurricular activities to supply them well. At the core of his police was a tight crew of experienced fighters and lieutenants that he treated like family. Between them, Gul Mullah and Omar Jan commanded 800 police and local police. In 2014, Gul Mullah had boasted proudly, "The Taliban cannot return to Marjah while we live. Without the Afghan army or police, we can still hold Marjah on our own."[54]

By summer 2015, the now-familiar cracks had begun to afflict central Helmand. The total number of soldiers, police, and local police in Helmand was supposed to be 28,400. The actual number was closer to 19,000. Heavy police and army losses in the fighting in the northern half of the province stretched the center's defenses thin and weakened morale.[55] Gereshk's police chief, Hekmatullah, another of Helmand's best and son of powerful Barakzai parliamentarian Malim Mir Wali, was killed on a mission near Sangin by an improvised explosive device. He would be missed in the ensuing months.

The departure of the United States had allowed mismanagement and corruption to rise. Without US supervision, police and army commanders engaged in widespread selling of their ammunition to the Taliban. They also created more "ghost soldiers," the practice of putting names of people who were absent from the ranks on the rolls of a unit. Commanders pocketed their salaries or passed them up the chain to Kabul, where officials demanded a cut.[56] The exact number of ghost soldiers midway through the summer is unknown.

The new commander of the army in Helmand (215th Corps) was General Dadan Lawang. He had won minor fame in 2013 for confronting Pakistani troops aggressively (some thought unwisely) at the Goshte border crossing in Nangarhar. He and his immediate subordinates were former communists— professionals but tired and short on political influence. Whatever aggressiveness Lawang possessed stayed behind in Nangarhar. He preferred life in his headquarters at Camp Bastion, the old British and marine base in the desert (renamed Camp Shorab), disconnected from his soldiers. When a whole battalion fled Nowzad in early 2015, shedding most of its equipment and all its artillery, Lawang was sleeping in, oblivious of the defeat until Kabul called him at 10:00 a.m. Concerned about Helmand, General Campbell placed a special forces team and detachment of US advisors with Lawang's headquarters to rebuild and retrain several Afghan army battalions rendered combat ineffective in the fighting in the north.[57]

The tribally affiliated Afghan local police suffered in this environment. Out of neglect and greed, the province skimped on salaries and ammunition resupply.[58]

As month after month went by, the local police had fewer and fewer bullets. Tribal leaders were left improvising to pay salaries—one reason that poppy cultivation had risen in 2014.[59] Tribal unity also weakened. Tribal leaders watched the defeats of the army in northern Helmand. Confidence in the government dropped, leading a few to try to appease the Taliban.[60]

Mullah Abdur Rahim Manan, the Taliban governor of Helmand, gathered forces from northern Helmand for the offensive against the center, flush from his 2014 successes in northern Helmand. As a fellow Ishaqzai tribesman, Mansour trusted him. Manan was an inveterate enemy of the United States. Scornful of US presence in Afghanistan, Manan once told an interviewer, "The front against the proud and unmanageable Crusader occupation, which rubbed America's nose in the dirt, is the Islamic Emirate."[61] He accepted peace only on the Taliban's terms: "Our vision is clear, and our policy clear, and our attitude consistent towards the issue of peace in Afghanistan, which would be not to accept peace in Afghanistan as long as the occupation continues."[62]

Manan carried on regular telephone conversations with former member of parliament Maulali Ishaqzai. She tried to expose him to the virtues of democracy.[63] He accepted elections but rejected democracy, saying, "The United States brought democracy so the United States is actually the government."[64] When she suggested that he lay down his arms and move to Kabul, he laughed. She said, "Manan was all about jihad. Jihad, jihad, jihad."[65] Manan exhibited a fatalistic mentality increasingly common among Taliban battlefield commanders. One of his Ishaqzai lieutenants commented, "The commander's belief is that he will be martyred in jihad."[66]

Manan raised thousands of fighters, largely from the Ishaqzai, Alizai, and Noorzai tribes of northern Helmand. He set up a training camp in southern Sangin that could feed trained fighters to the front to the south.[67] Mansour sent reinforcements from Pakistan as well. The total number of Taliban in Helmand was somewhere between 8,000 and 14,000, roughly the same number of Taliban that had been *in all of Afghanistan* in 2006. An estimated 1,800 would be the assault force across Nad Ali, Marjah, Lashkar Gah, and central Gereshk. Manan met with his commanders to plan the operation. He then issued orders for how it would be carried out.[68]

The Taliban staged in the desert settlements around Gereshk, Nad Ali, and Marjah. The large canal—known as the *boghra*—divided the government-controlled irrigated land from the desert settlements.[69] The settlements and their poppy fields had grown under the eyes of the marines and British in the wake of the battle of Marjah, blooming white, pink, and purple in the spring. Their existence allowed Taliban cadres to form up right next to the government positions instead of in the open desert with fewer places to hide.[70] The defeats of the surge had not lessened their ardor. Gul Mullah's ally, Gul Mohammed, reported: "The Taliban are in the desert surrounding Marjah. They control the desert communities. Their morale there is good. Poor people go to the Taliban because they are uneducated. Or people go to them because they believe the United States will leave."[71] One settlement elder told a survey team, "The Taliban are always against government. And they told us their reason: If even one ISAF remain, we will fight against the government."[72]

Manan's offensive first hit Babaji, the seam between Nad Ali and Gereshk districts, a weak spot in the government defensive array less than 20 kilometers from Lashkar Gah.[73] Roughly 155 soldiers, police, and local police (35 soldiers, 60 police, and 60 local police) opposed 200 Taliban. More police had originally been in the front line but Hamid Gul, the new Gereshk police chief, had gotten

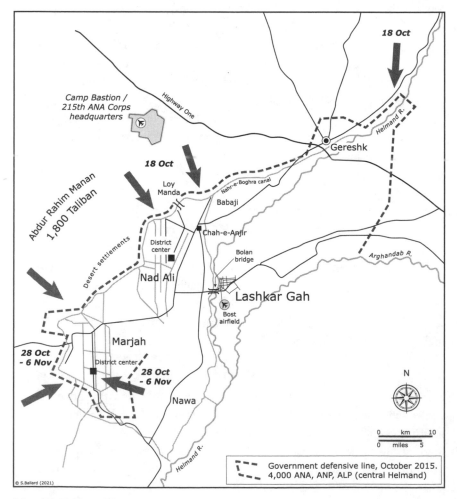

Map 20 Taliban offensives in central Helmand

wind of the Taliban massing and had withdrawn scores of his men to Gereshk bazaar, stripping out the defenses.[74]

To enter the irrigated land, the Taliban had to cross the *boghra* canal, approximately 4 meters deep and 15 meters wide. The best crossing point was a wide dirt culvert—something of a land bridge—at Loy Manda, at the far eastern edge of Omar Jan's front, on the seam with Gereshk itself. Omar Jan had emplaced a post with 30 police directly atop the land bridge. It was the main target of Manan's assault. On the night of October 18, 60 turbaned and prayer-capped fighters overwhelmed the dusty blue defenders with a hail of RPGs. Sixteen police were killed. Manan's men breached directly into Nad Ali and Babaji.[75]

Army and police officers reported that the Taliban advanced aggressively, readily firing upon the police and local police. Manan bypassed heavily armed army posts and concentrated against the police. Afghan local police retreated, even though they had ammunition. The army then also retreated, as did the rest of the police.[76] By the end of the day, 14 posts had fallen. The Taliban penetrated to within 10 kilometers of Lashkar Gah. In the words of one Helmand provincial security official, "Something went wrong."[77]

Omar Jan was constantly on his cell phone and police radio. He was furious with his men for falling back when they had ammunition. He was furious at the army for not racing forward to help. In addition to Loy Manda, several of his posts had fallen in the village of Chah-e-Anjir, strategically located on the axis of advance toward Lashkar Gah. Concerned the entire defense was the verge of collapse, he spearheaded his own counterattack in his blue armored Humvee against Chah-e-Anjir, berating his young driver, Sultan, "*Dzoo! Dzoo!* Go! Go! If we die it doesn't matter. We have to take the village!"[78] Omar Jan burst into the village at the forefront of his men. He shouldered an RPG and fired it at the Taliban. The blast gained him a foothold as Taliban fighters reeled back. The Taliban repeatedly rushed Omar Jan and his police, who ensconced themselves in mud homes. Eventually, Omar Jan retook the whole village, but Manan still had a wedge-shaped salient within 10 kilometers of Lashkar Gah.[79]

The next phase of Manan's offensive was at the very end of October against Marjah—Marjah the great victory of the first year of the surge, Lashkar Gah's strongest bulwark. Two thousand soldiers, police, and local police, including Gul Mullah's 105 fighters, defended the district. Morale, which had been high in the past, was shaky from news of the Babaji breakthrough.[80] Three days before the Taliban assault, 100 special police from Kabul (Afghan Civil Order Police) walked from their posts, Humvees and ammunition intact inside.[81]

The front line held for a week. Then, on November 3, Manan concentrated against the local police of Haji Moto Khan, a Noorzai tribal leader who defended a key position. He had relatives in the Taliban and supposedly made a deal and retreated with all his men. As word of a breakthrough spread, hundreds of soldiers, police, and local police abandoned the front line wholesale and stumbled rearward. The Taliban captured stocks of heavy machine guns, ammunition, and armored Humvees from the army. Tougher local police fought. They were on their own. Gul Mullah lost 25 of his 105 men, including his son and another brother, fighting on the front line for four days. The Taliban reduced the holdouts one by one. With some exaggeration, Omar Jan, who was watching from Nad Ali and speaking with his brother Gul Mullah several times per day, cursed: "They ran. Two thousand men. They had everything they needed—numbers, arms, ammunition—and they gave up!"[82]

By November 6, government forces had fallen back to the district center or to Lashkar Gah. Gul Mullah's 70 remaining men managed to hold his compound on the main road for a few days before retreating to Lashkar Gah.[83] Thousands of civilians took refuge there.[84] From the point of view of a Taliban commander from Nad Ali who participated in the attack, "We captured many areas from the government in Helmand and specifically in Nad Ali and Marjah, and the large Marjah operation that the foreigners conducted, has in the end had no result. Now only the Marjah district government building is with the Afghan soldiers. Complete control is with us."[85]

Campbell and Ghani reacted quickly. On Ghani's instructions, the ministry of defense deployed two army battalions and four commando companies to Helmand on October 24. Campbell permitted select and carefully targeted air strikes in support of the Afghan army and police. The arrival of Afghan commandos and a US special forces team rescued the Marjah district governor's compound—but like Sangin it was just a besieged island surrounded by an empty bazaar and Taliban. General Lawang, out in the desert, indulged in a rosy assessment of the situation.[86] In the words of an Afghan villager, "I saw with my own eyes government forces leave checkpoints.... I don't think the government can push the Taliban back. They don't fight.... We see the Americans supporting the government forces when they are trying to retake checkpoints, but then it's too late."[87]

Marjah was the signal defeat of the Helmand campaign. The Afghan forces in Helmand were a wreck. Total casualties were roughly 2,000, plus an unknown number of desertions. The casualties of the Afghan local police, fighting for their homes and families, were two to three times heavier than those of the regular police and army.[88] Campbell convinced the ministry of defense to take six Afghan army battalions out of the line as ineffective, over half the total in the province.[89] The defeat demoralized the other defending forces throughout the province. "No one thought the government and army would collapse so quickly," said Ayub Omar, district governor of Garmser.[90]

In early November, Campbell sent US special operations forces into Lashkar Gah to stiffen the defense. Ghani changed out the army leadership. With some media fanfare, he sent down General Moeen Faqir who would supposedly clean up corruption. Faqir would later be found guilty of pocketing money designated for food and provisions. One exasperated and high-ranking Helmand security leader complained, "The problem is Afghan leaders. They are corrupt and have no military organization. . . . We are very tired. We want American help and cooperation."[91]

The same story of attrition and exhaustion was true of the police and army throughout Afghanistan. Over 20,000 Afghan soldiers and police had been killed or injured in 2015, compared to 15,000 in 2014. US special forces teams with the Afghan commandos were critical to staving off defeat. So was close air support. But the use of air strikes was restrained because of the *in extremis* rule. The average in Afghanistan was 80 per month into 2016, less than a quarter of the average 340 air strikes per month of 2012. In October 2015, the height of the battles for Kunduz and central Helmand, the United States carried out 203 air strikes, compared to 500 or more per month in Iraq and Syria against a comparable adversary.

The strength of the army and police declined. Casualty and attrition rates spiked with the battles of autumn 2015 while recruitment plummeted. Suddenly, more soldiers and police were dropping from the rolls—either through combat losses, desertion, or refusal to re-enlist—than were enlisting. Whole battalions and district police forces dissolved or went combat-ineffective. Since attrition exceeded replacements, cumulative net losses grew and grew. The army and police got smaller and smaller. Campbell's headquarters discovered the recruiting base had shrunk as the Taliban had captured more and more ground. Danger further deterred young men from joining.[92] Net losses in the police were generally less than those in the army but were also rising.

The army and police were caught in a vicious cycle. As defeats mounted, morale tanked. In 2014, the police and army had been defeated after months of hard combat. Those defeats stoked fear. Soldiers and police stopped expecting success. In 2015, they often decided to flee, the military version of a run on banks.[93] Retreat became habitual, the accepted course of action. Over and over again, well-equipped soldiers and police facing inferior numbers of Taliban retreated after barely putting up a fight. The superior morale of the Taliban, compounded by corruption and dilatory US air support, is the primary explanation for the defeats of 2015, the year of the Taliban's greatest successes since 2006.

The violence in 2015 led to a series of changes in US policy. Obama had decided in May 2014 to keep 9,800 troops in Afghanistan in five main bases until the end of 2015 and then 5,500 troops around Kabul until the end of 2016, after which there would be only the embassy. America's war would end. In May 2014, circumstances seemed propitious. International terrorism appeared to be on the ropes. Bin Laden's death had crippled al-Qaʻeda. The Iraq withdrawal had been manageable and could be cited as a model for Afghanistan.

A month later, the strategic context shifted. The Islamic State swept up Mosul and instituted its caliphate. The event rattled the White House. Obama had not expected terrorists to return to Iraq and take over a third of the country. The Iraq withdrawal had resuscitated the terrorist threat to the United States. The Islamic State's propaganda machine drew volunteers from all over the world. A spate of terrorist attacks rocked Europe. As the strategic context shifted so did the domestic political context. The post–bin Laden relief turned into renewed domestic concern over terrorism. The percentage of Americans who feared they could be a victim of a terrorist attack jumped from 36 percent in 2011 to 49 percent in 2015.[94]

Campbell petitioned the White House to abort the planned drawdown and retain the bases outside Kabul. He contended that the United States needed to stay in these locations for five to ten years. Furthermore, he advised sending reinforcements for a total of 15,000 US troops. His proposal won him few friends at the White House.

General Joseph Dunford became chairman of the joint chiefs of staff in September 2015, after less than a year as commandant of the Marine Corps. The chairman was both the top position in the US military and the senior military advisor to the president. Dunford had wanted to remain commandant but Obama preferred he become chairman. Obama did not always agree with Dunford but trusted him to be thorough, apolitical, and rarely in the press. With nearly two years' experience in Afghanistan, Dunford doubted the government could fight on its own any time soon. On the other hand, he was wary of the terrorist threat. He thought it poor advice to tell the president simply to let Afghanistan fall. Intelligence assessments read, as they had in 2014, that terrorists would return and confront the United States with a more difficult challenge. With this in mind, Dunford argued that the military drawdown should be delayed.

The virtue of Obama's drawdown schedule was that he had given himself time to adjust course. Obama was reluctant to amend the plan to go to 5,500 at the end of the year. He certainly was not going to send reinforcements. Yet forced to return to war in Iraq and enter war in Syria, Obama did not want to repeat the experience in Afghanistan. He recognized that Afghanistan was vulnerable, especially after the attack on Kunduz. In early October 2015, Obama decided to leave the 9,800 troops in place until the end of 2016. After that, there would be 5,500, with bases in Kandahar, Helmand, Khost, Jalalabad, and Bagram. Obama accepted Campbell and Dunford's advice that this number would be necessary to target terrorists effectively. He gave no timeline for the withdrawal of the 5,500.

General John Nicholson succeeded Campbell in March 2016. Nicholson had extensive Afghanistan experience. After his time as the brigade commander for eastern Afghanistan and Kunar in 2006 and 2007 when the Korengal fighting had started, he had served as the operations officer for regional command south, the director of the Afghanistan-Pakistan cell on the joint staff in the Pentagon, and then the operations officer for all US and allied forces in Afghanistan. His wife had worked for years for non-governmental organizations in Afghanistan. Nicholson cared deeply for the Afghan people and had many Afghan friends.

Nicholson asked the White House for authorization to conduct air strikes more freely than *in extremis*. By the time Afghan formations were on the verge of defeat, it was too late for air strikes to save them. Therefore, Nicholson asked for "strategic effects" authorization. "Strategic effects" would permit him to conduct air strikes in support of the police and army when casualties or loss of terrain could endanger the government's position in a province. It would also permit him to send US advisors with Afghan police and soldiers on operations against the Taliban, though not participate in combat themselves. Dunford considered Nicholson's request the most important thing that could be done to slow Taliban momentum. The Taliban gains convinced Obama. In June, he gave Nicholson "strategic effects" authorization.[95] *In extremis* had been a tactical miscalculation. The strategic consequence was the destruction of much of the Afghan army and police at a time when terrorism had unexpectedly returned to threaten America. Fortunately, Obama was again flexible enough to adjust.

At the same time, Nicholson thought that more than 5,500 troops should stay in Afghanistan indefinitely after 2016. The idea was poorly received at the White House. Debate carried on for three months, framed by the upcoming US presidential election. It was a secret and out of the news. Dunford strictly controlled all information about the military planning. In meetings, Dunford dispassionately laid out the risks and military options in a way that Obama appreciated. The range of options was between 5,500 and 9,800 troops. Obama strongly desired to draw down or even to revert to a full withdrawal by the end of the year.[96] He came close to pulling the plug.

In the end, Obama did not want to bequeath an imminent military disaster to his successor. White House staffers thought it was hard to say no when Defense Secretary Ashton Carter and General Dunford sincerely believed there was a terrorist threat and had designed reasonable options to handle it. Iraq also weighed on Obama, not only the physical damage from terrorist attacks but the popular reaction attacks could trigger. The Islamic State had inspired a terrorist shooting in San Bernardino, California, in December 2015 that had killed 14. Donald Trump was running for president and used the attack to stir up hysteria over terrorism and immigrants. Obama worried that a major attack could cause Americans to persecute Muslims, a blow to tolerance within the United States. Minimizing the chance of a terrorist attack on American soil became important for the sake of civil liberties.[97] Obama therefore decided to do enough to avert near-term catastrophe in Afghanistan. That July he announced that 8,400 US troops would stay after 2016, again with no end date on the deployment.[98] Again, the Taliban resurgence had caused Obama to amend his withdrawal strategy.

The decision ended three years of deliberation over US withdrawal from Afghanistan. Obama and Biden had been inclined to leave. Obama had dramatically changed US strategy from deploying tens of thousands of troops with the goal of defeating the Taliban to a small presence of a few thousand with the minimalist goals of suppressing terrorists and preventing the government from falling. What he could not accomplish was getting out. The threat of terrorism had trapped him. This was the conundrum of the post–September 11 era. US presidents had to choose between spending resources in places of very low geostrategic value or accepting some unknown risk of a terrorist attack. Obama erred on the side of insuring against that risk by leaving forces in place. The intention to get out had met reality and blinked.

The defeats of 2015 positioned the Taliban to attack multiple provincial capitals in 2016. After a year of capturing army and police stockpiles and equipment, the Taliban now had plenty of vehicles, ammunition, and machine guns and RPGs. Mansour's new reaction forces, the *keetaq muntazaree*, were in place across the country, equipped with night vision goggles and optical sights. During the first half of the year, the Taliban pressured four provincial capitals—Tarin Kowt in Uruzgan, Farah City in Farah, Kunduz City in Kunduz, and Lashkar Gah in Helmand.

Taliban struck the government positions around Lashkar Gah almost daily. After two successful fighting seasons, the reputation of Manan, the Taliban governor, soared. Taliban outside Helmand described him as a "victorious man" who had "fought a great deal."[99] Manan spent almost all his time in Helmand. He was able to control the various commanders within the province, who were each now running various major operations. His commanders viewed him as "a very strong military person."[100] Every month, his forces bit off sections of the front line.

In Nad Ali, Omar Jan was still fighting. Despite being lightly wounded by an improvised explosive device in early 2016, he managed to keep 600 police and local police in the field along an ever-shrinking perimeter.[101] The army battalion in Nad Ali had dwindled from 600 to 150 soldiers. Omar Jan had supplied his men well over the years. He was now living off those evaporating savings. He desperately tried to get ammunition and replacement weapons from Lashkar Gah. The provincial police headquarters had little to offer.

Combat was fierce in May at the outset of the fighting season. Omar Jan had warned General Faqir that a big attack was imminent. Faqir, sitting safely at the army corps headquarters in the desert, refused to do anything.[102] Omar Jan fought alone. Twenty of his men died defending a single post. Omar Jan was pushed back from his front line 7 kilometers from the district center.[103] At times he was surrounded when Taliban cut the road to Lashkar Gah.

Morale became harder and harder to sustain. Parts of his force ceased wanting to fight at all. Cooperation with the army was poor. When Omar Jan's army counterpart blamed the police for the losses, Omar Jan shot back in the press, "The police are fighting in the front line and suffer heavy casualties more than any other forces."[104] The battles tired Omar Jan. He had seen two of his brothers and more than ten of his closest police die. His crew was like family to him. It is what made them effective. Their deaths hit home.

In July 2016, Omar Jan pleaded with me in Kabul, "If America just helps with air strikes and getting me supplies, we can win. My weapons are worn from shooting. My ammunition stocks are low. I do not need advisors. I just need someone to call when things are really bad." His voice growing soft, he confided, "But, if America will not help, if everyone else is retreating, I have to retreat too. I cannot sacrifice everything if there will be no help. I will have no choice." What he meant was he had a duty to care for his family. It was antithetical for a tribal Pashtun to sacrifice family on behalf of any government.[105]

In August, Mullah Naim Barech, the Taliban's former Helmand provincial governor who now worked with Manan, swept up Nawa and Garmser—the southern defenses of Lashkar Gah that had endured for seven years. The Taliban advanced 200 kilometers in less than three weeks. Ten thousand people abandoned their homes and sought refuge in Lashkar Gah.[106] The soldiers, police, and tribal leaders in these districts had heard all about the defeats in Sangin, Marjah, and Gereshk. They knew they were twisting in the wind. Men who had repeatedly defeated hundreds of Taliban in 2014 and 2015 now expected to be defeated themselves.

In Garmser, aided and abetted by a sympathetic Noorzai faction, 400 Taliban defeated roughly 1,000 police and soldiers. An entire army battalion headquarters surrendered after its commander was killed, replete with six shipping containers of guns and ammunition.[107] The police and local police forces disintegrated. Five US air strikes finally arrived during the last days of the battle, once more too few and too late to stem the tide. The first Friday after his victory, Naim strode through Garmser's Lakari bazaar for Friday prayers.[108]

At the beginning of October, the Taliban simultaneously attacked four provincial capitals: Tarin Kowt (Uruzgan), Kunduz City (Kunduz), Farah City (Farah), and Lashkar Gah (Helmand). In each, Taliban fighters took over whole neighborhoods. Nicholson initially hesitated to authorize air strikes because of lingering concerns about upsetting Obama. Eventually he had no choice. He permitted 205 air strikes.[109] In Tarin Kowt, a massive Taliban attack from all directions overran two-thirds of the police and army posts and captured all the roads, seizing several kilometers of the highway to Kandahar City. Kandahar police chief Abdul Razziq had to launch a major counteroffensive with US assistance and air strikes to prevent Tarin Kowt from falling. In Farah, where the Taliban had long controlled most of the districts, the attacks were mainly on the outskirts of the city and did not get very far.

In Kunduz, Mullah Salam again attacked Kunduz City. A good part of the police and army broke and ran. Salam briefly captured the traffic circle at the center of the city and torched the governor's home. An obstinate NDS detachment in the town center prevented the recurrence of the wholesale rout of the year prior.[110] Nicholson flew in hundreds of reinforcements, including Afghan commandos and US special forces. Over the course of a week, the commandos re-secured the city.

At Lashkar Gah, Mullah Manan attacked from three directions. In a few places, Taliban suicide bombers used captured police uniforms and Ranger pickups to infiltrate into the city and surprise police and army defenders. The police and army barely resisted. Six hundred soldiers in one battalion surrendered.[111] The police chief, General Qatooz, fled to the airfield at Bost. Governor Hayatullah Hayat and other officials sped all the way to Kandahar. Army corps commander General Faqir was safely at his headquarters in Camp Bastion. The highest-ranking commander left in town was Mir Hamza, the wily deputy NDS intelligence chief who had been fighting in Helmand since 1995. He refused to run, partly because he worried Razziq in Kandahar would call him a coward. Mir Hamza took charge of the police, local police, soldiers, and NDS forces that were sticking it out. Omar Jan joined him.

Police and local police west of the Helmand River were cut off. Manan besieged 100 soldiers and police at Chah-e-Anjir. A request for safe passage to retreat to Lashkar Gah may or may not have been granted. But when the soldiers and police moved out of their defenses, the Taliban opened fire in what the government soon claimed was a massacre. Manan disclosed his version of what happened in an interview with *al-Samoud*, the Taliban's news magazine:

> The responsibility for the defeat belongs to the [government] leadership. They were playing with the lives of their soldiers and left them in places from where there was no way to escape and made no attempt to relieve them. Because the leadership did not allow them to withdraw, they fell under siege by the mujahedin. The mujahedin several times asked them to surrender and lay down their arms and abandon the fight for the occupation and its agents. They rejected these calls, until the fighting broke out, killing a large number of them. . . . Some of them even fought to the death. Others surrendered to the mujahedin after

running out of ammunition and facing an uncertain fate. . . . The dead bodies lay scattered across the battlefield.[112]

Taliban swept to the Bolan bridge over the Helmand River—the same place Zakir had attacked in 2008—and shot at the governor's office 300 meters away. With Omar Jan's help, Mir Hamza counterattacked across the bridge. Manan was with the Taliban on the other side. Mir Hamza got on the radio with Manan and dared, "I am Director Mir Hamza. *Radza!* Come on! If I am martyred or captured!" Manan charged Mir Hamza's men seven times. Mir Hamza called the US advisors and bargained with them for two drone strikes—the only two thus far in the battle—and used the cover for another counterattack. A bullet hit Mir Hamza in the leg during the last charge and he had to be evacuated.[113] He and Omar Jan had bought enough time to save Lashkar Gah.

Three hundred commandos reinforced the town. General Nicholson and Minister of Defense Abdullah Habibi visited Lashkar Gah repeatedly to invigorate the defense. Ghani fired General Faqir. The new corps commander, General Wali Mohammed Ahmedzai was a commando and ten years younger than his predecessor. Sixteen years of US special forces mentorship showed. Upon arriving, he ditched his headquarters in the desert and flew immediately to Lashkar Gah. There, he grabbed his sergeant major and led 100 soldiers in a counterattack that finally drove Manan away from the western bank of the Helmand River. The general then planted himself in Lashkar Gah and ran the battle. Around 100 US special operations forces and advisors headquartered themselves in the town.[114]

In the middle of the fighting, Omar Jan escorted a convoy with his revered elder brother Gul Mullah and Marjah tribal leader Baz Gul—two leaders who had helped the marines so much in 2010. Manan was targeting Gul Mullah. One of his suicide bombers hit the convoy. The explosion killed Gul Mullah. Omar Jan was distraught. His men had halved from 600 to 300. Now his elder brother was gone. Only one brother was left. The war had destroyed his family. He lost hope.[115] He retreated into mourning at his compound in Lashkar Gah and prepared his resignation. Three years of defeat had ground down the government's best commanders.

Nicholson had saved them, but Tarin Kowt, Farah City, Kunduz City, and Lashkar Gah remained besieged. The army and police were too weak to push the Taliban out of the surrounding countryside. Government casualties in 2015 and 2016 exceeded 40,000 police and soldiers. The police and army had taken so much damage and were so demoralized that few units could hold ground. The defense depended on the commandos and US air strikes.

Taliban casualties are unknown. The government exaggerated Taliban losses at two or three times its own. The reality was certainly fewer than 40,000. The

Taliban were in their strongest position since 2009. They held large amounts of countryside in at least 16 of Afghanistan's 34 provinces. They were ready to reap an unprecedented acreage of poppy. They also had access to hundreds of thousands more young men for recruitment. With their expanded territory, the Quetta Shura moved as many as 16 of its members responsible for southern and western Afghanistan into Helmand. They reestablished their judicial system and allowed government schools and clinics to be open. One district governor warned me, "The people do not believe Ghani or the Ministry of Defense.... The people are starting to think the Taliban will be here forever."[116]

Since 2009, US policy in Afghanistan had sought to enable the Afghan government, its army, and its police to stand on their own so that the United States could eventually withdraw. This goal had justified Obama's surge and drawdown policy. In spite of years of effort and assistance, the defeats of 2015 and 2016 mark the failure of that endeavor, as well as the failure of Obama's endeavor to find an exit.

Omar Jan's story is not quite finished. After his brother's death, friends came to his house and implored him to return to command. Mohammed Fahim, the former district governor of Gereshk and longtime colleague who was also from Marjah, called him and told him that the people would lose hope if he quit. So Omar Jan picked himself up and fought on. He took his crew back to the Nad Ali main bazaar and his headquarters near an old crumbling mud fort that was the army base, which was all but surrounded.

Then, in spring 2017, marines under Brigadier General Roger Turner replaced US army soldiers as advisors in Helmand. Their return breathed new life into Omar Jan. The deputy commander was Colonel Matt Reid, a good friend. It was as if America had not let him down. For five months, he darted about Nad Ali, guiding his men, mending weak points, organizing reinforcements, calling for air strikes, constantly on his cell phone. In one firefight, he was a few meters from incoming rounds and RPGs, taking cover behind his blue Humvee, calling Colonel Reid on his iPhone, and wildly waving at the sky for marines to drop bombs. As he had promised a year prior, with air strikes, the line could hold.

On the evening of Saturday, September 23, Omar Jan was driving from Lashkar Gah back to the Nad Ali district center with a few of his trucks, having spent Friday, the holy day, with his family. Manan guessed he might be on the road and ambushed him. An RPG sailed into Omar Jan's truck and killed him.

I am not entirely sure why Omar Jan fought to the end. Most other police and army commanders had given up. He went beyond what honor demanded by sacrificing himself and his family. He left one lone brother to care for the sons, daughters, and widows of himself, Gul Mullah, and two other deceased brothers. With the risk of death so high, Omar Jan could have resigned and devoted himself to them in Lashkar Gah. Was his determination the extreme of irresponsibility? Or was it the epitome of Pashtunwali, following honor to self-destruction?

Whatever the case, there was no escape for Omar Jan. He exemplifies the tragedy of the US intervention. We propelled a good man to fight for his country. We convinced good people to take risks. He and his family earned money and some stature. But their modest roots barred them from ever ascending to true power. With his record of distinction, Omar Jan should have been provincial chief of police. That was never in the cards. Even Ghani, whom the family saw as a champion for their values, did not bat an eye for them. He probably did not even know their names. Omar Jan and his family were destroyed in the process. Little was left of them. Or America's victories in Afghanistan. Omar Jan was one of the last surviving achievements of the surge in Helmand. His death symbolizes the end of the remnants of that era.

19

The Trump Administration

The Taliban had scored resounding victories in 2015 and 2016. For the next two years the United States tried to staunch the bleeding while terrorism and extremism grew in Afghanistan.

During spring 2016, Taliban emir Mullah Akhtar Mohammed Mansour was unresponsive to attempts by President Ashraf Ghani to negotiate. His heart may have wanted to negotiate but in the wake of the succession struggle he towed a hard line. He also was more anti-Pakistan than ever. He diversified Taliban relations with foreign countries and regularly traveled to Iran in order to increase the armaments and support the Taliban had been receiving from that country for the past few years. He may have even been interested in reaching out to Russia. In March, in rejection of pressure from Pakistan Chief of the Army Raheel Sharif, Mansour publicly declared the Taliban would not participate in any negotiations.[1]

In the middle of his last year in office, Obama did something unprecedented. For years, he had withheld from striking Taliban leaders in Pakistan. When an opportunity arose to strike Mansour, Obama seized it. On May 21, a US drone killed Mansour as he was driving in western Baluchistan near the Afghan border, returning from a trip to Iran.[2]

Unlike the announcement of Mullah Omar's death ten months earlier, no succession struggle ensued. On May 23, a few key leaders from the Quetta Shura met to select Mansour's successor. More would have attended if not for of fear of further air strikes. Within a day, the group unanimously chose Maulawi Haybatullah, one of Mansour's two deputies. Sirajuddin Haqqani and Mullah Omar's son Yaqub were chosen as Haybatullah's deputies.[3]

Maulawi Haybatullah was a Noorzai from Panjwai, Kandahar. Rumored to be 47 years old, he had a stern look and long black beard with strands of white, mildly frayed at the edges. The title "Maulawi" signified status as a true religious scholar. He was also known as "Shaykh al-Hadith," which implies mastery of the sayings of the Prophet. He had lived much of his life in Pakistan and had trained at a madrasa there. Relatively unknown outside the Taliban, Haybatullah had been an early member of the movement but had been young and never in a senior position in the first regime. He served as a distinguished judge on a variety of provincial and military courts, a traditional job of a religious scholar. After 2001, he was the head judge (*qazi al-qazat*) of the Taliban's high court, located in Pakistan.

The fact that Haybatullah was a religious scholar and a judge enhanced his credibility. He had numerous students and an extensive network within the Taliban movement. He was known for "walking well" among the community. Other Taliban could not match his reputation for calm temperament and arduous study.[4] He was said to be more intelligent than Mullah Omar or Mansour. His position as head judge had brought him into sensitive decisions, so he was trusted. Haybatullah had been one of the first two senior leaders whom Omar's son and brother had entrusted with news of his death. He had handled the release of the information to Mansour and had guided him to hide the secret. He and three others then issued the fatwa that allowed Mansour temporarily to lead.[5]

Haybatullah was mindful of the leadership crisis that had followed the announcement of Mullah Omar's death. He consolidated power quickly. He used his Noorzai tribal affiliation to reach out to those disaffected by the primacy of Ishaqzai under Mansour. He brought back Baz Mohammed and his men, the most powerful of the remaining splinter factions. He also won over Abdul Qayum Zakir, Mansour's rival. To buy consensus, Haybatullah granted the military commanders greater autonomy. Haybatullah lacked Mansour's poppy funds to buy influence.[6] Compromise diluted discipline a bit. In contrast to the time of Mullah Omar, there were more political disputes and competition over resources (poppy) but the movement did not devolve into feuding factions.

President Donald Trump took office in January 2017, the third US president to handle the Afghan War. Elected on a wave of populism, Trump was profoundly skeptical of foreign interventions. He questioned why the United States should do anything in Afghanistan. His instinct was to get out. He had also, however, campaigned on decisive action against terrorism and had criticized President Obama's methodical strategy to defeat the Islamic State in Iraq and Syria. He vowed to crush terrorism while refocusing resources on the United States, to "make America great again."

Trump's Secretary of Defense was James Mattis, the retired marine general who had commanded the 1st Marine Division in its 2003 blitzkrieg on Baghdad and later led Central Command. The slight 5-foot-6 "warrior monk" was renowned in the US military for aggression on the battlefield and study of history at home. He dedicated his entire being to war and did not suffer the notion of defeat lightly. Three months after being sworn in, he traveled to Afghanistan. The Afghan army struck him as "slow and clumsy" and "club-footed." What he saw convinced him that the United States was losing.

General Dunford's term as chairman of the joint chiefs of staff spanned the Obama and Trump administrations. Dunford and Mattis were unbreakably close. Dunford had been one of Mattis's regimental commanders in 2003 and later his chief of staff. General Nicholson was still commander of US forces and ISAF in Afghanistan.

The new administration began a review of Afghanistan and Pakistan strategy in March. Nicholson proposed a new strategy. The ultimate goal was to compel the Taliban to negotiate a peace settlement. The components of the strategy were as follows: 3,800 reinforcements, a larger number of advisers, a program to double the size of the Afghan special operations forces, increased air strikes, greater political and economic pressure on Pakistan, and efforts to fragment the Taliban. Nicholson thought 80 percent of the population could be brought back under the government and that doing so could drive the Taliban to reconcile. Trump's national security advisor, Lieutenant General H.R. McMaster, agreed with Nicholson. Both believed a harsher Pakistan policy was overdue. Both hoped the Taliban could be brought to the negotiating table and a peace settlement could be reached that preserved the Afghan government and allowed some US forces to remain in Afghanistan.

Dunford was more pessimistic. His judgment was unaltered. No amount of resources could be expected to make a difference in Afghanistan. It was unrealistic to think the United States could foster lasting improvements in the Afghan government. He doubted Pakistan's orientation could be fundamentally changed or that peace talks would come about, as much as he was willing to give them a try. Yet nor could the United States get out. "If left alone, there are people in this region who will follow us home," he told marines on a visit to Helmand.[7] The potential for terrorism from Afghanistan would be too great a political risk for any US leader ever to bear. Therefore, the realistic choice was to invest enough forces—and no more—to suppress the terrorist threat. The United States was only covered for as long as troops were invested into the country. In his analogy of term life insurance, once payments stop, so do the benefits. The best he was willing to forecast was that "maybe in four years, things change and we will have opportunities."

Until June, Trump offered no guidance. Mattis, McMaster, and Dunford did not anticipate the intensity of his antipathy for Afghanistan. On June 12, the first national security council meeting on Afghanistan assembled. It was explosive. Trump was furious at the idea of fighting in Afghanistan and refused to decide on the strategy. Mattis and Dunford spent the next month refining the strategy and trying to answer the president's concerns.

A second meeting convened on July 19 in the "Tank," the secure conference room of the joint chiefs of staff in the Pentagon. Trump was even angrier and ruled the United States was losing. He wanted all assistance to Pakistan cut off. He derided Mattis and Dunford as bad advisors and demanded Nicholson be fired for failing to win.[8] A follow-up meeting the next day was less antagonistic. Trump was most interested in some way to win and get out. Total withdrawal was also put on the table. Once more, no decision came out of the meeting.

Over the next month, intelligence officials briefed Trump on the terrorist threat. The military and intelligence community assessed that withdrawing from Afghanistan would increase the chances of a terrorist attack on the United States. Trump conferred with a variety of people outside government about Afghanistan as well: former special operations forces, former intelligence agents, defense contractors, media executives. Many warned him that terrorists would attack the United States if Afghanistan fell. Rupert Murdoch, owner of Fox News, and Steve Feinberg, owner of the defense contractor DynCorp, allegedly advised him to stay.

Other than Trump, no cabinet member or participant in a national security council meeting argued that the United States should leave Afghanistan. All agreed that the United States could not walk out. Even Steve Bannon, the president's most isolationist advisor, who damned Nicholson's strategy as the same old tired thinking, concurred that the United States would have to stay.

The terrorist threat convinced Trump to go along. On August 18, he approved the new strategy and an increase of 3,900 troops, bringing the total US troops in Afghanistan to roughly 14,000.[9] The decision would never rest comfortably with Trump. He would later blame McMaster, Dunford, and Mattis, whom he called "the generals."

Trump announced the new strategy on August 21, highlighting its main characteristics. He promised greater pressure on Pakistan and greater authority for US commanders to use military force. He stressed that there would be no timeline; it would be a conditions-based approach. Eschewing any dream the Afghan government could stand up on their own, Trump's goals were realistic: "Attacking our enemies, obliterating ISIS, crushing al-Qaʻeda, preventing the Taliban from taking over Afghanistan, and stopping mass terrorist attacks against America before they emerge."[10] A political settlement was the most ambitious goal but Trump promised nothing: "Someday, after an effective military effort, perhaps it will be possible to have a political settlement that includes elements of the Taliban in Afghanistan, but nobody knows if or when that will ever happen."[11] The concept matched Dunford's thinking more than that of Nicholson, McMaster, or even Mattis. To many the speech sounded scripted, detached from Trump's true feelings. The speech's stand-out line was, "My original instinct was to pull out, and historically, I like following my instincts."[12]

Everyone picked up on the line. The new strategy was born under the threat that Trump could change his mind, possibly in a spur-of-the-moment message over social media. At any hour, Trump could put out a tweet pulling out all US forces and the whole endeavor would be over. Or as Pentagon officials liked to say in reference to Greek myth, "The Tweet of Damocles."

The most important outcome of the new strategy was that it prioritized peace talks. Both the Pentagon and the State Department saw talks leading to a political settlement—the parameters of which were left ambiguous—as the goal of the strategy. This created an impetus to invest greater resources into negotiations and to find the right diplomat to lead the effort. A year would pass before that effort would truly be underway.

On the battlefield, Nicholson used US military power to slow Taliban momentum after the disasters of 2015 and 2016. As the Islamic State was defeated in Iraq and Syria, Mattis reassigned drones, dozens of AH-64 attack helicopters, and a squadron of A-10 attack aircraft to Afghanistan. Where advisors were present, a crippling weight of air strikes could be called. Going beyond "strategic effects," Trump permitted Nicholson to strike Taliban whether or not the army and police were in danger. More ordnance would be delivered in 2018—841 air strikes in September 2018 alone—than any time since 2010. That did a lot to blunt Taliban attacks. In Kunduz, Mullah Abdul Salam, the capable Taliban governor, was killed in an air strike in February 2017. In Helmand, the inspiring new Afghan general, Wali Mohammed, and Brigadier General Roger Turner's 300 new marine advisors enabled the Afghan army and police to drive the Taliban a dozen or so kilometers from Lashkar Gah. As Brigadier General Watson (Turner's successor in Helmand) put it, "Afghans are grinding it out in small positions everywhere" and "holding what they took by their finger nails."[13] According to one of Mullah Manan's commanders, "Many of our friends have been martyred. We have expectation to miss them completely and in war always have trust in Allah."[14]

Toward the end of the unproductive 2017 fighting season, Haybatullah traveled to northern Helmand with members of the Quetta Shura and held a strategy meeting in Musa Qala. Haybatullah ordered a change in tactics because of increased US air strikes. Taliban cadres were not to defend against army and police offensives but to engage from standoff distances and fall back. Taliban attacks on posts were to be at night. Suicide bombings and assassinations within the towns and cities were to increase. Major offensives would shift to poorly defended provinces rather than Nangarhar, Helmand, or Kandahar.[15]

As he staved off Haybatullah's cadres, Nicholson could not fix deeper problems in the battered Afghan army and police. Attrition continued to exceed replacements. Advisors helped reduce desertion by tracking pay, supplies, and leave but only so much. They could not change the reluctance of young men to volunteer. US government investigation of automated pay records, ghost soldiers, and losses revealed that the true size of the army and police was 250,000 out of 352,000 and dwindling. On-hand strength in the field was even lower. Its adversaries' numbers were steady, at 60,000 to 80,000 Taliban and 5,000 Islamic State.

Ghani devoted time to the military situation to a degree that Karzai never had, often penning reforms late into the night. He was committed to expanding the power of the central government and marginalizing regional powerbrokers, such as Mohammed Atta, Ismael Khan, Abdul Razziq, and his own vice president Abdur Rashid Dostum, whom he viewed as parasites on society. He surrounded himself with young, educated, English-speaking Afghans. They shared his devotion to progress and his lack of military experience. Too many of their reforms impractically assumed merit could supplant tribal politics.

Very early in his tenure, Nicholson identified poor army and police leadership as a root of army setbacks. Every week, Nicholson spent hours advising Ghani on the selection of commanders and officials, careful not to offend by being too forceful. Ghani instituted a well-meaning reform to replace poor leaders with good ones, named the "Inherent Law." Five thousand overage or unqualified colonels and generals were to be retired from the army and police within two years, a goal easier set than met. Over 2017 and 2018, Ghani retired 1,215 army officers and 989 police officers.[16] Many were corrupt. Others were political opponents. Finding good replacements was a problem. In Helmand, for example, Ghani replaced three of four brigade commanders after a year of lobbying by Nicholson. The marines rated only one of the new ones as effective. The process was thickly immersed in politics. Powerbrokers jockeyed over new appointments. Ghani often had to weigh in personally to overcome the patronage networks in the ministries of defense and interior.[17]

Ghani's political instincts were his own worst enemy. Ghani wanted to put in his own subpar loyalists—often old hands with ignominious records, eastern Pashtuns, or former communists. With some justification, he distrusted Tajik officers. In an election, they might help Tajik political candidates. In a political crisis, they might desert. In August 2017, Ghani shipped General Wali Mohammed Ahmedzai out of Helmand to the north to do his political bidding where Mohammed Atta (governor of Balkh) and other Tajik leaders might try to exploit their connections in the army. In Helmand, Wali Mohammed's mediocre deputy was promoted to command the corps.

The makeup of the Afghan army morphed over Ghani's tenure. Ghani gradually dismantled the Tajik leadership network of Bismullah Khan, former minister of defense and chief of staff, within the army. Eastern Pashtuns gained influence.

Tajiks lost out. Eastern Pashtuns supportive of Ghani joined or stayed in the army while Tajiks became disinterested in serving in an organization they no longer led, fighting for a president opposed to their interests. By the end of 2018, 58 percent of the army was from Pashtun-dominated eastern Afghanistan, with 36 percent from Nangarhar, home of many of Ghani's strongest supporters. Only 2 to 4 percent of the force were from Kabul and less than 1 percent were from Panjshir or Balkh—Tajik strongholds.[18]

The open-ended US commitment in Trump's new strategy emboldened Ghani to move against his rivals. Between November 2017 and March 2018, he mired himself in an extended political crisis with the Tajiks by removing the powerful Mohammed Atta from the governorship of Balkh. Atta refused to step down until Ghani agreed to appoint one of Atta's protégés as the new governor. The crisis distracted from fighting the war. It was a textbook example of political science principal-agent theory in which an agent (Ghani) uses the assistance of a principal (the United States) to go after its own domestic political interests instead of the common but less politically valued interests shared with the principal (in this case waging the war).

After the disaster in Kunduz in 2015, violence continued across northern Afghanistan. Nicholson sought to pay greater attention to the region. He recognized that Americans had never operated enough in the north to build a strong collective knowledge, as we had in the east and south.

Kunduz province was almost entirely controlled by the Taliban. Spring and autumn Taliban assaults on Kunduz City became a staple of the war. The death of Mullah Salam and US special operations forces and air strikes precluded things from being as bad as 2015 or 2016. Pashtun communities in Baghlan, Faryab, and Sari Pul were Taliban hotspots. Attempts by certain Tajik and Uzbek warlords to seize Pashtun lands inflamed Pashtun support. Taliban influence spread into the Uzbeks and Tajiks in these provinces as well. The Taliban even had enclaves in Takhar and Badakhshan, a Tajik and Jamiat-Islami stronghold. Mansour and then Haybatullah appointed Tajiks and Uzbeks to be provincial governors and field commanders in order to reach into their respective communities.

For Nicholson, the persistence of Taliban in the heartland of the traditionally anti-Taliban Tajiks and Uzbeks was distressing. A leading Kabul journalist commented that after years of influence in the government and Kabul, "The Tajiks became bourgeois. They don't want to fight for Ghani. Bismullah Khan was way more effective. The Tajiks don't trust Atmar [Ghani's national security advisor]."[19] Related to their disinterest, over the years, too many of the old Tajik and Uzbek Northern Alliance warlords had too often neglected to help and spread their wealth to their own communities, farmers, and villagers. The Taliban exploited the resulting grievances.

Ghani's controversial first vice president, Abdur Rashid Dostum, mobilized his Uzbek "Junbesh" militia, which still numbered in the thousands, to defend his territory in Faryab and Jowzjan. His forces suffered 60 killed and dozens injured fighting the Taliban.[20] The grizzled old Uzbek warlord had even directed a clearing operation in August 2015 in a camouflage uniform from an armored personnel carrier, bringing along two sons as a sign of his family's commitment. Dostum's courage garnered admiration in the press but he could not eliminate the Taliban. His militia's heavy-handed tactics, beating and indiscriminately shooting at Pashtuns, underlined the divisions in the north. "I was in my house when about 200 Ranger cars of Junbesh militia came into the village," said one villager in Faryab, "They were carrying guns like Kalashnikovs and shouting 'You're Taliban!' and firing as people came out of their homes."[21] A 50-year woman from another village that the militia frequented recounted that they beat her with the butts of their rifles and yelled, "You are Pashtuns, you cannot say anything—you have no rights."[22] Dostum himself was forced out of Afghanistan in May 2017 amid Western outrage for brutalizing a rival at a buzgashi match (the traditional Afghan horse-riding sport).

Between politics, heavy-handedness, and Taliban inroads into the Tajiks and Uzbeks, the government and the old Northern Alliance was unable to reassert control of the north. Atta's influence buffered Mazar-e-Sharif and prevented the Taliban from closing in on the north's main city. Government influence and anti-Taliban attitudes similarly protected the western city of Herat from the Taliban.

In summer 2018, before turning over command, Nicholson reported to Mattis that he had achieved a stalemate. The intelligence community was less charitable. The last months of the 2018 fighting season went worse than expected. While Nicholson had enough advisors to protect key provincial capitals, others were still vulnerable. The peanut butter could only be spread so thin. The Taliban nearly captured Farah City in May and then Ghazni City in August. The latter was a bloody mess. One thousand Taliban, headquartered out of Andar district, stormed its center. Two Afghan helicopters were shot down attempting to land at the army base within the town. The Afghan corps commander for the area was General Dadan Lawang, the same who had lost most of Helmand in 2015, a clear sign Ghani was failing to emplace competent leaders. At his headquarters in Paktiya, Lawang was out of the loop and did not even request assistance from Nicholson until the news media publicized the attacks. US and Afghan special operations forces recaptured the heart of Ghazni city but Taliban could move freely in its neighborhoods. The defeat frightened Afghans and chopped away at confidence in the government. American newspapers used the battle to cast doubt on the whole strategy. Mujib Mashal reported in the *New York Times*, "The Ghazni assault has demonstrated a stunning display of Taliban tenacity that belies the official Afghan and American narrative of progress in the war and the possibility for peace talks. It also has revealed remarkable bumbling by the Afghan military."[23]

As the government struggled, the Islamic State and the Taliban were radicalizing. After being thrashed by the Taliban, Afghan army and militias, and US special operations forces in 2015 and 2016, the Islamic State (also known as the Islamic State in the province of Khorasan) staged a comeback in 2017 and 2018. Islamic State members and individuals inspired by them continued to plot attacks in the United States and Europe.[24]

Mattis and Dunford paid attention to the campaign against the Islamic State. Worldwide, the Islamic State was rated the gravest threat to the US homeland. In Iraq and Syria, the US military was enabling Iraqi and Kurdish forces to clear the Islamic State out of the cities of Mosul and Raqqah during 2017. Trump wanted the Islamic State defeated. Mattis and Dunford viewed their branch in Afghanistan in the context of the wider campaign. Dunford traveled to Afghanistan regularly and received briefings on the Islamic State and sometimes visited Nangarhar. Because of the terrorist threat and the wider campaign, early in 2017, Mattis ordered Nicholson to annihilate the Islamic State in Afghanistan.

The US counter–Islamic State campaign targeted Nangarhar. It was the main effort of Nicholson's whole strategy. In the Spin Ghar mountains of southern Nangarhar and its foothills, Islamic State cadres had survived after 2016 in valleys in four districts on the Pakistan border and were infiltrating into the districts closer to Jalalabad. They had training camps in the mountains in Nangarhar, as well as in the mountains of Kunar. Nicholson arrayed US special forces with Afghan commandos, militia, and local police against the Islamic State in southern Nangarhar. The loose string of dusty outposts amid ridgelines cordoned the Islamic State fighting cadres.

The special forces teams orchestrated unrelenting offensives and drone strikes. Southern Nangarhar was the only place in Afghanistan where US soldiers were directly in combat on a regular basis. Islamic State cadres disposed themselves in caves, stone sangars, and compounds to shoot at the US and Afghan outposts. The special forces teams defended their posts, raided Islamic State positions, laid ambushes, and patrolled with the Afghan special operations forces, border police, and militia through the valleys. Nicholson estimated that the Islamic State suffered hundreds of casualties in the fighting.[25]

Hundreds of bombs fell on southern Nangarhar per month. US soldiers overheard one Islamic State fighter radioing to his comrades, "They've destroyed everything even my clothes."[26] Famously, on April 13, 2017, Nicholson employed the "mother of all bombs," an 11-ton explosive that could turn a village into a crater. The giant bomb killed 94 fighters and 4 commanders.

The Islamic State's senior leaders were constantly targeted. Their first leader, Hafez Sayid Khan, had been killed by a drone strike in July 2016. A special operations raid eliminated his successor, Shaykh Abdul Hasib, in late April 2017. The next leader, Abu Sayed, a former Pakistani Taliban from Bajaur, Pakistan, displaced to Kunar to survive.[27] A drone strike got him in July. The fourth leader, Abdul Rahman, lasted a month before being killed by a US air strike.

US military operations damaged the Islamic State and probably prevented its leaders from realizing their intent to attack the United States. The Islamic State clung by their fingernails to their sanctuaries in the mountains of southern Nangarhar and Kunar. Fresh recruits from the Pakistani Taliban replaced some of the combat losses. Islamic States cadres often fled across the spine of the Spin Ghar from US operations and hid in Pakistan, later creeping back into Afghanistan once the special forces pulled back.[28] Years of war had taught the American commanders the folly of trying to control a mountain range. They wisely settled for containment. General Nicholson reported, "ISIS has proven to have a degree of resilience in southern Nangarhar. They're tough fighters and they'll be steadily reduced and we're going to continue the fight until it's complete."[29] Unfortunately, the movement's ideas found new places to thrive.

Social media and the internet enabled the Islamic State to inspire new recruits in places otherwise under government control. The Islamic State could leapfrog the containment of their cadres. Far more important than the combat in the mountains, the idea of the Islamic State was enough for new cells and supporters to sprout in Jalalabad, Kabul, and northern Afghanistan. In the heart of government support, they became by far the greater peril.

Islamic State cells expanded in Jalalabad city during 2017. They found recruits among the tens of thousands of Pashtun refugees fleeing Pakistani military operations.[30] The Afghans naturally allowed the refugees, including Islamic State converts, to enter the city or live in nearby camps. From there, Islamic State cells could recruit urban Afghans. They spread propaganda among the youth, especially in the high schools and university, where young men were more connected to the internet and Islamic State propaganda. Sympathetic teachers and professors created their own curriculum that supported Islamic State ideas.[31] Afghans who had been fighting for the Islamic State in Syria and Iraq started returning in 2017. They served as trainers and commanders. Arab trainers may have also arrived. The incoming cells had abundant funds to buy assistance.

The Islamic State's idea of a caliphate across all Muslims appealed to certain people in Jalalabad. Mullahs in mosques and teachers and professors at high schools and Jalalabad University were willing to help Islamic State cells. "University groups encourage extremism," Shaharzad Akbar, a leading youth leader, had reported years earlier. "They use social media and celebrate suicide attacks in Kabul."[32] Sympathetic teachers and professors disregarded the government curriculum and spread Islamic State teachings. Jalalabad University provided a large number of recruits.[33] Salafist Afghans originally from Kunar and Nuristan who followed Wahabi teachings—the form of Islam linked to al-Qaʻeda and the Islamic State and distinct from the Taliban's Deobandism and acceptance of Sufism—were often inclined to shelter the Islamic State.[34]

At first, the Islamic State cells concealed themselves and left the police alone. Ghani appointed Ghulab Mangal, the highly respected former governor of Helmand, to be governor of Nangarhar. Based on his experience, Governor Mangal came in set to drive coordination between the army, police, and NDS and institute programs to counter extremism. Mangal tried to capture the Islamic State cells but the NDS and the police disrespected his authority and Ghani would not, or could not, help him. With Americans no longer helping on the civilian side, his authority was hollow. Few funds existed. Ghani administered appointments and programs from Kabul. Instead of being treated as "part of the solution," Mangal was "micromanaged" and then bore the brunt of the public's blame as the Islamic State became active.[35] The Islamic State reaped the benefits of a centralized yet divided government.

In 2018, the Islamic State shifted from clandestine preparations to open terrorism. Islamic State suicide bombings buffeted Jalalabad, targeting government workers and offices. Hundreds of civilians were killed and wounded during the year.[36] Ministry offices and schools were frequent targets. The education department was hit twice in one month. The Islamic State even attacked the school for midwives. Eighty schools in the city and surrounding area closed because of Islamic State intimidation. Infuriated with Ghani, Mangal resigned in May 2018 after an Islamic State suicide bombing on the Nangarhar customs departments left approximately 40 dead and wounded. Ghani put the army in charge of security in Jalalabad.

The silver lining was that the danger to Jalalabad was so high that over the following year the NDS upped its game. Nazr Ali Wahidi, an experienced old Soviet-trained intelligence hand, from Garmser, became the provincial NDS director. With something of a dictatorial streak, he decreed and executed his own security measures, regardless of what anyone else wanted, and had the resources to do it. The Islamic State cells were not eradicated but neither did they overturn government control of Jalalabad.

The Islamic State also launched a suicide campaign in Kabul. Activists had been recruiting in the city since 2014. On March 8, 2017, an Islamic State suicide bomber and five gunmen killed 49 and wounded 90 in a horrific massacre at the Kabul main military hospital. Later in the year they hit the ministry of rural rehabilitation and development, leaving 7 killed and 15 wounded. Hatred of Hazaras was widespread among Islamic State members, based on the movement's view of Shiʻa as heretics. Hazara mosques, hospitals, and communities were often targeted. Across 2018, the Islamic State rocked Kabul with 24 attacks that caused at least 275 casualties, surpassing the activity of Haqqani network and its well-planned operations in the capital.[37]

As in Jalalabad, educated young men were susceptible to the Islamic State's internet propaganda. Young people chalked up walls around the city with pro-Islamic State graffiti calling for a caliphate. The group recruited out of Kabul University and other schools. The NDS arrested three lecturers in 2019. Unlike within the Taliban, a large percentage of Islamic State volunteers were young Tajiks from well-off families who were drawn to the Islamic State's image and idea of a caliphate that would encompass all Muslims throughout the world. Kabuli women were known to have joined the group as well. Researcher Borhan Osman interviewed eight women, who explained women worked on recruiting, social media, and spreading teachings at female madrasas. They even told stories of women participating in attacks.[38]

Well-funded Islamic State cells paid criminal gangs for access to the city and to transport materials. The cells lived in well-to-do neighborhoods, sometimes hiding as guests of prosperous families, affording them cover from government surveillance. One high-level government official complained to me, "My village is packed with Daesh."[39]

Perhaps most disturbing, the Islamic State received support from some Tajiks and Uzbeks of northern Afghanistan, communities thought to be pro-government. The allegiance of the Islamic Movement of Uzbekistan (IMU), an Uzbek militant group, was an early inroad but other Tajiks and Uzbeks aligned with the Islamic State as well. From 2010 to 2014, the Taliban had encouraged Salafists to found madrasas in northern Afghanistan and teach young Tajiks and Uzbeks. Some of these youth were open to the influence of the Islamic State and joined them. Key commanders also broke from the Taliban and went to the Islamic State, such as Qari Hekmatullah, an Uzbek commander known for his brutal ways.[40] By 2017, the Taliban reversed course and tried to shut down the Salafist madrasas because of the amount of support they were feeding to the Islamic State.[41] That year a Taliban versus Islamic State war consumed Jowzjan, with Manan's Taliban fighters from Helmand reinforcing local cadres.

In August, Qari Hekmatullah overran the Hazara valley of Mirza Olang within Jowzjan and massacred 54 civilians and local police for being Shi'a. The news of the Mirza Olang massacre disturbed the country and caused President Ghani to proclaim "the nature of war had changed."[42] A US air strike killed Qari Hekmatullah in April 2018.

Countrywide, the Islamic State numbered around 5,000 in 2018, compared to 2,500 in 2016. Suicide attacks climbed higher and higher throughout Afghanistan, reaching unprecedented heights every year. In 2018, they caused 886 deaths and 1,923 injuries to civilians, the highest ever, up 22 percent from

2017, and 135 percent from 2009. Two-thirds were attributed to the Islamic State.[43]

In short, the Islamic State was something new in Afghanistan, an evolution of the extremism that had been growing since 1979. The Taliban had always been generally Pashtun, traditionalist, rural, and isolationist, generally foreign to the cities, generally uninterested in the affairs of the wider world. The Islamic State went where the Taliban had been constrained. They thrived in disordered cities. They reached into the young and the educated. They crossed ethnic and gender boundaries. Their supporters subscribed to a larger transnational vision. Most of all, the Islamic State was more malignant. Theirs was a crueler, more destructive, form of sacrificial violence. The very radical nature of the Islamic State may have contained the group's size. They were nonetheless deadly and resilient.

The most dangerous effect of the Islamic State was on extremism. Their presence radicalized the Taliban. From 2015 onward, fighters amenable to the Islamic State's message and dissatisfied with the aggressiveness of the Taliban moved to the Islamic State. Members of the Quetta Shura believed this was occurring because the Taliban had been distancing itself from al-Qa'eda and other radical groups. By moderating from 2007 onward, they believed they had disadvantaged the movement. It was like free-market competition in terror. The Taliban now had a competitor. Buyers could choose between products. The Taliban had to make their product as appealing to as many as possible, to reach out to extremist fighters, not moderate or marginalize them. Consequently, the Quetta Shura increased support for al-Qa'eda and suicide attacks.[44]

Al-Qa'eda was weaker than ten years earlier. Obama's drone strikes and the death of bin Laden had crippled the organization, which probably declined to the hundreds in Afghanistan and Pakistan. The Islamic State was far larger and more potent. Ayman al-Zawahiri, the aging leader of al-Qa'eda, was hiding out in Pakistan, along with various colleagues. Bin Laden's 30-year-old son, Hamza bin Laden, tried to be the new face of al-Qa'eda until a drone strike killed him in Kunar sometime between 2017 and 2019.[45]

Al-Qa'eda nevertheless survived, with plans to someday resume attacks on the United States. International funding allowed them to help the Taliban. A few cells hung on in Kunar and Nuristan. Heartier offshoots were in Ghazni and southern Afghanistan. Kandahar police chief Abdul Razziq and US special operations forces had raided one of their training camps in the desert of southern Kandahar in 2015 where dozens embedded with the Taliban.[46] Smaller branches took root in Badakhshan, Kunduz, Logar, Nangarhar, and Paktiya. In all, 400 to 600 al-Qa'eda fighters probably dwelt in Afghanistan.[47]

Stories exist that in the last year of his life Mansour counseled the Quetta Shura that the Taliban should further distance themselves from al-Qa'eda. He saw the relationship as an impediment to peace talks and relations with the international community. Haybatullah followed a different course. Haybatullah's representatives told Afghan peace activists that the Taliban needed allies and that if it was an Islamic war and al-Qaʿeda was fighting for Islam, then dropping them would delegitimize the Taliban movement.[48] Several high-level Taliban commanders cooperated with the terrorist organization to a degree unseen since the time of Mullah Dadullah.

Haybatullah encouraged extreme ways of fighting.[49] He differed from Mullah Omar in both religious training and willingness to embrace the most radical methods. He was more ideological, even doctrinaire. He believed in martyrdom and suicide bombing. In 2008, when advising Mullah Omar, he had argued that Islam justified a wider use of suicide bombings. Amir Khan Motaqi, one of Haybatullah's chief assistants, explained to me in 2019, "Suicide bombers are very cheap for us. Just a few suicide bombers thwart all the forces, expenses, and technology of the United States."[50]

With Haybatullah's blessing, his own 23-year-old son trained to be a suicide bomber. In 2017, his son blew himself up in a car bomb during an attack in Helmand, recording a video before setting off on the mission.[51] Although rumors whispered the young man was actually adopted, no other Afghan leader had martyred a son, adopted or otherwise. The act was a sign of commitment that according to various reports won Haybatullah popularity. Taliban religious scholar Maulawi Mohammed Noor said Haybatullah did it "as a signal to show he is serious about instituting Islam and Islamic law. He wants people to know that he supports harsh punishments and that women will be forced to be covered and go to segregated schools. He wants to show how he is determined that Afghanistan will be ruled solely under Islamic law."[52]

The act also signified how the Taliban values were changing. Traditionally, sons were to be cherished, not cast aside needlessly. In tribal culture, honor demanded battle and possible death, but not outright suicide. Such sacrifice did wanton harm to the family and its survival. A Taliban leader had never endorsed suicide attacks in such a way. By doing so, Haybatullah both proved that he shared the sacrifice of other Afghan families of suicide bombers and set an example for others to follow. Suicide bombing and terrorism within Afghanistan had slowly become part of what it meant to be Taliban. In one meeting Abdul Salam Zaeef admitted to me that suicide bombing was a lasting idea within the Taliban that could be "a problem" if the Taliban won the war—implying the practice had assumed a life of its own.[53]

Disillusionment in Kabul and within the government was spreading. Endless casualties bore down on the government and its supporters. More than 100 soldiers and police were dying per week. In 2018, 282,000 Afghans left their homes to take refuge in the cities. Saad Mohseni, owner of the powerful Tolo

Television, remarked, "People are starting to think they need the Taliban to save them from violence. Afghans are kind of giving up."[54] Maryam Durrani, a Kandahar provincial councilwoman, surveyed 17- and 18-year-old girls at six Kandahar high schools on whether the United States should leave Afghanistan. "The majority said the United States should go," she discovered. "Then, in their opinion, the war would end."[55] Professor Fayz Mohammed Zaland of Kabul University explained, "So many soldiers and police are dead every day that people want peace."[56] Zaland himself believed the war had ceased to be in the interests of Afghans. "Take the chance on peace with the Taliban," he begged me. "All the deaths will end. War keeps killing people. Whatever comes with the Taliban won't be so bad. The risk of an attack on America is very small. Why do hundreds of Afghans have to die every week because 2,000 Americans died on 9/11?"[57]

A US government survey in September 2018 reflected Zaland's impression. Only 55 percent supported the presence of US forces in Afghanistan, down from 2008 when about 90 percent of Afghans supported US presence. Those who opposed US presence largely felt that US forces no longer helped security. Nearly half of all respondents believed the Taliban's war against US presence was legitimate.

The years of war had different effects on different Afghans, including on women. As the Taliban gained influence, elite Afghan women grew more vocal. "I fear the Taliban will return again," said Helmand parliamentarian Nasima Niyazi. "They will force me to stay in my home. It is oppression for a daughter to stay in the home. Being given away to a man is oppression. Not being allowed to go to the bazaar is oppression."[58] In Kandahar, Maryam Durrani stated, "Women need the United States. The Taliban cannot be trusted."[59] Many women hunted for a way out, searching for visas or education abroad. Sarina Faizy, an outspoken young Kandahar provincial councilwoman of remarkable promise, warned US military advisors at the end of 2018, "If I stay two or three more years here I will die." She left for the United States two months later.

Women in the countryside had less of a say. They had few freedoms, whether under the Taliban or the government. They sometimes confided to researchers or Afghan women leaders that they were tired of fighting and wanted no more deaths.[60] Unlike women in the city, they were likely to believe the United States needed to leave. They did not want to lose their sons. Their ability to do anything about it was limited. Many felt they could not demand an end to the fighting or impose on a son's career.[61] "Every household is different in the countryside," explained Nasima Niyazi. "Women have power in some, not in others. Sometimes they can influence their sons. . . . Often they are not even consulted. In some cases, they are happy if their son joins the Taliban. In other cases, they are not asked."[62] In the worst cases, described Maryam Durrani, "women in the countryside have no right to tell sons what job to take. Sons would not even go to their mother. The mother would not be happy. She would cry. It would make no difference if the son was going to the police or the Taliban."[63] Frequently, women knew the family needed the wages.[64] Nasima Niyazi said, "In both the city and the countryside, people need money. There are no jobs. Education brings nothing. There are no doctor, teacher, or lawyer jobs. War is the only way to make money so a young man must join one side or the other. Women must accept."[65]

Parliamentary elections finally occurred in autumn 2018 after a three-year delay. A new generation of younger leaders were elected along with a few older, such as Arif Khan Noorzai and Maulali Ishaqzai. Maulali, now 49, played her tribal card to great effect. She had frequently visited her tribesmen in the Kandahar countryside. She convinced prestigious Ishaqzai tribal leaders to back her. Then she called Mullah Manan, Taliban governor of Helmand, who was Ishaqzai too. He wanted influence in parliament and dispatched 300 registered voters to Spin Boldak to vote for her.[66] While Maulali staged her return to parliament, Fawzia Koofi could not run. Ghani's electoral complaints commission unfairly banned her from running for working with militia leaders of the north. She was still part of Jamiat Islami and involved herself in peace efforts. Shukria Barakzai, who like Maulali and Koofi had first been elected to parliament in 2005, was already ambassador to Norway and had given up her seat.

General Nicholson's tour concluded in September 2018. At two and a half years, he had outlasted every other US commander. General Scott Miller succeeded him. Miller was America's premier special operator. He was beloved by the military and civilian officials alike, a peerless athlete, lethal with a pistol or an M-4 assault rifle, morally conscientious. Captain America. He had been a special operator in 1993 in Mogadishu and in the middle of McChrystal's dismantlement of Zarqawi's network in Iraq in 2006. He had multiple tours in Afghanistan, including his time establishing the Afghan local police in 2010 and then as head of all special operations in Afghanistan in 2013 and 2014. He had gone on to command the vaunted Joint Special Operations Command (JSOC) and defeat the Islamic State in Syria. In military tactics, Miller was unsurpassed. He had also nurtured strong friendships with many Afghan leaders, including Asadullah Khalid, Massoum Stanekzai, Mohammed Atta, and Abdul Razziq, the most effective commander in Afghanistan.

Amid the defeats in Helmand, Kunduz, Ghazni, Uruzgan, and elsewhere, Kandahar had remained a government safe haven. The government ruled most of the territory that had been recaptured during the surge: Zharey, Panjwai, Arghandab, Spin Boldak, and the city itself—the majority of the province's population. Periodic Taliban probes had been repulsed. Mansour and then Haybatullah had postponed major offensives against Kandahar because the defenses were so strong. Mullah Shirin, the Taliban governor for Kandahar, ordered his commanders to wait three years because Razziq was too powerful.

Through this time, Razziq had been police chief. He was now 39 or 40 years old. The people of Kandahar both admired and feared him. Nearly 10,000 police and border police fell under him. His thorough security measures and unflagging energy created a critical mass of popular support even while torture, secret prisons, and extrajudicial killings upset the international community and much of the same Kandahar people. Educated Kandaharis despised his brutal ways but were scared to go without him. Throughout Afghanistan, Razziq had attained a sort of mythic status, reminiscent of Ahmed Shah Massoud, for his military prowess and open guerrilla war with Pakistan. Rumors abounded that he was conducting his own hits inside Pakistan against Taliban leaders and the ISI. His border police were always getting into skirmishes with the Pakistani military. Razziq delighted in telling off Pakistani generals in any public meeting or parlay. Afghans could look to Razziq as a fearless protector.

Ghani hated Razziq for his human rights abuses and power. Razziq criticized Ghani and aligned with other powerbrokers at odds with the president, especially Mohammed Atta in the north. Ghani could not move against Razziq without risking the support of the Karzais and the Americans. Razziq even told the press in early 2018 that Ghani had no right to remove him because he ruled by the will of the people of Kandahar.

The Taliban and Pakistan also hated Razziq. Razziq had survived multiple hits, many of which were said to be ISI plots. In 2017, a bomb was placed under Razziq's chair during a meeting in the governor's palace with the UAE ambassador. When it went off, he had luckily stepped out of the room. The deputy governor and the ambassador were killed, the governor severely wounded.

In August 2018, the Taliban leaders in Quetta placed an operative known as "Abu Dujana" inside the governor's palace to try to kill Razziq.[67] The ISI helped devise and execute the plot. Razziq's intelligence was too good for them to get anyone into the police headquarters itself. Kandahar governor Zalmay Wesa was less thorough. His security guards were not vetted by Razziq. Abu Dujana was just 17 or 18. He had trained for months in Pakistan for a suicide mission. One of the governor's security guards vouched for him.[68]

On October 18, 2018, two days before the long-delayed parliamentary elections, Razziq, General Miller, Governor Wesa, and several other officials met at the Kandahar governor's palace. Barely a month had passed since Miller had assumed command. Razziq was under the weather that morning but forced himself to get out of bed and attend. He dressed oddly in Western attire—khakis, a white open-collared shirt, tucked in, with a belt, and grey track shoes, quite the opposite of his favorite border police uniform or Kandahari chemise.

The meeting convened in the early afternoon. A Taliban leader in Pakistan spoke with Abu Dujana over the phone and told him it was time to strike. When the meeting broke up, Miller, Razziq, Wesa and the others stepped outside, talking and exchanging thoughts in a very Afghan fashion. Miller had known Razziq for years and Razziq always enjoyed seeing old friends. Abu Dujana, in an ill-fitting grey camouflage uniform, hovered alongside, waiting for an opening.[69] As the party walked toward Miller's helicopters to bid him farewell, Abu Dujana opened fire. Razziq was shot in the leg, stomach, and chest.[70] Abu Dujana then fired at the rest of the party, including Miller. Rounds struck Razziq's operations officer, the army corps commander, the provincial NDS intelligence director, and Governor Wesa. Two Americans were wounded. Miller's officers gunned down Abu Dujana. They then rendered first aid to the victims and evacuated the wounded. They helped save the governor's life. Miller himself was unscathed. Razziq's men, adoring their leader, carried him into a truck and sped to the Kandahar hospital, where he died.[71]

The attack shocked the people of Kandahar and Afghans throughout the country. Fear and anxiety worsened. An educated former policeman said, "It was the worst thing to happen to Kandahar and southern Afghanistan people. Losing Razziq is a major blow to the security in Kandahar . . . in such a critical time. I talked to two dozen people from last night to now. Everyone was nervous and concerned about the situation in the future."[72] Another Kandahari, who worked in civil society and was educated in Britain, reflected, "With all our differences, I don't think Razziq deserved what happened to him. We all have heard that he was brutal but we also know that he had saved Kandahar from collapsing to the Taliban. . . . I think without Razziq the situation will deteriorate in Kandahar and I am afraid that Kandahar might experience what happened in Ghazni or Farah. I really am afraid."[73]

Not everyone was distraught. Rumor had it that Ghani's young technocratic advisors cheered when they heard the news. Razziq's Noorzai rivals were gratified. A feud was a feud. Maulali Ishaqzai, ever the defender of her tribe, smiled and exclaimed with a touch of hyperbole, "*Dzalum.* Oppression. Razziq was killing people. Imprisoning them. When he died, people raised their voices in praise and greeted each other with *Mubarak*, congratulations, as if it was a religious holiday."[74]

America's unsolved moral dilemma in Kandahar had come to an end. Razziq was gone. Life is short in Afghanistan. American generals tended to say that Razziq was irreplaceable. Journalists and Western aid workers tended to say his human rights violations set the stage for a greater disaster. Time never told. As

Razziq foresaw, he never grew old. How should Americans remember Razziq? A model to be copied? Or a moral stain to be shunned? Therein lies his legacy. Razziq should be remembered as neither charismatic military genius nor bloody murderer but as one of the most complex unanswered questions of Afghanistan. His role in America's war is a story to be pondered rather than a guide to be followed.

20

Peace Talks

During early 2018, the United States, Afghan government, and Taliban began reexploring peace talks. The war had reached a withering intensity. The United States was facing an endless commitment if peace talks did not happen. The Afghan government was in a bad spot. The army and police were suffering crippling losses. Unlike 2010, US generals and the defense department now accepted talks as the goal of military strategy in Afghanistan. On the other side, the Taliban leaders were interested in talks as a way to secure a US departure. The possibility of a peace process, dormant other than the brief stirring in 2015, was returning.

On February 14, the Taliban issued an open letter to the American people in which they conveyed a willingness to enter talks with the United States as long as the Afghan government was excluded. Two weeks later, Ghani offered talks with the Taliban at any time in a speech at the "Kabul process" conference, a Russian initiative. The Quetta Shura refused to answer. The United States attempted its own feelers with various Taliban interlocutors. The Taliban political commission relayed to them and to other Westerners in unofficial meetings that they only wanted to talk with the United States and complete US withdrawal was sine qua non for any deal. No talks commenced but the letter and Ghani's speech were the first steps on a road to a new peace process.

Midway through 2018 a startling event catalyzed progress. The Taliban accepted a proposal by Ghani for a ceasefire over Kuchinay Eid, the celebration at the end of Ramadan. From June 16 to 18, on order of Taliban leader Maulawi Haybatullah, no attacks occurred. Haybatullah sent a message that it is wrong for Muslims to kill each other on Eid.[1] He seems to have been confident that the movement could benefit from a gesture of peace amid military strength. Precedent was for Taliban to rest over Eid anyway.

For three days, Taliban and soldiers and police left their sangars to greet each other. All over the television and internet were Taliban—long hair, wispy beards, kohl-lined eyes, *patoo* (traditional Afghan shawl) pulled tightly over heads—next to Afghan soldiers and police—shaven and cropped, sometimes draped in Afghan flags. Praying together, eating together, embracing. A Taliban fighter cruising into Kabul on a motorcycle shouted, "We want peace. I have fought for eight years!"[2]

In Nangarhar, Taliban fighters met with soldiers and police at a tree-lined crossroads—Humvees, pickups, and motorcycles, a mix of white Taliban and government black-red-green Afghan flags. A Taliban fighter with a chest rig, captured M-16, and a *kalima* headband exclaimed, "I am very happy. This is like a second *akhtar*. We will come together." Taliban fighters and people cheered: "We want peace." An Afghan soldier reported, "I could not come to my village for years because security was bad. There was no guarantee. I am happy to be in my own village. It is a historic garden. For six years I have not been able to be inside it," while Taliban fighters beamed as they cried, "We haven't been in Jalalabad for nine years. We say 'Akhtar Mubarak,' congratulations, at every government post. We are very happy we can go see it today. We will not sleep."[3]

The euphoria was intoxicating. General Dunford and Defense Secretary Mattis thought the ceasefire augured well for peace talks. Underneath the surface, things were less rosy. When Kabul University professor Fayz Mohammed Zaland met with the Taliban deputy governor for Logar and a group of leaders and mullahs, he was reminded that Haybatullah had ordered that peace would only occur when US forces left and that the Taliban would not talk with the government. His hosts said that the Taliban would not extend the ceasefire and were ready to go back to fighting. Similarly, a Taliban commander who entered Kabul boasted to a Voice of America reporter, "We fight jihad for Allah. As long as Americans are here, our war will continue. . . . Peace cannot happen until Americans leave. After Americans leave we can speak about peace." A Taliban commander in Nangarhar echoed him: "Our great obstacle before us is foreign occupation. Until occupation ends, the ceasefire will have very little benefit. For all Afghans, it will have little benefit because they are bombing our homes. When that is distant, when we have our own home, we will have no problem."[4]

Professor Zaland observed "The Taliban are not tired, from my conversations. They are happy to fight more. They have more money and supplies than ever before." It was the soldiers and police who were tired: "After the ceasefire, police asked 'Why fight? We are brothers.' The Taliban were different. They said: 'Three days. We fight on the fourth. We'll kill you.' And that is what they did."[5]

President Trump had never bought into his own Afghan strategy. For him, Afghanistan would always be a fool's errand. The cost of the war was an especially sore point—$27 billion per year in military spending, far less than the $110 billion of 2011 but still substantial.[6] In late March 2018, Trump had told Mattis that he had until August to turn things around. Over the year he informed businessmen that he wanted out of the Middle East and Afghanistan, that the United States never should have gone in. Rumors spread of angry outbursts in the West Wing in which Trump shouted "Where is my deal?! Why do I not have a deal yet!?!" Confidantes passed word that Trump would sooner withdraw unilaterally than go into the 2020 election with the Afghan War.

After a year of discussions about peace negotiations and visits by high-ranking officials to Afghanistan, the White House finally appointed an envoy for peace talks in September 2018. The envoy was none other than former ambassador Zalmay Khalilzad, negotiator of the Bonn agreement. The grayed 67-year-old Afghan American who had been present at the creation reappeared christened to preside over the end. Khalilzad had relinquished official duties in Afghanistan in 2005. After that he had been a frequent visitor, as ambassador to the United Nations and then a private citizen. In 2013, he had tentatively explored running for president of Afghanistan. Defense Secretary James Mattis and Secretary of State Mike Pompeo concurred that Khalilzad should talk directly to the Taliban. His discussions were to be a stepping stone to negotiations between the Taliban and the Afghan government.

Khalilzad was all energy. Telling everyone that he had only nine months to reach a settlement, he flew about madly to Doha, Dubai, Kabul, and Islamabad. Lean, with slicked-back hair, clad in expensive suits, in a meeting he barely stopped talking—or moving. He shook hands with everyone, patted backs, and constantly proposed ideas. Khalilzad met with everyone he could: the Taliban political commission, other Taliban, and just about every politician in Kabul. He was always on the lookout for a conversation, preferably one-on-one. Ghani distrusted him. Karzai was happy to have him back. Khalilzad's own staff could not keep track of him. He barely slept. He was the right man for the time.

Secretary of State Pompeo backed Khalilzad to a degree greater than any secretary of state had the previous peace envoys. Pompeo was closer to Trump than other cabinet members because he executed the president's wishes scrupulously. He knew that the president's patience was running out and that progress toward peace had to be quick. Pompeo empowered Khalilzad to act as he saw fit .

The military also backed Khalilzad. While Petraeus had opposed peace talks, General Dunford, as chairman of the joint chiefs of staff, and General Miller, as commander of all US and allied forces in Afghanistan, supported them. Dunford repeatedly instructed, "State Department has the lead on Afghanistan. We are in support of Khalilzad." Dunford thought peace talks were a long shot. Because of the terrorist threat, he forecast a long, low-level commitment to be the most likely future for America. But he saw no reason not to try. It would be a victory if Khalilzad could end the war. Miller tailored his operations to align with Khalilzad's diplomacy. Some friction naturally occurred between the military and Khalilzad's team. Pentagon officials were especially uncomfortable with

Khalilzad's impetuousness. That was manageable. Dunford and Miller would always endorse his initiatives.

The US negotiating goals at this point were largely unchanged from 2012: an end to violence, an Afghan political settlement, Taliban renunciation of al-Qaʻeda, and long-term presence of intelligence assets and special operations forces in Afghanistan for counterterrorism operations. Mattis and Dunford opposed offering any kind of timeline to zero because of their counterterrorism concerns. The negotiations had to be "Afghan led," meaning major issues would be discussed between the Taliban and government, not between the Taliban and the United States. Khalilzad's writ was to lead the Taliban into a multilateral "Afghan-owned, Afghan-led" process where the substantive issues, including withdrawal of US forces, would be negotiated. Withdrawal of US forces was not to be discussed early in the process when the Taliban could sweep it up as a unilateral concession and give nothing in return.

Khalilzad sought to convince the Taliban, Afghan government, and other leading Afghans to negotiate a new political settlement for the country that would include a new government and constitution and would supersede the Bonn agreement. An interim government of leading Afghans would probably be needed and Ghani would probably have to step down. Khalilzad was optimistic that once the Afghans sat across the table from each other a deal would quickly follow. "Intra-Afghan negotiations would be historic," he would say. To get the Taliban to agree, US troops would eventually have to draw down, though Khalilzad preferred to leave some number as a check on terrorism. He did not want to play the withdrawal card early since it was a big bargaining chip. Fundamentally, Khalilzad believed a political settlement needed to precede a drawdown. Otherwise, with US troops out of the way, the Taliban would be tempted to renege on any commitments and try to seize power by force.

The Taliban goal was to secure a complete US withdrawal and then enforce their own political settlement. Their position had hardened from 2011 when they had been willing to talk with the Afghan government early in a process. Taliban leader Maulawi Haybatullah was much less compromising than his predecessor—the pragmatic Mansour. In 2012 and 2013, Haybatullah had supported opening a peace office in Qatar and had convinced the Quetta Shura that peace talks were permitted in Islamic law.[7] But he had only wanted an agreement that removed all foreign troops and put the Taliban in power. Months after becoming emir he demanded that the United States announce full withdrawal from Afghanistan as a precondition for negotiations. Although that precondition fell by the wayside, Haybatullah envisioned negotiations solely with the United States. Haybatullah and other senior leaders spurned words or actions that might acknowledge the Kabul government.[8] On al-Qaʻeda, Haybatullah was willing to repeat Mullah Omar's promise that the Taliban would not support attacks on other countries without naming al-Qaʻeda or undertaking any action against them. Senior Taliban leaders were split about abandoning the organization.

A sense of military momentum was widespread. Borhan Osman, a researcher, had interviewed dozens of Taliban and reported,

> The Taliban foot soldiers showed no sense of urgency for talks, and said they were determined to fight for a long time. They considered "martyrdom" and the continuation of "jihad" until achieving the goal of establishing an Islamic system free of foreign military presence, both as equally desirable outcomes. Belief in a soon-to-come victory was not ubiquitous, but all believed it would ultimately come should the opposite side continue fighting and no political settlement was achieved.[9]

One former Afghan government official met with the Taliban political commission in October 2018. The Taliban told him that they thought Trump would withdraw any day. They were waiting for that. Kabul would then be captured. They were convinced the old Northern Alliance would concede and no civil war would occur. They said they would "grab the throats of the Northern Alliance like chickens and cast them about."[10] The Quetta Shura supposedly sent a commission to a few provinces to ask their commanders about peace. Fifty percent said they would obey an order to accept peace. Fifty percent opposed peace and said that they would ignore any such order, hardly a sign of flagging morale.[11] The future looked to be on the Taliban's side.

Internationally, the Taliban were receiving unprecedented support. Iran had grown into a major patron, challenging Pakistan's influence. Iranian financial assistance to the Taliban rose from minor levels during 2006–2011 to exceed $100 million per year after 2012 and roughly match Pakistan. Iran invited the Taliban to open an office in the western city of Mashad. The Islamic Revolutionary Guard Corps (IRGC) quietly increased its military assistance to the Taliban, especially in Helmand and Farah. They provided night vision devices, sights, drones, and other sophisticated equipment to Mullah Manan in Helmand and taught his men how to use them.

The increase in support was ostensibly to counter the Islamic State. In reality, the Iranians wanted to use the Taliban to attack the Afghan army and police and constrain US military activity anywhere near their border. Iranians encouraged the Taliban attacks on Farah City. Iran was playing both sides, supporting its longtime Tajik and Hazara allies while helping the Taliban. The country's leaders did not want a Taliban state and were unlikely to betray the Tajiks and Hazaras but fueling the war served their interests. They did not want the Taliban to concede to a long-term US military presence in Afghanistan.[12]

Neither did Russia. Russian diplomats opened their own channel to the Taliban political commission and provided funds and possibly weaponry. Like the Iranians, Russians claimed their interest was combating the Islamic State. Like the Iranians, they were more concerned that US presence was a strategic threat. A reasonable guess for the initiation of Russian support to the Taliban is 2014 or 2015, since the Islamic State appeared over those years, but support also may have started earlier. In 2017, Mattis noted reports of Russian activity in public testimony. According to press reports, intelligence later suggested the Russians transferred sums to Taliban leaders in 2018 and 2019 to attack US forces.[13]

More visible were Russian president Vladimir Putin's attempts to interfere in negotiations. On November 9, 2018, Russian Foreign Minister Sergey Lavrov hosted a peace conference in Moscow and invited the Taliban political commission, which accepted. Iran and Pakistan attended as well. Piqued, Ghani only sent low-level, unofficial, representatives. At the conference, the Taliban political commission and its head, Sher Mohammed Abbas Stanekzai, expressed their vision of a one-sided peace (Tayeb Agha had stepped down in 2015 in the wake of the news of Mullah Omar's death). Lavrov let the Taliban delegation call themselves representatives of "the Islamic Emirate of Afghanistan," the title that had infuriated Karzai and shuttered the Doha office back in 2013. Photographed next to Lavrov, Stanekzai was beside himself. After years of international opprobrium, Iran and Russia had granted the Taliban international recognition. The upswing encouraged harsh negotiating demands.

Relations between Ghani and Pakistan were strained. After his early attempt to find common ground, President Ghani became as caustic as Karzai ever was. As suicide bomber after suicide bomber ravaged Kabul, Ghani strengthened ties with New Delhi. Afghanistan and India traded a series of high-level visits. India transferred a small number of attack helicopters to the Afghan army. Ghani welcomed the opening of a trade route to India via the Iranian port of Charbahar.[14] None of this pleased Pakistan army chief Qamar Javed Bajwa. Pakistani military support for the Taliban flowed unimpeded.

After the approval of the South Asia strategy in August 2017, the Trump administration quickly turned up the heat on Pakistan, issuing a laundry list of demands from supporting negotiations to cutting off the Taliban to reducing tension with India. In January 2018, Trump announced that security assistance would be suspended. Congress followed up on the threat by rescinding $500 million, nearly the entirety of US security assistance.[15] For assistance to resume, Pompeo demanded that Pakistan deny safe haven to the Taliban and press them into a political settlement. The restriction of US economic assistance was problematic for Pakistan at this time. Pakistan was running a significant debt because of its large military and new infrastructure projects. It needed US money and a bailout from the International Monetary Fund, which were also unlikely without US support.

Bajwa's solution to this predicament was to resist the Trump administration's maximalist demands and concede on peace talks. Pakistan was not going to abandon the Taliban. Bajwa was confident that the Taliban could win and that China would help Pakistan regardless of US actions. Pakistani generals often boasted to US generals and diplomats that the Taliban were winning the war.

Bajwa was amenable, however, to negotiations. Pakistan military leaders had long wanted the United States to talk directly with the Taliban. In Islamabad in September 2018, newly elected Prime Minister Imran Khan and Bajwa were pleased when Khalilzad, Dunford, and Pompeo introduced their plans to talk with the Taliban bilaterally. They told their guests that the Taliban would re-veal themselves to be great friends of the United States and recommended that the United States offer complete military withdrawal. Nor were Bajwa and Imran Khan going to upset the United States by spoiling a process that could well die of its own accord. Negotiations were at a very early stage and likely to fail. Better to try to please the United States. Friendship with the United States meant something. Having two great power supporters—China and the United States—multiplied Pakistan's geostrategic options and leverage. Marginalized by the United States as a sort of state sponsor of terror was not how the Pakistani leadership desired to be viewed on the international stage.

Moreover, Bajwa and Imran Khan could live with a compromise peace if it met their terms—Taliban predominance over an Afghan government committed to neutrality and recused from the India-Pakistan rivalry. They did not necessarily want the Taliban to win the war by force. Compromise could be better. Taliban victory brought its own risks. In a struggle for survival against the Taliban, the former Northern Alliance would turn to India for the arms needed to save Kabul, presenting Pakistan with the distinct chance of a long-term proxy war with India in Afghanistan or, worse, a rump Kabul protectorate of India. For Pakistan, such an outcome would be worse than a compromise peace. Khalilzad's willingness to rewrite the Afghan constitution was enticing. Pakistanis considered the Bonn constitution to be faulty. A fresh constitution, created with Pakistani input, was of interest. So the chance of a compromise peace that enshrined Pakistani influ-ence and constrained India could be entertained, especially if doing so might relieve Trump's economic pressure.[16]

Khalilzad met with the Taliban political commission three times between October and the end of December. Neither side got what it wanted. Khalilzad refused to give on withdrawal. The Taliban refused to give on meeting the Afghan government or cutting ties with al-Qaʻeda. Stanekzai, head of the Taliban political commission, told visiting Afghans at the time that the Taliban did not need to distance itself from al-Qaʻeda. He said al-Qaʻeda was part of their organization and would obey instructions not to operate in or out of Afghanistan. He also said that the Taliban would stop violence only when the last Americans had left.[17] Things were proceeding slowly.

Then, Trump single-handedly changed the direction of negotiations. The November 2018 mid-term elections were approaching. Trump's patience was frayed. Right before them, he told Mattis that Khalilzad had nine months to get a deal in Afghanistan. If there was no deal by then, he said he would pull out. The terrorist threat impressed Trump less than had been the case a year before. When mentioned to him, he would mutter, "That's what everyone says. . . . " On November 8, the national security council met on Afghanistan for the first time in over a year in the Oval Office. It was another combative meeting. Trump laid into the generals, "Strategy was wrong, and not at all where I wanted to be. We've lost everything. It was a total failure. It's a waste. It's a shame."[18] The meeting concluded without a clear decision. Mattis and Dunford walked away certain Trump would withdraw within a year.

On December 10, the long-feared event occurred. Trump called Mattis and Dunford to the White House and ordered all forces, including everything involved in counterterrorism operations, out of Afghanistan within weeks. He said he would make an announcement in January. Mattis and Dunford told Trump that it would be a disaster. Trump beat them over the head with the "failure" of their strategy.[19] Having been given orders, Mattis and Dunford directed the preparation of a withdrawal plan.

Things heated up a week later when Trump announced he would pull all US troops out of Syria, where they had been fighting the Islamic State. Mattis and Dunford had no prior warning of the announcement. On top of this, the media got a story that Trump planned to withdraw 7,000 troops from Afghanistan. The information was not entirely accurate; Trump was after complete withdrawal. The world nevertheless came to understand that Trump was looking for a way out of Afghanistan.

Never one for losing wars, Mattis refused to be bullied. He believed that the United States should be in Afghanistan and was even more determined when it came to Syria, where the Islamic State posed a greater threat than the Taliban. Congress and the media admired Mattis as a bulwark against Trump's most dangerous impulses. Rather than kowtow, Mattis resigned in a public letter, scathing in its criticism of the president. Congress and the media expressed grave concern about the president's behavior. Trump relented on an immediate withdrawal from Afghanistan. He was still intent on getting out but was willing to give Dunford, Miller, and Khalilzad several months.

With Mattis's departure, Secretary of State Pompeo became the policy heavyweight. Pompeo agreed with Trump that the United States should leave Afghanistan. The war did not interest him. He often dismissed concerns about a renewed terrorist safe haven by saying, "We'll go back in if we have to," implying the United States could leave, be willing to absorb any terrorist attack, and then retaliate. But he thought a precipitous withdrawal would be a disaster and after the December 10 meeting counseled Trump to move slowly.

Pompeo informed Khalilzad of Trump's decision several days after the December 10 meeting. He ordered Khalilzad not to return from Doha without a deal. Khalilzad cast aside the old US negotiating position. He would initiate substantive negotiations with the Taliban. "Afghan-led" talks would be a goal for later. The long-standing goal of a permanent presence of intelligence and special operations forces in a counterterrorism mission was jettisoned as well. Khalilzad wanted to start negotiations by giving the Taliban a timeline for withdrawal if they would meet other US concerns. With the concurrence of Dunford and acting Defense Secretary Patrick Shanahan, Pompeo permitted Khalilzad to negotiate a withdrawal of US forces to zero with the Taliban.[20]

For years, Pentagon officials had refused to let State Department diplomats discuss withdrawal officially with the Taliban, let alone proffer a withdrawal timeline. They thought it a glaring signal of weakness that would convince the Taliban they were on the road to battlefield victory and thus hamstring negotiations. Dunford too had been unready to discuss withdrawal. Now, he decided that offering concessions could be better for US interests and for the Afghan people than a precipitous withdrawal alone. The possibility that thousands of Afghans could suffer in a collapse into a worse civil war weighed on his mind. The change in position was a result of Trump's intent. Dunford, Shanahan, and the Department of Defense were now willing to risk much more in pursuit of a settlement.

Khalilzad met with Stanekzai and the Taliban political commission on January 21, 2019. Khalilzad threw withdrawal of all US forces on the table. The Taliban were surprised. Khalilzad asked for an Afghan political settlement and a general ceasefire in return. Stanekzai rejected those requests but came back with an offer to renounce external terrorism and implement any enforcement mechanisms the United States desired. They promised no group or individual would be allowed to use Afghan soil to threaten another country. Khalilzad refused to make a deal that excluded a settlement and ceasefire but now solid ground existed between the two sides. Khalilzad's progress pleased Pompeo.

Khalilzad envisioned a US-Taliban agreement with four main components: first, a Taliban guarantee that Afghanistan would not be used by any group or individual to attack another country; second, a timeline for a complete US withdrawal; third, a Taliban promise to reach a political settlement with the government; fourth, a general ceasefire. In his wording, "Peace requires that we find common ground on four interconnected issues: troop withdrawal, counterterrorism assurances, intra-Afghan dialogue and negotiations, and reduction in violence leading to comprehensive ceasefire."[21] "Nothing is agreed until everything is agreed," Khalilzad would repeat over and over. The Taliban political commission was noncommittal on the four components. In public, they only spoke of the first two: withdrawal in return for counterterrorism assurances.[22]

While negotiations were accelerating, a related Khalilzad initiative came to fruition. Back in September, Khalilzad had judged that the Quetta Shura did not take the Taliban political commission seriously. Khalilzad wanted Pakistan's help in pressuring the Quetta Shura to appoint a high-ranking senior leader as his lead interlocutor. He knew whom he wanted: Abdul Ghani Baradar, former deputy of the entire Taliban, imprisoned by Pakistan in 2010. Karzai had gotten Pakistan to release Baradar to house arrest in September 2013, where he had been living since. Pompeo and Khalilzad pressured Pakistan army chief Bajwa and Prime Minister Imran Khan to free him entirely, which they did in October. For Bajwa and Imran Khan, releasing Baradar may have been a way of appeasing Trump without endangering critical Pakistani interests.

As the once anointed deputy of Mullah Omar, Baradar was deeply respected within the Taliban. At the end of January, Haybatullah appointed Baradar deputy for political affairs and had him oversee Stanekzai and the negotiating effort. Although mildly weakened from years in captivity, age deepened his reputation of old. A few strands of gray dignified his once fully black beard. Narrow, square-rimmed librarian glasses rested on his slightly slanting nose, accentuating the sharp mind his eyes had always exuded. Like many older Afghans, Baradar suffered from diabetes, which suppressed his activity level. He was so soft-spoken that Khalilzad sometimes had to strain to hear him in meetings. He wanted peace and was inclined to compromise to get there. The broad strokes of a deal were much more important to him than fine details, which he often brushed aside with a wave of his hand. He had a natural honesty that won a degree of trust from Americans while holding firmly to Taliban goals. He was nobody's fool.

Other Taliban joined the Taliban political commission for the first time as well. Most visible were the five former Guantanamo detainees who had been living in Qatar since 2014. They had all been senior leaders in 2001, including former army chief Mohammed Fazl and former Balkh governor Nooriullah Noori, who had commanded in Mazar-e-Sharif. All carried tremendous status within the movement. Another important addition was Amir Khan Motaqi, chief of staff of the office of the Quetta Shura. He had been close with Mullah Omar and had spoken at the 2001 ulema shura that endorsed jihad against a US invasion and been a key official since then, traveling into Afghanistan from time to time to relay instructions to commanders. Motaqi had a politician's touch in making friends and building consensus.[23]

President Ashraf Ghani opposed Khalilzad's effort. He demanded that the Taliban negotiate only with his elected and internationally recognized Afghan government, accept the constitution, and lay down arms. The Afghan presidential election was approaching, set for September 28. Khalilzad's public statements that progress in peace talks could cancel the election threatened Ghani's aspirations for a second presidential term. Ghani lobbied every American leader he knew for the election to happen on time. He frequently argued with Khalilzad. He was at first in the dark as to Trump's intent to get out and when informed did not believe it for months. Many US officials in Washington and on the national security council staff were Ghani's friends. Contrary to Trump's guidance, word came from them that the United States would never let Afghanistan become a vacuum for terrorists to occupy. Ghani was convinced that there was little reason to negotiate.

Karzai, on the other hand, wanted peace. Now living in Kabul, he spoke out in the press and organized political leaders in support of the peace process. Khalilzad was in regular touch. Even the Taliban listened to Karzai thanks to his inveterate criticism of the United States. Karzai led an Afghan delegation to two Moscow conferences and met face to face with the Taliban political commission. Unlike Ghani, Karzai insisted that all US military forces leave Afghanistan, believing foreign forces did not belong. He was also interested in an interim government. Karzai hoped that as a byproduct he could be renamed president or appointed to a titular chief of state role. He viewed himself as "father of the nation." Personal ambitions aside, Karzai was willing to put far more on the table than Ghani on behalf of peace.

Dr. Abdullah (who was now running for president for his third time) and the Tajik leaders were also willing to consider peace talks, though largely because of the possibility of an interim government that would improve their political position. Their attitude toward the Taliban was unflinching. They believed any deal should protect the long-term strategic relationship with the United States and disapproved of concessions. Mohammed Alam Ezedyar, senator from Panjshir and deputy of the Meshrano jirga, criticized that the peace process had given the Taliban "legitimate recognition" and that in return "we have nothing to show to our people, nothing tangible." "I hope you don't come to regret this peace process because of Taliban deceit," he told US officials.[24] Kamil Bek Hussaini, senator from Badakhshan, stated, "We won't accept Taliban resurgence. We want people to have rights and freedom."[25] Northern Alliance commanders and certain Pashtun tribal leaders—Alikozai, Achekzai—vowed to fight with or without the United States. The Taliban had killed their family members. They knew what could be coming.

The sudden momentum toward peace intensified worries among Afghans who had experienced life away from the Taliban. Government leaders feared the United States was about to abandon them. The new parliament convened hearings that criticized Trump for using Afghanistan for his own election purposes and surrendering to the Taliban. Women in the cities were especially worried. Even newly reelected parliamentarian Maulali Ishaqzai, with her Taliban tribesmen, did not want the Taliban intruding on her politician-tribal-pirate way of life: "I will not accept an emirate. Women want to walk freely and in color. The Taliban will never allow it."[26]

Within the United States, defenders of Afghan women's rights viewed the negotiations skeptically. Senators, representatives, and think tank scholars called for the protection of human rights and criticized the absence of Afghan women representation in the talks. Senator Jeanne Shaheen, a New Hampshire Democrat on the Senate Foreign Relations Committee, said that "Afghan women have made it loud and clear they want peace without oppression. . . . Their rights and future must not get lost in these negotiations."[27] Views like hers added to skepticism about the talks in Washington. Women's rights had always been an ideal of the intervention.

US military strategy adjusted to support negotiations. General Scott Miller had come to Afghanistan in 2018 convinced that US military operations could be more efficient. On his own accord, he sent 2,000 troops home that he assessed were superfluous to the mission and cut $650 million in funding to the Afghan army and police.

Miller created what he called his "operational design."[28] Over the winter, he focused strike aircraft, drones, intelligence collection assets, and special operations forces on killing Taliban leadership in order to disrupt preparations for offensives later in the year. Employing techniques from his time as commander of Joint Special Operations Command (JSOC), Miller maximized efficient use of these capabilities. Miller's officers dubbed the combination of assets "the black cloud" for its lethality.[29] The first success was Mullah Manan, Taliban governor of Helmand. On December 1, 2018, a drone strike hit Manan and two subordinates in his hometown of Nowzad—at least the third attempt to kill him in an air strike. The missiles wounded Manan. His fighters drove him to a nearby clinic where he succumbed to his wounds. Next, Pir Agha, the quick reaction force commander who had killed Mansour Dadullah, was struck in Paktika. He survived but his operations were disrupted for months. Other strikes killed multitudes of Taliban district governors and a few other provincial governors.

The operational design was one of Miller's improvements. Another was better leadership. Miller's predecessors had been leery of pressing Ghani or Karzai to appoint ministers and generals whom Americans evaluated as capable. Not so Miller. He convinced Ghani to appoint a wide range of generals and ministers. Most notable was former Kandahar governor and NDS director Asadullah Khalid to Minister of Defense. Khalid had recovered from his wounds in the 2012 suicide bombing. Although he could tire easily and spoke in slow measured sentences, his drive to destroy the Taliban and his political wisdom were undiminished. Unlike too many other Afghan generals and politicians, he wanted to get things done. Miller also convinced Ghani to appoint Massoud Andarabi as Minister of Interior. Andarabi was known as the most capable NDS intelligence operator.

In the summer, Miller adjusted his operational design to the Taliban summer offensive. Even with full authority to use air power, defending against the Taliban was a shell game. US and Afghan commanders never knew exactly where the Taliban would attack. The problem was compounded by the fact that Afghan defenders often failed to communicate an attack was occurring or fled rather than defend themselves.

Miller rose to the challenge. First, he shifted assets from killing Taliban leadership to defending posts. He optimized placement of aircraft, intelligence and surveillance assets, and special operations forces on the basis of strategic importance of a particular area and indications and warning of an attack. Second, he streamlined communications between Afghan posts, their higher headquarters, and US advisors. Over time, the Afghans learned how to send the Americans important information in a timely fashion. Third, he deployed special operations forces to provincial capitals under threat in order to stiffen defenses as well as target Taliban leadership.

The 2019 summer campaign was hard fought. The Afghan army and police suffered higher casualties than any year before. The Taliban suffered as well. According to a BBC independent report, approximately 1,000 Taliban fighters were killed in August, compared to 850 police and soldiers.[30] In Doha, Motaqi admitted that US air strikes killed many Taliban and that their forces could not take ground in the face of it; in fact, he forecast they would lose ground in Helmand.[31] The Taliban delegation spent weeks trying to work a deal in which air strikes would be suspended.

Khalilzad met with the Taliban for another round in late February. Baradar was present with full authority over negotiations. The two formed a warm relationship, often joking with each other. Baradar appreciated Khalilzad's efforts to release him from Pakistani arrest. Although Baradar was in charge, Stanekzai handled the day-to-day negotiations. The Taliban delegation tried to walk back their promise to implement counterterrorism measures and rejected talks with the Afghan government or a ceasefire. At one point, they insisted that al-Qaʻeda was not behind the September 11 attacks and refused to condemn the group publicly. The rhetoric was highly concerning to the US side. Khalilzad's team was already worried about the sincerity of the Taliban promise not to let terrorist groups use Afghan soil; Mullah Omar had promised the same thing nearly verbatim before September 11. Khalilzad threatened to walk. That compelled the Taliban grudgingly to specify that they would forbid al-Qaʿeda from conducting external operations from Afghanistan, a notable concession.[32] The US-Taliban agreement was to be public so the world and al-Qaʿeda would know what the Taliban had promised.

A follow-on round of US-Taliban negotiations in early May was equally difficult. The Taliban conceded a few more points on counterterrorism but talks never delved into a ceasefire or a political settlement. The Taliban delegation refused to allow any reference to the Afghan government in the US-Taliban agreement whatsoever and demanded they themselves be referred to as the Islamic Emirate of Afghanistan.[33]

Over the course of negotiations, Taliban were reluctant to break with al-Qaʿeda completely. According to the United Nations, Quetta Shura members consulted with al-Qaʿeda senior leaders behind the scenes and assured them that ties would remain intact. Al-Qaʿeda leader Zawahiri himself may have spoken with members of the Haqqani family.[34]

At Doha, the members of the Taliban delegation frequently claimed that the Taliban had never helped al-Qaʿeda or that al-Qaʿeda did not exist in Afghanistan—obvious denials of reality. Their spokesman, Sohail Shaheen, said to CBS News that he knew of no proof that al-Qaʿeda was responsible for September 11.[35] The delegation resisted detailed actions against al-Qaʿeda beyond the verbal promise to prevent external attacks. They barely conceded to banning fundraising, recruiting, and training, and they rejected any precise steps, let alone severing their relationship.

I was with Khalilzad's delegation at the time and heard these things firsthand. One university-educated member of the political commission lectured me that the Taliban were right not to turn over bin Laden in 2001 because the US request did not follow international law on extradition. He unconvincingly advised, "The Taliban are not with al-Qaʿeda. We will not attack another country. Our word alone will be enough." Another Taliban delegate asked me a disturbingly illuminating set of questions:

- Will the United States want the Taliban to separate themselves from people who were once al-Qaʿeda but have since left the organization?
- What if there is a group of former al-Qaʿeda? Will the United States let them live in Afghanistan?
- What about Arabs or other foreigners? Does the United States see them all as al-Qaʿeda? Afghanistan should be a home for Muslims rejected by their own countries.

- What about Taliban who had ties to al-Qaʻeda? Are they supposed to leave Afghanistan?
- And what about Taliban leaders who had ties to al-Qaʻeda? Are we to turn against them?

The questions hinted at just how close the Taliban and its leadership were to al-Qaʻeda.

Taliban intransigence raised deep concerns in Washington about the prospects for an agreement. These concerns did not alter the president's directions. Trump was irked that the drawdown had not already begun. He often complained about the cost of the war to Pompeo, Bolton, Shanahan, and Dunford and asked why US troops were there, conveying his personal disdain for terrorism as a justification. He accused them of trapping him in Afghanistan. In a set of meetings in July, he relayed that he would pull out all US troops in nine months—a time frame Trump had used from time to time that was fairly arbitrary, though in this case would remove all troops by April 2020, ahead of the US presidential election that year. On July 24, Trump met with Pakistani army chief Bajwa and Prime Minister Imran Khan in the White House. He once more exclaimed that the United States would be getting out. The two Pakistanis surely passed that to the Taliban.

Trump was not oblivious to the terrorist threat. Frequently he said he wanted out. Sometimes he said he wanted a long-term counterterrorism presence. On June 20, roughly a week before the seventh round of negotiations in Doha, Trump mused in an interview with *Time* magazine that the United States was "doing fine" in Afghanistan and troops would soon be down from 14,000 to 8,000, in effect telling the Taliban that they did not need to concede to halve US troop presence.[36] A week later Trump repeated the statement in an interview with *Fox News* but added that he would not reduce any further and would leave a very strong intelligence presence because Afghanistan was the "Harvard for terrorists."[37] The statements did not shake the policy to get a deal to withdraw to zero but suggest that Trump had a few doubts as he drew closer to an agreement.

Under guidance from Pompeo to get a deal, Khalilzad boldly pushed for an agreement before the end of the summer. The 2019 Afghan presidential election, scheduled for September 28, also pressured him. If the election occurred, the peace process would be delayed as a new government was seated. Worse, the election could lead to a political crisis like 2014, which would further delay peace talks. Better to complete a US-Taliban agreement and be on the road toward an Afghan political settlement before the election could be a problem.

On June 20, Khalilzad passed Baradar a paper that laid out a path to resolve all the major issues by September 1, with the announcement of a US-Taliban agreement on July 14 and the beginning of "intra-Afghan" negotiations between the Taliban, government, and other Afghan parties on July 22. Those intra-Afghan negotiations were to produce a roadmap by September 1 on necessary steps to lead to a full political settlement, possibly including an interim government. Pompeo set September 1 as a goal for political progress in a speech in July. Khalilzad's schedule would not be met but the basic steps became the consensus for how a peace process would proceed. Baradar and his delegation accepted Khalilzad's schedule in theory, pending agreement on the US withdrawal time-line. They even accepted that the government would be included in the political settlement, though they would not say so formally.[38]

In public, Taliban officials rejected officially meeting with the government. In private, several members of the Taliban political commission assured members of Khalilzad's team that they would negotiate with the Afghan government once the United States announced a withdrawal timeline.[39] Baradar supposedly said, "It does not matter if they [participants in intra-Afghan negotiations] are gov-ernment, just that they want good for Afghanistan and peace."

The Taliban political commission claimed the Taliban did not seek to mo-nopolize power and would settle for an Islamic "structure" to the government. Islamic structure was undefined. Sometimes it seemed to be a synonym for the old emirate. Other times it seemed to mean a state run according to the Taliban interpretation of Islamic law with a centralized state structure that could also be a democracy led by any Afghan. If asked, Taliban leaders and scholars tended to say the definition was for Afghans to decide among themselves.[40] The Taliban may also have been willing to countenance greater flexibility on education, health, women's rights, and human rights than had been the case during their first regime. The political commission's behavior suggested a more realistic ap-praisal of Afghan society.[41]

As much as the Taliban political commission foreswore monopoly, the emirate featured so strongly in their rhetoric that their true intent was impos-sible to discern. One member of the Taliban political commission detailed to me, "We want an emirate. We control seventy percent of Afghanistan. This is our chance to lead. We will be upset if we are not in charge. We will see if we return to violence if that happens." The leading religious scholar on the political commis-sion professed that the emirate and an Islamic structure were inseparable: "The Emirate is the Islamic structure of government. The Islamic structure of gov-ernment is the Emirate." How the government's democracy could be reconciled with the Taliban's emirate was unexplored territory.[42]

An important signal of Taliban willingness to meet with the government transpired on July 7 and 8 when a Stanekzai-led Taliban delegation met with roughly 40 government, Northern Alliance, and other Afghan representatives in an "intra-Afghan conference" organized by the Germans and Qataris. Although technically an "unofficial" event, for all intents and purposes participants negotiated with each other in an official capacity. Ghani's representatives—Nader

Naderi and Matin Bek—talked directly with Stanekzai and Motaqi, and hammered out a joint resolution.

Fawzia Koofi, influential even though she had left the parliament as the representative for Badakhshan, attended the conference and interrogated the Taliban delegates. After hearing their comments, she called out Stanekzai and the Taliban representatives: "You have not changed, don't pretend."[43] Since 2013, her belief had been that the only way to protect women's rights was for women to confront the Taliban face to face. "We women are not a piece of decoration," she had told Dunford in 2013, "Taliban say they will bring women's Islamic rights. Women need to be involved in peace to know."[44] In Doha, she was the toughest person on the government side. She corralled the Afghan women representatives and forced Khalilzad, who was present on the margins, to hear their concerns about the US and Taliban negotiations.

The final joint resolution called for peace talks that involved all Afghans to commence as soon as possible. The conference signaled to the US diplomats that the Taliban would actually meet with the government and other Afghans in the future, a noteworthy confidence-building measure.

The US withdrawal timeline and a ceasefire were the remaining major issues in the US-Taliban negotiations. Khalilzad had already agreed that the United States would go to zero. He had also agreed on the timeline for the initial phase of the drawdown. Forces would draw down to 8,600 and five bases would close in the first 135 days following the announcement of an agreement.[45] The timeline for the rest of the drawdown was up for discussion. The Taliban delegation sought a rapid US departure, preferably in less than a year. Khalilzad bargained for something much longer. Baradar and his colleagues told Khalilzad and other members of the US delegation that they had been listening to Trump's comments and believed the United States would be leaving no matter what and therefore they did not have to offer concessions. Two of his subordinates taunted me: "Your president wants to pull all US troops out of Afghanistan. He is going to do it."

Changing the Taliban's position would have required walking away from the table. Pompeo, attuned to Trump's impatience, did not want to wait. He instructed Khalilzad to negotiate any timeline with the Taliban and get an agreement as soon as possible.

For Khalilzad, the withdrawal timeline and guarantees on counterterrorism were less important than intra-Afghan negotiations. A political settlement would naturally suppress the terrorist threat and remove the need for US troops. Khalilzad believed the sides could actually reach an agreement quickly as had occurred at Bonn. He often reminded skeptics, "At Bonn, there was an agreement in ten days. It is easy."[46] He saw little risk in trading a short timeline for the initiation of negotiations, reasoning that the United States would be committed to nothing if the Taliban failed to meet their obligations in the agreement. Pompeo agreed. On August 4, Khalilzad convinced Baradar to accept a 14-month time-line for withdrawal, contingent upon the Taliban meeting their obligations.[47] If the Taliban did not distance themselves from terrorist groups, enter into peace talks with the government, and reach a peace settlement, the United States would delay or cancel its withdrawal—or so was the hope.

The ceasefire was the last major issue. The Taliban never formally agreed to one. The nature of jihad affected the Taliban negotiating position. In their minds, the movement could lose legitimacy if it stopped fighting the infidel occupier or its puppets. Taliban delegates repeatedly said that if they accepted a compre-hensive ceasefire (or openly broke with al-Qa'eda) that many fighters would go to the Islamic State. One Taliban told me, "We need the United States to an-nounce a withdrawal in order to prove to our fighters that the jihad has been won. Otherwise what was sacrifice for? We are very worried that that fighters will go to Daeesh or other groups." The most the Taliban formally offered was safe passage for US forces withdrawing from the country.[48] The question of an actual formal ceasefire was punted to the agenda of intra-Afghan negotiations.

The US-Taliban draft agreement was finished on September 1. Each side brought it to their respective leadership for approval. Khalilzad and Baradar set a tentative date of September 23 for the initiation of intra-Afghan negotiations in Oslo.[49] Khalilzad went to Kabul and declared that the draft was completed and being confirmed by President Trump.

The US military was uncomfortable with the agreement but went along. Dunford was on the edge: "I'm 51 percent in favor." He did not think the Taliban would seriously act against al-Qa'eda. Nor did Miller. Dunford's opposition to the agreement could have sunk the whole thing. What won over Dunford as well as Miller was the reasoning that if the Taliban fell through on their commitments, if they refused to reach a political settlement, the United States could walk away from a deal and continue the war. The United States could test Taliban sincerity.

If the virtue of the agreement was that the United States could walk away, the weakness was that it promised the United States precious little up front. The vi-ability of the agreement depended on the willingness of the United States to call off the drawdown in the future in order to enforce conditions.

In early September, it looked like an announcement was pending, the election would be delayed, and "intra-Afghan" negotiations for an Afghan political settle-ment would start within a month. Speaking with Tolo News, Khalilzad said, "In principle, on paper, yes we have reached an agreement—that it is done. . . . But it is not final until the president of the United States also agrees to it."[50] He spoke openly of five US bases closing within 135 days of an announcement. Trump toyed with a dramatic summit at Camp David with Baradar and Ghani, where he would personally announce the peace deal and the start of intra-Afghan negotiations.[51]

As US-Afghan negotiations concluded, Taliban emir Maulawi Haybatullah drastically escalated violence. He may have been trying to pressure Trump into confirming the agreement. Or he may have been trying to frighten the army, police, and Afghan leaders into conceding in later talks as his spokesman proclaimed, "They must . . . understand that we are not weak and if we enter talks . . . we enter from a strong position."[52] Or he may have been trying to get in his last licks before an announcement and some reduction in violence.

Haybatullah and the Taliban political commission did not foresee how escalation could trigger retaliation. Trump had never signaled that he wanted a reduction in violence before an announcement. Under pressure to get a deal, neither had Khalilzad. Baradar felt that violence should indeed be reduced beforehand but other Taliban leaders did not share his concern. In negotiations, the Taliban political commission had been very clear that violence would slacken only *after* an announcement and they never promised it would cease. From their perspective and in reality the United States had never said that escalation would violate the agreement.

Haybatullah launched three major offensives against Kunduz, Baghlan, and Farah, starting on August 31. The most substantial was the three-sided attack on Kunduz City. Minister of Defense Khalid, Minister of Interior Andarabi, and General Miller received early warning and flew up to direct the defense. The army, police, Afghan special operations forces, and air strikes turned the Taliban back within a day. The Taliban took twice as many casualties as the police and army. Fighting lasted longer in Baghlan and Farah and the army and police suffered heavier losses before the Taliban retreated.

In Kabul, two Taliban suicide bombings killed large numbers of soldiers and civilians. On September 2, a truck bomb blasted "green village," a compound where US and foreign officials and contractors quartered. Ten Americans were killed and another four were wounded, in addition to five Afghan civilians killed and 119 wounded. Another suicide bombing near the US Embassy on September 5 killed one US soldier, a Romanian soldier, and ten Afghan civilians. Forty-two Afghan civilians were wounded. The same day, just south of Kabul in Logar, a suicide car bomb against a US base wounded nine US soldiers and killed four Afghans. In the course of a week, 24 Americans were killed or wounded. All told, throughout Afghanistan 107 civilians were killed and 374 had been wounded.

Trump was enraged. He had expected violence to abate in the prelude to an announcement and felt betrayed. Leading Republicans, such as Senator Lindsey Graham and Representative Liz Cheney, were already disparaging the deal. Nine former US ambassadors had cowritten a critique.[53] The American losses, especially the one soldier who had been killed, were too humiliating. Khalilzad and

Miller returned to Doha to denounce the violence. Two days later Trump called off negotiations, tweeting:

> [A]n attack in Kabul . . . killed one of our great great soldiers, and 11 other people. I immediately . . . called off peace negotiations. What kind of people would kill so many in order to seemingly strengthen their bargaining position? They didn't, they only made it worse! If they cannot agree to a ceasefire during these very important peace talks, and would even kill 12 innocent people, then they probably don't have the power to negotiate a meaningful agreement anyway. How many more decades are they willing to fight?[54]

Trump opposed any delay or cancellation of the Afghan election. He suspended any drawdown of forces to 8,600 and ordered Miller to intensify military pressure.[55] The next day Pompeo recalled Khalilzad to the United States and announced on a series of Sunday talk shows that negotiations would not resume until the Taliban reduced violence and agreed to talk directly with the Afghan government, including Ghani. The day after that Trump clarified to reporters at the White House that peace talks were "dead" and would not resume.

It was an amazing turnabout, far from out of character. For all his distaste for Afghanistan, Trump also cared about his own reputation and a "good deal."[56] He did not want to be called a fool for believing a bunch of Taliban. And he was concerned about a terrorist safe haven reappearing in Afghanistan on his watch. As Khalilzad had closed on his agreement, Trump had frequently asked whether others thought it a "good deal." On August 29, he had speculated on Fox News that a deal was "getting close" but "who knows if it's going to happen." About going to zero, he was noncommittal: "We're going down to 8,600 and then we'll make a determination from there," adding that a "high intelligence presence" would stay in the country.[57]

Trump recognized that a terrorist threat out of Afghanistan could damage him politically. There was risk in accepting an agreement that appeared reckless, that his political supporters might interpret as a surrender document. His old political advisor, Steve Bannon, warned him that a terrorist attack coming out of Afghanistan would be a catastrophe for his reelection campaign; better to keep troops in Afghanistan to prevent any attacks. Pompeo thought Trump was worried that a written promise to go to zero could draw criticism from his supporters. In policy meetings since the spring, Trump had evinced concern that voters would hold him accountable for an attack on the United States. On August 30, he had asked his national security council, "How bad will this deal make me look?" and "Is this agreement salable?"[58] Furthermore, those Republicans who supported the war—Senate Majority Leader Mitch McConnell and Senate

Armed Services Committee chairman James Inhofe, in addition to Lindsey Graham and Liz Cheney—mattered. Trump needed the Republican Senate united behind him to check the Democrat-controlled House of Representatives, especially since information on his Ukraine dealings, which would lead to his impeachment, was coming out in the press. When Haybatullah attacked and killed an American, Trump decided he was being made into a fool and getting a bad deal that could harm his political position. "You can't do that," Trump swore to the press. "You can't do that with me."[59]

As the conservative *Wall Street Journal* editorial page succinctly explained two days after Trump's tweet,

> There is no domestic political clamor for the U.S. to withdraw all troops, especially with casualties low. The political harm for Mr. Trump would be far greater if a pullout triggered the collapse of the Afghan government and a humanitarian tragedy. A revived terrorist sanctuary in Afghanistan would also erase the political benefit for Mr. Trump from destroying the ISIS caliphate in Syria. The jihadist movement worldwide would declare a great victory.[60]

Like Obama before him, Trump had to worry about a withdrawal that might leave him guilty of permitting a terrorist threat to America.

The Afghan presidential election occurred as scheduled on September 28. Turnout was a paltry 1.8 million voters, by far the lowest of any Afghan presidential election. After four months of counting, the independent election commission announced that Ashraf Ghani, now 70 years old, had been reelected. He had won 50.6 percent of the vote, scraping by to avoid a second round. Abdullah rejected the result. He executed his threat of 2014 to declare a parallel government. But the rage of the northerners was less than 2014. Few protests broke out in the streets. Abdullah's political support was so weak that little happened to challenge Ghani's authority following the declaration of a parallel government. Nearly eight months after the election, after extensive international mediation, Ghani and Abdullah came to another unity government agreement on May 17. It recognized Ghani as president and divided up the ministries and provincial governorships with Abdullah. Abdullah's chief executive position disappeared but the unity government effectively continued.

Khalilzad did not wait for the result of the election to try to restart negotiations. Haybatullah, Baradar, and the political commission were taken aback by Trump's walkout. They had not expected it. On October 3, Khalilzad met with Baradar and a Taliban delegation in Islamabad on the side issue of trading Taliban prisoners for two American University in Afghanistan professors, Kevin King and Timothy Weeks, who had been kidnapped in 2016. Pakistan prime minister, Imran Khan, and chief of the army, Bajwa, moderated. One of the Taliban prisoners was Anas Haqqani, younger brother of Sirajuddin Haqqani, leader of the Haqqani network. Both were sons of the famed Jalaluddin Haqqani, founder of the Haqqani network. Anas had been detained in Dubai in 2013. The Haqqanis had long sought his release and were gratified that Khalilzad was willing to make a trade. The exchange took place on November 19. At the same time, possibly trying to encourage the resumption of peace talks, the Taliban ceased all suicide and other major attacks in cities. Few attacks of any kind by Taliban, including the Haqqani network, happened in Kandahar, Kabul, Mazar, or Herat.

Shortly after the prisoner exchange, Khalilzad and the Taliban delegation resumed talks on the peace agreement in Doha. Conveying Trump's intent, Secretary of State Pompeo demanded the Taliban stop violence nationwide before the announcement of a deal. Because of the walkout, the political commission put greater credence behind Khalilzad's words and demands. Haybatullah retreated from the August position. At the end of December, he and the Quetta Shura agreed to propose a 7-to-10-day temporary reduction of attacks that would occur once the agreement with the United States had been announced. In mid-January, Baradar gave Haybatullah's proposal to Khalilzad. Pompeo wanted more. Negotiations slowed in late January. The political commission complained about how the United States had raised its demands but the Taliban seemed to take Khalilzad seriously in light of the September walkout.

Pompeo did not capitalize on the walkout to raise other issues in the original agreement and ask for more up front, such as better guarantees on counterterrorism the initiation of peace talks with the Afghan government, or a timeline for progress in those peace talks.

Haybatullah, Baradar, Sirajuddin Haqqani, and other Taliban leaders worried Trump might walk again. In the backdrop was the ongoing war. The Taliban were far less exhausted than the government but seemed to prefer removing the United States via agreement to seeing if Trump would withdraw of his own accord. If a deal was not sealed before the fighting season, Taliban leadership would face greater difficulty reeling back fighters amid operations. In a bold public relations move, Sirajuddin penned an op-ed in the *New York Times*. "Everyone is tired of war. I am convinced the killing and the maiming must stop," he wrote. "The withdrawal of foreign forces has been our first and foremost demand."[61] In the second week of February, Haybatullah agreed to the pre-announcement reduction in violence. On February 13, Secretary Pompeo described a "pretty important breakthrough" in negotiations. For seven days, Taliban attacks were to cease in the cities, in the provincial capitals, on the highways, and on US and Afghan army headquarters. US and Afghan forces were to halt offensive operations and go into a defensive posture.

The seven-day reduction in violence began at midnight on February 22. Although the Taliban attacked a number of outlying areas, overall violence dropped dramatically. Throughout the seven days, the United States conducted no air strikes. Afghan civilians were relieved. People moved about freely on the highways and in the towns and cities. In Jalalabad, people were dancing in the streets. "The people out in the city are a great many," said one Kandahar shopkeeper to a Voice of America reporter, "Happiness is greater. Everyone that you see is happy." A Kandahari mullah exclaimed, "All the people, the big and the small, all are happy to come to peace... If Afghan or not. Peace, safety, security— the happiness of all people is peace."[62] But the joyous intermingling of the June 2018 ceasefire was missing. Taliban did not walk in the cities or visit Afghan soldiers and police and treat them as brothers. Mullah Yakub, Mullah Omar's son and one of Haybatullah's three deputies, instructed Taliban commanders to inform all their "mujahedin... know that what happened last time, in the ceasefire, should not happen again. Mujahedin must stay in their own place. They must not go to the enemy's area. Permission does not exist... They do not have permission to go to Kabul."[63]

Trump was now willing to accept an agreement. The reduction in violence insulated him against domestic criticism over the content of the deal. To further distance himself, he left the signing ceremony to Khalilzad and Pompeo.

The signing ceremony took place in the Sheraton hotel in Doha before a large audience of diplomats from across the world. Thirty countries and organizations attended, including Pakistan, Germany, Russia, Qatar, and the United Nations. The text of the peace agreement was the same as in September. Trump and Pompeo were satisfied that the Taliban had shown a commitment to reducing violence. The entire agreement was public, including the US timeline to withdraw within 14 months and the Taliban commitment to immediately "prevent any group or individual, including al-Qa'ida, from using the soil of Afghanistan to threaten the security of the United States and its allies" and "prevent them from recruiting, training, and fundraising."[64] The agreement stipulated intra-Afghan negotiations between all Afghan sides were to begin on March 10. Before that the Afghan government was to release up to 5,000 prisoners in exchange for 1,000 soldiers and police that the Taliban were holding.

Finally, after nearly 18 months of talks, at 4:00 p.m. on February 29, the United States and the Taliban signed their agreement. Ambassador Khalilzad signed for the United States. Mullah Baradar signed for the Taliban. Secretary of State Pompeo was present as a witness. On March 3, Trump congratulated Baradar over the phone.

The US-Taliban agreement was Afghanistan's best opportunity for peace since 2001 and America's best opportunity to get out. The agreement came about after war had ruled for nearly two decades. US leaders had gradually come to a consensus that the United States should risk significant concessions to the Taliban in an attempt to leave under the right conditions. The hopes of the surge and drawdown had long since expired.

Grinding stalemate helped compel the United States to come to the negotiating table. The battlefield situation had settled into a costly stalemate and clarified itself. US leaders could see that little was going to change any time soon. Unlike 2010, US generals no longer argued against talks. Years of war had nudged Dunford, Nicholson, and then Miller to coalesce behind negotiations as a possible solution to the war and to support State Department efforts in a way their predecessors had resisted. They may have preferred carrying with a small, sustainable number of forces but were not going to oppose a diplomatic effort or the instincts of the president.

Another important factor was the skill of the diplomats at the table. Zalmay Khalilzad drove peace talks forward relentlessly. He was too good to be thrown off course by the vagaries of diplomacy, bureaucratic resistance in Washington, or complaints in Kabul. Potholes, road bumps, and miscommunication no longer overturned negotiations. No diplomat equaled him in energy, stature, and Afghan relationships. On the opposite side, if different in character, Baradar was also effective. His patience and willingness to champion peace combined with his political weight repeatedly drew the Taliban political commission to compromise. They otherwise would have defaulted to hard-line positions when facing uncertainty in order to please the military commanders in Afghanistan and Quetta.

The biggest reason the peace agreement came about, however, is not the battlefield stalemate or diplomatic prowess. It is Donald Trump. He preferred to withdraw from Afghanistan. Although concerned about the domestic political ramifications of the terrorist threat, more than any other US politician, he was willing to buck criticism and demand that the United States leave. His anger forced US diplomats and generals to risk the appeasing position that jump-started negotiations. He pressed the US government and military inexorably toward withdrawal.

By the same token, Trump was too impatient to sponsor a well-structured peace agreement. His impatience stampeded Khalilzad into giving a lot while the Taliban promised little and gave even less. If Trump had been a bit more patient, Khalilzad possibly could have negotiated a survivable deal. The rush was unnecessary given that Trump himself walked out of negotiations in September and convinced the Taliban to concede on a reduction in violence. Instead of demanding tangible Taliban actions up front, such as immediate intra-Afghan peace talks, Khalilzad was forced to gamble that in return for a withdrawal timeline the Taliban would live up to their verbal and written assurances. His leverage was that if they tarried, the United States could halt the withdrawal. That leverage depended on Trump's willingness to start and stop the withdrawal in relation to progress in the peace process—a gamble on top of a gamble. The United States had found a path to peace. Unfortunately, its navigation depended on patience and consistency over what was sure to be an extended process.

After the signing, the process immediately stalled over prisoner releases. The March 10 deadline for intra-Afghan negotiations came and went. Months passed as Khalilzad shuttled between the Taliban and Ghani. Intra-Afghan negotiations finally commenced on September 12, with Mullah Baradar leading an Afghan delegation and Dr Abdullah leading the government and Afghan society delegation. In a repeat of February, everything stalled. The hope, a hope that I shared, that anything could happen once Taliban and government negotiators sat across from each other at the table, that they could spontaneously agree to a political settlement, was proven hollow.

General Miller completed the drawdown to 8,600 on June 18, 2020, ahead of the 135-day schedule. Disregarding damage to his leverage in the stalled negotiations, Trump then further reduced the number to 4,500 in time for the presidential election.

The Taliban exploited the decreasing number of US troops and redoubled their offensives, seemingly confident that the government was about to be all alone. On October 27, at the beginning of the pomegranate harvest, 1,000 or more Taliban advanced to the edge of Kandahar City. They seized most of Panjwai, Zharey, and the government stronghold of Arghandab, the districts that had been firmly in government hands since the US surge of 2009 to 2011. A few Afghans from the province told me there were just "too many for the police to handle."

Taliban commanders on the ground throughout the country widely declared that peace would come when they controlled the government. One commander told Jane Ferguson of the PBS News Hour: "We all know Ashraf Ghani and his whole government were brought here by the Americans, and they follow the orders of the Americans. After the Americans leave, they cannot do anything. They cannot carry on . . . The emirate is alive now, but once it comes to full power, everyone will accept it and respect it."

For all his bluster, Trump flinched from complete withdrawal. In October, he tweeted he would have all US troops out of Afghanistan by Christmas. In the end he reversed course. On November 17, after his election defeat, the Department of Defense announced that 2,500 troops were to remain in Afghanistan when Trump left office in January 2021.

21

Looking Back

Donald Trump lost the White House to Joseph Biden in the November 2020 presidential elections. The new year opened to a new policy debate in Washington over what to do in Afghanistan. Trump had left Biden with the unenviable choice of following through with the May 1 deadline amid a stalled peace process or staying in Afghanistan in an unending and escalating war.

Another event had impacted the war as well. Days after the signing of the US-Taliban agreement on February 29, 2020, the coronavirus pandemic had struck the United States, Afghanistan, and the entire world. The ensuing crisis locked down the United States in quarantine and absorbed the attentions of Trump and most other US leaders. The coronavirus altered America's outlook on the war. Between February and the end of 2020, 350,000 Americans died from the virus. The possible losses from a terrorist attack paled in comparison. At the height of the pandemic, more Americans were dying per day than had died on September 11. The US economy entered its worst economic crisis since the Great Depression of the 1930s, worse than the 2008–2009 recession that Obama had managed. To save the economy, Trump and Congress passed an unprecedented $2 trillion relief package. The importance of Afghanistan as a US interest decreased. The pandemic further tempted Trump to get out of Afghanistan in order to save money and to prevent troops from dying of coronavirus. Officials reported to the press in late April, "Trump complains almost daily that US troops are still in Afghanistan and are now vulnerable to the pandemic."[1] Upon assuming office, Biden faced the same challenges. He had to energize the government campaign to counter the pandemic, distribute vaccinations, and push forward another $1.9 trillion in spending to help the economy.

Biden had long been opposed to the war, somewhat viscerally after years of seeing American fallen and wounded. As much as his instincts told him to withdraw, senior officials described him as torn. He was said to be concerned about terrorist threats and to have described the possible collapse of Afghanistan as "haunting." During his presidential campaign, he had spoken of leaving a small number of forces for counterterrorism. Others in his administration worried about what would happen to women. Biden wisely waited and gave time for deliberations. The passing weeks clarified the damage Trump had inflicted on the peace process and difficulties of waging a war with only 2,500 troops on the ground. After a series of discussion with his principal cabinet members and advisors, Biden followed his instincts and decided to go out the door that Trump's agreement with the Taliban for a May 1 withdrawal had opened.

On April 14, 2021, President Biden announced that US military forces would begin their final withdrawal before May 1 and complete it by September 11 of that year. He said terrorism was no longer a major threat from Afghanistan, "Our presence in Afghanistan should be focused on the reason we went in the first place, to ensure Afghanistan would not be used as a base from which to attack our homeland again. We did that. We accomplished that objective." The changing strategic environment underpinned the decision: "Rather than return to war with the Taliban, we have to focus on the challenges that are in front of us . . . We have . . . to meet the stiff competition . . . from an increasingly assertive China . . . We have to defeat this pandemic and strengthen global health systems to prepare for the next one because there will be another pandemic." America's war in Afghanistan was at a close.

Scott Miller, the most skilled general of the Afghan War, oversaw the withdrawal and was the last commander of US forces in Afghanistan. General Joseph Dunford had retired in October 2020. General Mark Milley, a three-time Afghanistan veteran, succeeded him. Dunford's strategy of staying in Afghanistan with as few forces as possible—"term life insurance"—had won out in practice over six years, up until February 2020, even when official strategy envisioned withdrawal, military victory, or peace talks. His strength as a strategist was in never getting carried away. Obstacles to victory and to withdrawal stood out to him. Wisdom entertained dreams of neither. He focused on the central US interest—protecting the United States from terrorist attacks—with the minimum of forces. He kept the main thing the main thing. The rest of the list of America's Afghanistan generals also faded away—Stanley McChrystal as a business consultant, John Allen as the US envoy to fighting the Islamic State, David Petraeus as a fallen hero. Karl Eikenberry had perhaps the most satisfying retirement as a scholar at Stanford, eased by the fact that time had borne out many of his predictions.

On the Afghan side, Ghani started his second term, now with greater authority over the powers of the presidency but confronting peril without America. He was outshone by Karzai. Surveys showed that his popularity far exceeded Ghani's. Karzai had brought Afghans together under his "big tent," minded the perils of foreign intervention, protected the innocent, and dedicated himself to peace. In the eyes of the Afghan people, he was a kingly figure. "People trust in Karzai. Regardless if weak or poor. He has great influence." said Maryam Durrani.[2] As much as he grated on Americans with his harsh criticism, Karzai was actually good for US interests. After 2019, Karzai continued to campaign for peace, with one eye on again playing a leading role in the fate of Afghanistan.

Life for women between 2001 and 2021 had begun with great hope and ended with trepidation. Shukria Barakzai convalesced in Norway for years. Fawzia Koofi and Maulali Ishaqzai campaigned on for their peoples, Koofi undeterred by a minor injury in an ambush outside Kabul while serving as a member of Afghanistan's negotiating team. Two decades of reform for women had brought progress yet oppression continued. Diminishing American influence and the possible return of the Taliban threatened everything that had been gained.

On the other side of the hill, Taliban rule was steady. Having consolidated power, Haybatullah reigned as emir. Rivalries within the Taliban were minor. Sirajuddin, leader of the Haqqani network, also remained. Government losses of senior leaders—Omar Jan, Gul Mullah, Mullah Naqib, Abdul Razziq, and many, many more— were less than the Taliban's toll—Osmani, Dadullah Lang, Abdul Salam, Abdur Rahim Manan, and Akhtar Mohammed Mansour, not to mention the natural deaths of Mullah Obaidullah and Mullah Omar. One of the few original leaders to survive it all, the charismatic Mullah Baradar, resided in Doha, talking to diplomats and Khalilzad who were trying to energize peace talks.

Al-Qa'eda, the group that had incited all this misery, barely survived, its grayed leader Ayman al-Zawahiri in permanent hiding. The organization had been shredded in the maelstrom it had unleashed and ultimately surpassed by the Islamic State, the more extreme version of itself. Violence begat violence. Extremism begat extremism.

The Afghan War is the longest in American history, at nearly 20 years, almost six years longer than Vietnam. In total, 2,488 US troops died; 20,722 were wounded.[3] Afghan casualties are unknown. Half a million dead and wounded is probably conservative. Over 65,000 police and soldiers were killed; at least another 135,000 were injured. Taliban casualties were probably greater: roughly 100,000 killed and 150,000 injured.[4] The civilian toll was more than 120,000 killed and wounded. Hundreds of thousands more became refugees or internally displaced within Afghanistan. At the height of the war in 2015, more than 1,170,000 people had fled their homes.[5]

America's war was part of a larger period of revolutionary change engulfing Afghanistan. Since 1978, civil war had afflicted Afghanistan. No stable rule had been accepted. Other than short breaks in the fighting, Afghans had not known peace. Over America's involvement, the civil war extended to 40 years in length, a great gash across Afghanistan's history. Never before had the country been unable to rule itself or faced violence for so long.

In the course of America's war, Afghanistan witnessed wide-ranging social and political change. The country enjoyed a bout of reconstruction. Renewed violence tarnished the results but improvements were real. Foreign assistance paved roads, opened schools and clinics, ushered in a vibrant free press, and granted women greater rights and representation than ever before. The average child in 2013 was likely to receive ten years of schooling, compared to six in 2001.[6] Life expectancy rose from 56 to 65 years of age between 2001 and 2018. Perhaps the biggest social change was the acceleration of urbanization. Millions migrated to Jalalabad, Kandahar, Mazar-e-Sharif, and Herat. Kabul swelled to 5 million people. With urban growth came a new class of educated young people. And the country experienced its first democracy. Four presidential and three parliamentary elections established something of a precedent of voting and peaceful transition of power. Ambassador Zalmay Khalilzad liked to say "Afghanistan's encounter with the United States has been extremely beneficial." The flaw was Afghan democracy's centralization of power into the hands of the president. Without the consensus-minded Karzai, competing factions lacked an avenue to share power in an effective manner. The product was a weak declining democracy.

Islamic rule retrenched alongside democracy. Outside the cities, Taliban values, organization, and unity proved enduring. Their justice appealed to those oppressed, their order to those tired of violence, their piety to all Afghans. Girded by their notions of unity and Afghan identity, the Taliban surmounted two leadership transitions and the rise of the Islamic State. The Taliban were the most powerful political force in Afghanistan, the most successful Islamic movement in the country's history. Never before had an Islamic movement had such a long-standing and dominant political role.

Afghanistan cleaved into an urban democracy and a rural Islamic order. Democracy appears to have had the harder go of it. By 2016, violence had risen to a level that portended the return of the dark times of the early 1990s. For many, the Taliban again seemed the only salvation, bringing to mind an insight from David Edwards's *Heroes of the Age*: "Islam migrates better than honor or nationality. As a transportable system of belief and practice whose locus is personal faith and worship, it can be adapted to a variety of contexts and situations."[7]

The Taliban's order had a dark side: a deepening of extremism. In 2001, Afghanistan was a haven for external terrorist groups. Afghans themselves were more conservative than extremist. As war heated up, Afghans changed. The Taliban summoned forth thousands of Afghan suicide bombers. The tactic victimized Afghanistan's youth, devalued life, and became an engine of violence. In this atmosphere, Afghanistan opened itself to the Islamic State, which glorified more brutal forms of extremism and spread into urban youth formerly interested in democracy.

The war affected the United States as well. Its military changed dramatically. The green if well-trained peacetime force of 2001 transformed into battle-tested echelons on indefinite combat duty. By 2014, army and marine infantry officers and senior enlisted as a rule had multiple tours in Afghanistan under their belts. A whole new set of capabilities—counterterrorism tactics, surveillance and intelligence techniques, drone strikes, and advising—became ingrained. Special operations forces—whether Ranger, Delta Force, SEAL, or Green Beret—were lionized as the best an American warrior could be. Along with experience came the pain of post-traumatic stress and tens of thousands of wounded veterans.

In terms of foreign policy, Afghanistan, along with Iraq, convinced the American people and their leaders to shun large-scale interventions. The disappointment and expense of the Afghan surge did it more than anything else. After 2011, presidents and generals refused to send large numbers of troops into conflicts. American foreign policy ambitions receded. The idea of building democracies and changing regimes fell dead. President Obama and then President Trump shifted to a more isolationist foreign policy.

By 2016, the US military was trying to focus on larger-scale wars and innovation. Russia and China were rising threats. Secretary James Mattis's 2017 National Defense Strategy recognized that the US military's edge was dulling. Mattis reprioritized maintaining an advantage in "great power competition" over fighting terrorists. The never-ending Afghan War had diverted military assets from preparing for great power competition. The cost of the war from 2001 to 2019 was nearly $1 trillion, funds that might otherwise have been spent to modernize the US military or invest in research and development.

It is too early to say how Americans will remember the war. The idea of it as the "good war" wore off shortly after President Obama's 2008 election campaign. From 2011 onward, the popular verdict was that the United States had failed. In 2019, the *New York Times* dubbed the war a "lost cause."[8] Senator Elizabeth Warren bluntly stated in a Democratic primary debate that year, "What we're doing right now in Afghanistan is not helping the safety and security of the United States. It is not helping the safety and security of the world. It is not helping the safety and security of Afghanistan."[9] In polls from 2014 to 2018, between 49 and 56 percent of Americans said that the war was a failure. Where the good war remained was the memory of the initial response to September 11. A sense existed that war had been the only choice, regardless of the mistakes that followed.[10]

The bigger story is probably how little the war featured in national life.[11] Failure or success, Afghanistan was unimportant. Less than 0.3 percent of the population, including diplomats and contractors, served there. As combat writer Bing West regularly pointed out, Afghanistan had very low salience among the American people. Although comparisons were often made between the two, Afghanistan was not the searing national trauma of Vietnam. Afghanistan warranted few protests, no counterculture, and no meaningful political opposition. Congress approved executive budget requests and rarely pressed for withdrawal. State of the Union and inaugural addresses came and went with nary a word of Afghanistan. The omission should not be surprising. In Vietnam, the draft was in place; 2.7 million troops served, half a million at its height; and 58,000 were killed. Afghanistan was not a war of that magnitude. The sad truth is that few Americans paid much attention to the war or later remembered much of it.

Memory of Afghanistan is by far deepest within the small self-selected body of America's volunteer military. Approximately 800,000 served in Afghanistan.[12] In surveys of veterans in 2018 and 2019, the majority believed the 2001 invasion the right thing to have done but 40 to 58 percent responded that the longer war had not been worth fighting.[13] I personally have encountered a mix of memories. I know generals who believe we had to win: "I'm not going to be remembered as defeated like all those guys from Vietnam!" I know captains or gunnys who are proud of what they accomplished. I know others who see the sacrifice as a waste: "How we could be in Afghanistan for so long, and I could be there for seven months. . . . What came of my time there and our experience and the casualties? What benefit came from that? It's hard to think of any real benefit. There's just some kind of level of absurdity about it."[14] I know SEALs and Green Berets who think we should have left and pummeled any terrorists from afar. I know other SEALs and Green Berets who almost reveled in the war as a spartan fixture of their lives. I know soldiers and marines who hate the Afghans, love the Afghans, or don't even know the Afghans. And I know a lot of retired corporals and sergeants who are unsure what to make of the experience and value their brotherhood with each other above all else. "Even as we want it all to stop, we know on some level that it won't," writes Thomas Gibbons-Neff, the decorated marine sniper who went on to report for the *New York Times*. "After any peace deal—now, later, in another decade—we'll still be fighting the war in one place: Our heads."[15]

The popular verdict that America failed contains a fair bit of truth. The United States accomplished its major goals of eliminating Osama bin Laden and preventing terrorist attacks on the homeland but was unable to prevail over the Taliban. It was trapped in a protracted and costly war with no end in sight. Worse, the never-ending war incubated extremism and never-ending counterterrorism operations. The cost of the war in lives and treasure hardly seems worth the gains.

Why then did the United States and the Afghan government "fail"? The question underlies almost any discussion of the Afghan War. It drives the story, carrying us to a final conclusion, shaping what we see as important and unimportant, judging who was wise and who was foolish.

Foremost is the well-worn argument that the government and its warlord allies treated Afghans poorly, instinctively stealing in order to help themselves and their communities in the unending competition for survival, fomenting insurgency in the process. Evidence appears starkest in the early years of the war when mistreatment pushed certain tribes into the arms of the Taliban, giving the movement numbers and territory from which to attack. Without such support, the Taliban would have been much weaker.

Also weighty is the common argument that Pakistan prevented the United States from defeating the Taliban. Freedom to operate in Pakistan, protected from US strikes, enabled the Taliban to attack Afghanistan repeatedly, even after crushing defeats. After 2001, the Taliban leadership reorganized the movement there. Recruits for the 2006 offensive came from Afghan communities there. Suicide bombers trained there. During the worst of the surge, the movement sheltered there. In short, the engine of war cannot be reconstructed without Pakistan. A long succession of US leaders tried to change Pakistani policy, all to no avail because that policy was a function of Pakistan's immutable rivalry with India. Pakistani leaders—from Musharraf to Kayani to Bajwa—would never risk their influence in Afghanistan, their backyard and strategic depth.

We should look at why the Afghan government put up such a poor showing as well. If the army and police had regularly defeated the Taliban on the battlefield, the Taliban may have been unable to reemerge with the power that they did. Military effectiveness requires unity—and the government and its tribal allies did not have it. The army and police and tribal militias and their commanders fought as separate actors, with separate interests—and sometimes did not fight at all. In the worst cases, the army refused to help the police. This discord can be attributed to competition inherent in the tribes allied with the government. There was no overarching hierarchy within a tribe, let alone between them, that might have enforced cooperation. The discord can also, however, be attributed to the structure of the government itself, which was designed to prevent any leader from actually being in charge in any region. The arrangement was catastrophic in 2014 and 2015 when the army repeatedly refused to come to the aid of the police. Whatever their own set of rivalries, compared to the tribes and the government, the Taliban were cohesive. They were able to suppress internal competition to such a degree that it did not impede military effectiveness.

For all this, my overarching argument has been that something else, something fundamental, was equally at play in American failure. The answer that surfaces in the war's long history is that the Taliban stood for what it meant to be Afghan. The Taliban embraced rule by Islam and resistance to occupation, values that ran thick in Afghan history and defined an Afghan's worth. As a senior Taliban leader told Western researchers in 2015, "There is a considerable number of military chiefs and the long-fighting foot soldiers who fight for resurrection of an Islamic Emirate."[16] Resistance to occupation motivated sacrifice. Tainted by its alignment with the United States, the government had a much weaker claim to these values and thus a much harder time motivating supporters to go to the same lengths. The average soldier and policeman simply wanted to fight less than his

Taliban counterpart. Many could not reconcile fighting for Afghanistan along-side an infidel occupier and against a movement that represented Islam.

The explanation courses through the second half of the war. In battle after battle, numerically superior and well-supplied police and soldiers in intact de-fensive positions made a collective decision to throw in the towel rather than go another round. At decisive moments—Sangin, Kunduz, Nad Ali–Gereshk, Marjah, Lashkar Gah—the army and police had numerical superiority and at least equal amounts of ammunition and supply—even after the effects of corruption—yet retreated without putting up much of a fight. When under du-ress, police and soldiers too often just gave up. The Taliban's battlefield successes can be tied to evidence of purposeful Taliban who believed in something versus rudderless soldiers and police. So can the frightening resolve of suicide bombers, who killed leader after Afghan leader. Without the willingness to fight against su-perior numbers and kill themselves in devastating suicide bombings, the Taliban movement could have been contained. Islam and resistance to occupation is a necessary, albeit not sufficient, condition for the outcome of the war.

None of this is to say that government was unsupported, or that its troops were miserable and depressed, or that no one would fight. Little could be farther from the truth. The people supported the government in many, many places, as shown by polls and hundreds of thousands of volunteers for the army and police. *Jobs* More Afghans liked the government than the Taliban. And more Afghans were willing to serve on behalf of the government than the Taliban. But more Afghans were willing to kill and be killed on behalf of the Taliban. The Taliban had an edge in inspiration. That edge made a difference.

The risk of this explanation is substantial. The power of identity and religion can be miscast as evidence that Islam is inherently violent. The explanation comes uncomfortably close to Trump's hints that Islam is terrorism. A dem-agogue can deform appreciation of the perils of intervention into justifica-tion for hatred. The thrust of the explanation is not that Islam is violent. True enough, various Taliban—Mullah Dadullah Lang and Maulawi Haybatullah, for example—interpreted Islam in a way that intensified violence. But others had reservations, Mullah Baradar and Mullah Omar among them. The thrust of the explanation is that foreign occupation ran against national identity and Islam and inspired people to fight. It was not Islam that incited violence.

These powerful conditions inhibited the United States and the Afghan govern-ment from prevailing. But was failure inevitable? Conditions carried outcomes like a current but may not have determined the destination. There were chances for history to have taken a different course. At certain points, the United States could have made different decisions that might have averted failure or at least led to a far less costly stalemate.

Opportunity was widest early on, from 2001 to 2005. Popular support for the new Afghan government was high, as was patience with foreign presence, and the Taliban were in disarray. Unfortunately, American decisions foreclosed paths that might have avoided the years of war that followed.

The first was the Bush administration decision to exclude the Taliban from the post-invasion settlement, disregarding Churchill's advice of magnanimity in victory. The Taliban had demonstrated willingness to take part in the new settlement—the 2001 letter and later outreach to Karzai. Each time, Karzai was open to the idea. Each time, Rumsfeld or Cheney, maybe channeling Bush himself, angry over September 11 and overconfident after the initial quick victory, would have none of it. The new government was set up and a constitution was written without the Taliban at the table. We do not know if Mullah Omar and the entire movement truly would have settled. But enough major Taliban leaders were interested—Baradar, Obaidullah, Mansour—that future violence could have been delayed or diluted.

Bush and his team then built an army and police to defend Afghanistan far too slowly. Dismissive of the Taliban threat, by 2006 (ample time to recruit an army in other countries) only 26,000 Afghan army soldiers had been trained. When the Taliban attacked in 2006, there was little to stop them. A full army could have opened new opportunities. The Taliban were at best a fifth of their 2015 strength and popular support for the government and US presence was high. Even an uneven showing by a better army could have slowed Taliban momentum. And a Taliban movement with less territory and their own uneven record of success would have rallied fewer recruits. The government would have been more credible, and the burden on the United States would have been lighter. Between rejecting peace feelers and neglecting to build a strong army and police, like the Treaty of Versailles the post-2001 peace arrangement both punished the defeated too harshly and failed to safeguard the victors against future violence.

During this early period, other US mistakes assisted the return to war. Overly aggressive and poorly informed US counterterrorism operations upset Afghans and drove former Taliban back to violence. The same effect was had by the refusal of the Bush administration to curb the abusive practices of Karzai's government and its warlord allies. And Bush turned his attention to Iraq, which distracted from the growing problems in Afghanistan and denied the operational flexibility to better counter the future Taliban offensives.

These mistakes were avoidable. Bush could have reached out to the Taliban and could have built a better military quicker. There are plenty of historical examples of both. Nor did such decisions require in-depth knowledge of Afghanistan that was lacking at the time—these were principles of history and good foreign policy.

Later in the war opportunities to reach a better outcome narrowed. The war acquired a momentum of its own. The 2006 Taliban offensive dramatically escalated the conflict and overruled simple solutions. Further defeats damaged morale and induced further defeat. Extremist violence justified more extremism. The Americans who had been welcomed turned into an unwanted burden. Years of war bred disillusionment. It is hard to see any decision that could have resulted in a government victory. Nevertheless, a few points stand out where the United States might have cleared a path to a less violent future.

The surge was one of them. Given that its successes washed away and its costs were substantial, the United States would have been better served never to have surged at all. If Obama's campaign promises to right the "good war" obligated some number of reinforcements, Obama still might have deployed fewer, such as the initial tranche of 21,000. Petraeus and McChrystal did not present Obama with such an option. During the surge debate, their case that defeat was on the horizon and their overconfidence in counterinsurgency crowded out the practical alternative of foregoing further reinforcements. If Obama had, America's casualties and expenses would have been lower while the situation probably would have looked about the same as it did by 2016 anyway.

A separate opportunity came with the US drawdown and the government's 2014-onward showdown with the Taliban. The United States and its allies had done their utmost to ready the army and police. Having repulsed earlier attacks, the army and police were not yet broken. At this moment things went south. Close-run defeat in 2014 was quickly followed by one-sided defeat in Kunduz, Helmand, and elsewhere in 2015, a downward spiral of morale that led to more defeat. Obama was sucked back into the war. The whole cycle might have been defused early on if Obama had been much freer with the use of air strikes. He likely would have arrested the Taliban tide in 2014 or 2015. The defeats of Kunduz and Helmand that reverberated throughout the country, frightening thousands, setting a habit of military defeat instead of victory, probably would not have happened. An effective defense may have dampened Taliban morale and weakened future offensives. Victory would have been unlikely but the Afghan government should have been able to survive at lower cost to the United States. As it was, the decision to use air strikes sparingly *in extremis* virtually ensured defeat.

A final opportunity to reach a better outcome was the peace negotiation of 2019. Earlier efforts had failed because the conditions had not been ripe—Mullah Omar was recently deceased, President Obama was occupied with other issues, negotiators were not political heavyweights. By 2019, those obstacles had passed, plus Trump was uniquely angry enough to leave. The result was the closest the United States had yet come to a political settlement. The talks between Khalilzad and Baradar had the potential to lead to an acceptable compromise, as long as the United States was patient enough to apply its leverage. If far from a government victory, the goal of an inclusive new Afghan government that constrained terrorist activity and extricated the United States from Afghanistan represented a worthy end to the war. Unfortunately, Trump narrowed the opportunity by heedlessly pressing for withdrawal instead of giving Khalilzad the time to wring more out of the Taliban. The patience and care to exploit the opportunity was lacking, resulting in an agreement that was difficult to enforce and immediately derailed after the February 2020 signing.

Missing opportunities was human but consequential. US leaders did so for a variety of reasons. Perhaps the one common lesson is the value of forethought. US presidents and generals repeatedly saw their plans fall short when what they expected to happen did not: for Bush, when the Taliban turned out not to be defeated; for Petraeus and McChrystal, when the surge proved unsustainable; for Obama, when the terrorist threat returned; for Trump, when the political costs of withdrawing appeared steeper than assumed.

Habits that might have fostered forethought were missing. Information and intelligence that contradicted expectations were often neglected. Generals offered too few options to their civilian leaders and then placed too much faith in their own preferred course of action. For too long they searched for ways to win the war or, later, avoid losing it instead of supporting exploration of a broad range of options, especially negotiations. Civilians themselves oddly did not consider what might be necessary if their expected future failed to come to pass and how they might insure against that possibility. Presidents and their staffs preferred to insist on pursuing a policy, come what may. Relatively cheap precautions such as using the drawdown for leverage in negotiations or retaining authorities to strike Taliban were thus rejected. If America's civilian and military leaders had thought more about the different ways things could play out, then opportunities might not have been missed, options might not have been discarded, and America and Afghanistan may have experienced a less costly, less violent war, or even found peace.

The difficulty of changing the course of the Afghan War begs why the United States didn't just leave, curtail the expense, and end the tragedy for the Afghan people some time before 2020. Indeed, Rumsfeld worried about all this in 2001. His instinct was to hit and run. As much as Rumsfeld was later despised, by 2012 plenty of Americans thought that is exactly what should have been done. Yet three US presidents—two of whom were sorely tempted to get out—decided to stay. Rumsfeld himself ended up walking back from his own instincts.

Terrorism and domestic politics explain why they all stayed, assisted by the concern for human freedoms such as women's rights and the reluctance of generals to give up. The attacks of September 11 changed the international environment by igniting a fear that presidents could not ignore. Previously a minor irritation, terrorism transformed into a real threat to the United States, with the potential to involve chemical, biological, or nuclear weapons. In the early years the threat was palpable, the fear of subsequent attacks widespread. Bush never considered withdrawal at all.

The threat receded during Obama's presidency but he too could not ignore it. The political blowback to another attack, however decreasingly likely, was viewed as fatal. Obama shelved withdrawal during the surge debate and it was only after that experience that a zero option became a serious course of action. But he could never carry it out. Just as the wreck of al-Qa'eda was finally drifting into the distance and withdrawal appeared plausible, the rise of the Islamic State resurrected the threat and reinvigorated the political repercussions of an attack on the United States.

The same fate befell Trump, by far the US president most disgusted with Afghanistan. He too declared that all US forces would leave, only to reverse course. He succeeded in reducing forces to the lowest number yet but even the diminishing threat of terrorism dissuaded him from fulfilling his desire to get out. Even Biden deliberated before deciding to leave.

In another place and time, domestic pressure might have compelled a president to withdraw earlier in the war. As we have seen, Afghanistan never curried that kind of opposition. Presidents confronted little popular opposition to staying, however confused Americans were by Afghanistan. Not so with leaving. A president had to worry about political blowback to a terrorist attack on the homeland. Bush and Obama, if not Trump, also knew they would face disapproval from key political figures and groups when Afghan freedoms were quashed and women were severely oppressed. And any president would be walking out on their own without cover from the generals, who were reluctant to lose. The generals could be counted on to obey the decision but not to agree with it. If things went bad, the president could be accused of acting against the advice of the military. Leaving was more politically dangerous than staying. The possibility that a terrorist threat to the United States could revive, especially if the Kabul government fell, always turned out to be too much of a risk. It was one thing to look years out and coldly promise the United States would leave. It was another to peer over the brink as time drew nigh, see the uncertainties, and weigh the political fallout of a terrorist attack, and jump.

Such was the tragedy of America's Afghan War. The United States had few chances to succeed and few chances to get out. The idea that the war should have been abandoned is misleading. It presumes that a US president was free to pull the plug as he or she pleased when in reality getting out was nearly or equally as difficult as prevailing. A more realistic view might be that the Afghan War was always likely to veer toward something to be endured, an unwanted diversion in

American history with few opportunities to change course. Unlike their British and Soviet predecessors who lived before the era of international terrorism, American leaders had no easy way out.

The constraints of terrorism and public backlash were a feature of American society from 2001 to 2020. They defined an epoch. That epoch was fading long before 2020 but probably passed that year. The shadow of September 11 was receding and terrorism was losing its influence over US policy. Abu Bakr al-Baghdadi, leader of the Islamic State, was killed in a US special operations raid in October 2019. Great power competition against China and Russia was the rising concern in Washington. The coronavirus pandemic was a vast new threat and ushered in a new depression of unknown depths. It was no longer reasonable to assume terrorism demanded that the United States worry about Afghanistan. The constraints on leaving the war had weakened. In Biden's words, "We went to Afghanistan because of a horrific attack that happened 20 years ago. That cannot explain why we should remain."

None of that changes the preceding 19 years. Tragedy was greatest for the Afghan people. Historian John Lewis Gaddis writes in *The Landscape of History* that the purpose of the study of history is "to achieve the optimal balance, first within ourselves but then within society, between the polarities of oppression and liberation."[17] The moral question for Afghanistan boils down to whether intervention is just, how our presence harms a people, how innocents pay for our security: oppression juxtaposed against liberation. The United States exposed Afghans to prolonged harm in order to defend Americans from another terrorist attack. We resuscitated a state of civil war so that we could sleep a little sounder at home. Villages were destroyed. Families disappeared. It was inadvertent. US leaders never thought in terms of the terrible trade-off between the well-being of American citizens and the well-being of Afghans. They assumed life was better under a democracy. The intervention did noble work for women, education, and free speech. But that good has to be weighed against the tens of thousands of men, women, and children who died, as well as the fact that the good may wash away with time.

Foreign intervention was a blight on the peace and well-being of the people of Afghanistan. Forty years of civil war can be traced to it, starting with the Soviets. Their invasion upended a swift and relatively bloodless end to what would have been a minor civil war. The ensuing modern war wrought havoc on Afghans and their society. After the Soviet withdrawal, the Taliban regime managed to create stability after five years of brutal civil war. If their regime had survived, peace probably would have persisted in most of the country. The 2001 US intervention upset that balance. Nevertheless, by 2009, the Taliban were again reclaiming power. Only US escalation, in the form of the surge, pushed them back. And when the Taliban were succeeding again in 2015 and 2016, the United

States recommitted, putting wood back on the fire. The painful reality is that peace could have come a lot sooner without foreign intervention. Professor Odd Arne Westad wrote at the end of his magisterial work, *The Global Cold War*, that "Cold War ideologies and superpower interventions . . . helped put a number of Third World countries in a state of semipermanent civil war" and caused untold harm to their peoples in pursuit of marginal interests.[18] His words echo around us today.

NOTES

Chapter 1

1. Hamid Karzai Speech, Moscow Conference, Tolo News, https://www.youtube.com/watch?v=mdGIqTK7fpQ, February 2019.
2. William Dalrymple, *The Return of a King: The Battle for Afghanistan* (London: Bloomsbury, 2013).
3. Thomas Barfield, *Afghanistan: A Cultural and Political History* (Princeton, NJ: Princeton University Press, 2010), 41.
4. David Edwards, *Caravan of Martyrs: Suicide and Sacrifice in Afghanistan* (Berkeley: University of California Press, 2017), 148.
5. Samuel Huntington, *Political Order in Changing Societies* (New Haven, CT: Yale University Press, 2006).
6. "End the War in Afghanistan," *New York Times*, February 4, 2019.
7. Andrew Dugan, "Fewer in U.S. View Iraq, Afghanistan Wars as Mistakes," Gallup, www.gallup.com, June 12, 2015. R.J. Reinhart, "U.S. Views Mixed on War in Afghanistan," Gallup, www.gallup.com, September 11, 2019. Jim Golby and Peter Feaver, "It Matters if Americans Call Afghanistan a Defeat," *Atlantic*, August 17, 2019.

Chapter 2

1. Thomas Barfield, *Afghanistan: A Cultural and Political History* (Princeton, NJ: Princeton University Press, 2010), 32. "Afghanistan," World Bank: Data, https://data.worldbank.org/country/AF.
2. Barfield, *Afghanistan: A Cultural and Political History*, 24.
3. Barfield, *Afghanistan: A Cultural and Political History*, 160.
4. Abdul Karim Talib Rahimi, "Kandahar: The Courtyard of Great Promise and the Sangar of Prideful and Youthful Awakening," in *Kandahar: Extended History* (Kandahar, Afgh.: Kandahar Directorate of Culture, 2005), 82–83.
5. Mohammed Hassan Kakar, *My Selected Essays* (Kabul: Afghanistan Cultural Community, 2010), 82.
6. For a full discussion of Afghan identity see Joseph McCarthy, "The Enduring Heart of Central Asia: A Study to Understand Afghanistan's Survival," PhD dissertation, University of Nebraska, 2018.
7. Kakar, *My Selected Essays*, 78–80.
8. Asadullah Popal, "The Kandahar Sadozai," in *Kandahar: Extended History* (Kandahar, Afgh.: Kandahar Cultural Director, 2005), 263–266.
9. McCarthy, "The Enduring Heart," 175.
10. Abdul Bari Jehani, *Spelay* (Quetta, Pak.: Masaf Nisherati, 2010), 138–139.
11. Popal, "The Kandahar Sadozai," 263–266.

12. Discussion with Yusef Pashtun, former Kandahar governor, Kabul, August 3, 2013.
13. Barfield, *Afghanistan: A Cultural and Political History*, 60.
14. Michael Cook, *Ancient Religions, Modern Politics: The Islamic Case in Comparative Perspective* (Princeton, NJ: Princeton University Press, 2014), 220–222.
15. Olivier Roy, *Islam and Resistance in Afghanistan* (Cambridge, UK: Cambridge University Press, 1990), 139–141.
16. Richard Tapper, "Who are the Kuchi? Nomad Self-Identities in Afghanistan," *Journal of the Royal Anthropological Institute 14*, no. 1 (March 2008): 97–116.
17. Roy, *Islam and Resistance in Afghanistan*, 12..
18. Patricio Asfura-Heim, "Religious Leader Engagement in Afghanistan," CNA Research Memorandum, September 2012, 55.
19. For similar discussions, see Bernard Lewis, *The Crisis of Islam* (New York: Random House, 2003), 23.
20. Richard Bulliet, *Islam: The View from the Edge* (New York: Columbia University Press, 1994), 149.
21. Abdul Salam Zaeef, *Taliban: From Kandahar until Mazar* (Kabul, Afgh.: Aksos, 2018), 18.
22. David Edwards, *Heroes of the Age* (Berkeley: University of California Press, 1996), 136–137. Asfura-Heim, "Religious Leader Engagement in Afghanistan," 59, 63.
23. Discussion with senior Kunar religious scholar, Asadabad, Kunar, October 2, 2007.
24. Asfura-Heim, "Religious Leader Engagement in Afghanistan," 57.
25. Benazir Hotaki, "Bebe Zeneba, Zarghona Ana, and Maulali," in *Kandahar: Extended History* (Kandahar, Afgh.: Kandahar Cultural Director, 2005), 361.
26. Jenes Enevoldsen, *Sound the Bells, O Moon, Arise and Shine!: A Collection of Pashto Proverbs and Tappas* (Peshawar, Pak.: Interlit Foundation, 2000), 34.
27. Maulawi Mohammed Gul Shahid, *Religious Figures of Afghanistan* (Peshawar, Pak.: Maktabah Farooqiya, 2012), 562–563.
28. Enevoldsen, *Sound the Bells, O Moon, Arise and Shine!*, 39.
29. *Afghanistan: A Country Study* (Washington, DC: US Government Printing Office, 1986), xiv, 343.
30. Ibid., 85.
31. Ibid., 204, 350.
32. Ashley Edgette, "A Mecca for Militants: An Examination of the Development of International Terrorism in Peshawar, Pakistan, 1970–2010," *Hinckley Journal of Politics* (January 1, 2010): 16.
33. Carlotta Gall, *The Wrong Enemy: America in Afghanistan, 2001–2014* (New York: Houghton Mifflin Harcourt, 2014), 57.
34. Sheila Paine, *The Afghan Amulet: Travels from the Hindu Kush* (London: Tauris Parke Paperbacks, 2006), 69.
35. Laurent Gayer, *Karachi: Ordered Disorder and the Struggle for the City* (New York: Oxford University Press, 2014), 26.
36. "Pakistan," The World Bank: Data, https://data.worldbank.org/country/pakistan?view=chart.
37. "Pakistan: Armed Forces," National Intelligence Survey, October 1973, www.cia.gov.
38. Odd Arne Westad, *The Global Cold War* (Cambridge, UK: Cambridge University Press, 2005), 328.
39. Ibid., 354.
40. National Archives, RR-NSC: "US Policy Programs and Strategy in Afghanistan," National Security Decision Directive 166, March 27, 1985.
41. Peter Tomsen, *The Wars of Afghanistan: Messianic Terrorism, Tribal Conflicts, and the Failures of Great Powers* (New York: Public Affairs, 2011), 396.
42. National Archives, RR-NSC: "US Policy Programs and Strategy in Afghanistan," National Security Decision Directive 166, March 27, 1985.
43. For a discussion of mujahideen tactics, see Ali Jalali and Lester Grau, *The Other Side of the Mountain* (Quantico, VA: Marine Corps University Press,).
44. Tomsen, *The Wars of Afghanistan*, 440.
45. C. Christine Fair, "The U.S.-Pakistan F-16 Fiasco," *Foreign Policy*, February 3, 2011.

46. Amin Saikal, "The Rabbani Government, 1992–1996," in *Fundamentalism Reborn?*, edited by William Maley (New York: New York University Press, 1998), 33.

Chapter 3

1. Meeting with Kandahar religious leaders, Kandahar, March 29, 2014.
2. The term "warlords" can be misleading in Kandahar. It is meant to connote the fact these leaders fielded militias, funded themselves through poppy, and could not trace themselves to the lineage of a pre-1979 tribal leader. Yet the fact is that they were simply powerful tribal leaders. Each performed the traditional functions of a tribal leader of a robust tribal support base they had established. The war had created new avenues for advance that allowed young mujahideen to supplant the old leaders, many of whom had fled Afghanistan. This was a very normal shift of power within the tribes. Power is not necessarily hereditary; it is based on politics, skill, and resources. The "warlords" were simply tribal leaders with money and guns, just like Ahmed Shah and a host of other famous Afghan figures.
3. Abdul Salam Zaeef, *My Life with the Taliban* (New York: Columbia University Press, 2010), 60.
4. Wakil Ahmed Mutawakil, *Afghanistan and Taliban* (Kabul, Afgh.: Byeralai Pohaneon Lray, 2005), 11.
5. Zaeef, *My Life with the Taliban*, 60–63.
6. Zahidi Ahmedzai, *The Past and Future of the Islamic Emirate of Afghanistan* (Quetta, Pak.: Taliban Director of Culture, 2013), 95–96.
7. Zaeef, *My Life with the Taliban*, 65.
8. Zaeef, *My Life with the Taliban*, 65. Abdul Salam Zaeef, *Taliban: From Kandahar until Mazar* (Kabul, Afgh.: Aksos, 2018), 33–34.
9. Mutawakil, *Afghanistan and Taliban*, 14. Bette Dam, *The Secret Life of Mullah Omar*, Zomia Center, March 2019, 14.
10. David Edwards, *Before Taliban: Genealogies of the Afghan Jihad* (Berkeley: University of California Press, 2002), 293.
11. Zaeef, *Taliban: From Kandahar until Mazar*, 33. Carlotta Gall, *The Wrong Enemy: America in Afghanistan, 2001–2014* (Boston: Houghton Mifflin Harcourt, 2014), 41–42.
12. Alex Strick van Linschoten and Felix Kuehn, *Taliban Reader* (London: Hurst, 2018), 46–47.
13. Ahmed Rashid, *Taliban* (New Haven: Yale University Press, 2001), 25. Gall, *The Wrong Enemy*, 297.
14. Mutawakil, *Afghanistan and Taliban*, 16. Gall, *The Wrong Enemy*, 39. Discussion with Khairullah Khairkhwa, former Taliban governor of Herat, Doha, May 3, 2019.
15. Zaeef, *My Life with the Taliban*, 63.
16. The Taliban cultural commission's 2015 biography of Mullah Omar makes a point of his tribal ties to Mir Wais. "Biography of Mullah Omar," *Voice of the Jihad*, official Taliban website, April 4, 2015.
17. Discussion with Taliban founding member, Kabul, March 14, 2014.
18. Zaeef, *My Life with the Taliban*, 72.
19. Mutawakil, *Afghanistan and Taliban*, 15. Alex Strick van Linschoten and Felix Kuehn, *The Enemy We Created: The Myth of the Taliban* (New York: Columbia University Press, 2012), 119.
20. Rashid, *Taliban*, 95.
21. Mutawakil, *Afghanistan and Taliban*, 15. Strick van Linschoten and Kuehn, *The Enemy We Created*, 119.
22. Mutawakil, *Afghanistan and Taliban*, 11.
23. Naseem Ahmed, "Pakistan Taliban Policy 1994–1999," *Dialogue* (January 2012): 82. Anatol Lieven, *Pakistan: A Hard Country* (New York: Public Affairs, 2011), 406–407. James Dobbins, *After the Taliban: Nation-Building in Afghanistan* (Washington, DC: Potomac Books, 2008), 56.
24. Mutawakil, *Afghanistan and Taliban*, 17.
25. Gall, *The Wrong Enemy*, 43–44. Barfield, *Afghanistan: A Cultural and Political History*, 258. Rashid, *Taliban*, 45, 188.
26. Ahmedzai, *The Past and Future*, 97; Zaeef, *My Life with the Taliban*, 64. Mutawakil, *Afghanistan and Taliban*, 12, 13. Rashid, *Taliban*, 31.

27. Ahmedzai, *The Past and Future*, 107.
28. Zaeef, *Taliban: From Kandahar until Mazar*, 127.
29. Abdul Hai Mutmain, *Mullah Mohammed Omar, Taliban and Afghanistan* (Kabul: Afghan Publishing Community, 2017), 111.
30. Discussion with Raess Baghrani, Kabul, July 21, 2013.
31. Discussion with Kandahar City madrasa and religious leaders, Kandahar, December 22, 2018. They saw Mullah Omar regularly during the Taliban regime.
32. Mutawakil, *Afghanistan and Taliban*, 16, 26.
33. Rashid, *Taliban*, 41–42.
34. Ahmedzai, *The Past and Future*, 121.
35. Discussion with Taliban senior leader, Kabul, February 12, 2014.
36. Mutawakil, *Afghanistan and Taliban*, 16, 26.
37. Zaeef, *My Life with the Taliban*, 88.
38. Rashid, *Taliban*, 91.
39. Ibid., 59–60, 74.
40. Discussion with Mohammed Naim, Paktika tribal leader, Kabul, July 22, 2014.
41. Zaeef, *Taliban: From Kandahar until Mazar*, 33–34.
42. Edwards, *Before Taliban: Genealogies of the Afghan Jihad*, 293.
43. David Edwards, *Heroes of the Age: Moral Fault Lines on the Afghan Frontier* (Berkeley: University of California Press, 1996), 11, 30.
44. Ahmedzai, *The Past and Future*, 120.
45. Ibid., 144.
46. David Edwards, *Caravan of Martyrs: Sacrifice and Suicide Bombing in Afghanistan* (Berkeley: University of California Press, 2017), 86.
47. Zaeef, *Taliban: From Kandahar until Mazar*, 164–165.
48. Strick von Linschoten and Kuehn, *The Taliban Reader*, 114.
49. Zaeef, *Taliban: From Kandahar until Mazar*, 187–189.
50. Mustafa Hamid and Leah Farrall, *The Arabs at War in Afghanistan* (London: Hurst, 2015), 89–162.
51. Hamid and Farrall, *The Arabs at War in Afghanistan*, 1–3, 207, 216, 221.
52. Ibid., 222, 251.
53. Barfield, *Afghanistan: A Cultural and Political History*, 267.
54. Hamid and Farrall, *The Arabs at War in Afghanistan*, 224–226, 291.
55. Discussion with Mullah Abdul Salam Zaeef, Kabul, March 20, 2018.
56. Hamid and Farrall, *The Arabs at War in Afghanistan*, 243–244.
57. Ibid., 269.
58. Mutawakil, *Afghanistan and Taliban*, 47, 72. Strick von Linschoten and Kuehn, *Taliban Reader*, 169.
59. Romain Malejacq, "From Rebel to Quasi-State: Governance, Diplomacy, and Legitimacy in the Midst of Afghanistan's Wars (1979–2001)," *Small Wars & Insurgencies* 28, no. 4–5 (2017): 879.
60. Ibid.
61. Rashid, *Taliban*, 100.
62. *Offerings on the Occupation: The Islamic Emirates' Position, Messages, Announcements, and Interviews* (Islamic Emirate of Afghanistan Cultural Commission, 2012), 13.
63. Tajik leaders of 2002–2014.
64. Discussion with Taliban founding member, Kabul, March 14, 2014.
65. Edwards, *Heroes of the Age*, 232.
66. National Archives, Afghanistan, Records of the Office of Speechwriting (Clinton Administration): Madeleine Albright, Lecture at Emory University, December 3, 1998.
67. National Archives, Afghanistan, Records of the Office of Speechwriting (Clinton Administration): William Clinton, "Videotaped Remarks for the Feiminist Majority Foundation Campaign to Stop Gender Apartheid in Afghanistan," March 3, 1999.
68. George W. Bush, Address to the Joint Session of the 107th Congress, Washington, DC, February 27, 2001, in *Selected Speeches of President George W. Bush, 2001–2008*, georgewbush-whitehouse.archives.gov.

Chapter 4

1. Mustafa Hamid and Leah Farrall, *The Arabs at War in Afghanistan* (London: Hurst, 2015), 282. Robert Grenier, *88 Days to Kandahar* (New York: Simon & Schuster, 2015), 5.

2. George W. Bush, Address to the nation on the September 11 Attacks, Washington, DC, September 11, 2001, in *Selected Speeches of President George W. Bush, 2001–2008*, georgewbush-whitehouse.archives.gov.

3. Jack Lule, "Myth and Terror on the Editorial Page: The *New York Times* Responds to September 11, 2001," *Journalism & Mass Communication Quarterly* (June 1, 2002), 281.

4. Condoleezza Rice, *No Higher Honor: A Memoir of My Years in Washington* (New York: Crown Publishers, 2011), 83.

5. Rice, *No Higher Honor*, 86–87.

6. Bob Woodward, *Bush at War* (New York: Simon & Schuster, 2002), 33, 43, 192.

7. Woodward, *Bush at War*, 47, 59.

8. Ahmed Rashid, *Descent Into Chaos: The United States and the Failure of Nation Building in Pakistan, Afghanistan, and Central Asia* (New York: Viking, 2008), 26.

9. Abdul Salam Zaeef, *My Life with the Taliban* (New York: Columbia University Press, 2010), 147.

10. Bette Dam, *A Man and a Motorcycle: How Hamid Karzai Came to Power* (Amsterdam: Ipso Facto Publishers, 2014), 69.

11. Hamid and Farrall, *The Arabs at War in Afghanistan*, 276–277, 282.

12. Wakil Ahmed Mutawakil, *Afghanistan and Taliban* (Kabul, Afgh.: Byeralai Pohaneon Lray, 2005), 81.

13. Zaeef, *My Life with the Taliban*, 144.

14. Dam, *A Man and a Motorcycle*, 69. Abdul Hai Mutmain, Omar's Taliban biographer, tells a different version of the story. In his version, Mahmud brought a delegation of Pakistani religious scholars. Mutmain joined their meeting with Mullah Omar. When the religious scholars urged Omar to find a way out of war, Omar replied, "For the sake of my personal power, how can I push aside my responsibilities under Islamic law?" With tears in their eyes, the scholars agreed with him. "So if Islam has no punishment for this act," Mullah Omar reasoned, "I am forced to make every sacrifice of myself for this course. . . . Before every invader, I protect the religious obligation of jihad until my life has flowed by." Abdul Hai Mutmain, *Mullah Mohammed Omar, Taliban and Afghanistan* (Kabul: Afghan Publishing Community, 2017), 277–278.

15. Grenier, *88 Days to Kandahar*, 82–85.

16. George W. Bush, *Decision Points* (New York: Crown Publishers, 2010), 154.

17. Discussion with Amir Khan Motaqi, Doha, Kabul, August 8, 2019. Motaqi was at the council and spoke at it.

18. Abdul Salam Zaeef, *Taliban: From Kandahar until Mazar* (Kabul, Afgh.: Aksos, 2018), 311–312.

19. Zaeef, *Taliban: From Kandahar until Mazar*, 312.

20. Zahidi Ahmedzai, *The Past and Future of the Islamic Emirate of Afghanistan* (Quetta, Pak.: Taliban Director of Culture, 2013), 275.

21. Zaeef, *My Life with the Taliban*, 142, 143.

22. Grenier, *88 Days to Kandahar*, 116.

23. Ibid., 135.

24. Zaeef, *My Life with the Taliban*, 149, 152.

25. Hamid and Farrall, *The Arabs at War in Afghanistan*, 290.

26. Ibid., 283.

27. Woodward, *Bush at War*, 127.

28. A set of envelopes filled with anthrax spores had arrived at the Capitol building and other media offices from an unknown source. Intelligence also came in that bin Laden had recently met with Pakistani nuclear experts. Bush, *Decision Points*, 211. Steve Coll, *Directorate S: The C.I.A. and America's Secret Wars in Afghanistan and Pakistan* (New York: Penguin, 2018), 78.

29. Interview of former president George W. Bush, interviewed by Edmund Degen, Gregory Roberts, and Matthew Smith, OEF study group files, undated (post-2014).

30. "Attack on America: Key Trends and Indicators," www.gallup.com, December 18, 2001. Jeffrey Jones, "Americans View Afghans Favorably, but Not Taliban Government," www.gallup.com, October 19, 2001. October 5–6, 2001, poll in David Morse, "Public Overwhelmingly Backs Bush in Attacks on Afghanistan," www.gallup.com, October 8, 2001.

31. Woodward, *Bush at War*, 156, 186, 187, 192, 224.

32. Grenier, *88 Days to Kandahar*, 135.

33. Michael Howard, "What's in a Name?" *Foreign Affairs* 81, no. 1 (January–February 2002): 9–10.

34. Woodward, *Bush at War*, 51, 75, 78, 84.

35. Bush, *Decision Points*, 191.

36. Grenier, *88 Days to Kandahar*, 8, 90.

37. Woodward, *Bush at War*, 98, 101.

38. US drones may have had Mullah Omar under surveillance going from his home to a madrasa. There has since been debate about whether Omar could have been killed if only the drones had been allowed to strike. Coll, *Directorate S*, 72–75.

39. Chris Woods, *Sudden Justice: America's Secret Drone Wars* (Oxford, UK: Oxford University Press, 2015), 41.

40. Ahmedzai, *The Past and Future*, 195. Translated by author.

41. Mutawakil, *Afghanistan and Taliban*, 84.

42. Ahmedzai, *The Past and Future*, 195.

43. Bush, *Decision Points*, 198.

44. James Dobbins, *After the Taliban: Nation-Building in Afghanistan* (Washington, DC: Potomac Books, 2008), 32.

45. Gary Berntsen and Ralph Pezullo, *Jawbreaker: The Attack on bin Laden and Al-Qa'eda* (New York: Crown Publishers, 2005), 167, 191.

46. *Legion of Brothers*, CNN Films, 2017.

47. Berntsen and Pezullo, *Jawbreaker*, 90–111.

48. Hamid and Farrall, *The Arabs at War in Afghanistan*, 247. Berntsen and Pezullo, *Jawbreaker*, 128. Abdul Salam Zaeef, *My Life with the Taliban*, 155.

49. Berntsen and Pezullo, *Jawbreaker*, 111.

50. Discussion with Nazr Mohammed Mutmain, Kabul, August 25, 2019. Mutmain was an official in the Taliban regime and became an advocate for peace after 2010, maintaining relations with the movement.

51. Carlotta Gall, *The Wrong Enemy: America in Afghanistan, 2001–2014* (Boston, MA: Houghton Mifflin Harcourt, 2014), 4. Hamid and Farrall, *The Arabs at War in Afghanistan*, 290.

52. Mutawakil, *Afghanistan and Taliban*, 84. Ahmedzai, *The Past and Future*, 195.

53. *Legion of Brothers*, CNN Films, 2017.

54. Stephen Biddle, "Afghanistan and the Future of Warfare," Strategic Studies Institute monograph, November 2002, 18.

55. Doug Stanton, *Horse Soldiers* (New York: Scribner, 2009), 128, 216–217.

56. Ron Moreau and Sam Yousafzai, "The Taliban in Their Own Words," *Newsweek*, September 25, 2009.

57. Biddle, "Afghanistan and the Future of Warfare," 34.

58. Stanton, *Horse Soldiers*, 128, 236–245.

59. *Legion of Brothers*, CNN Films, 2017.

60. Ahmedzai, *The Past and Future*, 201.

61. Mutawakil, *Afghanistan and Taliban*, 85.

62. Mutmain, *Mullah Mohammed Omar*, 298. Translated by author.

63. Ahmedzai, *The Past and Future*, 215. Zaeef, *Taliban: From Kandahar until Mazar*, 320–321. Translated by author.

64. A Taliban official history says that the Taliban withdrew from all of Loya Paktiya. Mutawakil says they held authority there. Mutawakil, *Afghanistan and Taliban*, 85. Ahmedzai, *The Past and Future*, 215, 222, 223.

65. Mutmain, *Mullah Mohammed Omar*, 298.

66. Gall, *The Wrong Enemy*, 8.

67. Khalid Homayun Nadiri, "Old Habits, New Consequences: Pakistan's Posture toward Afghanistan since 2001," *International Security* (Fall 2014): 141. Gall, *The Wrong Enemy*, 8.

68. They would stay in Guantanamo until 2014 when they allowed to live in Qatar as part of the prisoner exchange for Bowe Bergdahl, the US soldier imprisoned by the Taliban.

69. Berntsen and Pezullo, *Jawbreaker*, 198, 237.

70. Zalmay Khalilzad, *The Envoy* (New York: St. Martin's Press, 2016), 63.

71. In a separate version of this story, the CIA came up with the plan for Karzai to enter Afghanistan and prompted him to go. Coll, *Directorate S*, 97.

72. Bette Dam, *A Man and a Motorcycle: How Hamid Karzai Came to Power* (Amsterdam: Ipso Facto Publishers, 2014), 50–51, 62, 73–75.

73. Dam, *A Man and a Motorcycle*, 102–105.

74. Ibid., 132–134, 137–143.

75. Interview with U.S. Army Captain Jason Amerine, Frontline, PBS, July 9 and 12, 2002, http://www.pbs.org/.

76. Dam, *A Man and a Motorcycle*, 132–134, 137–143.

77. Ibid., 97, 111.

78. Ibid., 163.

79. Bush, *Decision Points*, 197.

80. Jack Fairweather, *The Good War: Why We Couldn't Win the War or the Peace in Afghanistan* (London: Vintage, 2015), 36.

81. James Dobbins, *After the Taliban: Nation-Building in Afghanistan* (Washington, DC: Potomac Books, 2008), 83.

82. Dobbins, *After the Taliban*, 3–4.

83. Ibid., 57.

84. Ibid., 86.

85. Dam, *A Man and a Motorcycle*, 174.

86. Dobbins, *After the Taliban*, 90–93.

87. Dam, *A Man and a Motorcycle*, 71–72.

88. Grenier, *88 Days to Kandahar*, 215.

89. Hamid and Farrall, *The Arabs at War in Afghanistan*, 288.

90. Ahmedzai, *The Past and Future*, 223. Mutawakil, *Afghanistan and Taliban*, 85.

91. Hamid and Farrall, *The Arabs at War in Afghanistan*, 285, 287, 288. Gall, *The Wrong Enemy*, 33, 34.

92. Zaeef, *Taliban: From Kandahar until Mazar*, 323.

93. Alex Strick van Linschoten and Felix Kuehn, *Taliban Reader* (London: Hurst, 2018), 225–227.

94. Hamid and Farrall, *The Arabs at War in Afghanistan*, 288.

95. The delegation had evidently met with Mullah Omar earlier that day. At least one of the participants in the meeting claims Mullah Omar absolved himself of leadership of the movement and turned it over to Mullah Obaidullah. Several other sources, however, have Omar continuing to provide at least spiritual leadership of the movement. Bette Dam, *The Secret Life of Mullah Omar*, Zomia Center, March 2019, 6.

96. Anand Gopal, "The Taliban in Kandahar," in *Talibanistan: Negotiating the Borders between Terror, Politics, and Religion*, edited by Peter Bergen (New York: Oxford University Press, 2013), 11. Gall, *The Wrong Enemy*, 34.

97. Discussion with Raess Baghrani, Kabul, July 21, 2013.

98. Brian Knowlton, "Rumsfeld Rejects Plan to Allow Mullah Omar 'To Live in Dignity': Taliban Fighters Agree to Surrender Kandahar," *New York Times*, December 7, 2001.

99. Mutawakil, *Afghanistan and Taliban*, 86.

100. Sarah Chayes, *The Punishment of Virtue: Inside Afghanistan after the Taliban* (New York: Penguin, 2006), 45.

101. Dam, *A Man and a Motorcycle*, 186.

102. Gopal, "The Taliban in Kandahar," 11.

103. Fairweather, *The Good War*, 58.

104. Matt Kelley, "U.S. Warns Anti-Taliban Groups against Giving Leader Amnesty," *Associated Press*, December 7, 2001.

105. Zaeef, *Taliban: From Kandahar until Mazar*, 323.
106. Anand Gopal, "Rents, Patronage, and Defection: State-Building and Insurgency in Afghanistan," PhD dissertation, Columbia University, 2017.
107. Gall, *The Wrong Enemy*, 35–36.
108. Chayes, *The Punishment of Virtue*, 46.
109. One former Taliban, activist Nazr Mohammed Mutmain, was emphatic that "it is not true that Mullah Omar did not say he would start jihad against the United States. He never surrendered or concurred with the agreement with Karzai." Discussion with Nazr Mohammed Mutmain, Kabul, August 25, 2019. A 2017 biography of Mullah Omar by the former Taliban director of culture also says nothing on negotiations and depicts Omar as determined to fight to the end. It says that under the advice of his commanders he decided to leave the city and start a guerrilla war. As in the official history, it says that he told the Arab fighters at Kandahar airfield to retreat. Mutmain, *Mullah Mohammed Omar*, 298.
110. Ahmedzai, *The Past and Future*, 223.
111. Ibid. Zaeef confirms this message was sent out, except that he asserts Mullah Omar ordered a continuation of jihad against the United States instead of the initiation of guerrilla war. Zaeef, *Taliban: From Kandahar until Mazar*, 323.
112. Raees Baghrani himself has said that Omar fled to northern Helmand. Fairweather, *The Good War*, 106. Mutmain, *Mullah Mohammed Omar*, 300, 329.
113. Mohammed Gul Shahid, *Religious Figures of Afghanistan* (Peshawar, Pak.: Maktabah Farooqiya, 2012), 536–540. The book is a collection of biographies of Afghan religious scholars, *pirs*, and heroes (*ghazi*) from wars against the British and Soviets.
114. Mutawakil, *Afghanistan and Taliban*, 86.
115. Grenier, *88 Days to Kandahar*, 279.
116. Octavian Manea, Interview with Zalmay Khalilzad, *Small Wars Journal*, www.smallwarsjournal.com. May 11, 2016.
117. Donald Rumsfeld to Vice President Richard Cheney, "Decisions," Memorandum, Rumsfeld Library, papers.rumsfeld.com, September 3, 2002.
118. Bush, *Decision Points*, 187.
119. Hamid and Farrall, *The Arabs at War in Afghanistan*, 283.
120. Berntsen and Pezullo, *Jawbreaker*, 239–240, 271. Hamid and Farrall, *The Arabs at War in Afghanistan*, 9, 210, 283.
121. Woodward, *Bush at War*, 212.
122. Berntsen and Pezullo, *Jawbreaker*, 239–240, 271.
123. Hamid and Farrall, *The Arabs at War in Afghanistan*, 284.
124. Berntsen and Pezullo, *Jawbreaker*, 233, 265–266, 276–277, 284.
125. Ibid., 274–275, 280.
126. Elements of the two marine expeditionary units started arriving at FOB Rhino in Helmand on November 25.
127. Berntsen and Pezullo, *Jawbreaker*, 276–277, 290.
128. Hamid and Farrall, *The Arabs at War in Afghanistan*, 288. Berntsen and Pezullo, *Jawbreaker*, 284, 298–299, 307.
129. Hamid and Farrall, *The Arabs at War in Afghanistan*, 284–285, 289.
130. Berntsen and Pezullo, *Jawbreaker*, 298–299.
131. Ahmed Rashid, *Descent into Chaos: The United States and the Failure of Nation Building in Pakistan, Afghanistan, and Central Asia* (New York: Viking, 2008), 96.

Chapter 5

1. Carlotta Gall, *The Wrong Enemy: America in Afghanistan, 2001–2014* (Boston: Houghton Mifflin Harcourt, 2014), 239.
2. National Security Archive, George Washington University: Secretary Rumsfeld, Memo on "Directional Decisions," May 2002.
3. Afghanistan Papers, *Washington Post*: Interview with former National Security advisor Stephen Hadley, SIGAR, September 16, 2015. Douglas Feith, *War and Decision* (New York: Harper, 2008), 102. James Dobbins, John McGinn, Keith Crane, Seth Jones,

Rollie Lal, Andrew Rathmell, Rachel Swanger, and Anga Timilsina, *America's Role in Nation-Building: From Germany to Iraq* (Santa Monica, CA: The RAND Corporation, 2003). 137. Terrence Kelly, Nora Bensahel, Olga Oliker, *Security Force Assistance in Afghanistan: Identifying Lessons for Future Efforts* (Santa Monica, CA: RAND Corporation, 2011), 133.

4. Bob Woodward, *Bush at War* (New York: Simon & Schuster, 2002), 192, 237.

5. George W. Bush, *Decision Points* (New York: Crown Publishers, 2010), 186.

6. Interview of President George W. Bush, interviewed by Edmund Degen, Gregory Roberts, and Matthew Smith, OEF study group, undated (post-2014).

7. Stanley McChrystal, *My Share of the Task: A Memoir* (New York: Penguin, 2014), 77.

8. Terrorism polling trends, www.gallup.com.

9. James Dobbins, *After the Taliban: Nation-Building in Afghanistan* (Washington, DC: Potomac Books, 2008), 124.

10. Donald Rumsfeld, *Known and Unknown: A Memoir* (New York: Sentinel, 2012), 683.

11. The Rumsfeld Papers: Donald Rumsfeld to President George W. Bush, "Afghanistan," Memorandum, papers.rumsfeld.com, August 20, 2002. Woodward, *Bush at War*, 192, 237.

12. Dobbins, *After the Taliban*, 125, 130–131. Theo Farrell, *Unwinnable: Britain's War in Afghanistan, 2001–2014* (London: Bodley Head, 2017), 100.

13. Bush, *Decision Points*, 207.

14. National Security Archive, George Washington University: Secretary Rumsfeld to Undersecretary of Defense for Policy Doug Feith, Deputy Secretary of Defense Paul Wolfowitz, and chairman of the joint chiefs of staff General Richard Myers, April 17, 2002.

15. National Security Archive, George Washington University: Secretary Rumsfeld to Undersecretary of Defense for Policy Doug Feith, October 17, 2002.

16. National Security Archive, George Washington University: Secretary Rumsfeld, October 16, 2003.

17. Woodward, *Bush at War*, 192.

18. Bush, *Decision Points*, 205.

19. Interview of President George W. Bush, interviewed by Edmund Degen, Gregory Roberts, and Matthew Smith, OEF study group, undated (post-2014).

20. In August, Rumsfeld wrote to Bush that the critical problem was reconstruction but called for greater international coordination rather than commitment of US resources. The Rumsfeld Papers: Donald Rumsfeld to President George W. Bush, "Afghanistan," Memorandum, papers.rumsfeld.com, August 20, 2002. Dobbins, *After the Taliban*, 125, 135. David Rohde and David Sanger, "How a 'Good War' in Afghanistan Went Bad," *New York Times*, August 12, 2007.

21. Zalmay Khalilzad, *The Envoy* (New York: St. Martin's Press, 2016), 139.

22. Afghanistan Papers, *Washington Post*: Interview with former National Security advisor Stephen Hadley, SIGAR, September 16, 2015.

23. "Liberating the Women of Afghanistan," *New York Times*, November 24, 2001.

24. President George W. Bush, State of the Union Address, January 29, 2002.

25. Hillary Clinton, "New Hope for Afghanistan's Women," *Time*, November 24, 2001.

26. Sima Samaar, "Feminism, Peace, and Afghanistan," *Journal of International Affairs* (March 2019): 153.

27. Khalilzad, *The Envoy*, 132–133.

28. Ibid., 139.

29. Ibid., 84, 86–87, 150.

30. Khalilzad, *The Envoy*, 145–146.

31. Thomas Barfield, *Afghanistan: A Cultural and Political History* (Princeton, NJ: Princeton University Press, 2010), 297.

32. "Interview with Lieutenant General Karl Eikenberry" in *Eyewitness to War*, vol. 3, edited by Michael Brooks (Fort Leavenworth, KS: Combat Studies Institute Press, 2010), 30–56.

33. Rangin Dadfar Spanta, *Afghanistan Politics: Sense of the Time* (Kabul, Afgh.: Aazem Publications, 2017), 191.

34. Fahim also reportedly imprisoned Karzai in the early 1990s in Kabul when both were part of the Rabbani government. Karzai was the deputy foreign minister and Fahim was the intelligence chief. Fahim accused Karzai of spying. Karzai escaped when a rocket struck the

prison. Matthew Rosenberg, "Warlord Who Tamped Conflict as Afghan Vice President Dies," *New York Times*, March 10, 2014.

35. Barfield, *Afghanistan: A Cultural and Political History*, 300.
36. Meeting with Afghan women leaders, ISAF headquarters, Kabul, September 5, 2013.
37. Samaar, "Feminism, Peace, and Afghanistan," 153.
38. Khalilzad, *The Envoy*, 218.
39. Antonio Giustozzi, "The Struggle to Create an Afghan National Army," manuscript, February 2014, 123.
40. Afghanistan Papers, *Washington Post* (https://www.washingtonpost.com/graphics/2019/investigations/afghanistan-papers/documents-database/): Senior decisionmaker interview (Bush administration), Special Inspector General for Afghanistan, Lessons Learned Project, May 5, 2016.
41. Before the decision was made, the British had trained a single multiethnic battalion—"1st Battalion of the Afghan National Guard"—for security of the upcoming loya jirga.
42. National Security Archive, George Washington University: Secretary Rumsfeld to Larry Di Rita and chairman of the joint chiefs of staff General Richard Myers, July 20, 2002.
43. The Rumsfeld Papers: Donald Rumsfeld to Colin Powell and Condoleezza Rice, "U.S. Financial Commitments," Memo, papers.rumsfeld.com, April 8, 2002.
44. The Rumsfeld Papers: Donald Rumsfeld to Colin Powell and Condoleezza Rice, "U.S. Financial Commitments," Memo, papers.rumsfeld.com, April 8, 2002.
45. The Rumsfeld Papers: Donald Rumsfeld to Colin Powell and Condoleezza Rice, "U.S. Financial Commitments," Memo, papers.rumsfeld.com, April 8, 2002. Woodward, *Bush at War*, 321.
46. Afghanistan Papers, *Washington Post*: Senior decisionmaker interview (Bush administration), Special Inspector General for Afghanistan, Lessons Learned Project, May 5, 2016.
47. "The Exit Strategy from Afghanistan: Lessons from U.S. Efforts to Develop the Afghan National Defense and Security Forces," SIGAR Lessons Learned, Special Inspector-General for Afghanistan Reconstruction, June 19, 2017, 16.
48. Afghanistan Papers, *Washington Post*: Senior decisionmaker interview (Bush administration), Special Inspector General for Afghanistan, Lessons Learned Project, May 5, 2016.
49. Ahmed Rashid, *Descent into Chaos: The United States and the Failure of Nation Building in Pakistan, Afghanistan, and Central Asia* (New York: Viking, 2008), 134–135.
50. The Rumsfeld Papers: Donald Rumsfeld to Doug Feith and Condoleezza Rice, "Afghan Warlords," Memo, papers.rumsfeld.com, April 1, 2002. Discussion with Zalmay Rassoul, Minister of Foreign Affairs, March 16, 2014. Rassoul was present at the meeting.
51. National Security Archive, George Washington University: Secretary Rumsfeld to Undersecretary of Defense for Policy Doug Feith, Deputy Secretary of Defense Paul Wolfowitz, and chairman of the joint chiefs of staff General Richard Myers, June 25, 2002.
52. Afghanistan Papers, *Washington Post*: Senior decisionmaker interview (Bush administration), Special Inspector General for Afghanistan, Lessons Learned Project, May 5, 2016.
53. Afghanistan Papers, *Washington Post*: Zalmay Khalilzad interview, Special Inspector General for Afghanistan, Lessons Learned Project, 2016.
54. National Security Archive, George Washington University: Secretary Rumsfeld to General Tommy Franks, September 30, 2002.
55. National Security Archive, George Washington University: Secretary Rumsfeld to Condoleezza Rice, September 12, 2002.
56. His official title was Chief of the Office of Military Cooperation–Afghanistan. The Rumsfeld Papers: Donald Rumsfeld to President George W. Bush, "Afghanistan," Memorandum, papers.rumsfeld.com, August 20, 2002.
57. "Ambassador Eikenberry to Leave Afghanistan," Interview, National Public Radio, July 8, 2011.
58. Tommy Franks, Frank Hagenbeck, Dan McNeill, John Vines, Dave Barno, Karl Eikenberry, Dan McNeill, David McKiernan, Stanley McChrystal, David Petraeus, John Allen, Joseph Dunford, John Campbell, John Nicholson, Scott Miller.
59. The Rumsfeld Papers: Donald Rumsfeld to President George W. Bush, "Afghanistan," Memorandum, papers.rumsfeld.com, August 20, 2002.

60. Rashid, *Descent into Chaos*, 201.
61. Afghanistan Papers, *Washington Post*: Interview with former National Security advisor Stephen Hadley, SIGAR, September 16, 2015.
62. Bradley Graham, *By His Own Rules: The Ambitions, Successes, and Ultimate Failures of Donald Rumsfeld* (New York: Public Affairs, 2009), 433–434.
63. The Rumsfeld Papers: Donald Rumsfeld to Bill Luti, "Strmecki's Briefing," papers.rumsfeld.com, December 30, 2002.
64. Karl Eikenberry, presentation, United States Institute of Peace, March 16, 2015.
65. Khalilzad, *The Envoy*, 178, 182. Feith, *War and Decision*, 150. Interview with Karl Eikenberry, Donald Wright, OEF study group files, February 23, 2012.
66. Peter Tomsen, *The Wars of Afghanistan* (New York: Public Affairs, 2011), 631.
67. Khalilzad, *The Envoy*, 178, 182.
68. Rashid, *Descent into Chaos*, 201.
69. "Interview with Lieutenant General Karl Eikenberry," *Eyewitness to War*, 18.
70. Ibid., 48.
71. "The Exit Strategy from Afghanistan," 17.
72. "Interview with Lieutenant General Karl Eikenberry," *Eyewitness to War*, 24.
73. Khalilzad, *The Envoy*, 182, 193. Antonio Giustozzi, "The Struggle to Create an Afghan National Army," manuscript, February 2014, 124, 131. "The Exit Strategy from Afghanistan," 21.
74. "Interview with Lieutenant General Karl Eikenberry," *Eyewitness to War*, 17, 18.
75. Giustozzi, "The Struggle to Create an Afghan National Army," 127.
76. "Interview with Lieutenant General Eikenberry" in *Eyewitness to War*, 18.
77. Afghanistan Papers (https://www.washingtonpost.com/graphics/2019/investigations/afghanistan-papers/documents-database/): Interview with Former US Military Trainer who served in Afghanistan, 2003–2004, SIGAR, April 20, 2017.
78. The Rumsfeld Papers: Donald Rumsfeld to Paul Wolfowitz, General Dick Myers, General Pete Pace, and Doug Feith, "Afghanistan Funding," papers.rumsfeld.com, September 15, 2004.
79. Khalilzad, *The Envoy*, 193.
80. Giustozzi, "The Struggle to Create an Afghan National Army," 151, 204.
81. Ibid., 127.
82. Dobbins, *After the Taliban*, 137–138.
83. "The Exit Strategy from Afghanistan," 18–19.
84. "Interview with Lieutenant General Karl Eikenberry," *Eyewitness to War*, 24.
85. Ibid., 30–56.
86. Giustozzi, "The Struggle to Create an Afghan National Army," 134, 164.
87. David Edwards, *Heroes of the Age: Moral Fault Lines on the Afghan Frontier* (Berkeley: University of California Press, 1996), 103–104.
88. "Interview with Lieutenant General Karl Eikenberry," *Eyewitness to War*, 30.
89. The Rumsfeld Papers: Donald Rumsfeld to Undersecretary of Defense for Policy Doug Feith and chairman of the joint chiefs of staff General Richard Myers, "Afghanistan," papers.rumsfeld.com, May 2, 2003. Donald Rumsfeld to Doug Feith, "Ministry of Defense in Afghanistan," papers.rumsfeld.com, May 3, 2003. "Principles for Afghanistan—Policy Guidelines," Memorandum, Office of the Secretary of Defense (Policy), Rumsfeld Library, papers.rumsfeld.com, July 7, 2003. Donald Rumsfeld to Doug Feith and Paul Wolfowitz, "Afghan Army," papers.rumsfeld.com, October 22, 2003.
90. Dobbins et al., *America's Role in Nation-Building*, 137. Kelly, Bensahel, and Oliker, *Security Force Assistance*, 20, 26, 33, 37–38. Seth Jones, *In the Graveyard of Empires: America's War in Afghanistan* (New York: W.W. Norton and Company, 2010), 167–168, 176. Khalilzad, *The Envoy*, 200.
91. George W. Bush, *Decision Points*, 211.
92. Joseph Collins, *Understanding War in Afghanistan* (Washington, DC: CreateSpace, 2012), 50.
93. Kelly, Bensahel, and Oliker, *Security Force Assistance*, 33, 37–38, 50.
94. The Rumsfeld Papers: "Principles for Afghanistan—Policy Guidelines," Memorandum, Office of the Secretary of Defense (Policy), papers.rumsfeld.com, July 7, 2003. Dobbins et al, *America's Role in Nation-Building*, 146, 157, 158.

95. For a full discussion of the national solidarity program, see Jennifer Brick Murtazashvili, *Informal Order and the State in Afghanistan* (Cambridge, UK: Cambridge University Press, 2016) and Jennifer Brick, "Investigating the Sustainability of Community Development Councils in Afghanistan," Afghanistan Research and Evaluation Unit, February 2008.

96. Afghanistan Papers, *Washington Post*: Secretary of Defense Rumsfeld to Undersecretary of Defense for Policy Doug Feith, May 2, 2003.

97. Carter Malkasian and Gerald Meyerle, "Provincial Reconstruction Teams: How Do We Know They Work?," Strategic Studies Institute Monograph (March 2009): 32.

98. Barfield, *Afghanistan: A Cultural and Political History*, 281.

99. Rashid, *Descent into Chaos*, 243.

100. Abdul Hai Mutmain, *Mullah Mohammed Omar, Taliban and Afghanistan* (Kabul: Afghan Publishing Community, 2017), 316.

101. Steve Coll, *Directorate S: The C.I.A. and America's Secret Wars in Afghanistan and Pakistan* (New York: Penguin, 2018), 141.

102. The United States imprisoned him in Bagram for 18 months. Gall, *The Wrong Enemy*, 74.

103. Discussion with former Taliban ambassador to the United Nations Abdul Hakim Mujahed, Kabul, June 13, 2013.

104. Mutmain, *Mullah Mohammed Omar, Taliban and Afghanistan*, 326.

105. Talk by Barnett Rubin, United States Institute of Peace, Washington, DC, March 17, 2015.

106. Mullah Abdul Ghani Baradar is sometimes said to have been involved in writing this letter but in 2019 conversations he denied any contact with Karzai after 2001. Coll, *Directorate S*, 140–141.

107. Gall, *The Wrong Enemy*, 74–75.

108. The Rumsfeld Papers: "Principles for Afghanistan—Policy Guidelines," Memorandum, Office of the Secretary of Defense (Policy), papers.rumsfeld.com, July 7, 2003.

109. Khalilzad, *The Envoy*, 219.

110. Anand Gopal, "The Taliban in Kandahar," in *Talibanistan: Negotiating the Borders between Terror, Politics, and Religion*, edited by Peter Bergen (New York: Oxford University Press, 2013), 15.

111. Discussion with Mullah Manzoor, Kabul, July 26, 2019. Mullah Manzoor was a member of the first Taliban regime and participant in the movement's earliest meetings. He was governor of Baghdis in 2001 and later military commander for Highway One through Ghazni in 2010 and 2011.

112. Alex Strick van Linschoten and Felix Kuehn, *An Enemy We Created* (London: Hurst, 2012), 249.

113. *New York Times* journalist Carlotta Gall reported that 60 Taliban commanders (including one of Jalaluddin Haqqani's sons), Pakistani religious leaders, and certain experienced Pakistani military and ISI officers had met in Peshawar in December 2001 and then decided to wage a long guerrilla war against the United States. Carlotta Gall, *The Wrong Enemy: America in Afghanistan, 2001–2014* (Boston: Houghton Mifflin Harcourt, 2014), 19–21. See also Fairweather, *The Good War*, 113.

114. Discussion with former Taliban ambassador to the United Nations Abdul Hakim Mujahed, Kabul, June 13, 2013.

115. Ron Moreau, Michael Hirsh, John Barry, and Mark Hosenball, "If You Thought the Longtime Head of the Taliban was Bad, You Should Meet His No. 2," *Newsweek*, August 3, 2009; Gopal, "The Taliban in Kandahar," 15.

116. Discussion with former Taliban ambassador to the United Nations Abdul Hakim Mujahed, Kabul, June 13, 2013. Coll, *Directorate S*, 423–424.

117. Mutmain, *Mullah Mohammed Omar, Taliban and Afghanistan*, 349.

Chapter 6

1. Christina Lamb, *Farewell Kabul: From Afghanistan to a More Dangerous World* (London: William Collins, 2016), 312–313.

2. Dipali Mukhopadhyay, *Warlords, Strongman, Governors, and the State in Afghanistan* (New York: Columbia University Press, 2014), 76–165.

3. Zalmay Khalilzad, *The Envoy* (New York: St. Martin's Press, 2016), 201–203.
4. Mukhopadhyay, *Warlords*, 76–165.
5. Khan Mohammed of the Alikozai tribe was the nominal commander in Kandahar. Malim Mir Wali of the Barakzai was the nominal commander in Helmand.
6. Michael Bhatia and Mark Sedra, *Afghanistan, Arms and Conflict: Armed Groups, Disarmament, and Security in Post-War Society* (New York: Routledge, 2008), 237–241.
7. Abdul Latif Talebi, *Pashtuni Qabilay* (Kabul: Afghanistan Academy of Sciences International Center for Pashto Studies, 1991), 9.
8. Bhatia and Sedra, *Afghanistan, Arms and Conflict*, 228.
9. Thomas Barfield, *Afghanistan: A Cultural and Political History* (Princeton, NJ: Princeton University Press, 2010), 109.
10. *Legion of Brothers*, CNN Films, 2017.
11. Discussion with Dr. Najib, chief of staff of Kandahar governor's office, ISAF headquarters, Kabul, August 2, 2013.
12. Discussion with Mullah Sayid Mohammed Akhund, Kabul, October 27, 2013.
13. Discussion with Haji Babay Kakar, FOB Walton, Kandahar, November 9, 2013.
14. Zharey district profile, Tribal Liaison Office, 2009, 58.
15. Discussion with leading Alikozai tribal leader, Kabul, August 10, 2014.
16. Sherzai gerrymandered the new districts in such a way that the Noorzai were no longer the plurality in Zharey. His Alizai allies gained that position. Noorzai influence was effectively halved.
17. Meeting with Ishaqzai tribal leaders from Kandahar, Kabul, January 12, 2014. Discussion with Ishaqzai tribal leader, Kandahar, March 27, 2014. Discussion with leading Noorzai tribal leader, Kabul, August 5, 2013.
18. Dexter Filkins, Mark Mazzetti, and James Risen, "Brother of Afghan Leader Said to Be Paid by C.I.A.," *New York Times*, October 27, 2009.
19. Sarah Chayes, *The Punishment of Virtue* (New York: Penguin, 2006), 272–280, 294–295.
20. The 10th Mountain Division, under Major General Franklin Hagenbeck, had temporarily controlled US conventional operations since February 2002. That April, Hagenbeck launched 90 days of operations to eliminate Taliban and al-Qa'eda "remnants" in the east. McNeill's command later became Combined Joint Task Force 180 (CJTF-180).
21. Donald Wright, *A Different Kind of War: The United States Army in Operation Enduring Freedom, October 2001–September 2005* (Fort Leavenworth, KS: Combat Studies Institute Press, 2010), 184, 185
22. Wright, *A Different Kind of War*, 217.
23. Wright, *A Different Kind of War*, 190.
24. Ibid., 249.
25. Mark Moyar, *Oppose Any Foe: The Rise of America's Special Operations Forces* (New York: Basic Books, 2017), 271.
26. Charles Briscoe, Richard Kiper, James Schroder, and Kalev Sepp, *Weapon of Choice: ARSOF in Afghanistan* (Fort Leavenworth, KS: Combat Studies Institute, Press 2003), 206, 215, 358, 389.
27. Wright, *A Different Kind of War*, 211.
28. E.J. Degen, "The United States Army in Afghanistan: 2001–2014," OEF Study Group, US Army Lessons Learned Conference, July 2015.
29. Wright, *A Different Kind of War*, 214.
30. Steve Coll, *Directorate S: The C.I.A. and America's Secret Wars in Afghanistan and Pakistan* (New York: Penguin, 2018), 134–135.
31. Ibid., 161.
32. Mark Mazzetti and Philip Smucker, "On the Ground," *US News & World Report*, February 25, 2002.
33. Wright, *A Different Kind of War*, 220.
34. Gerald Meyerle, Megan Katt, and James Gavrilis, *Counterinsurgency on the Ground in Afghanistan* (Quantico, VA: Marine Corps University Press, 2011), 91.
35. "Interview with Master Sergeant Michael Threatt," in *Eyewitness to War*, vol. 3, edited by Michael Brooks (Fort Leavenworth, KS: Combat Studies Institute Press, 2010), 398.

36. Wright, *A Different Kind of War*, 220.

37. Anonymous, *Hunting al Qaeda: A Take-No-Prisoners Account of Terror, Adventure, and Disillusionment* (Minneapolis, MN: Zenith Press, 2009), 149.

38. Anand Gopal, "The Taliban in Kandahar," in *Talibanistan*, edited by Peter Bergen (New York: Oxford University Press, 2013), 26–27. Ahmed Rashid, *Descent into Chaos: The United States and the Failure of Nation Building in Pakistan, Afghanistan, and Central Asia* (New York: Viking, 2008), 142.

39. Meeting with Kandahar religious leaders, Kandahar, March 29, 2014. Discussion with police chief Abdul Razziq, Kandahar, March 30, 2014.

40. Bob Woodward, *Obama's Wars* (New York: Simon & Schuster, 2010), 66.

41. Anonymous, *Hunting al Qaeda*, 181.

42. Sean Maloney, *Fighting for Afghanistan* (Annapolis, MD: Naval Institute Press, 2011), 128. Elizabeth Rubin, "In the Land of the Taliban," *New York Times Magazine*, October 22, 2006. Gopal, "The Taliban in Kandahar," 26–27.

43. Discussion with Noorzai tribal leader, Kabul, April 8, 2014.

44. Another example were the small communities of Ghilzai tribes living on dry land near the desert. They had joined the Taliban in the 1990s but the fighters and commanders had mostly returned to their homes after 2001. Local militias and police forces arrested, harassed, or beat certain former Taliban, as well as village elders, accusing them of being active Taliban. Over time, both because of this harassment and the aforementioned land issues, many of these communities' leaders re-announced their fealty to the Taliban leadership in Pakistan. Zharey district profile, Tribal Liaison Office, 2009, 57.

45. Discussion with Ishaqzai member of Parliament, Kabul, March 5, 2014.

46. Meeting with Gul Agha Sherzai and Barakzai and Ishaqzai tribal leaders, Kabul, July 20, 2013.

47. Gopal, "The Taliban in Kandahar," 26–27.

48. Discussion with Maulali Ishaqzai, Kabul, January 13, 2014.

49. Meeting of Ishaqzai tribal leaders from Kandahar, Kabul, January 9, 2014.

50. Carlotta Gall, *The Wrong Enemy: America in Afghanistan, 2001–2014* (Boston: Houghton Mifflin Harcourt, 2014), 113–114.

51. Meeting with Ishaqzai tribal leaders from Kandahar, Kabul, January 12, 2014.

52. Abdul Hai Mutmain, *Mullah Mohammed Omar, Taliban and Afghanistan* (Kabul: Afghan Publishing Community, 2017), 313.

53. Gopal, "The Taliban in Kandahar," 14.

54. Scott Mann, *Game Changers: Going Local to Defeat Violent Extremists* (Leesburg, VA: Tribal Analysis Publishing, 2015), 47.

55. Historical polling results on terrorism, Gallup News, news.gallup.com, 2017.

56. He completed his tour as a lieutenant general and formed Combined Forces Command-Afghanistan (CFC-A). The command excluded US special operations forces that had a chain of command through US special operations command (SOCOM). Barno also moved his headquarters from Bagram to Kabul.

57. Rashid, *Descent into Chaos*, 243. Jack Fairweather, *The Good War: Why We Couldn't Win the War or the Peace in Afghanistan* (London: Vintage, 2014), 110.

58. According to Bette Dam, he lived in Qalat, the Zabul provincial capital, until 2004. Bette Dam, *The Secret Life of Mullah Omar* (Zomia Center, March 2019), 8–9.

59. Discussion with participant in Pugwash conferences with Taliban, Washington, DC, August 2, 2017. Discussion with Abdul Salam Zaeef, Kabul, March 20, 2018.

60. Bette Dam, *Op Zoek Naar de Vjiand* (Amsterdam: Bezige Bij, March 2019). Dam, *The Secret Life of Mullah Omar*.

61. See Alex Strick van Linschoten and Felix Kuehn, *An Enemy We Created: The Myth of the Taliban–Al Qaeda Merger in Afghanistan* (London: Hurst, 2012), 248. Alex Strick van Linschoten and Felix Kuehn, *Taliban Reader* (London: Hurst, 2018), 193.

62. Mutmain, *Mullah Mohammed Omar, Taliban and Afghanistan*, 299, 300.

63. Gall, *The Wrong Enemy*, 67.

64. Mutmain, *Mullah Mohammed Omar, Taliban and Afghanistan*, 319, 320, 330. Discussion with Abdul Salam Zaeef, Kabul, March 20, 2018. Discussion with Amir Khan Motaqi, Doha, Kabul, August 8, 2019.

65. Mutmain, *Mullah Mohammed Omar, Taliban and Afghanistan*, 319, 320.
66. Steve Coll, "Looking for Mullah Omar," *New Yorker*, January 23, 2012.
67. Discussion with religious scholar and former high-ranking Taliban official, Kabul, July 22, 2019.
68. Nazr Mohammed Mutmain, *Six Days with Taliban Leaders* (Kabul, Afgh.: Danish Publishing Community, 2019), 180.
69. Antonio Giustozzi, *The Taliban at War* (London: Hurst, 2019). Fairweather, *The Good War*, 114.
70. Linschoten and Kuehn, *An Enemy We Created*, 253.
71. Discussion with Abdul Salam Zaeef, Kabul, March 20, 2018.
72. Mutmain, *Mullah Mohammed Omar, Taliban and Afghanistan*, 319. Mullah Akhtar Mohammed Osmani was the one with whom CIA station chief Robert Grenier had tried to negotiate the Taliban surrender of bin Laden in September and October 2001. On the basis of a report from the Kandahar intelligence chief and the assumption that having been high up in the Taliban that he must now be "orchestrating a do-or-die fight," special forces hunted down Osmani in summer 2002. A team raided a compound four in Sangin (Helmand province) and picked up Osmani escaping on foot. He was imprisoned in Bagram until handed over to the Afghan government, which then released him to live in Pakistan. He went on to command Taliban operations in parts of the south in 2006 and 2007. Anonymous, *Hunting al Qaeda*, 23, 186.
73. Discussion with Amir Khan Motaqi, member of the Quetta Shura and Taliban political office, Doha, Kabul, August 8, 2019.
74. Rashid, *Descent into Chaos*, 242.
75. Abdul Salam Zaeef, *My Life with the Taliban* (New York: Columbia University Press, 2010), 87.
76. Zaeef, *My Life with the Taliban*, 87.
77. Discussion with Helmand provincial peace council executive, Lashkar Gah, June 7, 2014.
78. Zaeef, *My Life with the Taliban*, 87.
79. Discussion with Helmand provincial peace council executive, Lashkar Gah, June 7, 2014.
80. Rubin, "In the Land of the Taliban."
81. Strick van Linschoten and Kuehn, *An Enemy We Created*, 276.
82. Gall, *The Wrong Enemy*, 19–21. Fairweather, *The Good War*, 114.
83. Giustozzi, *The Taliban at War*.
84. Discussion with participant in Pugwash conferences with Taliban, Washington, DC, August 2, 2017.
85. Discussion with Ishaqzai tribal leader, Kandahar, March 27, 2014.
86. Giustozzi, *The Taliban at War*. Fairweather, *The Good War*, 114.
87. Ron Moreau and Sam Yousafzai, "The Taliban in Their Own Words," *Newsweek*, September 25, 2009.
88. Syed Saleem Shahzad, *Inside Al-Qaeda and the Taliban: Beyond 9/11* (Pluto Press, 2011), 21–22, 30–31.
89. Discussion with Taliban religious scholar, Kandahar, December 24, 2018.
90. Anne Stenersen, "The Relationship between al-Qaeda and the Taliban," in *Talibanistan: Negotiating the Borders between Terror, Politics, and Religion*, edited by Peter Bergen (New York: Oxford University Press, 2013), 73.
91. Anne Stenersen, "Al-Qaʻeda's Comeback in Afghanistan and Its Implications," *CTC Sentinel*, September 7, 2016.
92. Moreau and Yousafzai, "The Taliban in Their Own Words."
93. Mutmain, *Mullah Mohammed Omar, Taliban and Afghanistan*, 309–310.
94. Ibid., 320.
95. Giustozzi, *The Taliban at War*, 20.
96. Moreau and Yousafzai, "The Taliban in Their Own Words."
97. Antonio Giustozzi, "The Military Cohesion of the Taliban," Center for Research & Policy Analysis, www.cpraweb.org, July 14, 2017.
98. Ashley Edgette, "A Mecca for Militants: An Examination of the Development of International Terrorism in Peshawar, Pakistan, 1970–2010," *Hinckley Journal of Politics* (January 1, 2010): 19.

99. Laurent Gayer, *Karachi: Ordered Disorder and the Struggle for the City* (New York: Oxford University Press, 2014), 173.

100. Edwards, *Caravan of Martyrs*, 135, 140.

101. Mohammed Gul Sayid, *Scholars of Afghanistan* (Peshawar, Pak.: Maktabah Farooqiya, 2013), 536–540.

102. Rubin, "In the Land of the Taliban."

103. Rashid, *Descent into Chaos*, 243.

104. Gall, *The Wrong Enemy*, 65–67.

105. Anatol Lieven, *Pakistan: A Hard Country* (New York: Public Affairs, 2011), 412.

106. Ashley Tellis, "Pakistan's Record on Terrorism: Conflicted Goals, Compromised Performance," *Washington Quarterly* (Spring 2008): 10.

107. Muhammad Qasim Zaman, *Islam in Pakistan: A History* (Princeton, NJ: Princeton University Press, 2018), 258.

108. Lieven, *Pakistan: A Hard Country*, 390, 446–449.

109. Musharraf interview with *Guardian* newspaper, "Musharraf: Pakistan and India's Backing for 'Proxies' in Afghanistan Must Stop," *Guardian*, February 13, 2015. Rubin, "In the Land of the Taliban."

110. Anatol Lieven, "All Kayani's Men," *National Interest* (May/June 2010): 58–65.

111. Zach Constantino, "The India-Pakistan Rivalry in Afghanistan," United States Institute for Peace (December 2019).

112. "Musharraf: Pakistan and India's Backing." Ahmed Rashid, *Pakistan: On the Brink: The Future of America, Pakistan, and Afghanistan* (New York: Viking, 2012), 50. Gall, *The Wrong Enemy*, 89. Antonio's Giustozzi's research suggests Musharraf made the decision in 2004, rather than 2003, and took real action to support the Taliban in 2005. Musharraf himself is not specific as to the exact year in his comments to the media. Giustozzi, *The Taliban at War*, 34.

113. Presentation by former Minister of Interior Ali Ahmed Jalali, United States Institute of Peace, Washington, DC, March 16, 2015.

114. Steve Coll, "Looking for Mullah Omar," *New Yorker*, January 23, 2012.

115. Giustozzi, *The Taliban at War*. Fairweather, *The Good War*, 114.

116. Discussion with Deputy Minister of Justice Sayid Abdur Rassoul Halimi, Kabul, July 22, 2019. Halimi was a deputy minister of foreign affairs in the first Taliban regime. The United States imprisoned him in Bagram for a year. He then lived in Pakistan until May 2005 when he returned to Afghanistan and started to work with the Karzai regime.

117. Rashid, *Pakistan: On the Brink*, 50–51.

118. Alan Kronstadt, "Pakistan-U.S. Relations," Congressional Research Service, February 6, 2009, 2.

119. Rashid, *Descent into Chaos*, 149, 225.

120. Discussion with Nazr Mohammed Mutmain, Kabul, August 25, 2019. Mutmain was an official in the Taliban regime and became an advocate for peace after 2010, maintaining relations with the movement.

121. In early 2004, a special forces operation fought more than 100 Taliban in Zabul's Deh Chopan district. During the fight, they detected a well-defended cave where someone seemed to be hiding. They suspected it was Mullah Omar. "Interview with Master Sergeant Michael Threatt," 398. Mutmain, *Mullah Mohammed Omar, Taliban and Afghanistan*, 402.

122. In the winter of 2003–2004, five of seven districts in Zabul fell under Taliban control. Interview with Lieutenant Colonel Lee Knight, PRT Qalat commander (2004–2005), August 11, 2008.

123. The mosque was in Maiwand at the time. That part of Maiwand was tacked onto Zharey in 2003.

124. Panjwayi district profile, Tribal Liaison Office, 2009, 38–39.

125. Discussion with Afghan local police, Afghan local police post, Zharey, Kandahar, July 6, 2013.

126. Sean Maloney, "A Violent Impediment: The Evolution of Insurgent Operations in Kandahar Province 2003–07," *Small Wars & Insurgencies* 19, no. 2 (June 2008): 206.

127. Maloney, "A Violent Impediment," 207.

128. Discussion with Massoud Akhundzada, keeper of the cloak, Kabul, June 25, 2013.

129. Discussion with Mohammed Issa Samad Khan, Kandahar, January 17, 2019.

130. Discussion with District Governor Haji Faisal Mohammed and Jan Agha, Panjwai, May 23, 2013.

131. Discussion with Jan Agha, Ishaqzai tribal leader, FOB Walton, Kandahar, November 12, 2013.

132. Meeting with Ishaqzai tribal leaders from Kandahar, Kabul, January 12, 2014.

133. Discussion with Shafi Afghan, ISAF headquarters, Kabul, July 19, 2013. Discussion with Agha Lalay (Alikozai tribal leader), Kabul, August 10, 2014. Discussion with District Governor Haji Faisal Mohammed and Jan Agha, Panjwai, May 23, 2013.

134. Afghan Local Police shura, Panjwai District Center, July 5, 2013.

135. Moreau and Yousafzai, "The Taliban in Their Own Words."

136. Correspondence with David Wise, US political officer on Lashkar Gah PRT, 2005–2006, November 2011.

137. Discussion with District Governor Haji Faisal Mohammed and Jan Agha, Panjwai, May 23, 2013.

138. Zharey district profile, Tribal Liaison Office, 2009, 57.

139. Zalmay Khalilzad, *The Envoy* (New York: St. Martin's Press, 2016), 179. Rashid, *Descent into Chaos*, 202.

140. Secretary of Defense Donald Rumsfeld to Vice President Richard Cheney, "Marin Strmecki and Afghanistan Briefing," The Rumsfeld Papers, papers.rumsfeld.com, August 25, 2006. Bradley Graham, *By His Own Rules: The Ambitions, Successes, and Ultimate Failures of Donald Rumsfeld* (New York: Public Affairs, 2009), 435.

141. "Principles for Afghanistan—Policy Guidelines," Memorandum, Office of the Secretary of Defense (Policy), Rumsfeld Library, papers.rumsfeld.com, July 7, 2003.

142. "The Exit Strategy from Afghanistan: Lessons from U.S. Efforts to Develop the Afghan National Defense and Security Forces," SIGAR Lessons Learned, Special Inspector-General for Afghanistan Reconstruction, June 19, 2017, 22. Khalilzad, *The Envoy*, 186.

143. Discussion with Popalzai Member of Parliament from Kandahar, Kabul, November 2, 2013. Discussion with Barakzai Member of Parliament from Kandahar, Kabul, October 27, 2013.

144. Michael Bhatia and Mark Sedra, *Afghanistan, Arms and Conflict: Armed Groups, Disarmament and Security in Post-War Society* (New York: Routledge, 2008), 227.

145. Governor Sher Mohammed Akhundzada followed the same policy in Helmand, disarming his rivals. There, more than 2,000 armed men stood down.

146. Antonio Giustozzi, *Koran, Kalashnikov, and Laptop: The Neo-Taliban Insurgency in Afghanistan* (London: Hurst, 2007), 178, 179.

Chapter 7

1. Over 20 tribes lived in Helmand. Largest was the Alizai. The tribe had dwelt in rugged northern Helmand for centuries. Legend has it that the Alizai filled the Afghan ranks at the Battle of Maiwand in 1880, the historic defeat of a British army at the height of the Second Anglo-Afghan War. Sher Mohammed was scion of the leading Alizai family.

2. Most notably, Sher Mohammed used the disarmament, demobilization, and reintegration (DDR) program to disassemble the major Afghan Military Force militia in Helmand—the 1,200-man-strong "93rd Division"—because it was under his Barakzai rival, Malim Mir Wali. Carlotta Gall, *The Wrong Enemy: America in Afghanistan, 2001–2014* (New York: Houghton Mifflin Harcourt, 2014), 220.

3. Center for Military History: Interview with General Daniel McNeill, Brian Neumann and Colin Jay Williams, September 18, 2015.

4. Opening statement of Lt. Gen. Karl Eikenberry, Commander Combined Forces Command–Afghanistan, Testimony before the House Armed Services Committee, June 28, 2006, https://www.c-span.org/video/?193199-1/military-operations-afghanistan&start=8654&noClip=.

5. Ann Scott Tyson, "General Warns of Perils in Afghanistan," *Washington Post*, February 14, 2017.

6. Interview with Karl Eikenberry, Don Wright, OEF Study Group Files, February 23, 2012.

7. Ibid.

8. Ibid.

9. Interview with Karl Eikenberry, Don Wright, OEF Study Group Files, February 23, 2012.

10. E.J. Degen, "The United States Army in Afghanistan: 2001–2014," OEF Study Group, US Army Lessons Learned Conference, July 2015.

11. Michael Clarke, ed., *The Afghan Papers: Committing Britain to War in Helmand, 2005–06* (London: RUSI, 2011), 15–20.

12. CJTF-76 had replaced CJTF-180 in May 2004. Freakley and the 10th Mountain Division took over CJTF-76 in January 2006.

13. Rumsfeld sent the scholar Marin Strmecki to Afghanistan in spring 2006 to assess what could be done. His assessment was not briefed to Rumsfeld until halfway through 2006, by which time the Taliban offensive was well underway. Seth Jones, *In the Graveyard of Empires* (New York: W.W. Norton & Company, 2010), 177–178, 190.

14. One of its battalions (2nd Battalion, 4th Infantry Brigade) deployed was assigned to Zabul.

15. Ronald Neumann, *The Other War: Winning and Losing in Afghanistan* (Washington, DC: Potomac Books, 2009), 51–60.

16. "The Exit Strategy from Afghanistan: Lessons from U.S. Efforts to Develop the Afghan National Defense and Security Forces," SIGAR Lessons Learned, Special Inspector-General for Afghanistan Reconstruction, June 19, 2017, 29.

17. Karzai would later sack Daoud after he had a one-on-one meeting with Prime Minister Tony Blair. Karzai unfairly decided that Daoud was a British stooge. Christina Lamb, *Farewell Kabul: From Afghanistan to a More Dangerous World* (London: William Collins, 2016), 323. "Friendly Fire in Afghanistan," *Economist*, February 2, 2008, 62.

18. According to Sher Mohammed's own boasts, he released 3,000 of his tribesmen to join the Taliban and fight the British. This was certainly an exaggeration since his men were still in Musa Qala and Kajaki and his brother became deputy governor. But it is fair to assume that Sher Mohammed let a lot of fighters go do what they pleased. Emile Simpson, *War from the Ground Up: Twenty-First-Century Combat as Politics* (New York: Oxford University Press, 2013), 44.

19. Michael Martin, *An Intimate War: An Oral History of the Helmand Conflict* (London: Hurst, 2014), 197.

20. Discussion with Amir Khan Motaqi, Doha, Kabul, August 8, 2019.

21. Antonio Giustozzi, *The Taliban at War, 2001–2018* (New York: Oxford University Press, 2019), 61.

22. Gall, *The Wrong Enemy*, 127.

23. Discussion with Raess Baghrani, Kabul, July 21, 2013. Ron Moreau and Sami Yousafzai, "The Taliban in Their Own Words," *Newsweek*, September 25, 2009.

24. "Interview: Mullah Dadullah," Al Jazeera Television, May 2006.

25. Sean Maloney, "A Violent Impediment: The Evolution of Insurgent Operations in Kandahar Province 2003–07," *Small Wars & Insurgencies* 19, no. 2 (June 2008): 211, 212. Alex Strick van Linschoten and Felix Kuehn, *An Enemy We Created* (London: Hurst, 2012), 271, 274.

26. Dadullah himself publicly claimed he had 12,000 fighters countrywide. This could have been propaganda. The US military estimated 7,000–10,000. Peter Bergen, "The Taliban, Regrouped and Rearmed," *Washington Post*, September 10, 2006.

27. Theo Farrell and Antonio Giustozzi, "The Taliban at War: Inside the Helmand Insurgency, 2004–2012," *International Affairs* 89, no. 4, (2013): 850.

28. Discussion with Afghan local police commanders, Zharey district center, July 6, 2013.

29. "Maidan Village," in *Lights of the Jihadi Literature* (Quetta, Pak.: Islamic Emirate Cultural Commission, 2013), 141.

30. "Hazed, then Amu Firat," in *Lights of the Jihadi Literature* (Quetta, Pak.: Islamic Emirate Cultural Commission, 2013), 202.

31. Sean Maloney, *Fighting for Afghanistan* (Annapolis, MD: Naval Institute Press, 2011), 128.

32. A battalion of roughly 900 men was also in Zabul.

33. Center for Military History: Interview with Karl Eikenberry, Don Wright, February 23, 2012.

34. Michael Bhatia and Mark Sedra, *Afghanistan, Arms and Conflict: Armed Groups, Disarmament and Security in Post-War Society* (New York: Routledge, 2008), 227. Maloney, *Fighting for Afghanistan*, 54.

35. Ishaq's battalion, 1st Battalion, 3rd Brigade, rotated through on temporary tours of a month or two to help US special forces. It was a battalion originally trained by the special forces in 2002. OEF Study Group Files, Interview with Major Thomas Clinton, US Army Combat Studies Institute, March 12, 2007.

36. In Helmand, this estimate is based on 50 police each in ten of the districts, 200 police in Gereshk, 200 border police, 500 police in Lashkar Gah, and 500 police in Governor Daoud's untrained poppy eradication force. In Kandahar, the estimate is based on 300 police in the governor's special force under Zia Massoud, 300 border policemen under Abdul Razziq, 200 police (former militia) under Sherzai's brother, 500 police in the city, 100 police in Arghandab, and 50 police in Zharey, Panjwai, Khakrez, Maiwand, Dand, Daman, Spin Boldak, and Shah Wali Kot (it is unclear there was much of anything in the remaining districts). Antonio Giustozzi estimates there were 3,000 police in Kandahar at this time. Antonio Giustozzi, *Koran, Kalashnikov, and Laptop: The Neo-Taliban Insurgency in Afghanistan* (London: Hurst, 2007), 178, 179.

37. The international community also created a 500-man Afghan eradication force. Replete with specially trained Afghans, US and Gurkha ex-military contractors, and helicopters, the force was meant to eradicate poppy. It would be deployed on a questionable eradication mission in Helmand that upset local farmers just as the Taliban had started their offensive. Neumann, *The Other War*, 192.

38. The Rumsfeld Papers (papers.rumsfeld.com): "ANP Horror Stories," Combined Forces Command Briefing Slide, February 2005.

39. Correspondence with David Wise, US political officer on Lashkar Gah PRT, 2005–2006, November 2011.

40. Helmand PRT Weekly Report, May 5, 2006.

41. Ambassador Ronald Neumann, Kabul Embassy Cable, https://nsarchive2.gwu.edu/NSAEBB/NSAEBB358a/doc26.pdf, August 29, 2006

42. Ibid.

43. Gall, *The Wrong Enemy*, 126–127.

44. The police chief and his men were also rumored to kidnap little boys out of the bazaar. Jack Fairweather, *The Good War* (London: Vintage, 2015), 245.

45. Carlotta Gall, "Fighting Rages as U.S. and Afghans Hunt Taliban," *New York Times*, February 5, 2006.

46. Ahmed Rashid, *Descent into Chaos: The United States and the Failure of Nation Building in Pakistan, Afghanistan, and Central Asia* (London: Viking, 2008), 359. Giustozzi, *Koran, Kalashnikov, and Laptop*, 60. Fairweather, *The Good War*, 177. Theo Farrell, *Unwinnable: Britain's War in Afghanistan, 2001–2014* (London: Bodley Head, 2017), 173.

47. Command Sergeant Major Wesley Schutt, "Operations Carpi Diem, Riverdance, and Mountain Thrust, February 5, 2006–June 29, 2006," April 5, 2008.

48. National Counter Terrorism Center Incident Database, http://wits.nctc.gov/.

49. Gall, *The Wrong Enemy*, 129.

50. For part of its tour, the British task force operated under an unusual command-and-control arrangement in which Brigadier Butler did not have tactical control of his forces because Canadian Brigadier-General David Fraser in Kandahar was supposed to command all forces in the south. Instead, Butler assumed responsibility for administration and strategic oversight. It was all a bit of a show. Butler was really still in control and eventually the whole jumble was sorted so that Butler and the succeeding British brigadiers were in charge in both name and form.

51. The British went into Helmand with a plan to work with the people and win hearts and minds. The plan had been written by a team of army officers and civilian officials who had studied the province. Following established counterinsurgency practice, the plan concentrated forces in the center of the province around Lashkar Gah, from where they could radiate outward as security improved. Brigadier Butler and his commanders disregarded the plan and decided on their own to get into a fight in the hinterlands. Eager for battle, Butler criticized the plan as "pretty light on the military Line of Operation . . . drawn up by people who did not properly understand the Brigade's skill sets and capabilities." Farrell, *Unwinnable*, 171–178.

52. It is then that the Baghran district center actually fell. It had somehow been left around by the Taliban to this point.

53. Sean Rayment, *Into the Killing Zone: The Real Story from the Frontline in Afghanistan* (London: Constable, 2008), 44, 63–64. Discussion with Foreign and Commonwealth Office, October 24, 2008. Farrell, *Unwinnable*, 155–156, 171.

54. "In the Dark," *Economist*, February 2, 2008, 49.

55. Elizabeth Rubin, "In the Land of the Taliban," *New York Times Magazine*, October 25, 2006.

56. Lamb, *Farewell Kabul*, 273.

57. "Afghanistan—Decision Point 2008," Senlis Council Report, February 2008: 97.

58. Giustozzi, *Koran, Kalashnikov, and Laptop*, 179. Patrick Bishop, *3PARA* (London: Harper Perennial, 2007), 108.

59. Martin, *An Intimate War*, 200–201. Fairweather, *The Good War*, 200–203.

60. Discussion with British officers, Joint Service Command Staff College, Shrivenham, October 20, 2008. Farrell, *Unwinnable*, 174–175, 177.

61. Geoff Witte, "Epicenter Emerging in Afghan War," *Washington Post*, March 15, 2007.

62. Discussion with Ishaqzai tribal leader, Kandahar, March 27, 2014.

63. Sean Maloney, "A Violent Impediment: The Evolution of Insurgent Operations in Kandahar Province 2003–07," *Small Wars & Insurgencies* 19, no. 2 (June 2008): 210.

64. Discussion with Ishaqzai tribal leader, Kandahar, March 27, 2014.

65. Taliban Sources Repository (https://tsp.hf.uio.no): Mullah Abdul Manan martyr profile, *al-Samoud*, July 23, 2009.

66. Discussion with Afghan local police, Afghan local police post, Zharey, Kandahar, July 6, 2013.

67. Discussion with Zharey police chief Massoum Khan, Zharey district center, July 6, 2013.

68. Bhatia and Sedra, *Afghanistan, Arms and Conflict*, 231.

69. Kenneth Finlayson and Alan Meyer, "Operation Medusa," *Special Forces Magazine* (Spring 2008), 19, 20. Adnan Khan, "The View from Ambush Alley," *Maclean's*, September 11, 2006. Maloney, *Fighting for Afghanistan*, 226–227.

70. Maloney, *Fighting for Afghanistan*, 91, 95.

71. Ibid., 91–93, 147.

72. "Operation Mountain Thrust Continues Momentum in Afghanistan," American Foreign Press Service, June 19, 2008. Bishop, *3PARA*, 171, 201.

73. Fairweather, *The Good War*, 180–184.

74. Second Battalion, Eighty-Seventh US Infantry Regiment came down from regional command east to take part.

75. Discussion with Afghan local police, Afghan local police post, Zharey, Kandahar, July 6, 2013.

76. Discussion with Zharey Popalzai tribal leader, FOB Walton, Kandahar, March 28, 2014.

77. Elizabeth Rubin, "In the Land of the Taliban," *New York Times Magazine*, October 22, 2006.

78. Ibid.

79. Ibid.

80. Discussion with Abdul Wadood, Panjwai district center, July 5, 2013.

81. Carlotta Gall, "21 Killed by Suicide Bomber in Afghan South," *New York Times*, August 4, 2006.

82. Graeme Smith, "Talking to the Taliban," http://www.theglobeandmail.com/talkingtothetaliban/, 2007, accessedFebruary 1, 2009. The site, which had video and transcript of interviews with 42 Taliban, has since been taken down. For a write-up of the interviews, see Graeme Smith, *The Dogs Are Eating Them Now: Our War in Afghanistan* (Berkeley: Counterpoint, 2016): 199 – 215.

83. Maloney, *Fighting for Afghanistan*, 90.

84. Ambassador Ronald Neumann, Kabul Embassy Cable, https://nsarchive2.gwu.edu/NSAEBB/NSAEBB358a/doc26.pdf, August 29, 2006

85. Neumann, *The Other War*, 109–110, 144–145, 160–161.

86. Discussion with former Alikozai policeman and civil society activist, FOB Walton, Kandahar, November 10, 2013.

87. Discussion with Haji Agha Lalay, member of Kandahar provincial council, Kabul, November 16, 2013.

88. Lamb, *Farewell Kabul: From Afghanistan to a More Dangerous World*, 294–295.

89. In another episode, the Dutch had demanded Karzai remove his tribal backer Jan Mohammed from the governorship of Uruzgan before they would deploy there. Karzai

complied but, just as with Sher Mohammed, believed things would have been better had Jan Mohammed stayed. Lamb, *Farewell Kabul*, 315.

90. Discussion with former Afghan provincial advisor, Kabul, November 3, 2013.
91. Interview with Karl Eikenberry, Don Wright, OEF Study Group Files, February 23, 2012.
92. Lamb, *Farewell Kabul*, 320.
93. Ratnesar Romesh and Aryn Baker, "My Problem Is Perhaps That I'm Too Much of a Democrat for This Time of the Country's Life," *Time*, September 18, 2006.
94. Discussion with Yunis Qanooni, Kabul, April 23, 2014.
95. "Afghanistan Struggles to Create United Army," *Los Angeles Times*, November 1, 2006.
96. Discussion with Dr. Najib, Chief of staff of Kandahar governor's office, ISAF headquarters, Kabul, August 2, 2013.
97. David Fraser and Brian Hanington, *Operation Medusa* (Ottawa, CA: McClelland & Stewart, 2018), 121, 123.
98. Gall, *The Wrong Enemy*, 226.
99. Giustozzi, *Koran, Kalashnikov, and Laptop*, 48, 55.
100. "Today We Shall Die," Human Rights Watch Report, March 2015.
101. Maloney, *Fighting for Afghanistan*, 109.
102. Anand Gopal, "The Taliban in Kandahar," in *Talibanistan: Negotiating the Borders between Terror, Politics, and Religion*, edited by Peter Bergen (New York: Oxford University Press, 2013), 18.
103. Matthieu Aikins, "The Master of Spin Boldak," *Harper's*, December 2009.
104. Gopal, "The Taliban in Kandahar," 19.
105. Discussion with Noorzai tribal leader, Kandahar, January 17, 2019.
106. Carl Forsberg, "The Taliban's Campaign for Kandahar," Institute for the Study of War, Afghanistan Report #3, December 2009, 26. Gopal, "The Taliban in Kandahar," 18–19.
107. Farrell and Giustozzi, "The Taliban at War: Inside the Helmand Insurgency, 2004–2012," 858. Maloney, *Fighting for Afghanistan*, 302.
108. Fraser and Hanington, *Operation Medusa*, 116.
109. Smith, *The Dogs Are Eating Them Now*, 55.
110. Gall, *The Wrong Enemy*, 138.
111. Ibid., 139. Fairweather, *The Good War*, 209–211.
112. Fraser and Hanington, *Operation Medusa*, 125, 128.
113. Ibid., 143, 173.
114. Ibid., 116.
115. Fairweather, *The Good War*, 210.
116. Adam Day, "Operation Medusa: The Battle for Panjwayi," *Legion Magazine*, September 1, 2007.
117. Graeme Smith, *The Dogs Are Eating Them Now*, 61–62.
118. Rusty Bradley and Kevin Maurer, *Lions of Kandahar* (New York: Bantam Books, 2011), 2–6, 151, 215.
119. Bradley and Maurer, *Lions of Kandahar*, 2–6, 151, 215. Finlayson and Meyer, "Operation Medusa," 19, 20, 21.
120. Graeme Smith, "Talking to the Taliban," http://www.theglobeandmail.com/talkingtothetaliban/, accessed February 1, 2009..
121. Taliban Sources Repository (https://tsp.hf.uio.no): Mullah Abdul Manan martyr profile, *al-Samoud*, July 23, 2009.
122. Harjit Sajjon, "How the Taliban Gained a Foothold in Southern Afghanistan in 2006," Presentation to the Center for a New American Security, December 4, 2008. Greg Grant, "Tribal War," *Government Executive* 39, no. 3 (March 2007): 44. Bradley and Maurer, *Lions of Kandahar*, 238.
123. Gall, *The Wrong Enemy*, 140.
124. Lamb, *Farewell Kabul*, 309.
125. Sajjon, "How the Taliban Gained a Foothold." Grant, "Tribal War," 44. General David Richards Defense Department News Briefing, LDCH Political Transcripts, October 17, 2006. Discussion with Haji Agha Lalay, Alikozai provincial council member from Panjwai, ISAF Headquarters, April 2, 2013.

126. Discussion with Afghan local police commanders, Zharey district center, July 6, 2013.

127. Lamb, *Farewell Kabul*, 291.

128. Rayment, *The Killing Zone*, 123.

129. Fairweather, *The Good War*, 216–217.

130. Farrell, *Unwinnable*, 184–186.

131. Tom Coghlan, "Paras Almost Retreated under Taliban Assault," *Daily Telegraph*, October 3, 2006. Patrick Bishop, *3PARA* (London: Harper Perennial, 2007), 167, 235, 238, 240, 251–252.

132. Giustozzi, *Koran, Kalashnikov, and Laptop*, 212. Bishop, *3PARA*, 257–260.

133. Discussion with British officers, Joint Service Command Staff College, Shrivenham, October 20, 2008; Farrell, *Unwinnable*, 189. Coghlan, "Paras Almost Retreated under Taliban Assault". Bishop, *3PARA*, 260.

134. Thomas Donnelly and Gary Schmitt, "Musa Qala: Adapting to the Realities of Modern Counterinsurgency," www.smallwarsjournal.com, 2008. Bishop, *3PARA*, 267.

135. National Counter Terrorism Center Incident Database, http://wits.nctc.gov/.

Chapter 8

1. Sami Yousafzai and Ron Moreau, "Taliban Two-Step: Can't Sit Down Yet," *Newsweek*, November 10, 2008.

2. Abdul Hai Mutmain, *Mullah Mohammed Omar, Taliban and Afghanistan* (Kabul: Afghan Publishing Community, 2017), 330.

3. Mutmain, *Mullah Mohammed Omar, Taliban and Afghanistan*, 330.

4. Thomas Ruttig, "From Mullah Omar to Mansur: Change at the Taleban's Top Leadership," Afghan Analysts Network, https://www.afghanistan-analysts.org/en/reports/war-and-peace/from-mullah-omar-to-mansur-change-at-the-talebans-top-leadership/, July 31, 2015.

5. Mutmain, *Mullah Mohammed Omar, Taliban and Afghanistan*, 300.

6. Ibid., 335.

7. "InfoGuide: Taliban," Council on Foreign Relations, www.cfr.org, 2014. "The Taliban," Mapping Militant Organizations, web.stanford.edu, July 15, 2016. Antonio Giustozzi, *The Taliban at War* (New York: Oxford University Press, 2019), 278.

8. Anthony Cordesman, "Coalition, ANSF, and Civilian Casualties in the Afghan Conflict," Center for Strategic & International Studies, www.csis.org, September 4, 2012, 23–24; Anthony Cordesman and Jason Lemieux, "The Afghan War: A Campaign Overview," Center for Strategic & International Studies, www.csis.org, June 23, 2010, 1.

9. Andrew Garfield and Alicia Boyd, "Understanding Afghan Insurgents: Motivations, Goals, and the Reconciliation and Reintegration Process," Foreign Policy Research Institute, July 2013, 38–39.

10. Giustozzi, *The Taliban at War*, 157.

11. Discussion with British officers, King's College, London, October 23, 2008.

12. Theo Farrell and Antonio Giustozzi, "The Taliban at War: Inside the Helmand Insurgency, 2004–2012," *International Affairs* 89, no. 4 (2013): 854. Anand Gopal, "The Taliban in Kandahar," in *Talibanistan: Negotiating the Borders between Terror, Politics, and Religion*, edited by Peter Bergen (New York: Oxford University Press, 2013), 41.

13. Garfield and Boyd, "Understanding Afghan Insurgents," 42. This research is based on 78 interviews with Taliban over the winters of 2009–2010, 2010–2011, and 2011–2012.

14. Gopal, "The Taliban in Kandahar," 41.

15. Discussion with former Taliban Ambassador to the United Nations Abdul Hakim Mujahed, Kabul, June 30, 2013.

16. Discussion with Kandahari professional, Kabul, July 19, 2014.

17. Theo Farrell, *Unwinnable: Britain's War in Afghanistan, 2001–2014* (London: Bodley Head, 2017) 354.

18. He interviewed, through a local Afghan, 42 Taliban fighters from the south. Graeme Smith, *The Dogs Are Eating Them Now: Our War in Afghanistan* (New York: Counterpoint, 2014), 199–211.

19. Garfield and Boyd, "Understanding Afghan Insurgents," 7.

20. Ibid., 33.

21. Sixty-five percent reported sympathy in the east. "Afghanistan in 2009: A Survey of the Afghan People," Asia Foundation, asiafoundation.org, 2009, 65.

22. "Afghanistan in 2010: A Survey of the Afghan People," Asia Foundation, asiafoundation.org, 2010, 50, 52.

23. Mullah Omar, "Kuchinay Eid Message" (2008), in *Offerings on the Occupation: The Islamic Emirates' Position, Messages, Announcements, and Interviews* (Islamic Emirate of Afghanistan Cultural Commission, 2012), 20. For more on Taliban beliefs see Anand Gopal and Alex Strick van Linschoten, "Ideology in the Afghan Taliban," Afghan Analysts Network, June 2017.

24. *Poetry of the Taliban*, edited by Alex Strick van Linschoten and Felix Kuehn (London: Hurst, 2012), 13–14.

25. Ron Moreau and Sam Yousafzai, "The Taliban in Their Own Words," *Newsweek*, September 25, 2009.

26. Mohammed Hussein Mustasad, "Independence," in *Lights of the Jihadi Literature* (Quetta, Pak.: Islamic Emirate Cultural Commission, 2013), 191–192.

27. In their reading of Islamic law, pre-modern religious scholars could not justify a Muslim ruler aligning with an infidel state against a Muslim rival. The problem persists today. Michael Cook, professor of Islamic history at Princeton University, writes, "We live in a world in which mass mobilization and armed resistance are recurrent features of confrontations between native populations and rulers seen as foreigners or in league with foreigners. Where the native population is Muslim and the rulers, or [those] they are felt to be in league with, are not, jihad fits the situation like a glove: whatever costs it may carry in terms of relations with the world at large, it has strong domestic resonance." Michael Cook, *Ancient Religions, Modern Politics: The Islamic Case in Comparative Perspective* (Princeton, NJ: Princeton University Press, 2014), 223, 227.

28. "A Survey of the Afghan People in 2007," Asia Foundation, asiafoundation.org, 2014, 59, 78.

29. Discussion with Massoud Akhundzada, keeper of the cloak, Kabul, June 25, 2013.

30. Interview with Karl Eikenberry, Don Wright, Center for Military History, February 23, 2012.

31. For example, in early 2009, three Taliban in Zabul were feuding with each other over territory. Baradar heard of the issue and installed a new provincial governor (the famous Maulawi Ishmael from Ghazni) and personally delineated the territory under each commander's control. The feuding commanders stopped feuding. Ron Moreau, Michael Hirsh, John Barry, and Mark Hosenball, "If You Thought the Long-Time Head of the Taliban was Bad, You Should Meet his No. 2," *Newsweek*, August 3, 2009. Tsark magazine interview with Mullah Baradar (2009) in *Offerings on the Occupation: The Islamic Emirates' Position, Messages, Announcements, and Interviews* (Islamic Emirate of Afghanistan Cultural Commission, 2012), 39.

32. Edwards, *Heroes of the Age*, 153.

33. Al-Samoud interview with Jalaluddin Haqqani (December 31, 2008) in *Offerings on the Occupation: The Islamic Emirates' Position, Messages, Announcements, and Interviews* (Islamic Emirate of Afghanistan Cultural Commission, 2012), 73.

34. Mullah Omar, "Loya Eid Message," in *Offerings on the Occupation: The Islamic Emirates' Position, Messages, Announcements, and Interviews* (Islamic Emirate of Afghanistan Cultural Commission, 2012), 29–30.

35. Interview with Kandahar governor Mohammed Issa, *Tsark Magazine* (June 2010): 34.

36. Nir Rosen, "How We Lost the War We Won," *Rolling Stone* (October 30, 2008). Emily Winterbotham, "Legacies of Conflict: Healing Complexes and Moving Forward in Ghazni Province," AREU Case Study, October 2011, 18.

37. Aziz Ahmad Tassal, "Winning Hearts and Minds," Institute for War & Peace Reporting, November 27, 2007.

38. Graeme Smith, "Talking to the Taliban," http://www.theglobeandmail.com/talkingtothetaliban/, accessed February 1, 2009. Graeme Smith, *The Dogs Are Eating Them Now: Our War in Afghanistan* (New York: Counterpoint, 2014), 199–211.

39. Gopal, "The Taliban in Kandahar," 41. Garfield and Boyd, "Understanding Afghan Insurgents," 43.

40. Discussion with tribal leader with connections to smugglers and Taliban leadership, Kandahar, June 17, 2014.

41. These are the United Nations figures. David Mansfield, *A State Built on Sand: How Opium Undermined Afghanistan* (London: Hurst, 2016), 104, 237.
42. Giustozzi, *The Taliban at War*, 73, 75, 76.
43. Nir Rosen, "How We Lost the War We Won," *Rolling Stone* (October 30, 2008).
44. Christopher Dickey, "Afghanistan: The Taliban's Book of Rules," *Newsweek*, December 11, 2006. The code was issued in spring 2006.
45. Lrawbar website interview with Taliban spokesman Qari Yunis Ahmadi (2010) in *Offerings on the Occupation: The Islamic Emirates' Position, Messages, Announcements, and Interviews* (Islamic Emirate of Afghanistan Cultural Commission, 2012), 155.
46. Kate Clark, "The Layha, Appendix 1: Taliban Codes of Conduct," Afghan Analysts' Network (aan-afghanistan.com), June 2011, 26.
47. Discussion with Islamic bookstore owner, Kabul, December 8, 2013.
48. Discussion with Maulali Ishaqzai, Kabul, April 26, 2014.
49. Belquis Ahmadi and Sadaf Lakhani, "Afghan Women and Violent Extremism: Colluding, Perpetrating, or Preventing?," USIP Report, November 2016, 9.
50. Alex Strick van Linschoten and Felix Kuehn, *Taliban Reader* (London: Hurst, 2018), 135.
51. Hanifa Zahid, "The Art of My Village," in *Lights of the Jihadi Literature* (Quetta, Pak.: Islamic Emirate Cultural Commission, 2013), 69.
52. Belinda Badari, "The Corpse of a Maiden from Bala Baluk," in *Lights of the Jihadi Literature* (Quetta, Pak.: Islamic Emirate of Afghanistan Cultural Commission, 2013), 54.
53. Ashley Tellis, "Pakistan's Record on Terrorism: Conflicted Goals, Compromised Performance," *Washington Quarterly* (Spring 2008): 15.
54. David Sanger, "Cheney Warns Pakistan to Act on Terrorism," *New York Times*, February 26, 2007. "Taliban Leader 'Captured' in Pakistan," *Associated Press*, March 2, 2007.
55. Dan De Luce, "Is Trump Ready to Dump Pakistan," *Foreign Policy*, https://foreignpolicy.com/2018.03.26/is-trump-ready-to-dump-pakistan/, March 26, 2018.
56. Jack Fairweather, *The Good War* (London: Vintage, 2014), 229.
57. Giustozzi, *The Taliban at War*, 157.
58. Ken Ballen, Peter Bergen, and Patrick Doherty, "Public Opinion in Pakistan's Tribal Region," in *Talibanistan: Negotiating the Borders between Terror, Politics, and Religion*, edited by Peter Bergen (New York: Oxford University Press, 2013), 254, 259.
59. Garfield and Boyd, "Understanding Afghan Insurgents," 46.
60. Ibid.
61. Islamic Emirate Leadership Shura announcement on the investigation by the London School of Economics (2010) in *Offerings on the Occupation: The Islamic Emirates' Position, Messages, Announcements, and Interviews* (Islamic Emirate of Afghanistan Cultural Commission, 2012), 177.
62. Tayeb Agha, who was head of the Taliban political commission in 2013 and 2014, has said that Mullah Omar sent him to speak with the Russians in 2007. Evidently, the Russians rebuffed him. Discussion with Kabul University professor, Washington, DC, August 2, 2017.
63. Abdul Hai Mutmain, *Mullah Mohammed Omar, Taliban and Afghanistan* (Kabul: Afghan Publishing Community, 2017), 319.
64. Ron Moreau and Sam Yousafzai, "The Taliban in Their Own Words," *Newsweek*, September 25, 2009.
65. Giustozzi, *The Taliban at War*, 78–79.
66. Al-Samoud interview with Jalaluddin Haqqani (December 31, 2008) in *Offerings on the Occupation: The Islamic Emirates' Position, Messages, Announcements, and Interviews* (The Islamic Emirate of Afghanistan Cultural Commission, 2012), 72.
67. Ibid., 65.
68. Anand Gopal, Mansur Khan Mehsud, and Brian Fishman, "The Taliban in North Waziristan," in *Talibanistan: Negotiating the Borders between Terror, Politics, and Religion*, edited by Peter Bergen (New York: Oxford University Press, 2013), 145.
69. Musharraf actually told Bush about the arrangement in a meeting in September 2006 as an example of how to use ceasefires to reduce violence. He proposed to repeat it in southern Afghanistan. Fairweather, *The Good War*, 224.

70. Ron Moreau and Mark Hosenball, "Pakistan's Dangerous Double-Game," *Newsweek* (September 22, 2008).

71. VOA Pashto newscast, July 24, 2015. Mullah Omar, al-Qa'eda representatives, and Hekmatyar may have met before that July 2003. Gall, *The Wrong Enemy*, 73.

72. Alex Strick van Linschoten and Felix Kuehn, *An Enemy We Created: The Myth of the Taliban* (London: Hurst, 2012), 276. Sean Maloney, *Fighting for Afghanistan* (Annapolis, MD: Naval Institute Press, 2011), 43, 94–95, 227, 302. Peter Bergen, "The Taliban, Regrouped and Rearmed," *Washington Post*, September 10, 2006.

73. "Interview: Mullah Dadullah," Al Jazeera Television, www.aljazeera.com/news/asia/2007/05/ 200852518376440655.html, April 2007.

74. It is too much to accept Dadullah's claim that the Taliban fell under some master plan created by bin Laden. There is no doubt that the Taliban movement was independent. In fact, it was bin Laden who repeatedly reaffirmed al-Qa'eda's allegiance to Mullah Omar, not the other way around. Al-Qa'eda policy was for their operational commanders to swear allegiance to Omar. What Dadullah shows, however, is how much various Taliban commanders felt affinity to bin Laden. Anne Stenersen, "The Relationship between Al-Qaeda and the Taliban," in *Talibanistan*, edited by Peter Bergen (New York: Oxford University Press, 2013), 83.

75. Ron Moreau, Michael Hirsh, John Barry, and Mark Hosenball, "If You Thought the Long-Time Head of the Taliban Was Bad, You Should Meet His No. 2," *Newsweek*, August 3, 2009. Gopal, "The Taliban in Kandahar," 54.

76. See "Pashtun Rising," *Jane's Terrorism & Security Monitor*, January 16, 2008.

77. Mutmain, *Mullah Mohammed Omar, Taliban and Afghanistan*, 331.

78. Moreau et al., "If You Thought the Long-Time Head of the Taliban Was Bad."

79. Taliban Sources Repository: Mullah Omar, Statement on the Martyrdom of Mullah Dadullah, *al-Samoud*, https://tsp.hf.uio.no, 2007.

80. Discussion with Nazr Mohammed Mutmain, Kabul, August 25, 2019. Mutmain was an official in the Taliban regime and became an advocate for peace after 2010, maintaining relations with the movement.

81. Moreau et al., "If You Thought the Long-Time Head of the Taliban Was Bad."

82. Ibid.

83. Ibid.

84. Taliban Code of Conduct, 2009, 39.

85. The 2010 code of conduct clarified that cadre commanders, district governors, and governors had freedom of action. And they had the right to complain to a higher level if their immediate superior made objectionable changes to their organization. Taliban Code of Conduct (2010 version), section 7, paragraph 33.

86. Lrawbar website interview with Taliban spokesman Qari Yunis Ahmadi, *Offerings on the Occupation*, 155.

87. Ibid.,136.

88. "Afghanistan: Annual Report 2010, Protection of Civilians in Conflict Afghanistan," United Nations Assistance Mission Afghanistan, March 2011. "Afghanistan: Annual Report 2009, Protection of Civilians in Conflict Afghanistan," United Nations Assistance Mission Afghanistan, January 2010. "Afghanistan: Annual Report 2008, Protection of Civilians in Conflict Afghanistan," United Nations Assistance Mission Afghanistan, January 2009. "Afghanistan: Annual Report 2007, Protection of Civilians in Conflict Afghanistan," United Nations Assistance Mission Afghanistan, 2008.

89. Jason Lyall, Graeme Blair, and Kosuke Imai, "Explaining Support for Combatants during Wartime: A Survey Experiment in Afghanistan," *American Political Science Review* (November 2013).

90. Quetta Shura, "Announcement on the Comments of Obama to the Islamic World," (2009) in *Offerings on the Occupation: The Islamic Emirates' Position, Messages, Announcements, and Interviews* (Islamic Emirate of Afghanistan Cultural Commission, 2012), 88.

91. Office of Director of National Intelligence website: Letter from Osama bin Laden to unknown recipient on the situation in Pakistan and Afghanistan, Captured Osama bin Laden files from Abbottabad, undated, https://www.dni.gov/index.php/features/

bin-laden-s-bookshelf?start=3. The context of what bin Laden writes in the letter would date it in 2009 or 2010.

92. Mutmain, *Mullah Mohammed Omar, Taliban and Afghanistan*, 320.

93. Afghan Islamic Agency interview with Mullah Baradar (December 2009) in *Offerings on the Occupation: The Islamic Emirates' Position, Messages, Announcements, and Interviews* (Islamic Emirate of Afghanistan Cultural Commission, 2012), 128.

94. Syed Saleem Shahzad, *Inside Al-Qaeda and the Taliban Beyond 9/11* (London: Pluto Press, 2011), 32.

95. Gopal, Mehsud, and Fishman, "The Taliban in North Waziristan," 134, 142–144.

96. Ibid., 142–144.

97. Mullah Omar, "Loya Eid Message," (2008) in *Offerings on the Occupation: The Islamic Emirates' Position, Messages, Announcements, and Interviews* (Islamic Emirate of Afghanistan Cultural Commission, 2012), 22.

Chapter 9

1. E.J. Degen, "The United States Army in Afghanistan: 2001–2014," OEF Study Group, US Army Lessons Learned Conference, July 2015.

2. David Mansfield, A State Built on Sand: How Opium Undermined Afghanistan (London: Hurst, 2016), 141.

3. Interview with Karl Eikenberry, Don Wright, Center for Military History, February 23, 2012.

4. First Brigade, 82nd Airborne Division ("Task Force Devil") covered the east. It had five battalions. The five battalions included at any time one of a series of marine battalions that rotated through.

5. Interview with Colonel Chris Cavoli, unpublished interview, Combat Studies Institute, March 5, 2009.

6. Interview with Karl Eikenberry, Don Wright, Center for Military History, February 23, 2012.

7. Nuristan, Provincial Handbook, IDS, 2008, 4.

8. Straddling the border itself were a separate set of Pashtun tribes—the Salarzai, Mushwani, Mamund, and famous Mohmand. Important elements resided in Pakistan. This could induce divided loyalties. It also facilitated cross-border smuggling. The Shinwari are a separate powerful tribe along the northern stretch of the Kunar River. In the northernmost corner of Kunar is the Gohar community, non-Pashtuns with roots in Pakistan. Finally, along the Kunar River are communities of Tajik farmers ("dehgan"). Asger Christensen, "The Pashtuns of Kunar: Tribe, Class, and Community Organization," *Afghanistan Journal* 7, no. 3 (1980).

9. Chapa Dara district shura, Chapa Dara district center, November 6, 2007. Discussion with District Governor Mohammed Rahman, Shigal district center, November 5, 2007. Discussion with District Governor Mohammed Zalmay, Korengal Outpost, November 6, 2007. Discussion with shop-owners, Nangalam, October 31, 2007.

10. Conversation with US Army PRT member, anthropological expert, Watapur district, Kunar, February 18, 2008. For more on the Safis, see David Edwards, *Heroes of the Age* (Berkeley: University of California Press); and *Before Taliban* (Berkeley: University of California Press).

11. Anthropologists find this fascinating legend unlikely. Nuristanis are thought to be an Indo-Iranian-speaking people. Nuristan, Provincial Handbook, IDS, 2008, 9.

12. Salafists in Kunar and Nuristan are often called Wahhabis. Wahhabism and Salafism are very similar but the former applies to a specific way of interpreting Islam from Saudi Arabia. Technically, the Salafists in Kunar and Nuristan did not consider themselves Wahhabists. See David Edwards, *Before Taliban: Genealogies of the Afghan Jihad* (Berkeley, Calif.: University of California Press, 2002), 270–272.

13. Discussion with religious leaders, Asadabad, Kunar, October 27, 2007.

14. Discussion with Parliamentarian for Kunar, Wolesi Jirga, Kabul, February 5, 2014.

15. Bill Roggio, "ISAF Captures al Qaeda's Top Kunar Commander," *Long War Journal*, longwarjournal.org, April 6, 2011.

16. Jack Fairweather, *The Good War: Why We Couldn't Win the War or the Peace in Afghanistan* (London: Vintage, 2014), 182.

17. Ibid.
18. Wesley Morgan, "Meet the Next Commander in Afghanistan, Who Has Deeper Experience There Than Almost Any U.S. General," *Washington Post*, January 28, 2016.
19. Michael Coss, "Operation Mountain Lion: CJTF-76 in Afghanistan, Spring 2006," *Military Review* (January–February 2008): 22–29.
20. "Campaign Design and COIN Model," "Spartan Review" draft manuscript, history of the deployment of 3rd Brigade, 10th Mountain Division, May 2007, 3.
21. "Ambassador Eikenberry to Leave Afghanistan," interview, National Public Radio, July 8, 2011.
22. There was one brigade in the east in 2006. In late 2006 (or 2007), a second brigade was assigned.
23. The posts in the Kamdesh Valley went up in October 2006.
24. Sebastian Junger, *War* (New York: Twelve, 2010), 20.
25. Discussion with Saleh Mohammed, Parliamentarian for Kunar, Wolesi Jirga, Kabul, February 5, 2014.
26. UNHCR estimated 20,000 people lived in the Korengal Valley.
27. Asger Christensen, "The Pashtuns of Kunar: Tribe, Class, and Community Organization," *Afghanistan Journal* 7, no. 3 (1980).
28. Discussion with Korengali elders, Kunar government center, March 12, 2008.
29. David Kilcullen, *The Accidental Guerrilla: Fighting Small Wars in the Midst of a Big One* (New York: Oxford University Press, 2009), xiv.
30. Discussion with provincial government chief administrator, Asadabad, March 23, 2008.
31. Discussion with CJTF-82 assessments cell, Bagram Air Base, September 23, 2007.
32. Discussion with Afghan army company commander, Korengal outpost, Kunar, October 6, 2007.
33. Discussion with Korengali elders, Kunar government center, March 12, 2008.
34. Discussion with Task Force Bayonet, Jalalabad Airfield, September 26, 2007.
35. Discussion with Korengali elders, Kunar government center, March 12, 2008.
36. Discussion with Battle Company, 2nd Battalion, 503rd Infantry Regiment, Korengal Outpost, October 5, 2007.
37. Discussion with Battle Company, 2nd Battalion, 503rd Regiment, Korengal Outpost, April 5, 2008.
38. Discussion with Battle Company, 2nd Battalion, 503rd Regiment, Korengal Outpost, October 5–7, 2007.
39. Discussion with Korengali elders, Kunar government center, March 12, 2008.
40. Discussion with Afghan army company first sergeant, Korengal outpost, Kunar, April 1, 2008.
41. Junger, *War*, 194.
42. Ibid., 19.
43. The political decisions behind these deployments are described in chapter 10.
44. Discussion with CJTF-82, Bagram Air Base, September 24, 2007.
45. Douglas Cubbison, Wanat OP Draft evaluation paper, US Army Combat Studies Institute, 31.
46. Interview with Colonel Chris Cavoli, unpublished interview, Combat Studies Institute, March 5, 2009. Wesley Morgan, *The Hardest Place* (New York: Random House, 2021).
47. The US Army and Marine Corps were short on field grade officers to run units in Afghanistan due to war in Iraq. The US Navy and Air Force volunteered to send their top officers to run the provincial reconstruction teams.
48. Interview with Karl Eikenberry, Don Wright, Center for Military History, February 23, 2012.
49. Discussion with Shuryak tribal elders, Asadabad, March 23, 2008.
50. Discussion with advisory team, Camp Able Main, Watapur, Kunar, February 19, 2008.
51. For a detailed analysis of the Pech road see Kilcullen, *The Accidental Guerrilla*, 39–115.
52. Michael Phillips, "Close Contact," *Wall Street Journal*, April 9, 2007.
53. Discussion with elders of Kandagal Village, Pech district, Kunar, October 31, 2007.
54. Discussion with the Director of the Ministry Rural Rehabilitation and Development, Asadabad, October 28, 2007.
55. Discussion with Korengali elders, Kunar government center, March 12, 2008.

56. "Campaign Design and COIN Model," "Spartan Review" draft manuscript, history of the deployment of 3rd Brigade, 10th Mountain Division, May 2007, 13.
57. Discussion with T.F. Bayonet, Jalalabad Airfield, September 26, 2007.
58. Bing West, *The Wrong War: Grit, Strategy, and the Way Out of Afghanistan* (New York: Random House, 2011), 46.
59. Matt Trevithick and Daniel Seckman, "Heart of Darkness: Into Afghanistan's Taliban Valley," *Daily Beast*, www.dailybeast.com, November 15, 2014.
60. Discussion with T.F. Bayonet, Jalalabad Airfield, September 26, 2007.
61. Maneer Ahmed Nafeez, "Rebels," *Shah Mat* (Taliban magazine), February 2010, 39.
62. Tarun bore the same name as the 25-year-old district governor of Ghaziabad district of Kunar whose police chief was suspected of helping insurgents, which begs whether the two are the same.
63. Samiullah Tarun, "I Touch My Forehead in Affection for Islam," in *Lights of the Jihadi Literature* (Quetta, Pak.: Islamic Emirate of Afghanistan Cultural Commission, 2013), 92–94.
64. Discussion with Dr. Mohammed Durrani, Nangarhar provincial council member, Kabul, April 2, 2014.
65. Discussion with Abdul Basir Ghulab, Nangarhar provincial council member, Jalalabad, April 20, 2014.
66. Discussions with US Training and Assistance Command, East (TAAC-E), FOB Fenty, Jalalabad, September 21, 2013.
67. David Mansfield, *A State Built on Sand: How Opium Undermined Afghanistan* (London: Hurst, 206), 144, 161–163.
68. Discussion with Ismatullah Shinwari, Nangarhar representative to the Wolesi Jirga, Kabul, April 16, 2014.
69. David Mansfield, *A State Built on Sand*, 144, 161–162, 183–188.
70. Discussion with Zadran religious leader, November 27, 2013.
71. Commander Dave Adams, Presentation to CNA, May 21, 2008. Ann Marlowe, "A Counterinsurgency Grows in Khost," *Weekly Standard* (May 19, 2008).
72. Kael Weston, *Mirror Test: America at War in Iraq and Afghanistan* (New York: Knopf, 2016), 309.
73. Weston, *Mirror Test*, 308–309.
74. Discussion with Commander John Wade, Khost PRT commander (2006–2007), Alexandria, Virginia, January 11, 2008; Weston, *Mirror Test*, 217–219.
75. Discussion with Zadran religious leader, November 27, 2013. In 2010 and 2011, the Zadran tribe staged an uprising against Haqqani when the network went too far and attempted to impose itself upon their territory.
76. Discussion with legal advisor to Khost governor, Kabul, July 24, 2013.
77. Comments of Khost Provincial Security council chairman, Khost, October 2007.
78. Thom Shanker, "Top Officials Greet Gates in Kabul with Pleas," *New York Times*, December 5, 2007.
79. Douglas Cubbison, Wanat OP Draft evaluation paper, US Army Combat Studies Institute, 2009, 123.
80. Cubbison, Wanat OP Draft evaluation paper, 109.
81. Ibid., 151.
82. Cubbison, Wanat OP Draft evaluation paper, 47. Mark Bowden, Vanity Fair, 2011.

Chapter 10

1. Interview of President George W. Bush, interviewed by Edmund Degen, Gregory Roberts, and Matthew Smith, Army OEF Study Group, undated (post-2014).
2. Robert Gates, *Duty: Memoirs of a Secretary at War* (New York: Knopf, 2014), 205.
3. Ronald Neumann, *The Other War: Winning and Losing in Afghanistan* (Washington, DC: Potomac Books, 2009), 109–110, 144–145, 160–161.
4. Gates, *Duty*, 198–200.
5. Neumann, *The Other War: Winning and Losing in Afghanistan*, 109–110, 144–145, 160–161.

6. McNeill technically did not command US forces directly. He was the NATO commander. US conventional forces fell under the American commander of Regional Command East (RC-E), then Major General David Rodriguez. US forces, however, habitually adhered to McNeill's guidance, given his rank. US special operations forces had their own separate reporting chains as well. US conventional forces would fall under the ISAF commander, another American, from 2008 onward. The special operations command arrangement stayed in place until 2012 when all US special operations forces were put under a single general.

7. Sardar Ahmad, "Forces in Afghanistan Shift Focus to Taliban Leaders," Agence France Presse, January 2, 2007.

8. Interview of General Dan McNeill, unpublished papers, Army OEF Study Group,, April 24, 2009.

9. ISAF spokesman Richard E. Nugee quoted in Alisa Tang, "Key Taliban Leaders, About 50 Fighters Killed so Far in Southern Operation, NATO Says," Associated Press, December 20, 2006.

10. Osmani was killed in an air strike in December 2006. Jason Straziuso, "Senior Taliban Leader Killed in US Airstrike in Afghanistan, Military Says," Associated Press, December 24, 2006.

11. See "Pashtun Rising," Jane's Terrorism & Security Monitor, January 16, 2008.

12. Fifty-four security-related incidents were reported in September 2008, compared to 31 in the same month of the previous year, and 31 in the same month a year before that. Three hundred seventy-nine casualties were recorded in comparison to 236 in the same month of the year prior, and 182 in the same month a year before that. These numbers were calculated using data obtained through the NCTC Worldwide Incidents Tracking System: http://wits.nctc.gov/.

13. Ron Moreau, Michael Hirsh, John Barry, and Mark Hosenball, "If You Thought the Long-Time Head of the Taliban Was Bad, You Should Meet his No. 2," Newsweek, August 3, 2009.

14. Taliban Sources Repository: Interview with Mullah Baradar, al-Samoud, https://tsp.hf.uio.no, April 6, 2008.

15. "War without end," Economist (October 27, 2007): 50.

16. Discussion with British officers, Joint Service Command Staff College, Shrivenham, October 20, 2008.

17. Taliban Sources Repository: Interview with Mullah Baradar, al-Samoud, https://tsp.hf.uio.no, April 6, 2008.

18. Andrew Garfield and Alicia Boyd, "Understanding Afghan Insurgents: Motivations, Goals, and the Reconciliation and Reintegration Process," Foreign Policy Research Institute, July 2013, 44.

19. They set up a few new posts in the eastern corner of Panjwai and continued to sortie into other districts in larger force to disrupt Taliban activities. Their companies repeatedly cleared parts of Panjwai and other districts without being able to stay and hold ground.

20. Anand Gopal, "The Taliban in Kandahar," in Talibanistan: Negotiating the Borders between Terror, Politics, and Religion, edited by Peter Bergen (New York: Oxford University Press, 2013), 44.

21. Joshua Partlow, A Kingdom of their Own: The Family Karzai and the Afghan Disaster (New York: Knopf, 2016), 110.

22. Ibid.

23. Lunch with President Hamid Karzai, Kabul, August 24, 2014.

24. Rangin Dadfar Spanta, Afghanistan Politics: Sense of the Time (Kabul, Afgh.: Aazem Publications, 2017), 236.

25. Spanta, Afghanistan Politics: Sense of the Time, 442.

26. Discussion with UNAMA, Kandahar Air Force Base, July 4, 2013.

27. Discussion with Wolesi Jirga member (1) from Kandahar, Kabul, October 29, 2013. Discussion with Alikozai tribal leader, Kabul, June 23, 2014. Discussion with Alikozai tribal leader, Kandahar, March 29, 2014. Discussion with Ishaqzai tribal leader, Kandahar, March 27, 2014.

28. Dexter Filkins, Mark Mazzetti, and James Risen, "Brother of Afghan Leader Said to be Paid by C.I.A.," New York Times, October 27, 2009.

29. Discussion with US officer assigned to the Kandahar government center from 2010–2011, Kabul, March 21, 2014.
30. Discussion with Kandahar tribal leaders, provincial council members, and Kalimullah Naqib, Kabul, November 20, 2013.
31. Discussion with member of Kandahar provincial council, Kabul, June 25, 2013.
32. Discussion with Alikozai tribal leader, Kandahar, March 27, 2014.
33. Discussion with district governor, Kabul, May 31, 2013.
34. Discussion with Wolesi Jirga member (2) from Kandahar, Kabul, October 27, 2013.
35. Discussion with Maulali Ishaqzai, Kabul, January 14, 2014.
36. *Kandahar Provincial Handbook*, (Arlington, VA: IDS International, 2008), 25.
37. Carlotta Gall, *The Wrong Enemy: America in Afghanistan, 2001–2014* (New York: Houghton Mifflin Harcourt, 2014), 232.
38. Discussion with Kandahar tribal leaders, provincial council members, and Kalimullah Naqib, Kabul, November 20, 2013.
39. Discussion with Barakzai tribal leader, Kabul, June 19, 2013.
40. Discussion with Noorzai tribal leader, Kabul, February 1, 2014.
41. Shah Wali Kot and Khakrez, two northern Kandahar districts, are almost entirely Barakzai, Popalzai, and Alikozai. They should have been government bastions. Ahmed Wali and Karzai allowed Popalzai district governors and police chiefs to be installed who discriminated against the other two tribes and even killed a few of their village elders. Consequently, these Barakzai and Alikozai communities opened their own private war against the Popalzai, refused to work with the government, and allied with Taliban cadres. Discussion with Alikozai politician and former policeman from Arghandab, Kabul, December 7, 2013.
42. Sarah Chayes, "A Mullah Dies, and War Comes Knocking," *Washington Post*, November 18, 2007.
43. Arghandab enjoyed a higher income per capita than most other districts in the south. Tribal Liaison Office Report on Arghandab, 2009, 22.
44. Chayes, "A Mullah Dies, and War Comes Knocking."
45. Tribal Liaison Office Report on Arghandab, 2009, 22.
46. Ahmed Wali Karzai soon bought land in Arghandab with water rights and access to water. Professor Thomas Johnson, "Afghanistan Trip Observations: May–June 2009," Naval Postgraduate School, Powerpoint Presentation. Discussion with leading Alikozai tribal leader and member of Kandahar provincial council, Kabul, November 16, 2013. Discussion with Alikozai former policeman and civil society activist, FOB Walton, Kandahar, November 12, 2013.
47. Discussion with leading Alikozai tribal leader and member of Kandahar provincial council, Kabul, June 25, 2013.
48. Chayes, "A Mullah Dies, and War Comes Knocking."
49. Discussion with Ishaqzai tribal leader, Kandahar, March 27, 2014. Discussion with Kandahar peace council chairman, Kandahar City, March 29, 2014. Chayes, "A Mullah Dies, and War Comes Knocking". Gopal, "The Taliban in Kandahar," 48.
50. Chayes, "A Mullah Dies, and War Comes Knocking."
51. Discussion with Arghandab district governor, Kabul provincial government center, November 11, 2013. Discussion with former Alikozai policeman and civil society activist, FOB Walton, Kandahar, November 12, 2013. Discussion with leading Alikozai tribal leader and member of Kandahar provincial council, Kabul, June 25, 2013. Discussion with leading Alikozai tribal leader and member of Kandahar provincial council, Kabul, November 16, 2013. Omar El Akkad and Graeme Smith, "Mullah's Death Leaves Kandahar Exposed," *Globe and Mail*, October 13, 2007. Chayes, "A Mullah Dies, and War Comes Knocking". Discussion with former Alikozai policeman and politician, Kabul, December 7, 2013.
52. Discussion with Kalimullah Naqibi, Kabul, August 19, 2014.
53. Discussion with Alikozai tribal leader and provincial council member, Kandahar City, June 18, 2014.
54. Discussion with Arghandab district governor, Kabul provincial government center, November 11, 2013. Discussion with NDS, Daman district center, Kandahar, November 13, 2013. Garfield and Boyd, "Understanding Afghan Insurgents," 4, 18.

55. Discussion with Arghandab district governor, December 20, 2018. Discussion with Police advisory team interpreter, FOB Walton, Kandahar, November 12, 2013.

56. *Kandahar Provincial Handbook*, (Arlington, VA: IDS International, 2008), 64.

57. Suicide Attack Database, Chicago Project on Security and Threats, University of Chicago, http://cpostdata.uchicago.edu, accessed in 2014. The data was offline at the time of publication of this book and expected to come back online shortly. See https://dss.princeton.edu/catalog/resource1057.

58. Graeme Smith, "Inside the Taliban Jailbreak," *Globe and Mail*, July 3, 2008. Graeme Smith, "It's a Bust," *New York Post*, July 6, 2008.

59. Carlotta Gall, "Taliban Fighters Infiltrate Area Near Southern Afghan City," *New York Times*, June 17, 2008.

60. Discussion with police, Dand district center, Kandahar, November 10, 2013; Discussion with police precinct deputy, Kandahar City, June 19, 2014. Discussion with shopowners (Hazara), Kandahar City, March 30, 2014; Afghan local police shura, Panjwai District Center, July 5, 2013.

61. Discussion with Kandahar Provincial Coordination Center, Kandahar City, November 9, 2013.

62. Discussion with Zarghona Baluch, Kabul, December 4, 2013.

63. Discussion with teachers at Safi School, Cholay neighborhood, Kandahar City, March 30, 2014.

64. Discussion with shop-owner (tribe unknown), Kandahar City, March 30, 2014.

65. Discussion at SOTF-S, Kandahar Air Force Base, July 5, 2013.

66. In October 2007, Mullah Abdul Salem, a mid-level Taliban leader in Musa Qala, approached the government and said he was ready to turn against the Taliban in return for the district governorship. The British seized the opportunity. Under the command of British Brigadier Andrew MacKay, three Afghan army battalions, a British battalion-size force, a reserve US battalion from the 82nd Airborne Division (1st Battalion, 508th Parachute Infantry Regiment), and US Special Forces teams cleared Musa Qala in November and early December 2007. Mullah Salem became the new district governor and 300 police re-formed under Commander Koka, the old militia commander and inveterate enemy of the Taliban. One Afghan army battalion with British advisors stayed to watch over the town. Discussion with Major Hart, Operations Officer, 40 Commando, Royal Marines, Taunton, UK, October 22, 2008. Discussion with Brigadier MacKay, DCDC, October 21, 2008. Discussion with British officers, Joint Service Command Staff College, Shrivenham, October 20, 2008. Discussion with Brigadier MacKay, DCDC, October 21, 2008.

67. A British battalion eventually replaced the marines. Discussion with British officers, Joint Service Command Staff College, Shrivenham, October 20, 2008.

68. Discussion with Kandahar Police Chief Abdul Razziq, Kandahar police headquarters, June 18, 2014. Discussion with Helmand provincial peace council executive, Lashkar Gah, June 7, 2014.

69. The militia's senior commander, Tor Jan, died in the fighting. Rumors spread that Abdur Rahman Jan, angry at the poppy eradication, then let his militia stand down. In September, Marjah fell. Nad Ali followed a few weeks later. Whether an irate Abdur Rahman Jan had truly made a deal with the Taliban is unknown. Whatever the case, yet another piece on the chessboard had been lost and the path was open to Lashkar Gah. *Helmand*, Provincial Handbook, IDS International, October 2008, 40, 42.

70. Tom Coghlan, "Taleban Stage Audacious 'Tet-Style' Attack on British HQ City," *Times*, October 13, 2008. Theo Farrell, *Unwinnable: Britain's War in Afghanistan, 2001–2014* (London: Bodley Head, 2017), 246–248.

71. Among the reinforcements were Commander Koka and his men from Musa Qala. Discussions with 2nd Battalion, 7th Marine Regiment, Twenty-Nine Palms, February 23, 2009. Coghlan, "Taleban Stage Audacious 'Tet-Style' Attack."

72. Bing West, *The Wrong War: Grit, Strategy, and the Way Out of Afghanistan* (New York: Random House, 2011), 51.

73. Interview of Brigadier General Mark Milley, unpublished interview, OEF Army Study Group, August 18, 2009. Wesley Morgan, The Hardest Place (New York: Random House, 2021).

74. Poor governance afflicted Ghazni as well. Between the summer of 2006 and the summer of 2008, four governors had held office—two were fired for corruption, the third for poor performance.

75. Carlotta Gall, "Taliban Fighters Infiltrate Area Near Southern Afghan City," *New York Times*, June 17, 2008. Candace Rondeaux and Javed Hamdard, "Taliban Seizes Seven Afghan Villages," *Washington Post*, June 17, 2008. "Still in the Fight," *Economist*, June 21, 2008.

76. "Afghanistan on Fire," *New York Times*, August 20, 2008.

77. Robert Gates, *Duty: Memoirs of a Secretary at War* (New York: Knopf, 2014), 222.

78. Steve Coll, *Directorate S: The C.I.A. and America's Secret Wars in Afghanistan and Pakistan* (New York: Penguin, 2018), 332.

79. Kenneth Katzman, "Afghanistan: Post-Taliban Governance, Security, and U.S. Policy," Congressional Research Service, April 9, 2013, 19.

80. McKiernan would ask for more reinforcements in February 2009, for a grand total of 30,000. Gates, *Duty*, 219–221.

81. West, *The Wrong War*, 91–112.

82. Wesley Morgan, "Meet the Next Commander in Afghanistan, Who Has Deeper Experience There Than Almost Any U.S. General," *Washington Post*, January 28, 2016.

83. Quetta Shura announcement, April 26, 2011, in *Offerings on the Occupation: The Islamic Emirates' Position, Messages, Announcements, and Interviews* (Islamic Emirate of Afghanistan Cultural Commission, 2012), 271.

84. Discussion with Saleh Mohammed, Parliamentarian for Kunar, Wolesi Jirga, Kabul, February 5, 2014.

85. Matt Trevithick and Daniel Seckman, "Heart of Darkness: Into Afghanistan's Taliban Valley," *Daily Beast*, www.dailybeast.com, November 15, 2014.

86. Bill Roggio, "ISAF Captures al-Qaeda's Top Kunar Commander," *Long War Journal*, longwarjournal.org, April 6, 2011.

87. Charles Bremner and Michael Evans, "British Envoy Says Mission in Afghanistan Is Doomed," *Times*, October 2, 2008.

Chapter 11

1. Michael Hastings, *The Operators* (New York: Blue Rider Press, 2012), 22.

2. President Barack Obama, First Inaugural Address, January 20, 2009, www.obamawhitehouse.archives.gov.

3. Barack Obama, *A Promised Land* (New York: Crown, 2020), 436.

4. Robert Gates, *Duty: Memoirs of a Secretary at War* (New York: Knopf, 2014), 323.

5. President Barack Obama, First Inaugural Address, January 20, 2009, www.obamawhitehouse.archives.gov.

6. *The U.S. Army-Marine Corps Counterinsurgency Field Manual* (Chicago: University of Chicago, 2007), 37.

7. Ibid., 39.

8. Steve Coll, *Directorate S: The C.I.A. and America's Secret Wars in Afghanistan and Pakistan* (New York: Penguin, 2018), 350.

9. Ian Livingston and Michael O'Hanlon, "Afghanistan Index," Brookings Institution, November 30, 2011.

10. White Paper of the Interagency Policy Group's Report on U.S. Policy toward Afghanistan and Pakistan, March 27, 2009.

11. Obama, *A Promised Land*, 677.

12. Bob Woodward, *Obama's Wars* (New York: Simon & Schuster, 2010), 71, 72, 79, 80–81, 97–98, 102.

13. Obama, *A Promised Land*, 321.

14. White Paper of the Interagency Policy Group's Report on U.S. Policy toward Afghanistan and Pakistan. Stanley McChrystal, *My Share of the Task: A Memoir* (New York: Penguin, 2014), 285.

15. Fred Kaplan, *The Insurgents: David Petraeus and the Plot to Change the American Way of War* (New York: Simon & Schuster, 2013), 300.

16. Katzman, "Afghanistan: Post-Taliban Governance, Security, and U.S. Policy," 19.
17. Woodward, *Obama's Wars*, 332–333.
18. "Ambassador Eikenberry to Leave Afghanistan," Interview, National Public Radio, July 8, 2011.
19. McChrystal, *My Share of the Task*, 294.
20. Greg Jaffe, "The war in Afghanistan shattered Joe Biden's faith in American military power," *Washington Post*, February 23, 2020.
21. President Barack Obama, Remarks on a New Strategy in Afghanistan and Pakistan, https:// obamawhitehouse.archives.gov, March 27, 2019.
22. Innocent Malou, "Should America Liberate Afghanistan's Women," *Survival* 53, no. 5 (October/November 2011): 31–52. Catherine Powell, "Women's Rights Remain in Peril," Council on Foreign Relations, www.cfr.org, August 8, 2014.
23. Transcript of Pelosi and Delegation Press Conference on Visit with Troops in Afghanistan, May 11, 2010.
24. Rangin Dadfar Spanta, *Afghanistan Politics: Sense of the Time* (Kabul, Afgh.: Aazem Publications, 2017), 264.
25. Spanta, *Afghanistan Politics*, 526.
26. Joshua Partlow, *A Kingdom of Their Own: The Family Karzai and the Afghan Disaster* (New York: Knopf, 2016), 23.
27. United Nations Assistance Mission to Afghanistan, Human Rights Unit, *Afghanistan: Annual Report on Protection of Civilians in Armed Conflict*, 2008, ii.
28. Barry Bearak, "Karzai Calls Coalition 'Careless,'" *New York Times*, June 24, 2007.
29. Carlotta Gall, "Afghan Leader Criticizes U.S., Calling Arrests and Casualties Too High," *New York Times*, April 26, 2008.
30. Discussion with CJTF-82 assessments cell, Bagram Air Base, September 23, 2007.
31. See the 2009 Afghanistan poll conducted by ABC/BBC, 10. Online at http://news.bbc. co.uk/1/shared/bsp/hi/pdfs/05_02_09afghan_poll_2009.pdf.
32. Discussion with Haji Hafizullah, former Helmand provincial governor and Hezb Islami leader, Kabul, November 28, 2013. Discussion with Senator Haqwayoon, member of Meshrano Jirga, Parliament, December 5, 2013. Discussion with Islamic bookstore owner, Kabul, December 8, 2013. Discussion with Shazada Shahid, member of Wolesi Jirga, Kabul, February 9, 2014.
33. Discussion with Maulawi Baluch, Kabul, March 25, 2013.
34. Discussion with Gul Agha Sherzai, Kabul, July 26, 2013.
35. McChrystal, *My Share of the Task*, 310.
36. ISAF Tactical Directive unclassified guidance, July 6, 2009.
37. McChrystal, *My Share of the Task*, 312.
38. C.J. Chivers, "Warriors Vexed by Rules for War," *New York Times*, June 23, 2010.
39. "Irreversible Damage: The Strategic Impact of Civilian Harm in Afghanistan and Lessons for Future Conflicts," Open Society Foundations, June 2016, 27. Ian Livingston and Michael O'Hanlon, "Afghanistan Index," Brookings Institution, April 26, 2013. Sherard Cowper-Coles, *Cables from Kabul: The Inside Story of the West's Afghanistan Campaign* (London: Harper Press, 2011), 256. See also Joseph Felter and Jacob Shapiro, "Limiting Casualties as Part of a Winning Strategy: The Case of Courageous Restraint," *Daedalus* (Winter 2017).
40. McChrystal, *My Share of the Task*, 350.
41. Jim Hoagland, "Obama's Afghan Hopes Meet Reality," *Washington Post*, September 10, 2009.
42. Jim Hoagland, "Obama's Afghan Hopes Meet Reality," *Washington Post*, September 10, 2009.
43. Spanta, *Afghanistan Politics*, 262.
44. Rajiv Chandrasekaran, *Little America: The War within the War for Afghanistan* (New York: Knopf, 2012), 261–262.
45. Discussion with independent directorate of local governance, Kabul, February 3, 2014.
46. White House Press Release, Press Briefing by Bruce Riedel, Ambassador Richard Holbrooke, and Michelle Flournoy on the New Strategy for Afghanistan and Pakistan, March 27, 2009.
47. McChrystal, *My Share of the Task*, 366–367.
48. Woodward, *Obama's Wars*, 355.
49. "Irreversible Damage," 32.

50. New America Foundation, Drone Wars Pakistan: Analysis, https://www.newamerica. org/international-security/reports/americas-counterterrorism-wars/the-drone-war-in-pakistan/.
51. Peter Bergen and Jennifer Rowland, "CIA Drone Strikes and the Taliban," in *Talibanistan*, edited by Peter Bergen and Katherine Tiedemann (New York: Oxford University Press, 2013), 229.
52. Coll, *Directorate S*, 338–341, 354–360, 530–537.
53. Terrence Kelly, Nora Bensahel, Olga Oliker, "Security Force Assistance in Afghanistan: Identifying Lessons for Future Efforts," RAND Corporation, 40.
54. Paul Miller, *Armed State Building: Confronting State Failure, 1898–2012* (Ithaca, NY: Cornell University Press, 2013), 165.
55. General Stanley McChrystal to Secretary of Defense Robert Gates, COMISAF's Initial Assessment, August 30, 2009.
56. "Reconstructing the Afghan National Defense and Security Forces: Lessons from the U.S. Experience in Afghanistan," Special Inspector General for Afghanistan Reconstruction (September 2017), 97.
57. Discussion with CJTF-82 assessments cell, Bagram Air Base, September 23, 2007.
58. Terrence Kelly, Nora Bensahel, Olga Oliker, "Security Force Assistance in Afghanistan: Identifying Lessons for Future Efforts," RAND Corporation, 48.
59. Antonio Giustozzi, "The Afghan National Army: Unwarranted Hope?," *Survival* (January 2010): 36–42.
60. Spanta, *Afghanistan Politics*, 389, 559.
61. Spanta, *Afghanistan Politics*, 291.
62. Chandrasekaran, *Little America*, 91–94.
63. McChrystal, *My Share of the Task*, 342.
64. "Ambassador Eikenberry to Leave Afghanistan," Interview, National Public Radio, July 8, 2011.
65. Gates, *Duty*, 341. Cowper-Coles, *Cables from Kabul*, 211, 235.
66. Gates, *Duty*, 358.
67. For a detailed discussion of the 2009 elections, see Noah Coburn and Anna Larson, *Derailing Democracy in Afghanistan: Elections in an Unstable Political Landscape* (New York: Columbia University Press, 2014), 96–177.
68. Hastings, *The Operators*, 103–105.
69. Jim Hoagland, "Obama's Afghan Hopes Meet Reality," *Washington Post*, September 10, 2009.
70. "Ambassador Eikenberry's Cables on U.S. Strategy in Afghanistan," http://documents. nytimes.com/eikenberry-s-memos-on-the-strategy-in-afghanistan.
71. Rangin Dadfar Spanta, *Afghanistan Politics: Sense of the Time* (Kabul, Afgh.: Aazem Publications, 2017), 199–200.
72. A separate Gallup Poll showed Karzai's popularity dropped from 54 to 44 percent from September 2009 to March 2010. Because this line of questioning was not continued, it is impossible to know whether this was a temporary or more long-lasting drop. Julie Ray and Rajesh Srinivasan, "Afghans' Approval of Their Leadership Falls to 33%," Gallup, www.gallup. com, March 2010.
73. "Afghanistan in 2010: A Survey of the Afghan People," Asia Foundation, 2010, 5, 6, 73, 119.
74. McChrystal, *My Share of the Task*, 291
75. "Terrorism: The War in Afghanistan and C.I.A. Interrogations," CBS News Poll, September 1, 2009.
76. Jeffrey Jones, "Americans Split on Whether Goals in Afghanistan Will Be Met, December 4, 2009, https://news.gallup.com/poll/124565/americans-split-whether-goals-afghanistan-met.aspx.
77. Gates, *Duty*, 349.
78. General Stanley McChrystal to Secretary of Defense Robert Gates, COMISAF's Initial Assessment, August 30, 2009.
79. Woodward, *Obama's Wars*, 161.
80. General Stanley McChrystal to Secretary of Defense Robert Gates, COMISAF's Initial Assessment, August 30, 2009.

81. Stanley McChrystal, *My Share of the Task*, 330.

82. General Stanley McChrystal to Secretary of Defense Robert Gates, COMISAF's Initial Assessment, August 30, 2009.

83. David Ignatius, "What a Surge Can't Solve in Afghanistan," *Washington Post*, September 28, 2009.

84. Chandrasekaran, *Little America*, 126.

85. McChrystal, *My Share of the Task*, 323.

86. Gates, *Duty*, 375.

87. Rory Stewart, Testimony to the Senate Foreign Relations Committee, https: www.foreign. senate.gov, September 16, 2009.

88. Hastings, *The Operators*, 134.

89. Leon Panetta, *Worthy Fights*, 255.

90. Obama, *A Promised Land*, 436–437.

91. Gates, *Duty*, 362–363.

92. Gates, *Duty*, 342.

93. Woodward, *Obama's Wars*, 110.

94. Martin Feldstein, "The Fed's Unconventional Monetary Policy," *Foreign Affair* 95, no. 3 (May/June 2016): 108–109.

95. Woodward, *Obama's Wars*, 166–168, 251.

96. Jonathan Alter, *The Promise: President Obama, Year One* (New York: Simon & Schuster, 2011), 376.

97. Woodward, *Obama's Wars*, 184, 277–278, 336.

98. Gates, *Duty*, 498. Karen DeYoung, "U.S. Urgently Reviews Policy on Afghanistan," *Washington Post*, October 9, 2008.

99. McChrystal, *My Share of the Task*, 359.

100. President Barack Obama, "West Point Speech," www.cnn.com, December 2, 2009.

101. Ibid.

102. Ibid.

103. Ibid.

104. Carter Malkasian, *War Comes to Garmser: Thirty Years of Conflict on the Afghan Frontier* (New York: Oxford University Press, 2013), 246.

105. Office of Director of National Intelligence web-site: Letter from Osama bin Laden to Mullah Omar, Captured Osama bin Laden files from Abbottabad, November 5, 2010, https://www. dni.gov/index.php/features/bin-laden-s-bookshelf?start=3.

106. "Announcement of the Islamic Emirate about the Obama's New Strategy" (December 7, 2009), in *Offerings on the Occupation: The Islamic Emirates' Position, Messages, Announcements, and Interviews* (Islamic Emirate of Afghanistan Cultural Commission, 2012), 90.

107. "Last Year, Recent War," *Shah Mat* (Taliban magazine), February 2010, 3–4. Yet another article in same issue argued the opposite; the announcement was a ruse to hide America's intention to stay in Afghanistan; the United States had no intention of leaving whatsoever; "People, Every Armed Man, Foreign Occupation," *Shah Mat* (Taliban magazine), February 2010, 12.

108. McChrystal, *My Share of the Task*, 358.

109. Coll, *Directorate S*, 369, 425–426.

110. Ibid., 401. Woodward, *Obama's Wars*, 186, 228. Alter, *The Promise*, 374.

111. Biden may have toyed with pulling out without ever proposing it. Cowper-Coles, *Cables from Kabul*, 201.

112. Jeffrey Jones, "In U.S., Fears of Terrorism after Afghanistan Pullout Subside," Gallup, www. gallup.com, June 29, 2011.

113. Woodward, *Obama's Wars*, 166–168.

114. The closest pieces of evidence are in Woodward and Gates. Woodward recounts one occasion when Obama contemplated sending only 10,000 new reinforcements and then disregarded the idea because he worried that Gates might resign. In his own book, Gates wrote that he sent Obama a memo on Afghanistan strategy in September in which, among several other points, he briefly urged him not to consider withdrawal from Afghanistan as an option. Both incidents are still a far cry from showing that Obama or anyone else actually

was considering withdrawing from Afghanistan. Lastly, I should note that I have heard multiple rumors that Biden wanted to withdraw completely but knew it was politically infeasible and therefore never raised it; no hard evidence exists to prove these rumors. Woodward, *Obama's Wars*, 303–304. Gates, *Duty*, 365.

115. Alter, *The Promise*, 367.

Chapter 12

1. Discussion with RC-South headquarters, Kandahar Air Force Base, August 31, 2009.
2. These figures include the breakdown of the 4,000 advisors sent in March 2009 (4th Brigade, 82nd Airborne Division) that are usually not covered in figures on the surge. At least 2,000 of the 4,000 additional troops for advising the Afghan army, sent in March 2009, went to Kandahar.
3. Rajiv Chandrasekaran, *Little America: The War within the War for Afghanistan* (New York: Knopf, 2012), 59. Discussion with RC-South headquarters, Kandahar Air Force Base, August 31, 2009.
4. Stanley McChrystal, *My Share of the Task: A Memoir* (New York: Penguin, 2013), 323.
5. Discussion with Lashkar Gah provincial reconstruction team, Helmand, May 30, 2013.
6. "Operation Enduring Freedom Afghanistan, May 2009–April 2010," 2nd Marine Expeditionary Brigade brief, 2010.
7. Ibid.
8. Frank Biggio, *The Wolves of Helmand: A View from Inside the Den of Modern War* (Brentwood, TN: Forefront Books, 2020), 59.
9. Ibid, 59.
10. Bing West, *The Wrong War: Grit, Strategy, and the Way Out of Afghanistan* (New York: Random House, 2011), 152.
11. Discussion with RC-South headquarters, Kandahar Air Force Base, August 31, 2009.
12. Discussion with Helmand PRT representative, United States, July 2009.
13. At first, both 2nd Marine Expeditionary Force and Task Force Helmand reported to Regional Command South, the ISAF headquarters in Kandahar. In mid-2010, the marines would assume authority over all Helmand, reporting directly to the military command in Kabul. The British would then fall under the marine command. Discussion with RC-South headquarters, Kandahar Air Force Base, August 31, 2009.
14. Discussion with Helmand Provincial Reconstruction Team, Lashkar Gah, September 3, 2009.
15. Carter Malkasian and Jerry Meyerle, "Provincial Reconstruction Teams: How Do We Know They Work?" Strategic Studies Institute Monograph (Carlisle: Strategic Studies Institute, 2009).
16. Two US representatives (Marlin Hardinger from the State Department and Rory Donohoe from USAID) had been with the provincial reconstruction team since 2008.
17. *Helmand*, Provincial Handbook, IDS International, October 2008, 39.
18. Brief by Lieutenant Colonel Justin Holly, Camp Lejeune, March 17, 2009. Sherard Cowper-Coles, *Cables from Kabul: The Inside Story of the West's Afghanistan Campaign* (London: Harper Press, 2011), 191.
19. Chandrasekaran, *Little America*, 81–82.
20. A Norwegian delegation exploring peace talks claimed to have met with someone believed to be Omar in March 2009 near Karachi. If it was truly Omar, the Norwegians were struck by his sickly appearance—he was overweight and slurred his speech. They suspected he had diabetes. The meeting does not appear in Taliban histories and conflicts with their post-2015 assertion that Omar never left Afghanistan. As with everything to do with Omar, the truth is elusive.
21. Abdul Hai Mutmain, *Mullah Mohammed Omar, Taliban and Afghanistan* (Kabul: Afghan Publishing Community, 2017), 332.
22. Thomas Ruttig, "From Mullah Omar to Mansur: Change at the Taleban's Top Leadership," Afghan Analysts Network, www.afghanistan-analysts.org, July 31, 2015.
23. Mujib Mashal, "How Secret Peace Talks Between Afghanistan and the Taliban Foundered," *New York Times*, December 27, 2016. Bette Dam, *The Secret Life of Mullah Omar*, Zomia Center, March 2019, 9, 15.

24. "Islamic Emirate Announcement on the Start of Operation Nasrat (2009) in *Offerings on the Occupation: The Islamic Emirates' Position, Messages, Announcements, and Interviews* (Islamic Emirate of Afghanistan Cultural Commission, 2012), 40.

25. Ron Moreau, "America's New Nightmare," *Newsweek*, August 3, 2009.

26. Interview with Taliban religious leader from Helmand, Survey of Taliban, August 2014.

27. Discussion with Helmand provincial peace council executive, Lashkar Gah, June 7, 2014.

28. Ron Moreau, Michael Hirsh, John Barry, and Mark Hosenball, "If You Thought the Long-Time Head of the Taliban Was Bad, You Should Meet His No. 2," *Newsweek*, August 3, 2009.

29. Discussion with Kandahar Police Chief Abdul Razziq, Kandahar police headquarters, June 18, 2014. Discussion with Alizai tribal leader, Lashkar Gah, June 4, 2014.

30. Marjah reunion roundtable, Quantico, VA, March 2015.

31. In December 2008, the Royal Marines had retaken the Nad Ali district center.

32. Later in the year, the British continued operations to clear Nad Ali. Michael Martin, *An Intimate War* (London: Hurst, 2014). McChrystal, *My Share of the Task*, 318, 321. Theo Farrell, *Unwinnable: Britain's War in Afghanistan, 2001–2014* (London: Bodley Head, 2017), 244–262.

33. West, *The Wrong War*, 164.

34. South of Garmser, Nicholson deployed his light armored reconnaissance battalion to Khaneshin to reduce the movement of Taliban northward from the Pakistan border.

35. West, *The Wrong War*, 180, 195.

36. Helmand PRT Progress Report, February 10, 2010.

37. Discussion with Helmand PRT representative, United States, July 2009.

38. David Mansfield, *A State Built on Sand: How Opium Undermined Afghanistan* (London: Hurst, 2016), 217–218.

39. Helmand Provincial Reconstruction Team Food Zone Update, March 15, 2010.

40. Mansfield, *A State Built on Sand*, 236.

41. Cynthia Clapp-Wincek, "The Helmand Valley Project in Afghanistan," A.I.D. Evaluation Special Study No. 18, U.S. Agency for International Development, December 1983, 17.

42. Mansfield, *A State Built on Sand*, 248.

43. Discussion with Gul Mohammed, Marjah tribal leader, January 27, 2014.

44. Discussion with 2nd Marine Expeditionary Brigade, Camp Leatherneck, September 1, 2009.

45. McChrystal, *My Share of the Task*, 364–365.

46. Theo Farrell and Antonio Giustozzi, "The Taliban at War: Inside the Helmand Insurgency, 2004–2012," *International Affairs* 89, no. 4 (2013): 857.

47. Afghan Islamic Agency interview with Mullah Baradar (December 2009) in *Offerings on the Occupation: The Islamic Emirates' Position, Messages, Announcements, and Interviews* (Islamic Emirate of Afghanistan Cultural Commission, 2012), 127.

48. Chandrasekaran, *Little America*, 286.

49. Marjah reunion roundtable, Quantico, VA, February 12, 2015.

50. James Clark, "For Those Who Fought in Marjah, It Was More Than Just a Battle," *Task & Purpose*, February 13, 2015. https://taskandpurpose.com/fought-marjah-just-battle.

51. The last companies did not link up in southern Marjah until May 15.

52. McChrystal, *My Share of the Task*, 373.

53. Rangin Dadfar Spanta, Afghanistan Politics: Sense of the Time (Kabul, Afgh.: Aazem Publications, 2017), 355.

54. Zahir had spent years living in Germany and supposedly had been imprisoned there for trying to kill his stepson. Kabul would replace Zahir in early July with Abdul Mutalab, an NDS veteran. Mutalab was far more attuned to the realities of war. Poor Zahir would be assassinated in 2011. Chandrasekaran, *Little America*, 143.

55. David Mansfield, Helmand Counter Narcotics Impact Study May 2010, July 20, 2010, 9.

56. C.J. Chivers, "In Ambush, a Glimpse of a Long Afghan Summer," *New York Times*, May 19, 2010.

57. District conference, Garmser, May 13, 2010.

58. West, *The Wrong War*, 220.

59. C.J. Chivers, "What Marja Tells Us of Battles Yet to Come," *New York Times*, June 10, 2010.

60. Todd Pitman, "Lessons from Marjah, Afghanistan," *Orange County Register*, October 28, 2010.

61. Kyle Carpenter, *You Are Worth It: Building a Life Worth Fighting For* (New York: William Morrow, 2019), 92–93
62. Todd Pitman, "Marines in Marjah Find Firefights All Over," *NBC News*, October 7, 2010. http://www.nbcnews.com/id/39562801/ns/world_news-south_and_central_asia/t/marines-marjah-find-firefights-all-over/.
63. Discussion with District Governor Mohammed Fahim, Garmser, May 29, 2010. Fahim's family was from Marjah. His family members were in their village during this period.
64. Discussion with District Governor Mohammed Fahim, Garmser, May 29, 2010. Discussion with Mohammed Asif, Garmser, September 25, 2010. Mohammed Asif is not to be mistaken with the militia commander of the same name who became one of the biggest commanders in Marjah.
65. Discussion with District Governor Mohammed Fahim, Garmser, September 24, 2010.
66. Provincial reconstruction team conference, Lashkar Gah, April 21, 2010. Comments by Colonel Kyle Ellison (former battalion commander of 2nd Battalion, 6th Marine Regiment, which served in central Marjah between June 2010 and January 2011), Fort Bragg, May 8, 2017.
67. Heidi Vogt, "Afghan Army Struggles with Ethnic Divisions," *Associated Press*, July 27, 2010.
68. Discussion with Lieutenant Colonel Brian Christmas, FOB Delhi, Garmser, Helmand, May 2010.
69. I was working in Garmser at the time and got to know the family as well as other Marjah tribal leaders. Both Omar Jan and the Garmser district governor, Mohammed Fahim, were from Marjah and frequently introduced me to their relatives and friends.
70. Discussion with Gul Mullah, Marjah tribal leader, Lashkar Gah, June 6, 2014.
71. Discussion with Gul Mohammed, Marjah tribal leader, Kabul, February 24, 2014.
72. Discussion with Gul Mohammed, Marjah tribal leader, Kabul, November 25, 2013.
73. Discussion with Gul Mullah, Marjah tribal leader, Lashkar Gah, June 6, 2014.
74. Marjah district support team daily report, November 10, 2010. Brett Van Ess, "The Fight for Marjah: Recent Counterinsurgency Operations in Southern Afghanistan." *Small Wars Journal*, smallwarsjournal.com, September 30, 2010. Discussion with Colonel Cal Worth, Kabul, March 22, 2018.
75. Discussion with Gul Mohammed, Marjah tribal leader, Kabul, November 25, 2013. Brian Mockenhaupt, "The Living and the Dead," *Best American Magazine Writing* (New York: Columbia University Press, 2013), 482.
76. Comments by Colonel Kyle Ellison (former battalion commander, 2nd Battalion, 6th Marine Regiment), Fort Bragg, May 8, 2017.
77. Marjah district support team report, November 5, 2010. Mockenhaupt, "The Living and the Dead," 463–482.
78. Discussion with Gul Mohammed, Marjah tribal leader, Kabul, November 25, 2013.
79. Andrew Johnston, "Marines Host Stability Shura in Marjah," 2nd Marine Expeditionary Force website, October 31, 2010.
80. Marjah district support team reports, September and October 2010.
81. Marjah district support team report, November 5, 2010.
82. Marjah district support team daily report, November 8, 2010.
83. Discussion with Gul Mohammed, Marjah tribal leader, Kabul, November 25, 2013.
84. Marjah district support team report, November 5, 2010.
85. Discussion with Mohammed Asif, Garmser, September 25, 2010.
86. "Life in Helmand after the British Withdrawal," *BBC Pashto*, July 22, 2015. Jon Boone, "Afghans Fear Return of the Warlords as Anti-Taliban Militias Clash," *Guardian*, February 16, 2011.
87. Rajiv Chandrasekaran, "In Afghanistan, Why Does Counterinsurgency Work in Some Places But Not Others?," *Washington Post*, July 25, 2010. Marjah DST Daily report, January 20, 2011.
88. Marjah reunion roundtable, Quantico, VA, February 12, 2015.
89. AVIPA Plus Weekly Activity Report, July 12, 2010.
90. The marines had already deployed units to northern Helmand. Advisory teams had served in Sangin, and Musa Qala, and Nowzad. In December 2009, the marines conducted an operation to clear out the Nowzad bazaar.

91. Bing West, *One Million Steps: A Marine Platoon at War* (New York: Random House, 2014), 27. Farrell, *Unwinnable*, 261. Chandrasekaran, *Little America*, 214–215.

92. From July to the end of September, 3rd Battalion, 7th Marine Regiment, had worked in Sangin with Royal Marine 40 Commando to try to reduce violence before the arrival of 3rd Battalion, 5th Marine Regiment. A 400-man Afghan army battalion stayed to work with the marines.

93. Marjah reunion roundtable, Quantico, VA, February 12, 2015.

94. West, *One Million Steps*, 35.

95. West, *One Million Steps*, 43, 72, 141. Mark Moyar, "The Third Way of COIN: Defeating the Taliban in Sangin," Orbis Operations, July 2011, 37.

96. Farrell, *Unwinnable*, 358–359.

97. Ibid.

98. The Alikozai had fought the Taliban in 2006 and staged an ill-fated uprising in 2007 (the Taliban had quickly suppressed the outnumbered rebels, executing five of their leaders and forcing the tribesmen to live quietly at home or flee).

99. Helmand PRT Weekly Report, January 3, 2011. Moyar, "The Third Way of COIN," 48.

100. West, *One Million Steps*, 192–193. Moyar, "The Third Way of COIN," 46, 50. Rod Nordland and Taimoor Shah, "Afghans Say Taliban Are Nearing Control of Key District," *New York Times*, September 6, 2014.

101. Helmand Monitoring and Evaluation Program, District Reports, September 25, 2011, 9–21.

102. Malim Mir Wali, the Barakzai tribal leader of Gereshk, would have been an exception. He still influenced a large number of militia in Gereshk.

103. HMEP Periodic Review, Helmand Monitoring and Evaluation Program survey, Coffey international development, October 1, 2011, 4-28.

104. HMEP Periodic Review, Helmand Monitoring and Evaluation Program survey, Coffey international development, October 1, 2011, 4-18, 4-19.

105. Matthew Lesnowicz, "Gendarmerie de Marjah," *Marine Corps Gazette* 98, no. 2 (February 2014): 30–36.

106. Mansfield, *A State Built on Sand*, 236.

107. Ibid., 267–270.

108. Taliban commanders and mullahs administered land allocation and permissions for drilling wells. "The Political Economy of the Dashte," Coffey International Development, August 2013, 5, 6, 9, 12, 13, 14, 18, 19, 21, 27, 39, 50.

109. "The Political Economy of the Dashte," 53, 54.

110. "The Political Economy of the Dashte," 23.

111. Giustozzi, *The Taliban at War*, 156.

112. J. Kael Weston, *The Mirror Test: America at War in Iraq and Afghanistan* (New York: Alfred A Knopf, 2016), 371.

Chapter 13

1. Professor Thomas Johnson, "Afghanistan Trip Observations: May–June 2009," Naval Postgraduate School, PowerPoint Presentation.

2. These figures include the breakdown of the 4,000 advisors sent in March 2009 (4th Brigade, 82nd Airborne Division) that are usually not covered in figures on the surge. Task Force Fury—4/82 ABN, Operation Enduring Freedom X, August 2009 to September 2009, Briefing to panel, dodccrp.org

3. Colonel Harry Tunnell, Memorandum for Secretary of the Army John McHugh, August 20, 2010.

4. Personal observations, Regional Command South Headquarters, Kandahar Air Base, August 2009.

5. Rajiv Chandrasekaran, *Little America: The War Within the War for Afghanistan* (New York: Knopf, 2012), 154–161.

6. Carter oversaw operations in Helmand, Uruzgan, Zabul, and Kandahar.

7. Discussion with Governor Toorayalai Wesa, Kandahar City, November 10, 2013.

8. Dexter Filkins, Mark Mazzetti, and James Risen, "Brother of Afghan Leader Said to be Paid by C.I.A.," *New York Times*, October 27, 2009.

9. Chandrasekaran, *Little America*, 310–314.

10. Carlotta Gall, *The Wrong Enemy: America in Afghanistan, 2001–2014* (Boston: Houghton Mifflin Harcourt, 2014), 233.

11. Rod Nordland, "Afghanistan Strategy Focuses on Civilian Effort," *New York Times*, June 8, 2010.

12. Rangin Dadfar Spanta, *Afghanistan Politics: Sense of the Time* (Kabul, Afgh.: Aazem Publications, 2017), 307.

13. Peter Tomsen, *The Wars of Afghanistan: Messianic Terrorism, Tribal Conflicts, and the Failures of Great Powers* (New York: Public Affairs, 2011), 679–680.

14. Chandrasekaran, *Little America*, 261–262.

15. Benazir Hotaki, "Bebe Zeneba, Zarghona Ana, and Maulali," in *Kandahar Da Tarikh Pah Uzgdo Kay* (Kandahar, Afgh.: Kandahar Cultural Director, 2005), 360.

16. Deb Riechmann, "Karzai: Ramping Up Security Is a 'Go' for Kandahar," *Associated Press*, June 14, 2010. For Karzai's comments, see "US and NATO Commander and Karzai Seek Support from Locals," Associated Press, https://www.youtube.com/watch?v=RbgT-BpxZEI, posted July 24, 2015.

17. Dexter Filkins, "In Visit to Kandahar, Karzai Outlines Anti-Taliban Plan," *New York Times*, June 13, 2010.

18. Michael Hastings, "The Runaway General," *Rolling Stone*, June 22, 2010.

19. Barack Obama, *A Promised Land* (New York: Crown, 2020), 579.

20. Paula Broadwell, *All In: The Education of General David Petraeus* (New York: Penguin, 2012), 59.

21. Christina Lamb, *Farewell Kabul: From Afghanistan to a More Dangerous World* (London: William Collins, 2015), 536. Broadwell, *All In*, 282–283.

22. Ian Livingston and Michael O'Hanlon, "Afghanistan Index," Brookings Institution, November 30, 2011. Chandrasekaran, *Little America*, 277.

23. Spanta, *Afghanistan Politics*, 400.

24. Steve Coll, *Directorate S: The C.I.A. and America's Secret Wars in Afghanistan and Pakistan* (New York: Penguin, 2018), 444–445.

25. Gall, *The Wrong Enemy*, 162.

26. Dexter Filkins, "Pakistanis Tell of Motive in Taliban Leader's Arrest," *New York Times*, August 22, 2010.

27. Thomas Ruttig, "Negotiations with the Taliban," in *Talibanistan: Negotiating the Borders between Terror, Politics, and Religion*, edited by Peter Bergen (New York: Oxford University Press, 2013), 444–445. Lyse Doucet, "Pakistan Arrests Halt Secret UN Contact with Taliban," *BBC News*, March 19, 2010.

28. Filkins, "Pakistanis Tell of Motive in Taliban Leader's Arrest."

29. Correspondence with Afghan peace activists who met with Baradar on November 15, 2019.

30. Baradar was released from prison in 2013 and put under house arrest. Baradar would appear sickly to friends, relatives, and Afghan diplomats. Rumors spread that the Pakistanis had beaten and drugged him.

31. Discussion with Ishaqzai tribal leader, February 8, 2014. Mohammed Alyas Khan, "Short Biography of Mullah Akhtar Mohammed Mansour," *BBC Pashto*, May 22, 2016.

32. Wakil Ahmed Mutawakil, *Afghanistan and Taliban* (Kabul, Afgh.: Byeralali Pohaneon Lray, 2005), 53. Mohammed Alyas Khan, "Short Biography of Mullah Akhtar Mohammed Mansour," *BBC Pashto*, May 22, 2016.

33. Mutawakil, *Afghanistan and Taliban*, 53. Mohammed Alyas Khan, "Short Biography of Mullah Akhtar Mohammed Mansour," *BBC Pashto*, May 22, 2016.

34. Anand Gopal, "The Taliban in Kandahar," in *Talibanistan: Negotiating the Borders between Terror, Politics, and Religion*, edited by Peter Bergen (New York: Oxford University Press, 2013), 14–15.

35. Khan, "Short Biography of Mullah Akhtar Mohammed Mansour."

36. Muhammad Qasim Zaman, *Islam in Pakistan: A History* (Princeton, NJ: Princeton University Press, 2018), 247.

37. Mansour used his poppy wealth to purchase land and property in Karachi. He owned two apartments and four homes there. "The Former Taliban Lead Mullah Mansour's Land Dealings in Karachi," *VOA Pashto*, July 27, 2019.

38. From Quetta, Mansour received hundreds of tribal leaders who came from Afghanistan to hear his guidance. Most likely as part of his consolidation of power in May 2010, Mansour issued a third version of the Taliban code of conduct. The new code explicitly limited the authority of the military commission under Zakir and further stressed the chain of command, reiterating that every governor report solely to Mansour. He was responsible for solving disputes that they could not resolve on their own. Those he could not solve would go to the "leadership," meaning Mullah Omar. Taliban Code of Conduct (2010 version), in Kate Clark, "Calling the Taliban to Account," Afghan Analysts Network, June 2011, 69. My translation of the code differs from that of the Afghan Analysts Network. I translated *tanzimi raees* as organization director, Mansour's position, instead of regional commander.

39. Discussion with members of Taliban political commission, Doha, Qatar, August 26, 2019.

40. Carl Forsberg, "Counterinsurgency in Kandahar," *Institute for Understanding War* (December 2010), 14.

41. Interview with Kandahar governor, Mohammed Issa, *Tsark Magazine* (June 2010): 30, 33, 34.

42. Discussion with police sergeant, Malajat, June 19, 2014. Gall, *The Wrong Enemy*, 223, 225.

43. Taimoor Shah and Rob Nordland, "Near Kandahar, the Prize Is an Empty Town," *New York Times*, September 1, 2010.

44. Joshua Partlow and Karen Bruillard, "US Operations in Kandahar Push Out the Taliban," *Washington Post*, October 25, 2010.

45. Gall, *The Wrong Enemy*, 227.

46. Interview with Kandahar governor Mohammed Issa, *Tsark Magazine* (June 2010): 30.

47. Matthieu Aikins, "The Master of Spin Boldak," *Harper's*, December 2009.

48. Discussion at SOTF-S, Kandahar Air Force Base, July 4, 2013.

49. Gall, *The Wrong Enemy*, 227.

50. Discussion with police post sergeant, Kandahar City, June 19, 2014.

51. The 300 Afghan soldiers that had previously been in the district rotated out.

52. David Flynn, "Extreme Partnership in Afghanistan: Arghandab District, Kandahar Province, 2010–2011," *Military Review* (March–April 2012): 29–30.

53. Interview with 1st Lieutenant Scott Hendrickson (Platoon Leader, D Company, 1st Battalion, 66th Armored Regiment), unpublished interview OEF Study Group, , April 25, 2012.

54. Heidi Vogt, "Afghan Army Struggles with Ethnic Divisions," *Associated Press*, July 27, 2010.

55. Discussion with police advisory team interpreter, FOB Walton, Kandahar, November 12, 2013. Discussion with District Governor Shah Mahmud, Kandahar provincial government center, November 11, 2013.

56. Scott Mann, *Game Changers: Going Local to Defeat Violent Extremists* (Leesburg, VA: Tribal Analysis Publishing, 2015), 75.

57. Announcement on the investigation into the Arghandab incident (June 21, 2010) in *Offerings on the Occupation: The Islamic Emirates' Position, Messages, Announcements, and Interviews* (Islamic Emirate of Afghanistan Cultural Commission, 2012), 179.

58. Discussion with Mirza, Arghandab, March 18, 2014. Discussion with Ibrahim Arghandabi, former Alikozai policeman, Kabul, December 7, 2013.

59. Discussion with Arghandab Afghan local police coordinator, Arghandab, March 18, 2014.

60. Discussion with District Governor Shah Mahmud, Kandahar provincial government center, November 10, 2013.

61. The initial idea for special forces to work with villages to create tribal militia had been created by Miller's predecessor, Brigadier General Ed Reeder and Dr. Seth Jones from the RAND Corporation.

62. Afghanistan Papers (*Washington Post*): Interview with Major General Edward Reeder, SIGAR, undated.

63. Linda Robinson, *One Hundred Victories: Special Operations and the Future of American Warfare* (New York: Public Affairs, 2013), 25.

64. Spanta, *Afghanistan Politic*, 381.

65. Robinson, *One Hundred Victories*, 14–30. In Helmand, the marines filled this role. The existing tribal militias of Garmser and Marjah were converted into local police.
66. Discussion with Kohaq teacher, Arghandab, March 18, 2014.
67. Discussion with Khaliq Dod, Arghandab, March 18, 2014.
68. Discussion with Mirza, Arghandab, March 18, 2014.
69. Ibid.
70. Kohaq shura, Arghandab, March 18, 2014.
71. Discussion with Colonel Richard McNorton, ISAF headquarters, Kabul, August 2, 2013.
72. Discussion with Alikozai tribal leader and provincial council member, Kandahar City, June 18, 2014. Discussion with Colonel Richard McNorton, ISAF headquarters, Kabul, August 2, 2013. Robinson, *One Hundred Victories*, 42.
73. Mohammed Kochai, "Karzai: Do Not Leave Your Own Region to the Taliban," BBC Pashto, October 20, 2010. Ahmed Ludin, "From Arghandab, Karzai Calls on the People of Arghandab to Bring Taliban to Peace," Benawa, October 9, 2010.
74. Discussion with Agha Lalay, Alikozai tribal leader, Intercontinental Hotel, Kabul, November 16, 2013. Discussion with Colonel Richard McNorton, ISAF headquarters, Kabul, August 2, 2013.
75. Discussion with Arghandab Afghan local police coordinator, Arghandab, March 18, 2014.
76. Joshua Partlow and Karen Bruillard, "U.S. Operations in Kandahar Push Out Taliban," *Washington Post*, October 25, 2010.
77. Chandrasekaran, *Little America*, 274–276, 284. Spencer Ackerman, "Why I Flattened Three Afghan Villages," Wired.com, February 1, 2011.
78. Kevin Sieff, "Years Later, a Flattened Afghan Village Reflects on U.S. Bombardment," *Washington Post*, August 25, 2013.
79. Discussion with Haji Hafizullah, Alikozai tribal leader and provincial council member, Kandahar City, June 18, 2014.
80. "Quetta Shura Announcement on the Badr Spring Offensive" (2011) in *Offerings on the Occupation*, 276–277.
81. Andrew Garfield and Alicia Boyd, "Understanding Afghan Insurgents: Motivations, Goals, and the Reconciliation and Reintegration Process," Foreign Policy Research Institute, July 2013, 39.
82. Discussion with District Governor Shah Mahmud, Kandahar provincial government center, November 10, 2013.
83. Interview with Captain David Burgio (former platoon leader, D Company, 3rd Battalion, 66th Armored Regiment), unpublished interview, OEF Study Group, June 19, 2012.
84. Discussion with Kandahar police advisory team, FOB Walton, Kandahar, November 12, 2013.
85. Discussion with police post sergeant, Kandahar City, June 19, 2014.
86. Discussion with senior US military advisor to Kandahar Police Chief, FOB Walton, Kandahar, November 9, 2013.
87. Discussion with Kandahar Police Chief Abdul Razziq, Kandahar police headquarters, July 5, 2013.
88. Discussion with UNAMA, Kandahar Air Force Base, July 4, 2013.
89. Michael Hastings, *The Operators* (New York: Blue Rider Press, 2012), 22.
90. Discussion with Kandahar educated professional, Kabul, January 11, 2014.
91. Discussion with Kandahar Police Chief Abdul Razziq, Kandahar police headquarters, June 18, 2014.
92. Gall, *The Wrong Enemy*, 228.
93. Forsberg, "Counterinsurgency in Kandahar," 16.
94. Discussion with teachers at Safi School, Cholay neighborhood, Kandahar City, March 30, 2014.
95. Discussion with Zarghona Baluch, Kabul, December 4, 2013.
96. Discussion with Maryam Durrani and her father, Kabul, November 26, 2013.
97. Discussion with Kandahar religious leaders, June 24, 2014. Discussion with Kandahar University student, Kabul, May 26, 2014. Discussion with Kandahar City street vendor

(Alizai tribe), Kandahar City, March 30, 2014. Discussion with Kandahar Provincial Coordination Center, Kandahar City, November 9, 2013.

98. Discussion with educated Kandahari professional, Kabul, July 19, 2014.

99. Discussion with Ishaqzai tribal leader, Kandahar, March 28, 2014.

100. Each Afghan battalion had 350 to 550 men.

101. Broadwell, *All In*, 86.

102. Megan McCloskey, "Kandahar: Safer for Good or Just Safer for Now?," *Stars and Stripes*, February 3, 2011.

103. Marian Eide and Michael Gibler, eds., *After Combat: True War Stories from Iraq and Afghanistan* (Omaha: University of Nebraska Press, 2018), 138–140.

104. Kevin Hymel, "Toe to Toe with the Taliban: Bravo Company Fights in Makuan," *Vanguard of Valor II: Small Unit Actions in Afghanistan*, edited by Donald Wright (Fort Leavenworth, KS: Combat Studies Institute Press, 2012), 4–25.

105. Colonel Art Kandarian, interviewed by Lieutenant Colonel Greg McCarthy and Lieutenant Colonel Butch Welch, Army OEF Study Group, October 5, 2010.

106. Forsberg, "Counterinsurgency in Kandahar," 28.

107. Kevin Hymel, "Trapping the Taliban at OP Dusty: A Scout Platoon in Zhari District," *Vanguard of Valor: Small Unit Actions in Afghanistan*, edited by Donald Wright (Fort Leavenworth, KS: US Army Center for Military History Press, 2012), 164.

108. Hymel, "Trapping the Taliban at OP Dusty: A Scout Platoon in Zhari District," 166.

109. "Quetta Shura Announcement on the Badr Spring Offensive" (2011) in *Offerings on the Occupation*, 276–277.

110. Ibid.

111. Conversation with Colonel Douglas Sims, battalion commander in Eastern Panjwai in 2010 and 2011, Kandahar Air Force Base, November 8, 2013.

112. Conference on counterinsurgency, Center for a New American Security, Washington, DC, February 17, 2012.

113. James Russell, "Learning Cycles in War: The 3/2 Arrowhead Brigade and the 1st Battalion, 23rd Infantry Operations in Kandahar, 2012," *Journal of Strategic Studies* (forthcoming).

114. Andrew Garfield and Alicia Boyd, "Understanding Afghan Insurgents: Motivations, Goals, and the Reconciliation and Reintegration Process," Foreign Policy Research Institute, July 2013, 39.

115. Jonathan Addleton, *Dust of Kandahar* (Annapolis, MD: Naval Institute Press, 2016).

116. Discussion with Kandahar civilian platform, telephone conversation, Kabul, March 24, 2013.

117. Discussion with UNAMA, Kandahar Air Force base, July 4, 2013.

118. Fewer than 50 local police were recruited in Panjwai in 2011.

119. Discussion with US headquarters, Kandahar Air Force Base, July 4, 2013. Robinson, *One Hundred Victories*, 149–150.

120. From 2005 to 2011, the Canadians had suffered 162 killed and 2,000 wounded. By early 2012, the battle for Zharey and Panjwai was under its third commander. Carter had left in late 2010; Terry in late 2011; now Kandahar was under Major General James Huggins and his aggressive deputy, Marty Schweitzer. They wanted to finish the battle. In January 2013, two US infantry battalions were in Panjwai; an infantry battalion, two armored battalions, a Stryker battalion, and a military police battalion were in Zharey. Robinson, *One Hundred Victories*, 148–149.

121. Discussion with Greg Solewin, Commander's Advisory and Assistance Team, FOB Walton, Kandahar, November 8, 2013.

122. Interview with Colonel Brian Mennes, unpublished interview, OEF Study Group, November 2, 2012.

123. Russell, "Learning Cycles in War."

124. Schweitzer vectored in the additional teams.

125. Discussion with Zharey police chief Massoum Khan, Zharey district center, July 6, 2013.

126. Discussion with Kandahar police chief Abdul Razziq, Kandahar police headquarters, July 5, 2013.

127. Discussion with Afghan local police class, Afghan local police training center, Zharey, July 6, 2013.

128. Discussion with Kandahar police chief Abdul Razziq, Kandahar police headquarters, July 5, 2013.

129. Western Panjwai is where on March 11, 2012, Staff Sergeant Robert Bales had left his post and murdered 16 Afghans in a village. Four months later in Zharey, 1st Lieutenant Clint Lorance ordered his platoon to kill four Afghan civilians. Greg Jaffe, "'The Cursed Platoon,'" *Washington Post*, July 2, 2020.

130. Discussion with Achekzai tribal leader from Panjwai, Panjwai district center, Kandahar, July 5, 2013. Discussion with Zharey tribal leader, FOB Walton, Kandahar, March 28, 2014.

131. Discussion with Afghan local police commanders, Zharey district center, July 6, 2013.

132. Discussion with Afghan local police, Afghan local police post, Zharey, Kandahar, July 6, 2013. Discussion with Sayid Habib and Imam Abdul Bari Akhund (Kandahar City religious leaders), Kandahar, December 22, 2018.

133. Discussion with Noorzai tribal leader, Kabul, January 2, 2019.

134. Discussion with Ishaqzai tribal leader, Kandahar, March 28, 2014.

135. The postscript to the Zharey and Panjwai story is February 2013. That month, an "uprising" broke out in the western reaches of Panjwai, where the Taliban had stubbornly held on. In February, Taliban killed a water manager (the local mirab), kidnapped three young men who supported the government, and tried to kill the son of a local tribal leader. Razziq noticed what was happening and took advantage of it. An enclave of his own Achekzai tribesmen lived in the area. He had them instigate discontent. A few days after the kidnapping, a local Achekzai tribal leader, Abdul Wadood, whose son had been threatened, organized a rally of hundreds of people, waving Afghan flags and declaring they would no longer tolerate the Taliban. Alikozai and certain Noorzai tribesmen joined them. Razziq gave them guns, ammunition, and supplies. Total local police numbers in Panjwai soared from 150 to 450. Discussion with Haji Faizal Mohammed, Panjwai district governor, Panjwai district center, July 5, 2013; Afghan local police shura, Panjwai district center, July 5, 2013. Discussion with Abdul Wadood, Panjwai district center, July 5, 2013.

136. Discussion with Governor Toorayalai Wesa, Kandahar City, November 11, 2013.

137. Nazr Mohammed Mutmain, *Six Days with Taliban Leaders* (Kabul, Afgh.: Danish Publishing Community, 2019), 151.

138. Antonio Giustozzi, *The Taliban at War* (New York: Oxford University Press, 2019), 117.

139. Discussion with Helmand tribal leader, Lashkar Gah, June 4, 2014.

140. Giustozzi, *The Taliban at War*, 117–118, 278.

141. Discussion with Amarullah Saleh, Kabul, March 16, 2014.

Chapter 14

1. Anne Stenersen, "The Relationship Between al-Qaeda and the Taliban," in *Talibanistan: Negotiating the Borders between Terror, Politics, and Religion*, edited by Peter Bergen (New York: Oxford University Press, 2013), 73. Audrey Kurth Cronin, "Why Drones Fail," *Foreign Affairs* 92, no. 4 (July–August 2013): 45.

2. Office of Director of National Intelligence website: Letter from Osama bin Laden to unknown recipient on the situation in Pakistan and Afghanistan, Captured Osama bin Laden files from Abbottabad, undated, https://www.dni.gov/index.php/features/bin-laden-s-bookshelf?start=3. This letter mentions the Pakistani Taliban which means the letter was written no earlier than 2007.

3. Bill Roggio, "ISAF Captures al Qaeda's Top Kunar Commander," *Long War Journal*, longwarjournal.org, April 6, 2011.

4. Gordon Lubold, "Airstrikes Said to Hit al Qaeda Leaders," *Wall Street Journal*, October 27, 2016.

5. Paula Broadwell, *All In: The Education of General David Petraeus* (New York: Penguin, 2012), 248.

6. Bob Woodward, *Obama's Wars* (New York: Simon & Schuster, 2010), 338. See also Michael Hastings, *The Operators* (New York: Blue Rider Press, 2012), 136.

7. Robert Gates, *Duty: Memoirs of a Secretary at War* (New York: Knopf, 2014), 474, 483.

8. Gates, *Duty*, 488.

9. Ibid., 488.

10. The high casualty number was largely associated with the increase in US troops. Normalized figures are 0.0044 for 2008, 0.0049 for 2009, 0.0049 for 2010, and 0.0042 for 2011, suggesting the intensity of combat per unit was roughly the same.

11. Rangin Dadfar Spanta, *Afghanistan Politics: Sense of the Time* (Kabul, Afgh.: Aazem Publications, 2017), 296.

12. Spanta, *Afghanistan Politics*, 436.

13. Chandrasekaran, *Little America*, 321–323.

14. Jeffrey Jones, "Americans More Positive on Afghanistan After Bin Laden Death," Gallup, https://news.gallup.com/poll/147488/americans-positive-afghanistan-bin-laden-death, May 11, 2011. Gates, *Duty*, 492.

15. Michael Gordon and Bernard Trainor, *The Endgame: The Inside Story of the Struggle for Iraq, from George W. Bush to Barack Obama* (New York: Pantheon Books, 2012), 668.

16. Barack Obama, *A Promised Land* (New York: Crown, 2020), 323–325.

17. Chandrasekaran, *Little America*, 321.

18. President Obama on the Way Forward in Afghanistan, White House, https://obamawhitehouse.archives.gov/blog/2011/06/22/president-obama-way-forward-afghanistan, June 22, 2011.

19. Jeffrey Jones, "In U.S., Fears of Terrorism After Afghanistan Pullout Subside," Gallup, www.gallup.com, June 29, 2011.

20. "Islamic Emirate announcement on Obama's Plan to Withdraw US Troops" (2011) in *Offerings on the Occupation: The Islamic Emirates' Position, Messages, Announcements, and Interviews* (Islamic Emirate of Afghanistan Cultural Commission, 2012), 292.

21. Discussion with Ishaqzai tribal leader and in-law of Mansour, Kandahar, 2013.

22. Alissa Rubin and Rod Nordland, "Departing U.S. Envoy Sees progress in Afghanistan, and Pitfalls Ahead," New York Times, July 4, 2011.

23. Julie Ray and Rajesh Srinivasan, "Pakistanis More Sour on U.S. After Bin Laden Raid," Gallup Poll, www.news.gallup.com, May 20, 2011.

24. Spanta, *Afghanistan Politics*, 300.

25. Zach Constantino, "The India-Pakistan Rivalry in Afghanistan," United States Institute for Peace (December 2019).

26. Nazr Mohammed Mutmain, *Six Days with Taliban Leaders* (Kabul, Afgh.: Danish Publishing Community, 2019), 368.

27. Matthew Rosenberg, "U.S. Disrupts Afghans' Tack on Militants," *New York Times*, October 28, 2013.

28. Gates, *Duty*, 361. Chandrasekaran, *Little America*, 127.

29. Mutmain, *Six Days with Taliban Leaders*, 173.

30. Ibid., 175.

31. Ibid., 175.

32. Mutmain, *Six Days with Taliban Leaders*, 175.

33. Ibid., 175.

34. Ibid., 175.

35. Discussion with Ishaqzai tribal leader and in-law of Mansour, Kandahar, 2013. Discussion with former Taliban ambassador, Kabul, October 1, 2013. Discussion with Ishaqzai parliamentarian, Kabul, April 10, 2011. Discussion with Noorzai tribal leader, Kabul, April 22, 2014.

36. Discussion with Raees Baghrani, Kabul, April 11, 2014.

37. This same month the United States was embarrassed when another reputed Taliban contact turned out to be an imposter, having pretended to be Mullah Omar's new deputy, Mullah Mansour.

38. Steve Coll, *Directorate S: The C.I.A. and America's Secret Wars in Afghanistan and Pakistan* (New York: Penguin, 2018), 563–564.

39. Borhan Osman and Anand Gopal, "Taliban Views on a Future State," New York University, Center on International Cooperation, July 2016, 14–15.

40. Correspondence with Chris Kolenda, former Defense Department liaison to the peace talks, June 26, 2020.
41. Afghanistan Papers (www.washingtonpost.com): Interview with Ryan Crocker.
42. Correspondence with Chris Kolenda, former Defense Department liaison to the peace talks, June 26, 2020.
43. Michael Petrou, "Another Civil War?", *Maclean's*, June 27, 2011, 32–35.
44. Correspondence with Chris Kolenda, former Defense Department liaison to the peace talks, June 26, 2020.
45. Mutmain, *Six Days with Taliban Leaders*, 174.
46. Discussion with members of Taliban political commission, Doha, Qatar, August 26, 2019. Discussion with Maulali Ishaqzai, Kabul, August 1, 2019.
47. Borham Osman and Anand Gopal, "Taliban Views on a Future State," New York University, Center on International Cooperation, July 2016, 14.
48. Discussion with members of Taliban political commission, Doha, Qatar, August 26, 2019. Discussion with Maulali Ishaqzai, Kabul, August 1, 2019.
49. Discussion with former Taliban ambassador, Kabul, October 1, 2013.
50. Discussions at ISAF headquarters, Kabul, February to June 2013.
51. Coll, *Directorate S*, 636–637.
52. Interview with former Secretary of Defense Leon Panetta, OEF Study Group, 2016.

Chapter 15

1. "Special Forces; Remembering the Soldiers Who Died in Wardak," *Wall Street Journal*, August 8, 2011.
2. "The Insurgency in Afghanistan's Heartland," Crisis Group Asia Report No. 207, June 27, 2011, 17.
3. Discussion with Ismael Khan, Khost district governor, Washington, DC, April 12, 2012.
4. "Kabul's Day of Terror," *Guardian*, January 18, 2010.
5. "The Insurgency in Afghanistan's Heartland." Crisis Group Asia, 8.
6. David Montero, "US Drone Attacks Bombard Haqqani Network in Pakistan," *Christian Science Monitor*, September 15, 2010.
7. Qasim Nauman and Safdar Dawar, "Drone Strike in Pakistan Killed Senior Afghan Militant, Others," *Wall Street Journal*, June 12, 2014. "Pakistan Drone Strike Kills Top Haqqani Network Commander Maulawi Ahmed Jan at Islamic Seminary," CBS News, November 21, 2013. Bill Roggio, "Mullah Sangeen Zadran, Al Qaeda Commander Reported Killed in Drone Strike," *Long War Journal*, https://www.longwarjournal.org, Septepmber 6, 2013.
8. Paula Broadwell, *All In: The Education of General David Petraeus* (New York: Penguin, 2012), 324.
9. It was 3rd Battalion, 187th Infantry Regiment, and then 2nd Battalion, 2nd Infantry Regiment. Both operated in Andar and Deh Yak districts.
10. Paul Watson, "Behind the Lines with the Taliban," *Los Angeles Times*, January 11, 2009. Nir Rosen, "How We Lost the War We Won," *Rolling Stone* (October 30, 2008).
11. Rosen, "How We Lost the War We Won". Emily Winterbotham, "Legacies of Conflict: Healing Complexes and Moving Forward in Ghazni Province," AREU Case Study, October 2011, 18.
12. Watson, "Behind the Lines with the Taliban."
13. Winterbotham, "Legacies of Conflict," 18, 21.
14. Ibid., 25, 30.
15. Emal Habib, "Who Fights Whom in the Andar Uprising?," Afghan Analysts' Network, August 10, 2012.
16. M. Hassan Kakar, *A Political and Diplomatic History of Afghanistan, 1863–1901* (Boston: Brill, 2006), 34.
17. Discussion with Ghazni provincial councilman, Kabul, October 17, 2013.
18. Kakar, *A Political and Diplomatic History of Afghanistan, 1863–1901*, 89–95.
19. Fazl Rahman Muzhary, "One Land, Two Rules: Delivering Public Services in Insurgency-Affected Andar District in Ghazni Province," Afghan Analysts Network, www.afghanistan-analysts.org, June 13, 2019.

20. Discussion with Ghazni provincial councilman, Kabul, October 17, 2013.
21. Andar security shura, Andar district center, Ghazni, June 5, 2013. Discussion with Andar tribesman, Kabul, August 19, 2013. Rosen, "How We Lost the War We Won." Discussion with Governor Mohibullah Samimi, Kabul, October 19, 2013. Sebastien Trives, "Roots of the Insurgency in the Southeast," in *Decoding the New Taliban: Insights from the Afghan Field*, edited by Antonio Giustozzi (New York: Columbia University Press, 2009), 104.
22. Christoph Reuter and Borhan Younus, "The Return of the Taliban in Andar District: Ghazni," in *Decoding the New Taliban: Insights from the Afghan Field*, edited by Antonio Giustozzi (New York: Columbia University Press, 2009), 112, 116.
23. Discussion with Andar police sergeant (who worked in Andar from 2006 to 2012), Andar district center, Ghazni, September 29, 2013.
24. Watson, "Behind the Lines with the Taliban. Winterbotham, "Legacies of Conflict," 29. Nir Rosen, *Aftermath: Following the Bloodshed of America's Wars in the Muslim World* (New York: Nation Books, 2010), 445.
25. Jeffrey Stern, "Lost in the Land of the Taliban," *Esquire* (December 10, 2007).
26. "Taliban Leader Confirms Infighting and Vows Revenge," *Long War Journal*, www.longwarjournal.org/archives/2012/05/taliban_leader_confi.php, May 12, 2012. Anand Gopal, "Serious Leadership Rifts Emerge in Afghan Taliban," *CTC Sentinel* 5, no. 11, https://www.ctc.usma.edu/posts/serious-leadership-rifts-emerge-in-afghan-taliban, November 28, 2012. Discussion with Noorzai tribal leader, Kabul, March 8, 2014.
27. Discussion with Ghazni provincial council member from Andar, Kabul, October 17, 2013.
28. Discussion with Governor Mohibullah Samimi, Kabul, October 20, 2013.
29. Mullah Rahmatullah, "The Ghazni People's Uprising: Lessons and Teachings," written story, 2013.
30. Rosen, "How We Lost the War We Won."
31. Discussion with former governor Khayl Mohammed Husayni and Andar uprising leaders, ISAF headquarters, Kabul, August 26, 2013.
32. Reuter and Younus, "The Return of the Taliban in Andar District: Ghazni," 114.
33. Habib, "Who Fights Whom in the Andar Uprising?"
34. Rahmatullah, "The Ghazni People's Uprising."
35. Shura in Andar, Andar district center, Ghazni, September 29, 2013.
36. Habib, "Who Fights Whom in the Andar Uprising?"
37. Tufail Ahmad, "Anti-Taliban Uprisings Gaining Strength in Southeastern Afghanistan," Middle East Media Research Institute, August 8, 2012.
38. Discussion with Anti-Taliban movement post commander, Andar district center, Ghazni, September 29, 2013.
39. One story is that after the Taliban killed Rahmatullah's brother, they cut the dead body into pieces, and threw them in a field, breaking the rules of a proper Muslim burial. Discussion with Andar tribesman, Kabul, August 19, 2013.
40. Discussion with three anti-Taliban uprising commanders, Kabul, August 13, 2014.
41. Discussion with friend of Asadullah Khalid, June 12, 2013.
42. David Young, "Anatomy of a Tribal Uprising," AfPak Channel, September 12, 2012.
43. Andar security shura, Andar district center, Ghazni, June 5, 2013.
44. Discussion with Logar provincial governor, Arsala Jamal, Pul-e-Alam, Logar, June 5, 2013.
45. Shura in Andar, Andar district center, Ghazni, September 29, 2013. Rahmatullah, "The Ghazni People's Uprising."
46. Discussion with former governor Khayl Mohammed Husayni and Andar uprising leaders, ISAF headquarters, Kabul, August 26, 2013.
47. Discussion with former governor Khayl Mohammed Husayni, ISAF headquarters, Kabul, June 22, 2013.
48. Discussion with Ghazni provincial council member from Andar, Kabul, March 8, 2014.
49. Discussion with Anti-Taliban movement post commander, Andar district center, Ghazni, September 29, 2013.
50. There was a rumor that the Taliban had killed Ismael for stealing money and speaking with the United Nations but these turned out to be false. Discussion with 1st Battalion, 87th

Regiment, FOB Arian, Qara Bagh, Ghazni, June 5, 2013. Gopal, "Serious Leadership Rifts Emerge in Afghan Taliban."

51. Andar security shura, Andar district center, Ghazni, June 5, 2013.
52. Discussion with leading Ali Khel tribal leader from Muqor, Kabul, August 28, 2013.
53. Discussion with former governor Khayl Mohammed Husayni and Andar uprising leaders, ISAF headquarters, Kabul, August 26, 2013. Discussion with leading Ali Khel tribal leader from Muqor, Kabul, August 28, 2013.
54. Discussion with Ghazni provincial council member from Andar, Kabul, July 17, 2016.
55. Discussion with Kabul University professor from Andar tribe, Kabul, July 15, 2016. The professor spoke with Afghan soldiers fighting in Andar.
56. Discussion with Ghazni provincial council chair, Jami Jami, Kabul, February 18, 2014.
57. Discussion with three anti-Taliban uprising commanders, Kabul, August 13, 2014. This conversation was duly brought to the attention of the staff judge advocate for investigation and action. A year later, the uprising commander was killed in a firefight with the Taliban in Andar.
58. Discussion with three anti-Taliban uprising commanders, Kabul, August 13, 2014. See also Matthieu Aikins, "A US-backed Militia Runs Amok in Afghanistan," Al Jazeera, www.america. aljazeera.com, July 23, 2014.
59. Discussion with professional from Andar tribe, Kabul, March 2, 2016.
60. Discussion with Kabul University professor from Andar tribe, Kabul, March 2, 2016.
61. Discussion with Ghazni provincial council member from Andar, Kabul, July 17, 2016.
62. In February 2016, some local people would be upset enough to take part in a protest in Ghazni City against the uprising fighters. Taliban were there too and may have helped organize the protest but the grievances that brought average people were real. When the Taliban executed 11 police and soldiers a few months later, no protests happened. Discussion with Kabul University professor, Kabul, March 2, 2016.

Chapter 16

1. Discussion with Kandahar NDS director, Kandahar, June 18, 2014.
2. Ian Livingston and Michael O'Hanlon, "Afghanistan Index," Brookings Institute, November 30, 2011, 8.
3. Discussion with Dai al-Haq, Deputy Minister of Hajj and Endowments, Kabul, March 15, 2014.
4. Discussion with Fawzia Koofi and Amarullah Saleh, Kabul, March 16, 2014.
5. Discussion with Dai al-Haq, March 15, 2014.
6. "Reconstructing the Afghan National Defense and Security Forces: Lessons from the U.S. Experience in Afghanistan," Special Inspector General for Afghanistan Reconstruction (September 2017), 79.
7. Antonio Giustozzi and Artemy Kalinovsky, Missionaries of Modernity: Advisory Missions and the Struggle for Hegemony in Afghanistan and Beyond (London: Hurst, 2016), 292.
8. "Reconstructing the Afghan National Defense and Security Forces," 116.
9. Discussion with Regional Command Southwest, Camp Leatherneck, May 28, 2013.
10. Giustozzi and Kalinovsky, Missionaries of Modernity, 294.
11. Discussion with Colonel Gallahue, Logar, June 5, 2013. Discussion with Lieutenant Colonel Hadley, Pul-e-Alam, Logar, June 4, 2013.
12. Discussion with Brigadier General Burke Whitman, Officer in Charge, Police Advisory Group, Kabul, July 1, 2014.
13. Discussion with Ashraf Ghani and Deputy Minister of the Interior for Policy Siddiq Siddique, Kabul, June 2, 2013.
14. Discussion with Kandahar police chief Abdul Razziq, Kandahar police headquarters, June 18, 2014.
15. Steve Coll, "Looking for Mullah Omar," New Yorker, January 23, 2012.
16. Discussion with former Helmand police chief Baqizoi, Kabul, July 27, 2014.
17. Aoliya Atrafi, "Taliban Territory: Life in Afghanistan under the Militants," BBC, June 8, 2017.
18. The Alikozai ability to hold Arghandab until the death of Mullah Naqib in 2007 and the Andar uprising of 2012 are two other examples.

19. "A Survey of the Afghan People in 2014," Asia Foundation, asiafoundation.org, 2014, 45, 46, 47, 197. Sample size was 9,200.
20. "A Survey of the Afghan People in 2012," Asia Foundation, asiafoundation.org, 2012, 60. Sympathy for the Taliban was primarily Pashtun. Surveys showed much higher levels of support for the Taliban in Pashtun provinces. The Taliban's inspiration was limited by ethnic boundaries. That, however, does not change the fact that the Taliban consistently held a critical mass of support among the Pashtuns. These numbers go a long way toward explaining why the Taliban could find at least one or two communities in any district willing to shelter or join them. Afghans also report that they have very high confidence in their religious leaders, between 2011 and 2014 roughly tied with the media and community shuras for the top rank, and far higher than confidence in ministers, NGOs, and parliament. "A Survey of the Afghan People in 2014," Asia Foundation, asiafoundation.org, 2014, 89.
21. Interview with Taliban religious leader from Paktiya, Survey of Taliban, August 2014.
22. Interview with Taliban religious leader from Laghman, Survey of Taliban, August 2014.
23. Interview with Taliban commander from Zabul, Survey of Taliban, August 2014.
24. Mullah Omar's 2011 Loy Eid message in *Offerings on the Occupation: The Islamic Emirates' Position, Messages, Announcements, and Interviews* (Islamic Emirate of Afghanistan Cultural Commission, 2012), 340.
25. Discussion with Abdul Hakim Mujahed, former Taliban ambassador to the United Nations, Kabul, January 18, 2014.
26. Discussion with Maulawi Mohammed Noor, Kandahar, December 24, 2018.
27. Remarks by Governor Mohammed Atta, Governors' conference, Kabul, June 13, 2013.
28. Discussion with Abdul Bari Barakzai, Kabul, February 26, 2014.
29. Discussion with Shafi Afghan, FOB Walton, Kandahar, November 12, 2013.
30. Discussion with Kandahar Police Chief Abdul Razziq, Kandahar police headquarters, June 18, 2014.
31. Andrew Garfield and Alicia Boyd, "Understanding Afghan Insurgents: Motivations, Goals, and the Reconciliation and Reintegration Process," Foreign Policy Research Institute, July 2013, 46–47.
32. Theo Farrell and Antonio Giustozzi, "The Taliban at War: Inside the Helmand Insurgency, 2004–2012," *International Affairs* 89, no. 4 (2013): 853. The study interviewed 53 Taliban commanders and fighters in Helmand and another 49 interviews with Taliban from elsewhere in Afghanistan.
33. Ibid.
34. Hollings Conference, Istanbul, August 6, 2015.
35. Ashley Jackson, "Perspectives on Peace from Taliban Areas of Afghanistan," Special Report, no. 229, United States Institute of Peace, May 2019, 4, 12–13; interviews with Taliban were conducted between October 2018 and February 2019.
36. Jackson, "Perspectives on Peace from Taliban Areas of Afghanistan," 13.
37. Olivier Roy, *The Failure of Political Islam* (Cambridge, MA: Harvard University Press, 1998), 158–159.
38. Luke Mogelson, "Which Way Did the Taliban Go?," *New York Times Magazine* (January 20, 2013), 33.
39. Antonio Giustozzi, "The Struggle to Create an Afghan National Army," manuscript, February 2014, 203.
40. Giustozzi, "The Struggle to Create an Afghan National Army," 203.
41. Kandahar Survey Report, Human Terrain System, Glevum Associates, March 2010, 35.
42. Robert Zaman and Abdul Hadi Khalid, "Trends of Radicalization among the Ranks of the Afghan National Police," Afghan Institute for Strategic Studies, November 2015, 15–17.
43. Zaman and Khalid, "Trends of Radicalization," 15–17, 19–20.
44. Discussion with Dr. Attaullah Wahidyar, Kabul, December 12, 2018.
45. Discussion with Kakar tribal leader, FOB Walton, Kandahar, November 9, 2013.
46. Bill Roggio and Lisa Lundquist, "Green-on-Blue Attacks in Afghanistan: The Data," www.longwarjournal.org, January 30, 2015. http://www.longwarjournal.org/archives/2012/08/green-on-blue_attack.php. Report on Progress Toward Stability and Security in Afghanistan (Department of Defense, December 2012), 34.

47. Roggio and Lundquist, "Green-on-Blue Attacks in Afghanistan."
48. Ibid.
49. Zaman and Khalid, "Trends of Radicalization," 21.
50. Matthew Rosenberg, "An Afghan Soldier's Journey From Ally to Enemy of America," *New York Times*, January 3, 2013.
51. Emma Graham-Harrison, "Afghan Jailer Helps NATO Soldier's Killer Escape," *Guardian*, July 15, 2013. Jonathan Addleton, *The Dust of Kandahar* (Annapolis, MD: Naval Institute Press, 2016).
52. Zaman and Khalid, "Trends of Radicalization," 18.
53. Discussion with police precinct commander, Kandahar City, June 19, 2014.
54. Roggio and Lundquist, "Green-on-Blue Attacks in Afghanistan."
55. Maggie Ybarra, "Afghan Soldier Who Killed U.S. General Was Disgruntled, Not Taliban: Report," *Washington Times*, December 4, 2014.
56. Conference on Afghanistan, Istanbul, August 6, 2015.
57. Twelve Democrat Members of the House of Representatives, Letter to Barack Obama regarding protection of women's rights, July 15, 2013, www.ebjohnson.house.gov (website of Congresswoman Eddie Bernice Johnson).
58. A July 2013 law unfortunately reduced seats for women from 25 to 20 percent of seats in the provincial councils. "A Survey of the Afghan People in 2013," Asia Foundation, 2013, 66.
59. "A Survey of the Afghan People in 2013," Asia Foundation, 2013, 105.
60. "A Survey of the Afghan People in 2014," Asia Foundation, 2014, 60.
61. Human Development Index, United Nations Development Programme, hdr.undp.org, 2019.
62. "A Survey of the Afghan People: Afghanistan in 2019," Asia Foundation, 2019, 223.
63. "A Survey of the Afghan People in 2013," Asia Foundation, 2013, 66.
64. "A Survey of the Afghan People in 2014," Asia Foundation, 2014, 60.
65. Alex Strick von Linschoten and Thomas Kuehn, *The Taliban Reader* (London: Hurst, 2018), 345.
66. Atia Abawi, "Afghanistan 'Rape' Law Puts Women's Rights Front and Center," CNN, www.cnn.com, April 6, 2009.
67. Fawzia Koofi, "Where Afghan Law Fails Women," Al Jazeera, www.aljazeera.com, January 1, 2015.
68. Torunn Wimpelmann, *The Pitfalls of Protection: Gender, Violence, and Power in Afghanistan* (Berkeley: University of California Press, 2017), 68.
69. Ibid., 68.
70. Ibid., 67.
71. Ibid., 67.
72. Ibid., 77.
73. Meeting with Afghan women leaders, ISAF headquarters, Kabul, September 5, 2013.
74. Azam Ahmed and Habib Zahori, "Despite West's Efforts, Afghan Youths Cling to Traditional Ways," *New York Times*, July 31, 2013.
75. The shrine is named for a warrior who helped bring Islam to Afghanistan.
76. Alissa Rubin, "Women's War: Flawed Justice After a Mob Killed an Afghan Woman," *New York Times*, December 26, 2015.
77. Ibid.
78. Ibid.
79. Rangin Dadfar Spanta, *Afghanistan Politics: Sense of the Time* (Kabul, Afgh.: Aazem Publications, 2017), 506.
80. Ibid., 507.
81. Ibid., 498, 509.
82. Ibid., 513.
83. Ibid., 558–561.
84. Remarks by Minister of Defense Bismullah Khan and Governor Mohammed Atta, Governors' conference, Kabul, June 13, 2013.
85. Discussion with Dai al-Haq, Deputy Minister of Hajj and Endowments (Panjshiri leader), Kabul, November 27, 2013.
86. Discussion with Karim Khalili, Kabul, August 4, 2013.

87. Meeting with Afghan women leaders, ISAF headquarters, Kabul, September 5, 2013.
88. Discussion with Fawzia Koofi, Kabul, January 20, 2014.
89. Discussion with former provincial governor, Kabul, March 3, 2014.
90. Discussion with member of Wolesi Jirga from Badakhshan, Kabul, October 2, 2013.
91. Susan Rice, *Tough Love: My Story of the Things Worth Fighting For* (New York: Simon & Schuster, 2019), 391.
92. Discussion with member of parliament, Kabul, February 9, 2014. The member was a committee head and important within the Tajik political hierarchy.
93. See David Edwards, *Heroes of the Age: Moral Fault Lines on the Afghan Frontier* (Berkeley: University of California Press, 1996), 78–125.
94. Discussion with Haji Hafizullah, former Helmand provincial governor and Hezb Islami leader, Kabul, November 28, 2013.
95. Discussion with Hezb Islami leader, Kabul, February 7, 2014.
96. Spanta, *Afghanistan Politics*, 562.

Chapter 17

1. ISAF meeting, Kabul, June 10, 2013.
2. "U.S. Considers Faster Pullout in Afghanistan," *New York Times*, July 9, 2013. "Weighing a Quicker Exit from Afghanistan," *New York Times*, July 10, 2013. Matthew Rosenberg, "Impasse with Afghanistan Raises Prospect of Total U.S. Withdrawal in 2014," *New York Times*, October 4, 2013.
3. Abdul Hai Mutmain, *Mullah Mohammed Omar, Taliban and Afghanistan* (Kabul: Afghan Publishing Community, 2017), 337. Steve Coll, "Looking for Mullah Omar," *New Yorker*, January 23, 2012.
4. I heard this story in the 2019 US-Taliban peace talks in Doha, Qatar.
5. Office of Director of National Intelligence website: Letter from Osama bin Laden to unknown recipient regarding Afghanistan, Captured Osama bin Laden files from Abbottabad, undated, https://www.dni.gov/index.php/features/bin-laden-s-bookshelf?start=3. This letter repeatedly refers to ten years of war in Afghanistan, meaning it was written in 2011. It also refers to the Islamic Emirate and asks the recipient not to appoint a new leader, strongly implying the recipient was Mullah Omar.
6. Jonathan Addleton, *The Dust of Kandahar* (Annapolis, MD: Naval Institute Press, 2016).
7. A.H. Mutmain, *Mullah Mohammed Omar*, 337–338.
8. "Taliban: There Is Trust in the Agreement and the Way Is Not Shut," *BBC Pashto*, August 7, 2015.
9. Discussion with Raees Baghrani, Kabul, February 10, 2014.
10. Discussion with US Marine advisors, Camp Bastion, Helmand, October 10, 2013.
11. Discussion with Matt Treadgold, political officer, Sangin district support team, November 20, 2013. Treadgold was the last US official on a district support team in Afghanistan.
12. Angar had been police chief in 2010 and 2011 and then transferred. When northern Helmand went bad, the Ministry of the Interior sent Angar back.
13. Discussion with Omar Jan, Nad Ali police chief, October 5, 2013. Discussion with Mohammed Fahim, Gereshk district governor, September 23, 2013. Discussion with Helmand NDS, Camp Bastion, October 10, 2013. Discussion with Provincial Police Chief Hakim Angar, Camp Bastion, October 10, 2013.
14. Discussion with Malim Mir Wali, Kabul, October 9, 2013.
15. His father had actually been Pashtun but his mother was Tajik and Abdullah had spent his life in the Panjshir Valley and Kabul. Everyone thought of him as a Tajik.
16. Discussion with Member of Parliament Balakarzai, Kabul, March 2, 2014.
17. Discussion and Fawzia Koofi and Amarullah Saleh, Kabul, March 16, 2014.
18. Discussion with Amarullah Saleh and Hanif Atmar, Kabul, March 16, 2014.
19. The one Tajik with a Pashtun candidate—Ahmed Zia Massoud, brother of Ahmed Shah, who was with Ghani—won over few Tajiks.
20. Survey of religious and Taliban opinion, June 14 to July 7, 2014.
21. Discussion with Kandahar police chief Abdul Razziq, Kandahar, June 18, 2014.

22. Discussion with Alizai tribal leader, Lashkar Gah, June 4, 2014. Discussion with Noorzai tribal leader, Kabul, April 8, 2014.
23. Discussion with Helmand provincial peace council executive, Lashkar Gah, June 7, 2014.
24. President Barack Obama, Statement by the President on Afghanistan, Office of the Press Secretary, The White House, https://obamawhitehouse.archives.gov/the-press-office/2014/05/27/statement-president-afghanistan, May 27, 2014.
25. Meeting between Ashraf Ghani and Western Ambassadors, Kabul, June 15, 2013.
26. Rangin Dadfar Spanta, *Afghanistan Politics: Sense of the Time* (Kabul, Afgh.: Aazem Publications, 2017), 294.
27. Discussion with Ashraf Ghani, Kabul, August 20, 2017.
28. Discussion with Pashtun member of the Wolesi Jirga, Kabul, May 28, 2014.
29. Discussion with Minister Yusef Pashtun, Kabul, April 8, 2014.
30. Discussion with Maulali Ishaqzai, Kabul August 14, 2014. Discussion with southern Helmand tribal leaders, Kabul, August 18, 2014.
31. Discussion with pro-Ghani tribal leader in Helmand, June 5, 2014. Discussion with pro-Ghani tribal leader in Ghazni, June 2, 2014. Discussion with pro-Ghani youth leader, Kabul, July 19, 2014.
32. Nazr Mohammed Mutmain, *Six Days with Taliban Leaders* (Kabul, Afgh.: Danish Publishing Community, 2019), 82. Discussion with Abdul Salam Zaeef, Kabul, March 20, 2018.
33. Discussion with religious scholar from Paktiya, Kabul, June 23, 2014.
34. Discussion with pro-Abdullah Meshrano Jirga senator, Kabul, June 25, 2014.
35. At that time I was still in Kabul with General Dunford. My job during the election was to monitor what various political leaders were saying and thinking about the political crisis, meeting with actors from all sides and especially trying to work out how army and police commanders might align themselves.
36. Discussion with Abdullah campaign member, Kabul, June 27, 2014.
37. Discussion with pro-Abdullah member of parliament and campaign member, Kabul, July 1, 2014.
38. Ibid.
39. Discussion with Fawzia Koofi, Kabul, July 12, 2014.
40. Discussion with parliamentarian (member of the Abdullah campaign), Kabul, July 8, 2014. Discussion with parliamentarian (member of the Ghani campaign), Kabul, July 8, 2014.
41. Discussion with parliamentarian (member of Abdullah's inner circle), Kabul, July 9, 2014.
42. Discussion with relative of Ahmed Shah Massoud, Kabul, August 5, 2014.
43. Discussion with parliamentarian (member of the Ghani campaign), Kabul, July 8, 2014.
44. Discussion with Tajik religious scholar Dai al Haq (member of the Abdullah campaign), Kabul, July 9, 2014.
45. Discussion with Fawzia Koofi, Kabul, July 12, 2014.
46. John Kerry, *Every Day is Extra* (New York: Simon & Schuster, 2018), 422.
47. Kerry, *Every Day is Extra*, 422.
48. Interview with Taliban commander from Ghazni, Survey of religious and Taliban opinion, July 20 to August 20, 2014.
49. Taliban commander from Paktiya, Survey of religious and Taliban opinion, July 20 to August 20, 2014.
50. Discussion with Maulali Ishaqzai, Kabul, August 14, 2014.
51. Discussion with Maulali Ishaqzai, Kabul, August 14, 2014. Discussion with southern Helmand tribal leaders, Kabul, August 18, 2014.
52. Discussion with provincial police chief Abdul Razziq, Kandahar, June 17, 2014.
53. Interview with Taliban religious leader from Ghazni, Survey of Taliban, August 2014.
54. N.M. Mutmain, *Six Days with Taliban Leaders*, 57. Dilawar was a member of the Taliban political commission in Doha from 2013 onward.
55. Discussion with district police chief Omar Jan, Lashkar Gah, June 5, 2014.
56. Conversation with Helmand provincial chief of police, Lashkar Gah, June 5, 2014. Conversation with Afghan Army 215 Corps staff, Camp Bastion, June 4, 2014.
57. Presentation by Provincial Police Chief Hakim Angar, Camp Bastion, October 10, 2013.
58. Discussion at Regional Command South West, Camp Bastion, July 2, 2014.

59. Azam Ahmed, "Afghan Army Struggles in District Under Siege," *New York Times*, September 11, 2013.
60. Discussion with former Helmand police chief Baqizoi, Kabul, July 27, 2014.
61. Discussion with General Malouk, Camp Bastion, Helmand, June 4, 2014.
62. Remarks by Minister of Defense Bismullah Khan, Governors' Conference, Kabul, June 13, 2013.
63. Discussion with Alikozai tribal leaders, FOB Nolay, Sangin, August 9, 2014.
64. Interview with Taliban religious leader from Helmand, Survey of Taliban, July 20 to August 20, 2014.
65. Discussion with Helmand security official, July 10, 2014.
66. Survey of religious and Taliban opinion, July 20 to August 20, 2014.
67. Discussion with Alikozai local police post commander, FOB Nolay, Sangin, August 9, 2014. Discussion with Afghan local police commander, FOB Nolay, Sangin, August 9, 2014.
68. Discussion with Alikozai Afghan local police commander, FOB Nolay, Sangin, August 9, 2014.
69. Ibid.
70. Taliban commander in Helmand, Survey of religious and Taliban opinion, July 20 to August 20, 2014.
71. Commanders' conference, ISAF headquarters, Kabul, July 26, 2014.
72. Discussion with Alikozai Afghan local police commander, FOB Nolay, Sangin, August 9, 2014.
73. Discussion with Helmand security officials, telephone, June 30, 2014.
74. *BBC Pashto* news reports, June 28, 2014.
75. A week after the Sangin battle had begun, the Taliban launched a secondary offensive against Marjah and Gereshk in central Helmand. At least 300 Taliban were involved. The local police in Marjah and Gereshk were well supplied and the tribal leaders were very active. Coordination with the Afghan army, at this point, was still good. Together, they repulsed the Taliban attack without losing any ground. Taliban attacks in Garmser similarly gained little ground.
76. Taliban commander in Helmand, Survey of religious and Taliban opinion, July 20 to August 20, 2014.
77. Discussion with former Helmand police chief Baqizoi, Kabul, July 27, 2014.
78. Discussion with Afghan local police commander, FOB Nolay, Sangin, August 9, 2014.
79. Discussion with police officer, FOB Nolay, Sangin, August 9, 2014.
80. Discussion with Alikozai and Barakzai tribal leaders, FOB Nolay, Sangin, August 9, 2014.
81. Discussion with Helmand police chief Juma Gul Popalzai, FOB Nolay, Sangin, August 9, 2014.
82. Discussion with police officer, FOB Nolay, Sangin, August 9, 2014.
83. Discussion with Zharey tribal leader, telephone, August 1, 2014. Discussion with Alikozai tribal leader from Kandahar, telephone, August 1, 2014. Discussion with Ishaqzai tribal leader from Kandahar, telephone, August 1, 2014.
84. Interview with two Taliban commanders and a Taliban religious leader in Kandahar, Survey of religious Taliban opinion, June 15 to July 7, 2014.
85. Two Taliban commanders in Kandahar, Survey of religious and Taliban opinion, July 20 to August 20, 2014. Taliban commander and Taliban religious leader in Kandahar, Survey of religious Taliban opinion, June 15 to July 7, 2014.
86. Two Taliban commanders in Kandahar, Survey of religious and Taliban opinion, July 20, to August 20, 2014.
87. Two Taliban commanders in Kandahar, Survey of religious and Taliban opinion, July 20 to August 20, 2014.
88. Telephone conversation with Panjwai tribal leader and businessman, August 1, 2014.
89. Discussion with 3rd Battalion, 61st Cavalry Regiment, FOB Passab, Zharey, July 28, 2014.
90. Discussion with 3rd Battalion, 61st Cavalry Regiment, FOB Passab, Zharey, July 28, 2014.
91. Antonio Giustozzi, *The Taliban at War* (New York: Oxford University Press, 2019), 190.
92. Discussion with advisor for Police Chief Abdul Razziq, phone conversation, August 5, 2014.
93. Survey of religious and Taliban opinion, July 25 to August 14, 2014.

94. Discussion with 3rd Battalion, 61st Cavalry Regiment, FOB Passab, Zharey, July 28, 2014.
95. Interview with Taliban commander from Helmand, Survey of religious and Taliban opinion, July 20 to August 20, 2014.
96. Interview with Taliban religious leader from Nangarhar, Survey of Taliban, August 2014.
97. Protection of Civilians in Armed Conflict, UNAMA 2014 Report, February 2015.
98. Protection of Civilians in Armed Conflict, UNAMA 2014 Report, February 2015, 51–55.
99. Declan Walsh, "Powerful Police Chief Puts Fear in Taliban and Their Enemies," *New York Times*, November 8, 2014.
100. Aazem Arash, "Baghlan Police Chief: No Mercy for Taliban," *Tolo News*, August 13, 2014. Upon questioning, Tolo Television could produce no evidence that Razziq made this statement but he still may have done so.
101. "Kandahar: Life around the Home of Mullah Mohammed Omar," *BBC Pashto*, www.bbc.co.uk/pashto, November 15, 2014.

Chapter 18

1. George Packer, "The Theorist in the Palace," *New Yorker*, July 4, 2016.
2. Ashraf Ghani and Clare Lockhart, *Fixing Failed States: A Framework for Rebuilding a Fractured World* (New York: Oxford University Press, 2009), 4.
3. Discussion with US logistics advisor, Kabul, March 2, 2016.
4. "Conquering Chaos," *Economist*, January 7, 2017, 46. Security and Stability in Afghanistan, 1225 Report, US Department of Defense, December 2015, 81.
5. A Survey of the Afghan People, Asia Foundation, 2015. A Survey of the Afghan People, Asia Foundation, 2016, 18, 103–104, 126.
6. Borhan Osman, "Bourgeois Jihad: Why Young, Middle-Class Afghans Join the Islamic State," United States Institute of Peace (June 2020): 8.
7. Najibullah Quraishi, "ISIS in Afghanistan," FRONTLINE, https://www.pbs.org/wgbh/frontline/film/isis-in-afghanistan/transcript/, November 17, 2015.
8. Casey Garret Johnson, "The Rise and Stall of the Islamic State in Afghanistan," United States Institute of Peace Special Report, November 2016, 4.
9. Ibid.
10. Daoud Azimi, "Why Do the Afghan Taliban 'Special Forces' Fight against the Islamic State?," *BBC Pashto*, December 18, 2015.
11. Nangarhar district governor and district police chief meeting, FOB Fenty, Nangarhar, September 23, 2013.
12. Discussion with Governor Attaullah Ludin, Nangarhar, April 19, 2014.
13. Antonio Giustozzi, *The Islamic State in Khorasan: Afghanistan, Pakistan and the New Central Asian Jihad* (London: Hurst, 2018), 139–145.
14. Quraishi, "ISIS in Afghanistan."
15. Discussion with Tactical Advisory and Assist Command East, FOB Fenty, Jalalabad, March 3, 2016; VOA Pashto newscast, www.pashtovoa.com, July 2, 2015. Gordon Lubold, "Airstrikes Said to Hit al Qaeda Leaders," *Wall Street Journal*, October 27, 2016. Johnson, "The Rise and Stall of the Islamic State in Afghanistan," 2, 5.
16. Azimi, "Why Do the Afghan Taliban 'Special Forces' Fight against the Islamic State?"
17. Discussion with Tactical Advisory and Assist Command East, FOB Fenty, Jalalabad, March 3, 2016. Azimi, "Why Do the Afghan Taliban 'Special Forces' Fight against the Islamic State?". Johnson, "The Rise and Stall of the Islamic State in Afghanistan," 12.
18. Giustozzi, *The Islamic State in Khorasan*, 56.
19. Johnson, "The Rise and Stall of the Islamic State in Afghanistan," 2.
20. Ibid., 13.
21. Discussion with members of Taliban political commission, Doha, Qatar, August 26, 2019. Discussion with Maulali Ishaqzai, Kabul, August 1, 2019.
22. Borham Osman and Anand Gopal, "Taliban Views on a Future State," New York University, Center on International Cooperation, July 2016, 14.
23. Barnett Rubin, "What Could Mullah Mohammad Omar's Death Mean for the Taliban Talks?," *New Yorker*, July 29, 2015.

24. Margharita Stancati, "Taliban Confirms Death of Mullah Omar," *Wall Street Journal*, July 1, 2015; Abdul Hai Mutmain, *Mullah Mohammed Omar, Taliban and Afghanistan* (Kabul: Afghan Publishing Community, 2017), 342.
25. Barnett Rubin, "What Could Mullah Mohammad Omar's Death Mean for the Taliban Talks?," *New Yorker*, July 29, 2015.
26. *VOA Pashto* newscast, September 5, 2015.
27. "The Taliban New Leader's Spoken Message, 'Jihad Will Continue,'" *BBC Pashto*, August 1, 2015.
28. "Mullah Omar's Brother and Son Swore Allegiance to Mullah Mansour," *Pashto VOA*, www.pashtovoa.com, September 16, 2015.
29. During this time, Zakir was rumored to have gone to live in northern Helmand. He supposedly stopped leading anything and was not commanding Taliban operations in Helmand, which fell under Manan.
30. Azimi, "Why Do the Afghan Taliban "Special Forces" Fight against the Islamic State?"
31. Sami Yousafzai, "The Cruelest Taliban," *Daily Beast*, www.thedailybeast.com, February 11, 2016.
32. Discussion with Kabul University professor, Kabul, March 2, 2016.
33. Discussion with Deputy Minister of the Interior Ayub Salangi, Kabul, August 23, 2015.
34. A Survey of the Afghan People, Asia Foundation, 2016, 51.
35. Analysis of International Intervention to Train, Advise, and Assist Afghan National Police: A Four Year Case Study in Kunduz, Cooperation for Peace and Unity, May 29, 2016.
36. Niels Terpstra, "Rebel Governance, Rebel Legitimacy, and External Intervention: Assessing Three Phases of Taliban Rule in Afghanistan," *Small Wars & Insurgencies* 31, no. 6 (May 2020). Quoted interview is from 2018 but would appear relevant to 2015.
37. Discussion with leader of human rights NGO from Kunduz, Kabul, April 3, 2013.
38. Joseph Goldstein, "A Taliban Prize, Seized in a Few Hours after Years of Strategy," *New York Times*, October 1, 2015.
39. "Unhappy Anniversary: Afghanistan and a Resurgent Taliban," *Economist*, October 3, 2015.
40. Analysis of International Intervention to Train, Advise and Assist Afghan National Police, 34–36.
41. "Saleh: Weakness in Leadership."
42. "Saleh: Weakness in Leadership."
43. Conversation with General Abdul Hamid, Kandahar, December 21, 2018.
44. Jessica Donati, *Eagle Down: The Last Special Forces Fighting the Forever War* (New York: Public Affairs, 2021), 50–120.
45. Security and Stability in Afghanistan, 1225 Report, US Department of Defense, December 2015, 60. Mujib Mashal and Fahim Abed, "Afghan Forces, Their Numbers Dwindling Sharply, Face a Resurgent Taliban," *New York Times*, October 13, 2016.
46. Donati, *Eagle Down*, 50–120.
47. CENTCOM redacted report on Kunduz, https://www.centcom.mil/MEDIA/PRESS-RELEASES/Press-Release-View/Article/904574/april-29-centcom-releases-investigation-into-airstrike-on-doctors-without-borde/, April 29, 2016.
48. Matthieu Aikins, "Doctors with Enemies: Did Afghan Forces Target the M.S.F. Hospital?", New York Times Magazine, May 7, 2016.
49. Ibid.
50. A Survey of the Afghan People, Asia Foundation, 2016, 41.
51. Phone conversation with civil society professional from Kandahar, March 16, 2016.
52. Mullah Idris led this attack. His men seriously wounded police chief engineer Lutfullah and killed one of the leaders of the uprising. The road from Andar to Ghazni city was then choked off. Total numbers of local police and uprising fighters dropped from 450 to 160. Lutfullah had to go to India for medical care. A key victory was Idris's ambush of an army foray into his territory. His men killed roughly 15 soldiers and took all their equipment. The victory stunned government supporters and allowed Idris to take more ground. By early autumn, district governor Disewal and the local police and uprising fighters controlled at best a third of the district. When Kunduz fell, 1,000 Taliban, under Idris, assaulted Ghazni city. Unlike Kunduz, the Afghan army corps responsible for Ghazni, under General Yaftali, responded

rapidly and with the help of a few US air strikes managed to defend the town. Like Kunduz, the provincial capital was now surrounded. Phone conversation with Ghazni provincial council member, October 29, 2015. Discussion with Ghazni provincial council member from Andar, Kabul, July 17, 2016.

53. Joseph Goldstein and Taimoor Shah, "Taliban Strike Crucial District in Afghanistan," *New York Times*, June 18, 2015. In 2014, the Taliban had basically captured northern Helmand. In the first months of the 2015 fighting season, they mopped up much of what remained, overrunning the Nowzad and Musa Qala district centers and completely besieging the Sangin and Kajaki district centers. The Nowzad district center fell in May. Musa Qala fell in August. The government maintained detachments nearby until February 2016 when it became too hard. The Sangin district center remained under siege. Government forces at the Kajaki dam were cut off from the south.

54. Discussion with Gul Mullah, Marjah tribal leader, Lashkar Gah, June 6, 2014.

55. Phone conversation with Helmand provincial security official, November 3, 2015.

56. Conversation with Omar Jan, Nad Ali police chief, March 2, 2016.

57. Camp Bastion was in the desert outside Lashkar Gah's defensive rings. Thus neither the advisors nor the army leaders were in a good position to command. They were too far away to understand what was happening on the front line or to coordinate with the governor and provincial police chief in Lashkar Gah. Donati, *Eagle Down*, 126.

58. Phone conversation with Ayub Omar, December 11, 2015.

59. Discussion with Gul Mullah, Marjah tribal leader, Lashkar Gah, June 6, 2014.

60. Discussion with Gul Mohammed, Marjah tribal leader, Kabul, November 25, 2013.

61. Interview with Mullah Abdur Rahim Manan, *al-Samoud Magazine*, November 2016.

62. Ibid.

63. She herself had been disillusioned with democracy in 2014 but was always adept at shifting her position.

64. Meeting with Maulali Ishaqzai from Kandahar, Kabul, December 14, 2018.

65. Ibid.

66. Interviews with four Taliban commanders from Kandahar and Helmand, December 2018.

67. Rahmatullah Amiri, "Helmand (2): The Chain of Chiefdoms Unravels," Afghan Analysts Network, www.afghanistan-analysts.org/helmand-2-the-chain-of-chiefdoms-unravels, March 11, 2016.

68. Telephone conversation with Helmand provincial security official, July 16, 2016.

69. Police only entered the desert settlements for brief raids. Taliban checkpoints controlled movement. The Taliban based their cadres, at least partly composed of outside fighters, in the settlements to provide security and lay IEDs in the canal zones.

70. Discussion with Omar Jan, Nad Ali police chief, Lashkar Gah, June 6, 2014.

71. Discussion with Gul Mohammed, Marjah tribal leader, Kabul, February 24, 2014.

72. "The Political Economy of the Dashte," Coffey International Development, August 2013, 55.

73. Babaji was a perennial headache for the government. The southern part of the community was Barakzai, living on fertile soil irrigated by the Helmand River, strongly against the Taliban. The northern part was a mixed population of immigrants, many poor and landless, occupying drier land closer to the desert, forbidden from drawing water from canals. They conflicted with the land-owning Barakzai tribe, who had tried to kick them off the land. The mixed population had long supported the Taliban. The government defenses and posts were in this northern community, edging right up against the Taliban desert settlements. Phone conversation with Helmand security official, November 3, 2015. Discussion with Emile Simpson, Arlington, VA, March 11, 2016. Michael Martin, *An Intimate War* (London: Hurst Publishers, 2014). Amiri, "Helmand (2)."

74. Discussion with Gereshk district governor, Kabul, December 10, 2018.

75. Discussion with Nad Ali police captain, Lashkar Gah, December 27, 2018.

76. VOA Pashto, October 18, 2015. Conversation with Omar Jan, Nad Ali police chief, March 3, 2016.

77. Phone conversation with Helmand security official, November 3, 2015.

78. Discussion with Nad Ali police captain, Lashkar Gah, December 27, 2018.

79. Conversation with Omar Jan, Nad Ali police chief, March 2, 2016. Phone conversation with Helmand security official, November 3, 2015.
80. Telephone conversation with Helmand security official, November 3, 2015.
81. Discussion with Gereshk district governor, Kabul, December 10, 2018.
82. Conversation with Omar Jan, Nad Ali police chief, March 2, 2016.
83. Phone conversation with Gul Mullah, March 8, 2016. Conversation with Omar Jan, Nad Ali police chief, March 2, 2016. Phone conversation with district governor Ayub Omar, December 11, 2015.
84. Azizullah Popal, "Taliban Capture Many Areas of Marjah District," *VOA Pashto*, November 7, 2015.
85. Interviews with four Taliban commanders from Kandahar and Helmand, December 2018.
86. Telephone conversation with Helmand security official, November 3, 2015. Correspondence with US security evaluation team, December 20, 2015. Jessica Donati, *Eagle Down*, 126.
87. Sune Engel Rasmussen, "First Helmand, Then Afghanistan," *Foreign Policy*, September 21, 2016.
88. The army corps was down to 11,200 of 18,000 total soldiers, the police to 4,900 out of 8,000 men and the local police to 1,200 of 2,400. According to provincial council chairman, 1,200 police and soldiers were killed or wounded in October and November alone.
89. A handful of British advisors arrived in Bastion shortly thereafter as well.
90. Discussion with Garmser district governor, Kabul, June 27, 2017.
91. Phone conversation with high-ranking Helmand security official, July 16, 2016.
92. Discussion with Kabul University professor from Andar tribe, Kabul, July 15, 2016.
93. Discussion with Garmser district governor, Kabul, June 27, 2017.
94. Gallup Poll, June 2–7, 2015, www.gallup.com.
95. Phil Stewart, "Obama Approves Broader Role for U.S. Forces in Afghanistan," Reuters, June 10, 2016.
96. Peter Bergen, *Trump and His Generals* (New York: Penguin, 2019), 130.
97. Jonathan Finer and Tom Malley, "The Long Shadow of 9/11: How Counterterrorism Warps U.S. Foreign Policy," *Foreign Affairs* 97, no. 4 (July/August 2018): 61.
98. In reality, roughly 11,000 US troops were in Afghanistan. Various waivers, temporary duty assignments, and the flow of reliefs accounted for the surplus. Secretary of Defense James Mattis released the true numbers in 2017.
99. Interviews with four Taliban commanders from Kandahar and Helmand, December 2018.
100. Ibid.
101. Local tribesmen continued to volunteer to fight. Their tribal leaders had decided to defend their homes. Their support buoyed police morale. The local police after all were tribal militia.
102. Discussion with Garmser district governor, Kabul, June 27, 2017.
103. Telephone conversation with Omar Jan, July 15, 2016.
104. Mujib Mashal, "Afghanistan Forces Struggle to Hold Firm Against Taliban in South," *New York Times*, August 14, 2016.
105. Telephone conversation with Omar Jan, July 15, 2016.
106. Azizullah Popal, "With the Help of Foreign Advisors, Afghan Soldiers Begin Military Operation in Helmand," *VOA Pashto*, October 15, 2016.
107. Telephone conversation with former district governor Ayub Omar, August 12, 2016. Telephone discussion Alizai tribal leader, August 13, 2016.
108. Telephone conversation with Alizai tribal leader and local police commander, August 13, 2016.
109. Josh Smith, "U.S. Air Strikes Spike as Afghans Struggle Against Taliban, Islamic State," Reuters, October 26, 2016.
110. Gul Rahman Nyazman, "Fighting in Kunduz Moves from the Center to the Outskirts of the City," *VOA Pashto*, October 4, 2016.
111. Discussion with Governor Yaseen Khan, December 18, 2018.
112. Interview with Mullah Abdur Rahim Manan, *al-Samoud Magazine*, November 2016
113. Discussion with Helmand security official, Kabul, December 28, 2018.

114. A month earlier, Nicholson had shown the foresight to deploy 100 US soldiers to Lashkar Gah's airfield. Over 900 advisors and other US and coalition troops were now in Helmand. Azizullah Popal, "Fresh Reinforcements Have Arrived in Lashkar Gah," *VOA Pashto*, October 11, 2016. Thomas Gibbons-Neff, "Afghans' Reliance on U.S. Strikes Increasing," *Washington Post*, October 17, 2016.

115. Phone conversation with Omar Jan, November 3, 2016.

116. Discussion with Garmser district governor, Kabul, June 27, 2017.

Chapter 19

1. Discussion with members of Taliban political commission, Doha, Qatar, August 26, 2019.

2. Hamid Shuja, "Why Did Taliban Leader Mullah Mansour Check in with His Family a Few Moments Before He Was Killed?," *BBC Pashto*, www.bbc.com/pashto, August 29, 2017.

3. Sayid Abdullah Nizami, "Taliban Begins Selection of a New Leader," *BBC Pashto*, May 23, 2016.

4. Sayid Abdullah Nizami, "Maulawi Haybatullah Akhundzada, from Madrasa to Leader," *BBC Pashto*, May 24, 2016.

5. Abdul Hai Mutmain, *Mullah Mohammed Omar, Taliban and Afghanistan* (Kabul: Afghan Publishing Community, 2017), 338

6. Discussion with members of Taliban political commission, Doha, Qatar, August 26, 2019.

7. Visit to Task Force South West, Camp Shorab, Helmand, Afghanistan, March 22, 2018.

8. Carol Lee and Courtney Kube, "Trump Says U.S. 'Losing' Afghan War in Tense Meeting with Generals," *NBC News*, August 2, 2017.

9. Obama had officially left 8,400 but had allowed another 2,000 to remain in theater on temporary duty or other uncounted status, meaning that the total number in early 2017 was closer to 10,000. Secretary Mattis ended the murky accounting procedures and started reporting the true numbers of US troops in Afghanistan.

10. Transcript of Speech on Afghanistan Policy, President Donald Trump, August 21, 2017.

11. Ibid.

12. Ibid.

13. Teleconference with Brigadier General Ben Watson (Commanding General, Task Force Southwest), May 15, 2018.

14. Interviews with four Taliban commanders from Kandahar and Helmand, December 2018.

15. Teleconference with Brigadier General Ben Watson (Commanding General, Task Force Southwest), May 15, 2018.

16. Discussion with senior Ministry of the Interior official, May 9, 2018.

17. Teleconference with Brigadier General Ben Watson (Commanding General, Task Force Southwest), May 15, 2018.

18. Resolute Support Assessments Data, July 2019.

19. Conversation with Kabul-based journalist, Washington, DC, November 15, 2016.

20. Discussion with Batur Dostum, Washington, DC, March 29, 2017.

21. "Afghanistan: Forces Linked to Vice President Terrorize Villagers," Human Rights Watch, hrw.org, July 31, 2016.

22. Ibid.

23. Mujib Mashal, "Why the Taliban's Assault on Ghazni Matters," *New York Times*, August 13, 2018.

24. Paul Lushenko, Lance Van Auken, and Garrett Stebbins, "ISIS-K: Deadly Nuisance or Strategic Threat," *Journal of Small Wars & Insurgencies* (May 2019): 265–275.

25. Michael Phillips, "In Afghan Valley U.S. and ISIS Square Off," *Wall Street Journal*, May 16, 2018. Jessica Donati, "Islamic State Leader in Afghanistan Killed," *Wall Street Journal*, May 8, 2017.

26. Andrew Quilty and Wolfgang Bauer, "Faint Lights Twinkling Against the Dark," Afghan Analysts Network, https://www.afghanistan-analysts.org/en/reports/war-and-peace/faint-lights-twinkling-against-the-dark-reportage-from-the-fight-against-iskp-in-nangrahar/, February 19, 2019.

27. Borhan Osman, "Another ISKP Leader 'Dead,'" Afghan Analysts Network, www.afghanistan-analysts.org, July 23, 2017.

28. Phillips, "In Afghan Valley U.S. and ISIS Square Off,".
29. Quilty and Bauer, "Faint Lights Twinkling Against the Dark."
30. Sean Withington and Hussain Ehsani, "Islamic State Wilayat Khorasan: Phony Caliphate or Bona Fide Province?," Afghan Institute for Strategic Studies, 2020, 43–44.
31. Discussion with former Governor Ghulab Mangal, Kabul, September 6, 2018.
32. Discussion with Shaharzad Akbar, Kabul, August 17, 2013.
33. Borhan Osman, "Bourgeois Jihad: Why Young, Middle-Class Afghans Join the Islamic State," United States Institute of Peace (June 2020): 11.
34. Casey Garrett Johnson, "The Rise and Stall of the Islamic State in Afghanistan," United States Institute of Peace Special Report, November 2016, 3.
35. Discussion with former Governor Ghulab Mangal, Kabul, September 6, 2018.
36. "Afghanistan: Protection of Civilians in Armed Conflict, Annual Report 2018," United Nations Assistance Mission in Afghanistan, February 2019, 34.
37. Thomas Gibbons-Neff, "U.S. Special Forces Battle Against ISIS Turns to Containment, and Concern," New York Times, June 14, 2019.
38. Osman, "Bourgeois Jihad," 8, 11, 13.
39. Correspondence with Ministry of Education official, August 2019.
40. Discussion with Jawad Hamid, researcher from Mazar-e-Sharif, Doha, July 6, 2019. Obaid Ali, "Qari Hekmat's Island: A Daesh enclave in Jawzjan," Afghan Analysts Network, https://www.afghanistan-analysts.org, November 10, 2017.
41. Discussion with Massoud Khairokhel, Tribal Liaison Office (NGO), Kabul, July 17, 2019.
42. Niamatullah Ibrahimi and Shahram Akbarzadeh, "Intra-Jihadist Conflict and Cooperation: Islamic State-Khorasan Province and the Taliban in Afghanistan," Studies in Conflict & Terrorism 43, no. 12 (January 2019): 1086–1107.
43. "Afghanistan: Protection of Civilians in Armed Conflict, Annual Report 2018," United Nations Assistance Mission in Afghanistan, February 2019, 22–23.
44. Discussion with participant in Pugwash meetings with Taliban, Washington, DC, August 2, 2017.
45. Alex Horton, "Osama bin Laden's Son, a Young Face of al-Qaeda, killed in U.S. operation," Washington Post, September 15, 2019.
46. Anne Stenersen, "Al-Qa-'ida's Comeback in Afghanistan and Its Implications," CTC Sentinel 9, no. 9 (September 2019). Bill Roggio, "Taliban Supplies al Qaeda with Explosives for Attacks in Major Afghan Cities," Long War Journal, September 16, 2019.
47. Eleventh Report of the Analytic Support and Sanctions Monitoring Team, United Nations Security Council, May 27, 2020, 11–14.
48. Discussion with Kabul University professor, February 2, 2018.
49. Mujib Mashal and Taimoor Shah, "Taliban Say Top Leader's Son Carried Out a Suicide Attack," New York Times, July 22, 2017.
50. Discussion with Amir Khan Motaqi, Doha, Kabul, August 8, 2019.
51. "Taliban: The Mullah Haybatullah's Son Conducted a Suicide Attack in Helmand," BBC Pashto, https://www.bbc.com/pashto/afghanistan-40690561, July 22, 2017. Mujib Mashal and Taimoor Shah, "Taliban Say Top Leader's Son Carried Out a Suicide Attack," New York Times, July 22, 2017.
52. Discussion with Maulawi Mohammed Noor, Kandahar, December 24, 2018.
53. Discussion with Abdul Salam Zaeef, Kabul, March 20, 2018.
54. Discussion with Saad Mohseni, October 9, 2018.
55. Discussion with Maryam Durrani, Kandahar, December 20, 2018.
56. Discussion with Kabul University Professor, Washington, DC, August 1, 2018.
57. Ibid.
58. Discussion with Nasima Niyazi, Helmand member of parliament, Kabul, July 31, 2019.
59. Discussion with Maryam Durrani, Kandahar, December 20, 2018.
60. Conversation with Kandahar female leader, Kandahar, January 17, 2019.
61. Ashley Jackson, "Perspectives on Peace from Taliban Areas of Afghanistan," Special Report, no. 229, United States Institute of Peace, May 2019, 10.
62. Discussion with Nasima Niyazi, Helmand member of parliament, Kabul, July 31, 2019.
63. Discussion with Maryam Durrani, Kandahar, December 20, 2018.

64. Ibid.
65. Discussion with Nasima Niyazi, Helmand member of parliament, Kabul, July 31, 2019.
66. Conversation with Maulali Ishaqzai, Kabul, December 14, 2019.
67. His real name was Zahibullah.
68. Azizullah Popal, "General Abdul Razziq's Funeral in Kandahar, Laid to Rest," *VOA Pashto*, October 19, 2018. Bill Roggio, "General Raziq's Assassin Trained at a Taliban Camp," *Long War Journal*, longwarjournal.org, October 21, 2018. Mujib Mashal and Thomas Gibbons-Neff, "How a Taliban Assassin Got Close Enough to Kill a General," *New York Times*, November 2, 2018.
69. Information presented by NDS director Massoum Stanekzai, Kandahar governor's palace, *VOA Pashto*, October 22, 2019.
70. Taimoor Shah and Mujib Mashal, "An Afghan Police Chief Took on the Taliban and Won. Then His Luck Ran Out," *New York Times*, October 18, 2018.
71. The guard who had vouched for Abu Dujana fled Kandahar City. Mashal and Gibbons-Neff, "How a Taliban Assassin Got Close Enough to Kill a General."
72. Correspondence with former Kandahar policeman, October 18, 2018.
73. Correspondence with Kandahari civil society professional, October 19, 2019.
74. Discussion with Maulali Ishaqzai, December 14, 2018.

Chapter 20

1. Interviews with Taliban in Nangarhar, *VOA Pashto*, June 17, 2018.
2. *VOA Pashto*, June 16, 2018.
3. *VOA Pashto*, June 16, 2018.
4. Interviews with Taliban in Nangarhar, *VOA Pashto*, June 17, 2018.
5. Discussion with Kabul University professor Fayz Mohammed Zaland, Washington, DC, August 1, 2018.
6. An incorrect number of $50 billion was reported in the press and was often used in the White House. "Facing U.S. Withdrawal, Afghan Leader Pitches Trump Cost Savings," *CBS News*, www.cbsnews.com, February 1, 2019.
7. Discussion with Abdul Salam Zaeef, Kabul, March 20, 2018. Discussion with members of Taliban and Taliban associates, August 2019.
8. Discussion with Professor Fayz Mohammed Zaland, Kabul, December 7, 2018.
9. Borhan Osman, "A Negotiated End to the Afghan Conflict: The Taliban's Perspective," United States Institute of Peace, February 2018.
10. Discussion with Afghan government official, Kabul, December 12, 2018.
11. The commission conducted this survey in early 2019. Discussion with Massoud Khairokhel, Tribal Liaison Office (NGO), Kabul, July 17, 2019.
12. Antonio Giustozzi, *The Taliban at War* (New York: Oxford University Press, 2019), 210–211, 255, 270. "The Taliban Governor for Helmand, Mullah Manan, Has Been Killed in An Air Strike," *BBC Pashto*, December 2, 2018.
13. In June 2020, US intelligence linked Russian military intelligence to Taliban funds that were allegedly bounties to kill US troops, paid between 2018 and 2020. Charlie Savage, Mujib Mashal, Rukmini Callimachi, Eric Schmitt, and Adam Goldman, "Money Transfers Bolstered Belief in Russian Scheme," *New York Times*, July 1, 2020.
14. Zach Constantino, "The India-Pakistan Rivalry in Afghanistan," United States Institute for Peace, December 2019.
15. The money would be reprogrammed that September.
16. Conversation with Pakistani senior general, 2017.
17. Discussion with Professor Fayz Mohammed Zaland, Kabul, December 7, 2018.
18. John Bolton, *The Room Where It Happened: A White House Memoir* (New York: Simon & Schuster, 2020), 215.
19. Ibid., 218–219.
20. Author involvement in events, USFOR-A headquarters, Kabul, December 10–15, 2018.
21. "Has the Peace Process Failed?," *Daily Outlook Afghanistan*, September 16, 2019.

22. Mujib Mashal, "U.S. and Taliban Agree in Principle to Peace Framework, Envoy Says," *New York Times*, January 28, 2019.
23. Nazr Mohammed Mutmain, *Six Days with Taliban Leaders* (Kabul, Afgh.: Danish Publishing Community, 2019), 98.
24. Discussion with Deputy Speaker of the Wolesi Jirga Ezedyar and Badakhshan parliamentarian Kamil Bek, Parliament, Kabul, July 23, 2019.
25. Ibid.
26. Discussion with Maulali Ishaqzai, Kabul, August 1, 2019.
27. Lara Jakes, "Afghan Women Fear Losing Rights in Peace Deal," *New York Times*, August 17, 2019.
28. Discussion with General Scott Miller, Arlington, Virginia, August 16, 2018.
29. Kevin Maurer, "Witness to a War," *Washington Post Magazine*, September 15, 2019.
30. "Afghanistan War: Tracking the Killings in August 2019," *BBC News*, September 16, 2019.
31. Discussion with Amir Khan Motaqi, Doha, Kabul, August 8, 2019.
32. "No Retreat," *Economist*, September 14, 2019. Mujib Mashal, "2 Weeks of U.S.-Taliban Talks End with 'Progress' but No Breakthrough," *New York Times*, March 12, 2019.
33. "Has the Peace Process Failed?," *Daily Outlook Afghanistan*, September 16, 2019.
34. Eleventh Report of the Analytic Support and Sanctions Monitoring Team, United Nations Security Council, May 27, 2020, 11–14.
35. Sohail Shaheen interview, *CBS News*, August 21, 2019.
36. "Donald Trump's Interview with TIME on 2020: Read the Transcript," *TIME*, June 20, 2019.
37. Donald Trump television interview with Tucker Carlson, *Fox News*, foxnews.com, July 1, 2019.
38. Luke Mogelson, "The Afghan Way of Death," *New Yorker*, October 28, 2019.
39. "Talking Chop," *Economist*, September 14, 2019.
40. See Borhan Osman and Anand Gopal, "Taliban Views on a Future State," New York University, Center on International Cooperation, July 2016, 14.
41. See Ashley Jackson, "Perspectives on Peace from Taliban Areas of Afghanistan," Special Report, no. 229, United States Institute of Peace, May 2019, 10.
42. In November 2019, Baradar would tell an independent Afghan delegation of peace activists that a shura of all Afghans, arranged in the intra-Afghan negotiations, should decide the new form of government and the constitution. He asserted the Taliban did not want a monopoly and would accept the decision of a shura.
43. Mogelson, "The Afghan Way of Death."
44. Meeting with Afghan women leaders, ISAF headquarters, Kabul, September 5, 2013.
45. "No Retreat," *Economist*, September 14, 2019.
46. Ambassador Khalilzad to Afghan delegation, Intra-Afghan conference, Doha, July 7, 2019.
47. Mujib Mashal, "To Start Afghan Withdrawal, U.S. Would Pull 5,400 Troops in 135 Days," *New York Times*, September 2, 2019.
48. "No Retreat," *Economist*.
49. Brakkton Booker and Diaa Hadid, "Pompeo on Ending U.S. Taliban Talks," *National Public Radio*, www.npr.org, September 8, 2019.
50. Mashal, "To Start Afghan Withdrawal."
51. Baradar never agreed to attend any meeting with Ghani, especially without an announcement of a US timeline for withdrawal. His position and that of the political commission was that intra-Afghan negotiations would only begin after the US and Taliban had finalized and announced their agreement. Even then, they refused to admit they would officially meet with the government. A highly public summit at Camp David was never likely.
52. Rahim Faiez and Cara Anna, "Shattering Taliban Attack in Kabul Even as US Deal Nears," *Associated Press*, September 3, 2019.
53. James Dobbins, Robert Finn, Ronald Neumann, William Wood, John Negroponte, Earl Anthony Wayne, Ryan Crocker, James Cunningham, and Hugo Lorens, "US-Taliban Negotiations: How to Avoid Rushing to Failure," The Atlantic Council, September 3, 2019.
54. President Donald Trump, tweet, @realDonaldTrump, September 7, 2019.
55. "No Retreat," *Economist*.

56. In Washington and in the press, a separate popular argument was that Trump actually cancelled talks because the Taliban had refused his request to meet at Camp David. This is possible but matches little available information. The question also is not terribly significant. Whether because of Camp David or US losses, Trump called off negotiations. In both cases, the Taliban took an action that caused an unexpected (from their point of view) reaction by Trump that scuttled the deal. See Peter Baker, Mujib Mashal, and Michael Crowley, "How Trump's Plan to Secretly Meet with the Taliban Came Together, and Fell Apart," *New York Times*, September 8, 2019.

57. Deb Riechmann, "Trump: Taliban Deal Close, U.S. Troops to Drop to 8,600," *Associated Press*, August 29, 2019.

58. Bolton, *The Room Where It Happened*, 215–216.

59. Karen DeYoung, Josh Dawsey and Missy Ryan, "Trump Pronounces Taliban Agreement 'Dead' and Peace Talks Over," *Washington Post*, September 9, 2019.

60. "Trumping the Taliban," *Wall Street Journal*, September 9, 2019.

61. Sirajuddin Haqqani, "What We, the Taliban, Want," https://www.nytimes.com/2020/02/20/opinion/taliban-afghanistan-war-haqqani.html, February 20, 2020.

62. *Pashto VOA* television newscast, February 22, 2020.

63. Taliban ceasefire announcement, February 22, 2020.

64. Agreement for Bringing Peace to Afghanistan, February 29, 2020, on National Public Radio website, https://www.npr.org/2020/02/29/810537586/u-s-signs-peace-deal-with-taliban-after-nearly-2-decades-of-war-in-afghanistan.

Chapter 21

1. Carol Lee and Courtney Kube, "Trump Tells Advisers U.S. Should Pull Troops as Afghanistan COVID-19 Outbreak Looms," *NBC News*, April 27, 2020.

2. Discussion with Maryam Durrani, Kandahar, December 20, 2018.

3. Security and Stability in Afghanistan, 1225 Report, US Department of Defense, December 2015, 23. Casualty Status Report, January 6, 2020, www.defense.gov.

4. Antonio Giustozzi, *The Taliban at War* (New York: Oxford University Press, 2019), 261. Giustozzi did not have data past 2016. I repeated the 2016 figure for 2017–2019.

5. United Nations High Commission for Refugees, data2.unhcr.org.

6. Human Development Index, United Nations Development Programme, hdr.undp.org, 2019.

7. David Edwards, *Heroes of the Age: Moral Fault Lines on the Afghan Frontier* (Berkeley: University of California Press, 1996), 232.

8. "End the War in Afghanistan," *New York Times*, February 4, 2019.

9. Siobhán O'Grady, "Here's What Democratic Candidates Said They'd Do about the War in Afghanistan," *Washington Post*, September 13, 2019.

10. Andrew Dugan, "Fewer in U.S. View Iraq, Afghanistan Wars as Mistakes," Gallup, www.gallup.com, June 12, 2015. R.J. Reinhart, "U.S. Views Mixed on War in Afghanistan," Gallup, www.gallup.com, September 11, 2019. Jim Golby and Peter Feaver, "It Matters if Americans Call Afghanistan a Defeat," *Atlantic*, August 17, 2019.

11. John Vandiver, "Many Americans Say US Has Mostly Failed in Afghanistan, Poll Says," *Stars and Stripes*, October 5, 2018.

12. Dan Lamothe, "How 775,000 U.S. Troops Fought in One War: Afghanistan Military Deployments by the Numbers," *Washington Post*, September 11, 2019.

13. Ruth Igielnik and Kim Parker, "Majorities of U.S. Veterans, Public Say the Wars in Iraq and Afghanistan Were Not Worth Fighting," Pew Research Center, pewresearch.org, July 10, 2019. Jim Golby and Peter Feaver, "It Matters if Americans Call Afghanistan a Defeat," *Atlantic*, August 17, 2019. Survey of US military veterans, active duty, and U.S. people, Charles Koch Institute, October 8, 2018.

14. Marian Eide and Michael Gibler, eds., *After Combat: True War Stories from Iraq and Afghanistan* (Omaha: University of Nebraska Press, 2018), 205.

15. Thomas Gibbons-Neff, "A Marine Looks Back at His Battles in Afghanistan," *New York Times*, September 16, 2019.

16. Borhan Osman and Anand Gopal, *Taliban Views on a Future State*, New York University, Center on International Cooperation, July 2016, 14.
17. John Lewis Gaddis, *The Landscape of History: How Historians Map the Past* (Oxford, UK: Oxford University Press, 2002), 147.
18. Odd Arne Westad, *The Global Cold War* (New York: Cambridge University Press, 2005), 396–407.

GLOSSARY AND ABBREVIATIONS

ALP	Afghan local police, an official militia
AK-47	Russian-designed assault rifle, also known as the Kalashnikov
ANA	Afghan National Army
ANP	Afghan National Police
ANSF	Afghan National Security Force
arbakai	tribal militia
bayt	religious oath of allegiance
BCT	brigade combat team
CENTCOM	Central Command
CERP	commander's emergency response program, a US military fund for development projects
Chinook	CH-47 dual-rotor helicopter
COIN	abbreviation for counterinsurgency
COP	combat outpost
CT	abbreviation for counterterrorism
Daesh	informal term for the Islamic State
district	the subdivision of a province within Afghanistan, akin to a county within the United States
district center	the government capital of a district, usually made up of the district governor's office, the police headquarters, and a bazaar
DShK (pronounced "dish-ka")	Russian-designed heavy-machine gun
Durrani	Pashtun tribal confederation that included the traditional ruling elites
fatwa	religious edict
fitna	civil war
FOB	forward operating base
Ghilzai	Pashtun tribal confederation that was traditionally excluded from power
ghazi	Islamic warrior who has killed an infidel
Hadith	tradition or saying associated with the Prophet Mohammed
HESCO	dirt-filled basket used for fortfications
Hezb Islami	Islamist political party and insurgent group led by Gulbuddin Hekmatyar
Humvee	standard US military truck
IEC	Independent Election Commission
IED	improvised explosive device

ISAF	International Security Assistance Force, Afghanistan; the military command for US and international forces in Afghanistan
ISI	Inter-Services Intelligence; Pakistan's military intelligence organization
Jamiat Islami	Islamist political party composed primarily of Tajiks that was the center of the Northern Alliance
jihad	holy war
kandak	battalion (unit of 200-600 personnel) in the Afghan army
jirga	council
Kalashnikov	Russian-designed assault rifle, also known as the AK-47
Koran	the book of Allah's revelations to the Prophet Mohammed
Loya Jirga	A large nationwide council called for decisions or advice on major national issues for Afghanistan
M-4	US-issued assault rifle
M-16	US-issued assault rifle, carried by the Afghan army
madrasa	religious school
maulawi	religious scholar
mujahideen	holy warrior
MOI	Ministry of Interior
MOD	Ministry of Defense
mullah	village religious leader
NATO	North Atlantic Treaty Organization
NCO	Non-commissioned officer, such as a corporal or sergeant
NGO	non-governmental organization
NSC	National Security Council (United States)
NDS	National Directorate of Security, Afghanistan's intelligence organization
OEF	Operation Enduring Freedom
OP	observation post
Pashtunwali	code of the Pashtuns
PK	Russian-designed medium-machine gun
PRT	provincial reconstruction team
qazi	judge
Ramadan	holy month of fasting
RC	regional command
RPG	rocket-propelled grenade
Salafi	Islamic movement calling for interpretation of belief solely through strict adherence to the Koran and the Hadith
sangar	South Asian term for a fighting position such as a dugout, trench, or bunker
shahid	martyr
sharia	Islamic law
shura	council
SOF	special operations forces
ulema	the community of religious leaders
UN	United Nations
UNAMA	United Nations Assistance Mission in Afghanistan
USAID	United States Agency for International Development
Wahhabi	school of religious thought often associated with Saudi Arabia and al-Qa'eda
zakat	religious donation

SELECT BIBLIOGRAPHY

Addleton, Jonathan. *Dust of Kandahar*. Annapolis, MD: Naval Institute Press, 2016.

Afghanistan: A Country Study. Washington, DC: US Government Printing Office, 1986.

"Afghanistan: Annual Report 2010, Protection of Civilians in Conflict Afghanistan." United Nations Assistance Mission Afghanistan, March 2011.

"Afghanistan in 2016: A Survey of the Afghan People." Asia Foundation, asiafoundation.org, 2016.

Ahmadi, Belquis, and Sadaf Lakhani. "Afghan Women and Violent Extremism: Colluding, Perpetrating, or Preventing?" USIP Report, November 2016.

Ahmed, Azam. "Afghan Army Struggles in District Under Siege." *New York Times*, September 11, 2013.

Ahmed, Naseem. "Pakistan Taliban Policy 1994–1999." *Dialogue* (January 2012).

Ahmedzai, Zahidi. *The Past and Future of the Islamic Emirate of Afghanistan*. Quetta, Pak.: Taliban Director of Culture, 2013.

Aikins, Matthieu. "The Master of Spin Boldak." *Harper's*, December 2009.

Aikins, Matthieu. "A US-Backed Militia Runs Amok in Afghanistan." *Al Jazeera*, www.america.aljazeera.com, July 23, 2014.

Alter, Jonathan. *The Promise: President Obama, Year One*. New York: Simon & Schuster, 2011.

Alyas Khan, Mohammed. "Short Biography of Mullah Akhtar Mohammed Mansour." *BBC Pashto*, May 22, 2016.

Amiri, Rahmatullah. "Helmand (2): The Chain of Chiefdoms Unravels." Afghan Analysts Network, www.afghanistan-analysts.org/helmand-2-the-chain-of-chiefdoms-unravels, March 11, 2016.

"Analysis of International Intervention to Train, Advise, and Assist Afghan National Police: A Four Year Case Study in Kunduz." Cooperation for Peace and Unity, May 29, 2016.

Anonymous, *Hunting al Qaeda*. Minneapolis: Zenith Press, 2009.

Arash, Aazem. "Baghlan Police Chief: No Mercy for Taliban." *Tolo News*, August 13, 2014.

Asfura-Heim, Patricio. "Religious Leader Engagement in Afghanistan." CNA Research Memorandum, September 2012.

Azimi, Daoud. "Why Do the Afghan Taliban "Special Forces" Fight against the Islamic State?" *BBC Pashto*, December 18, 2015.

Barfield, Thomas. *Afghanistan: A Cultural and Political History*. Princeton, NJ: Princeton University Press, 2010.

Bergen, Peter. *Trump and His Generals*. New York: Penguin, 2019.

Bergen, Peter, ed. *Talibanistan: Negotiating the Borders between Terror, Politics, and Religion*. New York: Oxford University Press, 2013.

Berntsen, Gary, and Ralph Pezullo. *Jawbreaker: The Attack on bin Laden and Al-Qaʿeda*. New York: Crown Publishers, 2005.

Bhatia, Michael, and Mark Sedra. *Afghanistan, Arms and Conflict: Armed Groups, Disarmament and Security in Post-War Society*. New York: Routledge, 2008.

Biddle, Stephen. "Afghanistan and the Future of Warfare." Strategic Studies Institute monograph, November 2002.

Biggio, Frank. *The Wolves of Helmand: A View from Inside the Den of Modern War*. Brentwood, TN: Forefront Books, 2020.

Biography of Mullah Omar, *Voice of the Jihad*, official Taliban website, April 4, 2015.

Bishop, Patrick. *3PARA*. London: Harper Perennial, 2007.

Bolton, John. *The Room Where It Happened: A White House Memoir*. New York: Simon & Schuster, 2020.

Bradley, Rusty, and Kevin Maurer. *Lions of Kandahar*. New York: Bantam Books, 2011.

Brick, Jennifer. "Investigating the Sustainability of Community Development Councils in Afghanistan," Afghanistan Research and Evaluation Unit, February 2008.

Brick Murtazashvili, Jennifer. *Informal Order and the State in Afghanistan*. Cambridge, UK: Cambridge University Press, 2016.

Briscoe, Charles, Richard Kiper, James Schroder, and Kalev Sepp. *Weapon of Choice: ARSOF in Afghanistan*. Fort Leavenworth, KS: Combat Studies Institute Press, 2003.

Broadwell, Paula. *All In: The Education of General David Petraeus*. New York: Penguin, 2012.

Brooks, Michael. *Eyewitness to War* 3. Fort Leavenworth, KS: Combat Studies Institute Press, 2010.

Bulliet, Richard. *Islam: The View from the Edge*. New York: Columbia University Press, 1994.

Bush, George W. *Decision Points*. New York: Crown Publishers, 2010.

Carpenter, Kyle. *You Are Worth It: Building a Life Worth Fighting For*. New York: William Morrow, 2019.

Chandrasekaran, Rajiv. *Little America: The War within the War for Afghanistan*. New York: Knopf, 2012.

Chayes, Sarah. "A Mullah Dies, and War Comes Knocking." *Washington Post*, November 18, 2007.

Chayes, Sarah. *The Punishment of Virtue: Inside Afghanistan After the Taliban*. New York: Penguin, 2006.

Chivers, C.J. "Warriors Vexed by Rules For War." *New York Times*, June 23, 2010.

Chivers, C.J. "What Marja Tells Us of Battles Yet to Come." *New York Times*, June 10, 2010.

Christensen, Asger. "The Pashtuns of Kunar: Tribe, Class, and Community Organization." *Afghanistan Journal* 7, no. 3 (1980).

Clapp-Wincek, Cynthia. "The Helmand Valley Project in Afghanistan." A.I.D. Evaluation Special Study No. 18, U.S. Agency for International Development, December 1983.

Clark, Kate. "The Layha, Appendix 1: Taliban Codes of Conduct." Afghan Analysts' Network (aan-afghanistan.com), June 2011.

Clarke, Michael, ed. *The Afghan Papers: Committing Britain to War in Helmand, 2005–06*. London: RUSI, 2011.

Clinton, Hillary. "New Hope for Afghanistan's Women." *Time*, November 24, 2001.

Coburn, Noah, and Anna Larson. *Derailing Democracy in Afghanistan: Elections in an Unstable Political Landscape*. New York: Columbia University Press, 2014.

Coghlan, Tom. "Taleban Stage Audacious 'Tet-Style' Attack on British HQ City." *Times*, October 13, 2008.

Coll, Steve. *Directorate S: The C.I.A. and America's Secret Wars in Afghanistan and Pakistan*. New York: Penguin, 2018.

Coll, Steve. *Ghost Wars*. New York: Penguin, 2005.

Coll, Steve. "Looking for Mullah Omar." *New Yorker*, January 23, 2012.

Collins, Joseph. *Understanding War in Afghanistan*. Washington, DC: CreateSpace, 2012.

Constantino, Zach. "The India-Pakistan Rivalry in Afghanistan." United States Institute for Peace (December 2019).

Cook, Michael. *Ancient Religions, Modern Politics: The Islamic Case in Comparative Perspective*. Princeton, NJ: Princeton University Press, 2014.

Cordesman, Anthony. "Coalition, ANSF, and Civilian Casualties in the Afghan Conflict." Center for Strategic & International Studies, www.csis.org, September 4, 2012.

Coss, Michael. "Operation Mountain Lion: CJTF-76 in Afghanistan, Spring 2006." *Military Review* (January–February 2008): 22–9.

Cowper-Coles, Sherard. *Cables from Kabul: The Inside Story of the West's Afghanistan Campaign.* London: Harper Press, 2011.

Cubbison, Douglas. Wanat OP Draft Evaluation Paper. US Army Combat Studies Institute, 2009.

Dalrymple, William. *The Return of a King: The Battle for Afghanistan.* London: Bloomsbury, 2013.

Dam, Bette. *A Man and a Motorcycle: How Hamid Karzai Came to Power.* Amsterdam: Ipso Facto Publishers, 2014.

Dam, Bette. *The Secret Life of Mullah Omar.* Zomia Center, March 2019.

Degen, E.J. "The United States Army in Afghanistan: 2001–2014." OEF Study Group, US Army Lessons Learned Conference, July 2015.

Dobbins, James. *After the Taliban: Nation-Building in Afghanistan.* Washington, DC: Potomac Books, 2008.

Dobbins, James, John McGinn, Keith Crane, Seth Jones, Rollie Lal, Andrew Rathmell, Rachel Swanger, and Anga Timilsina. *America's Role in Nation-Building: From Germany to Iraq.* Washington, DC: The RAND Corporation, 2004.

Edgette, Ashley. "A Mecca for Militants: An Examination of the Development of International Terrorism in Peshawar, Pakistan, 1970–2010." *Hinckley Journal of Politics* (January 1, 2010).

Edwards, David. *Before Taliban: Genealogies of the Afghan Jihad.* Berkeley: University of California Press, 2002.

Edwards, David. *Caravan of Martyrs: Suicide and Sacrifice in Afghanistan.* Berkeley: University of California Press, 2017.

Edwards, David. *Heroes of the Age: Moral Fault Lines on the Afghan Frontier.* Berkeley: University of California Press, 1996.

Eide, Marian, and Michael Gibler. *After Combat: True War Stories from Iraq and Afghanistan.* Omaha: University of Nebraska Press, 2018.

Eikenberry, Karl. "The Limits in Counterinsurgency Doctrine in Afghanistan." *Foreign Affairs* (September–October 2013).

"The Exit Strategy from Afghanistan: Lessons from U.S. Efforts to Develop the Afghan National Defense and Security Forces." SIGAR Lessons Learned, Special Inspector-General for Afghanistan Reconstruction, June 19, 2017.

Fair, Christine. "The U.S.-Pakistan F-16 Fiasco." *Foreign Policy*, February 3, 2011.

Fairweather, Jack. *The Good War: Why We Couldn't Win the War or the Peace in Afghanistan.* London: Vintage, 2015.

Farrell, Theo. *Unwinnable: Britain's War in Afghanistan, 2001–2014.* London: The Bodley Head, 2017.

Farrell, Theo, and Antonio Giustozzi. "The Taliban at War: Inside the Helmand Insurgency, 2004–2012." *International Affairs* 89, no. 4 (2013).

Feith, Douglas. *War and Decision.* New York: Harper, 2008.

Feldstein, Martin. "The Fed's Unconventional Monetary Policy." *Foreign Affairs* 95, no. 3 (May–June 2016).

Felter, Joseph, and Jacob Shapiro. "Limiting Casualties as Part of a Winning Strategy: The Case of Courageous Restraint." *Daedalus* (Winter 2017).

Filkins, Dexter. "In Visit to Kandahar, Karzai Outlines Anti-Taliban Plan." *New York Times*, June 13, 2010.

Finer, Jonathan, and Tom Malley. "The Long Shadow of 9–11: How Counterterrorism Warps U.S. Foreign Policy." *Foreign Affairs* 97, no. 4 (July–August 2018).

Flynn, David. "Extreme Partnership in Afghanistan: Arghandab District, Kandahar Province, 2010–2011." *Military Review* (March–April 2012).

Forsberg, Carl. "Counterinsurgency in Kandahar." Institute for Understanding War (December 2010).

Forsberg, Carl. "The Taliban's Campaign for Kandahar." Institute for the Study of War, Afghanistan Report #3, December 2009.

Fraser, David, and Hanington, Brian. *Operation Medusa*. Ottawa: McClelland & Stewart, 2018.

Gall, Carlotta. *The Wrong Enemy: America in Afghanistan, 2001–2014*. New York: Houghton Mifflin Harcourt, 2014.

Garfield, Andrew, and Alicia Boyd. "Understanding Afghan Insurgents: Motivations, Goals, and the Reconciliation and Reintegration Process." Foreign Policy Research Institute, July 2013.

Gates, Robert. *Duty: Memoirs of a Secretary at War*. New York: Knopf, 2014.

Gayer, Laurent. *Karachi: Ordered Disorder and the Struggle for the City*. New York: Oxford University Press, 2014.

Ghani, Ashraf, and Clare Lockhart. *Fixing Failed States: A Framework for Rebuilding a Fractured World*. New York: Oxford University Press, 2009.

Gibbons-Neff, Thomas. "Afghans' Reliance on U.S. Strikes Increasing." *Washington Post*, October 17, 2016.

Giustozzi, Antonio. *Koran, Kalashnikov, and Laptop: The Neo-Taliban Insurgency in Afghanistan*. London: Hurst, 2007.

Giustozzi, Antonio. "The Military Cohesion of the Taliban." Center for Research & Policy Analysis, www.cpraweb.org, July 14, 2017.

Giustozzi, Antonio, *The Taliban at War*. London: Hurst, 2019.

Giustozzi, Antonio. "The Struggle to Create an Afghan National Army." Manuscript, February 2014.

Giustozzi, Antonio, ed. *Decoding the New Taliban: Insights from the Afghan Field*. New York: Columbia University Press, 2009.

Giustozzi, Antonio, and Artemy Kalinovsky. *Missionaries of Modernity: Advisory Missions and the Struggle for Hegemony in Afghanistan and Beyond*. London: Hurst, 2016.

Gopal, Anand. *No Good Men Among the Living: America, the Taliban, and the War Through Afghan Eyes*. New York: Metropolitan Books, 2014.

Gopal, Anand. "Rents, Patronage, and Defection: State-Building and Insurgency in Afghanistan." PhD dissertation, Columbia University, 2017.

Gopal, Anand, and Alex Strick van Linschoten. "Ideology in the Afghan Taliban." Afghan Analysts Network, June 2017.

Gordon, Michael, and Bernard Trainor. *The Endgame: The Inside Story of the Struggle for Iraq, from George W. Bush to Barack Obama*. New York: Pantheon Books, 2012.

Graham, Bradley. *By His Own Rules: The Ambitions, Successes, and Ultimate Failures of Donald Rumsfeld*. New York: Public Affairs, 2009.

Grenier, Robert. *88 Days to Kandahar*. New York: Simon & Schuster, 2015.

Hamid, Mustafa, and Leah Farrall. *The Arabs at War in Afghanistan*. London: Hurst, 2015.

Hastings, Michael. *The Operators*. New York: Blue Rider Press, 2012.

Hastings, Michael. "The Runaway General." *Rolling Stone*, June 22, 2010.

Hotaki, Benazir, "Bebe Zeneba, Zarghona Ana, and Maulali." In *Kandahar: Extended History*. Kandahar, Afgh.: Kandahar Cultural Director, 2005.

Howard, Michael. "What's in a Name?" *Foreign Affairs* 81, no. 1 (January–February 2002).

Huntington, Samuel. *Political Order in Changing Societies*. New Haven, CT: Yale University Press, 2006.

Ignatius, David. "What a Surge Can't Solve in Afghanistan." *Washington Post*, September 28, 2009.

"Interview: Mullah Dadullah." *Al Jazeera*, May 2006.

Interview with Kandahar governor Mohammed Issa. *Tsark Magazine*, June 2010.

Interview with Mullah Abdur Rahim Manan, *al-Samoud Magazine*, November 2016.

Jackson, Ashley. "Perspectives on Peace from Taliban Areas of Afghanistan." Special Report, no. 229, United States Institute of Peace, May 2019.

Jaffe, Greg. "The War in Afghanistan Shattered Joe Biden's Faith in American Military Power." *Washington Post*, February 23, 2020.

Jalali, Ali, and Lester Grau. *The Other Side of the Mountain*. Quantico, VA: Marine Corps University Press.

Jehani, Abdul Bari. *Spelay*. Masaf Nisherati, 2010.

Johnson, Casey Garret. "The Rise and Stall of the Islamic State in Afghanistan." United States Institute of Peace Special Report, November 2016.

Jones, Seth. *In the Graveyard of Empires: America's War in Afghanistan*. New York: W.W. Norton and Company, 2010.

Junger, Sebastian. *War*. New York: Twelve, 2010.

Kakar, Mohammed Hassan. *My Selected Essays*. Kabul: Afghanistan Cultural Community, 2010.

Kakar, Mohammed Hassan. *A Political and Diplomatic History of Afghanistan, 1863–1901*. Boston: Brill, 2006.

Kaplan, Fred. *The Insurgents: David Petraeus and the Plot to Change the American Way of War*. New York: Simon & Schuster, 2013.

Kelly, Terrence, Nora Bensahel, and Olga Oliker. "Security Force Assistance in Afghanistan: Identifying Lessons for Future Efforts." Santa Monica, CA: RAND Corporation, 2006.

Kerry, John. *Every Day Is Extra*. New York: Simon & Schuster, 2018.

Khalilzad, Zalmay. *The Envoy*. New York: St. Martin's Press, 2016.

Kilcullen, David. *The Accidental Guerrilla: Fighting Small Wars in the Midst of a Big One*. New York: Oxford University Press, 2009.

Kochai, Mohammed. "Karzai: Do Not Leave Your Own Region to the Taliban." *BBC Pashto*, October 20, 2010.

Koofi, Fawzia. "Where Afghan Law Fails Women." *Al Jazeera*, www.aljazeera.com, January 1, 2015.

Kronstadt, Alan. "Pakistan-U.S. Relations." Congressional Research Service, February 6, 2009.

Kurth Cronin, Audrey. "Why Drones Fail." *Foreign Affairs* 92, no. 4 (July–August 2013).

Lamb, Christina. *Farewell Kabul: From Afghanistan to a More Dangerous World*. London: William Collins, 2016.

"Last Year, Recent War." *Shah Mat* (Taliban magazine), February 2010, 3–4.

Legion of Brothers, CNN Films, 2017.

Lesnowicz, Matthew. "Gendarmerie de Marjah." *Marine Corps Gazette* 98, no. 2 (February 2014).

Lieven, Anatol. *Pakistan: A Hard Country*. New York: Public Affairs, 2011.

Lights of the Jihadi Literature. Quetta, Pak.: Islamic Emirate Cultural Commission, 2013.

Livingston, Ian, and Michael O'Hanlon. "Afghanistan Index," Brookings Institute, November 30, 2011.

Ludin, Ahmed. "From Arghandab, Karzai Calls on the People of Arghandab to Bring Taliban to Peace." Benawa, October 9, 2010.

Lule, Jack. "Myth and Terror on the Editorial Page: The *New York Times* Responds to September 11, 2001." *Journalism & Mass Communication Quarterly* (June 1, 2002).

Lyall, Jason, Graeme Blair, and Kosuke Imai. "Explaining Support for Combatants during Wartime: A Survey Experiment in Afghanistan." *American Political Science Review* (November 2013).

Malejacq, Romain. "From Rebel to Quasi-State: Governance, Diplomacy and Legitimacy in the Midst of Afghanistan's Wars (1979–2001)." *Small Wars & Insurgencies* 28, no. 4–5 (2017).

Maley, William, ed. *Fundamentalism Reborn?* New York: New York University Press, 1998.

Malkasian, Carter. "How the Good War Went Bad: America's Slow-Motion Failure in Afghanistan." *Foreign Affairs* (March–April 2020).

Malkasian, Carter. *War Comes to Garmser: Thirty Years of Conflict on the Afghan Frontier*. New York: Oxford University Press, 2013.

Malkasian, Carter, and Gerald Meyerle. "Provincial Reconstruction Teams: How Do We Know They Work?" Strategic Studies Institute Monograph. March 2009.

Maloney, Sean. *Fighting for Afghanistan*. Annapolis, MD: Naval Institute Press, 2011.

Maloney, Sean. "A Violent Impediment: The Evolution of Insurgent Operations in Kandahar Province 2003–07." *Small Wars & Insurgencies* 19, no. 2 (June 2008).

Malou, Innocent. "Should America Liberate Afghanistan's Women?" *Survival* 53, no. 5 (October–November 2011).

Mann, Scott. *Game Changers: Going Local to Defeat Violent Extremists*. Leesburg, VA: Tribal Analysis Publishing, 2015.

Mansfield, David. *A State Built on Sand: How Opium Undermined Afghanistan*. London: Hurst, 2016.

Martin, Michael. *An Intimate War: An Oral History of the Helmand Conflict*. London: Hurst, 2014.

Mashal, Mujib. "Afghanistan Forces Struggle to Hold Firm against Taliban in South." *New York Times*, August 14, 2016.

Mashal, Mujib. "How Secret Peace Talks between Afghanistan and the Taliban Foundered." *New York Times*, December 27, 2016.

Mashal, Mujib, and Thomas Gibbons-Neff. "How a Taliban Assassin Got Close Enough to Kill a General." *New York Times*, November 2, 2018.

McCarthy, Joseph. "The Enduring Heart of Central Asia: A Study to Understand Afghanistan's Survival." PhD Dissertation, University of Nebraska, 2018.

Meyerle, Gerald, Megan Katt, and James Gavrilis. *Counterinsurgency on the Ground in Afghanistan*. Quantico, VA: Marine Corps University Press, 2011.

Miller, Paul. *Armed State Building: Confronting State Failure, 1898–2012*. Ithaca, NY: Cornell University Press, 2013.

Mockenhaupt, Brian. "The Living and the Dead," *Best American Magazine Writing*. New York: Columbia University Press, 2013.

Mogelson, Luke. "The Afghan Way of Death." *New Yorker*, October 28, 2019.

Mogelson, Luke. "Which Way Did the Taliban Go?" *New York Times Magazine* (January 20, 2013).

Moreau, Ron, Michael Hirsh, John Barry, and Mark Hosenball. "If You Thought the Long-Time Head of the Taliban Was Bad, You Should Meet His No. 2." *Newsweek*, August 3, 2009.

Moreau, Ron, and Sam Yousafzai. "The Taliban in Their Own Words." *Newsweek*, September 25, 2009.

Morgan, Wesley. *The Hardest Place: The American Military Adrift in Afghanistan's Pech Valley*. New York: Random House, 2021.

Moyar, Mark. *Oppose Any Foe: The Rise of America's Special Operations Forces*. New York: Basic Books, 2017.

Mukhopadhyay, Dipali. *Warlords, Strongman, Governors, and the State in Afghanistan*. New York: Columbia University Press, 2014.

Mutawakil, Wakil Ahmed. *Afghanistan and Taliban*. Kabul, Afgh.: Byeralai Pohaneon Lray, 2005.

Mutmain, Abdul Hai. *Mullah Mohammed Omar, Taliban, and Afghanistan*. Kabul: Afghan Publishing Community, 2017.

Myerson, Roger. "How to Prepare for State-Building." *PRISM* 7, no.1 (September 2017).

Nadiri, Khalid Homayun. "Old Habits, New Consequences: Pakistan's Posture toward Afghanistan since 2001." *International Security* (Fall 2014).

Nafeez, Ahmed Nafeez. "Rebels." *Shah Mat* (Taliban magazine), February 2010.

Nazr Mohammed Mutmain. *Six Days with Taliban Leaders*. Kabul, Afgh.: Danish Publishing Community, 2019.

Neumann, Ronald. *The Other War: Winning and Losing in Afghanistan*. Washington, DC: Potomac Books, 2009.

Nizami, Sayid Abdullah Nizami. "Maulawi Haybatullah Akhundzada, from Madrasa to Leader." *BBC Pashto*, May 24, 2016.

Obama, Barack. *A Promised Land*. New York: Crown, 2020.

Offerings on the Occupation: The Islamic Emirates' Position, Messages, Announcements, and Interviews. Islamic Emirate of Afghanistan Cultural Commission, 2012.

Osman, Borhan. "Bourgeois Jihad: Why Young, Middle-Class Afghans Join the Islamic State." United States Institute of Peace (June 2020).

Osman, Borhan, and Anand Gopal. "Taliban Views on a Future State." New York University, Center on International Cooperation, July 2016.

Paine, Sheila. *The Afghan Amulet: Travels from the Hindu Kush*. London: Tauris Parke Paperbacks, 2006.

Partlow, Joshua. *A Kingdom of Their Own: The Family Karzai and the Afghan Disaster*. New York: Knopf, 2016.

"People, Every Armed Man, Foreign Occupation." *Shah Mat* (Taliban magazine), February 2010.

"The Political Economy of the Dashte." Coffey International Development, August 2013.

Popal, Asadullah. "The Kandahar Sadozai." In *Kandahar: Extended History*. Kandahar, Afgh.: Kandahar Cultural Director, 2005.

Popal, Azizullah. "Fresh Reinforcements Have Arrived in Lashkar Gah." *VOA Pashto*, October 11, 2016.

Popal, Azizullah. "With the Help of Foreign Advisors, Afghan Soldiers Begin Military Operation in Helmand." *VOA Pashto*, October 15, 2016.

"Protection of Civilians in Armed Conflict." UNAMA 2014 Report, February 2015.

Rahimi, Abdul Karim Talib. "Kandahar: The Courtyard of Great Promise and the Sangar of Prideful and Youthful Awakening." In *Kandahar: Extended History*. Kandahar, Afgh.: Kandahar Directorate of Culture, 2005.

Rashid, Ahmed. *Descent into Chaos: The United States and the Failure of Nation Building in Pakistan, Afghanistan, and Central Asia*. New York: Viking, 2008.

Rashid, Ahmed. *Pakistan: On the Brink: The Future of America, Pakistan, and Afghanistan*. New York: Viking, 2012.

Rashid, Ahmed. *Taliban*. New Haven, CT: Yale University Press, 2001.

Rayment, Sean. *Into the Killing Zone: The Real Story from the Frontline in Afghanistan*. London: Constable, 2008.

"Reconstructing the Afghan National Defense and Security Forces: Lessons from the U.S. Experience in Afghanistan." Special Inspector General for Afghanistan Reconstruction (September 2017).

"Report on Progress Toward Security and Stability in Afghanistan," 1225 Report, US Department of Defense, December 2015.

Rice, Condoleezza. *No Higher Honor: A Memoir of My Years in Washington*. New York: Crown Publishers, 2011.

Rice, Susan. *Tough Love: My Story of the Things Worth Fighting For*. New York: Simon & Schuster, 2019.

Roggio, Bill, and Lisa Lundquist. "Green-on-Blue Attacks in Afghanistan: The Data." http://www.longwarjournal.org/archives/2012/08/green-on-blue_attack.php, January 30, 2015.

Rohde, David, and David Sanger. "How a 'Good War' in Afghanistan Went Bad." *New York Times*, August 12, 2007.

Rosen, Nir. *Aftermath: Following the Bloodshed of America's Wars in the Muslim World*. New York: Nation Books, 2010.

Rosenberg, Matthew. "U.S. Disrupts Afghans' Tack on Militants." *New York Times*, October 28, 2013.

Roy, Olivier. *The Failure of Political Islam*. Cambridge, MA: Harvard University Press, 1998.

Roy, Olivier. *Islam and Resistance in Afghanistan*. Cambridge, UK: Cambridge University Press, 1990.

Rubin, Alyssa. "Women's War: Flawed Justice After a Mob Killed an Afghan Woman." *New York Times*, December 26, 2015.

Rubin, Barnett. *The Fragmentation of Afghanistan*. New Haven, CT: Yale University Press, 1995.

Rubin, Elizabeth. "In the Land of the Taliban." *New York Times Magazine*, October 25, 2006.

Rumsfeld, Donald. *Known and Unknown: A Memoir*. New York: Sentinel, 2012.

Russell, James. "Learning Cycles in War: The 3/2 Arrowhead Brigade and the 1st Battalion 23rd Infantry Operations in Kandahar, 2012." *Journal of Strategic Studies* (forthcoming).

Ruttig, Thomas. "From Mullah Omar to Mansur: Change at the Taleban's Top Leadership." Afghan Analysts Network, www.afghanistan-analysts.org, July 31, 2015.

"Saleh: Weakness in Leadership Was the Cause of the Collapse of Kunduz." *VOA Pashto*, November 21, 2015.

Samaar, Sima. "Feminism, Peace, and Afghanistan." *Journal of International Affairs* (March 2019).

Selected Speeches of President George W. Bush, 2001–2008, www.georgewbush-whitehouse.archives. gov.

Shahid, Mohammed Gul. *Religious Figures of Afghanistan.* Peshawar, Pak.: Maktabah Farooqiya, 2012.

Shahzad, Syed Saleem. *Inside Al-Qaeda and the Taliban: Beyond 9/11.* London: Pluto Press, 2011.

Shapiro, Jacob. *The Terrorist's Dilemma: Managing Violent Covert Organizations.* Princeton, NJ: Princeton University Press, 2013.

Shuja, Hamid. "Why Did Taliban Leader Mullah Mansour Check in with His Family a Few Moments before He Was Killed?" *BBC Pashto,* www.bbc.com/pashto, August 29, 2017.

Simpson, Emile. *War from the Ground Up: Twenty-First-Century Combat as Politics.* New York: Oxford University Press, 2013.

Smith, Graeme. *The Dogs Are Eating Them Now: Our War in Afghanistan.* New York: Counterpoint, 2014.

Smith, Graeme. "Talking to the Taliban," http://www.theglobeandmail.com/talkingtothetaliban/, 2007.

Spanta, Rangin Dadfar. *Afghanistan Politics: Sense of the Time.* Kabul, Afgh.: Aazem Publications, 2017.

Stanton, Doug. *Horse Soldiers.* New York: Scribner, 2009.

Stenersen, Anne. "Al-Qaʻeda's Comeback in Afghanistan and Its Implications." *CTC Sentinel,* September 7, 2016.

Strick van Linschoten, Alex, and Felix Kuehn. *The Enemy We Created: The Myth of the Taliban.* New York: Columbia University Press, 2012.

Strick van Linschoten, Alex, and Felix Kuehn. *Poetry of the Taliban.* London: Hurst, 2012.

Strick von Linschoten, Alex, and Felix Kuehn. *The Taliban Reader.* London: Hurst, 2018.

"Taliban: The Mullah Haybatullah's Son Conducted a Suicide Attack in Helmand." *BBC Pashto,* July 22, 2017.

"The Taliban New Leader's Spoken Message, 'Jihad Will Continue.'" *BBC Pashto,* August 1, 2015.

Talibi, Abdul Latif. *Pashtuni Qabilay.* Kabul: Afghanistan Academy of Sciences International Center for Pashto Studies, 1991.

Tapper, Richard. "Who are the Kuchi? Nomad Self-Identities in Afghanistan." *Journal of the Royal Anthropological Institute* (March 2008).

Tellis, Ashley. "Pakistan's Record on Terrorism: Conflicted Goals, Compromised Performance." *Washington Quarterly* (Spring 2008).

Terpstra, Niels. "Rebel Governance, Rebel Legitimacy, and External Intervention: Assessing Three Phases of Taliban Rule in Afghanistan." *Small Wars & Insurgencies* 31, no. 6 (May 2020).

Tomsen, Peter. *The Wars of Afghanistan: Messianic Terrorism, Tribal Conflicts, and the Failures of Great Powers.* New York: Public Affairs, 2011.

The U.S. Army-Marine Corps Counterinsurgency Field Manual. Chicago: University of Chicago, 2007.

West, Bing. *One Million Steps: A Marine Platoon at War.* New York: Random House, 2014.

West, Bing. *The Wrong War: Grit, Strategy, and the Way Out of Afghanistan.* New York: Random House, 2011.

Westad, Odd Arne. *The Global Cold War.* Cambridge, UK: Cambridge University Press, 2005.

Weston, Kael. *Mirror Test: America at War in Iraq and Afghanistan.* New York: Knopf, 2016.

Wimpelmann, Torunn. *The Pitfalls of Protection: Gender, Violence, and Power in Afghanistan.* Berkeley: University of California Press, 2017.

Winterbotham, Emily. "Legacies of Conflict: Healing Complexes and Moving Forward in Ghazni Province," AREU Case Study, October 2011.

Withington, Sean, and Hussain Ehsani. "Islamic State Wilayat Khorasan: Phony Caliphate or Bona Fide Province?" Afghan Institute for Strategic Studies, 2020.

Woods, Chris. *Sudden Justice: America's Secret Drone Wars.* Oxford, UK: Oxford University Press, 2015.

Woodward, Bob. *Bush at War*. New York: Simon & Schuster, 2002.

Woodward, Bob. *Obama's Wars*. New York: Simon & Schuster, 2010.

Wright, Donald. *A Different Kind of War: The United States Army in Operation Enduring Freedom, October 2001–September 2005*. Fort Leavenworth, KS: Combat Studies Institute Press, 2010.

Wright, Donald, ed. *Vanguard of Valor: Small Unit Actions in Afghanistan*. Fort Leavenworth, KS: US Army Center for Military History Press, 2012.

Wright, Donald, ed. *Vanguard of Valor II: Small Unit Actions in Afghanistan*. Fort Leavenworth, KS: Combat Studies Institute Press, 2012.

Young, David. "Anatomy of a Tribal Uprising." AfPak Channel, September 12, 2012.

Zaeef, Abdul Salam. *My Life with the Taliban*. New York: Columbia University Press, 2010.

Zaeef, Abdul Salam. *Taliban: From Kandahar until Mazar*. Kabul, Afgh.: Aksos, 2018.

Zaman, Muhammad Qasim. *Islam in Pakistan: A History*. Princeton, NJ: Princeton University Press, 2018.

Zaman, Robert, and Abdul Hadi Khalid. "Trends of Radicalization among the Ranks of the Afghan National Police." Afghan Institute for Strategic Studies, November 2015.

INDEX

For the benefit of digital users, indexed terms that span two pages (e.g., 52–53) may, on occasion, appear on only one of those pages.

Surnames starting with "al-" are alphabetized by remaining portion of name.

Figures and notes are indicated by f and n following the page number.